WORLD OF LANGUAGE

Betty G. Gray   Nancy Nickell Ragno   Marian Davies Toth

Contributing Author – Primary   Elfrieda Hiebert
Contributing Author – Vocabulary   Richard E. Hodges
Contributing Author – Poetry   Myra Cohn Livingston

Consulting Author – Thinking Skills   David N. Perkins

SILVER BURDETT GINN

NEEDHAM, MA   PARSIPPANY, NJ

Atlanta, GA   Irving, TX   Deerfield, IL   Santa Clara, CA

Acknowledgments

Cover: Gabriel

Contributing Writers: Sandra Breuer, Judy Brim, Gary Davis, Wendy Davis, Jack Dempsey, Anne Maley, Duncan Searl, Diana Sergis, Gerry Tomlinson

Contributing artists: Ernest Albanese, George Baquero, Robert Byrd, Sue Carlson, Jack Crane, Jim Cummins, John Cymerman, Allan Davis, Ric Del Rossi, Michele Epstein, Liane Fried, Robert R. Jackson, Susan Jakel, Pam Johnson, Phil Jones, Bruce Lemerise, Pam Levy, Greg Mackey, Claude Martinot, Lyle Miller, Nighthawk, Loughran O'Connor, Lisa O'Hanlon, Jose Reyes, John Rice, Ed Sauk, Sally Schaedler, Gary Undercuffler, Rhonda Voo, Fred Winkowski, Lane Yerkes

Picture credits: All photographs by Silver Burdett & Ginn (SB&G) unless otherwise noted **Unit 1** 2: UPI/Bettmann Newsphotos. 5: AP/Wide World Photos, courtesy Photo Cosmopress, Geneve. 9: Kurt Scholz/Shostal Associates. 15: Leonard Lee Rue III/Bruce Coleman. 17: North Wind. 18: *t.* The Bettmann Archive; *b.* The Granger Collection. 21: E.R. Degginger. 24: *Josephine and Mercie* by Edmund Charles Tarbell. The Corcoran Gallery of Art, museum purchase, gallery fund, 1909. 27: Photo Cosmopress, Geneve. 29: The Granger Collection. 41: Reprinted with permission of Charles Scribner's Sons, an imprint of Macmillan Publishing Company from *A Gathering of Days* by Joan W. Blos. Cover illustration by Ronald Himler. Copyright © 1979 Joan W. Blos. **Unit 2** 57: Culver Pictures. 65: Martha Swope. 70: *The Banjo Lesson* by Henry O. Tanner. Hampton University Museum, Hampton, Virginia. 74: Courtesy Pell and Alice Collins. 75: © Charmaine Lanham. 76: Courtesy Pell and Alice Collins. 84: Peter J. Menzel/Stock, Boston. 86: Martin Rogers/Stock, Boston. 90: Mark Ferri/The Stock Market of NY. 93: © Beth Bergman. 95: The Granger Collection. 96: Courtesy Pell and Alice Collins. 100: Dan De Wilde for SB&G. 104: Paul McAlpine/LGI, Inc. 105: *American Indian Music and Musical Instruments* by George S. Fichter. Reprinted with permission from George S. Fichter. **Unit 3** 116: *t.* Photo by Jill Oxendine, courtesy William Morrow & Co., Inc.; *b.* Photo by Cox Studios, courtesy Macmillan Publishing Company. 119: Historical Pictures Service. 125: © James Steinberg/Photo Researchers, Inc. 134: *Latest News* by Max Weber. The Nelson-Atkins Museum of Art, Kansas City, Missouri (Gift of Mr. J.S. Atha). 138: Jacket illustration by James McMullan from *M.C. Higgins, The Great* by Virginia Hamilton. Copyright © 1974 by Virginia Hamilton. 139: *l.* Photo by Jill Oxendine, courtesy William Morrow & Co., Inc.; *r.* Photo by Cox Studios, courtesy Macmillan Publishing Company. 145: © American Library Association. 152: Photo by Jill Oxendine, courtesy William Morrow & Co., Inc. 156: Dan De Wilde for SB&G. 161: *Magazine: Behind the Scenes at Sports Illustrated.* © 1983 by William Jaspersohn. Used by permission of Little, Brown & Company. **Unit 4** 176: Thomas Dimock/The Stock Market of NY. 177: Fred Bavendam/Peter Arnold, Inc. 179: Tom Stack/Tom Stack & Associates. 185: Buddy Jenssen/Leo deWys, Inc. 189: E.R. Degginger. 192: *A Shoal of Sperm Whales*, scrimshaw, photographed by Mary Anne Stets. The Mystic Seaport Museum, Inc. 209: Authenticated News International. 214: Dan De Wilde for SB&G. 218: Ed Cooper/H. Armstrong Roberts. 219: *Island of the Blue Dolphins* by Scott O'Dell. Used by permission of Dell Books, a division of Bantam, Doubleday, Dell Publishing Group, Inc. **Unit 5** 232: Owen T. Norman/Bruce Coleman. 235: Ted Horowitz/The Stock Market of NY. 239: The Bettmann Archive. 246: © 1990 Frank Fournier/Woodfin Camp & Associates. 252: *New York #2* by Charles Sheeler. Munson-Williams-Proctor Institute. 258: Rensselaer Polytechnic Institute Archives, Troy, New York. 259: *l.* The Granger Collection; *r.* Rensselaer Polytechnic Institute Archives, Troy, New York.

Silver Burdett Ginn
A Division of Simon & Schuster
160 Gould Street
Needham Heights, MA 02194

CONTENTS

INTRODUCTORY UNIT

Literature in Your World
Writing in Your World   **Introduction 1**

What Is a Writer?   **Introduction 2**

Introducing the Writing Process
Think, Read, Speak, Listen, Write   **Introduction 3**

Using the Writing Process
Write a Description   **Introduction 4**

Prewriting   Getting Ready to Write   **Introduction 4**

Writing   Putting Your Ideas on Paper   **Introduction 5**

Revising   Making Changes to Improve Your Writing   **Introduction 6**

Proofreading   Looking for and Fixing Errors   **Introduction 7**

Publishing   Sharing Your Writing with Others   **Introduction 7**

UNIT 1   EXPRESSING YOURSELF AS A WRITER

PART 1   LANGUAGE AWARENESS ◆ SENTENCES

Writing in Your Journal 3

Writing Four Kinds of Sentences 4
Parts of Speech in Sentences 6
Complete Subjects and Predicates 8
Simple Subjects and Predicates 10
Subject-Verb Order 12
Compound Subjects and Verbs 14
Simple and Compound Sentences 16
Avoiding Sentence Errors 18
VOCABULARY   Using the Thesaurus 20

Grammar-Writing Connection   How to Combine Sentence Parts 22

PART 2   COMPOSITION ◆ PERSONAL WRITING

Creative Writing   Fine Arts 25

LITERATURE   *Anne Frank: The Diary of a Young Girl,*
            translated by B. M. Mooyaart 26
SPEAKING and LISTENING   Group Discussions 32
WRITING   Identifying Purpose and Audience 34
WRITING   Choosing an Appropriate Form 36

Reading-Writing Connection   Focus on a Writer's Voice 38

Curriculum Connection   Composition 40

Books to Enjoy 41

Unit Review 42   Extra Practice 45
Language Puzzlers/Challenge 44

Literature Model: Anne Frank: The Diary of a Young Girl

UNIT THEME: Personal Writing

UNIT 2   USING LANGUAGE TO INFORM

PART 1 LANGUAGE AWARENESS ◆ NOUNS

Writing in Your Journal   55

Writing with Nouns   56
Common and Proper Nouns   58
Making Nouns Plural   60
Nouns with Special Plural Forms   62
Possessive Nouns   64
VOCABULARY Compounds   66

Grammar-Writing Connection How to Revise Sentences with Nouns   68

PART 2 A REASON FOR WRITING ◆ INFORMING

Creative Writing Fine Arts   71

CRITICAL THINKING A Strategy for Informing   72
LITERATURE ''Jug Bands'' by Steven Caney   74
SPEAKING and LISTENING Giving a Demonstration   80
WRITING Paragraphs   82
WRITING Developing a Paragraph by Facts   84
WRITING Developing a Paragraph by Examples   86
WRITING Organizing Ideas in a Paragraph   88
WRITING Paragraph Unity and Coherence   92

Reading-Writing Connection Focus on Clarity   94

WRITING PROCESS Writing a How-to Article   96
          Prewriting Writing Revising
          Proofreading Publishing

Curriculum Connection Writing for Music   104

Books to Enjoy   105

Unit Review   106   Language Puzzlers/Challenge   110
Cumulative Review   108   Extra Practice   111

v

UNIT THEME: The Art of Music

Literature Model: Jug Bands

UNIT 3   USING LANGUAGE TO PERSUADE

PART 1   LANGUAGE AWARENESS ◆ VERBS

Writing in Your Journal   117

Writing with Verbs   118
Verb Phrases   120
Linking Verbs   122
Verbs with Direct Objects   124
Verbs with Indirect Objects   126
Predicate Nominatives and Predicate Adjectives   128
VOCABULARY Idioms   130

Grammar-Writing Connection How to Revise Sentences with Verbs   132

PART 2   A REASON FOR WRITING ◆ PERSUADING

Creative Writing Fine Arts   135

CREATIVE THINKING   A Strategy for Persuading   136
LITERATURE *M.C. Higgins, the Great*, a review by Nikki Giovanni   138
SPEAKING and LISTENING Critical Listening   142
WRITING Persuasive Strategies   146
WRITING Developing a Paragraph with Reasons   148

Reading-Writing Connection Focus on Opinions   150

WRITING PROCESS Writing a Media Review   152
        Prewriting Writing Revising
        Proofreading Publishing

Curriculum Connection Literature   160

Books to Enjoy   161

Unit Review   **162**   Extra Practice   165
Language Puzzlers/Challenge   **164**

UNIT 4   USING LANGUAGE TO NARRATE

PART 1   LANGUAGE AWARENESS ◆ USING CORRECT VERB FORMS

Writing in Your Journal   173

Principal Parts of Verbs   174
Tenses of Verbs   176
Irregular Verbs   180
Active and Passive Voice   184
Troublesome Verb Pairs   186
VOCABULARY   Shades of Meaning   188

Grammar-Writing Connection   How to Revise Sentences with Verbs   190

PART 2   A REASON FOR WRITING ◆ NARRATING

Creative Writing   Fine Arts   193

CREATIVE THINKING   A Strategy for Narrating   194
LITERATURE   *The Black Pearl* by Scott O'Dell   196
SPEAKING and LISTENING   Telling About an Incident   202
WRITING   Using Dialogue   204
WRITING   Using a Journal   206

Reading-Writing Connection   Focus on Point of View   208

WRITING PROCESS   Writing a Personal Narrative   210
                      Prewriting   Writing   Revising
                      Proofreading   Publishing

Curriculum Connection   Writing for Social Studies   218

Books to Enjoy   219

Unit Review   220   Language Puzzlers/Challenge   224
Cumulative Review   222   Extra Practice   225

vii

UNIT THEME: The Sea Around Us

Literature Model: The Black Pearl

UNIT 5   USING LANGUAGE TO CLASSIFY

PART 1   LANGUAGE AWARENESS ◆ PRONOUNS

Writing in Your Journal   231

Writing with Pronouns   232
Pronouns and Antecedents   234
Possessive Pronouns   236
Interrogative and Demonstrative Pronouns   238
Reflexive and Intensive Pronouns   240
Indefinite Pronouns   242
Subject and Object Pronouns   244
Choosing Correct Pronouns   246
VOCABULARY   Formal and Informal Language   248

Grammar-Writing Connection   How to Revise Sentences with Pronouns   250

PART 2   A REASON FOR WRITING ◆ CLASSIFYING

Creative Writing   Fine Arts   253

CRITICAL THINKING   A Strategy for Classifying   254
LITERATURE   *The Brooklyn Bridge: They Said It Couldn't Be Built*
       by Judith St. George   256
SPEAKING and LISTENING   Discussing Characters   262
WRITING   A Character Sketch   264
WRITING   Comparison/Contrast Paragraphs   266

Reading-Writing Connection   Focus on Character Traits   270

WRITING PROCESS   **Writing a Comparison Essay**   272
       Prewriting   Writing   Revising
       Proofreading   Publishing

Curriculum Connection   Writing for Art   280

Books to Enjoy   281

Unit Review   **282**   Extra Practice   285
Language Puzzlers/Challenge   **284**

UNIT THEME: **Meeting the Challenge of Progress**

Literature Model: **The Brooklyn Bridge: They Said It Couldn't Be Built**

UNIT 6   USING LANGUAGE TO DESCRIBE

PART 1   LANGUAGE AWARENESS ◆ ADJECTIVES

Writing in Your Journal   293

Writing with Adjectives   294
Proper and Demonstrative Adjectives   296
Using Adjectives to Compare   298
Words as Different Parts of Speech   301
VOCABULARY   Context Clues   302

Grammar-Writing Connection   How to Expand Sentences with
Adjectives   304

PART 2   A REASON FOR WRITING ◆ DESCRIBING

Creative Writing   Fine Arts   307

CRITICAL THINKING   A Strategy for Describing   308
LITERATURE   *The Yearling* by Marjorie Kinnan Rawlings   310
SPEAKING and LISTENING   Giving Descriptive Details   316
WRITING   Sensory Details   318
WRITING   Figurative Language   320
WRITING   Organizing a Descriptive Paragraph   322

Reading-Writing Connection   Focus on Mood   324

WRITING PROCESS   **Writing a Description**   326
Prewriting   Writing   Revising
Proofreading   Publishing

Curriculum Connection   Writing for Science   334

Books to Enjoy   335

Unit Review   **336**   Language Puzzlers/Challenge   342
Cumulative Review   **338**   Extra Practice   343

UNIT THEME: People and Wildlife

Literature Model: The Yearling

UNIT 7   USING LANGUAGE TO IMAGINE

PART 1 LANGUAGE AWARENESS ◆ ADVERBS

Writing in Your Journal   349

Writing with Adverbs   350
Using Adverbs to Compare   354
Using Negatives Correctly   356
Using Adjectives and Adverbs   358
Troublesome Adjectives and Adverbs   360
VOCABULARY Suffixes   362

Grammar-Writing Connection How to Expand Sentences with Adverbs 364

PART 2 A REASON FOR WRITING ◆ IMAGINING

Creative Writing Fine Arts   367

CREATIVE THINKING A Strategy for Imagining   368
LITERATURE ''The Open Window'' by Saki   370
SPEAKING and LISTENING Having Conversations   376
WRITING Elements of a Short Story   378
WRITING Third-Person Point of View   380

Reading-Writing Connection Focus on Dialogue in Fiction   382

WRITING PROCESS Writing a Short Story   384
            Prewriting Writing Revising
            Proofreading Publishing

Curriculum Connection Literature   392

Books to Enjoy   393

Unit Review   394   Extra Practice   397
Language Puzzlers/Challenge 396

Literature Model: The Open Window

UNIT THEME: The Creative Mind

x

UNIT 8   USING LANGUAGE TO CREATE

PART 1 LANGUAGE AWARENESS ◆ PREPOSITIONS, CONJUNCTIONS, AND INTERJECTIONS

Writing in Your Journal   403

Writing with Prepositions   404
Prepositional Phrases as Modifiers   407
Using Prepositions Correctly   410
Writing with Conjunctions   412
Writing with Interjections   414
VOCABULARY   Prefixes from Latin   416

Grammar-Writing Connection   How to Combine Sentences   418

PART 2 A REASON FOR WRITING ◆ CREATING

Creative Writing   Fine Arts   421

CREATIVE THINKING   A Strategy for Creating   422
LITERATURE   Poetry   424
SPEAKING and LISTENING   Choral Reading   428
WRITING   Poets Use Details   430
WRITING   Ballads   432

Reading-Writing Connection   Focus on the Narrative Voice   434

WRITING PROCESS   Writing a Poem   436
    Prewriting   Writing   Revising
    Proofreading   Publishing

Curriculum Connection   Composition   444

Books to Enjoy   445

Unit Review   446   Language Puzzlers/Challenge   452
Cumulative Review   448   Extra Practice   453

UNIT 9   USING LANGUAGE TO RESEARCH

PART 1   LANGUAGE AWARENESS ◆ VERBALS AND COMPLEX SENTENCES

Writing in Your Journal   **459**

Verbals   **460**
Clauses   **462**
Complex Sentences   **464**
Correcting Sentence Errors   **466**
VOCABULARY   Homophones and Homographs   **468**

Grammar-Writing Connection   How to Combine Sentences   **470**

PART 2   A REASON FOR WRITING ◆ RESEARCHING

Creative Writing   Fine Arts   **473**

CRITICAL THINKING   A Strategy for Researching   **474**
LITERATURE   "Tribute to an Inventor: Cyrus McCormick"
         by Alice Hengesbach   **476**
SPEAKING and LISTENING   An Oral Report   **480**
STUDY SKILLS   Gathering Firsthand Information   **482**
STUDY SKILLS   Taking Notes   **484**
WRITING   Paraphrasing   **486**
WRITING   Structuring and Documenting a Report   **488**

Reading-Writing Connection   Focus on Main Idea   **492**

WRITING PROCESS   **Writing a Research Report**   **494**
         Prewriting Writing Revising
         Proofreading Publishing

Curriculum Connection   Writing for Science   **502**

Books to Enjoy   **503**

Unit Review   **504**   Extra Practice   **507**
Language Puzzlers/Challenge   **506**

UNIT 10   FOLKLORE

PART 1   LANGUAGE AWARENESS ◆ SUBJECT-VERB AGREEMENT

Writing in Your Journal   513

Making Subjects and Verbs Agree   514
Forms of *be, have,* and *do*   516
Agreement with Collective Nouns   518
Special Problems of Agreement   520
Special Problems of Agreement   522
VOCABULARY   Denotation and Connotation   524

Grammar-Writing Connection   How to Combine Sentences   526

PART 2   COMPOSITION ◆ THE TRADITION OF FOLKLORE

Creative Writing   Fine Arts   529

LITERATURE   "Tiger Story, Anansi Story" retold by Philip Sherlock   530
SPEAKING and LISTENING   The Oral Tradition   536
WRITING   Elements of a Folktale   538

Reading-Writing Connection   Focus on Your Growth as a Writer   540

Curriculum Connection   Writing for Social Studies   542

Books to Enjoy   543

Unit Review	544	Language Puzzlers/Challenge	550
Cumulative Review	546	Extra Practice	551

UNIT THEME: African and West Indian Folklore

Literature Model: Tiger Story, Anansi Story

WRITER'S REFERENCE BOOK

◆ Study Skills Lessons   **558**

◆ Dictionary of Knowledge   **576**

◆ Thesaurus   **588**

◆ Reports, Letters, Notes   **608**

◆ Spelling Guide   **613**

◆ Mechanics Lessons

    Capitalization   **616**

    Punctuation   **628**

◆ Diagraming Guide   **648**

◆ Grammar Handbook   **657**

◆ Glossary of Usage   **677**

◆ Writing and Computers   **683**

◆ Index   **691**

AWARD ◆ LITERATURE ◆ WINNING

The Black Pearl
by Scott O'Dell

The Brooklyn Bridge: They Said It Couldn't Be Built
by Judith St. George

The Yearling
by Marjorie Kinnan Rawlings

LITERATURE

JUG BANDS

from

Kids' America
by Steven Caney

The jug band is an American invention but no one is exactly sure just when or where in America these bands began. During the 1920's a record company asked a country jug band who played snappy rhythms to make a record. The band became a hit and featured a long jug solo which attracted attention. Soon people all over America (but mostly in the South) were listening to the country music of groups like the Memphis Jug Band, Cris Cannon and his Jug Stompers, and the Dixieland Jug Blowers.

There is no typical jug band or jug band music — almost any song can be played in the style. And the style depends on what instruments the band has to play music with: Jug band instruments include nearly any "real" instrument or any household object that can sound a note, beat, click, honk, tap, thump, or buzz. Jug band musicians have been known to play their music on washboards, hubcaps, home radiators, combs, cans, cowbells, spoons, whistles, and bicycle pumps, as well as the more traditional instruments for melody including the banjo, guitar, kazoo, harmonica, and fiddle.

LITERATURE: Nonfiction

Introductory Unit

Literature in Your World

In the *World of Language,* literature plays a key role. Literature unlocks your imagination. It opens your mind to the world of ideas. Through literature you can enter any time and any place. You can experience many different adventures, meet people you would never meet, share ideas with the greatest minds. Literature is indeed a key — to expanding your world and to enriching your world of language.

Writing in Your World

When you read literature, you enter the world of the writer. You bring to that world your knowledge and experiences. Often you respond to literature by writing. That is natural, for writing and reading are a team. They enhance each other although they are distinctly different.

Writing is a way of connecting yourself to the outside world and to your inner world of thoughts and dreams. Writing is talk written down, but it is more. Unlike spoken words, written words can be changed. They can be shaped and improved. Writing is thinking. Writing helps you understand your world, and it can help you change it! That is a powerful thought, but writing is powerful. It deserves a special place in your world and in the world of language.

What Is a Writer?

A writer is anyone who writes. You are a writer whenever you jot down a message, write a letter, or create a story. You do many kinds of writing, and you write for many reasons. Here are three kinds of writing that you will try this year.

Writing to Inform ◆ Writing can help you get something done in the world. You might write a business letter, for example, to someone to let them know about a particular problem.

Writing to Create ◆ You can use your imagination to write a poem, a play, or a story.

Expressive Writing ◆ You can use writing to express what you think or feel—to explore your ideas, plans, and impressions. It is a kind of talking to yourself.

Writing for yourself is a very important kind of writing. An ideal place for such writing is in a writer's journal.

Journal Writing

A journal is a writer's best friend. Carry one with you and you're always prepared to

- capture an idea by jotting it down
- experiment with all kinds of writing
- think things through and explain things to yourself
- note what you think about books, movies, music
- record your impressions and your experiences

A journal can be a special notebook, a section of another notebook, or a notebook made by stapling paper in a folder. Once you have your journal, use it as a writer. You will find many ideas for journal writing throughout this book.

Introducing the Writing Process

Sometimes you want to write something, make it really good, polish it, and then share it with others. To do this, focus on the *process of writing*. Take time to think, plan, get ideas, and make changes. Do not expect to write a perfect piece the first time. Take time to go through the writing process.

The writing process breaks writing into steps. For each step there are many *strategies* — ways of working — that you can learn. There are ways to get ideas and organize ideas. There are hints for how to get started and how to keep going. There are strategies for improving your writing and sharing it.

At the end of each unit, you will use the writing process to produce and ''publish'' a composition. You will be well prepared to do this by the other lessons in the unit. In each unit the following lessons lead up to the writing process.

- A **Thinking Skills** lesson gives you a thinking strategy to use in reading and writing.
- A **Literature** lesson gives you a model for the kind of writing you will do.
- A **Speaking and Listening** lesson enables you to first use oral language to develop the communication skills you need.
- The **Writing** lessons focus on the kind of writing you will be doing as you use the writing process.
- **Connection** lessons help you apply what you learn in grammar and literature lessons to writing.

Using the Writing Process

WRITER'S HINT

As you write, keep these two guidelines in mind.

1. Purpose Why are you writing? To tell a story? To persuade your readers? To give information?

2. Audience Who will read what you write? Someone your own age? Someone younger? An adult?

Write a Description

On the next four pages, you will have a preview of the five stages of the writing process: *prewriting, writing, revising, proofreading,* and *publishing*. You will try each one.

Writers often start with prewriting and end by publishing. They may, however, go back and forth among the other stages. With each stage there is an activity. When you have completed all five activities, you will have written a description.

Read the Writer's Hint now. For your description, your *purpose* is to describe an object so accurately your audience can "see" it. Your *audience* is your classmates.

1 Prewriting ◆ Getting ready to write

Have you ever said, "I don't know what to write about"? If so, you are not alone. Most writers feel that way before they start writing. How can you get the ideas you need? There are lots of ways. Here are just a few prewriting strategies for getting ideas for writing: brainstorm, make a cluster map, keep a journal, or read books or articles.

PREWRITING IDEA

Using Your Senses

You are a unique individual and you express your individuality in many ways. One way is through the things you own. Take your notebook, for example. Have you personalized it, perhaps by writing on the cover? Such an object is interesting to describe, for it reveals much about its owner.

Choose an object at hand to describe. Study it and write down every detail you notice. As you observe, think of the five senses. What does it look like? Does it make a sound if you drop it or open it? What does it feel like? Does it have a smell? As you observe, take notes. Your notes can just be words.

2 Writing ♦ Putting your ideas on paper

You have chosen the object you will describe. You have observed it carefully and taken notes. You have gathered some ideas. It's time to start writing — but you may not know how to get started. Sometimes once you start, you may not know how to keep going.

The important thing is just to start writing. Don't worry if your ideas are out of order or if you make spelling errors. You will be able to improve your writing when you revise and proofread.

WRITING IDEA

Starting with a Question

Put your prewriting notes in front of you before you begin writing your description. How can you begin? You might start with a question, such as *What does my notebook tell the observer about me, its owner?* As you write, use your notes to give details that tell exactly what makes the object you chose unique. You will not use all the details in your notes. Rather, you will choose those that suit your writing purpose. You may wish to end your description with a concluding sentence, such as *Anyone glancing at my notebook would know it could only belong to me.*

3 Revising ♦ Making changes to improve your writing

Reading to yourself is the first part of the revising strategy. As you read, think about your purpose. Did you stick to your purpose of describing an object? Did you forget to describe and start telling a story? Think about your audience. Were you writing for your classmates? Will they understand what you wrote?

The second part of the revising strategy is sharing with a partner. Read your writing aloud. Ask your partner to make suggestions and to ask questions. Think about your partner's suggestions. Then make only the changes *you* feel are important.

REVISING IDEA

Reading to Yourself and Reading to a Partner

First read your description to yourself. Did you really write a description? Will your classmates be able to "see" what you are describing? Make changes to improve your description. You can cross out words, write in new words, or draw arrows to show where to move words or sentences.

Your writing may look messy at this point. That is all right.

Next read your description to a partner. Ask "*What part did you like best? Is there any part that you would like to know more about?*" Listen to your partner's suggestions. Then make changes you think will improve your description.

4 Proofreading ♦ Looking for and fixing errors

After you have made sure your writing says what you want it to say, proofread for correctness. Check capital letters, punctuation, indenting, and spelling. Then make a clean copy in your best handwriting. A correct copy is a courtesy to your reader.

PROOFREADING IDEA

One Thing at a Time

It is hard to look for every kind of error at once. Check for one thing at a time. First check indenting, then capitalization, then punctuation. Check your spelling last.

5 Publishing ♦ Sharing your writing with others

There are many ways to share your writing. You may read it aloud to others. You may record it with a tape recorder or post it on a bulletin board. One of the best parts of writing is hearing or seeing your audience's response.

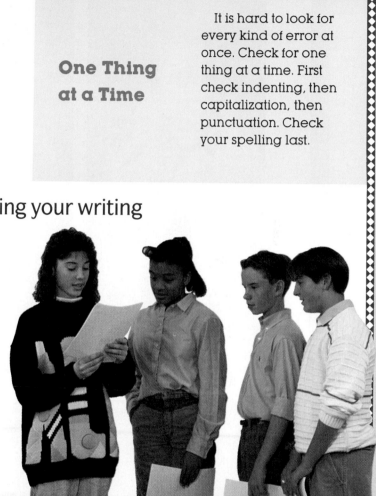

PUBLISHING IDEA

A Guessing Game

Take turns reading your descriptions aloud to each other. If several of you have described the same kind of object, such as a notebook, place those objects together on a table or desk. After you read your description, see if your classmates can use the details you gave to pick out your object among the "crowd".

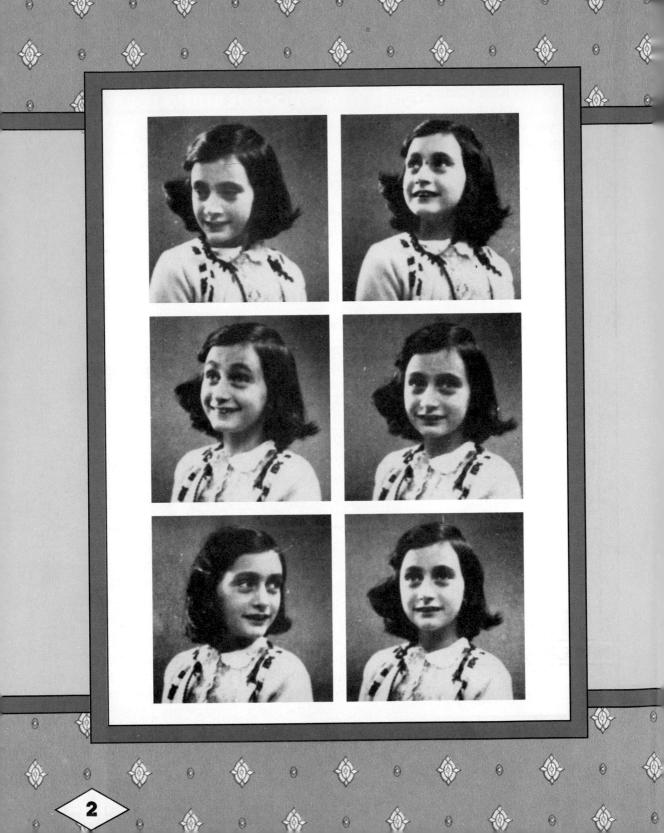

UNIT ONE

EXPRESSING YOURSELF AS A

WRITER

PART ONE

Unit Theme *Personal Writing*

Language Awareness Sentences

PART TWO

Literature *Anne Frank: The Diary of a Young Girl* translated by B.M. Mooyaart

Composition Personal Writing

Writing
IN YOUR JOURNAL

WRITER'S WARM-UP ◆ Many people write their thoughts and daily events in a journal. People have done this since writing began. Why might it be interesting to read an ancestor's diary? Write in your journal your ideas about personal writing. See how many reasons you can give as the benefits of personal writing.

Imagine you have just moved into a new neighborhood. What would you want to tell a new friend about yourself? How would you express your thoughts?

1 Writing Four Kinds of Sentences

A sentence expresses a complete thought. There are four kinds of sentences. The chart below will help you recognize and write each kind. Notice how each kind of sentence begins and ends.

Kind of Sentence	Purpose	End Mark	Example
Declarative	makes a statement	.	Anne Frank kept a fascinating diary.
Interrogative	asks a question	?	Why was Anne's diary so interesting?
Imperative	gives a command or makes a request	.	Read her diary to find out.
Exclamatory	expresses strong feeling	!	What an amazing story it tells!

If a statement, question, or command expresses strong feeling, it becomes an exclamatory sentence and ends with an exclamation mark.

■ **This is a great book! Did I like it! Don't miss it!**

> **Summary** ◆ A **sentence** is a group of words that expresses a complete thought. The four kinds of sentences are **declarative**, **interrogative**, **imperative**, and **exclamatory**. Always capitalize the first word in a sentence and use correct end punctuation.

Guided Practice

Name the kind of sentence each of the following is.

1. Anne Frank and her family hid from the Nazis in an attic.
2. Have you heard the story of their experience?
3. Read about Anne's thoughts and feelings in her diary.
4. What a remarkable record it is!

Practice

A. Write *declarative*, *interrogative*, *imperative*, or *exclamatory* to identify each sentence. Write the correct end punctuation mark.

5. Anne Frank lived in Holland during World War II
6. When did she and her family go into hiding
7. What she must have endured
8. Find out about her hopes and fears
9. How brave she was
10. I admire her courage and spirit
11. Please check the facts about her life
12. There is an Anne Frank museum in Amsterdam
13. What is on display at this museum
14. Don't miss the photographs of Anne and her family

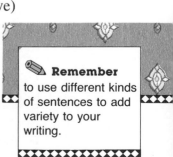

B. Rewrite each sentence, changing it to the kind of sentence indicated in parentheses.

EXAMPLE: Many people write diaries. (interrogative)
ANSWER: Do many people write diaries?

15. How revealing a diary can be! (declarative)
16. You can explore what you really think. (imperative)
17. It's like talking to a special friend. (exclamatory)
18. A diary is a daily account. (interrogative)
19. Could you ask someone to read it? (declarative)
20. Would you show it to anyone? (imperative)
21. Is a diary personal? (exclamatory)
22. You can illustrate your diary. (interrogative)
23. That's the truth. (exclamatory)
24. You should write something about yourself. (imperative)

Apply ◆ Think and Write

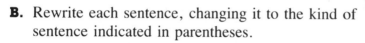

From Your Writing ◆ Add variety and interest to the writing you did for the Writer's Warm-up. Make some changes so that your writing includes the four different kinds of sentences. Discuss the two versions of your writing with a partner.

✎ **Remember** to use different kinds of sentences to add variety to your writing.

2 Parts of Speech in Sentences

Each word in a sentence works in a special way to help express a complete thought. Study the parts-of-speech chart below. Notice that a word is classified as one of eight parts of speech based on its function in a particular sentence. Find words that are used as examples for more than one part of speech.

Nouns name persons, places, things, or ideas. Sam kept a record of his march for freedom to Washington, D.C.
Pronouns take the place of nouns. Although the journal is his, Sam lets us read it.
Adjectives describe or modify nouns or pronouns. The worn pages contain a personal account of the freedom march.
Verbs express action or being. On August 28, 1963, Sam records, "Today we march to the Lincoln Memorial." There Martin Luther King cried, "We are free at last!"
Adverbs describe or modify verbs, adjectives, or other adverbs. I eagerly read the very moving story.
Conjunctions join words or groups of words. King wanted equality and justice, but he never used violence.
Prepositions relate nouns or pronouns to other words in a sentence. This picture of Sam appeared in the newspaper.
Interjections express emotion or feeling. Wow! He looks so different! My, what wonderful memories he saved!

Summary ◆ How a word is used in a sentence determines its part of speech. Understanding how words function helps you use them to communicate your ideas clearly.

Guided Practice

Tell the part of speech of each underlined word in the sentences below. Discuss your answer by using the chart on page 6.

1. Martin Luther King worked bravely for racial justice.
2. Both black and white people supported him and his crusade.
3. Oh, look at the number of people at this demonstration!

Practice

A. Complete each sentence below, using words from the list. Each word must function as the part of speech named in the blank.

met	only	at	in	loud	recent
him	well	oh	he	about	events

4. Not all diaries are (preposition) serious subjects.
5. For example, I kept a diary during a (adjective) trip.
6. I recorded the (noun) of each day.
7. One day my dog, Alf, (verb) a skunk.
8. Alf (adverb) barked (preposition) the skunk at first.
9. (interjection), how I hoped (pronoun) wouldn't rush at the skunk!

B. Read the rest of the diary entry. Write the part of speech that matches the way each underlined word is used in its sentence.

10. All three of us stood in a circle for a moment. 11. Then Alf circled the tree near the skunk. 12. I shouted at Alf to stop. 13. My shout pierced the air, and Alf froze in his tracks. 14. What a frozen moment in time that was! 15. Right then I slowly led Alf away. 16. It was definitely the right thing to do. 17. Alf could match any dog I know. 18. He was no match for a skunk!

Apply • Think and Write

Dictionary of Knowledge • Martin Luther King was awarded the 1964 Nobel Peace Prize. In the Dictionary of Knowledge read about the history of this prize and some of its famous recipients. Write several headlines announcing the award throughout the years. Can you identify the part of speech of each word in your headlines?

✏️ **Remember**
to use the parts of speech carefully to communicate your ideas clearly.

Invent an imaginary creature by combining two animal names. Then describe your creature's special abilities. For example: *An eaglephant dominates the world by its large size and keen eyesight.*

3 Complete Subjects and Predicates

Every sentence has two parts—a subject and a predicate. Each word in the sentence belongs to one of these two sentence parts. In the sentences below, all the words in the subject part are shown in blue. The words in the predicate part are shown in green. Notice that each of these sentence parts can be one or more words.

> Young Theodore Roosevelt went to Egypt with his family.
> He kept a diary during this trip.
> Every diary entry has the date and place of a visit.
> His accounts of this trip are entertaining.
> They inform.

All the words in the subject part of each sentence form the complete subject. The complete subject contains the topic of the sentence and any words that modify, or describe, it. The words in the predicate part together form the complete predicate, which tells what the subject of the sentence is or does.

> **Summary** ♦ The **complete subject** is all the words in the subject part of a sentence. It names someone or something. The **complete predicate** is all the words in the predicate part of a sentence. It tells what the subject is or does. Carefully choose the words you need in each sentence part to write about a topic clearly and accurately.

Guided Practice

Name the complete subject and the complete predicate in each sentence.

1. The personal writings of some famous people have become books.
2. Theodore Roosevelt's boyhood diaries were published.
3. He became the twenty-sixth President of the United States.

Think of a sentence that describes how a thing or a person did something. Then try to turn your sentences around.

EXAMPLE: *The plane rose swiftly. Swiftly rose the plane.*

5 Subject-Verb Order

The subject-verb order in English sentences is not always the same. Using variety in subject-verb order can make your writing more interesting for a reader.

Normal Word Order In most declarative sentences the subject comes before the verb. This is called normal word order.

■ Anne Frank's secret hiding `place` `was` in an office building.

Inverted Word Order In some sentences the subject follows the verb. This is called inverted word order.

■ Behind a hidden door `was` a secret `place.`

The subject may follow the verb when the sentence begins with *here* or *there*.

■ There `were` `people` in the secret hiding place.

In interrogative sentences the subject often follows the verb or comes between the parts of a verb.

■ `Were` `people` in this secret place?
■ `Were` `people` `hiding` in this secret place?

You (Understood) The subject of an imperative sentence is understood to be *you*, although the word *you* is not used.

■ `(You)` `Do` not `talk` loudly in the secret hiding place.
■ `(You)` Anne, `do` not `talk` loudly.

In the second sentence, *Anne* is not the subject. It is the name of the person being spoken to. Names used in this way are set off from the rest of the sentence by commas.

> **Summary** ◆ A subject may come before or after a verb. It may come between the parts of a verb or be understood.

Practice

A. Find the complete subject and the complete predicate in each sentence. Then write the complete subject.

4. Theodore Roosevelt visited Cairo, Egypt, in 1872.
5. He wrote in his diary about the pyramids there.
6. Theodore's family traveled for two hours to the site.
7. Great numbers of birds were sighted by him along the way.
8. The Sphinx was the first monument stop on the tour.
9. It is an ancient Egyptian figure with the body of a lion.
10. Its head is that of a man.
11. This giant figure should be seen from a distance.
12. A person of average height is about the size of its nose.
13. Theodore's keen observations of the figure were noted.

B. From the facts above, supply the missing sentence parts below. Label each part you supply *complete subject* or *complete predicate*.

14. _____ enjoyed his trip to Cairo.
15. _____ traveled with young Theodore.
16. _____ kept a diary during his travels.
17. The trip to the pyramids _____ .
18. _____ is an ancient Egyptian figure.
19. The size of the Sphinx _____ .
20. _____ cannot be appreciated up close.
21. The body of the Sphinx _____ .
22. The nose of the Sphinx _____ .
23. The head of the Sphinx _____ .

Apply ◆ Think and Write

An Ancient Riddle ◆ In the stories of ancient Greece, a Sphinx with the head of a woman would ask passersby this riddle: What has one voice and yet is four-footed first, then two-footed, and finally, three-footed?

Discuss possible answers to the riddle of the Sphinx. Carefully explain the best answer in your journal. Be sure each of your sentences has a complete subject and a complete predicate.

> ✎ **Remember** that every sentence needs a complete subject and a complete predicate.

Suppose you could speak in sentences of two words only. Build a chain story using only two-word sentences.

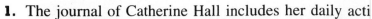

4 Simple Subjects and Predicates

How is a sentence built? All sentences are built on the same basic structure. Find the main word or words in the complete subject and the main word or words in the complete predicate. These words are called the simple subject and the simple predicate. They are often called just the subject and the verb. Together they form the base on which the sentence and its message are built.

Simple Subject, or Subject   This is usually a noun or pronoun. In each sentence below, the simple subject is shown in darker blue.

1. A young **girl** from New England wrote a historic journal.
2. **She** began it in 1830.
3. **Catherine Hall** was the name of this journal writer.

Note that in sentence **2**, the complete subject is just one word; it is also the simple subject. In sentence **3**, the simple subject is two words because it is someone's name.

Simple Predicate, or Verb   Of course, this is always a verb. The simple predicate is shown in darker green in each sentence below.

4. Catherine **lived** with her father and younger sister.
5. Her mother and baby brother **died**.
6. Her closest friend, Cassie, **did** not **keep** a journal.

Notice that in sentence **5**, the complete predicate is just one word; it is also the simple predicate, or verb. In sentence **6**, the verb is two words that are interrupted by the adverb *not*.

> **Summary** ◆ The **simple subject** is the main word or words in the complete subject. It is usually a noun or a pronoun. The **simple predicate** is the main word or words in the complete predicate. It is always a verb. Together the subject and the verb usually carry the main message in your writing.

Guided Practice

Can you find the basic parts of each sentence? Name th[e]
and the verb in each.

1. The journal of Catherine Hall includes her daily acti[vi]
2. She had usually written about her home and her sch[ool]
3. Her simple words create lasting images.

Practice

A. Write and label the simple subject and the verb in e[ach]

4. This interesting journal was really written by J[o]
5. Blos received a Newbery Medal for this fiction[al]
6. Her account of Civil War times is called *A Gat[hering of]
Days*.
7. Catherine finds a surprising message in her jou[rnal]
8. A runaway slave is asking her for help!

B. Expand each set of simple subject and verb into a c[omplete]
sentence.

9. author was awarded
10. journal is
11. she writes
12. writer researches
13. school is
14. fugitive n[
15. man has s[
16. message a[
17. story incl[u
18. words ma[

C. Write four sentences, using the words below. Choos[e]
that can work together as subject and verb, then ad[d]
words to build a sentence. Add endings to words if [you]
wish.

EXAMPLE: The mysterious **intruder tiptoed** silently up t[

plunge   gaze   tear   intruder   drizzle
tiptoe   rain   hawk   sparkle   dream

Apply ◆ Think and Write

A Journal Entry ◆ Write a journal entry telling about
something surprising, humorous, or exciting that you h[ave]
witnessed in the past week. Choose subjects and verbs [to]
tell the story clearly.

Guided Practice

Name the subject and verb in each sentence. Then tell if each sentence has *inverted word order*, *normal word order*, or *you* (*understood*) as the subject.

1. Read about Anne Frank in *The Diary of a Young Girl*.
2. Anne did not write in her diary every day.
3. Did Anne yearn for the outdoors?

Practice

A. Write each sentence, underlining the subject once and the verb twice. Write (*you*) as the subject before each imperative sentence. Identify the subject-verb order as *normal*, *inverted*, or (*you*) *understood*.

4. Anne missed flowers, birds, and the sky.
5. There was a window in her attic.
6. Anne gazed at the sun and the moon from there.
7. Can she enjoy nature through the window?
8. Imagine Anne's feelings.
9. Nature calmed Anne at times.
10. Anne wrote about the beauties of nature.
11. Do you use a journal to explore your feelings?

B. Rewrite the sentences below. Add variety by changing the sentences to inverted word order.

12. Anne Frank's thirteenth birthday arrived on June 14, 1942.
13. A small diary was among her favorite presents.
14. The record of an amazing survival was soon written between its red-checkered covers.
15. Deep feelings were written in Anne's diary.
16. The final diary entry was made on August 1, 1944.
17. Anne's diary remained in the attic with other books and papers.
18. The diary was found in Anne's room.

Apply • Think and Write

Sentence Variety ◆ In her diary, Anne Frank often tells how much she longs for the outdoors. Imagine staying indoors for two years! Write a paragraph about the things you would miss. Use variety in subject-verb order.

Remember to vary the subject-verb order in your sentences to make your writing more interesting.

Think of an action. Think of two persons or things that can perform that action. Use all three in a sentence.

EXAMPLES: *Boats and spirits can sink. Sheep and thoughts often wander.*

6 Compound Subjects and Verbs

The word *compound* means "composed of two or more parts." In a sentence the parts of a compound are joined by these connecting words, called conjunctions: *and*, *but*, *or*, *nor*.

Two or more simple subjects that share the same verb are called a compound subject. Notice the conjunction that joins the subjects in sentence **3** below. What verb do these subjects share?

1. ☐ Theodore Roosevelt ☐ valued ☐ natural resources.
2. ☐ John Muir ☐ valued ☐ natural resources.
3. ☐ Theodore Roosevelt ☐ and ☐ John Muir ☐ valued ☐ natural resources.

Two or more verbs that share the same subject are called a compound verb. Notice the conjunction that joins the verbs in sentence **6**. What subject do these verbs share?

4. ☐ John Muir ☐ was born ☐ in Scotland.
5. ☐ John Muir ☐ lived ☐ in the United States.
6. ☐ John Muir ☐ was born ☐ in Scotland but ☐ lived ☐ in the United States.

> **Summary** ◆ A **compound subject** is two or more simple subjects that have the same verb. A **compound verb** is two or more verbs that have the same subject. Use compound subjects and compound verbs to combine ideas in your writing.

Guided Practice

Name each compound subject and each compound verb. Name the conjunction that joins the parts of each compound.

1. John Muir visited Yosemite and stayed for six years!
2. Forests and parks are vital resources but are abused sometimes.
3. Young children or senior citizens may enter parklands without charge.

Practice

A. Write and label all compound subjects and compound verbs. Circle the conjunctions that connect parts of each compound.

4. Muir emigrated from Scotland to Wisconsin and went to college there.
5. He once walked from Indiana to the Gulf of Mexico and recorded his observations.
6. Wildlife and flowers were noted by him in a journal.
7. Yosemite National Park and Sequoia National Park were established largely through his efforts.
8. Redwoods and sequoias are found along the Pacific coast.

B. Use compound subjects or compound verbs to combine each pair of sentences.

9. Muir Woods was named after John Muir. Muir Woods was not donated by him.
10. It is located north of San Francisco. It contains many acres.
11. Evergreen ferns grow among the redwoods. Ladyferns grow among the redwoods.
12. Redwoods thrive in a damp climate. Ferns thrive in a damp climate.
13. This land is a national monument. This land is also for people's enjoyment.

C. Revise these short sentences to make them more interesting. Use either a compound subject or a compound verb to expand the meaning of each sentence.

14. Jack visited Yosemite National Park.
15. My friend Maria has hiked in Muir Woods.
16. Our class saw John Muir's journal.
17. Many people keep travel journals.
18. You could write about a trip.

Apply • Think and Write

Combined Ideas • Write about a park or space in your area or region of the country. Describe its natural landscape and its plants and wildlife. Use compounds to combine ideas in your writing.

✎ **Remember**
to use compound subjects and compound verbs to combine your ideas.

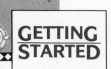
Make up a chain story. Begin with *"We found a boat, but. . . ."* The next person completes the sentence and says a new sentence, followed by *and*, *or*, or *but*. Each person adds to the story in this way.

7 Simple and Compound Sentences

Sometimes it is a good idea to join ideas in your writing, but be sure the ideas are closely related in meaning. Understanding how and when to join ideas in sentences can make your writing meaningful and interesting.

Simple Sentences   To express a single idea, use a simple sentence. A simple sentence is always built on one subject and one verb.

■ **Samuel Pepys** **was** **an English public official in the late 1600s.**

In a simple sentence, the subject or the verb or both may be compound, as shown in the sentence below.

■ **Writers** and **politicians** **study** and **admire** **his career.**
Notice that the compound parts of the verb share the same subjects.

Compound Sentences   You can join two or more simple sentences to form a compound sentence. Notice the different ways to connect two thoughts in the compound sentences below. Notice that each compound sentence has two complete thoughts—each with its own subject and verb.

> **MECHANICS ";?!"**
>
> Place a **comma** before the conjunction in a compound sentence unless the sentence is very short. A **semicolon** may take the place of the comma and conjunction. See pages 630–637 for more uses of the comma.

Pepys **wrote** a famous diary, **and** **he** also **served** in Parliament.
He **wrote** in code, **but** **it** **was** translated. **(Comma is optional.)**
The **diary** **tells** a personal story; **it** also **is** a historic record.

> **Summary** ◆ A **simple sentence** has one subject and one verb, either or both of which may be compound. A **compound sentence** consists of two or more simple sentences. Be sure to connect only complete thoughts that are closely related and to use appropriate punctuation.

Guided Practice

Identify the two simple sentences within each compound sentence. Tell how the complete thoughts are joined in each.

1. Pepys lived during a special period; it was the Restoration.
2. King Charles II was exiled, but then he was returned to power.
3. Trade was important during this time, and poetry was revived.

Practice

A. Write each sentence. Underline each subject once and each verb twice. Then label each sentence *simple* or *compound*.

4. Pepys lived in London and became head of the navy.
5. His last name is pronounced "peeps."
6. He kept a diary for nine years, and it fills nine volumes.
7. He wrote his diary in cipher, but it was decoded in 1819.
8. Cipher conceals meaning; it is a written code.

B. Revise these short, related simple sentences. Write a compound sentence to join each pair.

9. A diary is a personal record. It can be a public record.
10. It can be kept daily. It can be kept at frequent intervals.
11. Diaries and journals may be alike. They may be different.
12. A journal is often a public record. A diary is personal.
13. Pepys kept a personal diary. It told about political events.

C. Expand each simple sentence into a compound sentence. Be sure to join only related ideas.

14. Yoshio keeps a diary.
15. He describes his favorite places.
16. He imagines the details.
17. The reader can picture each sight.
18. All the senses are awakened.

19. Yoshio is a great observer.
20. He is a painter of words.
21. His pen is a paintbrush!
22. Yoshio shares his diary.
23. It is a pleasure to read.

Apply • Think and Write

A Reader's Choice • Suppose you could read any famous person's diary. Write a paragraph telling whose diary you would choose and why. Use both simple and compound sentences. Be sure that you have used correct punctuation in all your compound sentences.

✎ **Remember**
to use compound sentences to join related ideas in your writing.

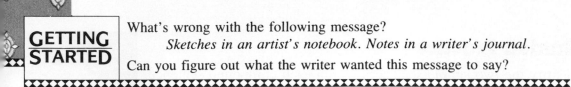

GETTING
STARTED

What's wrong with the following message?
Sketches in an artist's notebook. Notes in a writer's journal.
Can you figure out what the writer wanted this message to say?

8 Avoiding Sentence Errors

You can use what you know about sentence structure and punctuation to avoid the following common errors in writing.

Run-on Sentences   Sometimes two or more sentences are mistakenly written as one sentence. The two are separated by only a comma or do not have the necessary connecting word or semicolon. To correct a run-on sentence, make separate sentences or add a comma and a conjunction.

> **Run-on:** Leonardo da Vinci was a genius, he had great talents.
> **Correct:** Leonardo da Vinci was a genius. He had great talents.
> **Run-on:** He trained as a painter he was an excellent observer.
> **Correct:** He trained as a painter, and he was an excellent observer.

Sentence Fragments   Sometimes part of a sentence is mistakenly written as a sentence, beginning with a capital letter and ending with a punctuation mark. To avoid writing sentence fragments, make sure that every sentence contains a subject and a verb and expresses a complete thought.

> **Fragment:** He drew detailed plans. <u>For a flying machine.</u>
> **Correct:** He drew detailed plans for a flying machine.
> **Fragment:** <u>The design for hundreds of inventions.</u>
> **Correct:** Leonardo's notebooks contain the design for hundreds of inventions.

Summary ♦ Run-on sentences and sentence fragments are errors. Avoid these two serious errors in your writing.

Guided Practice

Tell whether each group of words is a sentence, a fragment, or a run-on sentence.

1. An artist, engineer, and scientist.
2. One of this Italian's famous paintings is the *Mona Lisa*.
3. This painting hangs in the Louvre museum many people view it.

Practice

A. Write each run-on sentence as two correct sentences.

4. He studied architecture, he drew plans for buildings.
5. He wrote his ideas in notebooks they show his many talents.
6. Leonardo was a sculptor he worked with different materials.
7. He studied anatomy his art reflects this knowledge.
8. He created great works of art, they are displayed worldwide.

B. The following notes about Leonardo da Vinci contain many fragments. Express the facts in complete sentences.

9. Leonardo's brilliant drawings. Powers of observation.
10. Sketches of flying machines. Plans for a parachute.
11. One of the great minds of all time.
12. Among Leonardo's most marvelous masterpieces.
13. Used backward handwriting. Need a mirror!

C. The paragraph below docs not contain beginning capitals or end punctuation. Write the paragraph correctly, using ten sentences.

(14–23) there are many kinds of artists they include musicians and writers creative people can be found in different fields of work many are in the performing arts some prefer the sciences Leonardo was a multitalented artist he was a rare individual for all times he filled many notebooks with his ideas great leaders pursued him they sought his advice on many topics.

Apply • Think and Write

Rewriting Notes ♦ Jot down some ideas for some project or hobby you might like to pursue. You may use fragments in your notes. Then rewrite your notes as sentences, avoiding run-ons and fragments.

> ✎ **Remember**
> not to use run-on sentences and fragments as sentences.

In two minutes think of as many words as you can that mean about the same thing as *happy*. Then do the same thing for *sad*.

VOCABULARY ◆
Using the Thesaurus

A **thesaurus** is a book of synonyms and antonyms. **Synonyms** are words with similar meanings. **Antonyms** are words with opposite meanings. In most thesauruses the entry words—the words that you look up—are arranged in alphabetical order. If you wish to replace a word in your writing or to find a word with a slightly different meaning, look up the original word in a thesaurus. Then choose the synonym or antonym that best expresses your desired meaning.

Study this entry for the word *urgent*.

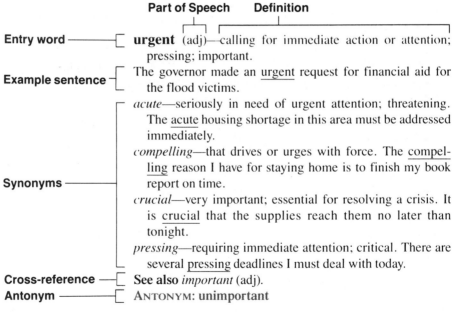

Part of Speech   Definition

Entry word ———— **urgent** (adj)—calling for immediate action or attention; pressing; important.

Example sentence — The governor made an <u>urgent</u> request for financial aid for the flood victims.

Synonyms —

acute—seriously in need of urgent attention; threatening. The <u>acute</u> housing shortage in this area must be addressed immediately.

compelling—that drives or urges with force. The <u>compelling</u> reason I have for staying home is to finish my book report on time.

crucial—very important; essential for resolving a crisis. It is <u>crucial</u> that the supplies reach them no later than tonight.

pressing—requiring immediate attention; critical. There are several <u>pressing</u> deadlines I must deal with today.

Cross-reference ——— See also *important* (adj).

Antonym ——————— ANTONYM: **unimportant**

Building Your Vocabulary

Create a sentence for each situation described below. Use a different synonym of *urgent* in each sentence.

1. You need help to fight a forest fire on the edge of town.

2. You are explaining to a friend why you cannot go to a movie.

3. You need to see a dentist because you have a toothache.

Practice

A. Study the Thesaurus entry on the opposite page and write answers to these questions.

    1. What part of speech is the entry word *urgent*?
    2. How many synonyms of *urgent* does the entry include?
    3. Which synonym means "driving one to do something?"
    4. What other entry word is related in meaning to *urgent*?
    5. What word is opposite in meaning to *urgent*?

B. The underlined words below are in the Thesaurus that begins on page 588. Rewrite each sentence. Follow the directions in parentheses and replace the underlined word.

    6. The fad of swallowing goldfish <u>disappeared</u> quickly. (Use slang.)
    7. We heard the <u>weak</u> sound of distant voices. (Use a synonym.)
    8. Some people <u>write</u> their names carelessly. (Fit the meaning.)
    9. Neatness counts; it is <u>important</u>. (Use an idiom.)
   10. Just <u>call</u> when you're ready to leave. (Use an informal word.)
   11. My aunt has an <u>easy</u> job with a travel agency. (Use slang.)
   12. Sam likes to <u>walk</u> for miles in the woods. (Fit the meaning.)

C. Imagine that you are stranded on a deserted island. You keep a journal while waiting for rescue. Write a paragraph telling of your experiences. Use synonyms of the following words in your journal entry.

       believe   careful   brave   fear   strong

Language Corner ◆ Word Meaning

At one time *brilliant* meant only "very bright" or "sparkling." Its meaning has expanded. Tell what *brilliant* means in the sentences below.

Rodin, a <u>brilliant</u> artist, sculpted *The Thinker*.
The young pianist gave a <u>brilliant</u> performance.
The <u>brilliant</u> on her finger sparkled in its simple setting.

How to Combine Sentence Parts

You know that every sentence contains a complete thought. Sometimes two sentences contain repeated information or related ideas. Such sentences can be combined to form one strong sentence. Notice how the two subjects in example **1** are combined in example **2**. Example **4** shows how the predicates in example **3** are combined.

1. Anne Frank lived in Holland. Her family lived in Holland.
2. Anne Frank and her family lived in Holland.

3. She hid from the Nazis. She kept a record of her experiences.
4. She hid from the Nazis and kept a record of her experiences.

Subjects and predicates are not the only parts of sentences that can be combined. Notice how the two short sentences in example **5** are joined to form the more efficient sentence in example **6**. Can you identify the parts of the sentences that are joined in example **6**?

5. Many people keep personal diaries. Many people keep journals.
6. Many people keep personal diaries and journals.

Simple sentences with related ideas can also be combined to form a compound sentence. Such sentences can be combined by adding a comma and the word *and, but,* or *or.* Notice how example **8** shows the relationship between the two sentences above it.

7. Many people read Anne's diary each year. They find it a deeply moving experience.
8. Many people read Anne's diary each year, and they find it a deeply moving experience.

The Grammar Game ◆ Create your own sentence examples! Write at least three pairs of sentences with parts that can be combined. Then exchange papers with a classmate and combine each other's sentences.

Working Together

As your group works on activities **A** and **B**, you will find that combining sentences can make your writing smooth and efficient.

In Your Group
♦ Encourage everyone to share ideas.   ♦ Address people by name. ♦ Listen carefully to each other.   ♦ Help the group finish on time.

A. Combine subjects, predicates, or other parts of sentences in each pair below. Write each new sentence.

1. Anyone can keep a diary. Anyone can record their experiences.
2. Diaries can be maintained for many years. Journals can be maintained for many years.
3. The diaries of famous people are interesting. The diaries of famous people are revealing.
4. I read a diary about a young student. I read a diary about his travels to India.
5. Most diaries are private. Some are made public.

B. Find pairs of sentences to combine in the paragraph below. Then write your new paragraph.

Martin began a diary several years ago. Each night he spends some time with it. He writes about the events of his day. He writes about his feelings and his ideas. He enjoys his diary. He likes keeping a record of his life.

WRITERS' CORNER ♦ Choppy Sentences

Using too many short, choppy sentences can make your writing boring and difficult to read.

CHOPPY: Martin went to his room. He closed the door. He wanted some privacy. It was time to write.

IMPROVED: Martin went to his room and closed the door. He wanted some privacy because it was time to write.

Read what you wrote for the Writer's Warm-up. Did you use too many choppy sentences? If you did, try to improve them.

JOSEPHINE AND MERCIE   painting by Edmund Charles Tarbell
The Corcoran Gallery of Art, Museum Purchase, Gallery Fund, 1909

UNIT
ONE

EXPRESSING YOURSELF
AS A

WRITER

═══════ **PART TWO** ═══════

Literature *Anne Frank: The Diary of a Young Girl,*
translated by B.M. Mooyaart

Composition **Personal Writing**

CREATIVE
Writing

FINE ARTS ◆ Study the painting "Josephine and Mercie " at the left. Then imagine that you find yourself in the painting. You are locked in time and cannot get out of the scene. What will you do? How will you explain your predicament to the two women? Record the conversation that will take place when the three of you try to find a solution to your problem.

LITERATURE

from

Anne Frank:
The Diary of a Young Girl

—translated by B.M. Mooyaart

At the end of World War II, the diary of a young Jewish girl was found in an old warehouse in the city of Amsterdam. In her diary, Anne Frank had recorded her deepest thoughts and feelings as well as the details of her daily life. Anne was thirteen when she started her diary in the summer of 1942. She was fifteen when she wrote the last entry in August, more than two years later.

Anne Frank and her family had moved to the Netherlands from Germany in 1933 to escape Adolf Hitler's anti-Jewish persecution. Anne and her sister Margot had lived there happily, and free. But when Germany invaded the Netherlands in 1940, new anti-Jewish laws severely restricted that freedom. By the time Anne began her diary, she could not attend public schools, go to movies, or even ride in trains. Yet, like many young people her age, Anne had more personal, deeper concerns. She was worried about finding ''a real friend.''

In 1941, Anne (third from right) walks with her father (center) and friends to a wedding.

Saturday, 20 June, 1942

I haven't written for a few days, because I wanted first of all to think about my diary. It's an odd idea for someone like me to keep a diary; not only because I have never done so before, but because it seems to me that neither I—nor for that matter anyone else—will be interested in the unbosomings of a thirteen-year-old schoolgirl. Still, what does that matter? I want to write, but more than that, I want to bring out all kinds of things that lie buried deep in my heart.

There is a saying that "paper is more patient than man"; it came back to me on one of my slightly melancholy days, while I sat chin in hand, feeling too bored and limp even to make up my mind whether to go out or stay at home. Yes, there is no doubt that paper is patient and as I don't intend to show this cardboard-covered notebook, bearing the proud name of "diary," to anyone, unless I find a real friend, boy or girl, probably nobody cares. And now I come to the root of the matter, the reason for my starting a diary: it is that I have no such real friend.

Let me put it more clearly, since no one will believe that a girl of thirteen feels herself quite alone in the world, nor is it so. I have darling parents and a sister of sixteen. I know about thirty people whom one might call friends—I have strings of boy friends, anxious to catch a glimpse of me and who, failing that, peep at me through mirrors in class. I have relations, aunts and uncles, who are darlings too, a good home, no—I don't seem to lack anything. But it's the same with all my friends, just fun and joking, nothing more. I can never bring myself to talk of anything outside the common round. We don't seem to be able to get any closer, that is the root of the trouble. Perhaps I lack confidence, but anyway, there it is, a stubborn fact and I don't seem to be able to do anything about it.

Hence, this diary. In order to enhance in my mind's eye the picture of the friend for whom I have waited so long, I don't want to set down a series of bald facts in a diary like most people do, but I want this diary itself to be my friend, and I shall call my friend Kitty. No one will grasp what I'm talking about if I begin my letters to Kitty just out of the blue, so albeit unwillingly, I will start by sketching in brief the story of my life.

My father was thirty-six when he married my mother, who was then twenty-five. My sister Margot was born in 1926 in Frankfort-on-Main, I followed on June 12, 1929, and, as we are Jewish, we emigrated to Holland in 1933, where my father was appointed Managing Director of Travies N.V. This firm is in close relationship with the firm of Kolen & Co. in the same building, of which my father is a partner.

The rest of our family, however, felt the full impact of Hitler's anti-Jewish laws, so life was filled with anxiety. In 1938 after the pogroms, my two uncles (my mother's brothers) escaped to the U.S.A. My old grandmother came to us, she was then seventy-three. After May 1940 good times rapidly fled: first the war, then the capitulation, followed by the arrival of the Germans, which is when the sufferings of us Jews really began. Anti-Jewish decrees followed each other in quick succession. Jews must wear a yellow star,[1] Jews must hand in their bicycles, Jews are banned from trains and are forbidden to drive. Jews are only allowed to do their shopping between three and five o'clock and then only in shops which bear the placard "Jewish shop." Jews must be indoors by eight o'clock and cannot even sit in their own gardens after that hour. Jews are forbidden to visit theaters, cinemas,

[1]To distinguish them from others, all Jews were forced by the Germans to wear, prominently displayed, a yellow six-pointed star.

and other places of entertainment. Jews may not take part in public sports. Swimming baths, tennis courts, hockey fields, and other sports grounds are all prohibited to them. Jews may not visit Christians. Jews must go to Jewish schools, and many more restrictions of a similar kind.

So we could not do this and were forbidden to do that. But life went on in spite of it all. Jopie used to say to me, "You're scared to do anything, because it may be forbidden." Our freedom was strictly limited. Yet things were still bearable.

Granny died in January 1942; no one will ever know how much she is present in my thoughts and how much I love her still.

In 1934 I went to school at the Montessori Kindergarten and continued there. It was at the end of the school year, I was in form 6B, when I had to say good-by to Mrs. K. We both wept, it was very sad. In 1941 I went, with my sister Margot, to the Jewish Secondary School, she into the fourth form and I into the first.

So far everything is all right with the four of us and here I come to the present day.

In July of 1942, everything changed for Anne and her family. Nazis were rounding up Jews in Amsterdam and sending them to concentration camps—and almost certain death. For Otto Frank and his family, the only escape was in hiding. With some Jewish neighbors, the Franks moved into what Anne called "the secret annex"— the top two floors of Mr. Frank's warehouse, behind a disguised door. For two years, these eight people lived secretly above the warehouse while work went on below. Friends brought food and other necessities to help them survive. An occasional glimpse through a crack in the window was all they saw of life outside for a long time. In the next diary entry, Anne expresses her feelings of frustration.

Saturday, 12 February, 1944

Dear Kitty,

    The sun is shining, the sky is a deep blue, there is a lovely breeze and I'm <u>longing</u>—so longing—for everything. To talk, for freedom, for friends, to be alone. And I do so long . . . to cry! I feel as if I'm going to burst, and I know that it would get better with crying; but I can't, I'm restless, I go from one room to the other, breathe through the crack of a closed window, feel my heart beating, as if it is saying, "Can't you satisfy my longings at last?"

    I believe that it's spring within me, I feel that spring is awakening, I feel it in my whole body and soul. It is an effort to behave normally, I feel utterly confused, don't know what to read, what to write, what to do, I only know that I am longing . . . !

Yours, Anne

Library Link ◆ *Although Anne Frank died in a concentration camp nearly fifty years ago, her story continues to reach millions of readers in many languages. Read more of Anne's entries in* The Diary of a Young Girl. *Anne Frank would be amazed that so many people are interested in a young girl's story.*

 ## Reader's Response

Do you think you would like to know Anne Frank? Why or why not?

Anne Frank:
The Diary of a Young Girl

 ## Responding to Literature

1. Try to imagine that you must hide in order to survive. How would you prepare for isolation from the world? In your journal, write about this unusual situation. Then share ideas from your journal entry with the class.

2. Anne said that, even with the restrictions, life was still bearable. What do you think made her so optimistic? What role might Anne's family have played in forming her attitude?

3. If, like Anne, you were going away for a long time and you were allowed to take only one book, which book would you choose? Tell why.

 ## Writing to Learn

Think and Discover ◆ Read this dictionary definition of *courage*. Then think about the courage of Anne Frank.

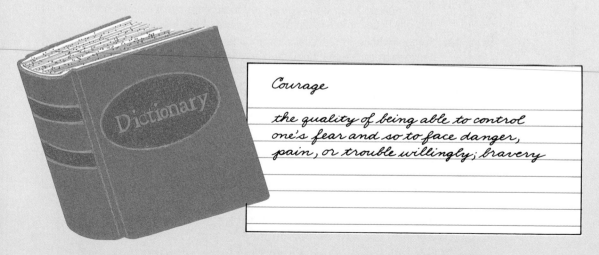

Dictionary

Courage

the quality of being able to control one's fear and so to face danger, pain, or trouble willingly; bravery

Write ◆ Write your own definition of courage.

Think of a topic that you like to talk about, such as your favorite pastime. State a few opinions on your topic. See how many classmates agree or disagree with your views.

SPEAKING and LISTENING ♦
Group Discussions

Working with others to solve a problem or to understand something requires good communication. This is true whether you are discussing an informal topic with friends or answering formal questions in the classroom. The following guidelines will help you make your contributions to discussions more meaningful.

Group Discussion Guidelines	
As a Speaker	1. First, remember that confidence in your personal views is essential to a good discussion.
	2. Thorough preparation, such as investigating facts, will help you contribute valuable, interesting insights to discussions.
	3. Prepare materials ahead of time that may help your discussion.
	4. Be prepared to state the topic and goal or to open the discussion about it. Do not worry about being "wrong" about a topic. Everyone has things to learn, and your effort will be appreciated.
	5. Speak honestly and politely. Refer to others by name as you build on or disagree with what has been said.
	6. Try to anticipate how others may disagree with your views.
	7. Remember to keep the focus on the topic. In a lively discussion, you can easily become excited and lose sight of the topic.
	8. Try to advance the discussion with what you say. This will build your confidence and also help stimulate others' thinking.
As a Listener	1. Make sure you and others understand the goal of the discussion.
	2. Be comfortable but maintain polite attention.
	3. Help others to make their views clear, even if you disagree with them. "Winning" is less important than the discussion's success.
	4. Listen carefully and critically. Evaluate what you hear and decide to support or disagree with it before you speak.

Summary ♦ Prepare as thoroughly as you can for a discussion. This will help you make and evaluate contributions that will benefit everyone involved in the discussion.

Guided Practice

Tell why you agree or disagree with each statement about discussions.

1. I am not sure my response is correct, but I'll say it anyway.
2. I am uneasy volunteering answers in class, so I won't bother.
3. If I disagree with someone, I should keep quiet.

Practice

A. Write *agree* or *disagree* for the attitude shown by each statement. Then write a sentence to explain your answers.

4. Tony thinks, "Why read the assignment? The story is dull, and I wouldn't have anything else to say about it."
5. "Well, that's my view," Carla says. "Let somebody else decide why it's right or wrong."
6. "Oh yeah?" Brad says in response to Sheila. "The truth is, you're never right about anything, Sheila."
7. "So that's my opinion," Juan replies, "and I don't care what anybody says. I won't change my mind about it."
8. "I've been listening carefully to what you said, Tim," Cathy says. "It was helpful, but I disagree because . . ."

B. Write how you would improve what each student does in a discussion. If no improvement is needed write *correct*.

9. Arnie suddenly breaks into the discussion to disagree, but he can't remember who had been speaking.
10. "I disagree," Oona says. "I'll read you this newspaper article that disproves those facts."
11. "Everyone seems to understand this topic more than I do," Brenda thinks. "I had better just keep quiet and agree."

C. Hold a group discussion with four or five of your classmates about a topic that interests you. As the discussion proceeds, follow the guidelines given in this lesson.

Apply ◆ Think and Write

Evaluating a Discussion ◆ Listen to a discussion at home or at school and take notes about it. Then write a paragraph about the discussion, explaining why it was or was not successful.

✎ **Remember** that your contributions are important in a group discussion.

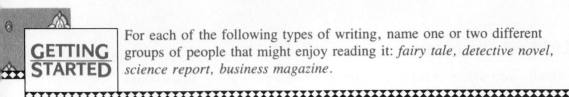

GETTING STARTED

For each of the following types of writing, name one or two different groups of people that might enjoy reading it: *fairy tale, detective novel, science report, business magazine.*

WRITING ♦
Identifying Purpose and Audience

Purpose In the early stages of writing, it is important to decide *why* you are writing. Defining a writing purpose helps you to communicate your ideas clearly.

Purpose is the reason for writing. It is your intent. For example, do you intend *to entertain* your readers with a play or a short story? Do you want *to persuade* them to accept your views through an editorial? Perhaps you want *to inform* them with a how-to essay. Or you may simply want *to express* your ideas.

What is the purpose for writing in each of the following forms?

a history textbook   a mystery novel   a journal entry

The textbook writer's purpose is *to inform*. The mystery novel writer's purpose is *to entertain*. The journal writer's purpose is *to express* thoughts.

Sometimes there is more than one purpose for writing a form. For example, an article describing ways to save energy in a home is written to persuade readers as well as to inform them.

Audience The audience, or people that you write for, should be identified. It is important to keep a specific audience in mind as you write. For example, writing a letter to a friend is very different from writing a composition for your teacher.

You often know the audience you are writing for, such as yourself, friends, relatives, or teachers. Sometimes, however, you write for a general audience. You may not know any member of such a group. In this case, it is helpful to choose one member of the group as a representative reader before you begin writing.

Summary ♦ Know your writing purpose and your audience. This will help you make effective writing choices.

Guided Practice

Identify a purpose and a possible audience for each form of writing.

1. reading textbook
2. book of nursery rhymes
3. editorial about an election
4. one-act play
5. advertisement for computers
6. encyclopedia
7. comic book
8. sports column

Practice

A. For each writing idea, write a purpose and a possible audience.

9. a story about a young artist struggling to fulfill her goals
10. an article that tells how to set up a small business at home
11. an essay about a school's most important needs by a young girl who wants a place on the student council
12. a fantasy story about animals that learn to talk
13. a poem about a memorable hero in a community

B. The purpose of the selection below is to persuade an audience through a letter to a newspaper. However, both the purpose and intended audience are unclear. Rewrite and improve the selection.

I have to wonder why doggies have to be leashed up in this town. My dog, Caliban, is an Irish setter and he never bothers anybody. He's the friendliest animal on four legs. I don't think it's kind at all to keep an animal chained up all the time. I mean, aren't dogs supposed to be people's best friends? Maybe kids or grown-up officials could have a kind of town meeting to discuss this again. I wonder what the real statistics show about towns where dogs aren't leashed.

Apply ◆ Think and Write

A Persuasive Article ◆ Persuade readers of the value of a product, such as a toy or a type of food. Decide who your audience will be before you begin writing.

✎ **Remember**
to set a purpose and identify an audience for your writing.

Think of an idea for a story. See if anyone can name a few different ways to write the story. For example, a story about a favorite athlete could be written as fiction, as a poem, or as an essay.

WRITING ♦
Choosing an Appropriate Form

Deciding what form to use in your writing is sometimes difficult. This becomes easier with practice, and as you become more aware of what forms other writers use. The more forms of writing you know, the more inventive you can be in combining them into new forms. For example, knowing how to express your opinions in an editorial can help you write a persuasive advertisement for a product.

As you think about what form to use, ask yourself questions about it. For example, "Is an article in the school newspaper an appropriate form for what I want to say? Or would a poster on the subject be more suitable?" Be sure the form you choose is right for your purpose and your audience. Do you want to entertain, inform, or persuade? For whom are you writing? What would they be interested in reading?

The chart below lists some of the forms of writing you can choose to use. Remember: You can adapt or combine these forms creatively to fit your writing needs.

Form of Writing	Appropriate Use
Diary	personal entries
Journal; Notebook	personal insights; creative writing ideas
News; Editorial Articles	to inform, persuade, report
Fliers; Stickers; Posters	to advertise, persuade, entertain
Fiction; Poetry; Songs	to entertain; to express personal views
Critical or Scholarly Papers	to evaluate, review, or share information
Personal or Formal Essays	reflections on specific subjects

Summary ♦ Choose the best form for your writing by considering your idea, your purpose, and your audience.

Guided Practice

What form would you use for each writing situation?

1. an interview with a surfing champion for classmates to read
2. what travelers might like to know about a trip to Japan
3. a campaign slogan for a local politician
4. facts about an issue on a voting ballot
5. your reaction to a work of art

Practice

A. Each selection below is part of a specific form. Write the name of the form for each selection.

   6. Voters in this city are ready for a change. They are weary of the current ineffective solutions to major problems.
   7. In the town lived a shy boy named Mark. Mark was so shy that he wrote notes to people instead of talking to them.
   8. The Roman emperor Claudius was an interesting man. In A.D. 20, Claudius made many important decisions.

B. Write a sentence that tells what is *not* appropriate about each writing situation below.

   9. a scientific report filled with personal opinions
   10. an account of a disaster in an entertaining feature
   11. an editorial that describes the facts on only one side of an issue
   12. a set of important safety instructions mixed with jokes
   13. a book on advanced physics theories for preschool children

C. Think of three ideas that you have for topics to write about. Write the ideas and the form you could use for each one.

Apply • Think and Write

Dictionary of Knowledge • Many authors are known for writing in more than one form, such as poetry and fiction. Eloise Greenfield was such an author. Read about her in the Dictionary of Knowledge. Use a form of your own choice to write a response to the article.

✎ **Remember** to choose a form of writing that is appropriate for your purpose.

Focus on a Writer's Voice

Many writers, young and old, keep personal diaries. A diary is a record of a person's activities, thoughts, and feelings. A journal is somewhat different. Although a writer may use a journal in the same way that a diary is used, a journal serves many other purposes as well.

Why do writers keep journals? Writers, like everyone else, need a place to

♦ express personal views that they wish to get down on paper;
♦ record facts, details, and insights;
♦ record writing ideas that can be used at a later time.

Not only is a journal a more reliable record than memory, it is also a spur to thinking. It can help you organize your thoughts and feelings and encourage self-examination. A journal can also help you to see the world in new ways.

What about the writer's voice? When you write a story or poem for others, you may wonder what people will think of your voice — of the style that reveals your personality. In a journal, you can practice using different styles for various audiences. A journal allows you to experiment with your writing and to develop a voice that you are comfortable with.

In a diary, you may use your writer's voice in a different way. A diary is more private than a journal and needs no formal style. The writing is usually spontaneous and free flowing. Because you rarely have a literary aim in a diary, there is no public reaction to worry about.

The Writer's Voice ♦ You have learned that many people in history kept personal diaries or journals. Why do you think that people such as Anne Frank or Nathaniel Hawthorne used diaries or journals to express themselves? How can this form of writing help you to get ideas for your stories?

Working Together

A diary or journal can be both a record of personal experience and a helpful tool for story ideas. As a group, work on activities **A** and **B**.

In Your Group
• Be sure people understand the task.   • Remember to listen. • Address people by their names.   • Value all contributions.

A. Read this passage from Anne Frank's diary. Discuss her state of mind. How would you describe the voice she uses in her diary?

> A lot of people are fond of nature...but few are so shut away and isolated from that which can be shared alike by rich and poor. It's not imagination on my part when I say that to look up at the sky...makes me calm and patient...Mother Nature makes me humble and prepared to face every blow courageously. [Entry for June 15, 1944]

B. Journal writing is an individual rather than a group activity. However, combining individual entries can be the start of an un- usual and humorous story. Write a journal entry covering what happened yesterday in school. Then, with your group, choose various contributions from the group and combine them into a single journal entry. You may wish to add to the entry until you have a story. Share the journal entry, or story, with the rest of the class.

THESAURUS CORNER ◆ Word Choice

Word choice reflects the writer's voice. Look up each entry word below in the Thesaurus. Write a sentence containing a synonym for each one. The sentence and the synonym should carry the feeling suggested by the accompanying phrase in parentheses.

1. crowd (lawless, like barbarians)
2. fear (doctor's diagnosis)
3. house (turrets and a moat)
4. leader (limitless power)
5. talk (pro and con)

Writing Across the Curriculum Composition

The author Henry Miller said ''Writing, like life itself, is a voyage of discovery.'' This statement is an extended definition—one that goes beyond the dictionary definition of the word *writing*. Like other writers, you can write extended definitions as a way of discovering your own special views on a subject.

Writing to Learn

Think and Discover What does writing mean to you? Write nonstop for three minutes. Capture your ideas in quick words and phrases.

Write Review your notes. Then write an expanded definition of writing to express what writing means to *you*.

Writing in Your Journal

In the Writer's Warm-up at the beginning of this unit, you began a personal journal. Throughout the unit you read about the journals of people such as Samuel Pepys, John Muir, and Anne Frank. Is journal writing important? In your own journal, express your views.

Read More About It

A Gathering of Days: A New England Girl's Journal, 1830–1832 *by Joan Blos*

Although fiction, this book takes the form of personal writing. The "journal" depicts the hardships and rewards of nineteenth century rural life.

Newbery Award

In Their Own Words *by Milton Meltzer*

Using short excerpts from the diaries, journals, letters, and other writing of many different people, the author presents a fascinating survey of black history in America.

Book Report Idea   Journal Entry

Have you ever wished you were a character in a book? The next time you give a book report, try writing it as the journal entry of a favorite fictional character.

Record the Events ◆ Choose one important incident from the book. You might want to relate the central problem of the plot. The entry should also hint at some of the things that have occurred or will take place in the book. Include details that will make others want to read the book. At the bottom of the journal page, write the title and author of the book.

Dear Journal,

Unit 1

Sentences *pages 4–19*

A. Write the sentences using correct end punctuation. After each sentence write *declarative*, *interrogative*, *imperative*, or *exclamatory*.

1. It is very hot today
2. Who turned off the fan
3. Check the thermometer
4. How thirsty I am

B. Write each underlined word and its part of speech.

5. The blue helium <u>balloons</u> rose <u>gracefully</u> to the ceiling.
6. <u>Red</u> and white air-filled balloons floated <u>to</u> the floor.
7. <u>Watch</u> <u>them</u> collide in patriotic splendor.
8. <u>Oh!</u> What a beautiful <u>sight</u> it is!

C. Write each complete subject. Then underline each simple subject.

9. Delegates in the convention hall grabbed at the balloons.
10. They wanted the balloons for souvenirs.
11. A small red, white, and blue flag was a souvenir for Juanita.
12. Some friends of mine watched the convention on TV.

D. Write each complete predicate. Then underline each verb.

13. A variety of stores have opened in the antiques mall.
14. Colorful rugs are displayed outside on a nice day.
15. Browsers as well as serious shoppers stop by.
16. Typical goods include antique cabinets, prints, and bowls.

E. Write each sentence. Then use one of these labels to identify the subject-verb order: *normal*, *inverted* or *(you) understood*.

17. There was a knock at the door.
18. Didn't you answer it?
19. Run to the window.
20. A neighbor is at the door.

F. Write and label all compound subjects and compound verbs in the sentences.

21. Zaire, Cameroon, and Senegal are all African nations.
22. Read and learn about them in an almanac.
23. Our teacher assigned a report and gave us some reference material.
24. My classmate and I gave an oral report about Cameroon.

G. Write *simple* or *compound* for each sentence.

25. We must follow the map, or we will get lost.
26. Africa is the second largest continent in the world.
27. Explorers and navigators charted its waterways.
28. The map is in an atlas, but I could not find the atlas on the bookshelf.

H. Add words to each fragment to make a complete sentence. Rewrite each run-on sentence as two correct sentences.

29. The best hitter in major league baseball.
30. No one can top him he is the home run king.
31. An athlete, businessman, and hobbyist.
32. His accomplishments are many the list seems endless.

Thesaurus   *pages 20–21*

I. Read the thesaurus entry at left and write answers to questions 33–37.

careful (adj) — having caution.

cautious — extremely careful
A <u>cautious</u> driver never tailgates.

conscientious — careful to do whatever is right

deliberate — done on purpose

judicious — having good judgment

ANTONYMS: **careless, hasty, negligent, reckless (adj.)**

33. What part of speech is *careful*?

34. Which synonym means "having good judgment"?

35. How many antonyms are listed for *careful*?

36. Which synonym means "extremely careful"?

37. In what kind of order are the synonyms listed?

LANGUAGE PUZZLERS

Sentence Ciphers

Here is a cipher system people have used to send secret messages. First a sentence is broken into five-letter groups.

Our agent arrives on the last flight.
Ourag / entar / rives / onthe / lastf / light.

Then each group is written backward, without punctuation or capitalization.

garuo ratne sevir ehtno ftsal thgil

Write the secret message enciphered below. Be sure to use correct punctuation and capitalization.

wonew twonk edieh ytitn ehtfo tnega
atahw kcohs sawti
oynac acolu neget tlare samoh
hllet ehtmi siyps dnuof

Pyramid Twisters

Write a pyramid of tongue-twister sentences like the one below. Start with a simple subject and one verb. Build up to a compound sentence that contains two compound subjects and two compound verbs.

Sofia sang.
Sam and Sofia sang.
Sam and Sofia sat and sang.
Sam and Sofia sat and sang, but Sara sulked.
Sam and Sofia sat and sang, but Seth and Sara sulked.
Sam and Sofia sat and sang, but Seth and Sara sulked and sighed.

Unit 1 Extra Practice

1 Writing Four Kinds of Sentences

p. 4

A. Write whether each sentence is declarative, interrogative, or imperative. Then write the correct end punctuation mark in parentheses.

EXAMPLE: Who wrote that story
ANSWER: interrogative (?)

1. Where is the magazine
2. Did you leave it on your desk
3. Here it is
4. Look at the table of contents for this issue
5. Every article discusses a famous discovery
6. Notice the title of this article
7. Why are you interested in that article
8. I have always admired Marie Sklodowska Curie
9. Read about the discovery of gold in California
10. Gold was also mined in Georgia

B. Rewrite each sentence, changing it into the kind of sentence indicated in parentheses.

EXAMPLE: She doesn't watch TV. (imperative)
ANSWER: Don't watch TV.

11. I shall listen to the news. (imperative)
12. She saves important news stories. (imperative)
13. They write letters to editors. (imperative)
14. News magazines are popular. (interrogative)
15. A journalist writes news stories. (interrogative)
16. Are there newscasts on radio? (declarative)
17. Was Lowell Thomas a newscaster? (declarative)
18. Does TV cover special events? (declarative)
19. Was there an earthquake? (exclamatory)
20. The television reporters ran. (exclamatory)
21. Is the story true? (declarative)

2 Parts of Speech in Sentences

A. Write the part of speech that answers each question. Do not repeat answers.

1. What expresses action or being?
2. What modifies a noun or pronoun?
3. What takes the place of a noun or nouns?
4. What expresses feeling or emotion?
5. What names a person, place, thing, or idea?
6. What modifies a verb, an adjective, or another adverb?
7. What relates a noun or pronoun to another word in the sentence?
8. What joins words or groups of words?

B. All the words in each group are examples of one part of speech. Write the part of speech of each group of words.

9. or, nor, but, and
10. now, twice, seldom, backward, extremely
11. did, had, could, build, operate, swim
12. we, she, him, them, whom, nothing, everyone
13. at, into, from, except, against, underneath
14. musicians, abilities, friendship, machine
15. big, small, careless, expensive, impossible
16. oh, gee, hey, wow, ouch, hooray

C. The lines in this poem, "Sight," by Cora Ball Moton are numbered **17-26.** Write each underlined word and its part of speech after the line number.

17. I see <u>skies</u> more bright <u>and</u> blue
18. Than <u>any</u> skies beheld <u>by</u> you,
19. I see <u>trees</u> so <u>tall</u> and high
20. Their <u>green</u> leaves brush <u>against</u> the sky,
21. I see <u>birds</u> (and hear <u>them</u> sing)
22. Like <u>rainbows</u> that <u>have taken</u> wing;
23. <u>I</u> see <u>flowers</u> fairer far
24. Than any <u>in</u> your garden are,
25. <u>These</u> lovely sights you'll <u>never</u> find
26. Because — my dear, you <u>see</u>; I'm <u>blind</u>.

D. Write the part of speech of the underlined word in each sentence.

27. The green bus will leave <u>last</u>.
28. Did the <u>last</u> chapter contain a summary?
29. Their lawn mower is <u>near</u> the shed.
30. Will the chipmunk come <u>near</u>?
31. This apple is <u>crisp</u> and juicy.
32. Can <u>you</u> read this?
33. We are going to the <u>library</u>.
34. I hope I can find my <u>library</u> card.
35. <u>Look</u> at that new skyscraper.
36. <u>I</u> wonder if that is enough food.
37. Write your name <u>below</u>.
38. There is little snow <u>below</u> the timberline.
39. At the next intersection turn <u>right</u>.
40. Everybody has the <u>right</u> to an education.

3 Complete Subjects and Complete Predicates

p. 8

A. Write each sentence. Underline the complete subject once and the complete predicate twice.

1. Many bird species make long migrations each year.
2. One bird outshines them all in endurance.
3. This particular creature is called the sooty tern.
4. Its flight takes it far out over the ocean.
5. Small, surface-swimming fish are its main food source.
6. The tern does not return to land at night.
7. Each bird soars continually for many days.
8. Its feathers are not water-repellent like a duck's.
9. The bird would soon drown in the water.

B. Write the sentence part indicated in ( ).

10. The terns stay aloft through heat and cold. (predicate)
11. The flocks search for nesting places on land. (predicate)
12. The high-flying birds can hang motionless in a breeze. (subject)
13. Incredible flights of 22,000 miles have been made by some arctic terns. (subject)
14. No other animal can match this astonishing feat. (predicate)

C. Write the word group and add the missing subject part or predicate part to make a complete thought. Underline the part you add and label it *subject* or *predicate*. Do not use any answer more than once.

EXAMPLE: has a colorful cover.
ANSWER: The magazine has a colorful cover. (subject)

15. Magazines
16. My favorite magazine
17. are usually kept longer than newspapers.
18. Many newsstands and bookstores
19. have weekly or monthly issues.
20. Beautiful color photography
21. Subscriptions for some magazines
22. have unforgettable photographs of animals, forests, and mountains.
23. is on the cover of that magazine.
24. had an article about bicycles.

4 Simple Subjects and Predicates   *p. 10*

A. Write the simple subject and the verb of each sentence. Draw one line under each subject and two lines under the verb.

1. Gold may bring happiness or sorrow.
2. The answer can be found in a famous myth.
3. Many people went into a stadium.
4. The fastest runner in the world had been challenged to a race.
5. Reporters were not allowed into the stadium.
6. The winner will be applauded.
7. The name of the great runner was Atalanta.
8. She had never been defeated on the track.
9. Her father had made the rules for the race.
10. The winner would become the husband of Atalanta.
11. Every loser would be executed.
12. One young man had trained for a long time for his race.
13. The challenger was Hippomenes.
14. The race soon began.
15. A golden apple rolled across the track.

B. Write the simple subject and verb in each sentence. Underline the subject once and the verb twice.

16. Hippomenes knew of Atalanta's love for gold.
17. Atalanta stopped for that golden apple.
18. Hippomenes dropped two more apples in her path.
19. Three delays by Atalanta won for Hippomenes both the great race and Atalanta.
20. Hippomenes' coach had been Venus.
21. The three golden apples had come from her.
22. This clever goddess had planned the marriage of Atalanta and Hippomenes.
23. Other unforgettable stories about athletic events exist in mythology.
24. You can look in your library today.
25. You should not overlook articles in magazines.

5 Subject-Verb Order

p. 12

A. Write each sentence. Underline the subject once and the verb twice. If the subject is understood, write (You).

1. Geography has always been my most challenging subject.
2. There are so many facts about the world.
3. Just look at the map on the wall.
4. In the center of the country lies Pierce County in North Dakota.
5. Does Alaska span the most territory of any state in the United States?
6. Along the Canadian-American border lie the Great Lakes.
7. Identify the city with the most annual rainfall.
8. Has snow ever fallen in the Sahara?
9. Can you keep all those names straight?
10. Was Sri Lanka once called Ceylon?
11. Ghana was once known as the Gold Coast.
12. Are some African nations new?
13. Name the capital of Nigeria.
14. Here is Lichtenstein, a very small country.
15. Is Wales a country or a part of Great Britain?
16. There are several oceans of remarkable beauty.

B. Rewrite the sentences below. Add variety by changing the inverted sentences to normal order and the normal sentences to inverted order.

17. Lists of my favorite magazines are here.
18. Out of the box rolled one rusty thumbtack.
19. There are mysterious lights in the sky now.
20. A picture of the cheerleaders is on the cover.
21. Soon came the sound of laughter.
22. In the center of the cake were two candles.
23. Not enough gravy was in the bowl.
24. Here is another good recipe for rye bread.

6 Compound Subjects and Verbs

p. 14

A. Write and label the compound subject or compound verb in each sentence. Underline the conjunction that connects the parts of each compound.

1. The mountaineers gasped and panted in the thin air.
2. One of them looked up and sighed.
3. "These rocks and crevices are tough!" he grumbled.
4. "There are no handholds or ledges anywhere!"
5. The mountain leveled but rose sharply again.
6. One climber inched upward and shouted to her partner.
7. "Grab and hold tight to that rope," she urged.
8. Strain and fatigue made her legs tremble.
9. Finally she gripped the summit and pulled herself over.
10. The exhausted woman looked around her and gasped.
11. Some scouts and their leader were having a picnic. ·
12. The leader walked over and shook the climber's hand.
13. "The scouts and I came up about an hour ago," she explained.

B. Rewrite each sentence, using and underlining either a compound subject or a compound verb.

14. The two adventurers crawled out of their tent.
15. There were three different animals in the clearing.
16. The animals seemed hungry.
17. Quickly, the partners took some measures.
18. The animals reacted in different ways.

C. Write the subject and the verb of each sentence in this article about rare minerals. Underline the subject. If either the subject or the verb is a compound, write *compound* after it.

> **EXAMPLE:** They located and collected minerals.
> **ANSWER:** They located, collected (compound)

19. Many articles in magazines and stories in newspapers have become books. **20.** Some chapters and sections of *In Suspect Terrain* by John McPhee first appeared in a magazine. **21.** The facts about the location of minerals surprised and amazed readers. **22.** In Indiana there are diamonds and gold. **23.** These precious minerals exist and can be found among rocks in part of the state. **24.** These valuable gems and stones were not always in Indiana. **25.** The last great glacier of the Ice Age carried or dragged the diamonds and the gold into that state. **26.** Either Ontario or Quebec may have been the original home of these minerals. **27.** Geologists studied and searched both of these Canadian provinces. **28.** Neither the original gold field nor the main diamond bed in Canada has yet been found.

7 Simple and Compound Sentences   *p. 16*

A. Write each sentence. Underline each subject once and each verb twice. Then label each sentence *simple* or *compound*.

1. Reporters write; students read.
2. The reporters on the staff of our school newspaper write clearly and accurately.
3. Reporters may interview many people, or they may search a library for information.
4. Nila or I will print the title or write it.
5. Rafael and Rena brought the papers, but we counted and distributed them.

B. Revise these short, related simple sentences. Write a compound sentence to join each pair.

6. We have bake sales. We have auctions.
7. Your writing is good. It could be better.
8. I told a joke. No one understood it.
9. Tara found paint. Archie borrowed brushes.

C. Write the sentence and underline each subject once and each verb twice. Label the sentence *simple* or *compound*.

10. Benjamin Franklin once owned a newspaper, but not everyone knows this.

11. Franklin corresponded with other journalists, and they shared their news with him.

12. He often lent them money; he also gave them practical suggestions and good advice.

13. The owner of a newspaper in South Carolina received great praise from Benjamin Franklin.

14. Elizabeth Timothy owned and edited the *South Carolina Gazette* in the city of Charleston.

15. Her husband had founded the paper, but she had learned business methods in her native Holland.

16. She did not sell the paper after his death in 1738, nor did she stop writing articles.

17. The *South Carolina Gazette* featured news; it sometimes carried reprints of famous poems.

18. Elizabeth Timothy encouraged many writers and published their work in her newspaper.

19. She successfully managed the newspaper and her family of seven children.

8 Avoiding Sentence Errors   *p. 18*

A. Each word group is a run-on sentence. Write each one as two sentences. Add a period and change one small letter to a capital letter.

1. Mr. Adams is our librarian he is always busy.

2. His youngest daughter is in my earth science class her name is Lee.

3. These stories are short you will like them.

4. Those magazines have finally been returned I can now finish my report for social studies.

5. Our class studied the card catalog later we examined the collections of reference books.

6. I will complete my note cards tomorrow I can write the report by Wednesday.

B. 7–23 Rewrite this article about Nellie Bly to correct the run-on sentences. Make seventeen sentences. Underline words in italics.

a popular novel in Nellie Bly's time was *Around the World in Eighty Days* by Jules Verne this book amazed and thrilled people because such a trip in so very few days seemed impossible hoping for more readers, the publisher of the New York *World* arranged an unusual publicity stunt he carefully studied timetables of American and foreign steamships and railroads then he purchased tickets for Nellie Bly and, on November 14, 1889, sent her on a trip around the world she would complete the journey in less than eighty days if all the ships and trains were on schedule the newspaper put her lively reports from Europe and Asia on its front page a special train was waiting for her when she reached San Francisco it whisked her to New York on the last lap of her journey Nellie Bly completed her trip around the world in seventy-two days and became nationally known

as she rushed around the world, Nellie Bly was in a race with another reporter the publisher of the San Francisco *Examiner* also wished to gain publicity he chose Elizabeth Bisland to make the globe-circling race while Bly was traveling east, Bisland went west everything went well until she reached Europe there Elizabeth Bisland missed her ship to America she finally completed her journey in seventy-six days

C. Rewrite each of the following sentences to eliminate fragments. If the sentence is correct, write *correct*.

24. Julius Caesar may have invented the newspaper for western civilization. **25.** Notices daily in public places by his order. **26.** Informed the citizens about new laws and current events. **27.** Before Caesar's time, people could hear the news, but they could not read it. **28.** A newspaper in China in the eighth century. **29.** In the fifteenth century, newspapers or newsletters were published in a few German cities, but each one was written by hand. **30.** The first newspaper in Europe in Venice about 1556. **31.** If Venetians wished a subscription, they paid a small fee called a *gazetta*. **32.** No newspapers in America until one in Boston in 1690. **33.** Royal authorities promptly stopped it because it criticized the government.

UNIT TWO

USING LANGUAGE
TO

INFORM

═══════ **PART ONE** ═══════

Unit Theme   *The Art of Music*

Language Awareness   Nouns

═══════ **PART TWO** ═══════

Literature   "Jug Bands" by Steven Caney

A Reason for Writing   Informing

WRITER'S WARM-UP ◆ What do you know about music? You probably have a favorite performer, but how many different kinds of music do you enjoy? What part does music play in your life? Write in your journal and tell why you like music. You might describe your favorite musical sounds.

Writing
IN YOUR JOURNAL

A folk song is a simple, thoughtful song about people and their daily lives. Think of words that name persons, places, things, or ideas you might hear about in a folk song.

1 Writing with Nouns

Every person, place, and thing has a name. *Student*, *lake*, and *radio* are names. An idea—something that cannot be seen, heard, or touched, such as *truth*—also has a name. All these names are nouns. The chart below shows examples of nouns.

Nouns	
Persons	**Places**
This songwriter was also a singer.	He was born in Oklahoma in 1912.
Have you heard of Woody Guthrie?	Cities welcomed him.
Many people admire him.	He loved this country.
Things	**Ideas**
He sang and played the guitar.	Social justice concerned him.
He wrote over 1,000 songs.	His ideals were high.
His name is well-known.	He achieved greatness.

Most nouns have a singular and a plural form. A noun that refers to one, such as *guitar*, is singular. A noun that refers to more than one, such as *songs*, is plural. Some nouns such as *Woody Guthrie* and *Oklahoma City* are more than one word.

Compare the sentences below. Which sentence do you think is more interesting and informative?

> **The man influenced many others through his work.**
> **Woody Guthrie influenced many performers, such as Bob Dylan, through his music.**

When you write, use nouns to provide more specific details. Exact nouns help create word pictures for your reader.

> **Summary** ◆ A **noun** names a person, place, thing, or idea. Use exact nouns to create clear word pictures in your writing.

Guided Practice

Name the nouns in each sentence.

1. Woody Guthrie wrote about working men and women.
2. Such people also wrote their own songs of work.
3. Sailors created chanteys about their work.

Practice

A. The sentences below give information about chanteys. Find the nouns and write them.

4. Some chanteys tell about life at sea.
5. Sailors would sing while at work.
6. A chantey has strong rhythm and contains several stanzas.
7. Parts of the chantey may be sung by a leader.
8. In other parts, the entire group joins in as a chorus.
9. Lumberjacks at work sing a different chantey.
10. Many songs cannot be traced to their original composers.
11. The popularity of chanteys was once limited to a locality.
12. Recordings have helped this music survive.
13. Now this music is played for the enjoyment of all people.

B. The sentences below tell about another form of folk music. Write the nouns and label each noun as *person*, *place*, *thing*, or *idea*.

14. Spirituals are songs of great beauty and power.
15. This music was sung at work and in worship.
16. Their lyrics bring forth deep emotion in people.
17. The musical patterns of Africa influenced some spirituals.
18. Their melodies often came from old religious songs.

C. Use the model below to write five sentences of your own.

19–23. A folk song from ____ might have ____ about ____ .

Apply • Think and Write

From Your Writing • Read what you wrote for the Writer's Warm-up. Write the nouns you used and label what each noun names. Then change or add nouns to provide more specific information.

> ✎ **Remember**
> to use exact nouns to give precise information.

Can you complete this musical analogy?

The Beatles : Ringo Starr :: group : _____

Now try making up some musical analogies of your own.

2 Common and Proper Nouns

The word *band* is a common noun. It is the general name for a group of musicians. The name *United States Marine Band* is a proper noun. It names a particular band. All names of specific persons, animals, cities, states, countries, and things are called proper nouns. Many proper nouns such as *Joanne* or *Louisiana* are composed of single capitalized words. Some proper nouns are composed of two or more words. Notice the examples of common and proper nouns below.

<table>
<tr><th>MECHANICS ";?!"</th><th>Common Noun</th><th>Proper Noun</th></tr>
<tr><td rowspan="7">A proper noun begins with a capital letter. If the noun is made up of two or more words, only the important words are capitalized. For more information on capitalization, see pages 616–625.</td><td>musician</td><td>Scott Joplin</td></tr>
<tr><td>country</td><td>United States of America</td></tr>
<tr><td>city</td><td>Memphis</td></tr>
<tr><td>song</td><td>"Maple Leaf Rag"</td></tr>
<tr><td>event</td><td>New York Jazz Festival</td></tr>
<tr><td>landmark</td><td>Statue of Liberty</td></tr>
<tr><td>story</td><td>"To Build a Fire"</td></tr>
</table>

When you write, use common nouns to give general information and use proper nouns to give particular details.

Summary ✦ A **common noun** is the general name of a person, place, or thing. A **proper noun** names a particular person, place, or thing. Use proper nouns to make your writing more specific.

Guided Practice

Name the common and proper nouns in these sentences.

1. A unique musical form that developed in America is jazz.
2. Jazz grew from the melodies of Europe and the rhythms of Africa.
3. Earlier in this century, jazz was popular throughout our nation.

Practice

A. The sentences below give general and specific information about jazz. Write the nouns in each sentence. Then label each noun *common* or *proper*.

4. New Orleans is regarded as the birthplace of jazz.
5. The blues developed as one form of jazz.
6. Its lyrics have an earthy, direct quality.
7. W.C. Handy, a composer, popularized the blues.
8. Handy toured the southern states as a bandleader.
9. His most important song was ''St. Louis Blues.''
10. Bessie Smith and Ma Rainey sang the blues.
11. After World War I, musicians migrated to find work.
12. Another style of jazz called swing originated in Chicago.
13. Large bands played the relaxed, rhythmic music of swing.

B. The sentences below tell about a special time in the musical history of the United States. Write the sentences, capitalizing each proper noun correctly.

14. The bands of count basie and duke ellington played swing.
15. ellington played at the cotton club in new york city.
16. Another notable bandleader of swing was benny goodman.
17. goodman and his band toured the united states.
18. His band had teddy wilson on piano and gene krupa on drums.

C. Write a proper noun for each common noun below. Then use each proper noun in a sentence.

19. singer **21.** city   **23.** song **25.** composer
20. state   **22.** musician **24.** event **26.** landmark

Apply • Think and Write

Musical Details • Think of a particular musical group you like. Write several sentences about the group, giving details about the musicians, the places where they perform, and the songs they play or sing. Remember to name names!

✎ **Remember**
to capitalize all the important words in proper nouns.

Pick a category such as animals or fruit. Begin with *one apple, two bananas*, and so on. How far through the alphabet can you go?

3 Making Nouns Plural

A **singular noun** names one person, place, thing, or idea. A **plural noun** names more than one person, place, thing, or idea. The basic rules for spelling plural nouns are given below.

Add *-s* to most singular nouns.

> **friend, friends**   **tape, tapes**   **idea, ideas**

Add *-es* to nouns ending in *ch, s, sh, ss, x,* or *z.*

> **coach, coaches**   **class, classes**   **box, boxes**

Add *-s* to nouns ending in a vowel and *y*. Change *y* to *i* and add *-es* to nouns ending in a consonant and *y*.

> **key, keys**   **melody, melodies**   **salary, salaries**

Add *-s* to nouns ending in a vowel and *o* and to musical terms ending in *o*.

> **zoo, zoos**   **stereo, stereos**   **piano, pianos**   **solo, solos**

The correct spelling of nouns ending in a consonant and *o* should be learned. Many such nouns have two acceptable spellings. Check your dictionary.

> **hero**   **motto**   **zero**   **tomato**
> **heroes**   **mottoes, mottos**   **zeros, zeroes**   **tomatoes**

Summary ♦ Most nouns are made plural by adding *-s* or *-es* to the singular form. Pay special attention to the spelling of plural nouns when you proofread your writing.

Guided Practice

Tell how you would spell the plural of each noun below.

1. survey   **3.** hero   **5.** soprano   **7.** wish
2. alto   **4.** ticket   **6.** license   **8.** comedy

Practice

A. The sentences below tell about careers in music. Write each sentence, using the plural form of the noun in parentheses.

  9. (Boy) and (girl) may pursue a variety of (career) in music.
 10. They may train to be (musician), (singer), or (composer).
 11. Other (area) of music offer different (opportunity).
 12. Disc (jockey) are radio (announcer) who introduce (record).
 13. Musical (conductor) lead (orchestra) and (band).
 14. Voice (coach) give singing (lesson) to student (performer).
 15. Instrument (maker) may craft (oboe) and (sax).
 16. (Repairer) may mend (flute) and (cello).
 17. Music (historian) write or lecture about (aspect) of music.
 18. Often they have university (degree) or technical (diploma).

B. One noun in each sentence should be made plural. Find that noun and write the sentence correctly.

 19. In an orchestra, string instruments do not include banjo.
 20. Woodwind instruments may include flutes and piccolo.
 21. Brass wind instruments may include tuba and trumpets.
 22. French horns and trombone are also in this category.
 23. Cymbals and xylophone are percussion instruments.

C. Use the plural forms of the nouns below to complete the paragraph. Write the paragraph.

ballet	city	form	picture	opera

   Most major (**24.** ＿＿) have symphony orchestras. They may play both classical and popular (**25.** ＿＿) of music. Such orchestras also accompany (**26.** ＿＿) and (**27.** ＿＿), and provide music for motion (**28.** ＿＿) and television productions.

Apply ◆ Think and Write

Dictionary of Knowledge ◆ Read about George M. Cohan, a star of American musicals, in the Dictionary of Knowledge. Write about souvenirs his fans might have collected. Use singular and plural nouns.

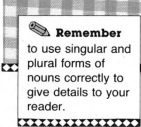

✎ **Remember**
to use singular and plural forms of nouns correctly to give details to your reader.

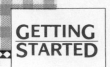
Some animal names change completely in the plural and some don't change at all. EXAMPLES: *One mouse—two mice; one moose—two moose.* If you can think of four more examples you're doing fine!

4 Nouns with Special Plural Forms

Some nouns have special plural forms. Use the rules below as a guide to spelling these forms. Use a dictionary when you are uncertain about the plural form of a word.

Add -*s* to many nouns ending in *f*, *fe*, or *ff*.

belief, beliefs   safe, safes   cliff, cliffs

For some nouns, drop the *f* or *fe* and add -*ves*.

calf, calves   shelf, shelves   leaf, leaves   wife, wives

A few nouns have irregular plural forms.

man, men	**tooth, teeth**	**mouse, mice**	**child, children**
foot, feet	**louse, lice**	**ox, oxen**	**goose, geese**

Some nouns have identical singular and plural forms.

deer, deer   series, series   Japanese, Japanese

For nouns formed from two or more words, make the most important word plural.

son-in-law, sons-in-law   board of health, boards of health
eyelid, eyelids   taxpayer, taxpayers

Add -*s* to nouns ending in *ful*.

handful, handfuls   mouthful, mouthfuls   cupful, cupfuls

Add an apostrophe and *s* ('*s*) to form the plural of a letter or numeral used as a noun.

A, A's   *2, 2's*   *i, i's*   *75, 75's*

Summary ♦ Some nouns have special forms. Check plural nouns carefully when you proofread your writing.

Guided Practice

Tell how you would spell the plural form of each noun below.

1. *12*   **2.** shelf   **3.** Chinese   **4.** child   **5.** bucketful

Practice

A. Write the plural form of each noun below.

6. half
7. roof
8. *100*
9. reindeer
10. Swiss
11. *B*

12. sister-in-law
13. bookcase
14. cuff
15. foot
16. woman
17. knapsack

18. teaspoonful
19. elf
20. videotape
21. tariff
22. chief of staff
23. board of education

B. One plural noun in each sentence about musicals is misspelled.
Write the misspelled words correctly.

24. Showsboat took musicals to the people of river frontiers.
25. Theater-in-the-rounds are good settings for musical comedies.
26. Showmans like George M. Cohan headlined early musicals.
27. The lifes of many people were enriched by his spirited shows.
28. Some of his songs reflected his patriotic believes.
29. Rock musicals are stepchilds of these early stage shows.

C. Complete these sentences about show costumes. Use the plural
forms of the nouns below.

child   armful   headache   kerchief   storeroom   shelf

30. Costume pieces like _____ and helmets are called headgear.
31. They are often kept backstage on hooks or on _____ .
32. Wardrobe personnel carry _____ of costumes to the actors.
33. Torn or ill-fitting costumes cause _____ for the seamstress.
34. The costumes are placed in _____ when the play ends.
35. _____ enjoy a backstage tour of the scenery.

Apply • Think and Write

Staging Sentences • Write several sentences about stage
props and costumes. Use the plural of each of the following
nouns in your sentences: mouse, wife, foot, child, leaf.

Remember
to spell special plural
forms of nouns
correctly.

Have fun with sentences that show relationships. You might say, *"Sam is Tom's sister's son's dog."* Can a partner explain, *"Sam belongs to the son of the sister of Tom"*? Try it.

5 Possessive Nouns

You have learned about singular and plural noun forms. Many nouns also have singular possessive forms and plural possessive forms. The possessive form of a noun shows ownership. It tells to whom or to what something belongs. A possessive noun is usually followed by the name of the thing owned. Study these rules.

To write the possessive form of a singular noun, add an apostrophe and *s* (*'s*).

the actor	Bob	an actress
the actor's costume	Bob's pen	an actress's script

To write the possessive form of a plural noun that ends in *s*, add only an apostrophe (').

some actors	all bosses	the Browns
some actors' lines	all bosses' orders	the Browns' seats

To write the possessive form of a plural noun that does not end in *s*, add an apostrophe and *s* (*'s*).

three women	the children
three women's songs	the children's dances

Do not confuse a noun's possessive form with its plural form. A possessive noun shows ownership. It always has an apostrophe.

Summary ◆ A **possessive noun** shows ownership. Use a possessive noun to show that something belongs to someone.

Guided Practice

Tell whether each noun is *singular*, *singular possessive*, *plural*, or *plural possessive*.

1. girls'   **2.** chief's   **3.** dancers   **4.** Kim's   **5.** men's

Practice

A. Write the noun. Label it *singular, singular possessive, plural,* or *plural possessive.*

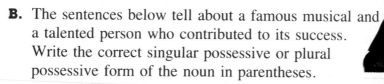

6. writers	**11.** children	**16.** adults
7. writer's	**12.** children's	**17.** Larry's
8. writer	**13.** adult's	**18.** singers'
9. writers'	**14.** Lois	**19.** witness's
10. child	**15.** Lois's	**20.** witnesses'

B. The sentences below tell about a famous musical and a talented person who contributed to its success. Write the correct singular possessive or plural possessive form of the noun in parentheses.

21. The (public) interest in a musical often centers on the dancing.
22. The (actors) roles in a musical require them to be good dancers.
23. A (choreographer) job is to create dance steps to go with music.
24. Jerome Robbins is one of (America) popular choreographers.
25. This (man) work with the musical *West Side Story* was superb.

C. Find the incorrectly written possessive in each sentence. Then write it correctly.

26. *West Side Story* captured this nations' attention.
27. The theme is based on Shakespeares play *Romeo and Juliet.*
28. The story and songs are about teenager's lives.
29. The womens roles were as intense as the men's roles.
30. The musicals' popularity caused it to be made into a film.

D. Write the plural possessive form for each of the singular possessive nouns below.

31. farmer's **32.** student's **33.** boss's **34.** nurse's **35.** woman's

Apply • Think and Write

An Informative List • Think about the kinds of items that might be left in an auditorium after a show. List possible forgotten items. Put an owner's name with each item, using singular and plural possessive nouns: Anita's scarf, men's gloves.

✏️ **Remember**
to use apostrophes correctly with possessive nouns.

Drumbeat and *bandstand* are each formed from smaller words. Name other words that contain the smaller words *drum*, *beat*, *band*, *stand*.

VOCABULARY ♦
Compounds

Words like *waterfall* and *offhand* are called compounds. A **compound** is a word formed from two or more words. Every compound functions as a unit, but not all compounds are written as single words. Some compounds are written as separate words, such as *house cat*. Other compounds are written with hyphens, such as *time-out*. Find the compounds in the sentence below.

> This afternoon Robin's brother-in-law bought her a tape deck
> for her birthday.

Compounding is the most common way in which new words are formed in English. Many compounds are nouns, but they may also be other parts of speech. Always use hyphens when writing compounds formed from three or more separate words, such as *merry-go-round*. Use a dictionary to check whether a compound is written as one word, with a hyphen, or as two words.

Building Your Vocabulary

Compounds are used to name many kinds of occupations, such as *police officer* and *cowhand*. Think of other compounds that name occupations.

Many informal and slang words are compounds, such as *copycat*, *butterfingers*, and *hothead*. List other slang and informal compounds.

Look at the picture puzzles below. What compounds do they form?

Practice

A. Later in this unit you will read about *jug bands*, or bands in which jugs and other objects are used as musical instruments. Match words in column **A** with words in column **B** to form five compounds that name possible musical instruments.

A	B
1. soda	cap
2. bicycle	board
3. wash	pump
4. cow	bottle
5. hub	bell

B. The vocabulary of music contains many compounds. Listed below are several incomplete compounds. Use the following words to complete the compounds. Write the compounds correctly.

glee   wind   house   key   leader
drum   song   snare   bag

6. wood_____   **9.** _____ drum   **12.** folk _____
7. _____ club   **10.** _____pipe   **13.** _____stick
8. opera _____   **11.** band_____   **14.** _____board

C. Many song titles contain compounds. Complete the song titles below.

15. "Rain_____ Keep Falling on My Head"
16. "Stars and Stripes For_____"
17. "Some_____ over the Rain_____"

Think of other song titles that contain compounds.

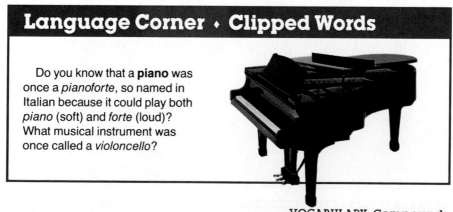

Language Corner ◆ Clipped Words

Do you know that a **piano** was once a *pianoforte*, so named in Italian because it could play both *piano* (soft) and *forte* (loud)? What musical instrument was once called a *violoncello*?

How to Revise Sentences with Nouns

You know that a noun can name a person, place, thing, or idea. Exact nouns can give important information to a reader. They can also make your writing clear and interesting. Which sentence below gives a better picture of what is happening?

1. The man played an instrument.
2. The musician played a trumpet.

Sentence **1** gives you an idea of what is happening, but sentence **2** gives more information. Sentence **2** not only tells you more about *who* is playing, it also tells you exactly *what* he is playing. The nouns *musician* and *trumpet* are more exact than the vague nouns *man* and *instrument*.

Proper nouns can also give specific information. Use them whenever you have a particular person, place, or thing in mind. Notice the difference between the two sentences below.

3. The musician was born in a southern city.
4. Louis Armstrong was born in New Orleans.

When you write, think carefully about what your reader needs to know. Choose common or proper nouns that will give that information. An exact noun can make the difference between a vague sentence and a specific one.

The Grammar Game ♦ Sharpen your noun sense! Quickly write as many exact nouns as you can for each noun below. Try to include at least one proper noun for each one. Then compare lists with a classmate. Did the two of you write any of the same nouns?

building	child	pet
relative	show	machine
vehicle	weather	athlete

Working Together

As you work with nouns in activities **A** and **B**, notice that using exact nouns makes your group's writing clear and interesting.

In Your Group

◆ Ask questions to prompt discussion.　◆ Record the group's ideas.
◆ Help the group stay on the job.　◆ Don't interrupt each other.

A. Write the sentences below, replacing the underlined words with more exact common nouns or proper nouns. Then write the sentences again, choosing different exact nouns to change the information given.

1. The <u>person</u> labored over the <u>work</u>.
2. Bill walked to the <u>room</u> to pick up his <u>belongings</u>.
3. Many <u>ingredients</u> are needed for this <u>recipe</u>.
4. The <u>sound</u> of the <u>animal</u> woke everyone in the <u>place</u>.
5. I found <u>clothes</u>, <u>jewelry</u>, and other <u>stuff</u> in the drawer.

B. As a group, rewrite the paragraph below, changing nouns to make the paragraph clearer and more exact.

There wasn't an empty place in the room, and everyone was impatient. Finally the place grew dark, and the group walked out on the stage. A woman raised her instrument slowly. It gleamed in the light as she nodded to the people around her. People tossed flowers onto the stage as the sound began.

WRITERS' CORNER ◆ Exact Information

Sometimes your reader may only need general information. However, if you want to give your reader more exact information, how exact do you want it to be?

GENERAL: **A famous athlete used to live in my neighborhood.**

EXACT: **A famous baseball player used to live in my neighborhood.**

MORE EXACT: **Babe Ruth used to live in my neighborhood.**

Read what you wrote for the Writer's Warm-up. Do the nouns you used give the information you intended? If they do not, change them.

THE BANJO LESSON   painting by Henry O. Tanner
Hampton University Museum, Hampton, Virginia

UNIT TWO

USING LANGUAGE
TO

INFORM

=== PART TWO ===

Literature   "Jug Bands" by Steven Caney

A Reason for Writing   Informing

CREATIVE
Writing

FINE ARTS ◆ Does Henry Tanner's "The Banjo
Lesson" remind you of an experience you thought
you had forgotten? Do you remember the first
song you could sing or the first tune you could
whistle? Write a story that recalls a favorite song
that makes you smile every time you hear it.

CRITICAL THINKING ♦
A Strategy for Informing

A GOAL/PLAN/OUTCOME CHART

A how-to article is one kind of informative writing. In it, the writer gives careful, step-by-step directions to help the reader achieve a goal. After this lesson you will read "Jug Bands," an article that tells how to make country music instruments. Later you will write your own how-to article.

Do you have a soda bottle or a cider jug at home? In this passage from "Jug Bands," the writer tells how you can turn them into musical instruments.

> To play a note, hold the bottle or jug with the rim straight up and against your puckered lips. Your bottom lip should be pressed against the side of the neck and be flush with the opening. Your top lip should arch over the opening a bit. Now blow across the opening. . . .

Actions, of course, have outcomes. What do you think the outcome would be if you blew across a bottleneck?

◆ Learning the Strategy

Problem solving is planning or taking actions to reach a goal. The outcome may be good or bad, expected or unexpected. Sometimes we study past problem-solving actions to help us plan future actions. For example, suppose you are on a committee to boost band concert attendance. You know that the band at another school has well-attended concerts. So you talk to the band leader there to find out what actions they took to achieve that outcome.

Now suppose your goal is to run a 10K race in under 50 minutes. You plan and follow a training schedule. When you plan for the future, of course, you don't know the outcome. You don't know if you will reach your time goal for the 10K or not.

CRITICAL THINKING: Problem Solving

Whether you are studying the past or planning for the future, a goal/plan/outcome chart can be useful. Here, for example, is a chart about the 10K race.

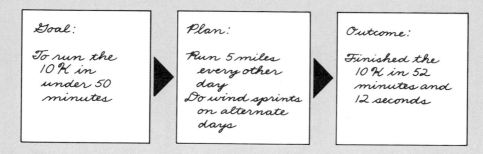

Goal:

To run the 10K in under 50 minutes

Plan:

Run 5 miles every other day
Do wind sprints on alternate days

Outcome:

Finished the 10K in 52 minutes and 12 seconds

What parts of the chart could have been filled in before the race? What could not have been filled in until after the race? Why not omit the "outcome" box? Are there any reasons for noting the outcomes of actions?

Using the Strategy

A. Almost everyone can improve what they eat or the way they eat for better health. Make a goal/plan/outcome chart. For "goal" write "To improve my nutrition." For "plan" write at least three actions you could take to achieve your goal. For "outcome" write the most likely result, or leave that box blank and fill it in one week from now.

B. In a jug band, the players play instruments made from common household objects. Before you read "Jug Bands," figure out your own jug band. Make a goal/plan/outcome chart. For "goal" write "To create instruments for six players." For "outcome" write "Instruments for the Rooter Tooter Band" (or whatever band name you make up). For "plan" list what household items you would use and how they would be played. Then read "Jug Bands" to see if your ideas were on target.

Applying the Strategy

- What is the likely outcome of the actions you planned for your nutrition goals in **A**? What makes you think so?
- When might it be useful to evaluate past goals, plans, and outcomes?

JUG BANDS

from

Kids' America
by Steven Caney

The jug band is an American invention but no one is exactly sure just when or where in America these bands began. During the 1920's a record company asked a country jug band who played snappy rhythms to make a record. The band became a hit and featured a long jug solo which attracted attention. Soon people all over America (but mostly in the South) were listening to the country music of groups like the Memphis Jug Band, Cris Cannon and his Jug Stompers, and the Dixieland Jug Blowers.

There is no typical jug band or jug band music — almost any song can be played in the style. And the style depends on what instruments the band has to play music with: Jug band instruments include nearly any "real" instrument or any household object that can sound a note, beat, click, honk, tap, thump, or buzz. Jug band musicians have been known to play their music on washboards, hubcaps, home radiators, combs, cans, cowbells, spoons, whistles, and bicycle pumps, as well as the more traditional instruments for melody including the banjo, guitar, kazoo, harmonica, and fiddle.

Playing the Jug

You might as well begin by learning to play the instrument that gives the jug band its name. A crockery jug will certainly look the best, but any jug or bottle with a skinny neck and opening will make a good instrument. Large soda bottles, ketchup bottles, cooking-oil bottles or laundry jugs will also work fine. The larger the jug, the lower the note it will sound, and vice-versa.

To play a note, hold the bottle or jug with the rim straight up and against your puckered lips. Your bottom lip should be pressed against the side of the neck and be flush with the opening. Your top lip should arch over the opening a bit. Now blow across the opening, but don't blow too hard; about the way you normally exhale is perfect. Keep adjusting your lips slightly until you get a deep vibrating note. After some practice you will learn exactly how to pucker and place your lips to play any jug or bottle.

FOOM FOOM

To play with the jug band just blow a note in time to each beat of the music. If you want to change the note for a particular song, either use another jug or fill your jug partially with water.

Making a Washtub Bass

The second most common instrument in a jug band, after the jug of course, is a washtub bass. The bass with its deep twangy sound adds a distinctive emphasis to the music, but unlike the one-note jug, you can actually play a melody on the washtub bass.

Materials

washtub — it is best to use a large, round, metal washtub. Washtubs were once very common in American homes, but in recent times they have been almost completely replaced by sinks, bathtubs, and automatic washing machines. However, you might still find one in your basement or maybe at your grandparents' home. You might also buy a new washtub at the hardware store. As a last resort you can look for one at a local garage sale.

Although a washtub will give the clearest, richest sounds, in a pinch you can also make a bass using a metal or plastic bucket, a large dishpan, or even a sturdy corrugated box. These containers probably won't sound as good as a metal washtub but they do work well enough for practice or an impromptu jam session.

old broom handle — a wooden closet rod, or a strong, straight branch will do for the neck of the bass. The exact length of the handle doesn't matter, but when it rests on top of the washtub, the handle should be about as high as your head. If the handle is longer or shorter it could make playing a bit more difficult.

strong nylon cord — or heavy fishing line will make a good bass string. A length of package twine or other cord may sound fine on the bass, but rough cord can make your fingers sore while playing. If you do use a rough cord, wear a glove on your plucking hand.

large washer — or some other object to tie to one end of the string.

tools

hammer

nail

pocketknife or small saw

1. To assemble the instrument, first turn the washtub upside down and hammer a hole in the bottom center using a fat nail. The bottom is now the top of your washtub. Now thread one end of the cord through the hole and tie a washer, bolt, nut, twig, or anything to it that will prevent the cord from pulling back through the hole.

2. Cut or whittle a small notch in one end of the broom handle or whatever you are using for the neck so that the rim of the washtub fits in this groove. Also cut or whittle a groove in the neck near the top.

3. Stand the neck on the rim of the washtub and lean the neck slightly toward the center of the tub. Hold the neck in that position and tie the free end of the cord tightly around the groove at the top of the neck so that the string is taut. This step is sometimes easier if you have a helper hold the neck while you do the tying. The washtub bass is now complete and ready to play.

Position the tub on the floor so you are standing directly behind the neck. Put one foot on the washtub rim to keep it from slipping, hold the top of the neck in one hand, and pluck the cord with your other hand.

You can raise or lower the pitch of the notes you play by pulling back on the neck to tighten the cord or slacking it slightly. With a little practice

you will figure out just how much to tighten or loosen the cord to get the notes you want.

Some washtub bass players use one hand to hold the string tightly against the neck while also keeping the string taut. By moving this hand a bit up and down the neck, the playing part of the string is made shorter or longer so that the other hand can get the notes they want.

Practice playing different notes on the washtub bass and try to play a steady rhythm. Even though you may be able to play a melody, most of the time a jug band bass player plucks out rhythm or bass notes that harmonize with the music being played by the other instruments. Practice some more, and play along to a record on the radio plucking the string in time to the music. As you play, "work" the neck to find what notes sound good with the tune being played. When you have finished playing leave everything connected and just rest the neck across the washtub.

Library Link ♦ *You can find other interesting projects like this one in the book* Kids' America *by Steven Caney.*

 Reader's Response

◆◆

Would you like to play in a jug band? Explain why or why not.

JUG BANDS

 ## Responding to Literature

1. Design a record cover for a jug band recording. Select a song that you could imagine a jug band playing. Then design a cover to entice people to buy the record. Include a short description of the instruments you would use.

2. What instrument would you play in a jug band? Would you play a jug, a comb, or a washtub bass? If you wish, you can design your own instrument. Write a paragraph to describe your instrument and how you feel when you play it.

3. What is your favorite type of music? What instruments are involved? Research your favorite instrument. Then write a short description of the instrument and how it is made.

 ## Writing to Learn

Think and Plan ♦ A Goal/Plan/Outcome chart will help you organize a plan of action to achieve a goal. If you were going to make a washtub bass, what plan of action would you take? What would your outcome be? Copy and complete the chart.

Goal: ▶ Plan: ▶ Outcomes:

Write ♦ Prepare a short paragraph and tell what you might learn from making a washtub bass.

GETTING
STARTED

Think of something you have made with your hands, such as a shelf or scarf. Describe how you made the object. Answer any questions your classmates may have.

SPEAKING and LISTENING ♦
Giving a Demonstration

When you give a demonstration, you show an audience how something works or how something is done. Oral directions are easier to follow when they are demonstrated, or shown, as well as spoken.

A successful demonstration depends on the participation of both the speaker and the listener. The speaker needs to be well prepared and to appear confident. The listener needs to be responsive and enthusiastic.

The following guidelines will help you as both a speaker and a listener during a demonstration.

Giving a Demonstration	1. Gather and arrange materials, including visual aids such as charts, in order to make the clearest presentation possible. 2. Practice what you will say and use effective body language. Look at your listeners, maintain good posture, and use gestures. Also, vary the tone of your voice and the rate of your speaking. 3. Relax and take your time with each step. Pause occasionally and ask for questions. This will help to involve your listeners. 4. Conclude your demonstration with a short review of the steps you covered. Be sure your listeners have understood the demonstration.
Being an Active Listener	1. As you listen, look at the speaker and show interest. Give courteous, enthusiastic attention. 2. Ask questions that will help the speaker make things clear to you. Also, be sure to choose appropriate moments during the demonstration to ask your questions. 3. Be sensitive to the speaker. Do not send "I am bored" messages, such as yawning. This weakens the demonstration. 4. Show appreciation with questions, comments, and applause.

Summary ♦ As a speaker, present a demonstration in a clear, lively style. As a listener, actively encourage the speaker by giving your full attention and asking appropriate questions.

Guided Practice

Tell whether you agree or disagree with the way each speaker or listener acts during a demonstration. Explain your answer.

1. Ted purposely varies his tone of voice as he speaks.
2. Lisa hurries because she is afraid people will be bored.
3. Leo is interested, but slouches down in his chair.

Practice

A. Write *agree* or *disagree* for each example of an action during a demonstration. Then write a sentence explaining your answer.

4. Sheila asks the speaker to explain a fact more clearly.
5. Tony never raises his eyes from the material before him.
6. Jill gives her demonstration without any practice.
7. Rosa shows extra visual aids for an unfamiliar subject.
8. Jack isn't interested in the subject, so he reads a book.

B. Working with a partner, discuss how the speaker (S) and listener (L) could make the following situations more successful.

9. S: "This is a synthesizer keyboard. Want to try it?"
   L: chats with person beside him
10. S: sets up keyboard and faces away from the audience
    L: silently watches the speaker's back
11. S: "I'd play the synthesizer but you wouldn't like it."
    L: loudly volunteers to play the synthesizer
12. S: finishes demonstration and sits down
    L: asks who will demonstrate next

C. Work with a partner in a speaker-listener team. One partner demonstrates a magic trick or other skill. The other partner acts as listener. After the demonstration, discuss how the demonstration could be improved.

Apply ◆ Think and Write

Evaluating a Demonstration ◆ Think of an effective demonstration you have witnessed. You may have seen the demonstration on a television commercial, at an amusement park, or in your classrooom. Write about why the demonstration was effective.

> ✎ **Remember**
> to be a lively speaker or an active listener during a demonstration.

GETTING STARTED

How would you complete the following sentence? *The world's best musical group is _____ .* Convince listeners of your choice in three sentences.

WRITING ◆
Paragraphs

A paragraph is a group of related sentences that introduces and develops a main idea. Paragraphs are the true "building blocks" of writing. They indicate that a writer has moved from one main idea to another. Paragraphs also make reading a page easier. The first line of a paragraph is indented slightly from the left margin.

In a paragraph you will usually find a **topic sentence** that states the main idea, **supporting sentences** that provide more detailed information, and when appropriate, a **clincher sentence**. The clincher sentence summarizes or restates the paragraph's main idea.

Topic Sentence

Supporting Sentences

Clincher Sentence

People in prehistoric times made music with simple instruments. The human voice was probably the first instrument. People enjoyed chanting and singing around a fire. They also beat rhythmically on hollow logs and shook rattles made of bone and pebbles. Eventually people found that a simple reed or hollow stick could produce musical sounds when air was blown into it. Such instruments provided the joys of music for our prehistoric ancestors.

> **Summary** ◆ A **paragraph** is a group of related sentences about one main idea.

Guided Practice

The sentences below make up a paragraph. Tell which sentence is the topic sentence. Then order the supporting sentences correctly.

1. He used electronic equipment to create sounds.
2. Since 1950, many composers have experimented with untraditional ways of making music.
3. The sounds may have any tone, pitch, loudness, and duration.
4. Edgàrd Vares, for example, was known for his electronic music.

Practice

A. Read the following paragraph. Then write an answer for each question below it.

The water drum is a unique musical instrument. It is a closed cylinder that is usually made of metal. Inside the drum is a certain amount of water that affects the drum's tone. By tilting the drum, the player shifts the water during or between each beat. The movement of the water raises or lowers the pitch of the drum beat and produces some very unusual sounds.

5. What is the paragraph's main idea?
6. What is the paragraph's topic sentence?
7. Which sentences develop the main idea?
8. Is there a clincher sentence?

B. Write a topic sentence for each topic below.

9. rock music
10. an interesting hobby
11. music in the future
12. a local radio station

C. Rewrite the following to make it meet the requirements of a good paragraph. Be sure to omit any sentences that do not develop the main idea. Add a clincher sentence.

Composer John Cage captured people's attention early in his career when he set up a piano in Cambridge's Harvard Square. That is near many other historical places. Cage sat down at the piano to play—but did not play. Instead he sat still while an assistant turned pages of music for him. The lunchtime audience was baffled for a long while. Arthur Fiedler was another famous musician from the Boston area. Then people realized what John Cage wanted them to hear. The real music this composer wanted to reveal to the world was the sound of Harvard Square's busy daily life.

Apply • Think and Write

Writing a Paragraph • Write about when and where you most often listen to music. Include a topic sentence and use supporting sentences to develop the main idea. Underline the topic sentence.

> ✎ **Remember**
> to use supporting sentences that relate to the main idea of a paragraph.

GETTING
STARTED

Think of a newspaper headline you have read recently. See how well you can ''prove'' the information in the headline to classmates.

WRITING ◆
Developing a Paragraph by Facts

Writers often use facts to develop paragraphs. A fact is information that can be proved to be true. A fact can be checked and verified. Each fact in a supporting sentence of a paragraph works to convince readers that the main idea is true.

Which paragraph below is more effective and believable?

> The banjo is a uniquely American instrument. You almost never hear foreign musicians play a banjo. There really is nothing quite like the banjo to make people tap their toes. The rhythms of ragtime and bluegrass music are hard to imagine without a banjo's brassy sound.

> The banjo is a uniquely American instrument. It was developed by black Americans over a century ago. It is commonly used in ragtime and bluegrass compositions. When plucked, its strings make a sound identified instantly as American.

The second paragraph is more effective than the first because there are facts that can be verified. Notice that most of the statements in the first paragraph are personal opinions.

> **Summary** ◆ Use facts to prove that the main idea of a paragraph is true.

Guided Practice

Tell which sentences support the following topic sentence with facts.

Ragtime music was very popular in America between 1900 and 1915.
1. There were many ragtime dancing contests during this time.
2. Some people probably enjoyed blues music more than ragtime music.
3. People often listened to Scott Joplin's ragtime tunes.

Practice

A. Write the topic sentence below. Then write only the statements that support the main idea of the topic sentence with facts.

The banjo was first developed by people of West Africa.
   4. Arabian merchants introduced guitars to the West Africans.
   5. West Africans had many of their own native instruments.
   6. The West Africans modified the design of Arabian guitars.
   7. With its many strings, the banjo is difficult to master.

B. Write the sentence that best supports each topic sentence with an appropriate fact.

Stringed instruments are the most versatile ones in orchestras.
   8. An orchestra's wind section has great range too.
   9. Plucked, bowed, and strummed strings all sound different.
   10. I would choose a cello over a drum any time.

The gong is one of the world's oldest musical instruments.
   11. The gong's sound reminds me of a crash of thunder.
   12. A gong is not appropriate to every kind of composition.
   13. Monks in ancient China may have invented the gong.

The bassoon was probably developed in medieval Italy.
   14. It is one of the largest wind instruments in the world.
   15. In 1539, an Italian "maestro" created its familiar shape.
   16. The bassoon produces a deep, mellow tone.

C. Read the topic sentences below. Then write three facts you could use to support each one.

   17. The piano is a difficult instrument to learn.
   18. Our school band needs more practice.
   19. Marilyn Vega is the best singer in our school chorus.

Apply • Think and Write

A Factual Paragraph ◆ What is your favorite musical instrument? Write a paragraph about the instrument. Include a topic sentence and at least three factual statements that support the main idea.

✎ **Remember**
that facts can help prove the main idea in a paragraph.

Complete this sentence: *I know a lot about* _____ . Then give a few examples that help to prove your statement.

WRITING ♦
Developing a Paragraph by Examples

An effective way to develop a paragraph is to use examples. Examples are specific cases that illustrate the main idea of a paragraph. They create word pictures that help readers understand the idea. Using examples is an especially good way to develop an explanatory paragraph—a paragraph that explains or proves a point.

Most fully developed paragraphs have two or three examples. However, one example is enough if it contains complete information. Notice how the examples in the paragraph below support the main idea and add specific details to the paragraph.

Jazz music has many forms. There is ragtime, an energetic style of piano playing noted for its strong rhythm. Blues is a type of jazz mainly identified by its mournful, sad melodies. Bop jazz began in the 1940s with such musicians as Dizzy Gillespie and Charlie Parker. These jazz musicians developed a long, dazzling style of jazz known for its many notes. Today many jazz musicians blend jazz and rock music into a form known as fusion. All of these unique styles have made jazz one of the most diverse types of music played today.

Summary ♦ Use clear, detailed examples in paragraphs to explain or prove a point. Be sure that each example supports the main idea of the paragraph.

Guided Practice

Tell which sentences are appropriate examples for a paragraph with the following topic sentence.

The term popular music refers to many diverse styles of music.
1. Some classical compositions have been adapted as popular music.
2. Jazz developed as a major form of popular music in the 1930s.
3. A nation's history can be told in its popular music.

Practice

A. Write the following topic sentence and the sentences below that would be appropriate examples for a paragraph.

    Our local radio station plays a wide variety of music.
4. Each evening, an hour of Beatles' hits can be heard.
5. The station goes off the air at midnight.
6. The melodious voice of Bing Crosby is played on weekends.
7. The rock music has many styles.
8. Some peppy jazz tunes by Benny Goodman are played each day.

B. Write two examples to develop each topic sentence.

9. Being able to play an instrument has many benefits.
10. Our school has many talented musicians.
11. I enjoy many different kinds of music.
12. All musicians should give free concerts.
13. Loud music can be harmful.

C. Choose one of the topic sentences from **Practice B** to develop into a paragraph. Add more examples to the paragraph. Include a clincher sentence.

Apply • Think and Write

A Paragraph Developed by Examples • Write about the best concert or other musical event, such as a play, that you have seen. Before you write, think about the specific details of the experience. Use examples to show why your experience was so memorable.

Remember that examples are a good way to explain or prove a point in a paragraph.

GETTING
STARTED

Do you have a certain daily routine? Describe the order in which you do things in a typical day. Add as many details as you can.

WRITING ◆
Organizing Ideas in a Paragraph

Once you know your purpose for writing and have chosen a form, you need to decide on a method for organizing your ideas. Paragraphs need a logical organization in order to give readers an effective and clear message. This lesson describes four different ways to organize ideas in a paragraph: time order, space order, order of importance, and climactic order.

Time Order   In time order organization, ideas are arranged according to the order in which they occur. This method is useful in giving directions, in describing a process or series of events, and in telling a story. Words such as *first, then*, and *later* often appear in time order paragraphs. This example from ''Jug Bands'' is written in time order.

> To assemble the instrument, first turn the washtub upside down and hammer a hole in the bottom. . . . The bottom is now the top of your washtub. Now thread one end of the cord through the hole and tie a washer, bolt, nut, twig, or anything to it that will prevent the cord from pulling back through the hole.

Space Order   Space order is useful in creating a word picture of a person, place, or thing. With this method you describe details in a particular spatial order to create a vivid picture in your paragraph. With your words, you will lead the reader to look from left to right, from inner to outer, from near to far, and so on. The following paragraph is an example of space order organization.

> This great composer's workroom was very unlike his orderly symphonies. As we entered, we saw his desk in the center of the room and a high stack of old papers directly behind the desk. On the left wall stood a huge, dusty bookshelf overflowing with books. A window to the right of the bookshelf let sunshine in. The piano, dark and silent, faced the desk from the far right corner.

Order of Importance   This method of organization arranges facts and ideas according to their importance, in descending order. The most important information comes first, as in a news story. The supporting sentences then give specific details of lesser importance that relate to the main idea. Study the following example.

A four-year-old boy named Wolfgang Mozart played harpsichord today for the royal family at Salzburg, Austria. The young genius delighted the court with four short pieces that he had written. Wolfgang's father, Leopold, accompanied his son on the violin. The Mozarts are planning a European tour.

Climactic Order   Use this method to build interest and suspense in your writing. To get this effect, arrange details in ascending order of importance. The most important detail is presented last. Climactic order is most often used in short stories and other forms of fiction. The following paragraph is written in climactic order.

Luisa got ready for school and thought about the shiny new guitar in the music store window. How she longed to own the guitar. She decided this was the day to ask her mother to help her buy the guitar. She nervously walked to the kitchen to greet her mother. There, on the kitchen table with a bright red bow, was the guitar of her dreams.

Summary ♦ Choose a method for organizing ideas in a paragraph that is based both on your purpose for writing and on the form you will use.

Guided Practice

Tell the best organization method—time order, space order, order of importance, or climactic order—for each paragraph topic.

1. a description of the stage setting for a school musical
2. a news bulletin about a local symphony orchestra concert
3. instructions on how to clean piano keys

Practice

A. Write *time order, space order, order of importance,* or *climactic order* to indicate the best organization method for each paragraph topic. Write a sentence explaining your choice.

   4. a major announcement by the leader to the school orchestra
   5. instructions on how to care for an upright bass
   6. the story of how Beethoven overcame his hearing impairment
   7. basic events in the life of pianist Clara Haskill
   8. a description of the famous Carnegie Hall building design

B. Read each paragraph. Write the organization method used in each.

   9. As soon as Leo saw the stage, he knew this would be a loud concert. Behind the waiting instruments, from one side of the stage to the other, a row of amplifiers hummed and glowed with small red lights. Towering up at each far side was a wall of huge black speakers. From overhead in the hall, the announcer's voice boomed.

   10. Israeli archaeologists have reported their discovery of an ancient zither, or cithara, near Haifa. The zither, a flat, stringed instrument made of wood, was found in the tomb of an ancient royal family. "It was in very good condition," one professor said.

11. Rhea took a deep breath. Behind her she could hear the orchestra members giving her just the right tempo. Her fingers danced up the violin's neck. The notes from Rhea's violin climbed and climbed. She was about to hit the most difficult part of the composition.

12. First Linda sang the two verses of the old blues song. Then she stepped back from the spotlight and let Rikki take over on guitar. Each long note sounded like a moan of misery. A moment later, Linda was back to accompany Rikki's mournful strings in a brilliant, melancholy finale.

13. Irene Kelly's latest musical opened last night on Broadway in New York City. As Ms. Kelly and the cast of ''A Musical Jamboree'' took their first of many curtain calls, the audience erupted with thundering applause. Critics noted that ''Ms. Kelly's melodies, lyrics, and story ideas are original and unforgettable.'' Theater managers expect the show to be sold out throughout the season.

14. To assure quality sound from your saxophone, the wooden reed should sometimes be changed. To do this, buy a proper replacement reed for the instrument. Unscrew the mouthpiece from the saxophone. Then remove the old reed from its metal holder. Simply insert the new reed and you are ready to play again.

C. Write a brief paragraph for one of the following topics. Before you begin, decide which organization method would work best for the topic.

how to play your favorite game
a description of your bedroom
an event that occurred recently in your town
a description of an exciting sporting event

Apply • Think and Write

Organizing Ideas • Imagine that you are the music reporter assigned to cover a musical event for your local newspaper. The event happens to be a concert featuring your favorite musical group. Write about the concert in two or more paragraphs. Use at least two of the organization methods learned in this lesson.

✎ **Remember** to organize ideas in paragraphs in a clear, logical way.

GETTING
STARTED
XXX

Complete this topic sentence: *There are many ways our class could help to* _____ . Take turns adding supporting sentences. Raise your hand if you hear a sentence that does not belong.

WRITING ♦
Paragraph Unity and Coherence

A paragraph with unity and coherence holds together and makes sense. All of its various sentences are unified to support the main idea clearly. Ideas are arranged in a logical order and flow smoothly.

Unity   To achieve unity in your paragraphs, you should first know your writing purpose. Then you can state your main idea in a topic sentence. Think about what you need to say to support the main idea. Each sentence should contribute to the whole. Do not include any unrelated or unnecessary thoughts. Notice the unrelated sentence in this paragraph.

> A musical group on tour is like a traveling corporation. In addition to band members and their families, many others are part of the company. An army of managers, security people, and technicians is needed to keep things running smoothly and to set up each show. Proper lighting is important for a concert.

Coherence   Certain words and phrases help you achieve coherence by bridging ideas within paragraphs and between paragraphs. These are called transitional words. Without transitions, your writing would be choppy and your ideas unclear. The paragraph below shows how using transitional words can create a coherent paragraph.

> First, the conductor lifted her baton. As she did this, the hall fell silent. Then she paused for a moment. The audience was full of anticipation. Paul, however, was asleep in his seat. He was snoring, so the conductor turned to him.

Summary ♦ In a unified paragraph, every sentence contributes to the main idea. Transitional words or phrases help you achieve coherence.

Guided Practice

Tell which sentence does not belong in a paragraph with the following topic sentence.

Beverly Sills is one of the greatest opera singers of our time.
1. Sills made her operatic debut in 1946.
2. Opera singers are noted for their rich, flexible voices.
3. She has performed different works by composers such as Verdi.

Practice

A. Read the following paragraph. Write the two sentences that do not support the main idea.

   The Italian composer Giuseppe Verdi wrote many operas that are among the world's best loved music. Verdi wrote a total of 26 operas. Writing an opera is a challenging task. His most productive years were between 1851 and 1871, in which he composed his major masterpieces. These include *Aida, Don Carlos*, and *Rigoletto*. An opera is a drama set to music. Many of the melodies that Verdi wrote for singers remain familiar throughout the world.

B. Rewrite the paragraph below to make it more unified and coherent. Add one or more transitions. Delete any unrelated details or sentences.

   There is a lot of hard work behind the glamour of producing records. You must know music. You must study music theory. You need to work in training studios to learn about recording technology, which some people say is too complex. Gradually, you will become acquainted with artists and technicians. You may receive larger roles in each record production project. Musical artists often prefer to do live performances.

Apply ◆ Think and Write

Dictionary of Knowledge ◆ The musical conductor is one of the most important persons in an orchestra. Read about the duties of a conductor in the Dictionary of Knowledge. Make notes on the facts that interest you most. Then write a unified, coherent paragraph that discusses why you think a conductor is important in an orchestra.

> ✎ **Remember**
> to use transitions to connect ideas in your paragraphs.

Focus on Clarity

In telling how to build a washtub bass, the author of "Jug Bands" (pages 74–78) gives precise information in the clearest possible way. You can write sentences and paragraphs of equal clarity. To do so, you will use some of the techniques the author uses.

First the author lists the parts needed to build the bass. Then, in **numbered steps**, he tells how to assemble the parts. His numbered steps put the directions in **time order**. Readers can follow the numbered steps easily.

1. Turn the washtub upside down.
2. Cut or whittle a small notch in one end of the broom handle.
3. Position the tub on the floor so you are standing directly behind the neck.

Directions can also be written in paragraph form. Instead of putting numbers at the beginning of sentences, you use special words. These are **time-order words**, such as *first* and *then*, which signal the end of one step and the beginning of the next step.

First turn the washtub upside down. **Then** drive a large nail through the bottom center of it. **Next**, put one end of the cord through the hole. **Finally**, tie something to the cord to prevent it from pulling back through the hole.

Sometimes, **diagrams** or other illustrations add clarity to the written instructions. If they are helpful, use them.

The Writer's Voice ◆ Time order is useful in various kinds of writing. For example, recipes are written in time order. So are many paragraphs in history books. What other kinds of writing use time order?

Working Together

One way to gain clarity in writing is to use time-ordered development when the material permits it. Be sure your steps are in order, and the transitions between them are clear as you do activities **A** and **B**.

In Your Group
♦ Contribute your ideas.   ♦ Agree or disagree in a pleasant way. ♦ Invite others to talk.   ♦ Record the group's ideas.

A. Which of the topics below are suitable for time-order development and which are not?

1. The Appearance of My Room

2. How to Hard-boil an Egg

3. Five Reasons to Go to College

4. An Exciting Day at the Beach

B. The following paragraph lacks clarity. As a group, revise it so that the events are in order.

Sousa played in Offenbach's orchestra when it toured America in 1876 and 1877. As a boy, he studied violin and harmony, working as an apprentice to the United States Marine Band. One of his best-known marches, "The Stars and Stripes Forever," was composed a year before the Spanish-American War broke out. John Philip Sousa was born in Washington, D.C., on November 6, 1854. While employed as a bandleader of the Marine Band, he composed "Semper Fidelis" (1888) and "The Washington Post" (1889).

THESAURUS CORNER ♦ Word Choice

Clarity in writing demands the right word — not, as Mark Twain said, "its second cousin." When choosing a synonym from the Thesaurus, you must choose one that has the exact meaning you want. Write a paragraph on any topic you wish. Use at least three nouns from the Thesaurus in your writing. (These do not have to be main entry words. They can be synonyms or antonyms.)

WRITING PROCESS
INFORMING

Writing a How-to Article

People read for many reasons. One of the best reasons is to learn how to do something. You might read about changing the oil in a car, bathing a pet, or how to play a computer game.

In "Jug Bands," you learned how to create your own jug band instruments. The directions for making a washtub bass, for instance, were clear and specific enough so that you could create the instrument after reading. The purpose of this kind of informative writing is to explain *how* clearly.

Know Your Purpose and Audience

In this lesson, you will write a how-to article. Your purpose will be to inform by explaining how to do something you do well.

What's MY PURPOSE

Who's MY AUDIENCE

Your audience will be your classmates. After you complete your articles, you and your classmates can give demonstrations for each other. You might also create a "How-to" column for your school newspaper.

1 Prewriting

Prewriting is getting ready to write. First choose your topic. Then use a strategy to help you gather ideas about your topic.

Choose Your Topic ◆ Start by making a list of all the things you know how to do. List everything you can remember. Then choose the topic your audience would enjoy the most.

Think About It

Think about the things you know how to do well. Perhaps you can bake bread, do beautiful stencil work, or do a triple dive. Choose the topic you know the most about and that will interest others most.

Talk About It

Choose an interview partner. Ask your partner about his or her hobbies. Find out which one is his or her favorite. Let your partner interview you in the same way.

Topic Ideas

do a triple dive
do counted cross stitch
grow tomatoes
mow the lawn
plow a field
(do stencils)
do gymnastics

Choose Your Strategy ♦ Here are two idea-gathering strategies. Read both. Then use what you think will work for you.

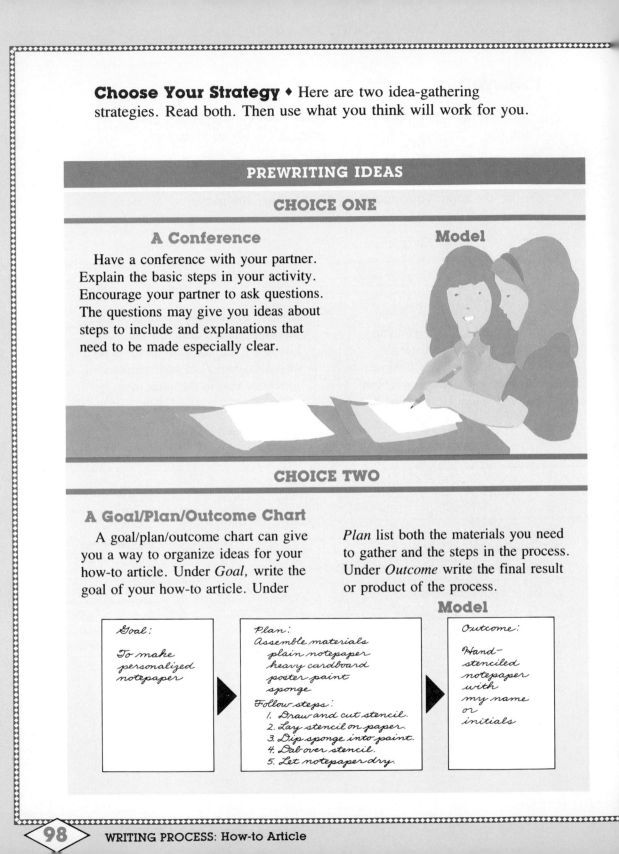

PREWRITING IDEAS

CHOICE ONE

A Conference   Model

Have a conference with your partner. Explain the basic steps in your activity. Encourage your partner to ask questions. The questions may give you ideas about steps to include and explanations that need to be made especially clear.

CHOICE TWO

A Goal/Plan/Outcome Chart

A goal/plan/outcome chart can give you a way to organize ideas for your how-to article. Under *Goal,* write the goal of your how-to article. Under *Plan* list both the materials you need to gather and the steps in the process. Under *Outcome* write the final result or product of the process.

Model

Goal:

To make personalized notepaper

Plan:
Assemble materials
  plain notepaper
  heavy cardboard
  poster paint
  sponge
Follow steps:
  1. Draw and cut stencil.
  2. Lay stencil on paper.
  3. Dip sponge into paint.
  4. Dab over stencil.
  5. Let notepaper dry.

Outcome:

Hand-stenciled notepaper with my name or initials

2 Writing

Writing is putting your ideas on paper. This organizational outline may help as you write your how-to article. Start with an introduction that identifies your topic and catches interest. The body may contain one or more paragraphs that list materials and steps in logical order. Transition words like *next*, *then*, and *after* can make the order of the steps clear. In your conclusion, give your readers encouragement or advice and bring your article to a logical close.

Sample First Draft ♦

Have you ever wanted notepaper with your name or initials on it? You can make it yourself with Homemade Stencils. Early Americans often stenciled furniture.

First assemble these materials: sheets of blank notepaper, a piece of cardboard, scissors a sponge, and poster paint. Next draw your name or initials in block letters on the cardboard. Cut the letters out the holes in the cardboard will be your stencil.

After you make the stencil, lay it on a sheet of notepaper. Next dip a part of the sponge into the paint. Pour some paint into a dish. The sponge should be damp, not wet. Dab it over the stencil onto the paper. Remove the stencil and let the letters dry.

Stenciling is one of my favorite hobbys. It isn't hard, but it takes practice. Once you've done it a few times, you'll be expert enough to decorate tee shirts, book covers, and canvas bags as well as notepaper.

Introduction
1. Identify topic.
2. Catch interest.
Body
1. List materials.
2. Explain steps in order.
Conclusion
1. Encourage and advise.
2. Close logically.

3 Revising

Revising is making changes to improve your writing. Most writers check over their first drafts to make sure that their meaning is clear. This strategy may help you.

REVISING IDEA

FIRST   Read to Yourself

As you read, think about your purpose. Did you inform your readers about how to do something? Will they understand and enjoy your how-to article? Will they be able to do the activity themselves?

Focus: Did you describe the steps clearly and in a logical order?

THEN   Share with a Partner

Ask a classmate to be your first audience. Read your article aloud to your partner and ask for feedback. These guidelines may help you and your partner.

The Writer

Guidelines: Read clearly and slowly. Listen to your partner's suggestions. Then decide what changes *you* feel are important.

Sample questions:
- Would someone unfamiliar with the process be able to follow it?
- **Focus question:** Are all the materials and steps given in a logical order?

The Writer's Partner

Guidelines: As the writer reads, try to visualize the process. Let the writer know where you have trouble visualizing it.

Sample responses:
- I think you need to explain more about how _____ .
- This part doesn't seem related to _____ .
- Is this step in the best order?

Revising Model ◆ In the sample draft below, revising marks show the changes the writer wants to make.

Revising Marks

delete ℓ

add ∧

move ⟲

Have you ever wanted notepaper with your name or initials on it? You can make it yourself with *I think you'll enjoy learning how to do it.* Homemade Stencils. ~~Early Americans often stenciled furniture.~~

First assemble these materials: sheets of blank notepaper, a piece of cardboard, scissors a sponge, and poster paint. Next draw your name or initials in block letters on the cardboard. Cut the letters out the holes in the cardboard will be your stencil.

~~After you make~~ the stencil, lay it on a sheet of notepaper. Next dip a *corner* ~~part of~~ the sponge into the paint. ⟮Pour some paint into a dish.⟯ The sponge should be damp, not wet. Dab it over the stencil onto the paper. Remove the stencil and let the letters dry.

Stenciling is one of my favorite hobbys. It isn't *difficult* ~~hard,~~ but it takes practice. Once you've done it a few times, you'll be expert enough to decorate tee shirts, book covers, and canvas bags as well as notepaper.

An unrelated idea was replaced with a related idea.

Corner is a more specific noun than *part*.

The writer's partner was confused by the order of the steps.

Difficult replaces the overused word *hard*.

Revising Checklist

☐ **Purpose:** Did I inform my readers about how to do something I do well?

☐ **Audience:** Will my classmates understand how to do the process themselves?

☐ **Focus:** Did I give all the steps clearly and in a logical order?

Read the how-to article above the way the writer has decided it *should* be. Then revise your own how-to article.

Grammar Check ◆ Specific nouns can help make your writing clear.

Word Choice ◆ Do you want to avoid overused words like *hard*? A thesaurus can help you improve your word choice.

4 Proofreading

Proofreading is looking for and fixing surface errors. A correct copy is a courtesy to your readers.

Proofreading Model ♦ Here is the draft of the how-to article on stenciling notepaper. Notice that proofreading changes in red have been added to the blue revisions.

Proofreading Marks

capital letter	≡
small letter	/
add comma	⌄
add period	⊙
indent paragraph	¶
check spelling	⬭

Proofreading Checklist

- ☐ Did I spell words correctly?
- ☐ Did I indent paragraphs?
- ☐ Did I use correct capitalization?
- ☐ Did I use correct punctuation?
- ☐ Did I type neatly or use my best handwriting?

¶ Have you ever wanted notepaper with your name or initials on it? You can make it yourself with *I think you'll enjoy learning how to do it.* Homemade Stencils. ~~Early Americans often stenciled furniture.~~

First assemble these materials: sheets of blank notepaper, a piece of cardboard, scissors a sponge, and poster paint. Next draw your name or initials in block letters on the cardboard. Cut the letters out the holes in the cardboard will be your stencil.

After you make the stencil, lay it on a sheet of notepaper. Next dip a ~~part of~~ *corner* the sponge into the paint. (Pour some paint into a dish.) The sponge should be damp, not wet. Dab it over the stencil onto the paper. Remove the stencil and let the letters dry.

Stenciling is one of my favorite (hobbys) *hobbies*. It isn't ~~hard~~ *difficult*, but it takes practice. Once you've done it a few times, you'll be expert enough to decorate tee shirts, book covers, and canvas bags as well as notepaper.

PROOFREADING IDEA

One Thing at a Time

Try reading for one thing at a time. Read once for grammar mistakes. Read again for misspelled words. Then check for errors in capitalization and punctuation.

Now proofread your how-to article and make a neat copy. Be sure to add a title.

5 Publishing

Publishing is sharing your writing with others. Try one of the ideas below for publishing your how-to article.

A Favorite Hobby

Have you ever wanted notepaper with your name or initials on it? You can make it yourself with homemade stencils. I think you'll enjoy learning how to do it.

First assemble these materials: sheets of blank notepaper, a piece of cardboard, scissors, a sponge, and poster paint. Next draw your name or initials in block letters on the cardboard. Cut the letters out. The holes in the cardboard will be your stencil.

After you make the stencil, lay it on a sheet of notepaper. Pour some paint into a dish. Next dip a corner of the sponge into the paint. The sponge should be damp, not wet. Dab it over the stencil onto the paper. Remove the stencil and let the letters dry.

Stenciling is one of my favorite hobbies. It isn't difficult, but it takes practice. Once you've done it a few times, you'll be expert enough to decorate tee shirts, book covers, and canvas bags as well as notepaper.

PUBLISHING IDEAS

Share Aloud	Share in Writing
Read your how-to articles aloud to each other. If you can, demonstrate your skill to the class or have a partner demonstrate as you explain.	Use your articles to create a how-to column for your school newspaper. Encourage readers to write and tell if they enjoyed trying the activities.

CURRICULUM CONNECTION

Writing Across the Curriculum   Music

In music, everyone has the same goal: to make good music. However, music lovers often disagree about whether a composer or musician has achieved that goal. Analyzing and evaluating music is part of the enjoyment for both music professionals and fans.

Writing to Learn

Think and Analyze   Why do some musical groups succeed and others fail? Choose your favorite group. Then make a goal/plan/outcome chart to record what the group tried to do and how it turned out.

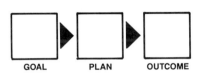

GOAL   PLAN   OUTCOME

Write   Use the information on your chart. Write a paragraph to explain why your musical group has succeeded or failed.

Writing in Your Journal

At the beginning of this unit, you wrote in your journal about why you like music and your favorite musical sounds. You went on to read more about music: folk music, jazz, careers in music, and musical theater. What new information about music did you learn in this unit? In your journal, express your answers to that question.

BOOKS TO ENJOY

Read More About It

American Indian Music and Musical Instruments *by George S. Fichter*

Mr. Fichter first gives us background information on American Indian tribes and what place music held in their lives. Then we learn all about the music—music of joy or sorrow, songs for curing sickness, even about lullabies. The book also contains a chapter on making Native American musical instruments, including full directions.

The Story of Folk Music *by Melvin Berger*

We all have some favorite folk songs. This book tells how and why this special music evolved in our country. The author has also included biographical information on popular folk singers of the past and the present.

Book Report Idea   Letter to the Author

Give a book report on a book you enjoyed in the form of a friendly letter to its author.

Dear Author ◆ Tell what you liked best about the main character and plot. Also share an opinion or two. If you have any questions about how the author came to write the story, include them. After you share your letter with classmates, you might want to mail it. Send it to the book's publishers. They will forward the letter to the author.

April 11, 1989

Dear Robin McKinley,

For the last three days I have not been able to put down your fantasy novel The Hero and the Crown. The main character, Aerlin, is exactly my idea of a hero, too. Thank you for letting me ride with her to do battle against the dragon and to wield the incredible power of the Blue Sword.

Unit 2

Nouns   *pages 56–65*

A. Write the nouns in each sentence. Then write whether each noun names a person, place, thing, or idea.

1. Many schools have personal computers.
2. Some students receive instruction to operate the machines.
3. Few instructors teach the skills in classrooms.
4. Most equipment is reserved for clerical purposes.
5. In the future, the principal will hold workshops.

B. Write the nouns in each sentence. Then write *common* or *proper* after each noun.

6. Alaska is the largest state in area of the United States.
7. Its capital is Juneau, but its largest city is Anchorage.
8. The first white settlers were Russians who were trappers.
9. Kodiak Island was the site of the first permanent Alaskan settlement.

C. Write the plural form of each noun.

10. piano
11. mystery
12. prize
13. bush
14. inch
15. pony
16. tax
17. tray

D. Write the correct plural form in parentheses.

18. life (lifes, lives)
19. leaf (leaves, leafs)
20. cupful (cupfuls, cupsful)
21. child (childs, children)
22. A (As, A's)
23. deer (deer, deers)

E. Write each noun. Label it *singular, singular possessive, plural,* or *plural possessive*.

24. Larry's
25. princess
26. wife's
27. dancers'
28. women
29. men's

Compounds   *pages 66–67*

F. **(30–34)** Use these ten words to write five compounds.

paper   dish
washer   fire
bulb   light
place   still
stand   weight

Paragraphs   *pages 82–83*

G. Read the paragraph. Then write an answer for each question below.

Baseball cards can be valuable investments for collectors. Stamp collecting is another possible investment. The value of a baseball card generally depends on the player featured, the year the card was issued, and the condition of the card. For example, if a 1910 baseball card featuring Honus Wagner is in mint condition, it may command more than $50,000 today. One way that a collector can make a profit is to select a young baseball player with potential and collect cards featuring this player. Then if the player has a good season, the value of his cards will rise. Baseball cards are almost always a solid investment.

35. What is the paragraph's main idea?
36. What is the paragraph's topic sentence?
37. Which sentences develop the main idea?
38. Which sentence does not support the main idea?
39. Is there a clincher sentence?

Organizing Ideas in a Paragraph   *pages 88–89*

H. Write the best organization method for each paragraph topic. Write *time order, space order, order of importance,* or *climactic order.*

40. A description of the exterior of the Taj Mahal in India.
41. A major announcement by the school principal.
42. A news story about a town's Independence Day celebration.
43. Instructions on how to care for your pet dog.
44. The story of how Frederick Douglass escaped from slavery.
45. The process of how to hook up a home computer.

CUMULATIVE REVIEW

UNIT 1: Sentences *pages 4–19*

A. Write the sentences, using correct punctuation. After each sentence write *declarative, interrogative, imperative,* or *exclamatory*.

1. Listen to this speech
2. Did you take notes
3. What a day this has been
4. I am next on the list

B. Write each complete subject. Underline each simple subject.

5. The skill of listening has helped many public speakers.
6. A good speaker can keep an audience's interest.
7. Some talented speakers have special styles.
8. The first step for a speaker is to get the audience's attention.

C. Write each complete predicate. Underline each verb.

9. Kim and Rita joined us in the cafeteria this afternoon.
10. All of the school's faculty members were also there.
11. An important school official made an announcement about the faculty meeting.
12. We will be playing a few games outside after lunch.

D. Write and label the compound subject or compound verb in each sentence.

13. Don, Chris, and I recently purchased school supplies.
14. Terri traveled alone but joined us later.
15. Gordon and his sister met us at the store.
16. They walked home or took the bus.

E. Write *simple* or *compound* for each sentence.

17. Please tie your shoe laces, or you will trip over them.
18. The laces are frayed, but you can still use them.
19. Sally and Paula prefer shoes with buckles.
20. I would rather slip into these moccasins or those slippers.

UNIT 2: Nouns *pages 56–65*

F. Write the nouns in each sentence. Then write whether each noun names a person, place, thing, or idea.

21. My house is located on a rural road far from the city.
22. Our family owns twenty acres of land.
23. Our neighbors recently built a barn and added a hayloft.
24. My father will soon acquire a tractor and a plow.
25. My goal is to be a successful farmer.

G. Write the nouns in each sentence. Then write *common* or *proper* after each noun.

26. The Brooklyn Bridge links the boroughs of Manhattan and Brooklyn.
27. This historic structure spans the East River in lower New York City.
28. Its strong cables were designed by John Roebling and his son.
29. The Verrazano-Narrows Bridge links Brooklyn and Staten Island, New York.
30. This bridge is named after Giovanni da Verrazano, the discoverer of New York Bay.

H. Write the plural form of each noun.

31. cello	**34.** gallery	**37.** oboe	**40.** entry
32. patch	**35.** wish	**38.** trench	**41.** surprise
33. history	**36.** decoy	**39.** article	**42.** ash

I. Write the correct plural form in parentheses.

43. handful (handfuls, handsful)
44. loaf (loafs, loaves)
45. 100 (100s, 100's)
46. wife (wifes, wives)
47. sheep (sheep, sheeps)
48. man (mans, men)

J. Write each noun. Label it *singular, singular possessive, plural,* or *plural possessive.*

49. thief's	**52.** women's	**55.** geese
50. the Garcias'	**53.** actress	**56.** Mr. Rogers's
51. children	**54.** Carmen's	**57.** chef

LANGUAGE PUZZLERS

Unit 2 Challenge

Word Clues

Write the word that can be used before or after each of the three words in the group to make a two-word proper noun. (Hint: Each missing word begins with a capital letter.)

1. Lady   Bell   Island   _ _ _ _ _ _ _
2. Arbor   Labor   Veterans   _ _ _
3. Guard   Barbary   Ranges   _ _ _ _ _
4. State   Hudson   Green   _ _ _
5. Lee   Assembly   Surgeon   _ _ _ _ _ _ _
6. League   Dipper   Stuart   _ _ _ _ _ _
7. Cross   Square   Sea   _ _ _
8. Nob   Bunker   Capitol   _ _ _ _
9. Nile   House   Mountains   _ _ _ _ _

Possessive Compounds

What possessive form is used in each of these compound nouns?

1. a pain brought on by excessive writing: _____ cramp
2. an international exposition: _____ fair
3. a plant that eats insects: _____-flytrap
4. a holiday honoring Washington and Lincoln: _____ Day
5. the center of a dart target: _____-eye
6. a short distance: _____ throw
7. a very simple task: _____ play
8. a game with string: _____ cradle

Unit 2 Extra Practice

1 Writing with Nouns

p. 56

A. Write the noun in each sentence. Then write whether it names a person, place, thing, or idea.

EXAMPLE: The bridge shook.
ANSWER: bridge, thing

1. Photographers arrived.
2. Cameras clicked.
3. Develop this film.
4. Visit my neighborhood.
5. Notice its beauty.
6. The model laughed.
7. Show more patience.
8. Is the lens dirty?
9. Never lose hope.
10. Our town is quiet.

B. Write each sentence. Then underline the nouns.

11. The principal signed the certificate during the assembly.
12. Our superintendent never lacks enthusiasm for her work.
13. Bill looked at the signature with delight.
14. At the entrance of the library was a large sign with a schedule of movies and lectures.

C. In this article about photography, there are twenty underlined words. Ten are nouns. Write each noun after its sentence number. Write *none* if the sentence has no underlined noun.

15. The first photographs were taken in the early nineteenth century. 16. For a camera a photographer used a huge wooden box. 17. Over a hole at one end was a large, thick lens. 18. The image was recorded on a metal plate coated with chemicals. 19. The camera had no gears, levers, or shutter. 20. The photographer covered the lens with his hand. 21. To take a picture, he simply took his hand away from the lens. 22. The earliest photographs are views of buildings, statues, or streets without people. 23. To make these pictures, the photographer left the lens uncovered for almost an hour. 24. Anything that moved became a smudge on these first photographs.

D. In this article there are thirty underlined words. Fifteen are nouns. Write each noun after its sentence number. Write *none* if a sentence has no underlined noun.

25. Fear and <u>pain</u> can be <u>seen</u> in the <u>faces</u> of the <u>first</u> men and women to be <u>photographed</u>. **26.** A session with a <u>photographer</u> was indeed a <u>strenuous</u> <u>experience</u>. **27.** The <u>only</u> light in the dingy, <u>odorous</u> studio came from <u>windows</u>.

28. A <u>person</u> had to remain <u>completely</u> motionless before a huge, ugly <u>camera</u> for as long as five <u>minutes</u>. **29.** Any <u>movement</u> ruined the <u>picture</u>. **30.** Usually a large metal clamp was <u>placed</u> behind the head to <u>keep</u> it still. **31.** <u>Nervous</u> <u>subjects</u> were sometimes tied in a chair. **32.** Lips were <u>firmly</u> closed, and eyes were <u>kept</u> wide open. **33.** Eventually <u>scientists</u> <u>developed</u> <u>chemicals</u> that <u>quickly</u> recorded an image on the metal plate <u>inside</u> the camera. **34.** <u>Then</u> <u>portraits</u> of lively <u>children</u> and <u>frisky</u> pets could be made.

2 Common and Proper Nouns

p. 58

A. Each set of words contains one proper noun. Write and capitalize it.

1. state, avenue, colorado, river, mountains
2. frankenstein, movie, book, story, doctor
3. festival, holiday, dinner, thanksgiving
4. coffee, forests, brazil, rivers, country
5. city, harbor, boston, college, museums

B. Write the nouns and label each noun *common* or *proper*.

6. Paris is the capital of France.
7. Alaska and Texas are our largest states.
8. A holiday in September is Labor Day.
9. The Amazon is a river in South America.
10. Many people read magazines.
11. Is Saturn the planet with rings?
12. The success of our team is assured.
13. Mark Twain was a famous American author.
14. Mr. Kim is the principal of our school.
15. Ms. Banks devotes much time to her work.
16. Gutzon Borglum worked high on Mount Rushmore.

C. Write this article, capitalizing each proper noun correctly.

17. Few photographers have been as famous in america as mathew b. brady. **18.** In 1849 he became the first photographer to make a portrait in the white house. **19.** His photograph of president james knox polk is historic. **20.** During the civil war brady had permission to take pictures of camps and battles, but he never gave military information to either side. **21.** His portraits of general ulysses s. grant and other generals are famous.

3 Making Nouns Plural

p. 60

A. Write each singular noun. After it, write its plural form.

1. bank	**6.** witness	**11.** cameo
2. tax	**7.** play	**12.** piano
3. donkey	**8.** echo	**13.** toe
4. factory	**9.** action	**14.** crutch
5. melon	**10.** brush	**15.** copy

B. Write each sentence. Use the plural form of each singular noun in parentheses.

16. Those (pencil) are not broken.

17. Your (reaction) seem to be normal.

18. Do you paint your (fence) yearly?

19. These (sandwich) certainly taste delicious.

20. There are new (dish) in the cupboard.

21. Do those (box) contain workbooks or textbooks?

22. Are the new (overpass) closed today?

23. Not one of the (library) has that book.

24. Their (ally) have surrendered.

25. Those dark (alley) lead nowhere.

26. The (display) of new books impress everyone.

27. These (community) need more bike paths.

28. Are the art (studio) on the fourth floor?

29. Sweet (potato) grow rapidly.

30. Do the (alto) know their parts?

31. Do any (auto) use kerosene?

32. Are the (hero) receiving any medals?

33. There are green (tomato) on the windowsill.

4 Nouns with Special Plural Forms p. 62

A. Write each singular noun. Under it, write its plural form.

1. cuff	**11.** belief	**21.** daughter-in-law
2. calf	**12.** thief	**22.** department of recreation
3. foot	**13.** tooth	**23.** assistant manager
4. woman	**14.** child	**24.** committee for civic pride
5. mouse	**15.** louse	**25.** lieutenant governor
6. series	**16.** goose	**26.** editor-in-chief
7. Japanese	**17.** deer	**27.** faculty assistant
8. notebook	**18.** teacup	**28.** division of motor vehicles
9. capful	**19.** bucketful	**29.** bureau of welfare
10. *U*	**20.** *12*	**30.** chief of staff

B. One noun in each sentence is misspelled. Write each misspelled word correctly.

31. The children filled boxes with leafs and twigs.

32. On those ranches were oxes, horses, and mules.

33. His sister-in-laws work in factories or stores.

34. The antlers of reindeers are quite large.

35. Friends, think about yourselfs for two minutes.

36. The jewelry and money are in those saves.

37. Put two handsful of stones in that terrarium.

38. Always dot your *is* when writing addresses.

39. The mouses were kept in large cages.

40. Scientists examined the fins, jaws, and tooths of the salmon.

41. That license plate has three *7s*.

42. They taped the two halfs of the paper together.

43. We built those shelves by ourselfs.

44. I bruised both my kneescap during the game.

45. All board of trades are closed on holidays.

C. Rewrite the following sentences, using the plural form of the underlined singular nouns. Make any other necessary changes.

46. The child fed the ox a forkful of hay.

47. The freshman received an A for his report on salmon.

48. My brother-in-law saved the life of a goose.

49. The man dug his foot into the side of the cliff.

50. The mouse knocked the dish onto the foot of the woman.

5 Possessive Nouns

A. Write each noun. Label it *singular*, *singular possessive*, *plural*, or *plural possessive*.

1. cousins	**6.** servants	**11.** children's
2. cousin's	**7.** servants'	**12.** Nicholas's
3. cousin	**8.** servant's	**13.** women's
4. cousins'	**9.** Lois	**14.** witness's
5. servant	**10.** Lois's	**15.** witnesses'

B. Write the appropriate possessive form of the noun in the prepositional phrase.

EXAMPLE: names of chiefs   (chief's, chiefs') names
ANSWER: chiefs'

16. uncle of the boy   (boy's, boys') uncle
17. wing of a bird   (bird's, birds') wing
18. faces of the girls   (girl's, girls') faces
19. hats of those men   (men's, mens') hats
20. pace of a snail   (snail's, snails') pace

C. Write the possessive form of each underlined noun.

21. We met Anns parents and Jims grandparents.
22. I always enjoy hearing her fathers stories about his childhood on a farm.
23. Many farmers sons and daughters have left the farm to live in cities.
24. Experts examined those artists paintings.
25. The childrens questions amazed the librarians.
26. Crowded parks spoil many families picnics.
27. These students desks were in that teachers room.
28. Nurses uniforms are made in this factory.
29. The womens club discussed the nations future.

D. Write the correct form of each underlined noun.

30. two coach	**34.** all child
31. all coach jackets	**35.** few child hearts
32. a pony hooves	**36.** many thief faces
33. ten pony lives	**37.** the thief mouth

UNIT THREE

USING LANGUAGE
TO

PERSUADE

PART ONE

Unit Theme *Mass Media*

Language Awareness Verbs

PART TWO

Literature Book Review of *M.C. Higgins, the Great*
by Nikki Giovanni

A Reason for Writing Persuading

Writing
IN YOUR JOURNAL

WRITER'S WARM-UP ◆ Hardly a day
passes that you do not watch TV or
listen to the radio. You read magazines,
newspapers, and books. How does the
mass media affect you? Select one form of mass
media communication to write about in your
journal. Tell how this medium could be improved,
in your opinion.

Describe a "mystery" person in your class by naming a few of his or her actions. For example: *She tells funny jokes, reads many books, and plays the trombone.* See if anyone can guess who the person is.

1 Writing with Verbs

Every sentence has a verb. The verb is the simple predicate of the sentence. It tells what the subject does or is.

Some verbs show action that is visible.

> Guglielmo Marconi <u>built</u> the first radio in 1895.
> In 1901 he <u>transmitted</u> a message across the Atlantic.

Other verbs show action that cannot be seen.

> Many people <u>heard</u> about this new invention.
> They <u>imagined</u> many uses for the radio.

Some verbs do not show action. Instead they show *being*. They state that someone or something exists. These verbs are called state-of-being verbs. The most common state-of-being verbs are forms of the verb *be*: *am, is, are, was, were, being,* and *been.*

> Radio broadcasting <u>was</u> experimental until 1920.
> Baseball games and election results <u>were</u> the first broadcasts.

Verbs that can replace a form of the verb *be* in a sentence are also state-of-being verbs. These verbs include *appear, become, feel, grow, look, remain, seem, smell, sound, stay, taste,* and *turn.*

> **remained**
> Radio ~~was~~ the major source of entertainment for years.

> **Summary** ♦ A **verb** expresses action or being. Use vivid verbs to describe actions clearly.

Guided Practice

Identify each verb as an action verb or a state-of-being verb.

1. The Golden Age of Broadcasting began in 1925.
2. Comedy and adventure shows were the core of this new medium.
3. The imaginative programs enriched the listeners' lives.

Practice

A. Write the verb in each sentence.

4. Soap companies sponsored many daytime radio dramas.
5. Some of these melodramatic "soap operas" ran for decades.
6. The lives of radio characters seemed fascinating.
7. Exciting adventure serials were favorite programs for many.
8. Families gathered together for "The Green Hornet" programs.
9. Each week this masked crusader stung another public enemy.
10. Radio comedies cheered America during difficult times.
11. Jack Benny remained a top comedian for many years.
12. He often played a violin during his comedy routine.
13. For most listeners, Jack Benny's gimmicks never grew stale.

B. Write the verb in each sentence and label it *action* or *state-of-being*.

14. President Franklin Delano Roosevelt spoke often on radio.
15. He discussed America's problems and possible solutions.
16. With these "fireside chats," Roosevelt became very popular.
17. "The War of the Worlds," a 1938 drama, was a major radio event.
18. This show described a Martian invasion of New Jersey.
19. The actor Orson Welles played a news reporter at the scene.
20. Panic was the result in many American homes.
21. Convincing sound effects were important in radio drama.
22. The right music also seemed necessary for setting the mood.
23. Listeners pictured the scenes with their imagination.

C. Write sentences that include the following verbs. Label each verb *action* or *state-of-being*.

24. was	**26.** think	**28.** decide
25. listened	**27.** seems	**29.** believe

> 📎 **Remember**
> that verbs can show actions in descriptive and specific ways.

Apply • Think and Write

From Your Writing List the verbs that you used in the Writer's Warm-up. Add or change some verbs to express your ideas more clearly.

Think of words to substitute for *might* in this sentence: *I might watch television*. List as many words as you can that will fit in the sentence.

2 Verb Phrases

A verb often consists of more than one word. When a verb has two or more words, it is called a verb phrase.

Verb: Television broadcasts <u>began</u> in the late 1930s.

Verb Phrases: Television <u>has become</u> a popular medium.
Some studios <u>have been producing</u> shows for years.

The most important verb in a verb phrase is the **main verb**. The other verbs are **helping verbs**. The chart lists common helping verbs.

Helping Verbs							
am	was	being	has	does	could	shall	might
is	were	been	had	did	will	should	must
are	be	have	do	can	would	may	

Some helping verbs can also be used as main verbs in sentences.

Main Verb: The first television shows <u>were</u> popular.

Helping Verb: They <u>were</u> *shown* only in certain areas.

Words can interrupt verb phrases. Notice in the following sentences that *not* and *n't* are not parts of the verbs.

We <u>are</u> not <u>reading</u> about the early TV programs today.
<u>Doesn't</u> this early TV set <u>look</u> small?

Summary ♦ A **verb phrase** is made up of a main verb and one or more helping verbs.

Guided Practice

Name the helping verbs and main verbs in these sentences.

1. In 1945 no more than 10,000 TV sets could be found in our land.
2. Dozens of people might gather around one set.
3. Within a few years new TV stations had sprung up everywhere.

Practice

A. Write the verb phrase in each sentence. Underline the main verb.

4. By 1950 the number of TV sets had soared to six million.
5. The early shows were broadcast in black and white.
6. Color television wouldn't begin until 1953.
7. Milton Berle could be described as TV's first star.
8. His zany comedy show would run from 1948 to 1956.
9. It was watched by over 80 percent of all TV viewers.
10. TV shows for children were also gaining in popularity.
11. "The Howdy Doody Show" did appear in most areas after 1948.
12. The show's puppetry and humor had enchanted viewers.
13. Viewers were also enjoying the antics of Lucille Ball in "I Love Lucy."

B. Write appropriate helping verbs that complete the sentences.

14. Many shows ____ produced live in TV's early days.
15. By the mid-1950s, however, videotaping ____ become a major method of production.
16. Picture and sound quality ____ constantly improving due to continuing technological advances.
17. Today, audiences ____ watch wall-size or pocket-size TV's.
18. The first communication satellite ____ launched in 1965.
19. Satellites ____ made worldwide communications possible.
20. In the future, cable TV ____ continue its rapid growth.
21. VCR's ____ giving TV owners even greater flexibility.
22. Families ____ now record home movies with video cameras.
23. We ____ soon see even more exciting changes.

C. Write sentences that include the following main verbs with appropriate helping verbs.

24. enjoyed **25.** watching **26.** made **27.** seen

Apply • Think and Write

Creative Writing • Imagine what television might be like forty years from now. Describe some TV programs of the future. Underline all the verb phrases that you use and circle the helping verbs.

✎ **Remember**
to use helping verbs
to express your
meaning accurately.

GETTING STARTED

Play "I am a . . . ." In your mind, complete the sentence with the name of an object, such as *table*, *flag*, or *mailbox*. Act out the object and see if anyone can guess what you are.

3 Linking Verbs

A state-of-being verb often acts as a linking verb. It connects, or links, the subject of a sentence with a word or words in the predicate.

> Many television shows <u>are</u> comedies.
> Adventure shows <u>are</u> lively.

In the first example, the linking verb *are* connects the subject *shows* with the word *comedies*, which renames the subject. In the second example, *are* links *shows* with *lively*, a word that describes the subject.

The most common linking verbs are listed below.

Forms of *Be*	Other Linking Verbs
am, is, are, was, were, being, been	appear, become, feel, grow, look, remain seem, smell, sound, stay, taste, turn

A verb phrase in which the main verb is a form of *be* also is a linking verb.

> ■ Some reruns <u>have been</u> popular for decades.

Many linking verbs can also be used as action verbs.

Linking Verb: These shows <u>look</u> informative.
Action Verb: We <u>look</u> at these shows.

Notice that the linking verb *look* connects the subject *shows* with *informative*, a word that describes the subject. The action verb *look* does not connect the subject with a word in the predicate.

> **Summary** ◆ A **linking verb** connects the subject with a word or words in the predicate.

122 GRAMMAR: Linking Verbs

Guided Practice

Name the linking verb in each sentence.

1. Action and comedy shows are the mainstays of network television.
2. These types of shows seem the most popular.
3. Many dramatic shows have also been successful and appreciated.

Practice

A. Write the linking verb in each sentence.

    4. Coverage of newsworthy events is one of TV's roles.
    5. With TV, people can grow more aware of current events.
    6. On TV, distant places and events somehow feel close at hand.
    7. News analysis by experts seems increasingly popular too.
    8. Documentaries are informative television programs.
    9. For many children, TV has been an early teacher.
    10. ''Sesame Street'' is a favorite show among young children.
    11. Movies remain a major part of the TV schedule.
    12. Some movies seem worthy of a second viewing.

B. Write the verb in each sentence. Write *LV* if it is a linking verb or *AV* if it is an action verb.

    13. A wide variety of sports programming appears on TV.
    14. We looked at a football game.
    15. The players looked strong.
    16. The television sportscaster sounded excited.
    17. The officals sounded the horn to start the game.

C. Write each sentence, completing it with a linking verb and a word or words that rename or describe the subject of the sentence.

    18. My favorite situation comedy _____ .
    19. The actors in this sitcom _____ .
    20. Television sportscasts _____ .
    21. One problem with television _____ .

Apply ◆ Think and Write

A Viewer's Choice ◆ What is your favorite television show? Write about the show, describing the basic plot and regular characters. Underline the linking verbs that you use.

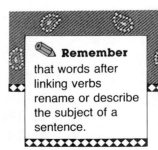

✎ **Remember** that words after linking verbs rename or describe the subject of a sentence.

Describe a few events using this pattern: noun-verb-noun. Begin most of the words of each sentence with the same letter.

Applesauce attracts ants.   Bees bothered Ben.   Cal caught a cold.

4 Verbs with Direct Objects

Every sentence has a predicate. If the verb in the predicate is an action verb, the sentence may need a direct object to complete its meaning. The direct object answers *Whom?* or *What?* after the verb and receives the action. It is usually a noun or pronoun.

Subject	Verb	Direct Object(s)
Television	employs (employs whom?)	many <u>workers</u>.
Television shows	require (require what?)	<u>writers</u> and <u>editors</u>.

In most sentences, the direct object follows the verb. Other words may stand between a verb and the direct object. Two or more direct objects form a compound direct object.

When an action verb has a direct object to complete its meaning, it is a **transitive verb**. An action verb that has no direct object is an **intransitive verb**.

Transitive: Writers <u>prepare</u> scripts. (Prepare what? scripts)
Intransitive: Some viewers <u>laugh</u> loudly. Others <u>frown</u>.

Many action verbs can be either transitive or intransitive.

Transitive: Some scripts <u>entertain</u> viewers.
Intransitive: Some scripts <u>entertain</u>.

Since linking verbs do not convey action and do not have direct objects, they are always intransitive.

Summary ◆ The **direct object** receives the action of the verb.

Guided Practice

Name the direct objects in the sentences.

1. Many workers create a show for TV.
2. The producer chooses a script and a director.
3. The director makes many artistic and technical decisions.

Practice

A. Write the subject, the verb or verb phrase, and the direct object in each sentence. Write *DO* above each direct object.

4. Creative designers have planned the sets.
5. A camera operator moves the camera to different positions.
6. The technical crew plans each position beforehand.
7. Audio technicians follow the dialogue and actions closely.
8. They mix the sound of voices, music, and sound effects.
9. The actors must reach their locations on cue.
10. All performers must know their parts well.
11. A manager directs traffic in the studio.
12. Stagehands move props to the right locations.
13. Technicians in the control booth operate other equipment.

B. Write the verb in each sentence and label it *transitive* or *intransitive*. If a verb is transitive, write its direct object.

14. Television reporters often work hard.
15. These journalists gather news at the scene of the event.
16. A camera and sound crew often goes along.
17. TV journalists prepare short, clear reports for newscasts.
18. An anchorperson in the studio introduces each news report.

C. Write each sentence, completing it with a direct object.

19. A news reporter witnesses ____ .
20. An anchorperson describes ____ .
21. A journalist interviews ____ .
22. The camera crew films ____ .
23. Viewers see ____ .

Apply ◆ Think and Write

An Investigator's View ◆ Write about a situation in your neighborhood or town that you would like to investigate for a televised report. Describe why you think the situation would make an interesting or important story. Circle all the direct objects in your sentences.

✎ **Remember** that direct objects provide useful information to your readers.

GETTING STARTED

Add words to complete this sentence: *I gave____ the____ .* For example: *I gave John the book.* Then move the last word and add another: *I gave the book a title.* How many sentences can you form in this way?

5 Verbs with Indirect Objects

Some sentences have two different kinds of objects after the verb. A direct object receives the action of the verb. An indirect object tells to whom or for whom something is done. To find an indirect object, ask "to whom (or what?)" or "for whom (or what?)" after the verb.

■ The reporter gave <u>us</u> a tour of the newspaper office.

In the sentence above, *tour* is the direct object and *us* is the indirect object. *Us* tells to whom the reporter gave the tour. Notice that the indirect object comes before the direct object.

Although an indirect object tells to whom or for whom, it is not preceded by the words *to* or *for*.

| She showed <u>us</u> the computer. (indirect object)
She showed the computer to us. (no indirect object)

Two or more indirect objects form a compound indirect object.

■ We asked the <u>editor</u> and the <u>reporters</u> many questions.

These verbs often have indirect objects: *bring*, *buy*, *give*, *lend*, *offer*, *owe*, *sell*, *send*, *show*, *teach*, *tell*, and *write*.

> **Summary** ♦ The **indirect object** comes before the direct object. It tells to whom or for whom the action of the verb is done. You can use indirect objects to complete the meaning of sentences.

Guided Practice

Name the indirect objects in the sentences.

1. Many citizens write the editors letters.
2. Writers tell them their feelings about current events and problems.
3. The editorial pages give people and the editors the opportunity to express their opinions.

Practice

A. Write each indirect object in the sentences.

4. News reporters hand the editors stories about local events.

5. The reporters have asked eyewitnesses and experts many questions about these news events.

6. News services sell the editors stories from distant places.

7. Feature groups offer every newspaper various items.

8. A book critic showed our class his latest review.

9. A review tells the public a book's strengths and weaknesses.

10. Other critics offer readers opinions on drama, film, and TV.

11. Editors show layout artists the positions of stories.

12. We gave our editor some suggestions for catchy headlines.

13. The layout artist showed us different page designs.

B. Write the sentences and label the verbs *V*, the indirect objects *IO*, and the direct objects *DO*.

14. Some workers gave the visitors information about their jobs.

15. A printer showed us the printing plates and presses.

16. An advertising department sells businesses space for ads.

17. People also give the paper short classified ads.

18. The circulation department sends stores and news-carriers their papers on time.

C. Write each sentence, completing it with an indirect object.

19. I gave _____ information about the new park.

20. Later, we wrote _____ a letter.

21. The reporter mailed _____ a copy of the story.

22. A reporter told _____ news about an important event.

23. A group of us offered _____ help in working on the story.

Apply • Think and Write

Dictionary of Knowledge • Joseph Pulitzer was a noted American newspaper publisher who established the prestigious Pulitzer Prizes. Read about Pulitzer in the Dictionary of Knowledge. Imagine trying to write a prize-winning news story. Describe what you would write about. Include an indirect object in at least one of your sentences.

> **Remember**
> that you can use indirect objects before direct objects to express complete thoughts.

Make up a riddle using linking verbs. For example: *I am a writer. I can be sharp at times. But I grow smaller every day. What am I?* Say your riddle aloud and see if anyone can guess your identity.

6 Predicate Nominatives and Predicate Adjectives

As you know, a linking verb does not show action. Rather, it connects the subject with a word in the predicate. If this word in the predicate is a noun or pronoun, it is called a predicate nominative. A predicate nominative functions differently from a direct object. It renames or identifies the subject. A direct object does not.

> Book publishing is an important <u>industry</u>. (predicate nominative)
> Book publishing attracts many creative <u>people</u>. (direct object)

If the word linked to the subject describes the subject, it is a predicate adjective.

> ■ Books can be quite <u>enjoyable</u> to readers.

In the sentence above, the adjective *enjoyable* describes the subject *books*.

You may use compound predicate nominatives and compound predicate adjectives in your sentences.

> Many of the workers in publishing are <u>editors</u> or <u>designers</u>.
> This book is <u>delightful</u> and <u>attractive</u>.

> **Summary** ♦ A **predicate nominative** is a noun or pronoun that follows a linking verb and renames or identifies the subject of the sentence. A **predicate adjective** follows a linking verb and describes the subject of the sentence.

Guided Practice

Identify each predicate nominative or predicate adjective.

1. A publishing house is a bookmaking company.
2. Over 18,000 publishing companies are successful in our country.
3. The publisher is the director of a publishing house.

Practice

A. Write the linking verb in each sentence. Then write and label each predicate nominative (*PN*) or predicate adjective (*PA*).

4. The job of selling a manuscript is often difficult.
5. A literary agent is an author's representative.
6. An author may be original and creative.
7. Editors are the preparers of manuscripts.
8. An edited manuscript should be clear and orderly.
9. A copy editor is an authority on proper style.
10. Researchers must be certain of the facts in a book.
11. A book's design should appear attractive to readers.
12. Modern printing presses seem gigantic.
13. A royalty is the author's share of a book's profits.

B. Write each sentence, underlining the verb. Then label each direct object (*DO*), predicate nominative (*PN*), or predicate adjective (*PA*).

14. Bookstores sell mainly trade books.
15. Examples of trade books are novels and biographies.
16. An educational publisher is a producer of textbooks.
17. Textbook use has become widespread across the nation.
18. Reference books should present current information.

C. Write each sentence, completing it with a predicate adjective (*PA*) or a predicate nominative (*PN*). Add any other words you need to complete your idea.

19. A good book can become a (PN) .
20. The best writing sounds (PA) .
21. My favorite novel is probably (PN) .
22. Reference books such as encyclopedias are (PA) .
23. A textbook can be a (PN) .

Apply • Think and Write

An Author's Plan • Imagine that you have been asked to write a book for a famous publishing company. Write about the type of book that you would like to have published. Briefly describe the content. Include one sentence with a predicate nominative and one sentence with a predicate adjective.

Remember to use predicate nominatives and adjectives that describe the sentence subject.

GETTING STARTED

What does *brought up* mean in these sentences? *Bill brought up some firewood. Beth brought up a problem. Old Mother Hubbard brought up her children.*

VOCABULARY •
Idioms

If a person tells you "It's raining cats and dogs," should you call the animal catcher or get your umbrella? If someone asks you "What's up?" do you check to see what's above your head? Phrases like these are called idioms. **Idioms** are expressions whose meanings cannot be understood by simply combining the meanings of their individual words.

Most native speakers of English easily understand many idioms. We understand them because we have heard them used over and over again. People whose first language is not English, however, often have difficulty understanding idioms. Imagine hearing the expressions below for the first time. What would you think they meant?

Marcia really <u>fell for</u> our trick.
Sometimes I'm <u>all thumbs</u>.
It's important to <u>stand up for your rights</u>.
Terry is <u>up to his neck</u> in work.

Idioms, when used well, add clarity and color to writing and speech. When overused, idioms make writing and speech dull and "muddy." Learn to recognize idioms in speech and writing, and use the ones that best express your meaning.

Building Your Vocabulary

Match the idioms in column **A** with their meanings in column **B**. Create sentences that include the idioms.

A	**B**
1. to be done in	to be finished with
2. to drop a line	to be exhausted
3. to go all out	to fail to remember
4. to draw a blank	to write a letter
5. to be through with	to quit
6. to give up	to try hard

Practice

A. Rewrite the sentences. Replace the underlined idioms with words whose meanings might be clearer to a new speaker of English.

EXAMPLE: We asked the boys to <u>pitch in</u>.
ANSWER: We asked the boys to *help with the job*.

1. In his bright-orange shirt, Jack <u>stands out</u>.
2. My father really <u>blew his stack</u> last night.
3. The campers woke up at <u>the crack of dawn</u>.
4. The teacher asked the noisy students to <u>pipe down</u>.
5. After plowing the field, the farmer <u>called it a day</u>.
6. Janet was <u>in the doghouse</u> after breaking two dishes.
7. We worked on the engine all day but <u>got nowhere</u>.
8. We just couldn't <u>figure out</u> what was wrong.
9. After three hours everyone <u>ran out of</u> ideas.
10. The actor feels <u>at home</u> on the stage.

B. Clichés are expressions that have become "worn out" through overuse. Some idioms are also clichés. Rewrite the story below, replacing the underlined clichés with clearer language.

Jimmy J. James, our new mayor, who speaks to reporters <u>once in a blue moon</u>, held a press conference today at town hall. He <u>didn't beat around the bush</u>. "I'm not going to try to <u>pull the wool over your eyes</u>," he said. "This town is <u>going to the dogs</u>. So far, we've done nothing but <u>shoot the breeze</u>; now it's time for action. Our laws are going to be tougher. I want lawbreakers to know I'm going to <u>throw the book at them</u>. In this town, it's going to be <u>shape up or ship out</u>. As long as I'm mayor, this town is going to be <u>as clean as a whistle</u>."

Language Corner · Brand Names

The brand names of some products have been used so much that they became everyday words. Here are a few: *zipper, kerosene, aspirin, nylon*.

What are some other brand names that you use in everyday language?

How to Revise Sentences with Verbs

In this unit you have learned more about verbs and how they function in sentences. Choosing the best possible verbs for your sentences can make a difference in your writing. Exact verbs can enliven your writing and turn a dull sentence into an interesting one. Read the following sentences.

1. The children came into the room and looked at the visitor.
2. The children raced into the room and stared at the visitor.

Both sentences tell *what* the children did, but sentence **2** tells more than just what happened. The exact verbs *raced* and *stared* tell the reader exactly *how* the children acted. The children could have come into the room and looked at the visitor in an entirely different manner.

3. The children sauntered into the room and glanced at the visitor.

Choosing the best verb for a sentence usually involves finding the most precise verb to give your reader the most complete information possible. Sometimes this could be a matter of deciding whether to use an action verb or a linking verb. In most cases, an action verb can state an idea more directly and clearly than a linking verb. For example:

4. Comedians were the stars of many early radio shows.
5. Comedians starred in many early radio shows.

The Grammar Game ♦ Concentrate on verbs! Replace the underlined verbs in the sentences below with more exact verbs. Write each sentence at least twice, substituting exact verbs that differ in meaning.

It <u>rained</u> today.
Maria <u>spoke</u> to her friend.
I <u>hurt</u> my finger.

The child <u>cried</u>.
I <u>went</u> to school.
Joe <u>laughs</u> a lot.

Working Together

Use exact and active verbs to enliven your writing as you work with your group on activities **A** and **B**.

In Your Group

- Be sure everyone understands the task.
- Show appreciation for others' ideas.
- Contribute your ideas.
- Agree or disagree pleasantly.

A. Rewrite the sentences below, substituting action verbs for linking verbs. Be sure to make all necessary corrections.

1. Radio was enjoyable for millions of people during the 1930s.
2. George Burns and Gracie Allen were a source of entertainment for people of all ages.
3. Sound effects were responsible for providing much of the action.
4. Crews were able to imitate the sound of horses by pounding rhythmically on wood.

B. Rewrite the paragraph below, using more exact or active verbs of the group's choice.

Early television comedians were masters of visual humor. Milton Berle went around the stage in outlandish costumes. Jackie Gleason made and did an entire cast of characters for his shows. Ernie Kovacs used props for humor. Furniture and lamps were sources of movement around the sets. These comedians were the delight of television viewers everywhere.

WRITERS' CORNER • Overused Verbs

Avoid repeating the same verbs too often in a piece of writing. Overused verbs can make your writing monotonous and hard to read.

Television became very popular during the 1950s. Radio and movies became less important. Television personalities became overnight celebrities. Television became a big business.

Improve a few of the sentences above by using different verbs. Then read what you wrote for the Writer's Warm-up. Did you overuse any verbs? If you did, choose a few sentences to improve.

USING LANGUAGE
TO
PERSUADE

═══ **PART TWO** ═══

Literature   Book Review of *M.C. Higgins, the Great*
by Nikki Giovanni

A Reason for Writing Persuading

CREATIVE
Writing

FINE ARTS ◆ Imagine that one of the men in Max
Weber's painting came to life for one hour. You are
asked to interview him. What would the man say
about his life? What would he say about the
medium with which he shares the painting? Write
a transcript of the interview you have with him.

CREATIVE THINKING ◆
A Strategy for Persuading

A CLUSTER MAP

Persuading means getting someone to agree with you. One kind of persuasive writing is a review. The reviewer states his or her opinion of a book or movie, for example. Then the reviewer supports that opinion with persuasive details. After this lesson you will read Nikki Giovanni's review of the book *M.C. Higgins, the Great* by Virginia Hamilton. Later you will write a review of a television program or movie.

One thing a reviewer often does is summarize a story plot. Nikki Giovanni packs a number of details into this one sentence from her review of *M.C. Higgins, the Great*.

> His great-grandmother Sarah had traveled to this mountain with a baby on her hip and the hounds of the slavemaster at her heels some hundred years ago.

Details are important in a review. In her review, Nikki Giovanni summarizes details of the plot. She also elaborates, or tells in detail, what she thinks of the book.

Learning the Strategy

How can you gather or generate and record ideas? What if you were on a committee that was planning a local teen television show. What is a way of thinking up and keeping track of ideas for the show? Suppose you have been assigned to interview your new principal for the school paper. How can you organize the facts you gather from your interview? Imagine that you are preparing an oral report about the Olympic Games. How can you round up the information you already have and add new facts you find out from research?

A cluster map is a strategy that has several uses. It can help you round up facts. It can help trigger new ideas. It is also a way to organize ideas into related groups.

A cluster map about the Olympic Games might look like the one below. The red circle in the center contains the topic. Subtopics are in blue circles attached to the topic circle. Details are in green circles attached to the subtopic circles. What do you know about the Olympics? What facts might you add to this cluster map?

Using the Strategy

A. Make a cluster map about yourself. Put your name in the topic circle. Add subtopics such as ''my favorite things'' or ''my talents.'' Add detail circles about each subtopic. If you like, use your cluster to write an entry about yourself for a class ''Who's Who.''

B. In her review of *M.C. Higgins, the Great* Nikki Giovanni gives her opinion of what makes this story worth reading. What do you think makes a story enjoyable? Make a cluster map. In the topic circle write ''What is good fiction?'' Subtopics might include ''plot,'' ''characters,'' and ''setting.'' In the detail circles, write what you look for in a story. Is it a fast-moving plot? Realistic characters? An exotic setting? As you read Nikki Giovanni's review, compare your ideas with hers.

Applying the Strategy

◆ How does a cluster map help you think of new ideas?
◆ Describe one time this week when you have had to or will have to round up or generate facts or ideas.

M.C. HIGGINS,
the Great

M.C.
HIGGINS,
THE GREAT
Winner of the
NEWBERY MEDAL
Virginia
Hamilton

Book Review by Nikki Giovanni

They say the pity of youth is that it's wasted on the young. Since we're well into our thirties and because we love the stories of Virginia Hamilton we must agree. Before motherhood descended upon us we could curl up in a corner with "Zeely" or "The Planet of Junior Brown" and cry all alone remembering…wishing…hoping about a childhood of our dreams. Now we gather child, dog, and gerbils (after we have extracted their promise not to chew the book) around us on the couch, under the quilt, with a big bowl of popcorn and share *M.C. Higgins, the Great*. Actually we're proud to share Virginia Hamilton with our family. They should know the good things.

Nikki Giovanni

Virginia Hamilton

M.C. Higgins is a very nice dude. He's just beginning to recognize girls as different from boys and basically worthy of kissing. But M.C. also has come into a recognition of responsibility. His family lives on Sarah's Mountain which, because of strip mining, is in danger of being deluged by the waste. M.C. doesn't quite understand that strip mining will forever change the countryside he has grown so used to but he does know his way of life is in danger. He dreams and ultimately plans a way to save his mountain.

The dream involves his mother. Banina Higgins has the best voice in the state and another dude with a tape recorder is coming to "take his mother's voice" and make her a star. M.C. is sure when the dude hears her sing that's exactly what he will do. But Ben Killburn isn't so sure. Ben is M.C.'s best friend though they have to keep that a secret since the Killburns are "strange people" and M.C.'s father, Jones, wants nothing to do with them.

Into M.C.'s and Ben's life comes Lurhetta, a girl who works all year during school so that she can roam the countryside in the summer. She is, as neither Ben nor M.C. are even likely to know, free. But with free-

Review

dom comes always a price. The ability to take care of yourself, to follow your own wishes also compels you to travel alone. M.C. can leave Sarah's Mountain, can leave his stubborn father, can be free from watching his younger brothers and sisters but he will also be without roots. His great-grandmother Sarah had traveled to this mountain with a baby on her hip and the hounds of the slavemaster at her heels some hundred years ago. Could he, should he really turn that land over to those who only see the coal beneath…not the love…the sacrifice…the history the hill represents? Once Jones had hauled a pole home. Forty feet high and planted it. M.C. somehow got a bicycle to the top. He sits atop it balancing between the summer of his promise and the winter of his youth. Lurhetta leaves M.C. a knife as she folds up her tent to travel on alone: a shiny new pointed shaft that can be used or put away — that can plow or ply. It's M.C.'s choice whether to dream realities or to escape into fantasies. Mayo Cornelius Higgins makes the only decision a truly great person could make.

Once again Virginia Hamilton creates a world and invites us in. *M.C. Higgins, the Great* is not an adorable book, not a lived-happily-ever-after kind of story. It is warm, humane and hopeful and does what every book should do — creates characters with whom we can identify and for whom we care. M.C.'s plight may cause some to reconsider our acceptance of strip mining. Without extra coal some may be a bit cooler but with the extra coal many will be homeless and worse, rootless. Is that really fair? We're glad M.C. decided to build his wall with the headstones of his ancestors. Old Sarah gave her great-grandson not only the mountain but the ability to claim it. Virginia Hamilton has joined the forces of hope with the forces of dreams to forge a powerful story. We're glad Miss Hamilton is a writer. It makes the world just a little bit richer and our lives just a little bit warmer.

Library Link ♦ *This review of* M.C. Higgins, the Great *appeared in the New York Times Book Review. Many local newspapers have daily or Sunday book reviews.*

 ## Reader's Response

Does Nikki Giovanni's review of *M.C. Higgins, the Great* make you want to read the book? Explain why or why not.

M.C. HIGGINS,
the Great

Book Review by Nikki Giovanni

 ## Responding to Literature

1. Of all the characters in the book, which one might become your favorite? Tell why that character may be the most interesting.

2. What is your opinion of a character who would put a bicycle on top of a forty-foot pole? What questions would you like answered? Work with a partner. Write five questions to ask M.C. Trade papers and answer your partner's questions as M.C. might answer them.

3. Nikki Giovanni says that "once again Virginia Hamilton creates a world and invites us in." Do you remember a book that opened a new world and invited you in? Write a journal entry. Tell the name and author of the book. Describe the world you discovered and how it made you feel.

 ## Writing to Learn

Think and Elaborate ◆ A cluster map can help you capture many of your ideas about *M.C. Higgins, the Great.* Put the book's name in a center circle and cluster words around it.

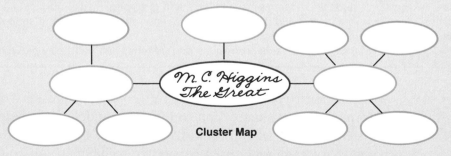

Cluster Map

Write ◆ Use your word cluster to write a paragraph about the book. Tell why you might or might not read it.

Name a product you prefer to others like it. Can you give some facts to explain why you prefer this particular product? If not, how can you explain your preference?

SPEAKING and LISTENING ♦
Critical Listening

Good listeners are critical listeners. They do not accept everything they hear. Instead, they evaluate, or judge, what they hear. To do this they have to be able to tell the difference between fact and opinion. A **fact** is a statement that can be proved to be true. An **opinion** is what a person *believes* or *thinks* about something. An opinion cannot be proved; however, it can be supported with facts. Sometimes facts and opinions may appear in the same sentence. If you listen critically and use common sense, you will be able to tell the difference between fact and opinion. Use the guidelines below to help you.

Being a Critical Listener	1. Are the statements facts or opinions or both? 2. Does the speaker support his or her statements or opinions with facts and examples? 3. Can those facts be proved in reliable sources, such as encyclopedias or almanacs, or by asking an expert to verify them?

It is important to remember that when you speak, your audience can also listen critically. Use the guidelines below to help you present information in a convincing and persuasive way.

Being an Effective Speaker	1. State your information clearly and honestly. 2. Support your statements with facts and examples. 3. If you are trying to persuade others of your opinion, be sure to support your opinion with facts. 4. Make sure your facts are reliable and that they can be readily proved.

Many areas of your life, such as TV, constantly present you with information to evaluate. You can use the guidelines to help you to listen critically as you view TV. A critical listener should also be aware of commonly used persuasive techniques. As you study the persuasive techniques on the next page, see if you can recall their use in any recent TV shows or commercials.

Recognizing Propaganda Techniques

Certain persuasive techniques are often found in propaganda. **Propaganda** is an organized effort to spread ideas about a person, product, or cause. Sometimes propaganda contains accurate information. Sometimes it does not. A critical listener is familiar with the following propaganda techniques and is not misled by them.

Loaded Words   This method uses words that appeal to your emotions. Using the word *patriotic* might stir you to vote for:
- Candidate Dithers—the choice of patriotic Americans!

Faulty Cause and Effect   This appeal assumes that one event causes another to happen. Actually, there is no real connection.
- We've been in business for 50 years. That makes us the best!

Bandwagon   This implies that you will miss something superb if you don't "jump on the bandwagon" and do what everyone else is doing.
- Don't be left out. Join millions of people at the Health Club.

Testimonial   This uses a famous person to recommend that you do, buy, or believe something.
- "Be a star like me. Use Slip 'n' Slide Face Cream."

Mudslinging   This tells you why competitors or others are "bad" but does not offer facts that can be verified.
- Subscribe to *Space* magazine. The others are cheap imitations.

Transfer   This shows you something you feel good about and tries to transfer those positive feelings to something else.
- If you love animals, you'll adore our fall fashion designs.

Summary ♦ Critical listening requires that you be able to distinguish between fact and opinion. Effective speaking requires that you support your message with facts. Use your awareness of propaganda techniques to help you evaluate persuasive appeals.

Guided Practice

Tell whether each statement is a fact or an opinion.

1. You can't expect to make it as a performer unless you have clean, bright, white teeth.
2. Of the people we surveyed, six out of ten plan to vote for Congressman Hardwater again.
3. Animal lovers support their local zoo. Visit it today!
4. Believe me, our cereal is the ultimate in crunchiness.
5. Scientists exploring Antarctica wore our down-filled vests.

Practice

A. Write *fact* or *opinion* for each statement below.

6. We couldn't be the most successful company in our field unless we were the best—the choice is obvious.
7. Over ten thousand tourists visited Sunnydale last year.
8. Larry's Lawnmowers want you to relax this summer.
9. Government research shows our sandwich is fat free.
10. You'll love the taste of our Super Sandwich.

B. Write the name of the propaganda technique used in each message. Then write how you recognized the technique.

11. "Hi! I'm Froth Gariell. I take a break from acting at the Klondike Vacation Spa. Believe me, it's the coolest spot."
12. Come on, admit it. You don't want those unattractive brains to ruin your social life. They're so unbecoming!
13. See how little others have to offer. Then buy from us!
14. Look at them—hundreds of acres of beautiful trees. What a fine sight! Shouldn't you buy Glee paper products?
15. Thousands of citizens support Senator Flack. Can you afford to ignore the majority? Reelect her next week.
16. There's no doubt that people are ready for a change. That's why you can't face the future without this book.
17. Before I started using Marvelous Mouthwash my life was dull. Now my life is exciting and I'm Mr. Popularity.
18. Don't be left out this summer. Join the happy crowds at Sizzling Shore Resorts.

C. Work with a partner. Take turns, each stating one fact and one opinion about the topics below. Then supply a fact to support your opinion. Listen critically to distinguish your partner's facts from his or her opinions.

clothes   rain   football   television

D. 19–20. Write two brief paragraphs about a topic you feel strongly about. Use only facts in the first paragraph, and use only opinions in the second paragraph. Do not identify your paragraphs as you read them to a classmate. Have your classmate explain which paragraph is more convincing, and why.

E. Working with a small group of classmates, recall advertisements you have heard on radio, seen on TV, or read in magazines, newspapers, or on billboards. Then discuss the questions below.
- Which ads are based on facts?
- Which ones mix facts and opinions?
- Do any of them use propaganda techniques? If so, which propaganda techniques are used?

F. Write a two-line advertisement for each item below. Use the propaganda technique indicated in parentheses.

21. vitamins (testimonial)
22. amusement park (bandwagon)
23. magazine (loaded words)
24. toothpaste (transfer)

AMERICAN LIBRARY ASSOCIATION

Apply • Think and Write

Dictionary of Knowledge • An almanac is a useful publication that many people use as a source for facts to support their statements. Read more about almanacs in the Dictionary of Knowledge. List five facts you could expect to find in an almanac.

> ✎ **Remember**
> to judge messages critically and to listen for the use of propaganda techniques.

Students should attend school twelve months of the year. Try to convince your classmates that this is an excellent idea. Then try to convince them that it is <u>not</u> an excellent idea.

WRITING ♦
Persuasive Strategies

A persuasive strategy is simply a plan you can use to convince readers of your opinion. Before you choose a strategy, know your audience so that what you write is appropriate, appealing, and understandable to that audience. Then, depending on your needs and situation, use one or more of the strategies below.

Persuasive Strategies

Give a Precedent   Use a precedent, a factual example from the past, that supports your view of the present situation. Your argument will seem easier to accept if there is a history behind it.

> **In my last term as class president we raised more funds for charity than any other class has in this school's history.**

Respond to Objections   Directly confront ideas that are opposed to yours. Anticipate how others will disagree with you and answer their objections in your statement.

> **I know everyone is fond of the old gymnasium. A new one will be costly. However, students' needs have changed, and we ought to invest in the school's future.**

Call for Fairness   Appeal to your readers' sense of fairness and ask them to consider what is just and reasonable. Nikki Giovanni used this strategy in her review of *M.C. Higgins, the Great.*

> **"Without extra coal some may be a bit cooler but with the extra coal many will be homeless and worse, rootless. Is that really fair?"**

Predict Results   Point out the results that could occur from deciding in your favor or not deciding in your favor.

> **If we build a new gymnasium, the overcrowding problem will be solved. Without a new gymnasium, we can't host sports events.**

Summary ♦ To convince readers of your opinion, use the **persuasive strategy** that is most appropriate to your audience and situation.

Guided Practice

Name the persuasive strategy used in each example below.

1. If the mountain is saved, the countryside will remain unchanged. If it is not saved, the countryside could change forever.
2. In the past, strip mining has caused serious environmental problems, such as soil erosion and mud slides.
3. True, strip mining does alter the landscape, but the government now requires that the landscape be restored.

Practice

A. Write *precedent*, *objection*, *fairness*, or *results* to identify the persuasive strategy used in each example below.

   4. If we spend all our energy on remodeling the gym, the art studio will have to go unrestored.
   5. Although it is often unwise to take on too many tasks at once, we could try to improve the gym and the art studio.
   6. Since different people have different interests, our school should support its artists as well as its athletes.
   7. Let's remember that, in the past, those concerned were polled before a decision was made.

B. Write a sentence that explains the persuasive strategy used in each example below.

   8. Yes, this is a difficult book. However, a good book challenges one's ideas. We students are ready for that.
   9. Recall the last time we voted to develop some public land. A shopping mall replaced our beautiful forest.
   10. Let's consider how our children and grandchildren will see us if we make the honorable choice right now.

Apply • Think and Write

A Letter to the Editor • Write a short letter to the editor of a newspaper or magazine. State your opinion on an issue that is important to you. Use the persuasive strategies best suited to your beliefs and to your audience, the publication's readers.

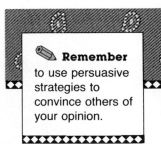

✎ **Remember**
to use persuasive strategies to convince others of your opinion.

GETTING STARTED

Think of a recent instance when you were persuaded to do something. What reasons were given that helped convince you? What reasons were used that were not convincing?

WRITING ♦
Developing a Paragraph with Reasons

When reading your writing or hearing you speak, people may ask you why you have a certain opinion. The answers you provide—your reasons—should be clear and persuasive. Reasons offer proof for the position a writer or speaker takes.

When writing a persuasive paragraph, state your opinion in the topic sentence. Then give three or more reasons that support your opinion. Conclude the paragraph with a sentence that restates your opinion.

Study the example paragraph below.

Children should be encouraged to enjoy books. First, books provide information on many different subjects. Sharing a book with your child encourages learning in a pleasant way. A child who appreciates the rich rewards of reading will be less content with TV and its often empty entertainment. Most important, reading develops a child's imaginative abilities. Let's make sure that our children learn to take pleasure in reading.

Notice how the guidelines below for writing a persuasive paragraph are reflected in the example paragraph you just read.

♦ Its topic sentence states the opinion.
♦ Its four solid reasons are organized in order of importance, from least to most important.
♦ It is written to appeal to a certain audience—to parents. Always choose reasons that your readers will find most convincing.

Summary ♦ A **persuasive paragraph** should begin with a clearly stated opinion and then be supported by at least three strong reasons. Consider what your particular audience will find most convincing and use those reasons.

Guided Practice

Suggest as many reasons as you can to **support each opinion** below.

1. Good manners are important.
2. People should have guidelines of **acceptable behavior.**
3. Behavior that is acceptable in one situation is **not always** acceptable in another situation.
4. The rules for proper manners should change as society changes.
5. The tradition of saying ''thank you'' after a kind action is a good one.

Practice

A. Write a sentence that gives a reason to **support each opinion.**

6. Children should be encouraged to **keep physically fit.**
7. Physical exercise is important to good **health.**
8. Getting enough sleep and eating **properly** also help children keep physically fit.
9. There are many activities that **people** can participate in that will allow **them** to exercise and also have fun.
10. People of all ages should get some form of exercise.

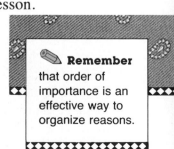

B. OPINION: *Schools should enforce stricter dress codes.* Write sets of three reasons in **support of** this opinion that would appeal to each audience shown below.

11–13. junior high students **14–16.** parents **17–19.** teachers

C. Write a persuasive paragraph on a subject you feel strongly about. Use your opinion as your topic sentence. **Check** to make sure that your completed paragraph follows **the guidelines in this lesson.**

Apply • Think and Write

Supporting an Opinion • Decide whether or not you agree with the opinion in **Practice B.** Write all your supporting reasons. Choose your three strongest reasons and write them in a ''manifesto''—that is, a statement of your belief on a subject.

> ✏️ **Remember**
> that order of importance is an effective way to organize reasons.

Focus on Opinions

You already know the difference between fact and opinion. A **fact** is a statement that can be proved true by observation or research. An **opinion** is a statement of personal feeling, judgment, or belief. No matter how well you state your opinion — or how many facts you base it on — an opinion remains your own personal view.

Opinions are valuable. They are also common; everyone has them. The editorial pages of newspapers contain opinions on current events. Newspaper and magazine columnists express their opinions on various topics of concern. Television, movie, and book reviewers give their opinions on screen and print offerings.

Earlier in the unit you read Nikki Giovanni's book review of *M.C. Higgins, the Great*. Giovanni states her opinion. She makes it clear that she likes Virginia Hamilton's story. She says the book is one of "the good things" of life. And she likes the fictional M.C. Higgins himself.

> M.C. Higgins is a very nice dude. He's just beginning to recognize girls as different from boys and basically worthy of kissing. But M.C. also has come into a recognition of responsibility....He dreams and...plans a way to save his mountain.

Notice that Giovanni supports her favorable opinion of the book with evidence drawn from the story. She does not merely say that it is "a powerful story." She shows *why* it is a powerful story, why it is "warm, humane and hopeful." She supplies specific evidence to show that "M.C. Higgins is a nice dude" and that Hamilton's story as a whole is a wise, thoughtful book.

The Writer's Voice ◆ What is some of the evidence from *M.C. Higgins, the Great* that Giovanni gives in order to show that M.C. has "come into a recognition of responsibility"? Look back at the review on pages 138–140. Can this supporting evidence be regarded as fact?

Working Together

The nature of opinions — and how a writer can support them with evidence — is important for you to know. As a group, discuss opinions as you do activities **A** and **B**.

In Your Group

♦ Encourage everyone to participate. ♦ Record people's ideas.
♦ Agree or disagree in a pleasant way. ♦ Express appreciation.

A. Read the following statements. Which ones state facts? Which ones state opinions? See if the members of your group agree on each answer and can explain their reasons.

1. "Strip-mining" means removing raw materials from the earth in a layer-by-layer process.

2. *M.C. Higgins, the Great* is not an adorable book, not a lived-happily-ever-after kind of story.

3. *M.C. Higgins, the Great* was published in 1974.

4. *M.C. Higgins, the Great*...does what every book should do — creates characters with whom we can identify and for whom we care.

B. As a group, choose one of the following topics and write an opinion about it that is acceptable to the group. Then assemble as much evidence as you can to support the opinion. Report your results to the rest of the class.

1. shopping malls   **3.** homework   **5.** popular music
2. air pollution   **4.** football   **6.** outdoor classes

THESAURUS CORNER ♦ Word Choice

Choosing the exact verb you need is critical to effective writing. Write three sentences stating your opinion on any topic. In each sentence, use one of the verbs below or a synonym. Check the Thesaurus to find the most appropriate verb.

believe know say give move question

WRITING PROCESS
PERSUADING

Writing a
Media Review

The media—newspapers, magazines, radio, and television—often carry reviews of works such as books, movies, and television programs. In a review, a critic gives opinions supported by reasons, facts, and examples from the work.

Nikki Giovanni's review of Virginia Hamilton's *M.C. Higgins, the Great* is an excellent example. She uses examples from the book to support her favorable opinion. Her review may persuade many readers to find a copy of the book and step into M.C. Higgins's world.

Know Your Purpose and Audience

What's MY PURPOSE

Now it is your turn to be a critic. In this lesson you will write a media review. Your purpose will be to review a movie or a television program, using reasons, facts, and examples to support your opinion.

Who's MY AUDIENCE

Your audience will be your fellow students. Later, you might read your reviews for a mock television show. You might also create a review column for your school newspaper.

1 Prewriting

First choose your topic—the movie or television program you want to review. Then use an idea-gathering strategy.

Choose Your Topic ◆ Congratulations! You have just been named the new media reviewer for a newspaper. What will you evaluate for your first review? Your choice of topic must interest your readers as well as yourself.

Think About It	Talk About It
Perhaps you have recently seen a movie or television program to which you reacted strongly. List several that you have strong feelings or opinions about. Choose the one you feel strongest about.	As a class, brainstorm a list of currently popular movies or TV shows. Do any of the titles mean something to you? Pick the title you know the most about.

Topic Ideas

Wild Kingdom
NOVA
(The African Queen)
The Birds
Dial M for Murder
Winds of War
Roots

Choose Your Strategy ♦ Following are two strategies for gathering ideas about your topic. Read both and then use what you think will work better for you.

PREWRITING IDEAS

CHOICE ONE

A Team Review

Find a partner who has also seen your movie or television program. Pretend to be a popular team of reviewers who appear on television. Exchange opinions, supporting them with reasons, facts, and examples. Feel free to disagree. Take notes to use when you write your review.

Model

CHOICE TWO

A Cluster Map

Write the name of your movie or television program in the topic circle of a cluster map. Add circles for subtopics such as *characters, plot, purpose, quality of acting,* and *my personal response.* In detail circles give your opinions plus reasons, facts, and examples.

Model

2 Writing

Review your prewriting notes. Then use the chart below as a guide to writing your review. You may want to write one paragraph for each part of the chart.

Sample First Draft ◆

Although it is quite old, the 1951 movie The African Queen is a classic film that everyone should see.

It is set in East Africa at the outbreak of World War I Rose Sayer played by Katharine Hepburn is a prim missionary in a remote jungle village. When the village is attacked by the Germans, she must escape. Enter Charlie Allnut, played by Humphrey Bogart. In his broken-down Riverboat, the African Queen, they move down a wild river. On the way, they encounter enemy troops and a treacherous waterfall. They keep going.

Hepburn and bogart shine in their performances. Hepburn visibly softens as she begins to fall in love with Bogart. Bogart makes it believable as the lazy drifter Charlie turns into a curagous hero. Viewers can't resist cheering them on and worrying about them at each suspenseful turn in the river.

The African Queen is a movie you won't want to miss.

Introduction
1. Identify the work.
2. State an overall opinion.

Summary
1. Briefly summarize the work.

Evaluation
1. Apply your criteria.
2. Give opinions.
3. Support them with reasons, facts, and examples from the work.

Conclusion
1. Conclude with your personal response to the work.
2. Make a recommendation to your readers.

3 Revising

Now that you have drafted your media review, you will probably need to polish it. This plan for revising may help you.

REVISING IDEA

FIRST   Read to Yourself

Review your purpose. Did you write a review of a movie or television program? Consider your audience. Will your classmates understand and perhaps be persuaded by your views? As you read, listen to the sounds of your writing. If you find yourself adding words as you read, you may need to make changes.

Focus: Have you clearly stated your opinion? Have you supported your opinion with facts, reasons, and examples?

THEN   Share with a Partner

Ask a partner to listen as you read your review aloud. Ask for his or her responses. These guidelines may help.

The Writer

Guidelines: Read clearly and slowly. Listen to your partner's feedback. Make the changes *you* think are necessary.

Sample questions:
• Do you understand the criteria I applied?
• **Focus question:** Did I support my opinions with facts, reasons, and examples?

The Writer's Partner

Guidelines: Be honest; be courteous. Be specific; refer to specific passages or details.

Sample responses:
• The part I liked best was ____.
• How did you feel about ____?

Revising Model ♦ Below is a draft review that is being revised. Revised drafts don't have to look neat. Words can be added, crossed out, or moved around.

Although it is quite old, the 1951 movie The African Queen is a classic film that everyone should see.

It is set in East Africa at the outbreak of World War I Rose Sayer played by Katharine Hepburn is a prim missionary in a remote jungle village. When the village is ~~attacked by~~ ~~the Germans~~, she must escape. Enter Charlie Allnut, played by Humphrey ~~Bogart.~~ In his broken-down Riverboat, the African Queen, they ~~move~~ *dash* down a wild river. On the way, they encounter enemy troops and a treacherous waterfall. *However* They keep going.

Hepburn and bogart shine in their performances. Hepburn visibly softens as she begins to fall in love with Bogart. Bogart makes it believable as the lazy drifter Charlie turns into a curagous hero. Viewers can't resist cheering them on and worrying about them at each suspenseful turn in the river. *I love this story of two ordinary people*

The African Queen is a movie you won't want *caught up in high adventure.* to miss.

The writer wanted to change from passive to active voice.

Dash is a stronger verb than *move*.

The writer added a transition word to connect ideas.

The writer's partner asked about the writer's personal response.

Read the review above with the changes the writer wants to make. Then revise your own media review.

Grammar Check ♦ Active voice verbs equal powerful writing.
Word Choice ♦ Some verbs, such as *move*, are overused. A thesaurus can help you find stronger synonyms.

4 Proofreading

Check for surface-level errors in spelling, capitalization, punctuation, and indentation.

Proofreading Model ♦ Here is the review of *The African Queen*. Proofreading changes have been added in red.

<table>
<tr><td colspan="2">Proofreading Marks</td></tr>
<tr><td>capital letter</td><td>≡</td></tr>
<tr><td>small letter</td><td>∕</td></tr>
<tr><td>add comma</td><td>⋏</td></tr>
<tr><td>add period</td><td>⊙</td></tr>
<tr><td>indent paragraph</td><td>¶</td></tr>
<tr><td>check spelling</td><td>◯</td></tr>
</table>

Proofreading Checklist

- ☐ Did I spell words correctly?
- ☐ Did I indent paragraphs?
- ☐ Did I use correct capitalization?
- ☐ Did I use correct punctuation?
- ☐ Did I type neatly or use my best handwriting?

¶ Although it is quite old, the 1951 movie The African Queen is a classic film that everyone should see.

It is set in East Africa at the outbreak of World War I. Rose Sayer, played by Katharine Hepburn, is a prim missionary in a remote jungle village. When the village is attacked by the Germans, she must escape. Enter Charlie Allnut, played by Humphrey Bogart. In his broken-down Riverboat, the African Queen, they move down *dash* a wild river. On the way, they encounter enemy troops and a treacherous waterfall. *However,* They keep going.

Hepburn and bogart shine in their performances. Hepburn visibly softens as she begins to fall in love with Bogart. Bogart makes it believable as the lazy drifter Charlie turns into a *curageous* hero. Viewers can't resist cheering them on and worrying about them at each suspenseful turn in the river.

I love this story of two ordinary people The African Queen is a movie you won't want *caught up in high adventure.* to miss.

PROOFREADING IDEA

Trading with a Partner | Ask a classmate to check your draft for errors. Return the favor. Sometimes it's easier to find someone else's mistakes.

After you have proofread your review, make a neat copy. Don't forget to add a title.

5 Publishing

Here are two ways to share your review with classmates.

Review of The African Queen

Although it is quite old, the 1951 movie The African Queen is a classic film that everyone should see.

It is set in East Africa at the outbreak of World War I. Rose Sayer, played by Katharine Hepburn, is a prim missionary in a remote jungle village. When the Germans attack the village, she must escape. Enter Charlie Allnut, played by Humphrey Bogart. In his broken-down riverboat, the African Queen, they dash down a wild river. On the way, they encounter enemy troops and a treacherous waterfall. However, they keep going.

Hepburn and Bogart shine in their performances. Hepburn visibly softens as she begins to fall in love with Bogart. Bogart makes it believable as the lazy drifter Charlie turns into a courageous hero. Viewers can't resist cheering them on and worrying about them at each suspenseful turn in the river.

I love this story of two ordinary people caught up in high adventure. The African Queen is a movie you won't want to miss.

PUBLISHING IDEAS

Share Aloud	Share in Writing
Have a mock television show or shows. Pretend to be the media reviewer for your local station. ''Broadcast'' your review to the class or to a small group of classmates. Have ''viewers'' call in and respond.	Suggest a media review column to your school newspaper editor. Propose a title such as ''Film Clips'' or ''Tune in . . . or Turn Off!'' Submit your media reviews for publication. Ask readers to write in and share their opinions.

CURRICULUM
·CONNECTION·

Writing Across the Curriculum   Literature

Authors title their works very carefully. Mulling over the title before you read can help you anticipate the story. During this unit you made cluster maps in response to *M.C. Higgins, the Great* and as a prewriting strategy. Cluster mapping is a strategy you can use to stimulate ideas about a story title.

Writing to Learn

Think and Elaborate   The title of a famous Jack London story is ''To Build a Fire.'' Write the key word, *fire*, in the center of your page. Ask yourself, ''What does this word suggest to me?'' Cluster your ideas around it. Let each response suggest another.

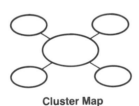

Cluster Map

Write   Use your cluster map to compose a paragraph about your responses to the word *fire*.

Writing in Your Journal

In the Writer's Warm-up, you wrote about mass media. Then you read about media such as radio, television, and newspapers. If you could interview someone in the mass media, who would it be? In your journal, write five questions you would ask that person.

BOOKS TO ENJOY

 ## Read More About it

Television: The First Fifty Years
by Jeff Greenfield
This is a witty, well-illustrated look at the history of TV. The author delves into the pluses and minuses of America's favorite medium.

Magazine: Behind the Scenes at Sports Illustrated *by William Jaspersohn*
Did you ever wonder how a magazine like *Sports Illustrated* gets written and printed every week? This book takes the reader through one busy week at the magazine.

 ## Book Report Idea   Roving Reporter

Be a roving book reporter. You'll need a tape recorder with a microphone.

Interview Readers ♦ Begin by asking people about the books they've been reading. If necessary, stimulate discussion with questions such as: "What's the setting? What did you like about the characters? How was the ending?" Be sure to get the title and author of each book, too. Close by giving a similar brief oral review of a book you've recently read. Then, when it's time to present a book report, you can simply play your tape.

UNIT REVIEW

Unit 3

Verbs   *pages 118–129*

A. Write each verb. Then identify each one by writing *action* or *state-of-being*.

   1. This crowd seems very restless.
   2. Please keep your seats during the game.
   3. The athletes sign autographs before and after the game.
   4. What is your favorite team?

B. Write each verb phrase. Underline the main verb.

   5. Who could it be at this hour?
   6. Dwight must have forgotten his keys.
   7. The noise will not disturb the baby.
   8. Little Jennifer is also sleeping.

C. Write the verb in each sentence. Write *LV* if it is a linking verb or *AV* if it is an action verb.

   9. The hero of the adventure show looks brave.
  10. He appears tall on television.
  11. What other shows with heroes appear on television today?
  12. People look at these shows for different reasons.

D. Write the verb in each sentence and label it *transitive* or *intransitive*. If a verb is transitive, write its direct object.

  13. Pets need constant care and attention.
  14. I often see other animals in my backyard.
  15. A squirrel jumped quickly from tree to tree in my neighbor's backyard.
  16. My friends joined me in a baseball game at Lincoln Park yesterday.

E. Write the indirect objects in the sentences.

17. Please give us news about the election.
18. I sent Maria a package on her birthday.
19. My neighbor offered me help with my science project.
20. I wrote the mayor and governor a letter recently.

F. Write and label each predicate nominative *PN* or each predicate adjective *PA* in the sentences.

21. The juniper is an evergreen tree or shrub.
22. Its needles are small and prickly.
23. The juniper berries taste spicy.
24. Did you become an authority on junipers?

Fact and Opinion *pages 142–145*

G. Write *fact* or *opinion* for each statement.

25. In the United States, some elections are held every four years.
26. This candidate would be a great president.
27. A vice-presidential candidate is known as the running mate.
28. Voter registration drives will help my candidate.

Persuasive Strategies *pages 146–147*

H. Write *precedent*, *objection*, *fairness*, or *results* to identify the persuasive strategy used in each item below.

29. Do not be fooled a second time. Last year we were promised a traffic light, but it was never installed. Vote "No" on the transportation bond issue this year.
30. I know that team uniforms cost a lot of money, but our school athletes deserve to wear their team colors when competing with other schools.
31. Try to plan ahead for future generations so that they will have beaches and parks to enjoy. After all, profit from land development is a short–term reward.
32. If we don't get uniforms for the teams, our athletes may not perform as well. If we do, their confidence on the playing field will be bolstered.
33. Do not forget what happened the last time we were overly confident about winning the game. This time, we shouldn't simply assume we can win without much effort.

Verb Transformations

What other verbs can you make from each of the following verbs by substituting only one letter?

EXAMPLE: know

ANSWERS: snow, knew

1. throw
2. steal
3. mutter
4. fall
5. move

6. take
7. gave
8. fly
9. rang
10. catch

Pyramid Verbs

Use the letter *A* to make a verb pyramid like the one below. Then start one with the letter *B*. Add only one letter at a time.

D
DO
DON
DONE

Now make a verb pyramid by adding two letters at a time.

E
EAT
EATS
FEAST
FEASTED

Unit 3 Extra Practice

1 Writing with Verbs

p. 118

A. Write the verb in each sentence.

1. Go to the door.
2. Strangers enter.
3. Learn their names.
4. Water evaporates.
5. Is it a cloud?
6. Remain quiet.
7. Are you brave?
8. What looks new?
9. There were cinders.
10. The plot thickens.
11. What trail is this?
12. The fog grew thick.
13. She ran home quickly.
14. Fasten your seat belt.
15. The plane landed early.
16. He was a friend.
17. That tastes sweet.
18. They never worry.
19. Memorize the rule.
20. He thinks clearly.

B. Write the verb in each sentence. Then write whether it is an action verb or state-of-being verb.

EXAMPLE: Velma is a good student.

ANSWER: is, state-of-being verb

21. Brian brought the groceries home.
22. Please open that can of spinach.
23. Who is your science teacher?
24. The cat leaped over the fence.
25. Lee seems very busy today.
26. We played basketball all afternoon.
27. That song sounds familiar.
28. There were hardly any empty seats in the entire auditorium.
29. That giant sequoia tree is 2,000 years old.
30. Who stood in the rain all day?
31. Those clouds look ominous.
32. Juanita traveled for more than four hours.
33. Dad cooked his favorite dish, beef stew with potatoes, carrots, and onions.
34. Tammy became ill after dinner.
35. Be on your best behavior.

C. Write this article. Then underline the ten verbs.

36. Many successful people began their careers early in life. **37.** Most great athletes and dancers practiced or rehearsed for hours after school. **38.** During school vacations the future business and political leaders often observed and learned about their fields of interest. **39.** Wise students use their time well. **40.** They improve their athletic skills, enrich their minds, enhance their talents, and increase their chances for success in the future.

2 Verb Phrases

p. 120

A. Write the verb phrase in each sentence. Underline the main verb.

1. Who could have written that story?
2. Jody must be the author.
3. It will be published soon.
4. Who might have informed him?
5. Everyone is asking questions.
6. Our library does need a new computer.
7. We should be having a paper sale.
8. Old telephone books can be contributed to the paper drive.
9. Do not bring loose papers or magazines.
10. Bundles should never be tied carelessly.

B. There is a verb or a verb phrase in each sentence in this article about Kurt Thomas. Write each verb or verb phrase.

11. Kurt Thomas is a great gymnast. **12.** He has made gymnastics popular in America. **13.** In 1978 he won a gold medal at a competition in France. **14.** An American had not placed first in an international gymnastics contest since 1932. **15.** Then in New York he defeated gymnasts from eighteen nations. **16.** In 1979 Kurt was honored with the James A. Sullivan Award. **17.** It is presented annually to America's best amateur athlete. **18.** No gymnast had ever been given that award. **19.** In 1980, at the age of twenty-four, he turned professional. **20.** Kurt's career had its start in Miami, Florida. **21.** Each day he would train for hours. **22.** He could not attend many parties. **23.** He followed a strict diet. **24.** Kurt Thomas was rewarded for this discipline. **25.** Now he enjoys fame.

C. Write each verb or verb phrase in this article after its sentence number. Underline the main verb in each verb phrase.

26. Many people have never heard of Lillian Leitzel. **27.** Her name does appear, however, in many books about famous athletes. **28.** As a child she had joined a circus. **29.** The acrobats and trapeze artists were her favorite performers. **30.** In her spare time she would watch them in rehearsal. **31.** She would then imitate their routines. **32.** Eventually Leitzel became a skillful aerialist.

33. As an adult she was just four feet nine inches tall. **34.** She weighed only ninety-five pounds. **35.** Nevertheless, she did have great strength.

36. One day in 1918, Leitzel went to a gym in Philadelphia. **37.** There, at the age of thirty-six, she broke the world's record for chin-ups with one hand. **38.** An Englishman had held the record. **39.** In 1878 he had done twelve chin-ups with one hand. **40.** On that day Lillian Leitzel did twenty-seven chin-ups in a row with her right hand. **41.** After a short rest she returned to the bar. **42.** This time she was using her left hand. **43.** She then did nineteen more chin-ups. **44.** A world's record had been broken twice in the same day by Lillian Leitzel. **45.** Achievements like hers will always be remembered by sports enthusiasts.

3 Linking Verbs

p. 122

A. Divide your paper into three columns. In the left column, write the subject of each sentence. In the middle, write the linking verb. In the right column, write the word in the predicate linked to the subject by the verb.

1. Space exploration is the subject of the television special.
2. For centuries it has been a dream of mankind.
3. H. G. Wells was a well-known writer of space adventures.
4. *The First Men in the Moon* is one of his early works.
5. That subject is no longer a fantasy.
6. The astronauts are ready for their launch.
7. Their mission is the construction of a space station.
8. Two astronauts are engineers.
9. It is two minutes till blast-off.
10. The weather is fine for a launch today.

B. Supply a linking verb other than a form of *to be* in each sentence. Write each complete sentence.

11. Each astronaut ____ confident.
12. Ground control ____ excited about the project.
13. The engines ____ thunderous.
14. After take-off, the rocket ____ smaller and smaller.
15. The crew ____ weightless in their capsule.
16. The earth ____ blue from space.
17. The space station's construction ____ the most important part of the mission.
18. The station gradually ____ a large silver ring.
19. The astronauts ____ happy at the station's completion.
20. Space exploration ____ an important part of progress.

C. Supply a linking verb and a word to rename or describe the subject in each sentence. Write each sentence.

21. My favorite science fiction story ____ .
22. Its exciting plot ____ .
23. My favorite character ____ .
24. The book's richly detailed setting ____ .
25. The meaning behind the story ____ .

4 Verbs with Direct Objects   *p. 124*

A. Write the subject, the verb, and the direct object in each sentence. Underline the subject once and the verb twice.

1. Their loyal fans showered them with praise at the end of the game.
2. Everyone must learn the words of this song before the next rehearsal.
3. We carefully read every notice on the bulletin board.
4. My mother and father repaired and repainted every chair and table in the family room.
5. The immense size of the faces of the four Presidents on Mount Rushmore always impresses each tourist or traveler in South Dakota.
6. We also enjoyed our visit to The Big Badlands.

B. Write the verb in each sentence and label it *transitive* or *intransitive*. If a verb is transitive, write its direct object.

7. Good luck does not always bring happiness. **8.** John Sutter owned a large ranch in the Sacramento Valley of California. **9.** He had many animals. **10.** In January of 1848 his carpenter was building a sawmill. **11.** In a river beside the mill, the carpenter discovered gold. **12.** This discovery of gold on his land delighted Sutter. **13.** Soon, however, his workers left their jobs. **14.** The news of the gold spread quickly in California. **15.** People abandoned their homes and businesses. **16.** Sailors deserted their ships. **17.** They rushed to the Sacramento Valley. **18.** Squatters gradually occupied Sutter's lands and streams. **19.** No one could remove the people. **20.** Soon thousands more from many distant places arrived at the ranch of John Sutter. **21.** Eventually Sutter lost everything.

5 Verbs with Indirect Objects

p. 126

A. Write the indirect object of each sentence.

1. Other languages have given the English language many important words.
2. A dictionary can teach a reader the history of some especially colorful words.
3. The English language owes the Arabic language thanks for one common but valuable word.
4. Arabic lent English its word for "storehouses," *makhāzin*.
5. That word offered publishers inspiration for the name of a special publication, the magazine.
6. A tour of Arabian storehouses gives a visitor hours of excitement and surprises.
7. Merchants in storehouses could sell shoppers almost anything from gold to goldfish.
8. A magazine can tell its subscribers many interesting and surprising things.
9. It provides them numerous articles on almost any subject from mythology to modern sports.
10. People often buy their friends subscriptions to magazines for birthdays and holidays.

B. Write the subject, verb, indirect object, and direct object of each sentence. Underline the indirect object once and the direct object twice.

11. I paid my friend a visit at the hospital.
12. We brought him some treats and games.
13. He showed the nurses his presents.
14. The doctor gave my friend a complete check-up.
15. Then she told him the good news.
16. "I promise you a speedy recovery."
17. He gave her a smile and a hearty handshake.

C. Rewrite each sentence, using each prepositional phrase in parentheses to make an indirect object. Underline the indirect object once and the direct object twice.

18. I handed the book (to him).
19. He threw a smile (to me).
20. The nurses showed a chart (to us).
21. I told a joke (to the nurses).
22. It gave a laugh (to them).
23. Have I told this one (to you)?
24. They gave a magazine (to me).
25. You must tell that story (to everyone).
26. We bought a bouquet of flowers (for Lolinda).

6 Predicate Nominatives and Predicate Adjectives

p. 128

A. Write the linking verb in each sentence. Then write and label the predicate nominative or the predicate adjective.

1. Her father was a successful rancher.
2. The winner of the prize was you.
3. The orange tasted sour.
4. She became a famous author of short stories.
5. We are not experts in oceanography.
6. The leaves on that shrub turned orange.
7. Pollution has become a problem.
8. The monitor sounded nervous.
9. The journey looked difficult.

B. Write each sentence, underlining the verb. Write whether the verb is followed by a direct object, predicate nominative, or predicate adjective.

10. The cover of the magazine impressed us.
11. Its design was truly beautiful.
12. The readers of that article were excited.
13. The writers of the article were she and I.
14. Sonja met a famous author of short stories.
15. They became regular correspondents.
16. A reporter for the magazine interviewed several scientists.
17. The sports columnists covered many different events.
18. Their favorite sports are tennis and basketball.
19. They attend matches and games regularly.
20. All the students enjoy our magazine.

C. Write the subject and the verb of each sentence in this article about John Sutter. Underline the subject once and the verb twice. If a sentence has a predicate nominative or a predicate adjective, write it after the verb.

21. John Sutter was a pioneer. **22.** He came to America from Switzerland at the age of thirty-one. **23.** His original name was Johann Suter. **24.** In 1834 he changed his name. **25.** He worked briefly in St. Louis. **26.** But the Pacific Ocean fascinated him. **27.** He had read much about it. **28.** Finally he went to Oregon. **29.** He became a successful trader. **30.** Sutter also visited Alaska. **31.** In 1839 he moved to California. **32.** He settled in the Sacramento Valley. **33.** Here he established a ranch. **34.** He even built a fort. **35.** Sutter became rich and powerful. **36.** But he was also kind. **37.** Newcomers received much help from him. **38.** Settlers were grateful. **39.** Valuable timber grew on his land. **40.** A sawmill became a necessity. **41.** James Marshall built a sawmill for him. **42.** Marshall found gold on the site of the excavation for the sawmill. **43.** News of the gold spread rapidly. **44.** Squatters soon destroyed Sutter's land and cattle. **45.** The sawmill was a complete failure. **46.** Further attempts were unsuccessful. **47.** He requested aid from Congress without success. **48.** Later the state of California granted him a small pension. **49.** In 1873 he moved to Pennsylvania. **50.** At his death in 1880, John Sutter was almost penniless.

UNIT FOUR

USING LANGUAGE
TO

NARRATE

=== **PART ONE** ===

Unit Theme   *The Sea Around Us*

Language Awareness   Using Correct Verb Forms

=== **PART TWO** ===

Literature   *The Black Pearl* by Scott O'Dell

A Reason for Writing   Narrating

Writing
IN YOUR JOURNAL

WRITER'S WARM-UP ◆ You probably know more about the sea than you think you do. Close your eyes and picture yourself there. Can you hear the roar of the waves and the call of the gulls? Now write in your journal about the sea. You could write about the creatures that live in the sea or how people enjoy the sea.

Think of the many activities you do within the span of one week. Describe an activity that occurs every day. Then describe an activity that you did yesterday and one that you are doing now.

1 Principal Parts of Verbs

Every verb has four principal parts, or basic forms. Study the principal parts of the verb *sail* below.

Present	**Past**	**Past Participle**	**Present Participle**
sail	sailed	(have) sailed	(are) sailing

Most verbs are **regular verbs**. Their past and past participles are the same and are formed by adding *-ed* to the present. The present participle is formed by adding *-ing* to the present.

The present and past forms of a verb are used alone. The past participle and present participle are used with helping verbs. The past participle usually uses a form of the verb *have*. The present participle uses a form of the verb *be*.

■ I **have sailed** in all types of boats.   I **am sailing** toward the shore.

Study the forms of the helping verbs *have* and *be* below.

Have		**Be**	
Present	**Past**	**Present**	**Past**
I, we, you, they have	had	I am	was
she, he, it has	had	she, he, it is	was
		we, you, they are	were

Some regular verbs require spelling changes when *-ed* and *-ing* are added to the present.

Final e Dropped: dive, dived, diving
Final Consonant Doubled: clap, clapped, clapping
Final y Changed to i: carry, carried, carrying

> **Summary** ♦ The **principal parts** of a verb are its basic forms. They are the present, the past, the past participle, and the present participle.

Guided Practice

Name the principal parts of these regular verbs.

1. talk   **2.** worry   **3.** paddle   **4.** grin   **5.** reply   **6.** open

Practice

A. The verbs below are regular verbs. Write the four principal parts of each verb.

7. mix   **9.** work   **11.** carry   **13.** delay   **15.** hurry
8. cry   **10.** raise   **12.** slip   **14.** change   **16.** climb

B. Write each sentence, completing it with the principal part of the verb indicated in parentheses.

17. Many people (earn, present) their living on the sea.
18. For thousands of years, people have (fish, past participle) the sea.
19. Most people eventually (turn, past) to modern scientific methods.
20. Many pearl fishers, however, still (use, present) age-old methods.
21. For ages, pearl fishers have (retrieve, past) pearls.
22. They (search, present) for beds of oysters under the water.
23. Divers have (remove, past participle) the valuable pearls.
24. Cultured pearls have (gain, past participle) in popularity.
25. Workers are (sort, present participle) the pearls by size.
26. A jeweler is (design, present participle) a lovely necklace.

C. Write sentences, using the following verbs. Use the forms of the verbs indicated in parentheses.

27. rain (present participle)   **29.** smile (present)
28. save (past participle)   **30.** happen (past)

Apply • Think and Write

From Your Writing • Choose three regular verbs you used in the Writer's Warm-up. Write the four principal parts of each verb.

> ✎ **Remember**
> to check the spelling of the principal parts of verbs.

Have you ever wished that you could predict the future? Predict some exciting things that will happen ten years from now.

2 Tenses of Verbs

The time expressed by a verb is called its tense. The tenses of a verb are formed from the verb's principal parts.

The **present tense** expresses an action taking place now.

- Coral reefs <u>form</u> in many parts of the world.

The **past tense** expresses an action that took place in the past.

- This reef <u>formed</u> off the Florida coast.

The **future tense** expresses an action that will occur in the future. It is formed by adding the helping verb *will* or *shall* to the present.

- More coral reefs <u>will form</u> in time.

The **present perfect tense** expresses an action that occurred at an indefinite time in the past and may still be going on. It is formed with the helping verb *have* or *has* and the past participle of the main verb.

- Most reefs <u>have formed</u> over hundreds of years.

The **past perfect tense** expresses an action that happened before another past action. It is formed with the helping verb *had* and the past participle.

- This coral reef <u>had formed</u> long before divers came here.

The **future perfect tense** expresses an action that will be finished before a stated time in the future. It is formed with *will have* or *shall have* and the past participle.

- Before long, another reef <u>will have formed</u> across the bay.

176 GRAMMAR and USAGE: Verb Tenses

Study the table below. It lists the tenses of the verb *work*. A list of all the forms of a verb, arranged by tense, is called a **conjugation**. To give such a list is to conjugate a verb. For a conjugation of the irregular verbs *be*, *have*, and *do*, see page 657.

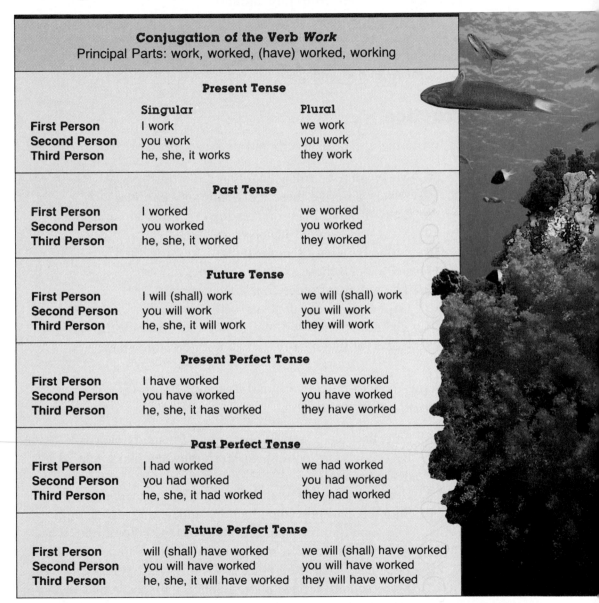

Conjugation of the Verb *Work*
Principal Parts: work, worked, (have) worked, working

Present Tense

	Singular	Plural
First Person	I work	we work
Second Person	you work	you work
Third Person	he, she, it works	they work

Past Tense

First Person	I worked	we worked
Second Person	you worked	you worked
Third Person	he, she, it worked	they worked

Future Tense

First Person	I will (shall) work	we will (shall) work
Second Person	you will work	you will work
Third Person	he, she, it will work	they will work

Present Perfect Tense

First Person	I have worked	we have worked
Second Person	you have worked	you have worked
Third Person	he, she, it has worked	they have worked

Past Perfect Tense

First Person	I had worked	we had worked
Second Person	you had worked	you had worked
Third Person	he, she, it had worked	they had worked

Future Perfect Tense

First Person	will (shall) have worked	we will (shall) have worked
Second Person	you will have worked	you will have worked
Third Person	he, she, it will have worked	they will have worked

Summary ♦ The **tense** of a verb shows time.

Guided Practice

Name the tense of each underlined verb.

1. Coral reefs <u>form</u> from tiny animals.
2. We <u>will study</u> these tiny creatures.
3. Various types of coral reefs <u>have developed</u> in the sea.
4. By next year, <u>we will have learned</u> more about coral reefs.
5. Coral reefs <u>had interested</u> me before we <u>started</u> this project.

Practice

A. Write the underlined verb and its tense: *present*, *past*, or *future*.

6. Many tourists <u>will view</u> coral reefs this year.
7. Divers <u>describe</u> these reefs as lovely gardens.
8. They <u>observe</u> many interesting creatures in coral reefs.
9. Most reefs <u>started</u> many years ago.
10. Millions of tiny sea creatures <u>linked</u> together.
11. People <u>call</u> these creatures *polyps*.
12. The polyps <u>produce</u> limestone deposits.
13. Over time, these deposits <u>will form</u> reefs.
14. The new polyps <u>will create</u> another reef miles away.
15. Coral formations often <u>assume</u> interesting shapes.

B. Write the underlined verb and its tense: *present perfect*, *past perfect*, or *future perfect*.

16. Scientists <u>have studied</u> coral reefs for many years.
17. Before modern equipment, early devices <u>had hindered</u> underwater study.
18. Heavy diving suits <u>had limited</u> divers' movements.
19. Snorkels <u>had prevented</u> lengthy underwater dives.
20. The aqualung <u>has changed</u> underwater exploration.
21. Scientists <u>have tried</u> miniature submarines under the sea.
22. They also <u>have used</u> other types of diving vehicles.
23. Some scientists <u>have photographed</u> the spectacular reefs with special cameras.
24. In the future, scientists <u>will have developed</u> other devices.
25. Scientists <u>will have investigated</u> many fascinating parts of the sea by then.

C. Write each sentence, using the underlined verb in the tense indicated in parentheses.

26. People <u>move</u> beneath the sea for thousands of years. (present perfect)
27. The ancient Greeks <u>search</u> for pearls and shells. (past)
28. Divers <u>use</u> many different devices. (present perfect)
29. In the 1300s, divers <u>create</u> special goggles out of clear tortoiseshell. (past perfect)
30. In the early 1700s, John Lethbridge <u>invent</u> a wood and leather diving suit. (past)
31. This suit <u>help</u> Lethbridge with salvage work. (past)
32. A German engineer <u>develop</u> a diving helmet as early as 1837. (past perfect)
33. Helmeted divers also <u>cover</u> themselves with airtight suits. (past)
34. Machines above the surface of the water <u>pump</u> air into the divers' helmets. (past)
35. Today, some divers still <u>use</u> similar helmets. (present)
36. Recently, however, most divers <u>rely</u> on scuba masks and tanks for underwater work. (present perfect)
37. Scuba equipment <u>provide</u> divers with more freedom. (present perfect)
38. Most divers <u>select</u> scuba tanks instead of helmets and diving suits. (future)
39. Scientists probably <u>devise</u> even more advanced diving devices before long. (future perfect)
40. By then, many people <u>enjoy</u> the pleasures of underwater exploration. (future perfect)

Apply ◆ Think and Write

Creative Writing ◆ Scientists use submersibles to study underwater life. These vehicles have large windows and can travel deep and far in the ocean. Write about an imaginary ride in a submersible. Above each verb or verb phrase, write its tense.

> 🖊 **Remember**
> to use the appropriate verb tense in each sentence.

Make up a silly, humorous story. Use some of the following words in your story: *fly, bite, catch, think, throw, swim, sink, ride, grow, eat.*

3 Irregular Verbs

Irregular verbs do not form their principal parts by adding *-ed*. However, many irregular verbs do follow other patterns.

Some irregular verbs form the past participle by adding *-en* to the past.

Present	Past	Past Participle	Present Participle
break	broke	(have) broken	(are) breaking
choose	chose	(have) chosen	(are) choosing
freeze	froze	(have) frozen	(are) freezing
speak	spoke	(have) spoken	(are) speaking

Some have the same present and past participle.

| come | came | (have) come | (are) coming |
| run | ran | (have) run | (are) running |

Some have the same past and past participle.

bring	brought	(have) brought	(are) bringing
feel	felt	(have) felt	(are) feeling
find	found	(have) found	(are) finding
sell	sold	(have) sold	(are) selling

Some have the same present, past, and past participle.

burst	burst	(have) burst	(are) bursting
cost	cost	(have) cost	(are) costing
hurt	hurt	(have) hurt	(are) hurting
put	put	(have) put	(are) putting

Learn the principal parts of the irregular verbs in the chart on the next page. Some verbs follow the patterns listed above. Some verbs do not follow a pattern. For these verbs, you may find it helpful to memorize their principal parts.

Irregular Verbs

Present	Past	Past Participle	Present Participle
become	became	(have) become	(are) becoming
begin	began	(have) begun	(are) beginning
bite	bit	(have) bitten	(are) biting
blow	blew	(have) blown	(are) blowing
catch	caught	(have) caught	(are) catching
do	did	(have) done	(are) doing
draw	drew	(have) drawn	(are) drawing
drink	drank	(have) drunk	(are) drinking
drive	drove	(have) driven	(are) driving
eat	ate	(have) eaten	(are) eating
fall	fell	(have) fallen	(are) falling
fly	flew	(have) flown	(are) flying
get	got	(have) gotten (got)	(are) getting
give	gave	(have) given	(are) giving
go	went	(have) gone	(are) going
grow	grew	(have) grown	(are) growing
know	knew	(have) known	(are) knowing
ride	rode	(have) ridden	(are) riding
ring	rang	(have) rung	(are) ringing
say	said	(have) said	(are) saying
see	saw	(have) seen	(are) seeing
shake	shook	(have) shaken	(are) shaking
sing	sang	(have) sung	(are) singing
sink	sank	(have) sunk	(are) sinking
steal	stole	(have) stolen	(are) stealing
swim	swam	(have) swum	(are) swimming
take	took	(have) taken	(are) taking
teach	taught	(have) taught	(are) teaching
think	thought	(have) thought	(are) thinking
throw	threw	(have) thrown	(are) throwing
wear	wore	(have) worn	(are) wearing
write	wrote	(have) written	(are) writing

Summary ♦ Some irregular verbs follow patterns when forming their principal parts. Others do not.

Guided Practice

Name the principal parts of these irregular verbs.

1. begin   **2.** drive   **3.** give   **4.** wear   **5.** ride   **6.** drink

Practice

A. Write the correct form of the verb in parentheses.

7. Unusual creatures have (swam, swum) in the sea for ages.
8. That fishing boat (catched, caught) a giant manta ray.
9. The captain (said, sayed) the ray was hard to catch.
10. The giant ray had (grew, grown) to almost five feet across.
11. With its huge ''wings,'' it (flew, flown) through the water.
12. What had the ray (ate, eaten)?
13. The crew (throwed, threw) a line around the fish.
14. The ray (shook, shaken) its wide, flat body on the boat's deck.
15. The crew has (took, taken) the ray onto the dock.
16. The captain (rang, rung) a bell to summon the crowd.
17. Have you (went, gone) to see the fish?
18. We (stole, stolen) a look from the dock.
19. Several of us have (drawed, drawn) pictures of the fish.
20. Has anyone here ever (saw, seen) a fish of this size?
21. A local newspaper has (wrote, written) about the giant ray.

B. Write the correct past or past participle of the verb in parentheses.

22. Sharks have (become) very famous sea creatures.
23. People have (write) hundreds of tales about sharks.
24. Few people have (get) a glimpse of a great white shark.
25. We (see) hammerhead sharks at the aquarium yesterday.
26. The hammerhead shark (eat) several small fish.
27. Some people have (catch) small sharks near the shore.
28. Swimmers have even (swim) alongside sharks.
29. I (think) sharks lived only in deep water.
30. Some people have (take) safety courses about sharks.
31. Experts at the aquarium (teach) us visitors important safety precautions.

C. Write each sentence, using the correct form—past, present, past participle or present participle—of the verb in parentheses.

32. Last week, Mrs. Henderson (teach) us about octopuses and some other unusual sea creatures.

33. She (say) a great deal about these eight-legged mollusks.

34. Several students have (write) reports about octopuses.

35. Today we are (see) a movie about these creatures.

36. Some people (catch) octopuses for food.

37. Divers now (swim) in search of octopuses under the water.

38. Have you ever (eat) octopus?

39. Yesterday, we (take) a trip to the aquarium.

40. The class (ride) to the aquarium on the train.

41. The trip (begin) with a lecture on octopuses and squid.

42. Guides had (give) us pictures of octopuses and squid.

43. We also (get) pictures of a giant squid.

44. Juan has (take) pictures of many creatures at the aquarium.

45. A guide (drive) us around the aquarium in an electric cart.

46. The class is (go) to the aquarium again on Wednesday.

D. For each present-tense verb, write a sentence that uses either the past tense or past participle of the verb.

47. shake **49.** blow **51.** drink **53.** wear **55.** ring
48. throw **50.** think **52.** fall **54.** steal **56.** sink

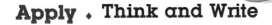

Apply ♦ Think and Write

Dictionary of Knowledge ♦ Jacques-Yves Cousteau is one of the most famous ocean explorers in the world. Read about Cousteau in the Dictionary of Knowledge. Describe some of the sights that Cousteau and his crew might encounter during an ocean exploration. Circle all the irregular verbs that you use.

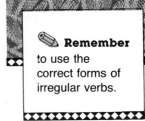

✎ **Remember**
to use the correct forms of irregular verbs.

Try to rearrange the following sentences to make them more forceful.
Several sea cucumbers were seen by the diver.
A playful sea otter will be fed by a friendly crowd.

4 Active and Passive Voice

In most sentences, the subject *performs* the action. When the subject of the sentence performs the action, the verb is in the active voice.

■ The fierce shark <u>frightened</u> the small cowfish.

In some sentences, the subject *receives* the action. In that case the verb is in the passive voice.

■ The small cowfish <u>was frightened</u> by the fierce shark.

A passive verb is a verb phrase made by using a form of the verb *be* and a past participle.

They <u>are</u> well <u>protected</u>.	We <u>were</u> <u>needed</u>.
It <u>will be caught</u>.	It <u>had been fed</u>.

Too many passive verbs can make writing wordy and weak. When you write, try to replace weak-sounding passive verbs with more direct and forceful active verbs.

Passive Voice: A stingray occasionally <u>is seen</u> by divers.
Active Voice: Divers occasionally <u>see</u> a stingray.

Summary ♦ A verb is in the **active voice** when the subject performs the action. A verb is in the **passive voice** when the subject receives the action.

Guided Practice

Name the verb. Tell whether it is in the active or passive voice.

1. Spotted eagle rays feed on various types of shellfish.
2. Many types of fish are consumed by sharks.
3. Moray eels have alarmed divers at times.

Practice

A. Write the verb in each sentence. Label it *active* or *passive*.

4. Many divers admire the lovely angelfish.
5. These fish are considered the loveliest of all fish.
6. One type is called the Queen angelfish.
7. The Queen angelfish's body is marked with yellowish bands.
8. These bands fade away with age.
9. Divers in the West Indies have discovered many types of angelfish.
10. The presence of divers frightens these fish.
11. They glide away from any divers in the area.
12. These fish often will be observed in small groups.
13. They are found swimming in deep water near reefs.

B. Rewrite each sentence, changing each passive verb to an active verb.

14. Various shellfish are seen by underwater explorers.
15. Spiny lobsters are found by divers in hidden places.
16. Divers are frequently watched by these odd-looking lobsters.
17. The banded coral shrimp can be discovered by divers near rocks and coral.
18. The shrimps' white antennae will be spotted easily by a trained eye.

C. Write two sentences for each of these verbs. In the first sentence, use the passive voice. In the second sentence, change to the active voice.

19. see **20.** visit **21.** discover **22.** experience **23.** enjoy

Apply ♦ Think and Write

An Active Adventure ♦ What other types of animals roam the vast seas? Imagine a day in the life of a sea animal, such as a shark, a blue whale, or a sea horse. Write about the adventures of the animal, using the passive voice. Then change most of your sentences to the active voice to make your writing more direct and forceful.

✎ **Remember**
to use the active voice to form strong sentences where possible.

Your friend's dog, Rufus, knows many tricks, but refuses to perform them. What is wrong with the orders? *Set Rufus! Sit the bone on the table! Lay on the floor! Lie your toy on the table!*

5 Troublesome Verb Pairs

Some verbs are often confused. The following explanations of these three pairs of verbs will help you avoid usage errors.

Sit, Set

The verb *sit* means "to move into a seat" or "to be in a place." Its principal parts are *sit, sat, sat, sitting*. It does not usually have a direct object.

Sit on the dock. Empty shells sat on the beach.

The verb *set* means "to put or place something." Its principal parts are *set, set, set, setting*. It usually has a direct object.

Set the anchor on the deck. He is setting the rope there, too.

Rise, Raise

The verb *rise* means "to get up" or "to go up." Its principal parts are *rise, rose, risen, rising*. It never has a direct object.

I rise before dawn. The sun rose slowly above the horizon.

The verb *raise* means "to lift" or "to move something higher." It is a regular verb. Its principal parts are *raise, raised, raised, raising*. It may have a direct object.

We raised the anchor. They are raising the sails.

Lie, Lay

The verb *lie* means "to rest" or "to recline." Its principal parts are *lie, lay, lain, lying*. It never has a direct object.

The captain lies in the hammock.	**The children are lying nearby.**
Yesterday we lay on the deck.	**A sail has lain here for years.**

The verb *lay* means to "put something down" or "to place." Its principal parts are *lay, laid, laid, laying*. It may have a direct object.

Lay the rope over there.	**We laid the sails on the dock.**

Summary ◆ Some verbs are often confused. Use *sit, set, rise, raise, lie,* and *lay* carefully in your speech and writing.

Guided Practice

Complete each sentence by naming the correct verb in parentheses.

1. Please (rise, raise) the sail. **3.** (Set, Sit) the map down.
2. The net (lays, lies) on the deck. **4.** (Lay, Lie) the bait here.

Practice

A. Write each sentence, using the correct form of the verb in parentheses.

5. Today, divers are (raise) chests from a sunken ship.
6. They wonder what has (lie) in the ship's chests.
7. The chests have (rise) slowly to the surface.
8. Powerful cranes are (set) them on the ship's deck.
9. Doubloons, jewels, and pearls are (lie) in the containers.
10. Archaeologists have (lay) the treasure in orderly rows.

B. Write the correct form of the verb in parentheses.

11. A sunken ship (lies, lays) on the bottom of the sea.
12. People are (rising, raising) the ship this year.
13. Divers have (sat, set) their equipment on a floating platform over the wreck.
14. Chests of old gold coins are (sitting, setting) in the ship's hull.
15. Divers have (lain, laid) the coins on the platform.
16. The divers (rose, raised) slowly from the bottom.
17. After the dive, the treasure (lay, laid) on the deck.
18. One diver (rose, raised) a heavy gold cup in his hand.
19. The group is (sitting, setting) the treasure in a vault.
20. The members of the expedition (sit, set) around the table.

C. Write a sentence for each of the following verbs.

21. lie **22.** lay **23.** sit **24.** set **25.** raise **26.** rise

Apply ⋅ Think and Write

A Narrative Adventure ⋅ You've been invited aboard a vessel that is searching for a lost Spanish galleon, a sailing ship from the sixteenth century. Write about your adventure, describing what you find. Use forms of *sit, set, lie, lay, rise,* and *raise* in your writing.

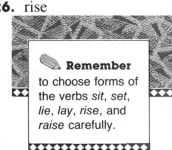

Remember
to choose forms of the verbs *sit, set, lie, lay, rise,* and *raise* carefully.

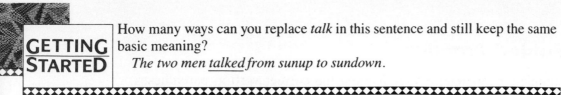

GETTING STARTED

How many ways can you replace *talk* in this sentence and still keep the same basic meaning?

The two men talked from sunup to sundown.

VOCABULARY ◆
Shades of Meaning

English has a rich variety of words that can be used to express many different meanings. Often, several words share the same basic meaning. These words are called **synonyms**. Rarely, however, do two synonyms mean exactly the same thing. The fine differences in meaning between synonyms are called **shades of meaning**.

Skillful writers understand these slight differences in meaning between related words. They choose the synonyms that express their meanings most accurately and vividly. Later in this unit you will read an excerpt from *The Black Pearl*. You will see how the author's careful choice of words helps you experience the boy's adventure.

Building Your Vocabulary

Water moves in different ways. Choose a word from the following list that you think best completes each sentence.

dripped   surged   flooded   spouted   cascaded

1. The ship rose and fell as the waves _____ .
2. During the storm, enormous waves _____ the shore.
3. Old Faithful _____ water high into the air as we watched.
4. Water _____ off the roof like a small waterfall during the cloudburst.
5. Water _____ slowly from the faucet all night.

Play the "I am _____" game. Here is how it works.
   I am <u>bold</u>, but Tom is <u>reckless</u>.
   I am <u>curious</u>, but Jill is <u>snoopy</u>.

Make up some "I am _____" sentences of your own. Then do the same with sets of three sentences.
   I am <u>relaxed</u>. He is <u>idle</u>. They are <u>lazy</u>.
   I am <u>amusing</u>. She is <u>silly</u>. They are <u>ridiculous</u>.

Practice

A. Write the word in parentheses that better fits the meaning of each sentence. Write each sentence.

1. Water (flowed, gushed) from the walls of the crumbling dam.
2. The seeds began to (grow, sprout) after the first rain fell.
3. He was (irritated, tormented) by the noise from the dripping water faucet.
4. As we approached the gate, the dog (barked, snarled) menacingly through its bared teeth.
5. From the mountain they could (observe, survey) the land and determine the best route through the valley.

B. Replace *threw*, *wrote*, or *written* in each sentence below with the synonym from the list that best fits the meaning of the sentence. Use a dictionary if you need help with meanings.

heaved   hurled   lobbed   drafted   inscribed   composed

6. They <u>threw</u> the heavy boulder over the cliff.
7. The softball pitcher <u>threw</u> the ball slowly across the plate.
8. The outfielder <u>threw</u> the ball forcefully to the catcher.
9. The senators <u>wrote</u> several versions of the bill.
10. The emperor's name was <u>written</u> on the ancient stone tomb.
11. Thomas Jefferson <u>wrote</u> the Declaration of Independence.

C. Write sentences for these synonyms of *throw* and *write*.

12. flip   13. cast   14. correspond   15. scrawl

Language Corner ◆ Collective Words

Some words are used to name groups of things. We speak of a *gaggle* of geese, a *pride* of lions, and a *kindle* of kittens.

Here are some made-up group names: a *pack* of movers, a *battery* of electricians, a *pile* of football players, a *batch* of bakers. Make up some group names of your own.

How to Revise Sentences with Verbs

Using verb tenses correctly can help make your writing more effective. As you know, verb tenses are used to tell the reader what time a particular event is taking place. It is important to keep your verbs in the same tense in a single piece of writing. Mixing present-tense verbs and past-tense verbs can confuse your reader. Read the following paragraph.

> As I walked along the beach, I noticed an old wreck partially buried in the sand. Grass grows between the cracks in the wood. Sea gulls perched on it familiarly. I began to wonder about what might have happened to this boat.

The paragraph is written in the past tense except for one sentence. Did you stumble over that sentence when you read it? Although it may seem like a small detail, that one sentence in the present tense disturbs the flow of the paragraph.

Using verbs in the active voice can also make your writing more direct and effective. Try to choose the active voice whenever possible. Use the passive voice only when the person or thing performing an action is unknown or relatively unimportant. Notice how changing to the active voice in sentence **2** makes the sentence more forceful.

1. The boat was battered and sunk by the storm.
2. The storm battered and sank the boat.

The Grammar Game ◆ Focus on verb tense! Quickly write the past tense of each verb below. Then exchange papers with a classmate. Did you both agree on all past-tense forms? If not, check with another classmate.

choose	put	shake	blow	buy
give	steal	bring	sink	cost
say	wear	sell	hurt	lay

Working Together

As your group does activities **A** and **B**, notice how choosing the active voice and verb tense can make your writing more direct and effective.

In Your Group

- ◆ Look at others when they speak.
- ◆ Respond to the ideas of others.
- ◆ Record ideas and suggestions.
- ◆ Help the group reach agreement.

A. Identify the tense of the verb in each sentence below. Then write the sentences, changing the verbs to different tenses.

1. Divers approached the wreck at noon today.
2. The team will explore many staterooms and the engine room.
3. They will have reached the ballroom before sundown.
4. Other groups before this have failed.
5. Poor equipment ruins many of these efforts.

B. Rewrite the sentences below, changing the verbs to the active voice. Then arrange the sentences to form a paragraph.

6. At one table a diver was greeted by an octopus.
7. Within minutes, the captain's quarters were discovered by a team.
8. In the ballroom, the divers were amazed at the beauty of the fixtures and the chandeliers.
9. Next, the dining rooms were explored by the group.
10. The deck of the ship was eagerly approached by the divers.

WRITERS' CORNER ◆ Sentence Variety

Avoid using too many sentences of the same length in a single paragraph. Too many short sentences are boring. Too many long sentences become difficult to read. Varying the length of your sentences will make your writing more interesting to read and easier to understand. This paragraph, for example, uses sentences of different lengths.

Read what you wrote for the Writer's Warm-up. Did you use too many short or long sentences in any of your paragraphs? Could you improve a paragraph by varying the length of the sentences?

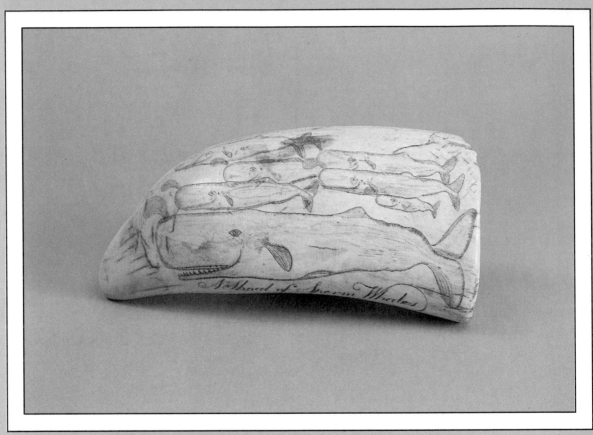

A SHOAL OF SPERM WHALES   *scrimshaw, photographed by Mary Anne Stets*
The Mystic Seaport Museum, Inc.

USING LANGUAGE
TO

NARRATE

PART TWO

Literature   *The Black Pearl* by Scott O'Dell
A Reason for Writing Narrating

CREATIVE
Writing

FINE ARTS ◆ The whale is used as a symbol of the sea in many decorative arts. Novels, songs, stories, and poems have been written about this huge creature. Look at the largest whale in this scrimshaw piece. What do you think it wants to say? Write a caption for the art. Speak for the whale.

CREATIVE THINKING ♦
A Strategy for Narrating

A THOUGHT BALLOON

Telling a story is often called narrating. After this lesson you will read part of *The Black Pearl* by Scott O'Dell. In it, a young pearl diver uses the words *I* and *me* to narrate the story from his point of view. Later you will write a personal narrative; that is, you will tell a true story from your own point of view.

In this passage from *The Black Pearl,* the boy is talking with an old man who is also a pearl diver. They are talking about an underwater cave inhabited by a manta ray.

> "You have fished everywhere in the lagoon," I said, "but not in the cave."
> "No," he said. "Nor did my father nor his father."
> "Big pearls may grow there."
> The old man did not answer . . . but suddenly he looked across the fire. It was a fleeting look that he gave me and yet its meaning was as clear as if he had spoken to me and said, "I cannot go . . . because I fear the Manta Diablo."

Do you understand the boy's eagerness to explore the cave? Can you understand the old man's reluctance? Have there been times when *you* have been eager to do something dangerous? Have there been times when *you* have been afraid? Your own life experiences can help you understand the viewpoints of both characters.

Learning the Strategy

It is often important to understand someone else's point of view. For example, suppose you have an after-school job. How might it be useful to know your boss's point of view about the qualities of a good employee? Imagine that your teacher has asked everyone to write an essay about the current President of the United States. Would you be surprised if someone expressed a viewpoint different from yours? Why or why not?

One way to understand someone else's point of view is to put yourself in his or her place. Imagine what you might think or say if you were that person. A thought balloon is one strategy that can help you do that. Imagine that you have invited a cousin who has never seen the ocean to go surfing with you. The thought balloon below shows what some of your cousin's reactions may be. What ideas might you add? Based on this thought balloon, do you think you will enjoy your day at the beach with your cousin?

You do _what_ with that little board?

I saw the movie _Jaws_ eight times.

Did I mention I'm allergic to sunlight?

How long do we have to stay?

cousin

Using the Strategy

A. Pretend you are one of a group of space voyagers who are colonizing a distant planet. Imagine what you might see. Imagine how you might feel. Make a thought balloon for yourself as you step onto the new planet. You may want to use your ideas as the basis for a science-fiction story.

B. Reread the passage from *The Black Pearl* on page 194. Make a thought balloon about exploring the cave for either the boy or the old man. Later, as you read the story, compare your ideas with what the story reveals about the two characters.

Applying the Strategy

- How do you figure out whether someone else has the same point of view as you do?
- Should you ever change your point of view to adopt someone else's?

THE BLACK PEARL

by Scott O'Dell

Ramón Salazar heard the strangest stories as he was growing up in the town of La Paz in Baja California Sur, Mexico. There were tales of a monstrous manta ray and a huge black pearl to be found in the Vermilion Sea. Of course, Ramón never believed he would see the Manta Diablo that was as big as a ship and had teeth as long as knives. But he always dreamed he would find the great Pearl of Heaven.

When he was sixteen, Ramón became a partner in his father's pearl business. His father taught him to weigh pearls, judge their worth, and be wary of his best diver, the fierce Sevillano. But Ramón's father refused to teach him the dangerous work of pearl diving. So an old Indian, Soto Luzon, secretly taught Ramón while his father was away.

The old man taught Ramón to dive in a quiet lagoon that made Ramón uneasy. The Manta Diablo lived there, the old man said, in a hidden cave. For three days, though, the lagoon was peaceful, the diving went well, and they found a few pearls of little value. On the fourth day, Ramón approached the hidden cave.

A red haze hung over the water as I floated the canoe on the morning of the fourth day and began to paddle toward the cave where the old man said the Manta Diablo lived.

The sun was up but the haze hung so thick that I had trouble locating the channel. After I found it I searched for almost an hour before I sighted the cave. It was hidden behind a rocky pinnacle and faced the rising sun, and the opening was about thirty feet wide and the height of a tall man, and curved downward like the upper lip of a mouth. I could not see into the cave because of the red mist, so I drifted back and forth and waited until the sun rose higher and the mist burned away.

I had talked to the old man the night before about the cave. We had eaten supper, and the women and children had gone to bed, and the two of us were sitting around the fire.

"You have fished everywhere in the lagoon," I said, "but not in the cave."

"No," he said. "Nor did my father nor his father."

"Big pearls may grow there."

The old man did not answer. He got up and put wood on the fire and sat down again.

"The great one itself, the Pearl of Heaven, may lie there," I said.

Still he did not answer, but suddenly he looked across the fire. It was a fleeting look that he gave me and yet its meaning was as clear as if he had spoken to me and said, "I cannot go to the cave to search for pearls. I cannot go because I fear the Manta Diablo. If you go there, then it is alone. El Diablo cannot blame me."

And that morning when I went down to the beach he did not go with me. "The wound on my hand hurts very much," he said, "so I will stay behind." And the look he gave me was the same I had seen the night before.

At last, about midmorning, the sun burned away the mist and I could see for a short distance into the cave. I paddled through the mouth and soon found myself in a vast vault-like room. The walls of the room were black and smooth and shone from the light that came in through the opening.

Near the mouth of the cave the water was very clear. I picked up my basket and sink stone, took a deep breath, and slipped over the side of the canoe, remembering all that the old man had taught me.

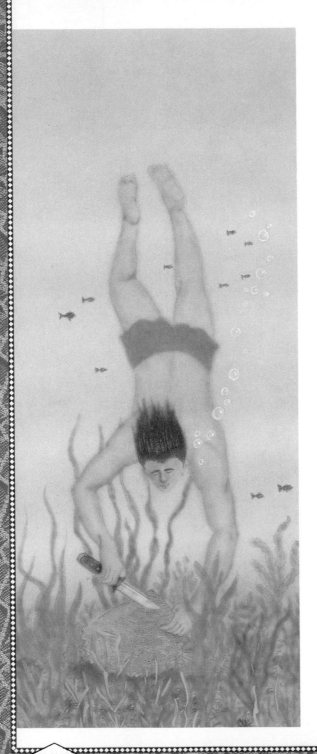

I reached the bottom after about a fathom and a half. I looped my foot in the rope tied to the sink stone and waited until the bubbles that had risen behind me disappeared and I could find the bed of shells I had noticed from above. The bed was five steps away toward the mouth of the cave. I walked carefully in the sand as I had learned to do.

The shells were the largest I had ever seen. They were half the length of my arm and thick through as my body and covered with weed that looked like a woman's hair. I chose the nearest one, which seemed to be easier to get at than the others. I took out my knife and worked quietly, but a school of small fish kept swimming in front of my eyes, so I failed to pry the shell loose before my lungs began to hurt and I had to go up.

On my second dive I had no sooner reached the bottom than a shadow fell across the bed where I was working. It was the shadow of a gray shark, one of the friendly ones, but by the time he had drifted away my breath was gone.

I dived six times more and worked quickly each time I went down, hacking away with my sharp knife at the base of the big shell where it was anchored to the rock. But it had been growing there for many years, since long before I was born, I suppose, and it would not come free from its home.

By this time it was late in the afternoon and the light was poor. Also my hands were bleeding and my eyes were half-blind with salt from the sea. But I sat in the canoe and thought of all the hours I had spent for nothing. And I thought too of the Sevillano and the great pearl he had found, or said he had found, in the Gulf of Persia.

I filled my lungs and took the sink stone and went down again. With the first stroke of my knife, the shell came free. It toppled over on one side, and I quickly untied the rope from the sink stone and looped it twice around the shell and swam back to the surface. I pulled up the shell, but it was too heavy for me to lift into the canoe, so I tied it to the stern and paddled out of the cave.

Across the lagoon I could see the old man standing among the trees. From time to time during the day I had caught glimpses of him standing there with his eyes fixed on the cave. I knew that I could drown and he would not try to save me, and that he was telling El Diablo all the while that he had not wanted me to go to the cave and that he therefore was not to blame. But I also felt that if I found a pearl he would be willing to take his share because he had nothing to do with finding it.

He came out from the trees as I paddled across the lagoon and strolled down to the beach as if he did not care whether I had found a pearl or not. I suppose this was to show El Diablo and his friends the fish and the long, gray shark that Soto Luzon was without blame.

"A big one," he said when I dragged the shell ashore. "In my life I have never seen such a monster. It is the grandfather of all oysters that live in the sea."

"There are many in the cave bigger than this one," I said.

"If there are so many," he answered, "then the Manta Diablo cannot be mad that you have taken only one of them."

"Perhaps a little mad," I said and laughed, "but not much."

The mouth of the oyster was closed and it was hard to put my blade between the tight edges of the shell.

"Lend me your knife," I said. "Mine is blunted from use."

The old man placed his hand on the hilt of his knife and pulled it from the sheath and then slipped it back again.

"I think it is better if you use your own knife," he said and his voice began to tremble as he spoke.

I wrestled a long time with the oyster. At last the hard lips began to give a little. Then I could feel the knife sink through the heavy muscles that held them together and suddenly the lips fell apart.

I put my finger under the frilled edge of the flesh as I had seen my father do. A pearl slid along my finger and I picked it out. It was about the size of a pea. When I felt again, another of the same size rolled out and then a third. I put them on the other half of the shell so they would not be scratched.

The old man came and leaned over me, as I knelt there in the sand, and held his breath.

Slowly I slid my hand under the heavy tongue of the oyster. I felt a hard lump, so monstrous in size that it could not be a pearl. I took hold of it and pulled it from the flesh and got to my feet and held it to the sun, thinking that I must be holding a rock that the oyster had swallowed somehow.

It was round and smooth and the color of smoke. It filled my cupped hand. Then the sun's light struck deep into the thing and moved in silver swirls and I knew that it was not a rock that I held but a pearl, the great Pearl of Heaven.

"Madre de Dios," the old man whispered.

I stood there and could not move or talk. The old man kept whispering over and over, "Madre de Dios."

Darkness fell. I tore off the the tail of my shirt and wrapped the pearl in it.

"Half of this is yours," I told him.

I handed the pearl to him, but he drew back in fear.

"You wish me to keep it until we reach La Paz?" I said.

"Yes, it is better that you keep it."

"When shall we go?"

"Soon," he said hoarsely. "El Diablo is away but he will come back. And his friends will tell him then about the pearl."

Library Link ◆ *Share more of Ramón's adventures by reading* **The Black Pearl** *by Scott O'Dell.*

Reader's Response

◆◆

Why do you think the old man was afraid of the lagoon and El Diablo?

THE BLACK PEARL

Responding to Literature

1. By entering the cave, the narrator of this story chose to violate established tradition. What do you believe will be the consequences of his action?

2. The boy could have lost his life in the darkness of the cave. What drives people to take dangerous chances in search of a dream? Give examples to explain your thoughts.

3. The setting of this story is vivid and clear. Draw a map of one important scene. Display your map and explain the events of the scene you chose.

Writing to Learn

Think and Decide ✦ What did the boy experience when he opened the shell? Try to imagine this experience from his point of view. Make a sketch of the diver. Above him, add a thought balloon. In it, write words and phrases to tell what he might have been thinking.

Thought Balloon

Write ✦ Write about the discovery from the diver's point of view. Tell what he may have thought when the tips of his fingers touched the magnificent pearl.

GETTING STARTED

Think of an amusing story that you have shared with a friend. Tell the story to listeners.

SPEAKING and LISTENING ◆
Telling About an Incident

You probably have a number of favorite stories that you enjoy telling people. These stories may be based on certain subjects you enjoy talking about, such as humorous incidents that happened in your childhood or at school.

When you choose a story that you like to tell, your enthusiasm usually affects your audience. Everyone seems to enjoy a lively story told with confidence. Telling a good story takes practice, but there are certain guidelines you can follow.

As an Effective Speaker	**1.** Establish story facts in a clear, lively style. Throughout the story, focus on your subject. **2.** During your story, describe specific events and actions. Give your listeners the feeling that they are actually witnessing the event. **3.** Balance your descriptions with dialogue, or bits of conversation. **4.** Use your voice to express yourself in a variety of ways. Stress important words and vary the speed at which you speak. **5.** Always make eye contact with your audience. Facial expressions and gestures also add meaning to your story. **6.** Repeat or summarize significant details whenever you can. This helps to maintain your listeners' interest.
As an Active Listener	**1.** Give polite attention and react positively to the speaker. **2.** Listen critically. Throughout the story, ask yourself whether the details, characters, plot, and theme are making sense. **3.** Applaud the speaker's efforts. Contribute honest responses to any discussion of the story.

Summary ◆ As a speaker, tell stories that are based on interesting and enjoyable incidents. As a listener, pay attention and evaluate what you hear.

Guided Practice

Read aloud each of the following sentences three times. Each time, change the way you use your voice to express yourself.

1. Is this really the way to keep a small sailboat on course?
2. I do hope we'll be sighting land again sometime soon.
3. You don't really seem to understand the problem.

Practice

A. Read how each student tells a story. Is the student using good storytelling techniques? Write *yes* or *no*. Explain your answer.

4. Karen doesn't ramble; she keeps her story on the subject.
5. Alvin tells his story in one great rush of details.
6. Juan pauses occasionally throughout his story.
7. Olga uses different voices to repeat a conversation.
8. Mark uses vivid expressions but forgets the ending.

B. Write answers to these questions: What are this student's errors in storytelling? How can they be corrected?

''Two merchant sailors were sitting by the dock,'' Tony began. ''The two sailors were talking about the greatest event in each one's career. It was sunny, and the dock was crowded with tourists waiting to go deep-sea fishing. One of them says he survived a shipwreck. The other one says he doesn't think that's very special. So the first one asks angrily what the other man does think is special . . .''

C. Think of a story that you like to tell. Tell the story to two classmates. Try to use dialogue in at least one part of the story. Have the classmates evaluate your storytelling techniques according to the guidelines in this lesson.

Apply • Think and Write

Evaluating a Story • Listen to a story told by a television or radio personality. A comedian, for example, often tells stories. Take notes on the story. Then write about it, describing why you did or did not enjoy the story.

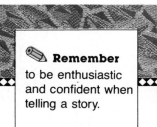

Remember to be enthusiastic and confident when telling a story.

WRITING ◆
Using Dialogue

In a story, dialogue is conversation between two or more characters. Dialogue is important because it can reveal a character's personality as well as move the action of the story forward. Dialogue involves the readers and places them in the center of the action. It also makes a story more like real life.

When you write, the world around you and your imagination are the main sources of ideas for dialogue. For this reason, it is helpful to jot down some of the many interesting phrases and bits of conversation you hear each day. This material can then be adapted as dialogue for your stories.

Below is an example of dialogue from *The Black Pearl*. Ramón has just shown Luzon a huge oyster that he found.

> "There are many in the cave bigger than this one," I said.
> "If there are so many," he answered, "then the Manta Diablo cannot be mad that you have taken only one of them."
> "Perhaps a little mad," I said and laughed, "but not much."
> The mouth of the oyster was closed. . .
> "Lend me your knife," I said. "Mine is blunted from use."
> The old man placed his hand on the hilt of his knife and pulled it from the sheath and then slipped it back again.
> "I think it is better if you use your own knife," he said and his voice began to tremble as he spoke.

In this dialogue, the writer keeps visual details to a miniumum and lets the characters talk. You feel as if you are actually there with the characters.

Here are some important hints for writing dialogue.

1. Use expressions that tell how things were said, such as *he whined*, or *she said with a laugh*. Avoid using only *he (she) said*. Also, try to capture people's real speech.
2. Begin a new paragraph each time a different person speaks.

3. Enclose the person's exact words in one set of quotation marks.
4. Capitalize the first word of the quotation and of each new sentence.
5. Separate the quotation from the rest of the sentence by a comma.

See pages 638–641 for more on punctuation of dialogue.

> **Summary** ♦ **Dialogue,** the conversation of characters in a story, is written in a special way.

Guided Practice

Create a short dialogue between the two persons in each situation.

1. Brian sees Manuel and wants him to join a group playing a game.
2. Amy tells Kris that the class field trip has been canceled.
3. Andrea asks her mother to help her plan a birthday party.

Practice

A. Choose one of the situations below. Write a dialogue between the two persons. Use words that tell how things were said.

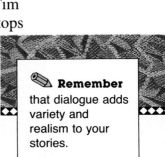

    4. a baseball player talking to an umpire
    5. two friends talking about a class they like
    6. two sisters discussing what movie to see

B. Rewrite this description of a conversation as direct dialogue, using quotation marks. Add any needed words to the dialogue.

    Donna wants Tim to go scuba diving with her and explore an undersea cave. Tim doesn't believe her. Donna points out that she has everything they need, such as flashlights and extra air tanks. Tim jokes that Donna must have planned ahead for this. Then he stops joking and tells her that he's afraid. Donna encourages him.

Apply ♦ Think and Write

Developing Dialogue ♦ Write an interesting conversation you have had or heard recently as a dialogue. Think of it as the opening for a story. Then write an outline for the possible story that could develop.

> ✎ **Remember**
> that dialogue adds variety and realism to your stories.

Imagine writing a fictional story about a day in the life of a friend. What would it be about? Name some ideas for the story.

WRITING ◆
Using a Journal

Where do writers get their ideas? Imagination is a major source. But writers also observe the world around them a great deal. They search for inspiring events and people. Before writing, they often spend time reflecting on personal thoughts and feelings.

A writer needs a place to collect and organize these valuable ideas for future reference. The author Nathaniel Hawthorne wrote many of his ideas for stories into journals. Here is one example:

"A story of the life, domestic and external, of a family of birds in a martin-house—for children."

You too can use a journal to organize your ideas.

Organizing a Journal You may wish to divide your journal into three sections. In the first section, write brief entries describing your ideas. You may want to provide space for separate categories, such as the following.

PLACES	(places you have either visited or imagined)
PLOTS	(outlines for scenes and stories)
CHARACTERS	(details about people)
DIALOGUE	(conversations you have had, heard, or imagined)
MOODS	(the right words for certain emotions)
IDEAS, THEMES	(everyday thoughts, feelings, opinions)
POETRY	(lines, verses, rhythms that come to you)

In the second section, write about what you are learning, such as various math and science concepts.

Use the third section for your writing experiments. You can also use this section to develop earlier entries from the first section. These entries will be a great help as you develop your stories.

> **Summary** ◆ Take time to organize your writing ideas by keeping a journal. Use your journal for experimenting with ideas.

Guided Practice

Suggest a brief writing idea for each category.

1. a plot   **2.** a character   **3.** a mood   **4.** a place

Practice

A. Write the category under which each journal entry might appear. Choose from the categories on the opposite page.

    5. Here, the sun shines almost daily. The huge trees along the beach sway and sigh like the ocean itself. The clean water glows bright blue. I feel I could make a home here.

    6. ''Now what?'' he asked. ''I've lost the directions, and they're expecting us at eight o'clock.''

    7. Grandmother came to America, 1905; settled and married in Texas; a family farm; what happened during the 1930s.

B. Write each of the sample entries below, completing it with ideas of your own. Also write what part of your notebook would be best for that entry.

    8. I wonder if the American colonists _____ .

    9. A woman who loves scuba diving discovers evidence of _____ during one of her dives. She feels afraid to tell _____ .

    10. When I am with _____ , I can't help but feel _____ . I think it's because he/she _____ . Unlike myself, _____ is _____ .

    11. Now I know why I like to go to _____ . It's because _____ .

C. Write an entry for one of the categories suggested for the first section of your journal. Then develop the entry into a longer piece of writing for the third section of your journal.

Apply ✦ Think and Write

Dictionary of Knowledge ✦ Many famous writers have used journals for their ideas. Nathaniel Hawthorne's journals were filled with observations and ideas. Read about Hawthorne in the Dictionary of Knowledge. Write about how Hawthorne's journals helped him form ideas for writing. Then describe how you will use your writer's journal.

✎ **Remember**
that your journal should be organized to fit your personal writing needs.

Focus on Point of View

In storytelling, **point of view** simply means "Who tells the story?" When you plan a story, you must answer that question. Your answer depends on what works best for you and what is most helpful in expressing your meaning. There are two basic points of view.

FIRST PERSON When you use **first-person** point of view, you tell the story as yourself ("*I* saw *my* friends") or through a character whom you pretend to be ("I saw the planet Krypton through a dim haze"). The key words are *I* and *we*.

THIRD PERSON When you use **third-person** point of view, you tell the story from the outside ("Jennifer was sure that she would get an A+ in calculus"). The key words are *he*, *she*, and *they*.

Author Scott O'Dell wrote *The Black Pearl* from the first-person point of view:

Also my hands were bleeding and my eyes were half-blind with salt from the sea. But I sat in the canoe and thought of all the hours I had spent for nothing.

O'Dell may or may not have dived for pearls, but he wanted to write about a character who had. Moreover, he wanted readers to know this man from the inside. Everything is presented from the "I" perspective. Throughout the story, the character's point of view remains consistent. We experience and know only what the storyteller does and knows.

With third-person point of view, the storyteller does not take part in the action. He or she only describes it.

The Writer's Voice ◆ What would the key word be in second-person point of view? Why is second-person point of view almost never used?

Working Together

First-person point of view can make your story believable and interesting. It could, however, limit you to the thoughts and observations of the storyteller. As a group, discuss activities **A** and **B**.

In Your Group	
◆ Encourage everyone to participate.	◆ Record people's ideas.
◆ Help the group stay on the job.	◆ Build on other ideas.

A. Find the sentences below that use first-person point of view. Discuss how to identify them. Then change the point of view of the other sentences from third person to first person.

1. When I sighted the cave, the first part of my search was over.
2. They had eaten supper, and the two of them talked by the fire.
3. Finding the bed of shells, he took out his knife.
4. On my second dive, I saw the shadow of a gray shark.
5. The size of the pearl startled him, and he stood there speechless.

B. Rewrite this story opening in first-person point of view. Decide which character to write about as "I" and make the appropriate changes throughout. Then add at least five new lines of dialogue.

   Rosa, inside the tiny submarine, was about to signal the research ship above that she wanted to come up. Suddenly there was Barry outside the porthole in his scuba gear.
   "Turn on your radio!" he signaled with his hands. "Big trouble!"

THESAURUS CORNER ◆ Word Choice

Each sentence contains a verb error. Rewrite each sentence, correcting the error. As you do so, use the Thesaurus and Thesaurus Index to replace the word in dark type with a suitable synonym.

1. "I **fathom**," she said, "that pearls is the gems of the sea."
2. If you were to **procure** pearls, you would wanted them to be round.
3. Leave me tell you that pearls are not as **solid** as other gems.

WRITING PROCESS
NARRATING

Writing a Personal Narrative

In *The Black Pearl* a fictional character, a young boy, tells how he found the Pearl of Heaven. The boy narrates the story in the first person, using the words *I* and *me*.

A personal narrative is also a first-person story. However, the narrator and the story are not fictional but true. In a personal narrative, you tell a story about something that really happened to you. You write as if you are talking to a friend who has said, "Tell me what happened," as friends often do.

Know Your Purpose and Audience

What's MY PURPOSE

In this lesson you will write a personal narrative, a true story about something that happened to you. Your purpose will be to engross or entertain the reader.

Who's MY AUDIENCE

Your audience will be your classmates. Later you can read your narratives aloud or display them and create awards for each other's narratives.

1 Prewriting

First you need to choose your topic—the event you will write about. Then you need to use an idea-gathering strategy.

Choose Your Topic ♦ Begin by deciding two different ways you might complete this sentence: "I'll never forget the time I ____." Tell something true that happened to you. Choose the most interesting event.

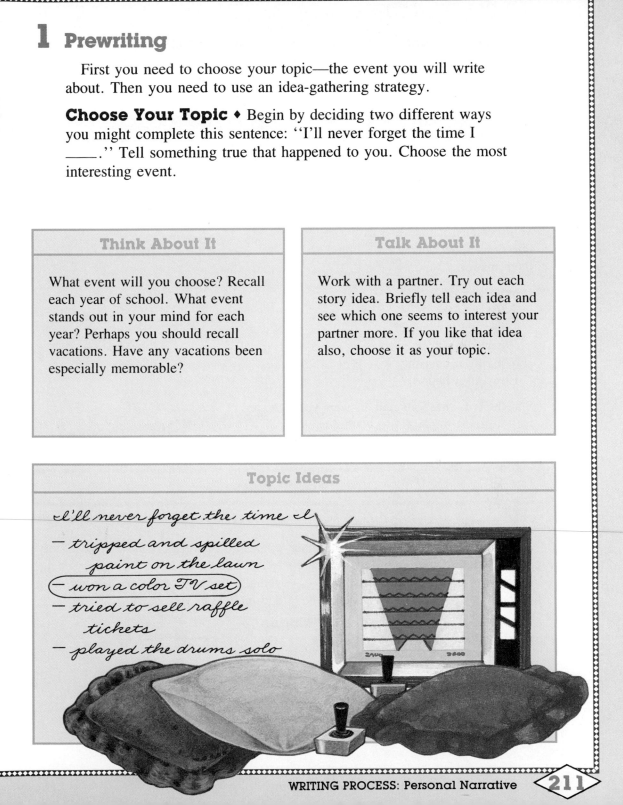

Think About It

What event will you choose? Recall each year of school. What event stands out in your mind for each year? Perhaps you should recall vacations. Have any vacations been especially memorable?

Talk About It

Work with a partner. Try out each story idea. Briefly tell each idea and see which one seems to interest your partner more. If you like that idea also, choose it as your topic.

Topic Ideas

I'll never forget the time I

— tripped and spilled paint on the lawn

— won a color TV set

— tried to sell raffle tickets

— played the drums solo

Choose Your Strategy ◆ The two strategies that follow can help you gather ideas about your topic. Read both, then use the idea you think will be more useful.

PREWRITING IDEAS

CHOICE ONE

Asking Questions

Questions can help you get ideas for your personal narrative. List the following questions about your topic along with their answers.

Who was involved?
What happened?
When did it happen?
Where did it happen?
Why did it happen?
How did it happen?

Star the two questions and answers you feel are most important to your story.

Model

* What happened?
  I won a color TV set.
* Why did it happen?
  I was trying to win a
  steak dinner.

CHOICE TWO

Thought Balloons

Look at events in your story from other points of view. What might other people have said or thought about what was happening to you? Think of people who witnessed or were involved in your story. Make thought balloons for them. Seeing yourself the way others see you can help add interest to your story.

Model

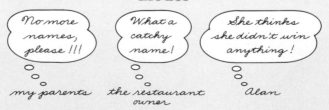

No more names, please!!!   *my parents*

What a catchy name!   *the restaurant owner*

She thinks she didn't win anything!   *Alan*

2 Writing

Review your prewriting notes. The two questions you starred may help you decide which parts to focus on and which parts require fewer details. Now write your story from beginning to end, nonstop if possible. Concentrate on getting down each event in correct order. Include dialogue and other points of view to add interest. Don't worry about effective sentences or surface errors at this point. They can be fixed later.

When you have finished writing, review your draft. Think:

♦ Do I need an introductory sentence or paragraph?
♦ Does the last event provide a sense of closure, or do I need to add a few concluding sentences?

Sample First Draft ♦

I'll never forget the contest I entered last year. I saw an anouncement about a new restaurant coming to town. The person who picked the best name for the restaurant would win a Color Television set. The next hundred best ideas would win a free steak dinner. Now I love steak, and I believed I could think up a name that would win a free meal. My parents began to groan when I opened my mouth. For weeks I thought of names. I kept saying names over and over again. Finally, I entered my favrits in the contest.

When the winners' list was posted my friend Alan and I scanned the list of meal winners. I was not on the list. I frowned, but Alan started to laugh. Then he pointed and said I had won first prize!

The Spice Palace got its name and I got a new television however I still dream about that free steak dinner. Maybe I'll enter another contest.

3 Revising

Now that you have drafted your personal narrative, you probably need to polish it. This strategy may help you.

REVISING IDEA

FIRST Read to Yourself

As you read, review your purpose. Will your personal narrative entertain an audience? Will your classmates enjoy your narrative? Put a pencil check in the margin to show where you want to make improvements.

Focus: Is your narrative written in the first-person point of view?

THEN Share with a Partner

Choose a partner to be your first audience. Read your narrative aloud and ask your partner to respond. These guidelines may help you work together.

The Writer

Guidelines: Read in a clear, conversational tone. Listen to your partner's feedback. Then make the changes you feel are needed.

Sample questions:
- What part did you enjoy most?
- Were there any parts that could be clearer?
- **Focus question:** Have I used first-person point of view consistently?

The Writer's Partner

Guidelines: Give your partner specific ideas rather than generalities. Use a courteous, helpful tone.

Sample responses:
- I really got a kick out of the part where _____ .
- I'm not clear about what happened when _____ .
- Maybe you could add dialogue to show what _____ said to you.

Revising Model ♦ As the model below shows, you can cross out, add, and move words around when you are revising.

Presumed conveyed the writer's meaning more precisely.

The order of these sentences was confusing.

The writer decided to vary the verbs for interest.

The writer's partner suggested inserting dialogue.

I'll never forget the contest I entered last year. I saw an anouncement about a new restaurant coming to town. The person who picked the best name for the restaurant would win a Color Television set. The next hundred best ideas would win a free steak dinner. Now I love steak, and I *presumed* believed I~~could think up a name that would win a free meal. My parents began to groan when I opened my mouth. For weeks I thought of names I kept saying names over and over again. *mumbled them, I wrote them, I sang them.* Finally, I entered my favrits in the contest.

When the winners' list was posted my friend Alan and I scanned the list of meal winners. I was not on the list. I frowned, but Alan started to laugh. Then he pointed and said I had won first prize. *"Kim!" he said. "Forget the meal. You won first prize!"*

The Spice Palace got its name and I got a new television however I still dream about that free steak dinner. Maybe I'll enter another contest.

Read the narrative above the way the writer has decided it *should* be. Then revise your own personal narrative.

Grammar Check ♦ Specific and varied verbs add sparkle to your writing.

Word Choice ♦ Are you searching for a word with a precise meaning? A thesaurus can help you find the right word.

Revising Checklist

☐ **Purpose:** Did I write a personal narrative to entertain an audience?

☐ **Audience:** Will my classmates understand and enjoy my personal narrative?

☐ **Focus:** Have I used the first-person point of view consistently?

4 Proofreading

Proofreading is checking for and correcting surface errors to make your writing more readable.

Proofreading Model ◆ Here is the draft narrative about winning a contest. Proofreading changes have been added in red.

Proofreading Marks

capital letter ≡

small letter /

add comma ⌄

add period ⊙

indent paragraph ¶

check spelling ⬭

Proofreading Checklist

☐ Did I spell words correctly?

☐ Did I indent paragraphs?

☐ Did I use correct capitalization?

☐ Did I use correct punctuation?

☐ Did I type neatly or use my best handwriting?

I'll never forget the contest I entered last year. I saw an *announcement* about a new restaurant coming to town. The person who picked the best name for the restaurant would win a color television set. The next hundred best ideas would win a free steak dinner. Now I love steak, and I *presumed* believed I could think up a name that would win a free meal. My parents began to groan when I opened my mouth. For weeks I thought of names. I *mumbled them, I wrote them, I sang them.* kept saying names over and over again. Finally, I entered my *favorites* favrits in the contest.

When the winners' list was posted, my friend Alan and I scanned the list of meal winners. I was not on the list. I frowned, but Alan started to laugh. Then he pointed and said I had won first prize! *"Him!" he said. "Forget the meal. You won first prize!"*

The Spice Palace got its name, and I got a new television; however, I still dream about that free steak dinner. Maybe I'll enter another contest.

PROOFREADING IDEA

Mechanics Check

Check the first letters of sentences and dialogue for capital letters. Dialogue begins with opening quotation marks. Then check the ends of sentences and dialogue for correct punctuation.

Now proofread your personal narrative and make a neat copy. Be sure to add a title.

5 Publishing

Here are two ideas for sharing.

The Contest Challenge

I'll never forget the contest I entered last year. I saw an announcement about a new restaurant coming to town. The person who picked the best name for the restaurant would win a color television set. The next hundred best ideas would win a free steak dinner.

Now I love steak, and I presumed I could think up a name that would win a free meal. For weeks I thought of names. My parents began to groan when I opened my mouth. I mumbled them, I wrote them, I sang them. Finally, I entered my favorites in the contest.

When the winners' list was posted, my friend Alan and I scanned the list of meal winners. I was not on the list. I frowned, but Alan started to laugh. Then he pointed. "Kim!" he said. "Forget the meal. You won first prize!"

The Spice Palace got its name, and I got a new television. However, I still dream about that free steak dinner. Maybe I'll enter another contest.

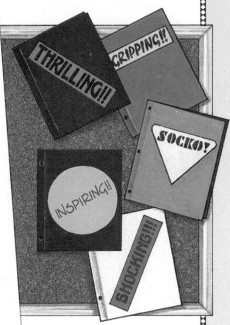

PUBLISHING IDEAS

Share Aloud

Read your personal narrative aloud within a small group. Have the group decide on an award for each narrative, such as Most Surprising, Silliest, Most Touching, or Most Thrilling.

Share in Writing

Display your narrative on a bulletin board. Read someone else's narrative and design a review word for it. A review word is a key word taken from a book review and reprinted in the front of a paperback. A word such as INSPIRING! describes the narrative's content. Write your word in fancy lettering. Attach it to the cover.

Writing Across the Curriculum Social Studies

Historians often contemplate how historic characters might have felt about their experiences and the times they lived in. You can enhance your study of history by doing the same kind of imagining about people from the past.

Writing to Learn

Think and Imagine By using your imagination, you can be a part of history. Look at this picture of the *Mayflower*. Imagine that you are one of its passengers. Fill a thought balloon with your thoughts upon reaching your destination.

Thought Balloon

Write Use your thought balloon to help you compose a letter from a *Mayflower* passenger to a friend in England.

Writing in Your Journal

In the Writer's Warm-up at the beginning of this unit, you wrote about the sea. Then you read about diving, coral reefs, sea animals, and other elements of the sea around us. What did you learn in this unit that you didn't know before? In your journal, write about what you have learned about the sea.

BOOKS TO ENJOY

Read More About it

Island of the Blue Dolphins *by Scott O'Dell*

In this haunting story, the author of *The Black Pearl* tells about Karana, a young Indian girl who is forced to spend eighteen months alone on an island off the coast of California.

Newbery Award

The Sea Around Us *by Rachel Carson*

Rachel Carson's lifelong interest in the sea is clearly reflected in this important book. A marine biologist, Carson skillfully describes the history, geography, and biology of the sea.

Treasure Island *by Robert Louis Stevenson*

The young hero, Jim Hawkins, sets sail with two dangerous pirates—Long John Silver and Blind Pew—on a hair-raising search for buried treasure.

Book Report Idea   Book Debate

Have you ever read a book that someone recommended highly only to discover you didn't like it? Consider giving a book debate.

Choose Sides ✦ To hold a book debate, you and one other student will need to have read the same book. To some extent, your opinions of the book should differ. Debate the points on which you differ. Support your opinions with strong passages from the book you both have read.

Unit 4

Verbs   *pages 174–187*

A. Write the four principal parts of each regular verb.

    1. fix   **3.** type   **5.** rip   **7.** walk

    2. hurry   **4.** stop   **6.** boast   **8.** stir

B. Write the underlined verb and label its tense: *present, past, future, present perfect, past perfect,* or *future perfect*.

    9. I <u>have researched</u> the topic in various books.

   10. Mandy <u>had reserved</u> a seat for me next to hers.

   11. Phil <u>volunteered</u> his help with the project.

   12. By next week, we <u>will have learned</u> more about the topic.

   13. This assignment <u>requires</u> hard work.

   14. The librarian <u>will help</u> me find more books later.

C. Write each sentence. Use the correct verb in parentheses.

   15. Has Laura (began, begun) her piano lessons yet?

   16. She (knowed, knew) about the schedule.

   17. Some people never (got, gotten) this opportunity.

   18. I have (wrote, written) some songs for her.

D. Write the verb in each sentence. Then write *active* or *passive*.

   19. Cactuses grow in dry, hot regions of America.

   20. One type is called the saguaro.

   21. It can be found in Arizona and neighboring regions.

   22. I admire cactuses with brightly colored flowers.

E. Write each sentence, using the correct verb form in parentheses.

   23. My father has (risen, raised) each morning at five for years.

   24. Don't (sit, set) your glass at the edge of the counter.

   25. Are the children (lying, laying) in their beds?

   26. Where have you (lain, laid) your notebook?

Synonyms *pages 188–189*

F. Write each sentence, replacing the verb *walked* with an appropriate synonym from the following list.

> **paced**   **rambled**   **trudged**   **strode**

27. The tired hikers walked over the hill toward their camp.
28. The worried parent walked the floor of the emergency room.
29. The winners walked toward the stage to collect their medals.
30. The stranded travelers walked through the airport shops.

Dialogue *pages 204–205*

G. Rewrite the following description as direct dialogue, using quotation marks. Add any needed words to the dialogue.

Aunt Nancy looked worried when Gary and Denise met her in front of the department store. She had been waiting an hour and a half for them. When they finally arrived, she wanted to find out what took them so long. Gary and Denise described their ride on a bus. The bus had engine trouble and required assistance. Aunt Nancy was relieved to see them and decided to treat them to lunch at a nearby restaurant.

Using a Journal *pages 206–207*

H. Write the category under which each journal entry might appear. Choose from the following categories: places, plots, moods, characters, dialogue, themes, or poetry.

31. The twins are fiercely independent. They never wear the same clothes. Although they are the best of friends, each twin has his own set of friends.
32. A woman climbs a ladder to retrieve a kite that is stuck on a second floor ledge. Suddenly a window loudly blows open. A cat timidly pokes its head out the window.
33. Another day of heavy rain; nothing to do; friends are away; I have traced the design on the bedspread twice!
34. The large, green leaves of the pumpkin plant have spread quickly across the patch of garden. Lovely yellow flowers poke through the tangle of greenery.

UNIT 1: Sentences *pages 4–19*

A. Write each complete subject. Underline each simple subject.

   1. The old empty warehouse was torn down last month.
   2. The civil engineer in charge supervised the project.
   3. Groups of employees watched the demolition.

B. Write each complete predicate. Underline each verb.

   4. Brenda is spending the weekend with her grandparents.
   5. Mr. and Mrs. Hall took her to a play last night.
   6. Brenda's parents phoned them today.

C. Write and label the compound subject or compound verb in each sentence.

   7. Mom and Dad gave me the idea for my play.
   8. They discussed possible ideas and finally agreed on one.
   9. I listened first then wrote down their suggestion.

D. Write *simple* or *compound* for each sentence.

   10. Three or four houses were damaged during the hurricane.
   11. The police alerted people, but some did not listen to warnings.
   12. Families were evacuated to the high school auditorium.

UNIT 2: Nouns *pages 56–65*

E. Write whether each noun is common or proper.

   13. Friday   **14.** person   **15.** Detroit   **16.** Dan   **17.** event

F. Write each noun. Label it *singular, singular possessive, plural*, or *plural possessive*.

   18. woman **19.** chief's **20.** mice **21.** classes' **22.** Charles's

UNIT 3: Verbs *pages 118–129*

G. Write the verb in each sentence. Write *LV* if it is a linking verb or *AV* if it is an action verb.

23. The road felt slippery.   **25.** The passengers were lucky.
24. A car skidded across.   **26.** They wore seat belts.

H. Write and label each direct object and indirect object in the sentence.

27. Please give me four quarters for a dollar.
28. The bus driver told the passengers some jokes.
29. Did you ask the doctor or nurse any questions?
30. She sent us a postcard from our nation's capital.

I. Write and label each predicate nominative *PN* or each predicate adjective *PA* in the sentences.

31. Frank seemed tense and unhappy this morning.
32. He is usually a cheerful person.
33. John became the president of our class this week.

UNIT 4: Verbs *pages 174–187*

J. Write the underlined verb and its tense: *present, past, future, present perfect, past perfect*, or *future perfect*.

34. Joanne received the radio that she had wanted for her birthday.
35. Amy has enjoyed herself at the school fair.
36. By August, I will have earned enough money for a new bike.
37. I think a red bike will look nice.

K. Write the verb in each sentence. Then write *active* or *passive*.

38. My class learned about American regional dialects.
39. We were also taught the origins of many words.
40. Word origins are called etymologies.

L. Write the correct form of the verb in each sentence.
41. (Sit, Set) the plant by the window.
42. The school flag is (risen, raised) every morning.
43. We (lay, laid) the bricks on the wet cement last month.

LANGUAGE PUZZLERS
Unit 4 Challenge

Verb Clues

Figure out each irregular verb form. (Hint: Draw blanks for the letters and number each blank.)

1. I am a past participle of seven letters.
My 7, 6, 4 catches butterflies.
My 1, 2, 6, 7 is a bird.
My 1, 3, 4 shows I'm smart.

2. I am a past participle of six letters.
My 2, 3, 5 is a garden tool.
My 1, 3, 6, 5 falls from pine trees.
My 4, 2, 3, 5 is on your foot.

3. I am a past participle of six letters.
My 1, 2, 6 is a kitty.
My 5, 3, 4 is an embrace.
My 5, 2, 6 belongs on your head.

A Troublesome-Verb Crossword

Copy the crossword graph. Then fill in the words.

Across
1. Jenny _____ the map on the table yesterday.
2. Eduardo _____ in last week's race.
3. The cat _____ by the fire all night.
5. The twins _____ down for a nap every afternoon.
6. Amy _____ the newspaper in our mailbox each day.
8. Melissa _____ down in the rocking chair.

Down
1. _____ your coats on the bed.
2. The sun will _____ the temperature of the room.
4. Water levels will _____ when the tide comes in.
6. _____ me help you wash the dishes.
7. You may _____ the packages on that chair.

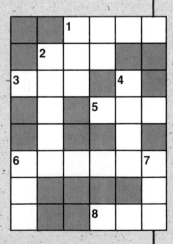

Unit 4 Extra Practice

1 Principal Parts of Verbs

p. 174

A. Each word below is either the past participle or the present participle of a regular verb. Write the present form of the verb.

1. lived	**7.** opened	**13.** saving	**19.** snowing
2. cried	**8.** rained	**14.** trying	**20.** humming
3. tapped	**9.** followed	**15.** dotting	**21.** spilling
4. smiled	**10.** obeyed	**16.** closing	**22.** creating
5. joked	**11.** laughed	**17.** hopping	**23.** playing
6. jogged	**12.** walking	**18.** happening	**24.** coughing

B. Write the four principal parts of each verb. All are regular verbs.

25. ask	**28.** flow	**31.** climb	**34.** suppose
26. use	**29.** drown	**32.** treat	**35.** roast
27. skid	**30.** sneak	**33.** attack	**36.** misspell

C. Write each sentence, completing it with the correct principal part of the verb in parentheses. Label the part *present*, *past*, *past participle*, or *present participle*.

37. For centuries people have (study) the skies. **38.** Among America's most brilliant astronomers, many scientists (name) Maria Mitchell. **39.** Born in 1818 in Massachusetts, she (live) on Nantucket Island. **40.** Her father (repair) and (adjust) clocks, but he also (study) the stars with his own telescope. **41.** From him Maria (learn) much about astronomy. **42.** Although she (work) as a librarian, the stars (remain) her chief interest. **43.** By the age of twenty-nine, she had (discover) a comet. **44.** This discovery (earn) Mitchell national and international praise. **45.** In 1865, Vassar Female College (appoint) her as its first professor of astronomy. **46.** During her lifetime she (receive) many awards from colleges and from scientific societies. **47.** Stories about people like Maria Mitchell are (provide) inspiration for many young men and women today.

2 Tenses of Verbs

p. 176

A. Write the underlined verb and its tense: *present*, *past*, or *future*.

1. Neil opened the four boxes of costumes.
2. Who will open that jar of pickles?
3. I shall close the letter with a funny story.
4. The state fair closes today.
5. We closed the show with a song.
6. Everyone looked through the new telescope.
7. It looks cold outside now.
8. The search team will look everywhere.
9. Ruthanne will answer the next question.
10. My little sister reads very well.

B. Write the underlined verb and its tense: *present perfect*, *past perfect*, or *future perfect*.

11. His answers have surprised us again.
12. The letter had arrived before we left.
13. We shall have finished it before midnight.
14. Robyn said that her brother had studied Portuguese for three years.
15. Who will have memorized it by June 3?
16. She has defined all the words in the lesson.
17. No one had noticed the new chair until today.
18. The librarians have moved the magazine rack.

C. Write each underlined verb and its tense.

19. A customer in a supermarket approaches the checkout counter. **20.** Soon the cash register will communicate with the customer. **21.** Many of the new cash registers seem almost human. **22.** They scan the price codes on boxes and cans. **23.** They display on a monitor the name and price of the product. **24.** Finally they thank the customer for his or her business. **25.** These cash registers have appeared in many stores. **26.** Not many years ago, however, engineers had dreamed of such machines. **27.** They experimented with many different kinds of models. **28.** Perhaps by the year 2000, engineers will have designed a cash register that also will wrap the customer's purchases. **29.** By then, will the supermarket itself have become obsolete?

3 Irregular Verbs

p. 180

A. Write the principal parts of each verb.

1. do	**3.** eat	**5.** catch	**7.** sing	**9.** steal
2. go	**4.** hurt	**6.** take	**8.** wear	**10.** shake

B. Write each sentence, completing it with the correct form (the past or the past participle) of the verb in parentheses.

11. Just before midnight the storm (begin). **12.** The moon had just (sink) behind the craggy hills. **13.** The wind (blow) fiercely. **14.** Many ancient trees (fall). **15.** Broken branches with jagged ends were (throw) about wildly. **16.** The old stone dam had (burst) a short time earlier. **17.** The swirling river had (become) a menace to the quiet village. **18.** Snakes had (swim) into flooded cellars. **19.** Bats had (fly) into broken windows in many houses. **20.** Frightened animals had been (drive) from the forest into the village streets. **21.** The howling wind (ring) the bell in the clock tower. **22.** In a noisy old automobile, a newspaper reporter (ride) into the village. **23.** She had (come) because of a mysterious telephone call. **24.** If she had (know) what lay ahead, would she have left the city?

25. Many programs on radio once (begin) with a scene like this one. **26.** People (think) such shows were fascinating. **27.** Their imaginations were (give) opportunities to grow. **28.** Helped by clever sound-effects technicians, listeners (see) in their minds what they heard. **29.** Using many gadgets, the technicians created the noises that had been (write) in the script. **30.** Of all the machines that talked, people (find) the radio the most interesting.

C. Complete the answers to these questions. Use only the past or past participle in your answers.

31. Did he throw it away? Yes, he _____ it away at once.
32. Did she drive that car? Yes, she _____ it several times.
33. Did they steal it? No, someone else must have _____ it.
34. Have you worn that? Yes, I have often _____ it.
35. Has the show begun? No, it has not yet _____ .
36. Have the guests gone? No, they have not _____ yet.
37. Have they taken the medicine? No, they have not _____ it.
38. Did anybody eat the salad? Yes, everybody _____ the salad.

4 Active and Passive Voice

p. 184

A. Write the verb in each sentence. Label it *active* or *passive*.

1. Computers are used in our school in many ways.
2. The vice-principal schedules students on a computer.
3. Attendance is reported on a computer-printed bulletin.
4. We compose stories and essays on personal computers in the writing center.
5. Our computer disks are handled very carefully.
6. The school newspaper printed my article about fly fishing.
7. The chess club was trained with computer software.
8. Adventure games are played in the computer room during the activity period.
9. Software is exchanged by a number of my friends.
10. Music students practice on electronic keyboards.

B. Rewrite each sentence, changing each passive verb to an active verb.

11. A speech was assigned yesterday by our English teacher.
12. A topic was chosen quickly by everyone.
13. Dan was not surprised by my choice.
14. Photography is enjoyed by both of us.
15. My first camera was given to me by my parents.
16. My landscapes have been exhibited by the library.
17. Half of the basement was turned into a darkroom by my dad.
18. Processing color slides will be discussed by other students.
19. Prizes for photos have been won by Dan.
20. That photo was awarded a ribbon by the judges.
21. Some slides have been made into prints by the photo lab.
22. One was purchased by my dentist for his office.
23. That slide was placed in the projector backwards by me.
24. Speeches will be evaluated by a student and the teacher.
25. Speeches will be presented by the class next week.

C. Write two sentences using each of these verbs. In the first sentence use the passive voice. In the second sentence change to the active voice.

26. win	**28.** write	**30.** use	**32.** choose	**34.** take
27. rip	**29.** argue	**31.** buy	**33.** wipe	**35.** bite

5 Troublesome Verb Pairs

p. 186

A. Write the correct form of the verb in parentheses.

1. Don't (raise, rise) the lid on that trunk.
2. The prices have (raised, risen) again.
3. Why did the club (raise, rise) its dues?
4. The teacher has (raised, risen) my grade.
5. Has the sun (raised, risen) yet?
6. Salute when the flag (raises, rises).
7. They (raised, rose) the flag at dawn.
8. Why did Nick (raise, rise) that question?
9. She (raised, rose) to her feet and spoke.
10. Where did you (set, sit) the ice cubes?
11. (Set, Sit) here and tell me another good story.
12. Don't (set, sit) the dessert on the table yet.
13. (Set, Sit) it there, please.
14. Don't let the dog (set, sit) on the couch.
15. I have never (set, sat) so long in one place.
16. (Set, Sit) this plant in a shady place.
17. They told us not to (set, sit) on that balcony.
18. She (set, sat) her package on that rack.
19. (Lay, Lie) those packages on the counter.
20. If you are tired, (lay, lie) down and rest.
21. In which pile do we (lay, lie) these ribbons?
22. Whose cap is (laying, lying) on that box?
23. Yesterday I (laid, lay) in the hammock.
24. Millions of leaves (laid, lay) on our lawn.
25. We (laid, lay) our money on the table last night.
26. They (laid, lay) their gifts there a week ago.
27. How long has the book (laid, lain) here?

B. Write the correct form of *lie or lay* to complete each sentence below.

28. Those tigers ____ down after they eat.
29. The cat has been ____ there for an hour.
30. The sunbather ____ on the beach and dozes.
31. The fawn ____ motionless in the underbrush and waited.
32. How long has that photograph ____ there?
33. No one has ____ a hand on it.
34. The children have always ____ their books there.

UNIT FIVE

USING LANGUAGE
TO

CLASSIFY

=== PART ONE ===

Unit Theme *Meeting the Challenge of Progress*

Language Awareness Pronouns

=== PART TWO ===

Literature *The Brooklyn Bridge: They Said It Couldn't Be Built* by Judith St. George

A Reason for Writing Classifying

Writing
IN YOUR JOURNAL

WRITER'S WARM-UP ◆ To make progress, people set goals and then work toward them. The challenge of progress is setting the right goals and then overcoming any obstacles. Think about a real situation in which progress was made. Then write about it in your journal. Tell what challenges were overcome.

Can you answer this riddle? What two-letter word can stand for *book*, *goat*, *sky*, *national park*, and *dish*?

1 Writing with Pronouns

Pronouns are words that take the place of nouns.

    She   **them**   **its**

■ ~~Ms. Lu~~ told ~~Jan and Richard~~ about the ~~Brooklyn Bridge's~~ history.

In the sentence above, the pronouns replacing the nouns are **personal pronouns**. The chart shows the forms of personal pronouns.

Person	Singular	Plural
First (the person speaking)	I, me, my, mine	we, us, our, ours
Second (the person spoken to)	you, your, yours	you, your, yours
Third (the person or thing spoken about)	he, him, his, she, her, hers, it, its	they, them, their, theirs

By using pronouns you can avoid repeating the same nouns again and again. Notice how pronouns can make a sentence shorter and easier to read.

                      she   **them**

■ Ms. Lu told the students ~~Ms. Lu~~ would show ~~students~~ the bridge.

> **Summary ◆** A **pronoun** takes the place of a noun or nouns. Using pronouns in your speaking and writing can help you avoid repeating the same words over and over.

Guided Practice

Name the pronouns in each sentence.

1. The students told Ms. Lu they liked her tour of the bridge.
2. She told them facts about its builder, John Roebling.
3. Roebling died before the bridge was finished, but his son completed it for him.

Practice

A. Write the pronouns from these sentences about the Brooklyn Bridge.

    4. It is a very famous bridge.

    5. Workers labored almost fourteen years to build it.

    6. They were very dedicated to the project.

    7. Thousands of people were on hand for its opening in 1883.

    8. People, wagons, and horses made their way across the bridge.

    9. They were amazed at its strength and beauty.

    10. ''The eighth wonder of the world'' was their name for it.

    11. We enjoy it just as much in our day.

    12. You may want to visit the bridge someday with your friends.

    13. I often ride my bike on the bridge's promenade.

B. Rewrite each sentence using a pronoun to take the place of the underlined word or words.

    14. John Roebling dreamed that <u>John Roebling</u> would build a bridge to link Manhattan and Brooklyn.

    15. When Roebling first published the plans, many people doubted <u>Roebling</u> would be able to build the bridge.

    16. Roebling asked other engineers to judge the plans, and <u>those engineers</u> approved the plans.

    17. Many people contributed <u>many people's</u> ideas to the project.

    18. Today, the Brooklyn Bridge is a famous landmark; <u>the Brooklyn Bridge</u> is admired by many people.

C. Write a pronoun to complete each sentence.

    19. Colonel Washington Roebling took charge of the bridge project after _____ father's death.

    20. Work on the bridge left _____ seriously ill.

    21. _____ turned to _____ wife for assistance.

    22. _____ nursed Roebling and helped manage the project.

    23. _____ courage and dedication inspired the engineers.

Apply • Think and Write

From Your Writing • Read what you wrote for the Writer's Warm-up. Look for nouns that you have repeated too often. See if you can replace any of those nouns with pronouns.

✎ **Remember**
that you can use pronouns to replace nouns you do not want to repeat.

GETTING STARTED

Why would people be confused by this bulletin? "The school is having her annual faculty baseball game on Thursday. The principal has announced its intention to manage the team!" Help clear up the confusion.

2 Pronouns and Antecedents

The words to which a pronoun refers are called antecedents. An antecedent can come before or after the pronoun that replaces it. An antecedent may even be in a different sentence.

> The *inventor* said that <u>he</u> has a plan.
> If <u>his</u> plan works, the *inventor* will become famous.
> *Inventors* and *builders* were very important in the 1800s.
> <u>They</u> helped create a better life for everyone.

Notice that an antecedent can also be more than one word.

When you write be sure to use a singular pronoun to refer to a singular antecedent, and a plural pronoun to refer to a plural antecedent.

Singular: *Tim* read about <u>his</u> favorite inventor, Alexander Graham Bell.
   Plural: Other *students* discussed <u>their</u> favorite inventors.

Always use a pronoun that agrees with its antecedent in gender.

Masculine: *Bell* met <u>his</u> wife Mabel at a school for the deaf.
 Feminine: *Mabel* was a courageous woman, and Bell admired <u>her</u>.
   Neuter: The *school* was known for <u>its</u> progressive ideas.

> **Summary** ✦ An **antecedent** is the word or words to which a pronoun refers. The antecedent for every pronoun should be clear, and the pronoun should agree with its antecedent in both gender and number.

Guided Practice

Name the antecedent for each underlined pronoun.

1. Alexander Graham Bell was known for <u>his</u> many inventions.
2. Bell had many ideas, and we benefit from <u>them</u> today.
3. Many people believe <u>they</u> have easier lives because of Bell.

Practice

A. Write each pronoun and its antecedent.

4. In 1874, while visiting his father, Bell developed the idea for the telephone.
5. Bell's family gave their support to the inventor in many ways.
6. Bell and Thomas Watson soon met. They began working together.
7. Bell and Watson worked hard building their first telephone.
8. The telephone was nearly completed in 1875, but it transmitted only sounds, not words.

B. Write the paragraph, using correct pronouns to complete the sentences. Underline the antecedent of each pronoun.

The telephone transmitted (**9.** _____) first clear words in 1876. Bell and Watson finally had (**10.** _____) first long-distance telephone conversation. Although (**11.** _____) did not participate in the telephone business, Bell was often called upon to appear in court. Some people claimed that (**12.** _____) had invented the telephone before Bell did. Bell testified that (**13.** _____) was the real inventor.

C. Write a sentence for each pronoun and antecedent below. Be sure that the pronouns and antecedents agree in number.

> **EXAMPLE:** people, them
> **ANSWER:** *People* usually have telephones installed for them.

14. Alexander Graham Bell, he
15. inventors, they
16. Bell and Watson, their
17. Thomas Watson, his
18. telephone, it
19. sound, its
20. Mabel Bell, her
21. experiment, it
22. people, their
23. family, they

Apply • Think and Write

Pronoun Replacements • What if Alexander Graham Bell had never invented the telephone? Write about what your family's life might be like without it. Then replace some of the nouns you used with pronouns and read the passage to a partner. See if your partner can identify the antecedents of the pronouns.

> ✏️ **Remember**
> to be sure that pronouns agree with their antecedents.

Think of a famous person, past or present, that you admire. Then give clues to see if anyone can guess the person's name. For example: *His team was the New York Yankees. His number was 3. Who was he?*

3 Possessive Pronouns

Like possessive nouns, possessive pronouns are used to show ownership or possession.

■ The <u>Romans'</u> bridges were sturdy. Many of <u>their</u> bridges still exist.

	Singular	Plural
First person	my, mine	our, ours
Second person	your, yours	your, yours
Third person	his, her, hers, its	their, theirs

The possessive pronouns *my*, *your*, *his*, *her*, *its*, *our*, and *their* are used before nouns.

■ <u>Our</u> country has many celebrated bridges.

The possessive pronouns *mine*, *yours*, *his*, *hers*, *ours*, and *theirs* are used alone. Notice that *his* can be used both with nouns and alone.

■ The house nearest the river is <u>mine</u>.

Do not confuse the possessive pronouns *its*, *their*, *your*, and *theirs* with the contractions *it's*, *they're*, *you're*, and *there's*. Remember that a **contraction** is a shortened form of two words. A contraction always has an apostrophe; a possessive pronoun does not.

■ <u>Their</u> house is near the bridge.   <u>They're</u> visiting friends.

> **Summary** ◆ A **possessive pronoun** shows ownership.

Guided Practice

Name the possessive pronouns.

1. My mother recently bought a book about famous bridges.
2. Her interest began when she read about the Brooklyn Bridge.
3. The books about European bridges are also hers.

Practice

A. Write each possessive pronoun. Then write whether it is used alone or with a noun.

    4. The teacher told our class about early Roman architecture.
    5. My favorite Roman structures are the arch bridges.
    6. Their most famous bridges were made of stone.
    7. The stone bridge in this picture is theirs.
    8. Its name is the Pons Fabricus.
    9. Fabricus, a Roman leader, gave his name to the bridge.
  10. The Emperor Trajan had his men build a bridge over the river.
  11. The result of their efforts was a bridge one-half mile long.
  12. Over a million stones were cut to make its twenty piers.
  13. These photographs of the bridge are mine.

B. Write the correct possessive pronoun for the underlined words.

  14. The emperor and the emperor's son designed a bridge.
  15. The emperor and his son's bridge lasted for centuries.
  16. The emperor's wife had the emperor's wife's name carved on the bridge.
  17. The bridge was sturdy because the bridge's walls and piers were made of stone.
  18. Soldiers built the bridge, and the soldier's efforts were well rewarded.

C. Choose the correct word in parentheses to complete each sentence. Write the paragraph.

    In my town stands a bridge modeled after a Roman arch bridge. (**19.** It's, Its) a well-traveled bridge. (**20.** Its, It's) span measures about 350 meters. (**21.** There's, Theirs) a park on the other side of the bridge. Many people drive (**22.** their, they're) cars to the park. (**23.** They're, Their) pleased that the park was built here.

Apply • Think and Write

Classifying Items • Write about a bridge you have crossed or one you have seen in a magazine or book. You might describe the bridge and the people and vehicles that use it. Use possessive pronouns in your writing.

> ✏️ **Remember**
> to avoid confusing possessive pronouns and contractions.

GETTING
STARTED

Ask trivia questions beginning with *who* or *what*. Answer using *that* or *those*. For example: *Who founded the Ford Motor Company? That was Henry Ford. What was a popular Ford car long ago? That was a Model T.*

4 Interrogative and Demonstrative Pronouns

Interrogative Pronouns There are five interrogative pronouns and they all begin with *w*: *who, whose, whom, which,* and *what.* Interrogative pronouns are often used to begin questions.

Who invented the phonograph?	Whom did people admire?
What was the kinetoscope?	Whose was it?
Which is the most famous invention?	

Demonstrative Pronouns The four demonstrative pronouns *this, that, these,* and *those* point out specific people, places, or things. Use *this* and *these* to point to people, places, and things that are nearby. Use *that* and *those* to point to people, places, and things far away.

This and *that* are singular pronouns. *These* and *those* are plural pronouns. Singular demonstrative pronouns point to singular antecedents. Plural demonstrative pronouns point to plural antecedents. Notice the tinted antecedents in the sentences below.

| That was Thomas Edison. | Those were his notes. |
| Is this the very first light bulb? | These are modern light bulbs. |

When you write, use demonstrative pronouns to point out persons, places, and things clearly.

> **Summary** ♦ An **interrogative pronoun** asks a question. A **demonstrative pronoun** emphatically points out its antecedent.

Guided Practice

Name each interrogative pronoun and demonstrative pronoun.

1. Who invented it? That is a wonderful machine.
2. This is an interesting old typewriter. Whose is it?
3. That is the first phonograph. These are early records.

Practice

A. Write and label each interrogative and demonstrative pronoun.

4. Who was the most famous inventor of the 1800s?
5. That was Thomas Alva Edison, the inventor of hundreds of different things.
6. Which was his most famous invention?
7. That was the light bulb, invented in 1879.
8. Who helped improve motion-picture equipment?
9. These are movies for Edison's early movie machine.
10. Soon this was the country's favorite form of entertainment.
11. That is a typewriter Edison improved using metal parts.
12. Those are special typewriter keys.
13. What do you think was Edison's most important invention?

B. Write the correct demonstrative pronoun to complete each sentence. Then write the antecedent of each pronoun.

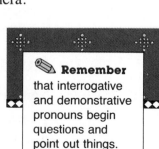

14. (This, These) is a picture of Edison's laboratory in Menlo Park, New Jersey.
15. (That, Those) are Edison's notes about the light bulb.
16. Are (these, this) the photographs of Edison?
17. Is (that, those) the cylinder used to record ''Mary Had a Little Lamb'' for the first phonograph?
18. (This, These) are examples of early phonographs.

C. Complete each sentence with the kind of pronoun indicated in parentheses. Write the sentence.

19. (Interrogative) was the most troublesome machine for Edison?
20. (Demonstrative) was the talking picture machine.
21. (Demonstrative) is an example of an early movie camera.
22. (Interrogative) are the original plans for the camera?
23. (Demonstrative) are some parts to the machine.

Apply ◆ Think and Write

Creating an Invention ◆ If you could create your own invention, what would it be? Write a paragraph about your invention, telling what it would do. Use demonstrative and interrogative pronouns in your paragraph.

> ✎ **Remember**
> that interrogative and demonstrative pronouns begin questions and point out things.

Think of some things that members of your family would do for themselves if they could. For example: *My father would give himself a raise. My sisters would teach themselves to type.*

5 Reflexive and Intensive Pronouns

Reflexive Pronouns   Reflexive pronouns end with *-self* or *-selves*. The singular reflexive pronouns are *myself, yourself, himself, herself,* and *itself.* The plural reflexive pronouns are *ourselves, yourselves,* and *themselves.* Reflexive pronouns refer back to a noun or pronoun in the same sentence, usually the subject. These pronouns are necessary to the meaning of the sentence.

■ **Jake imagined <u>himself</u> at the wheel of the antique automobile.**

Intensive Pronouns   Intensive pronouns also end in *-self* or *-selves.* They are used with a noun or another pronoun to intensify, or emphasize, the noun or pronoun. Intensive pronouns are not necessary to the meaning of a sentence.

■ **Henry Ford <u>himself</u> once drove the car through the streets.**

Do not use reflexive or intensive pronouns in place of personal pronouns. A reflexive or an intensive pronoun must always have an antecedent in the same sentence.

■ **Todd and <u>I</u> toured the museum.** (*not* Todd and <u>myself</u>)

When you write, be sure to use correct pronoun forms. Do not use *hisself, ourself,* and *theirselves.* Use *himself, ourselves,* and *themselves.*

> **Summary** ◆ A **reflexive pronoun** refers to a noun or pronoun in the same sentence, usually the subject. An **intensive pronoun** emphasizes another word in the sentence.

Guided Practice

Name each reflexive or intensive pronoun and its antecedent.

1. People eventually found themselves dependent on the automobile.
2. The automobile itself, however, was not always popular.
3. Can you picture yourself driving one of those old cars?

Practice

A. Write and label the reflexive or intensive pronoun in each sentence. Write the antecedent for each pronoun.

   4. Before automobiles, people often transported themselves by horses and wagons.
   5. One inventor built himself a steam-powered wagon.
   6. This wagon could propel itself rather well.
   7. Other people soon built themselves steam-powered automobiles.
   8. The most famous was the ''Stanley Steamer,'' built by the Stanley twins themselves.
   9. The steam-powered car was itself soon without supporters.
   10. Steam power did not lend itself to long-distance travel.
   11. We went ourselves to see early gasoline-powered cars.
   12. The gasoline-powered car itself was an engineering triumph.
   13. I myself construct models of early automobiles.

B. Write each sentence, using a reflexive or intensive pronoun.

   14. In the 1890s, inventors built ____ gasoline-powered cars.
   15. The first successful American gasoline car soon propelled ____ .
   16. The Duryea brothers were ____ responsible for this car.
   17. Henry Ford ____ drove a car he had built in Michigan.
   18. My mother bought ____ an antique Ford car.

C. If an incorrect reflexive or intensive pronoun is used, rewrite the sentence correctly. If the pronoun is correct, write *correct*.

   19. Americans soon found theirselves in love with the automobile.
   20. The cars themselves were expensive and difficult to make.
   21. Usually, one mechanic built an entire car hisself.
   22. My friends and myself rode in an antique automobile recently.
   23. We promised ourself to learn more about early automobiles.

Apply • Think and Write

Dictionary of Knowledge • Henry Ford not only created an early automobile but also pioneered mass production. Read about Henry Ford in the Dictionary of Knowledge. Write a paragraph telling about Ford and his work. Use intensive and reflexive pronouns in your paragraph.

> ✎ **Remember**
> to use reflexive and intensive pronouns correctly.

Make up newspaper headlines that use the words *everyone*, *no one*, *everything*, *anybody*, or *something*. For example: *No One Found at Scene*. Then invent stories to go with the headlines.

6 Indefinite Pronouns

A pronoun that does not always refer to a specific person, place, or thing is called an indefinite pronoun. Many indefinite pronouns, such as *many*, *few*, and *several*, express the idea of quantity. The chart below lists the common indefinite pronouns.

Singular			Plural
anybody	everybody	no one	both
anyone	everyone	nothing	few
anything	everything	one	many
each	neither	someone	others
either	nobody	something	several

Because they do not refer to particular persons, places, or things, indefinite pronouns often do not have antecedents.

■ **Many** rode bicycles for basic transportation years ago.

An indefinite pronoun may be the antecedent of a personal pronoun. Make sure that the personal pronoun agrees with the indefinite pronoun in number.

■ *Several* rode <u>their</u> bicycles. *Everyone* rode <u>her</u> bicycle today.

> **Summary** ♦ An indefinite pronoun does not always refer to a specific person, place, or thing.

Guided Practice

Name the indefinite pronouns in these sentences.

1. Many of the early bicycles had giant front wheels.
2. In 1885 someone invented a bicycle with equal-sized wheels.
3. This new invention could carry almost anyone safely.

Practice

A. Write each indefinite pronoun. Label it *singular* or *plural*.

4. The first bicycles looked very unusual, and many were even outlandish in appearance.
5. Few looked like today's sleek, lightweight machines.
6. Each of these early bicycles was very tall.
7. No one simply climbed onto these bicycles and rode off.
8. Several of these machines were very difficult to master.
9. Someone might need weeks of practice on an early bicycle.
10. The new, safer bicycles of the 1880s were welcomed by almost everyone.
11. Many used their bicycles only for pleasure.
12. Others rode their bicycles to work every day.
13. Bicycles were economical transportation for everybody.

B. Write an indefinite pronoun to complete each sentence.

14. _____ was more startling than the giant high wheeler bicycle.
15. _____ in these pictures looks at ease on these bicycles.
16. Unstable and dangerous, _____ of these high wheelers were very difficult to ride.
17. On a giant high wheeler, _____ traveled a great distance with each turn of the huge front wheel.
18. _____ on the streets was careful to avoid the enormous bicycles.

C. Write a sentence using each pair of words.

19. everyone, his
20. several, their
21. each, her
22. many, their
23. something, its
24. anybody, his

Apply • Think and Write

Classifying Reactions • Imagine yourself riding a giant high wheeler bike through your neighborhood. Write about your experience and the reactions of people on the streets, using several indefinite pronouns.

> ✎ **Remember**
> to be sure that personal pronouns agree with indefinite pronoun antecedents.

Ask "who" questions about historical figures. Each answer must include a fact about the person. For example: *Who was President of the U.S. in 1962? John Kennedy; he was our thirty-fifth President.*

7 Subject and Object Pronouns

Some pronouns have different forms, or *cases*. Pronouns in the nominative case are called *subject pronouns*. Pronouns in the objective case are called *object pronouns*. The form or case of a pronoun is determined by how it is used in a sentence.

The chart below lists the subject and object pronouns and rules for when to use these pronouns.

Subject Pronouns		Object Pronouns	
Singular	**Plural**	**Singular**	**Plural**
I	we	me	us
you	you	you	you
he, she, it	they	him, her, it	them
who	who	whom	whom
Use as the subject of verbs.		Use as direct objects.	
We visited an old factory. **Who led the tour?**		**Mr. Tomkins invited me.** **Whom did you invite?**	
Use as predicate nominatives.		Use as indirect objects.	
The tour guide was she.		**Mr. Chu asked her a question.**	

It is often difficult to choose between *who* or *whom* in a question. To decide, write an answer to the question using *he* for the pronoun *who*, or *him* for the pronoun *whom*.

(Who, Whom) wrote the report.   He wrote the report. (Use *Who*)
(Who, Whom) did you visit?   You visited him. (Use *Whom*)

> **Summary** ◆ Pronouns change form to show case. Be sure to use subject and object pronouns correctly in your speaking and writing.

Guided Practice

Name each subject and object pronoun.

1. People needed goods, and factories produced them.
2. They made various products.
3. Who worked in these factories?
4. A guide showed us a paper factory.
5. The foreman of the factory is he.

Practice

A. Write each pronoun and label it *subject* or *object*. There may be more than one pronoun in a sentence.

6. You can visit many old factories today.
7. We can also see them in photographs.
8. People in cities needed work; factories gave them jobs.
9. They found her a job in a nearby factory.
10. Whom does she know at the factory?

B. Write the correct pronoun in parentheses. Label each one *subject*, *predicate nominative*, *direct object*, or *indirect object*.

11. Jason showed (I, me) pictures of an early car factory.
12. (He, Him) found (they, them) in a history book.
13. (We, Us) studied (they, them) carefully.
14. (Who, Whom) designed those wonderful old cars?
15. The people in this photograph are (they, them).

C. Write the sentences replacing each underlined word or group of words with a pronoun. Label each pronoun as *subject* or *object*.

16. In the 1830s the factory system spread through the country.
17. The workers produced goods with various materials.
18. Marie showed her classmates pictures of an old factory.
19. In one picture, a woman is standing by a giant machine.
20. The woman is helping a young boy with his work.

Apply • Think and Write

A Picture Prompt • In a magazine or book, find a colorful photograph of people making something. Write a description of what is happening in the picture. Circle and label the subject and object pronouns that you use.

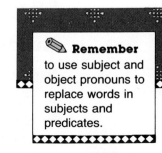

✎ **Remember**
to use subject and object pronouns to replace words in subjects and predicates.

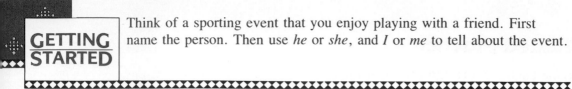

GETTING STARTED

Think of a sporting event that you enjoy playing with a friend. First name the person. Then use *he* or *she*, and *I* or *me* to tell about the event.

8 Choosing Correct Pronouns

Choosing between subject and object pronouns is often difficult. The simple tests in the chart below can help make it easier.

If a noun follows a pronoun in a sentence, test for the correct pronoun by leaving out the noun. **Mrs. Lane showed (we, us) students pictures of early immigrants.** **Mrs. Lane showed <u>us</u> pictures of early immigrants.**
If a pronoun is joined to a noun or another pronoun by *and* or *or*, test for the correct pronoun by leaving out the other element. **Joan and (I, me) will report on the lives of the immigrants.** **<u>I</u> will report on the lives of the immigrants.**
If two pronouns are joined by *and* or *or*, both must be either subject or object pronouns. **<u>She</u> and <u>I</u> will do more research on the topic. (not <u>Her</u> and <u>I</u>)**
Supply the missing words that are understood after *than* or *as* to choose the correct pronoun. **Janice has studied immigration more than (I, me).** **Janice has studied immigration more than <u>I</u> (have).**
Do not use an unnecessary pronoun after a noun. **The immigrants ~~they~~ came from many countries.**

> **Summary** ♦ Simple tests and guidelines can help you avoid pronoun errors.

Guided Practice

Name the correct pronoun in parentheses.

1. The guide gave (we, us) students a tour of the Statue of Liberty.
2. Kim has visited the Statue of Liberty more often than (I, me).
3. Eric and (I, me) have ancestors from the same country.

Practice

A. Write the correct pronouns for these sentences about immigration.

    4. Mrs. Lane showed (us, we) students a film about Ellis Island.

    5. My classmates and (I, me) visited a museum exhibit about immigrants of the 1890s.

    6. (We, Us) visitors enjoyed the whole museum.

    7. A guide showed (us, we) visitors photographs of immigrants.

    8. Karen knows more of the immigrants' experiences than (I, me).

    9. (She, Her) and (I, me) found a model of the immigration facilities at Ellis Island.

    10. She told Kevin and (I, me) stories of her great-grandparents' arrival in the United States.

    11. Kevin has visited Ellis Island more than (I, me).

    12. My grandparents and (I, me) often discuss their immigration.

    13. (They, Them) and other immigrants supported each other.

B. Find the pronoun errors and write the sentences correctly.

    14. Jana and me read about one family of immigrants.

    15. Her and I learned a great deal about these people.

    16. The immigrants they traveled by ship from Europe.

    17. Them and other people from their village arrived together.

    18. Some friends arrived two days earlier than them.

C. Complete each sentence with a correct subject or object pronoun. Write the pronoun.

    19. My cousins from Ireland showed _____ students photographs.

    20. _____ and their friends live in New York City.

    21. The book about the immigrants inspired Jana and _____ .

    22. Jana had already read more about the immigrants than _____ .

    23. She and _____ saw a film about the immigrants' experience.

Apply • Think and Write

Making Observations! • Imagine that you are an immigrant on a ship and you are seeing the American shore for the first time. Write about your observations and feelings. Check all pronouns in your writing for correct usage. Make any necessary changes.

Remember that you can use simple tests to avoid pronoun errors.

A moviegoer standing in the ticket line says, "Excuse me, but could you maintain my position in the queue whilst I acquire some sustenance?" "Translate" the moviegoer's message.

VOCABULARY •
Formal and Informal Language

The language you use for reports and other serious purposes is commonly called **formal language**. It is writing and speech that is dressed up for special occasions and audiences. It is language on its best behavior.

Everyday language, on the other hand, is called **informal language**. It is writing and speech used with friends and family. It is language that is relaxed.

How is formal language different from informal language? One difference is in the use of **slang**—words and phrases used in everyday speech but not accepted in more serious English. For instance, an employer might say that a worker was "chewed out" for coming in late, but in an official report the employer might write that the worker was "reprimanded." *Chewed out* is slang.

Another difference between formal and informal language is in the use of contractions and abbreviations. Contractions, such as *I'm* and *you'll*, are rarely used in formal language, and only the most common abbreviations (such as *Mr.*, *Mrs.*, *Ms.*, and *Dr.*) are used in formal writing.

Building Your Vocabulary

Express the meanings of the underlined phrases in formal language.

1. "You are expected to <u>hit the books</u> every weekend," declared the professor.
2. However, her tests were known to be <u>as easy as pie</u>.
3. The company stated that its new product was <u>going down the tube</u>.
4. The theatergoers decided to <u>hit the road</u> early.
5. The security guards asked the protesters to <u>cool off</u>.
6. The paper reported that the president and his wife <u>hung loose</u> at a seaside resort for the weekend.
7. The general instructed the men to <u>hit the deck</u>.

Practice

A. Rewrite the following sentences, substituting more formal language for the underlined words and expressions.

1. The accountant felt there were too many <u>top dogs</u> in the company.
2. His boss advised him to <u>clam up</u>.
3. "General Smith <u>Alive and Kicking</u>," the headline read.
4. The president stated he was <u>fed up</u> with his senior advisor.
5. "<u>Hold your horses</u>," the judge warned the impatient lawyer.
6. The citizens urged their mayor to <u>get cracking</u> on repaving the cracked roads.
7. The roads had been paved in a <u>slapdash</u> manner to begin with, they insisted.
8. The mayor asked the protestors on the lawn to <u>take a hike</u>.
9. "<u>What's cooking</u> here?" asked the police officer.
10. The lawyer stated that the accused had <u>clobbered</u> a student leaving the <u>dorm</u>.

B. Rewrite the following sentences, spelling out all contractions and abbreviations.

11. "It's the first st. on the left," the directions read.
12. "It'll be on TV tonight," the announcer said.
13. The phone was busy all night.
14. Who'll graduate on Feb. 3, '91?
15. They're arriving in fifteen min.

Language Corner • British English

Do you wear a **woolly** in the wintertime? In England you would. *Woolly* is an informal British word for "woolen sweater."

What do you think the underlined words mean in these sentences?

Carry a <u>brolly</u> in the rain.
Misers are <u>mingy</u> with money.
It's <u>beastly</u> hot today.

How to Revise Sentences with Pronouns

You know that pronouns are mainly used to take the place of nouns in sentences. Pronouns allow you to avoid repeating the same noun over and over in your writing. Notice how pronouns eliminate the repetition of *Samuel Morse* in sentence **2**.

> **1.** When Samuel Morse was still a boy, Samuel Morse decided that Samuel Morse would devote Samuel Morse's life to painting.
> **2.** When Samuel Morse was still a boy, he decided that he would devote his life to painting.

Every pronoun should have a clear antecedent. A pronoun without a clear antecedent can make a sentence vague and confusing. The following sentences contain pronouns without clear antecedents.

> **3.** Samuel and his father knew that he would go to England.
> **4.** At Yale College, they admired Samuel's drawings.
> **5.** You can study many drawing techniques at an art school.

In sentence **3**, the pronoun *he* could apply to either Samuel or his father. The pronouns *they* in sentence **4** and *you* in sentence **5** do not have clear antecedents either. The meanings of these sentences can be made clear by simply identifying who *he, they,* and *you* are.

> **6.** Samuel and his father knew that Samuel would go to England.
> **7.** At Yale College, Samuel's classmates admired his drawings.
> **8.** Students can study many drawing techniques at an art school.

The Grammar Game ♦ Fit them in! Write a sentence for each group of words. Be sure to construct your sentences so that all pronouns are used correctly!

we students	Does everyone have...?	us football fans
Whom...?	than us	between him and
as much as him	you and me	by herself

Working Together

As your group completes activities **A** and **B**, you will find that using pronouns correctly gives clarity to your writing.

In Your Group

- ◆ Encourage everyone to participate.
- ◆ Summarize after each discussion.
- ◆ Build on other people's ideas.
- ◆ Keep the group on the subject.

A. Write the sentences below, replacing all unclear pronouns.

1. Samuel Morse and his father agreed he would study in England.
2. In England they admired and praised Morse's paintings.
3. On its voyage back to America in 1832, Morse heard them talking about electricity.
4. Morse met the captain of his ship. He told him that he was determined to invent an electric telegraph system.
5. Morse showed a few systems to them in America, but they didn't appreciate them and wouldn't invest in them.

B. As you know, Samuel Morse's electric telegraph system was eventually a great success. For many years, messages and news were transmitted by Morse code. Work with the members of your group to write a paragraph that could be transmitted to a distant place. The subject could be a newsworthy person or event in your school. Use pronouns as often as possible, but be sure to use them correctly.

WRITERS' CORNER ◆ Exact Information

Be careful not to use too many indefinite pronouns in a piece of writing. Overusing indefinite pronouns can make your writing ineffective. Give exact information whenever possible.

VAGUE: **Everyone in our family, except a few, arrived on time.**

EXACT: **Everyone in our family, except Lee and Grandmother, arrived on time.**

Read what you wrote for the Writer's Warm-up. If you used too many indefinite pronouns, supply more exact information where possible.

NEW YORK #2   painting by Charles Sheeler
Munson-Williams-Proctor Institute

USING LANGUAGE
TO
CLASSIFY

=== **PART TWO** ===

Literature   *The Brooklyn Bridge: They Said It Couldn't Be Built* by Judith St. George

A Reason for Writing   Classifying

CREATIVE
Writing

FINE ARTS ◆ Study the most prominent building in the painting "New York #2." Look at it compared to the other buildings. Now give life to the building. Imagine what it might say to the rain, the stars, the birds, or the other buildings. Write a poem that speaks for the building.

CRITICAL THINKING ♦
A Strategy for Classifying

A VENN DIAGRAM

Classifying means sorting things into groups, putting together things that belong together. One way to classify things is to compare and contrast them, or notice their likenesses and differences. After this lesson you will read part of *The Brooklyn Bridge*. It is in part the story of two men, the bridge's designer John Roebling and his son Washington Roebling. The two men were alike in some ways, but as this passage suggests they were quite different in others.

John Roebling had been a perfectionist, short-tempered, formal and not terribly interested in people. Washington was . . . more even-tempered, lighthearted and kindly. Although he was quick and bright, neither he nor anyone else considered him to be the creative genius his father had been.

As different as they were, both men were successful civil engineers. They share credit for the completion of the famous bridge. Is it unusual, do you think, for parents and children to be both alike and different?

Learning the Strategy

Daily life is full of opportunities for comparing and contrasting. You do it often, probably without realizing it. For example, suppose you are reading newspaper ads for cassette players. How might you decide which one to buy? Suppose you want to make a scrapbook of today's most popular singers. How could you organize the scrapbook? Imagine your family is taking a trip to Canada. You plan to keep a journal of the trip. In what ways might you compare and contrast Canada and the United States?

A Venn diagram is one strategy for classifying likenesses and differences. It is two circles that overlap. The one below is about Canada and the United States. The words in the middle note likenesses, those on the outside note differences.

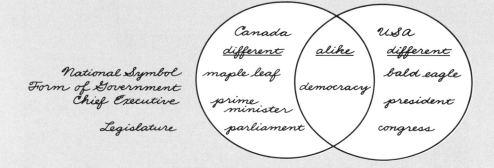

National Symbol
Form of Government
Chief Executive

Legislature

Canada
different
maple leaf

prime
minister
parliament

alike

democracy

USA
different
bald eagle

president

congress

What other facts might you add? What other pairs of topics might you be able to compare and contrast on a Venn diagram?

Using the Strategy

A. Compare and contrast yourself with a brother, sister, or friend. Make a Venn diagram to show how you and the other person are alike and different. You might want to use the information from your diagram to write a funny greeting card for that special person.

B. As you know, John and Washington Roebling were alike in some ways and different in others. Make a Venn diagram about this famous father and son, using the information on page 254. Then, as you read *The Brooklyn Bridge*, look for other ways to compare and contrast this father and son.

Applying the Strategy

• How did you think of both likenesses and differences between you and a friend or relative for **A** above?
• When might it be useful to notice likenesses and differences?

LITERATURE

from

THE

BROOKLYN

BRIDGE:

They · Said · It · Couldn't · Be · Built

by Judith St. George

The people of Brooklyn, New York, had long wanted a bridge across the East River to New York City. But everyone said that a bridge was "impossible." Then in 1852, a gifted engineer envisioned a bridge as he crossed the river by ferry. John Roebling was a bridge builder, and he knew that the "impossible" could be done.

John Roebling loved designing and building suspension bridges—bridges suspended from cables that pass over towers and fasten at either end. In 1857

he submitted his ingenious plan for a suspension
bridge across the East River. He persisted for twelve
years until his plans were approved in June 1869.

Within a few days John Roebling began work on
the bridge he had dreamed of for more than fifteen
years. But he had a tragic accident as he was checking
a building site at the Brooklyn ferry landing. He died
of complications arising from the injury on July 22,
1869, at the age of sixty-three, when his work was just
beginning.

Now what? John Roebling was the Brooklyn Bridge, and the Brooklyn Bridge was John Roebling. Was his death the death of the bridge as well? Not at all. John Roebling's vision lived on in the plans he had left behind. The only decision to make was who would be chief engineer to carry them out. That wasn't a difficult decision, either. A month after John Roebling's death, his thirty-two-year-old son, Washington Augustus, was appointed to the job.

Washington was a civil engineer who had not only seen action during the Civil War but had also built temporary suspension bridges for the army. He had risen from private to colonel in four years, been cited for gallantry three times and was known for his coolness under pressure. Forever after known as Colonel Roebling, Washington had not only worked closely with his father on two suspension bridges, but he had assisted him on the Brooklyn Bridge from the very beginning as well.

John Roebling drew this Brooklyn Bridge tower in 1857.
Rensselaer Polytechnic Institute Archives, Troy, New York

Father and son were very different. John Roebling had been a perfectionist, short-tempered, formal and not terribly interested in people. Washington was far more relaxed. He was better at working with people, more even-tempered, lighthearted and kindly. Although he was quick and bright, neither he nor anyone else considered him to be the creative genius his father had been.

Even their appearances were different. John Roebling was all bony thinness and harsh angles, with deep-set, penetrating blue eyes. Washington had a pleasanter, more open expression. His 1867 passport summed him up: "Stature 5 feet 9 inches; Forehead, broad; Eyes, light gray; Nose, short; Mouth, small; Chin, square; Hair, light; Complexion, fair."

John Augustus Roebling   Washington Roebling

Despite their differences father and son were both civil engineers, and as professionals, they shared important qualities of courage, determination, drive for perfection and complete confidence in their own ability. Faced now with the overwhelming task of building the Brooklyn Bridge, Colonel Roebling needed all the confidence he could muster. Luckily, as an officer, Colonel Roebling had worked and fought under pressure conditions during the war. Now he tackled the bridge the way a commanding officer would tackle a field assignment. It was as if he saw the bridge as a military adversary to be fought and conquered, an ongoing battle that he would wage on many fronts for a long time to come.

For now he had to order supplies and equipment, interview and hire assistants, get together a work force, evaluate manufacturers, attend to a hundred and one details. And just as he had had to give an accounting of his activities to his commanding officer in the army, so now he had to give an accounting of his every decision to the New York Bridge Company. From there his reports would be made public. He knew he would be held responsible for every step of the construction. He wrote later about that time in his life: "Here I was at the age of 32, suddenly put in charge of the most stupendous engineering structure of the age! The prop on which I had hitherto leaned had fallen; henceforth I must rely on myself."

The Brooklyn Bridge, the longest suspension bridge in the world, was built entirely under Washington Roebling's direction. Yet the often dangerous work exacted a heavy price. In 1872 Colonel Roebling contracted a crippling disease from working in an underwater enclosure. From that day he remained homebound—but still in command. He supervised the work through his wife, Emily. She became his chief assistant and communicator.

The heroic efforts of Washington and Emily Roebling guided the Brooklyn Bridge to its opening on May 24, 1883. In a huge celebration called People's Day, thousands of people walked across the bridge they said "could never be built." Today the Brooklyn Bridge is still as strong and structurally sound as on the day it opened. Its strength stands as a tribute to one family's courage.

Library Link ♦ Find out more about the fascinating history of the Brooklyn Bridge by reading *The Brooklyn Bridge: They Said It Couldn't Be Built* by Judith St. George.

 ## Reader's Response

Do you wish you could have helped build the Brooklyn Bridge? Why or why not?

THE BROOKLYN BRIDGE:

They • Said • It • Couldn't • Be • Built

Responding to Literature

1. As professionals, John Roebling and his son each possessed the important qualities of courage, determination, and drive for perfection. In your opinion, why were their professional attitudes so much alike?

2. When Washington Roebling became the chief engineer, he learned to rely on himself. In what ways do you think his background contributed to his confidence?

3. Imagine that you suddenly find yourself in charge of the "most stupendous engineering structure of the age," how would you feel? Write a journal entry telling what you are doing and how you feel about it.

Writing to Learn

Think and Compare • Now that you have read about John Roebling and his son, make a Venn diagram. Show their likenesses and differences completely.

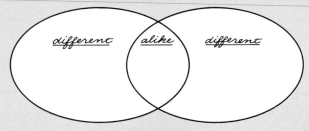

Venn Diagram

Write • Write a paragraph and express your opinion. Tell whether these two men were more alike than different, or more different than alike. Support your opinion with evidence from your completed diagram.

Think of a famous present-day figure whom you admire or perhaps do not admire. How many details about that person do you have to tell before your classmates are able to name the mystery person?

SPEAKING and LISTENING ◆
Discussing Characters

One way to gain a better understanding of characters in stories is through a class discussion. In a discussion you have the opportunity to share your views on characters with others and to have others share their views with you. The discussion may focus on characters within a single story or on characters from several stories.

Preparation is an important first step. Make sure you understand what characters will be considered in your class discussion. As you read, pay attention to all the clues the author or authors are giving about the characters. Jot notes on various items, such as a character's actions, appearance, and dialogue. Have your notes and page references ready so that you can speedily refer to them to support your views. Here are some guidelines to help enrich a discussion of story characters.

Discussing Story Characters	1. Participate actively in the discussion by sharing your facts and ideas about the characters. 2. Make sure your statements about the characters are brief and to the point. Refer to the words and actions of characters that support your ideas. Be polite even when you disagree. 3. Encourage others to respond to your views.
Being a Critical Listener	1. Listen attentively as others present their views on characters. 2. Give others time to cite specific examples that support their views on the characters. 3. Evaluate the information you hear and ask yourself how it compares with your perception and understanding of the characters.

Summary ◆ Before participating in a discussion of story characters, take time to understand the characters. During the discussion, give and listen for specific details about each character.

Guided Practice

Tell what is wrong with each behavior in the sentences below.

1. Gloria laughs loudly at Tina's suggestion about a character.
2. Dan bases his view of a character solely on actions.
3. Norm disagrees about a character but remains silent.

Practice

A. Read each item about discussing story characters. Take turns with a partner telling why you agree or disagree with each item.

> **4.** Preparation is a lot of trouble. Just try to remember something about the characters and take it from there.
> **5.** Notes that compare and contrast characters probably aren't very useful for such a discussion.
> **6.** When students share ideas about characters, they can learn and help others learn more about the characters.
> **7.** To invite disagreement shows that you're open to new ideas others may have about the characters.

B. Prepare for a class discussion that will compare two characters you have read about in recent units. Review the statements below and then follow the guidelines in this lesson. Participate in the discussion by responding to each of the statements.

> **8.** Although Anne Frank and Ramón Salazar lived in very different worlds, they were alike in many ways. Explain.
> **9.** Anne and Ramón each had a similar relationship with an older person. How would you describe that relationship?
> **10.** Both teenagers had a sense of frustration and both had a dream. Do you agree or disagree with this statement?

Apply • Think and Write

Contrasting • Recall a character that you really liked and one that you didn't like at all from stories you have recently read. Write about the differences between the characters.

Remember to give specific examples of a character's words and actions to support your views.

Name three things about yourself that tell what you are like. Try to describe "the real you."

WRITING ♦
A Character Sketch

Sometimes in your writing you may want to include a character sketch. The sketch may be of someone you have read about or of someone you know. In a character sketch a writer uses facts and observations to describe a person. The details included should give a clear picture of "who the person is."

Imagine that you are preparing to write a character sketch based on your personal observations. You might note the following characteristics of Mr. Bell, your neighbor, in your journal.

Appearance: Usually in old dungarees, sweatshirt, work clothes.
Habits and Mannerisms: Talks to himself. Often repeats this motto: "The future belongs to those who can fix it."
Words and Actions: Spent day fixing neighbor's car. Said, "You can practically do it yourself next time."
Voice Tones and Gestures: Speaks in warm, friendly way.

Your observations tell you that Mr. Bell is self-reliant and informal. He acts and speaks in a neighborly way. These details create a general impression. You can turn your general impression of Mr. Bell into an interesting topic sentence and then support it by using details. For example:

Mr. Bell is our neighborhood's example of friendly self-reliance. His motto is "The future belongs to those who can fix it." He wears old work clothes and always seems eager for the next do-it-yourself project. In fact, such work seems to be a pleasure for him. Recently he spent a day repairing a neighbor's car. He seemed glad to have shared his skill.

Summary ◆ In a **character sketch** use facts and examples to convey your general impression of a person.

Guided Practice

Tell what kind of characteristic each group of details below shows. Choose from the categories on the opposite page.

1. tousled hair, T-shirt, jeans, and unlaced sneakers
2. seemed to speak harshly but would often wink
3. tugs at ear when faced with a decision

Practice

A. For each group of observations below, write a topic sentence for a character sketch.

4. Irene is slim and physically strong. She jogs along the beach. "I sleep better with the sound of waves," she exclaims.

5. Seth has many interests, but his favorite is the computer. He often attends exhibits that show new computer technology. He encourages his friends to discover the fun of computers.

B. Write five notes about a person you know and admire. Use the questions below to help you recall specific details.

6. What do you notice immediately about his or her appearance?
7. What habit or mannerism always reminds you of him or her?
8. If you dropped in unexpectedly, what do you think you would find this person doing?
9. Does he or she have a favorite phrase or motto?
10. How is the person unlike what his or her appearance suggests?

C. Use your notes from **Practice B** to write a topic sentence for a character sketch. Then develop a paragraph by using the details you noted to support your topic sentence.

Apply ◆ Think and Write

Observing a Character ◆ Choose a character from a TV program you watch regularly. Jot down some of your observations about this person. Use your notes to write a character sketch.

> ✎ **Remember**
> to include specific details in your character sketch.

Would you prefer to live in the city or in the country? Why? Give several examples of how life in each place is different.

WRITING ◆
Comparison/Contrast Paragraphs

The words *comparison* and *contrast* are often used together. A comparison shows the <u>similarities</u> between two things. A contrast points out the <u>differences</u>. The word *comparison*, however, is often used to mean both similarities and differences.

Before writing a comparison paragraph or a contrast paragraph, look for categories. Find ways in which things can be grouped according to their similarities and differences. For example, if you are comparing characters, you might want to choose categories such as appearance and personality.

The chart below shows two useful methods of organizing comparison/contrast paragraphs.

Ways to Compare and Contrast	
Point-by-Point	**Block**
AB _____	A _____
_____	_____
_____ AB _____	_____
_____	_____
_____	_____
_____ AB _____	_____ B _____
_____	_____
_____	_____
_____ AB _____	_____

Point-by-Point Method   When you use the point-by-point method, you discuss one point about A and then the same point about B. You build your paragraph with pairs of facts that demonstrate differences or similarities. Use the point-by-point method to organize relatively simple information.

In the example below, Judith St. George begins with a topic sentence that states the main idea. She then contrasts John Roebling and his son Washington by the point-by-point method. One or two more pairs of facts would complete the paragraph.

Father and son were very different. John Roebling had been a perfectionist, short-tempered, formal and not terribly interested in people. Washington was far more relaxed. He was better at working with people, more even-tempered, lighthearted and kindly.

The block method described next is useful in organizing and presenting more complex information.

Block Method   When you compare or contrast two things using the block method, your first sentences tell all about A. This helps your reader to focus on one group of details. Then you use transition words to tell the reader "Now I'll show you how B is alike or different from A." You complete the paragraph with sentences that tell all about B. For example:

Girder bridges and suspension bridges have interesting differences. The roadways of suspension bridges hang from cables attached to supports at the ends of the bridges. Some suspension bridges are more than 4,000 feet long. Suspension bridges are built in places where the construction of additional supports would be very difficult—for instance, across a deep river or steep canyon. In contrast, girder bridges are made of beams called girders that rest directly on supports placed in the ground at intervals. Most girder bridges are less than 1,000 feet long. Girder bridges can be built in most places; many serve as highway bridges.

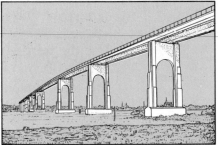

In this example, facts about suspension bridges appear first. The transition words *in contrast* signal the reader that now a new idea will be presented—all the facts about girder bridges. To try to give so much information point-by-point would probably be confusing to the reader. The block method gives clarity to this information.

Summary ✦ To **compare** or **contrast** two things, first look for similarities or differences. Then use the point-by-point method or the block method to organize ideas.

Guided Practice

Which two topic sentences below tell the reader that a paragraph of comparison or contrast is being introduced?

1. English is one of the world's main international languages.
2. Two of our newest poets see the future very differently.
3. Through my studies, I've come to realize that living underwater and living in outer space have much in common.

Practice

A. Read the point-by-point comparison below. Notice the transition words after the first pair of statements. Rewrite the paragraph, using the following transition words where needed.

just as   **in a like manner**   **similarly**

Learning to write is similar to learning a sport. To play most sports, you need certain pieces of equipment. In the same way, writing requires equipment—pencil or pen and paper. New players of a sport learn by watching professionals. Writers seek out the classic works to study. A new athlete must decide what position to play in the game. Hopeful writers decide on their point of view and favorite topics. Finally, athletes must practice again and again. Writers create and revise to sharpen their skills.

B. Use the pairs of facts below to write a clear point-by-point paragraph of contrast. Add transition words as needed. Begin with this topic sentence: *The greenhouse effect and a possible ice age will each challenge humanity in different ways.*

4. The greenhouse effect has increased because of pollution. An ice age is a natural part of Earth's history.
5. The greenhouse effect traps heat in the atmosphere and causes a rise in temperature. During an ice age, growing glaciers cool the air surrounding Earth.
6. An intensified greenhouse effect might cause oceans to rise. In an ice age, the seas would ''shrink'' by freezing.

C. The facts below contain complex information. Will a point-by-point or a block method make the facts more clear? Demonstrate your answer by creating a paragraph from these facts. Begin with this topic sentence: *Mars seems better suited than other planets for a human colony.*

7. A journey to Mars and back may take only about two years.
8. The climate on Mars is most like Earth's— neither too hot nor too cold for humans and their machines.
9. All the other planets in our solar system are farther away from Earth than Mars is.
10. We have already landed on Mars with un-manned probes.
11. On other planets the temperature is hot enough to melt lead or cold enough to freeze gases into solids.
12. Other probes have only photographed and flown by the more distant planets, such as Saturn.
13. People could move and work most easily on Mars, where the pull of gravity is most similar to that on Earth.
14. On huge planets with gravity like Jupiter's, a person would not even be able to stand up.

D. Write notes for a paragraph that will compare similarities in or contrast differences between one of the following pairs of topics. Then draft a topic sentence for the paragraph. Be prepared to explain whether you would use the point-by-point method or the block method of organization.

> **camping out on vacation/staying in hotels**
> **contributing to progress/preserving tradition**

Apply ◆ Think and Write

Dictionary of Knowledge ◆ Read about science museums in the Dictionary of Knowledge. Write a paragraph that contrasts the different types of exhibits that are displayed in science museums.

✎ Remember
to organize comparison/contrast paragraphs using the point-by-point or block method.

Focus on Character Traits

How do writers reveal an individual's personality? **Telling** about a person's character is the easiest way. A writer creates a precise word picture that tells how a person looks and acts.

* John Roebling was all bony thinness and harsh angles, with deep-set, penetrating blue eyes.
* John Roebling had been a perfectionist, short-tempered, formal and not terribly interested in people.

Notice how the author's careful word choices work together to create a clear image of the man: *bony, harsh, penetrating*. This short-tempered, formal perfectionist could hardly be "terribly interested in people." The details combine to form a clear picture of John Roebling.

Showing a person's character is often more convincing than telling about it. When a reader can see and hear a character in action, the experience is more like real life than merely being told "the facts."

For example, observe young Washington Roebling at his desk. The writer lets you in on the bridge builder's thoughts.

* It was as if he saw the bridge as a military adversary to be fought and conquered, an ongoing battle...

You can also show a person's character by letting other people in the story give their opinions about the person.

Both telling and showing depend upon careful observation, specific details, and thoughtful word choices. Your aim as a writer is to create a vivid word picture or impression of the person.

The Writer's Voice ◆ Look back at earlier literature excerpts in this book. Find at least three examples of *telling* and three examples of *showing*. What are the advantages of each method?

Working Together

A writer reveals character traits by telling or showing the reader what the character is like. Both methods help the reader *see* the person being described. As a group, work on activities **A** and **B**.

In Your Group

- Be sure people understand the task.
- Express appreciation for others' work.
- Invite others to talk.
- Record the group's ideas.

A. Discuss the statements below. List the ones that help the reader *see* the character. Work together to rewrite the other sentences so that they also give the reader a clear picture.

1. Kelly has sharp features and wavy auburn hair.
2. You would know Kelly instantly if you saw her in a crowd.
3. "She has the most striking green eyes I've ever seen," says Jo.
4. Kelly collects many items for her scrapbook.
5. Kelly's bright skirts and blouses match her cheery smile.

B. Use the following facts to write a paragraph that gives a clear impression of the person described. All the group members should contribute to the finished paragraph.

- A bride — not young, not pretty
- Riding on a train
- Wears a blue cashmere dress
- Sits very stiff, straight

THESAURUS CORNER · Word Choice

Rewrite the paragraph below. Use the Thesaurus and Thesaurus Index to replace each word in dark type with a good synonym. Write a pronoun above each underlined name.

Prior to the American Civil War, Clara Barton was a **careful** schoolteacher. The **compelling** wartime need for nurses changed that. Clara Barton soon became a symbol of the **gutsy** and **sturdy** women of the era. Clara Barton's **kind** care and attention saved many lives. After the war, Clara Barton organized the American Red Cross and was its **kingpin** for many years.

Writing a Comparison Essay

A writer can sometimes help the reader understand a subject by explaining how it is like another, more familiar subject. This is what a comparison essay does. It points out the likenesses of two different subjects.

In *The Brooklyn Bridge*, the author first introduces John Roebling, the bridge's famous designer. When John Roebling died, his son, Washington Roebling, directed completion of the bridge. The author introduces Washington Roebling by comparing and contrasting him with his father, whom the reader already knows. She compares and contrasts their physical characteristics, their personalities, and their professional experiences and abilities.

Know Your Purpose and Audience

What's
MY PURPOSE

In this lesson you will write a comparion essay. Your purpose will be to inform by explaining how two different people are alike.

Who's
MY AUDIENCE

Your audience will be your classmates. Later you and your classmates might hold a read-around or make a class chart of admirable character traits.

1 Prewriting

To get ready to write, first choose your topic—the two people you will compare. Then gather ideas about your topic.

Choose Your Topic ◆ Start by making a list of people you admire. You might list friends, relatives, or famous people. Choose the two people who make the most interesting pair.

Think About It	Talk About It
Look at the names you have listed. Consider the looks, personalities, interests, achievements, and values of each. Do any have similar traits? Circle the two that are the most alike.	Talk with a partner about people you admire. List three names each. Then trade papers and see if you can get an idea of your own from your partner's list.

Topic Ideas

Marian Love (mother)
Ann Fiedora (friend)
(Charles Love) (great-grandfather)
(Frank Eck) (neighbor)
George Washington (president)
Barbara Jordan
   (politician, leader)
Phillis Wheatley (poet)

Choose Your Strategy ♦ Here are two strategies for gathering ideas about your topic. Read both and use what you think will work for you.

PREWRITING IDEAS

CHOICE ONE

Brainstorming

Brainstorm character traits for each person. Jot down ideas quickly without organizing them. Then classify each trait by using a numbered list.

1. physical appearance
2. personality traits
3. interests and achievements
4. values

Model

Charles Love (great-grandfather)
believes in hard work — 4
funny, thoughtful — 2
was electricity pioneer — 3
values community service — 4

Frank Eck (neighbor)
helps troubled kids — 4
was computer pioneer — 3
friendly, helpful — 2
handsome — 1

CHOICE TWO

A Venn Diagram

Make a Venn diagram to show how your two people are alike and how they are different.

Model

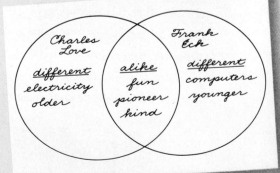

Charles Love
different
electricity
older

alike
fun
pioneer
kind

Frank Eck
different
computers
younger

2 Writing

As you write, remember to discuss only likenesses. Construct your essay by either the point-by-point method or the block method.

Sample First Draft ♦

My neighbor Frank Eck reminds me of my Great-Grandfather Charles Love. They have many traits in common.

My Great-Grandfather became an electrition in 1920. Although electricity was still a novelty to many granddad figured out how to use electricity to power factories. Like granddad, he worked with something new. In 1970 he became a computer enginear. Many people didn't know what computers could do. Frank invented a computerized object that guides airplanes.

Frank works at the community center each weekend, helping troubled boys. Both men value hard work they also believe in helping in the community. Granddad served on the school board for years. Frank and granddad are both fun to be with. Granddad is a good listener, and he loves to tell jokes. Frank is friendly and helpful.

Granddad and Frank Eck were both pioneers in their fields. I am proud to know these fine, interesting men.

	Point-by-Point Method	Block Method
Introduction Paragraph	Identify the people. Discuss one trait for both people.	Identify the people. Tell all about one person.
Paragraph	Discuss another trait for both people.	Tell all about the other person.
Conclusion	Sum up the likenesses.	Sum up the likenesses.

3 Revising

You have completed a draft of your essay. Now it's time to revise for clarity of meaning. This plan for revising may help you.

REVISING IDEA

FIRST Read to Yourself

As you read, review your purpose. Did you write a comparison essay? How are the two different people alike? Consider your audience. Will your classmates understand why these people are alike? Put a pencil check in the margin where you want to make improvements.

Focus: Did you reveal similar character traits of the two people? Did you discuss their personalities, interests, achievements, or values?

THEN Share with a Partner

Read your essay aloud to a classmate. Below are some guidelines you and your partner may use as you work together.

The Writer

Guidelines: Read clearly. Encourage comments. Then decide what changes *you* feel are important to make.

Sample questions:
- Did I focus on the likenesses of the two people?
- **Focus question:** Are there other character traits I could describe?

The Writer's Partner

Guidelines: Listen carefully and take notes if you like. Make specific suggestions in a kind way.

Sample responses:
- I like your description of these people's similar interests.
- Could you tell more about the values they share?

Revising Model ◆ A revised draft should show the changes the writer wants to make. It doesn't matter if it looks messy.

Revising Marks

delete   ℓ

add   ∧

move   ⟲

The antecedent of this pronoun was not clear.

Instrument is a more precise word than *object*.

The writer moved these sentences to clarify the point-by-point structure.

The writer's partner suggested adding an example of these character traits.

My neighbor Frank Eck reminds me of my Great-Grandfather Charles Love. They have many traits in common.

My Great-Grandfather became an electrition in 1920. Although electricity was still a novelty to many granddad figured out how to use electricity to power factories. Like granddad, ~~he~~ *Frank* worked with something new. In 1970 he became a computer enginear. Many people didn't know what computers could do. Frank invented a computerized *instrument* ~~object~~ that guides airplanes.

Frank works at the community center each weekend, helping troubled boys. Both men value hard work they also believe in helping in the community. Granddad served on the school board for years. Frank and granddad are both fun to be with. Granddad is a good listener, and he loves to tell jokes. Frank is friendly and helpful. *He often helps neighbors with home repairs.*

Granddad and Frank Eck were both pioneers in their fields. I am proud to know these fine, interesting men.

Read the draft comparison essay above with the writer's changes. Then revise your own comparison essay.

Grammar Check ◆ Your writing will be easier to read if the antecedents of all pronouns are clear.

Word Choice ◆ Use your thesaurus to find precise synonyms for vague words.

Revising Checklist

☐ **Purpose:** Did I write a comparison essay? Did I give information about how two people are alike?

☐ **Audience:** Will my classmates understand how these people are alike?

☐ **Focus:** Did I give information about the similar character traits of the two people? Did I discuss their personalities, interests, achievements, or values?

4 Proofreading

Fixing surface errors in spelling, punctuation, capitalization, and indentation will help make your essay clear.

Proofreading Model ◆ Here is the draft comparison essay. Proofreading changes have been added in red.

My neighbor Frank Eck reminds me of my Great-Grandfather Charles Love. They have many traits in common.

My Great-Grandfather became an *electrician* (electrition) in 1920. Although electricity was still a novelty to many granddad figured out how to use electricity to power factories. Like granddad, *Frank* he worked with something new. In 1970, he became a computer *engineer* (enginear) Many people didn't know what computers could do. Frank invented a computerized *instrument* object that guides airplanes.

Frank works at the community center each weekend, helping troubled boys. Both men value hard work they also believe in helping in the community. Granddad served on the school board for years. Frank and granddad are both fun to be with. Granddad is a good listener, and he loves to tell jokes. Frank is friendly and helpful. *He often helps neighbors with home repairs.*

Granddad and Frank Eck were both pioneers in their fields. I am proud to know these fine, interesting men.

PROOFREADING IDEA

Spelling Check

To catch spelling and other errors, read each sentence backward word-by-word.

Now proofread your comparison essay and make a neat copy. Don't forget to add a title.

5 Publishing

Here are two ways you can share your essay with classmates.

A Common Bond

My neighbor Frank Eck reminds me of my great-grandfather, Charles Love. They have many traits in common.

My great-grandfather became an electrician in 1920. Although electricity was still a novelty to many, Granddad figured out how to use electricity to power factories. Like Granddad, Frank worked with something new. In 1970 he became a computer engineer. Many people didn't know what computers could do. Frank invented a computerized instrument that guides airplanes.

Both men value hard work. They also believe in helping in the community. Frank works at the community center each weekend, helping troubled boys. Granddad served on the school board for years.

Frank and Granddad are both fun to be with. Granddad is a good listener, and he loves to tell jokes. Frank is friendly and helpful. He often helps neighbors with home repairs.

Granddad and Frank Eck were both pioneers in their fields. I am proud to know these fine, interesting men.

Admirable Character Traits
Kindness
Julia Galarza, Mr. Schmidt
Community Service
Frank Eck, Charles Love,
Sumiko Satow, Mary Nelson
Achievement
Nancy Chang, Melba Nor...
Frank Eck,
Charles Love

PUBLISHING IDEAS

Share Aloud

Organize team read-arounds. Form small groups. Arrange desks in a circle, and take turns reading your essays aloud. After each reading, ask the audience to name the ways in which the people are similar.

Share in Writing

You and your classmates may have found similar traits to admire in people. Read someone else's essay. Then work with your class to make a large chart of likenesses. List admirable traits and people who display those traits.

CURRICULUM
CONNECTION

Writing Across the Curriculum Art

Architects often base new architectural designs on designs of the past. Many fascinating books about the history of architecture can help you appreciate and evaluate the buildings around you.

Writing to Learn

Think and Compare Look at the two stadiums below—the modern Houston Astrodome and the ancient Roman Colosseum. Make a Venn diagram to compare and contrast the two structures.

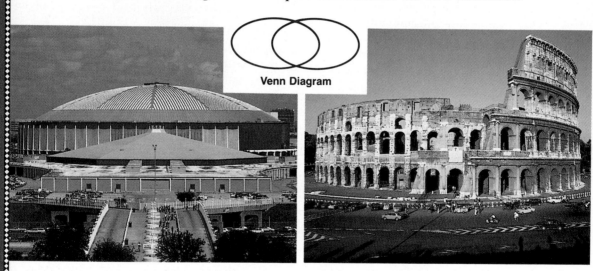

Venn Diagram

Write Use your Venn diagram to write about how the colosseum and the astrodome are alike and different.

Writing in Your Journal

In the Writer's Warm-up you wrote about an example of progress. During the unit you read about people who met the challenge of progress. What challenges do you think you will encounter in your lifetime? In your journal write about one such challenge and how you believe you may meet it.

BOOKS TO ENJOY

Read More About It

Cathedral: The Story of Its Construction
by David Macaulay
Building cathedrals presented tremendous challenges
to the workers of the Middle Ages. Using detailed
drawings, the author shows the step-by-step
construction methods by which these grand structures
were completed.   **Caldecott Honor Book**

Bert Breen's Barn *by Walter D. Edmonds*
If young Tom Dolan's family is to make any
progress on their farm, they'll need a barn. How
Tom buys, moves, and reassembles a sturdy old barn
presents a fine account of country life at the turn of
the century.   **National Book Award**

Book Report Idea   News Story Report

Newspaper reporters use catchy
headlines and interesting lead
paragraphs to gain their readers'
attention. Writing a book report
in the form of a news story might
be a way to interest a friend in a
good book.

Write a Headline ♦ Begin
with a headline that captures the
main idea of the book's plot. The
opening paragraph should give
some important details about the
story. Include a quotation from a
character who "witnessed" the
events in the book.

> *Youngsters Time-Travel
> Through Galaxy*
>   Three local youngsters
> recently returned from an
> incredible journey to another
> galaxy. The trio traveled by
> tesseract, a little understood
> form of time travel. "The trip
> was dangerous, but necessary,"
> explained Meg Murray, the
> group's leader. "We had to free
> my father from the evil
> forces of IT."

UNIT REVIEW

Unit 5

Pronouns   *pages 232–247*

A. Write the pronouns in the sentences.

1. Danielle drew a picture of me and my Siamese cat.
2. The cat with almond-shaped eyes was her best drawing.
3. She colored the cat's eyes blue and its coat white.
4. Are your cat's eyes blue, or are they green?

B. Write each pronoun and its antecedent.

5. A great inventor of his time, Edison had little formal education.
6. Workers pooled their skills in Edison's workshops.
7. The kinetoscope was important. It advanced motion pictures.
8. Edison's workshops were located in New Jersey. They were the forerunners of modern research labs.

C. Write each possessive pronoun. Then write whether it is used alone or with a noun.

9. My class recently visited the New York Public Library.
10. Many people use the library for its numerous reference books.
11. The notes in the margin are mine.
12. His book was written for a general audience.

D. Write and label each interrogative and demonstrative pronoun.

13. What was the box camera?
14. Who invented it?
15. That was George Eastman.
16. Was this the first camera?

E. Write and label the reflexive or intensive pronoun in each sentence. Write the antecedent for each pronoun.

17. You can serve yourself some refreshments.
18. The sandwiches were made by the students themselves.
19. I myself made the salad and the desserts.
20. Suddenly I found myself as the center of attention.

F. Write each indefinite pronoun. Label it *singular* or *plural*.

21. Did you find someone to replace me?
22. Few could play in the game yesterday.
23. Why were others left behind?
24. Explain each of the rules simply and clearly.

G. Write each pronoun and label it *subject* or *object*.

25. They told me about the Great Depression.
26. Who helped them find jobs in 1930?
27. We studied it thoroughly in school.
28. Whom did you interview for the story?

H. Write the correct pronouns in the sentences.

29. (He, Him) and I found arrowheads during the camping trip.
30. Mr. Betz told (we, us) the Iroquois once lived in the area.
31. (They, Them) and others lived in upstate New York.
32. Sheila knows more about their history than (I, me).

Formal and Informal Language   *pages 248–249*

I. Rewrite the following sentences, spelling out all contractions and abbreviations, and substituting more formal language.

33. The exam isn't scheduled til Friday.
34. I won't be going for three more min.
35. They're wearing tuxes to the dance.
36. Marsha has work to do in the science lab.
37. Bill hasn't seen his friend since Jan.

Comparison and Contrast Paragraphs   *pages 266–269*

J. Choose one of the following topics and write a paragraph contrasting the differences between the two things. Use the point-by-point method of organization or the block method. Use the following as a model for a topic sentence: *Traveling on an airplane is quite different from traveling on a train.*

38. water and air
39. spring and fall
40. cats and dogs
41. football and baseball

LANGUAGE PUZZLERS

Unit 5 Challenge

Hidden Pronouns

Find twenty-one personal pronouns hidden in the words below. (Hint: One small "i" doesn't count.)

weather	**thematic**	**yourself**	**flourished**
titmouse	**others**	**myriad**	**antihistamine**

Make a similar hidden-pronoun puzzle to share with two classmates. The first person to find all the pronouns wins.

A Pronoun Scramble

Can you find twenty indefinite pronouns in this puzzle? Make the pronouns by using letters that touch each other horizontally, vertically, or diagonally. No letter box may be used twice in the same word. To start you off, the pronoun *another* is shown.

p	e	r	n	x	b	o	d
z	h	e	m	o	s	t	y
y	t	o	a	l	l	e	v
d	i	w	n	w	d	y	e
o	f	e	y	o	t	h	r
b	o	n	b	n	h	e	a
y	v	e	j	e	a	r	l
r	e	h	t	i	c	h	d

Unit 5 Extra Practice

1 Writing with Pronouns

p. 232

A. Write the personal pronoun in each sentence.

1. Did he arrive?
2. Has she left?
3. They fell.
4. Sam wrote it.

5. She laughed.
6. Find them.
7. It broke.
8. Bill asked her.

B. Ten of the twenty underlined words in this article are pronouns. Write each underlined pronoun after its sentence number.

9. If your hobby is photography, it could win you fame as well as great enjoyment. **10.** In 1863, when she was forty-eight, Julia Margaret Cameron received her first camera as a gift from her husband. **11.** With his encouragement she became skilled in its use. **12.** They turned their home into a studio, where she invited British celebrities to be photographed. **13.** Her unusual close-up portraits were so exceptional that some became more famous than the people in them.

C. In her book, *The Story of Walt Disney*, Dianne Disney Miller, a daughter of Walt Disney, tells how Mickey Mouse was named. Ten of the underlined words are pronouns. Write each underlined pronoun after its sentence number. Write *none* if a sentence has no underlined pronoun.

14. Mice had been used in cartoons before, but until then they'd never been featured. **15.** "I think I've got something," Father told Mother. **16.** "It's a mouse. **17.** I'll call him Mortimer. . . . **18.** I like that, don't you?"
19. Mother thought it over and shook her head. **20.** "I like the mouse idea," she said, "but Mortimer sounds wrong. . . ."
21. "What's wrong with it?" Father asked. **22.** "Mortimer Mouse, Mortimer Mouse. It swings, Lilly."
23. But Mother didn't buy it. **24.** She couldn't explain why "Mortimer" grated on her. **25.** It just did.
26. "All right," Father said, "how about Mickey? Mickey Mouse?"

2 Pronouns and Antecedents

p. 234

A. Write each underlined pronoun. Then write the word or word group that is its antecedent.

1. The players said that <u>they</u> would practice.
2. My cousin told a joke. No one understood <u>it</u>.
3. Angela said, "<u>I</u> need more information."
4. "<u>We</u> want dessert," chanted Pat and Mike.
5. "What's following <u>me</u> now?" asked the driver.
6. Parents and teachers have <u>their</u> cards.
7. The plane is on <u>its</u> final approach.
8. Sir, may I see <u>your</u> driver's license?
9. <u>You</u> were the best speaker, Tanya.
10. "No one can beat <u>us</u>!" roared the Raiders.

B. In this article ten pronouns are omitted. Write the article, using appropriate pronouns from the list. Use some pronouns more than once. Write the antecedent(s) for each pronoun.

he   his   it   they   their

11. A treasured possession of some families is ____ collection of old photographs. **12.** ____ are the portraits of relatives who lived long ago. However, are all these pictures genuine? In the nineteenth century few people owned cameras. **13.** ____ were too costly. Not many people could go to photographers. **14.** ____ charged too much. **15.** Young soldiers wanted to be photographed in ____ uniforms. Some merchants knew this. **16.** ____ sold inexpensive copies of photographs of soldiers. **17.** A private with little cash would buy a picture of someone whose face resembled ____ face. **18.** Then ____ sent this picture home. **19.** The soldier's parents were thrilled to receive a reminder of ____ son. **20.** ____ was then put in the family album.

C. Write the pronoun in each sentence. Then write its antecedent.

21. The engineers knew they would succeed.
22. Laura asked, "May I use the abacus?"
23. Put the record back in its jacket.
24. Yours was excellent, Stuart.
25. "Are the tickets for us?" asked Amy and Vic.

3 Possessive Pronouns

p. 236

A. Write the possessive pronoun in each sentence.

1. Our pool is not very deep.
2. Have you ever swum in theirs?
3. Did everyone read her book report on *The Adventures of Tom Sawyer*?
4. Mine needs a catchy title like that one.
5. Cathy and Richard borrowed hers.
6. His nose is badly sunburned.
7. Their names are easy to spell.
8. Why was your dog barking?
9. Ours is either in the garage or in the attic.
10. Write her address on this envelope.

B. Complete each title with the correct word in parentheses. Write the title.

11. "This Nearly Was ____ " (my, mine)
12. "Hitch ____ Wagon to a Star" (your, yours)
13. "I Left ____ Heart in San Francisco" (my, mine)
14. "Smoke Gets in ____ Eyes" (your, you're)
15. "This Land Is ____ Land" (you're, your)
16. "You Are ____ Sunshine" (mine, my)

C. Read the following movie review. Write the correct pronoun for each blank. Write *possessive* after each possessive pronoun.

17. At the theater last night, ____ nearly lost a friend — ____ cousin, Jane. 18. ____ threatened to stop going to shows with ____ if ____ ever took ____ to such a boring movie again. 19. The picture ____ both saw was called, fittingly enough, *Evening of Horror*. 20. ____ was truly horrible. 21. The actors mumbled ____ lines as if sleepwalking, and director Marie Chall must have lost ____ copy of the script halfway through, because nothing happened after that. 22. Star Ron Redfern looked as if ____ had wandered in from another set, and ____ costar, Mae Runaway, forgot ____ French accent most of the time. The film had one benefit, though. 23. ____ cured ____ insomnia! 24. The film succeeded in putting ____ to sleep nine times! 25. Maybe ____ should be grateful for that.

4 Interrogative and Demonstrative Pronouns
p. 238

A. Write and label each interrogative and demonstrative pronoun.

1. Who is playing the piano?
2. Whom do you suspect?
3. Whose tapes are these?
4. This is a good solution to the problem.
5. Whom will they call for an answer?
6. Be sure to ask Pat about that.
7. Which of the three is the most interesting?
8. What did you like about the song?
9. These are the contest winners.
10. Would the judges prefer those?

B. Complete each sentence with a demonstrative pronoun. Then write the word to which it refers.

11. _____ turned out to be a good day for sailing.
12. _____ are your assignments.
13. Let's raise the jib. _____ are the ropes you pull on.
14. Was _____ a dragonfly?
15. Whose gloves are _____ ?
16. See the boats over there? _____ belong to the camp.
17. Is _____ your sailboat? It's beautiful!

5 Reflexive and Intensive Pronouns
p. 240

A. Write a reflexive pronoun to complete each sentence. Then write the word or words to which it refers.

1. Jan and I taught _____ to sail.
2. Al should not strain _____ launching the boat.
3. You should help _____ to the suntan lotion.
4. With this device, the boat can actually steer _____ .
5. All by _____ , Cynthia won the Tri-Lakes Sailathon.
6. We have to remind _____ about the racing rules.
7. Each sailor must look out for _____ or _____ .
8. I always wear a life jacket to protect _____ .
9. The wind seemed to be whipping _____ into a storm.

B. Write and label the reflexive or intensive pronoun in each sentence. Write the antecedent for each pronoun.

10. Our class performed scenes we ourselves had written about Anne Frank.
11. Anne herself wrote a number of essays and kept a diary.
12. The diary itself was a place for Anne to write about her feelings.
13. After we read some entries, we tried to imagine ourselves in Anne's situation.
14. Her family concealed themselves in an attic for years to escape the Nazis.
15. Mr. Frank himself taught his daughters their high school subjects.
16. I treated myself to a hardcover copy of Anne's *Diary*.

6 Indefinite Pronouns

p. 242

A. Write each sentence, using an indefinite pronoun that completes it appropriately. Use no indefinite pronoun more than twice.

1. _____ was in the corridor.
2. That certainly is not good for _____ .
3. _____ of it looks delicious.
4. We could not see _____ of them.
5. That dictionary defines almost _____ .
6. _____ seems wrong with the photograph.
7. Certainly _____ must be there by now.
8. _____ of them are excellent actors.
9. _____ of the projectors are in use today.
10. A low calorie diet may not be good for _____ .
11. _____ of us could have done more.
12. _____ of the machines had been repaired.

B. Write each pronoun. Then label it *demonstrative*, *reflexive*, *interrogative*, or *indefinite*.

13. Those are wild geese in the sky.
14. Did Ken weigh himself?
15. Who was inside the automobile?
16. Describe anything in the clearest manner.
17. Look at the geyser! That is spectacular!

7 Subject and Object Pronouns   *p. 244*

A. Write each pronoun. Then label it *subject* or *object*.

1. Do they know me?
2. She helped us.
3. We gave them food.
4. Di saw her and him.
5. He and I won an award.
6. They followed us.

B. Write a subject pronoun to replace each group of words in parentheses.

7. The secretary and (my father) read the letter.
8. I receive more mail than (your sister) does.
9. How did (the pioneers) mail letters?
10. Ken and (his friends) wrote invitations.
11. Among the great writers of letters was (Abigail Adams).
12. Willie or (Sara) might receive a phone call.

C. Write an object pronoun to replace each group of words in parentheses.

13. No one had shown (my mother) the letter.
14. Who sent Mary and (her brothers) this parcel?
15. Has anyone found (the addresses) yet?
16. Who telephoned (my grandfather) and me?
17. Their postcard surprised me more than it surprised (my aunt).
18. Did anyone notify the principal or (the students)?
19. Who told your cousin and (Angela) the news?

D. Write each underlined pronoun. Label it *subject* or *object*. Then write how it is used in the sentence: *subject, predicate nominative, direct object,* or *indirect object.*

20. My twin sister and I belong to a large family. **21.** On our birthday, relatives in almost every state send her and me cards. **22.** Uncle Lacey in Tulsa always remembers us in special ways. **23.** This year we didn't receive the usual card from him. **24.** He mailed us a cassette. **25.** On it he and Cousin Marla sang "Happy Birthday" and a few choruses of "Oklahoma." **26.** Then they read us one of her poems. **27.** In verse, Uncle Lacey and my cousin invited us to beautiful Oklahoma. **28.** Our most unforgettable relatives are he and Cousin Marla.

8 Choosing Correct Pronouns

p. 246

A. Test for the correct pronoun in parentheses by omitting the underlined words. Write the correct pronoun.

1. (We, Us) <u>the people</u> need more information.
2. The good news pleased (we, us) <u>football fans</u>.
3. Why are (we, us) <u>club members</u> proud today?
4. Give (me, us) <u>volunteers</u> more information.
5. How can (we, us) <u>teenagers</u> help our city?
6. Watch (we, us) <u>runners</u> in the big race.
7. Who told (we, us) <u>altos</u> to sing softly?
8. Should (we, us) <u>players</u> wear our uniforms?

B. Write the correct pronoun in each sentence.

9. Dad and (I, me) studied the recipes.
10. Grandmother told Jamie and (I, me) another joke.
11. Will Fred or (she, her) correct the papers?
12. The teachers and (they, them) will advise us.
13. The senator greeted them and (we, us) yesterday.
14. (We, Us) students checked each answer.
15. Will they or (we, us) be assigned the job?
16. How much did they and (she, her) prepare?
17. Give him and (she, her) the ballots.
18. Nobody could solve it as quickly as (she, her).
19. The members elected Pam and (I, mc) as captains.
20. Everyone gave (we, us) captains a cheer.
21. Will the players and (we, us) be allowed to go?
22. (She, Her) and I are the only ones left.
23. Jan helped Bill and (I, me) with the dishes.
24. (They, Them) and I work well together.
25. Clifford is as tall as (she, her).
26. They can run as fast as (we, us).
27. That joke amused them more than (we, us).
28. We liked that breakfast more than (they, them).
29. That squeak annoyed him as much as (I, me).
30. I will sell as many subscriptions as (he, him).
31. They hiked farther than (I, me).
32. It will help him less than (she, her).
33. Pete has more time than (I, me).

UNIT SIX

USING LANGUAGE TO
DESCRIBE

───── **PART ONE** ─────

Unit Theme *People and Wildlife*

Language Awareness Adjectives

───── **PART TWO** ─────

Literature *The Yearling* by Marjorie Kinnan Rawlings

A Reason for Writing Describing

Writing
IN YOUR JOURNAL

WRITER'S WARM-UP ♦ Humans have always had a special relationship with wildlife. Sometimes animals benefit most, sometimes humans do. What encounter with wildlife have you experienced or do you know about? Write about it in your journal. Describe the animal you know the most about.

Think of the best words you can to replace the word *good* in the following phrases: *A good ball player, a good apple, a good book, a good friend, a good dog, a good color.*

1 Writing with Adjectives

What words make these two word pictures different?

> Droopy gray trees lined the murky, sinister path.
> Sprightly young trees lined the breezy, sunlit path.

The two sentences have the same base: Trees lined the path. The words that change the basic picture are powerful descriptive words called adjectives. They change, or modify, the nouns *trees* and *path* to create two very different word pictures. One picture is gloomy and frightening, while the other is happy and inviting.

Adjectives answer the following questions. Notice that you can place adjectives before or after the words they modify.

> What kind? The area, <u>remote</u> and <u>primitive</u>, is <u>peaceful</u>.
> Which one? The <u>last</u> tree on the <u>third</u> hill marks the border.
> How many? <u>Many</u> trees in a group let in <u>few</u> rays of sun.
> How much? <u>Some</u> vegetation receives <u>no</u> light and dies.

Not all adjectives create word pictures. The words *a, an,* and *the* are special adjectives called **articles**. Because *the* is used to refer to specific persons, places, or things, it is called the **definite article**. Because *a* and *an* refer to any person, place, or thing, they are called **indefinite articles**.

> *the* river   *the* old river   *a* river   *an* overflowing river

> **Summary** ♦ An **adjective** modifies a noun or pronoun. Use specific adjectives to create vivid word pictures.

Guided Practice

Name the adjectives, including the articles, in each sentence.

1. Imagine a woodland setting with a variety of wild creatures.
2. Dim light creeps through the branches of stately trees.
3. The mysterious woods are alive with restless, shadowy forms.

Practice

A. Many adjectives in the sentences below supply details about the wilderness. List these adjectives along with the articles.

4. The wilderness is an unsettled, uncultivated region.
5. Many wildflowers grow there without any special care.
6. Gigantic trees stand on a carpet of green grass.
7. They are independent and untamed.
8. Long, snakelike streams wind along many uncharted paths.
9. Creatures, great and small, live together in natural harmony.
10. Some wilderness areas offer magnificent scenery.
11. Crystal lakes lie among the snowcapped mountains.
12. Other areas offer peaceful relaxation in attractive settings.
13. Careful and respectful visitors are welcome.

B. Rewrite the paragraph, adding adjectives that answer the questions in the blanks. Choose descriptive adjectives that create a unified word picture.

As I started out, the day already seemed (**14.** what kind?). A (**15.** what kind?) sun was just rising over the (**16.** which one?) hill. Traces of (**17.** how much?) (**18.** what kind?) fog lingered around the (**19.** which one?) path. A (**20.** what kind?) breeze stirred the (**21.** what kind?) trees and clouds tumbled together like (**22.** how many?) (**23.** what kind?) creatures.

C. The underlined words below are overused adjectives. Rewrite the sentences, using more specific and descriptive adjectives.

24. Gardens may be <u>nice</u> places for flowers to grow.
25. Yet I think flowers that bloom in the wilderness are <u>fine</u>.
26. The sun warms the blossoms on this <u>fine</u> day.
27. What a <u>good</u> time this is to watch the birds soar!
28. Wouldn't it be a <u>nice</u> way to travel?

Apply • Think and Write

From Your Writing • Read what you wrote for the Writer's Warm-up. Change or add adjectives to create vivid word pictures.

✎ **Remember**
that you can use adjectives to give details to your reader.

Think of a special contribution a nation has made to the world. Then connect that nation to its contribution in a phrase.

EXAMPLE: *Japan—Japanese cooking*

2 Proper and Demonstrative Adjectives

Proper Adjectives   When an adjective is formed from a proper noun, it is called a proper adjective. Notice that some proper adjectives have the same form as the proper noun. You can use a dictionary to check the form and spelling of proper adjectives.

> **MECHANICS "";?!""**
>
> Like a proper noun, a proper adjective is always capitalized. For other uses of capital letters, see pages 616–625.

Proper Nouns	Proper Adjectives
America	an American city
Palm Beach	a Palm Beach vacation
Australia	the Australian outback
New York	a New York newspaper

Demonstrative Adjectives   You have already learned about the demonstrative pronouns *this*, *that*, *these*, and *those*. When the same words are used to modify nouns, they are called demonstrative adjectives. Notice the difference below.

Demonstrative Pronoun: This is the Australian outback.
Demonstrative Adjective: This land is the Australian outback.

A demonstrative adjective points out a specific person, place, or thing and is more definite than any of the articles. Use *this* and *these* to point out someone or something near. Use *that* and *those* to point out something farther away.

Singular: this book   that star
Plural: these books   those stars

> **Summary** ♦ A **proper adjective** is formed from a proper noun. The **demonstrative adjectives**, *this*, *that*, *these*, and *those*, point out the nouns they modify. Use these kinds of adjectives to add specific details to your writing.

Guided Practice

Name each proper and demonstrative adjective.

1. This book, *The Yearling,* is about a boy, Jody, and a pet deer.
2. This story takes place in the Florida wilderness.
3. That setting may be unfamiliar to those Canadian students.

Practice

A. Write and label each proper and demonstrative adjective.

> **4.** Jody's deer seems like that white-tailed deer.
> **5.** These white-tailed deer are sometimes called Virginia deer.
> **6.** These deer are the most common North American deer.
> **7.** There is no such thing as an Australian deer.
> **8.** Those red deer are called Old World deer.
> **9.** This South American deer is called a pudu.

B. Rewrite this part of a conversation about *The Yearling.* Use the correct adjective from each set in parentheses.

"Here, look at (**10.** this, that) edition of *The Yearling.* See, (**11.** that, this) book has (**12.** those, these) great illustrations by the artist N.C. Wyeth. Look for (**13.** this, that) picture of Jody and his deer, Flag. (**14.** Those, These) trees are typical of the (**15.** Florida, florida) setting of (**16.** this, that) book. The land was primitive in (**17.** these, those) times in (**18.** this, that) part of Florida."

C. Rewrite more of this conversation about *The Yearling.* Fill each space with the kind of adjective indicated in parentheses.

"The author of (**19.** demonstrative) book, Marjorie Kinnan Rawlings, wrote for a New York newspaper before she settled in Cross Creek, Florida, in 1928. For the next ten years, she lived among the (**20.** proper) folk in (**21.** demonstrative) harsh (**22.** proper) scrub country. Rawlings used (**23.** demonstrative) land as the setting of *The Yearling.*"

Apply ◆ Think and Write

Neighborly Descriptions ◆ Write about the different kinds of people who came from around the world to settle in your community.

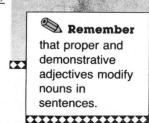

✎ **Remember**
that proper and demonstrative adjectives modify nouns in sentences.

What's your choice: vanilla or rocky road? the book or the movie of a favorite story? Defend each choice by comparing it to an alternative.
Vanilla ice cream is smoother than rocky road.

3 Using Adjectives to Compare

Adjectives change forms when we use them to make comparisons. The three forms, or degrees of comparison, are explained below.

Positive Degree: A horse is a <u>fast</u> animal.
Comparative Degree: An elk is <u>faster</u> than a horse.
Superlative Degree: The cheetah is the <u>fastest</u> animal of all.

To use comparative and superlative forms, learn the rules below.

Add *-er* and *-est* to most one-syllable adjectives and many two-syllable adjectives. Some spelling changes may occur. See the spelling rules on pages 613–614.

Positive	Comparative	Superlative
sharp	sharper	sharpest
big	bigger	biggest
busy	busier	busiest

Use *more* and *most* with some two-syllable adjectives and with all adjectives of three or more syllables.

Positive	Comparative	Superlative
careful	more careful	most careful
generous	more generous	most generous

Use irregular forms for some adjectives.

Positive	Comparative	Superlative
good	better	best
bad, ill	worse	worst
much, many	more	most
little	less	least

Summary ◆ Many adjectives have three forms, or **degrees of comparison**: positive, comparative, and superlative.

Guided Practice

Name the comparative and superlative forms of these adjectives.

1. warm   **2.** bad   **3.** lively   **4.** dangerous **5.** hopeful

The rules listed below will help you use adjectives correctly when you make comparisons.

Do *not* confuse comparative and superlative degrees.

If two are being compared, use the comparative degree.

Compared with city life, rural life is slower (not slowest).

If more than two are compared, use the superlative degree.

For Marjorie Rawlings, Cross Creek was the best (not better) of all places.

Do *not* use double comparatives or superlatives.

She wrote better (not more better) nature stories than news articles. I think *The Yearling* is the finest (not most finest) book she wrote.

Do *not* use awkward-sounding comparatives or superlatives.

Is *Cross Creek* more vivid (not vivider) than this book?

Use *than*, not *then*, when making comparisons. *Then* tells when.

***Cross Creek* is more autobiographical than (not then) *The Yearling*. First she wrote short stories, and then (tells when) she wrote novels.**

Summary ◆ Use the **comparative degree** to compare two. Use the **superlative degree** to compare more than two. Use adjectives carefully when you make comparisons.

Guided Practice

Choose the correct word or words in parentheses.

6. Rawlings is one of the (more, most) famous of all nature writers.
7. The wildlife in Florida became (more important, importanter) in her writing (than, then) other subjects.
8. The (nicest, most nicest) people she ever met were in Cross Creek.

Practice

A. Write each adjective. Label it C for *comparative* or S for *superlative*. Then write its positive form(s) under it.

9. newest	**12.** least	**15.** finer	**18.** simplest
10. better	**13.** flattest	**16.** worst	**19.** happiest
11. riper	**14.** busier	**17.** driest	**20.** easier

B. Write each positive degree adjective. Then write its comparative and superlative forms.

21. short	**23.** delicate	**25.** important
22. helpful	**24.** many	**26.** difficult

C. Choose the correct words in parentheses to complete the sentences about Marjorie Kinnan Rawlings. Write the sentences.

27. At first, Rawlings was (successfuler, more successful) with her writing (than, then) with her orange groves.

28. Her neighbors were the (nicest, most nicest) she had known.

29. They inspired her to write (better, more better) stories.

30. She observed and (than, then) wrote about what she had learned.

31. Of all the characters Martha is the (memorablest, most memorable).

D. Write the correct form of each adjective in parentheses.

32. *Cross Creek* is probably Rawlings's (good) work.

33. It was her (big) accomplishment.

34. What was her (bad) enemy there?

35. The snakes were (dangerous) than the mosquitoes.

36. The people were (precious) to her than those in the North.

Apply ◆ Think and Write

Dictionary of Knowledge ◆ Marjorie Kinnan Rawlings is best known for her descriptions of wildlife. Read about her accomplishments in the Dictionary of Knowledge. Use adjectives to make comparisons about some people or places that this author might have described.

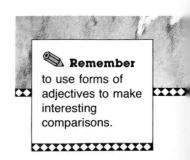

✎ Remember
to use forms of adjectives to make interesting comparisons.

Think of words that name different foods. Then use each word to describe something beginning with the same letter.
EXAMPLES: *Bread—bread box; pumpkin—pumpkin pie*

GETTING STARTED

4 Words as Different Parts of Speech

How a word is used in a sentence determines its part of speech.

Noun or Adjective? How is *nature* used in each sentence below?

■ Rawlings wrote about <u>nature</u>. Rawlings was a <u>nature</u> writer.

Pronoun or Adjective? The words *this*, *that*, *these*, and *those* are used as either demonstrative pronouns or demonstrative adjectives. How is *that* used in each sentence below?

■ <u>That</u> is beautiful!   <u>That</u> sunset is beautiful!

Many indefinite pronouns, such as *any*, *each*, *one*, *all*, *both*, and *few*, are also used as adjectives. How is *both* used below?

■ <u>Both</u> were written by her.   <u>Both</u> books were written by her.

> **Summary** ♦ Some words can function as various parts of speech. This allows you to use words flexibly in your writing.

Guided Practice

Tell whether the underlined word is a noun, adjective, or pronoun.

1. Did you cat the <u>orange</u>?
2. Is that an <u>orange</u> grove?
3. <u>All</u> crops are handpicked.
4. <u>All</u> are handpicked.

Practice

Rewrite each sentence, using the underlined word as an adjective.

5. Rawlings bought land to grow <u>citrus</u>.
6. <u>This</u> became a problem.
7. She hadn't anticipated the frost in <u>Florida</u>.
8. <u>All</u> had crop damage.

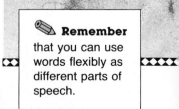

✎ Remember that you can use words flexibly as different parts of speech.

Apply ♦ Think and Write

Descriptive Writing ♦ Describe an ideal garden, using the names of various foods as adjectives. Example: tomato plants

GETTING STARTED

xxx

Find clues in these sentences for the meanings of the underlined words:
Have you ever tried to count to a googol? Was mischievous Huck Finn a scalawag? Do shoelaces unravel if the aglets fall off?

VOCABULARY ◆
Context Clues

English contains so many thousands of words that few people can hope to learn them all. One way to learn new words is to use a dictionary. Another way is to use the **context**, or the words that surround an unknown word, to determine a meaning.

Clues provided by context are called **context clues**. The chart below gives examples of different kinds of context clues.

Kinds of Clues	Examples
Direct definition	*Fern leaves are called* <u>fronds</u>.
Definition by apposition, a synonym phrase set off by commas	<u>Coniferous</u>, or *cone-bearing*, trees often stay green year-round.
Definition through description	*A tree's* <u>canopied</u> limbs *formed a roof over Jody's head.*

Building Your Vocabulary

For each sentence below, use the context to determine the meaning of the underlined word.

1. Travelers who first see a <u>prairie</u> are often surprised by the miles and miles of seemingly endless grass.
2. The vast frozen <u>tundra</u> also stretches for miles without a tree or hill in sight.
3. The <u>pampas</u> are very similar to prairies, except they are found in South America.
4. A <u>pine barren</u>, on the other hand, is crowded with trees—tall pine trees that thrive in the sandy soil.
5. The most densely packed woodland is the <u>rain forest</u>, crowded with tropical trees and undergrowth and fed by large amounts of rain.

Practice

A. Write *definition*, *description*, or *synonym* to name the type of context clue given for each underlined word.

1. As we climbed the mountain, the huge mass of ice that formed the <u>glacier</u> loomed before us and flowed down the mountain.
2. Our guide told us that the park was once part of an Indian <u>reservation</u>, an area of land set aside for the Indians.
3. She said that <u>valley glaciers</u> fill steep mountain valleys.
4. The other kind of glaciers, <u>continental glaciers</u>, are found at the poles and cover vast areas of land.
5. We also saw a beautiful <u>fiord</u> that had been dug out by the glacier and filled with ocean water many years ago.
6. As we surveyed this majestic scene, we felt a great <u>reverence</u>, or respect, for the wonders of the world.

B. Use context clues to determine the meaning of each underlined word. Write the meaning.

7. The student gave a <u>superlative</u> speech. It was one of the finest ever given.
8. We learned the <u>rudiments</u> of Latin, but found that even these basics took us several weeks to cover.
9. The carpenter is an <u>industrious</u> young man, always working hard and steadily to complete the job at hand.
10. The cat had an <u>unfathomable</u> way of always appearing whenever food was present. No one knew how she did it.

Language Corner • Word Origins

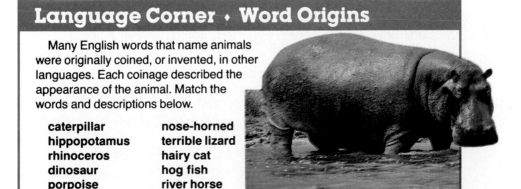

Many English words that name animals were originally coined, or invented, in other languages. Each coinage described the appearance of the animal. Match the words and descriptions below.

caterpillar	nose-horned
hippopotamus	terrible lizard
rhinoceros	hairy cat
dinosaur	hog fish
porpoise	river horse

How to Expand Sentences with Adjectives

As you know, using adjectives to modify nouns and pronouns can make a difference in your writing. Adjectives can add important details and information, and make your writing more interesting and colorful. Which sentence below is more detailed and interesting?

> **1.** The wind blew across the land.
> **2.** The bitter, arctic wind blew across the barren land.

Sentence **1** states a fact but does not give any information about the wind or the land. Adding the adjectives *bitter* and *arctic* in sentence **2** tells us exactly what kind of wind is blowing, and *barren* gives us a better picture of the land.

Adjectives give other kinds of information as well. For example, they can tell *how much, how many,* or *which one*. Notice the difference these kinds of adjectives made in the sentences below.

> **3.** The <u>entire</u> party huddled around the stove inside the tent.
> **4.** A <u>few</u> dogs remained outside.
> **5.** The <u>lead</u> dog sat proudly beside the sled.

A single, well-chosen adjective can give readers a great deal of information. When you use adjectives, however, be careful not to use the same ones over and over. Overused adjectives can make a potentially interesting piece of writing boring. Overused adjectives should be replaced with other, more effective ones.

The Grammar Game ◆ Create word pictures! Write pairs of adjectives for each word below. Then do it again, choosing adjectives to change the picture.

button	jacket	house	elephant	concert
movie	river	dinner	shoe	eyes

Working Together

Notice how adjectives make your sentences come alive as you complete activities **A** and **B** with your group.

In Your Group

- ◆ Contribute your own ideas.
- ◆ Help the group finish on time.
- ◆ Pay attention to all suggestions.
- ◆ Take turns recording information.

A. News headlines require an efficient use of language to describe stories to come. Choose a single, exact adjective to expand each headline. Then change each adjective to change the news.

1. **WEATHER AHEAD**
2. **JUDGE LECTURES JURY**
3. **ASTRONAUTS TRAIN**
4. **EXPLORERS DISCOVER ISLAND**
5. **MYSTERY SOLVED**
6. **CROWDS GATHER**
7. **TRAVEL TO PLACES**
8. **PAINTING FOUND**
9. **STORM HITS CITY**
10. **WOMAN WINS LOTTERY**
11. **DOG RESCUES CHILD**
12. **LOCAL TEAM WINS**

B. Imagine that you are approaching the front entrance of your school. Write a paragraph or two to describe what you see. Use the most exact adjectives possible. Group members must agree on the final product. Then exchange papers with another group. Do your descriptions give the same information?

WRITERS' CORNER ◆ Overusing Adjectives

Choose adjectives for nouns that need more description, but avoid stringing together too many adjectives to describe a noun. Overusing adjectives can make your sentences long, boring, and difficult to read.

EXAMPLE: The beautiful, small, narrow, rocky, uninhabited island was noted for its frequent, spectacular volcanic activity.

IMPROVED: The small, uninhabited island was noted for its frequent volcanic activity.

Read what you wrote for the Writer's Warm-up. Did you overuse adjectives in any of your sentences? If you did, try to improve them by using fewer, more effective adjectives.

AN OCTOBER DAY   *painting by Winslow Homer*
Sterling and Francine Clark Art Institute, Williamstown, Massachusetts

USING LANGUAGE
TO
DESCRIBE

PART TWO

Literature *The Yearling* by Marjorie Kinnan Rawlings
A Reason for Writing Describing

CREATIVE
Writing

FINE ARTS ◆ Imagine that developers are about to build a resort and a superhighway on the mountain in the background of Winslow Homer's painting. How do you feel about that? Write an editorial. State your case and give strong reasons for your opinions.

CRITICAL THINKING •
A Strategy for Describing

A VENN DIAGRAM

Describing is using details to paint word pictures. Making comparisons is one way to do this. For example, which is the more vivid image: "The sun poured down like hot butterscotch" or "The sun shone"? Saying that the sun is like hot butterscotch is making a comparison.

After this lesson you will read part of *The Yearling* by Marjorie Kinnan Rawlings. The author uses many comparisons to describe the characters and settings in her novel. Later you will write a description that may include comparisons.

There are lots of comparisons a writer could make to describe sunlight. Hot butterscotch is one. What does the author compare sunlight to in this passage from *The Yearling?*

> He stretched out one arm and laid his head on it. A shaft of sunlight, warm and thin like a light patchwork quilt, lay across his body.

Comparisons are often used in descriptive writing. When else might you want to compare one person or thing with another?

Learning the Strategy

Making comparisons and contrasts is an everyday occurrence. You often notice how two people or things are alike or different. Sometimes it's important to organize and remember these observations. Suppose there will be an election for student body president. You are going to listen to two candidates' speeches. How would you remember and compare or contrast what they say? Or imagine you had to write a report that compares and contrasts birds and

CRITICAL THINKING: Compare/Contrast

reptiles. How might you organize your facts? Or suppose you are writing a poem about a mountain. You want to describe it by comparing it to a giant. How can you think of comparisons?

A Venn diagram is one strategy for recording likenesses and differences. It is two circles that overlap. The one below is about birds and reptiles. The words in the middle note likenesses, those on the outside note differences. How could a diagram like this help you write your report?

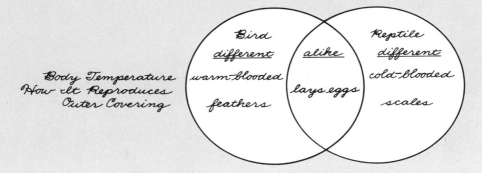

Using the Strategy

A. Do you remember what school was like in sixth grade? What is school like now? Make a Venn diagram to compare your sixth grade year in school with this year. You might use the information to write a description of school then and now.

B. The boy in *The Yearling* lived in a very rural area of the Florida Everglades over fifty years ago. You can't know all the details, but you can imagine how his life might have been like or different from yours. Make a Venn diagram to help get your mind set for reading. As subtopics use "surroundings" and "leisure-time activities." Fill in details you know about yourself and can imagine for him. Then read *The Yearling* to find out more about that boy from long ago.

Applying the Strategy

• Do you find making Venn diagrams hard or easy? Why?
• When might the ability to list likenesses and differences help you in your schoolwork?

LITERATURE

from

The Yearling

by Marjorie Kinnan Rawlings

It was a fine afternoon in April—too fine to waste hoeing corn, Jody thought. So he swung himself over the cabin fence and headed down the road for the glen. He ran the two miles quickly and soon came upon the magnolia tree where he had carved a wildcat's face. Then he plunged down a steep bank into the cool, shady glen around a spring. The cold, clear spring bubbled up out of the sand as Jody rolled up his pants and waded into the water. He waded through the shallows—cooling himself, watching for water animals, and enjoying this place that was all his own.

A breeze parted the canopied limbs over him. The sun dropped through and lay on his head and shoulders. It was good to be warm at his head while his hard calloused feet were cold. The breeze died away, the sun no longer reached him. He waded across to the opposite bank where the growth was more open. A low palmetto brushed him. It reminded him that his knife was snug in his pocket; that he had planned as long ago as Christmas, to make himself a flutter-mill.

He had never built one alone. Grandma Hutto's son Oliver had always made one for him whenever he was home from sea. He went to work intently, frowning as he tried to recall the exact angle necessary to make the mill-wheel turn smoothly. He cut two forked twigs and trimmed them into two Y's of the same size. Oliver had been very particular to have the cross-bar round and smooth, he remembered. A wild cherry grew half-way up the bank. He climbed it and cut a twig as even as a polished pencil. He selected a palm frond and cut two strips of the tough fiber, an inch wide and four inches long. He cut a slit lengthwise in the center of each of them, wide enough to insert the cherry twig. The strips of palm frond must be at angles, like the arms of a windmill. He adjusted them carefully. He separated the Y-shaped twigs by nearly the length of the cherry cross-bar and pushed them deep into the sand of the branch bed a few yards below the spring.

The water was only a few inches deep but it ran strongly, with a firm current. The palm-frond mill-wheel must just brush the water's surface. He experimented with depth until he was satisfied, then laid the cherry bar between the twigs. It hung motionless. He twisted it a moment, anxiously, helping it to fit itself into its forked grooves. The bar began to rotate. The current caught the flexible tip of one bit of palm frond. By the time it lifted clear, the rotation of the bar brought the angled tip of the second into contact with the stream. The small leafy paddles swung over and over, up and down. The little wheel was turning. The flutter-mill was at work. It turned with the easy rhythm of the great water-mill at Lynne that ground corn into meal.

Jody drew a deep breath. He threw himself on the weedy sand close to

JODY AND THE FLUTTER-MILL *Illustration by N.C. Wyeth*

LITERATURE: Story

the water and abandoned himself to the magic of motion. Up, over, down, up, over, down — the flutter-mill was enchanting. The bubbling spring would rise forever from the earth, the thin current was endless. The spring was the beginning of waters sliding to the sea. Unless leaves fell, or squirrels cut sweet bay twigs to drop and block the fragile wheel, the flutter-mill might turn forever. When he was an old man, as old as his father, there seemed no reason why this rippling movement might not continue as he had begun it.

He moved a stone that was matching its corners against his sharp ribs and burrowed a little, hollowing himself a nest for his hips and shoulders. He stretched out one arm and laid his head on it. A shaft of sunlight, warm and thin like a light patchwork quilt, lay across his body. He watched the flutter-mill indolently, sunk in the sand and the sunlight. The movement was hypnotic. His eyelids fluttered with the palm-leaf paddles. Drops of silver slipping from the wheel blurred together like the tail of a shooting star. The water made a sound like kittens lapping. A rain frog sang a moment and then was still. There was an instant when the boy hung at the edge of a high bank made of the soft fluff of broom-sage, and the rain frog and the starry dripping of the flutter-mill hung with him. Instead of falling over the edge, he sank into the softness. The blue, white-tufted sky closed over him. He slept.

When he awakened, he thought he was in a place other than the branch bed. He was in another world, so that for an instant he thought he might still be dreaming. The sun was gone, and all the light and shadow. There were no black boles of live oaks, no glossy green of magnolia leaves, no pattern of gold lace where the sun had sifted through the branches of the wild cherry. The world was all a gentle gray, and he lay in a mist as fine as spray from a waterfall. The mist tickled his skin. It was scarcely wet. It was at once warm and cool. He rolled over on his back and it was as though he looked up into the soft gray breast of a mourning dove.

He lay, absorbing the fine-dropped rain like a young plant. When his face was damp at last and his shirt was moist to the touch, he left his nest. He stopped short. A deer had come to the spring while he was sleeping. The fresh tracks came down the east bank and stopped at the water's edge. They were sharp and pointed, the tracks of a doe. They sank deeply into the sand, so that he knew the doe was an old one and a large. Perhaps she was heavy with fawn. She had come down and drunk deeply from the spring, not seeing him where he slept. Then she had scented him. There was a scuffled confusion in the sand where she had wheeled in fright. The tracks up the opposite bank had long harried streaks behind them. Perhaps she had not drunk, after all, before she scented him, and turned and ran with that swift, sand-throwing flight. He hoped she was not now thirsty, wide-eyed in the scrub.

He looked about for other tracks. The squirrels had raced up and down the banks, but they were bold, always. A raccoon had been that way, with his feet like sharp-nailed hands, but he could not be sure how recently. Only his father could tell for certain the hour when any wild things had passed by. Only the doe had surely come and had been frightened. He turned back again to the flutter-mill. It was turning as steadily as though it had always been there. The palm-leaf paddles were frail but they made a brave show of strength, rippling against the shallow water. They were glistening from the slow rain.

Jody looked at the sky. He could not tell the time of day in the grayness, nor how long he may have slept. He bounded up the west bank, where open gallberry flats spread without obstructions. As he stood, hesitant whether to go or stay, the rain ended as gently as it had begun. A light breeze stirred from the southwest. The sun came out. The clouds rolled together into great white billowing feather bolsters, and across the east a rainbow arched, so lovely and so various that Jody thought he would burst with looking at it. The earth was pale green, the air itself was all but visible, golden with the rain-washed sunlight, and all the trees and grass and bushes glittered, varnished with the rain-drops.

A spring of delight boiled up within him as irresistibly as the spring of the branch. He lifted his arms and held them straight from his shoulders like a water-turkey's wings. He began to whirl around in his tracks. He whirled faster and faster until his ecstasy was a whirlpool, and when he thought he would explode with it, he became dizzy and closed his eyes and dropped to the ground and lay flat in the broom-sage. The earth whirled under him and with him. He opened his eyes and the blue April sky and the cotton clouds whirled over him. Boy and earth and trees and sky spun together. The whirling stopped, his head cleared and he got to his feet. He was light-headed and giddy, but something in him was relieved, and the April day could be borne again, like any ordinary day.

Library Link ◆ *You can read more about Jody and his experiences in the Florida Everglades by reading* **The Yearling,** *the book from which this excerpt was taken.*

 ## Reader's Response

What was your favorite part of this selection? Why?

The Yearling

Responding to Literature

1. Jody remembers a day when "the air itself was all but visible, golden with the rain-washed sunlight." Do you remember a day when the beauty of it became so special that it etched a memory in your mind? Describe your day.

2. Jody's life is different from the life most of us experience. What would happen if you and Jody traded places for a day?

3. Review this selection and find a descriptive phrase that you particularly like. Print this phrase neatly in large letters and draw a frame around it. Display your framed phrase. Did any classmate choose the same phrase you chose?

Writing to Learn

Think and Compare ♦ Jody shows us a day in April at the glen near the spring. What would this same place look like in February? Show likenesses and differences in a Venn diagram.

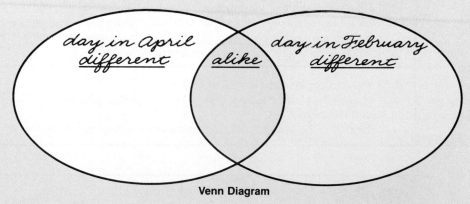

Venn Diagram

Write ♦ Write a journal entry about a visit to the glen in February. Tell how it is the same or different from the description in this selection.

Describe an object in your home without naming it. See how quickly someone can name what you are describing. The person who can guess the object then describes an object in his or her home.

SPEAKING and LISTENING ◆
Giving Descriptive Details

Think of how often you describe something to others in the course of a day. For example, in school you may describe to your teacher an idea for a project. At home you may describe to a family member something you saw on a class trip.

When you describe objects, events, people, or other types of information to others, it is important to use clear and vivid details. This helps your listeners "see" what you are describing.

Which sentence below helps you see the scene depicted?

> A furry squirrel jumped from branch to branch on a huge oak tree near my house.
>
> A squirrel was near my house.

The first description has more vivid details. These details help you to picture the squirrel in action.

Use the following guidelines when giving and listening for descriptive details.

Giving Details	1. Observe your subject carefully and have a clear picture of it before beginning your description. 2. Use appropriate words for specific details so that listeners can picture what you are describing. 3. Use gestures or drawings to enhance your description.
Listening for Details	1. Listen closely for each important detail. 2. For each detail, build a clear picture in your mind of what is being described. 3. Respond to the speaker with comments or by asking questions.

Summary ◆ Use specific, vivid details when describing something to others. Listen carefully to form a mental picture of what is being described.

Guided Practice

Describe two of the following subjects. Be sure to use specific details.

1. your bedroom
2. your favorite food
3. a flower
4. a bicycle
5. a person on television
6. your best friend

Practice

A. Write at least two specific details that would help a listener picture each of the following subjects.

7. a parade
8. your school building
9. the street you live on
10. your desk at school
11. one of your relatives
12. a favorite outfit
13. a rainy day
14. a beautiful place in nature

OSPREY'S NEST *painting by Winslow Homer*
Sterling and Francine Clark Art Institute
Williamstown, Massachusetts

B. Study the painting by the American artist Winslow Homer on this page. Then write as many descriptive details about the painting as you can. Read your description to a partner. Did you both include the same details?

C. Choose two photographs or illustrations from this or another textbook. Describe the photographs or illustrations to a partner without letting your partner see them. Be sure to use specific details in your descriptions. See if your partner can name the subjects you are describing.

Apply • Think and Write

Picturing Details • Ask a relative, such as a parent or grandparent, to describe a special event or incident from his or her childhood. Listen carefully to the details. Then list the details that helped you picture the description. Tell what you liked about the description.

✎ **Remember**
that specific details help listeners picture what you are describing.

Describe the smell, look, taste, and feel of a fruit, such as a banana. Ask if others can add more details to your description.

WRITING ◆
Sensory Details

One of the most common ways in which writers create effective descriptions is by using details that appeal to the five senses. They write about how something looks, feels, sounds, smells, or tastes in order to get readers involved in a story. These sensory impressions help the reader experience what the writer is describing.

Details that appeal to any of the five senses are called sensory details. These details convey particular sensations to a reader and help make your writing more concrete. Study these examples of sensory details from *The Yearling*.

Sight: He waded across to the opposite bank where the growth was more open.

Touch: It was good to be warm at his head while his hard calloused feet were cold.

Hearing: The water made a sound like kittens lapping.

Smell: He drew deep breaths of the pines, aromatic with wetness.

Taste: She laid out biscuits for him, and a plate of hash, and poured him a cup of sweet milk. She watched him eat.

When you write, choose words that are specific and colorful. Sometimes just one word can express the entire sensory impression you want to convey.

■ The water made a sound like kittens <u>drinking</u>.
■ The water made a sound like kittens <u>lapping</u>.

Notice that the word *lapping* gives a more vivid impression of how the water actually sounded.

> **Summary** ◆ Use **sensory details** to make your writing more specific and concrete.

Guided Practice

Tell which of your senses each of the following images appeals to.

1. The creamy chocolate pie melted in my mouth.
2. The sun sent beaming yellow rays through the front window.
3. The kitten's soft fur brushed against my skin.
4. Distant traffic hummed like a swarm of bees.
5. The odor of burnt toast permeated the air in the kitchen.

Practice

A. Write a sentence describing each subject below. Each sentence should appeal to one of the five senses.

6. an onion	**10.** fresh coffee percolating
7. honey on bread	**11.** a wild deer running
8. a forest brook	**12.** an earthquake occurring
9. a high mountain	**13.** a roasted marshmallow

B. For each item below, write two sentences.

14. how my pet looks	**17.** how a pine forest smells
15. how the sea sounds	**18.** how a silk scarf feels
16. how an orange tastes	**19.** how an old building looks

C. Choose one of the following topics. Write a paragraph that describes the scene. The paragraph should appeal to as many of the senses as possible.

a circus	a football game
a fishing trip	a fall leaf tour in New England
a museum	a stampeding herd of wild buffalo

Apply ◆ Think and Write

Dictionary of Knowledge ◆ Artists sometimes rely on writers' descriptions to help them create images. For example, N.C. Wyeth illustrated Jody with his flutter-mill, as shown on page 312, using details given in *The Yearling*. Read about N.C. Wyeth in the Dictionary of Knowledge. Write how you think sensory details helped Wyeth create beautiful illustrations for *The Yearling*.

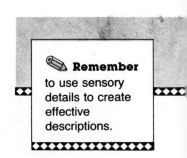

✎ **Remember**
to use sensory
details to create
effective
descriptions.

Describe your hair as if it were actually a person. For example:
My hair stood up when I heard the mysterious noise.
See how many "human" qualities you can give to your hair.

WRITING ♦
Figurative Language

As you know, using accurate details in your writing is important. Such details help to convey exact images to the reader. When you describe how things actually look, sound, or feel, you are using literal language. With literal language, you say precisely what you mean.

Sometimes, however, you may wish to describe images in a more imaginative way. You then use figurative language. Figurative language is not meant to be interpreted in a literal sense. Notice the difference between these examples.

Literal: Melanie had new ideas.
Figurative: Melanie broke ground with her new ideas.

Of course, Melanie did not actually break the ground. With figurative language, you say things in new ways.

You can also use figurative language to make comparisons. Similes, metaphors, and personification are types of figurative language that compare. A simile compares by using the words *like* or *as*.

■ **The bobcat was like a raging storm.**

A metaphor compares by saying that something *is* something else.

■ **The snow is a blanket on the rooftops.**

In personification, something nonhuman is given human qualities.

■ **The dancing snowflakes leaped to Earth.**

Later in this book, you will see how similes, metaphors, and personification are used in poetry.

> **Summary** ♦ Use **figurative language** to convey vivid images. **Similes**, **metaphors**, and **personification** help the reader see something in a new way.

Guided Practice

Tell whether each sentence is an example of simile, metaphor, or personification.

1. The rain slapped the concrete sidewalks.
2. The horse leaped like a graceful ballerina.
3. The moon was a round bouncing ball.

Practice

A. Write each sentence, underlining the example of figurative language in the sentence. Write whether it is an example of simile, metaphor, or personification.

4. The angry lion ran like a bolt of lightning.
5. A lazy river crawled through the lush valley.
6. The mountain groaned in pain during the earthquake.
7. Like an agile mountain goat, the climber scaled the slope.
8. He is a tiger in his devotion to endangered species.

B. Write a sentence to describe each subject. Use figurative language in your descriptions.

9. a trainer holding out a fish for a porpoise
10. a forest ranger aiding an injured deer
11. a fisher waiting for a bite on his line
12. a calm lake after vacationers have left
13. a forest after a heavy snowfall

C. The following sentences are written in literal language. Rewrite each sentence, using figurative language.

14. The plant grew very tall.
15. A friend came over to my house.
16. There was lightning in the sky.
17. The wind blew the leaves on the trees.
18. She walked to the park.

Apply • Think and Write

Describing an Object • Write a paragraph in which you describe one of your favorite possessions, such as a bicycle or a piece of clothing. Use figurative language to make the object vivid to the reader.

✎ **Remember**
to use figurative language to convey vivid images in your writing.

Think of someone in your school or community with whom classmates would be familiar. Use one important detail to describe the person. Continue adding details until someone guesses who the person is.

WRITING ◆
Organizing a Descriptive Paragraph

You have learned that using specific details in your writing can help a reader actually see what you are describing. However, you must organize the details into cohesive paragraphs to make them understandable. How you organize the details usually depends on your purpose for writing and what you are describing.

There are various methods for organizing a descriptive paragraph. Space order and order of impression are two common methods.

Space order is usually used to describe persons, places, or things in a logical order. For example, in writing a description of your home, you might begin by describing the outside of the home. Then you could go on to describe the inside of the home, room by room. In this way, readers would understand how all parts of the home are logically connected. A particular room might be described from left to right or from near to far.

In order of impression, you begin with details that might be noticed first. Then you describe details that might be noticed next. You continue in this way until the reader has a clear picture of the person or thing you are describing. Order of impression is used most often in describing people. For example:

> Tall, lanky Michele walked very fast to wherever she was going. She always seemed to be in a hurry. Her hair was dark and curly, and she was constantly brushing two annoying curls out of her eyes. Her eyes, blue and sparkling, danced with mischievous delight whenever she had an idea.

Summary ◆ A descriptive paragraph may be organized by **space order** or by **order of impression**.

Guided Practice

Tell which method of organization—space order or order of impression—each sentence illustrates.

1. At first glance, Mabel's expression looked angry.
2. As you enter, the dining room is on the left.
3. His hands twitched nervously as he waited.

Practice

A. Write the kind of organization you would use for each writing situation.

    4. a description of a woman who wears silly hats
    5. a letter describing a bird-watching trip to a friend
    6. a journal entry describing the new camp director
    7. an article describing certain flowers
    8. a paragraph about a man noted for his unusual strength

B. Read the paragraph below from *Roughing It* by Mark Twain. Then write which method of organization it uses.

We . . . sat down on a huge overhanging lava-shelf, tired but satisfied. The spectacle presented was worth coming double the distance to see. Under us, and stretching away before us, was a heaving sea of molten fire of seemingly limitless extent. . . . At unequal distances all around the shores of the lake were nearly white hot chimneys or hollow drums of lava, four or five feet high. . . .

C. Write a paragraph describing one of your friends or family members. Use order of impression in your description. Begin by describing the most noticeable details about the person.

Apply • Think and Write

Describing a Place • Think of a place that you have really enjoyed visiting, such as a park, museum, or zoo. Write about the place. Use space order to describe how the place looked and order of impression to describe people or animals that you saw.

Remember to organize ideas in descriptive paragraphs in a logical way.

Focus on Mood

Mood means atmosphere. A writer may create a mood in various ways. Sometimes a story's setting conveys the mood. Sometimes action does it, sometimes dialogue, and sometimes carefully chosen details. In *The Yearling,* which you read earlier, Marjorie Kinnan Rawlings's setting creates a mood of mystery.

- When Jody awakes, he is "in another world."
- The sun is gone, along with "all the light and shadow."
- He sees "no black boles of live oaks, no glossy green of magnolia leaves, no pattern of gold lace…"
- The world is "a gentle gray," and the rain is "a mist as fine as spray from a waterfall."

By noting the absence of familiar details like sun, trees, and leaves, Rawlings suggests something unusual, something mysterious. Later she focuses on action to produce a mood of confusion and fear.

- A doe scents Jody, and there is "a scuffled confusion in the sand where she had wheeled in fright."
- The tracks of the doe "had long harried streaks behind them."

Mood is created through details and through the words the writer chooses to present those details. A skillful writer such as Marjorie Kinnan Rawlings can make you feel the atmosphere of her story. Your goal as a writer is to do the same thing — to use words and details that convey exactly the mood you want.

The Writer's Voice ◆ Describe a natural setting in a way that suggests a calm mood. Use words that convey calmness — *quiet, peaceful, placid*, and so on. Then describe the same setting in a way that suggests a restless mood. Use words that convey restlessness — *jumpy, roving, troubled*, and so on.

Working Together

Mood in a story is often easier to feel than it is to explain. Creating the right mood in an original piece of writing can be an exciting challenge. As a group, work on activities **A** and **B**.

In Your Group
♦ Contribute your ideas.   ♦ Agree or disagree in a pleasant way.
♦ List responses.   ♦ Help the group finish on time.

A. Discuss the contrasting moods of the paragraph below. Find and list four words that are important in conveying the two moods.

I was happily whistling a tune as I walked outside the campground early one morning at Ngorongoro National Park in Tanzania. I was eagerly looking forward to seeing my first African wild animals from the safety of the tour car. The night before, I had wanted to camp out in my small tent instead of the lodge. The game warden, however, had told me it was not allowed. Now, alarmingly, a huge water buffalo charged across my path. Terrified, I retreated to the lodge. Now I understood the game warden's concern. The park was really a zoo without walls.

B. As a group, go over each sentence above. Change the four listed words, and any other necessary words to create a new and different mood or moods. Change or omit any sentences or parts of sentences that do not help to convey the new mood(s).

THESAURUS CORNER ♦ Word Choice

Fourteen of the main entry words in the Thesaurus are adjectives. Write them down. Use at least three of the adjectives (or synonyms for them) in a paragraph conveying a specific mood. For example, *brave, strong,* and *far* might fit into a paragraph with a mood of high adventure. In your paragraph, make sure the words from the Thesaurus fit naturally and logically. Underline them. If possible, use more than three adjectives or their synonyms from the Thesaurus.

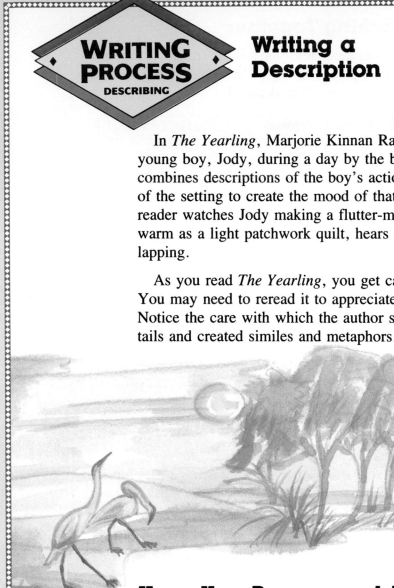

WRITING PROCESS

DESCRIBING

Writing a Description

In *The Yearling*, Marjorie Kinnan Rawlings describes a young boy, Jody, during a day by the bank of a stream. She combines descriptions of the boy's actions and descriptions of the setting to create the mood of that long-ago place. The reader watches Jody making a flutter-mill, feels the sun as warm as a light patchwork quilt, hears the water like kittens lapping.

As you read *The Yearling*, you get caught up in the story. You may need to reread it to appreciate the writer's craft. Notice the care with which the author selected sensory details and created similes and metaphors.

Know Your Purpose and Audience

In this lesson you will write a description. Your purpose will be to inform your audience about a place you know well. You will use sensory details and figurative language to create the mood you feel when you are there.

Your audience will be younger students. Later you can choose a way to share your description with an elementary school audience.

What's MY PURPOSE

Who's MY AUDIENCE

1 Prewriting

First choose your topic—the place you will write about. Then choose a strategy for gathering details about it.

Choose Your Topic ♦ Make a list of your favorite places. List every place that gives you a good feeling. Then choose the place that you can describe the most vividly.

Think About It

You might include a childhood hideout, a scenic park, or a historical site in your town. Then circle the one place you can remember best or that you can easily visit to observe.

Talk About It

With your class brainstorm a list of possible places. Seeing a long list of possible topics will help you get an idea for your own special place.

Topic Ideas

My favorite places:
— under the bridge beside
    the barn
— the apple orchard
— my bedroom
— the vegetable garden
— the corner chair in
    the library
— the fountain

Choose Your Strategy ◆ Read the strategies that follow. Then use one or both of the strategies for help in gathering ideas for your description.

PREWRITING IDEAS

CHOICE ONE

A Mental Movie

Run a mental movie. Pretend you are in the place you will describe. Let your experiences there run like a film across the screen of your mind. What do you see? What do you hear? How does it make you feel? Take notes about what you observe as you run your mental movie.

Model

CHOICE TWO

A Venn Diagram

Use a Venn diagram to develop a simile or metaphor. List one detail and something to compare it with. Fill in details about how the two things are alike or different. Use the alikes to help create a simile or metaphor.

Model

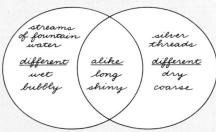

streams of fountain water

silver threads

different
wet
bubbly

alike
long
shiny

different
dry
coarse

Metaphor: long silvery threads of water

2 Writing

Start with a topic sentence that identifies your place and catches your readers' interest. These are examples.

- I am always drawn to Grandma's attic because it is filled with special family heirlooms.
- As a child, I had a special hideout on a rocky hill.

Naturally, you can't describe *everything* about your place. Instead decide on a single impression or one mood that you want to convey. Complete this sentence: My place makes me feel ____. Describe what people do in that place and the sensory details that contribute to the central impression or mood.

Sample First Draft ◆

The Frog Fountain at Symonds square is a cheerful spot. I sit there and watch the children. Nearby, grown-ups chat together on wooden benches. It's a restful place for a daydream and the noises of the city seem very far.

A giant Frog King made of gray stone stands in the middle of the fountain. He wears a golden crown that sparkles in the sun surrounding him is a circle of small frogs. Water streams from their mouths in long, silvery threads. The splashing water sounds like the aplause of a happy audience. Sometimes a playful breeze sprays glittering mist on passersby. Even when I'm feeling down, the Frog Fountain cheers me up. I pass the Fountain every day on my way home from school. I often stop there for a while.

3 Revising

Revise to sharpen your description and clarify your meaning. This plan for revising may help you.

FIRST Read to Yourself

As you read, review your purpose. Did you write a description of a place that you know well? Consider your audience. Would a younger student enjoy your description? Listen to the sounds of your writing. Are you hesitating or adding words? Put a pencil check to show where you may make revisions.

Focus: Have you selected details that contribute to a single impression or mood?

THEN Share with a Partner

Read your description aloud to a partner. These guidelines may help you.

The Writer

Guidelines: Read slowly and clearly. Then listen to your partner's responses.

Sample questions:
• What kind of details would a younger audience like to hear?
• **Focus question:** What would you say is the central mood of my description?

The Writer's Partner

Guidelines: As you listen, remember that the audience will be younger children. Give helpful ideas based on that knowledge.

Sample responses:
• Younger children might like to hear more about _____.
• This detail doesn't seem to go with the mood.

Revising Model ✦ Here is a draft description that the writer is revising. The marks show changes the writer wants to make.

Revising Marks

delete   ℓ

add   ∧

move   ⟋

The writer's partner thought a younger audience would enjoy this detail.

The writer decided the mood is cheerful rather than restful.

Remote is a more precise word than *far*.

Miniature is a more vivid adjective than *small*.

This sentence was moved to reinforce the mood at the end.

     The Frog Fountain at Symonds square is a cheerful spot. I sit there and watch the children. *sail paper boats in the reflecting pool* Nearby, grown-ups chat together on wooden benches. It's a restful place for a daydream and the noises of the city seem very far. *Everyone seems to have a good time* *and the cares* *remote*

     A giant Frog King made of gray stone stands in the middle of the fountain. He wears a golden crown that sparkles in the sun surrounding him is a circle of ~~small~~ frogs. *miniature* Water streams from their mouths in long, silvery threads. The splashing water sounds like the aplause of a happy audience. Sometimes a playful breeze sprays glittering mist on passersby Even when I'm feeling down, the Frog Fountain cheers me up. I pass the Fountain every day on my way home from school. I often stop there for a while.

Read the draft description above with the writer's revisions. Then revise your own description.

Grammar Check ✦ Vivid adjectives can enliven a description.
Word Choice ✦ Precise words convey meaning clearly. A thesaurus is a source of synonyms for vague words like *talk*.

Revising Checklist

☐ **Purpose:** Did I write a description of a place I know well?

☐ **Audience:** Will younger students enjoy my description?

☐ **Focus:** Did I select details that contribute to a single impression or mood?

4 Proofreading

Fixing surface errors is a courtesy to your readers. A correct copy is easier to read.

Proofreading Model ♦ Here is the draft description of Frog Fountain. Proofreading changes have been added in red.

Proofreading Marks

capital letter	≡
small letter	/
add comma	⌄
add period	⊙
indent paragraph	¶
check spelling	◯

Proofreading Checklist

- ☐ Did I spell words correctly?
- ☐ Did I indent paragraphs?
- ☐ Did I use correct capitalization?
- ☐ Did I use correct punctuation?
- ☐ Did I type neatly or use my best handwriting?

> The Frog Fountain at Symonds square is a cheerful spot. I sit there and watch the children. *sail paper boats in the reflecting pool* Nearby, grown-ups chat together on wooden benches. It's a restful place for a daydream and the noises of the city seem very far. *Everyone seems to have a good time and the cares remote*
>
> A giant Frog King made of gray stone stands in the middle of the fountain. He wears a golden crown that sparkles in the sun. surrounding him is a circle of small frogs. *miniature* Water streams from their mouths in long, silvery threads. The splashing water sounds like the aplause of a happy *applause* audience. Sometimes a playful breeze sprays glittering mist on passersby. Even when I'm feeling down, the Frog Fountain cheers me up. I pass the Fountain every day on my way home from school. I often stop there for a while.

PROOFREADING IDEA

Spelling Check

To catch errors, concentrate on one line of your draft at a time. Place a ruler under each line you read to block out the remainder of the text.

Now proofread your description and make a neat copy. Be sure to add a title.

5 Publishing

You and your classmates can read your descriptions aloud to each other in small groups. You can also post them on a bulletin board. Here are two ways of sharing them with a younger audience.

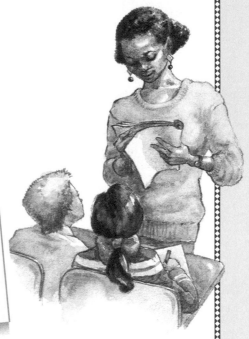

Frog Fountain

The Frog Fountain at Symonds Square is a cheerful spot. I sit there and watch the children sail paper boats in the reflecting pool. Nearby, grown-ups chat together on wooden benches. Everyone seems to have a good time, and the cares of the city seem very remote.

A giant Frog King made of gray stone stands in the middle of the fountain. He wears a golden crown that sparkles in the sun. Surrounding him is a circle of miniature frogs. Water streams from their mouths in long, silvery threads. The splashing water sounds like the applause of a happy audience. Sometimes a playful breeze sprays glittering mist on passersby.

I pass the fountain every day on my way home from school. I often stop there for a while. Even when I'm feeling down, the Frog Fountain cheers me up.

PUBLISHING IDEAS

Share Aloud

Your class might visit younger elementary school classes, two or three of you to each class. Pass out drawing paper and crayons. Then read your descriptions aloud. Have the children draw pictures of the place you describe. See how clear your description was by the details the children include.

Share in Writing

Send the class's descriptions to other elementary classrooms. Your teacher might ask the other teacher(s) to read the descriptions aloud. Ask if the younger children might send back ''picture postcards'' with a picture of one description on the front and a message on the back.

CURRICULUM
·CONNECTION·

Writing Across the Curriculum Science

Zoologists classify animals. Making Venn diagrams can help you "look over the zoologists' shoulders" as they decide how to group animals by likenesses.

Writing to Learn

Think and Compare The fish you see here live more than half a mile below the surface of the sea. Make a Venn diagram to compare the likenesses and differences of any two of the fish.

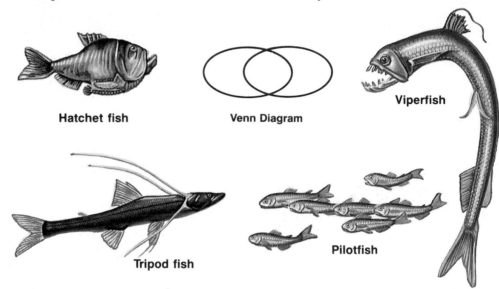

Hatchet fish   Venn Diagram   Viperfish

Tripod fish

Pilotfish

Write Use your Venn diagram to write about the characteristics of deep-sea fish that live in almost total darkness.

Writing in Your Journal

At the beginning of this unit, you wrote about wildlife. Then you went on to read about special relationships between people and animals. In your journal write why you believe it is or is not important to preserve animal species.

Read More About It

Rascal *by Sterling North*
This heart-warming tale tells of the adventures of a boy and his pet raccoon. Narrated in the first person, *Rascal* is based on the author's own experience.

Newbery Honor Book

Mrs. Frisby and the Rats of NIMH
by Robert O'Brien
When the lab rats at the National Institute of Mental Health are able to increase their learning ability, they use their intelligence to escape and set up their own society. The careful use of facts and details help make the science fiction aspects of this plot believable.

Newbery Award

Stranger at Green Knowe *by Lucy M. Boston*
Set in an English country house, this highly original story describes the understanding and affection that develops between a young refugee and a gorilla that has escaped from a zoo.

Book Report Idea   Character Questionnaire

A questionnaire is a practical way to find out information. For your next book report, you can design and complete a questionnaire that will tell others about a character you've met in a book. When writing your questionnaire, think of categories and questions that will explore the traits and interests of the book character.

> Date: January 15, 1774
> Name: Johnny Tremain
> Home: Boston, Massachusetts
> Interests: silversmithing;
>   horses; revolution
> Recent Accomplishments:
>   participation in Boston
>   Tea Party

Unit 6

Adjectives   *pages 294–301*

A. Write the adjectives in each sentence. Include the articles.

1. An eerie silence fell over the huge stadium.
2. Fans were standing now in several shady areas.
3. It was a wise choice, given the overwhelming heat.
4. Snakelike lines of thirsty people formed at the lone fountain.
5. A polite and patient crowd applauded the boisterous teams.

B. Write and label each proper and demonstrative adjective.

6. Who cooked these Chinese vegetables?
7. This recipe calls for Swiss chocolate.
8. That French dressing of oil and vinegar is seasoned with pepper and mustard.
9. We need those potatoes for the Irish stew.
10. Is this Hispanic festival a New York tradition?

C. Write the comparative and superlative forms of each adjective.

11. many
12. sad
13. little
14. peaceful
15. bad
16. sweet
17. good
18. angry
19. flexible

D. Write whether each underlined word is used as a noun, an adjective, or a pronoun.

20. Theresa is a <u>city</u> girl, and she prefers to remain in the <u>city</u>.
21. <u>Many</u> people enjoy the country, but <u>many</u> do not.
22. <u>This</u> happened yesterday, but I heard about it only <u>this</u> morning.
23. The old <u>desk</u> chair is too big for the new <u>desk</u>.
24. The <u>poetry</u> was selected from this <u>poetry</u> book.

Context Clues *pages 302–303*

E. Choose one of the following adjectives to complete each sentence. Use context clues and a dictionary for help. Write the sentence.

impoverished   paramount   benevolent   opulent

25. The ruler of that country is known as the ____ queen because she promotes the happiness of her people.
26. Some people in this movie are extremely poor; they look ____.
27. Look at that huge luxurious house; it must be ____.
28. Everyone listened carefully to the last announcement; it was of ____ significance.

Sensory Details *pages 318–319*

F. Write which of your senses each of the following images appeals to.

29. The distinct fragrance of roses filled the room.
30. A column of smoke swirled in the air.
31. A fly landed on my nose and tickled it.
32. I was awakened by the blast of a car radio.
33. The sweet and sour sauce was a delicious combination of flavors.

G. Write a sentence to describe each item below. Each sentence should appeal to one of the senses.

34. the sight of a newborn chick
35. the taste of oatmeal
36. the feel of a baseball glove
37. the smell of newly cut grass
38. the sound of a siren
39. the sight of a tornado

Figurative Language *pages 320–321*

H. Write each sentence. Underline each example of figurative language. Label it *simile*, *metaphor*, or *personification*.

40. The train roared through the station like an angry lion.
41. The young tree crouched in fear during the hurricane.
42. The sky was a blue sea.
43. My cat jumped like a leaping frog.

CUMULATIVE REVIEW

UNIT 1: Sentences *pages 4–19*

A. Write each sentence. Underline the simple subject once and the verb twice.

1. A baby whale was beached this summer.
2. Surprised and curious bathers had alerted authorities.
3. Several marine biologists towed the whale back to the ocean.
4. The startling event may be repeated next summer.

B. Write and label the compound subject or compound verb in each sentence.

5. Hungry bees and busy ants descended upon the picnic grounds.
6. People forgot their leftovers or discarded them.
7. Grounds workers gathered the trash and hauled it away.
8. Now signs or park workers remind people of their picnic duties.

C. Write *simple* or *compound* for each sentence.

9. Thousands of sandbags were flown to the flooded area.
10. The floodwaters rose dramatically, and then they receded.
11. The community could finally relax.
12. The danger was over, but the cleanup was ahead.

UNIT 2: Nouns *pages 56–65*

D. Write each noun. Label it *common* or *proper*.

13. Ann made a great effort in the recent debate.
14. She debated the issue of censorship with her opponent.
15. Then Charlie reported on the amazing travels of Marco Polo.

E. Write each noun. Label it *singular, singular possessive, plural*, or *plural possessive*.

16. Julie's
17. geese's
18. fringes
19. niece
20. goose's
21. empresses'

UNIT 3: Verbs   *pages 118–129*

F. Write each verb. Label it *LV* for linking verb or *AV* for action verb.

 22. Mars seems unreal.   **24.** You get it all.
 23. We spotted a deer.   **25.** The fish tasted salty.

G. Write each sentence. Then label all direct objects and indirect objects.

 26. Show my friend and me the new art supplies.
 27. Can you find the stray dog a good home?
 28. Sean bought his mother and grandmother flowers and candy.
 29. Dorothy pitched me an impossible curveball.

H. Write and label each predicate nominative *PN* or each predicate adjective *PA* in the sentences.

 30. This musical composition is a student's creation.
 31. It was an inspiration to all of us.
 32. The composer is creative and sensitive.
 33. The musicians are skillful.

UNIT 4: Verbs   *pages 174–187*

I. Write each underlined verb and its tense: *present perfect, past perfect*, or *future perfect*.

 34. In the next election many more citizens <u>will have voted</u>.
 35. The reporters <u>have followed</u> the candidates closely.
 36. They <u>had traveled</u> back and forth across the country.

J. Write the verb in each sentence. Label it *active* or *passive*.

 37. My family and I moved to this small town recently.
 38. Our home is located on a quiet, tree-lined street.
 39. The local high school boasts a championship football team.

K. Write the correct form of the verb in each sentence.

 40. The lazy cat is (lying, laying) on the sofa.
 41. Dad is (sitting, setting) the dishes on the table.
 42. Prices have (risen, raised) sharply this year.

UNIT 5: Pronouns *pages 232–247*

L. Write the sentences, underlining each possessive pronoun.

43. Please take your shoes from my closet and put them in yours.
44. When you're finished, we will separate our clothes.
45. How many of their books are in his house?
46. The skirt is hers, but it's not in its place.

M. Write and label each interrogative and demonstrative pronoun.

47. Are these the answers?
48. Who is at the door?
49. Which are your favorite desserts?
50. Those were left behind.

N. Write and label each reflexive or intensive pronoun and its antecedent.

51. We can save ourselves a lot of trouble this time.
52. The clown saw himself in the mirror and laughed.
53. She herself forgot the keys to the house.
54. Perhaps you yourself have misplaced something.

O. Write each indefinite pronoun. Label it *singular* or *plural*.

55. Many filled out the job application.
56. Someone called back several for an interview.
57. A few were highly qualified, but only one was hired.
58. The others went for interviews in different departments.

P. Write each sentence, underlining the pronouns. Label the pronouns *subject* or *object*.

59. Kim and I watched them at the press conference.
60. They were the astronauts for the next space shuttle mission.
61. Who will join us in the cheering section?
62. Whom did you recognize among the crew?

Q. Write the correct pronouns in parentheses.

63. (He, Him) and (she, her) play guitars in the band.
64. Do (they, them) play better than (we, us)?
65. Arturo and (she, her) watched (they, them) at the concert.
66. The audience gave (we, us) performers a round of applause after the first act.

UNIT 6: Adjectives   *pages 294–301*

R. Write the adjectives in each sentence. Include the articles.

67. The extraordinary book became an immediate success.
68. A dramatic and mysterious chain of events occurs in the book.
69. Vivid, likeable characters capture the imagination.
70. The exotic setting adds an adventurous and romantic mood to the story.
71. The creative writer wrote crisp, witty dialogue.

S. Write and label each proper or demonstrative adjective.

72. This Victorian mansion has Italian marble in several rooms.
73. There is Chinese furniture in that room.
74. Persian rugs adorn these hallways.
75. The African sculpture was placed in the English garden.
76. Those luxuries were added by a team of Hollywood decorators.

T. Choose the correct words in parentheses to complete the sentences. Write the sentences.

77. Mary Jane was the (happiest, most happiest) person in the neighborhood.
78. Her sick dog was getting (better, more better) every day.
79. The veterinarian is (hopefuller, more hopeful) today (than, then) yesterday about the dog's recovery.
80. For Mary Jane this news was the (better, best) she had ever heard.
81. Compared with today's doctor bill, last month's bill was (more expensive, most expensive).

U. Write whether each underlined word is used as a noun, an adjective, or a pronoun.

82. Those flowers are ordinary, but these are unusual.
83. Denise wants to be an investment banker and make an investment in her future.
84. One can do much work in one hour.
85. Computer magazines contain advertisements for all the latest computers.
86. This is a work of fiction, and this person is the fiction writer.

Parts-of-Speech Puzzler

Ten words in the passage below are used as two different parts of speech. Write the words and their different parts of speech.

This vacation Jessica decided to do something unusual. Her friend Danny asked her what vacation spots she had in mind. She told him that camping in a wilderness area was her first choice. He reacted with surprise.

"Wouldn't you mind surprise visits from wild animals in your tent at night? And how would you like tent living in a heavy rain?"

Jessica admitted those ideas didn't appeal to her, but she did want adventure.

"You've read too many adventure stories," Danny said. "For the wilderness you'll need rain gear, good camping equipment, and nerves of steel. Frankly, I don't find any appeal in the wild."

Verse Reversal

Six of the adjectives in this verse can also be used as nouns in sentences. Find the adjectives and use them as nouns in your own verse or in sentences about King Arthur.

When good King Arthur ruled this land,
The castle kitchen was a place so grand.
A dinner menu might include
A colossal array of royal food.
On the table lay greens from a vegetable plot,
And apple cobbler, steaming hot.
Yes, this generous king pleased family friends
And amazed town nobles with his culinary blends.

Unit 6 Extra Practice

1 Writing with Adjectives

p. 294

A. Write the adjective in each sentence.

1. All fans rejoiced.
2. Happy times came.
3. Wheat is plentiful.
4. Spend the money.
5. Buy new clothes.
6. They seem anxious.
7. Good pupils study.
8. Do each lesson.
9. Learn many things.
10. Make wise choices.
11. Days can be rainy.
12. Brown leaves fell.

B. In this article about a photograph, there are twenty underlined words. Ten are adjectives. Write each adjective after its sentence number.

13. One famous photograph was used to make a picture most Americans know well. **14.** On February 9, 1864, Abraham Lincoln walked from the White House to the photographic studio of Mathew Brady. **15.** Lincoln had an unusual face that challenged every photographer. **16.** Some pictures showed an ugly, ordinary man. **17.** His political enemies even used poor photographs of him to frighten voters. **18.** On that day in 1864, Brady took numerous pictures of the illustrious President. **19.** One picture especially revealed Lincoln's great dignity, anxiety, and tenderness. **20.** Later an engraver used that photograph to make the picture of Lincoln that is on every five-dollar bill.

C. Write each sentence. Then underline the adjectives.

21. High winds and stormy seas delayed the ship.
22. Flowers, bright and fragrant, bloomed there.
23. It was easy, painless, and profitable.
24. She gave complete answers to both questions.
25. A warm welcome awaits another new customer.
26. A short rest under a shady tree seemed appropriate.
27. The delightful day had taken us through miles of lush land.

D. Artist Francis Carpenter used the twenty-five adjectives in this article to describe Abraham Lincoln's face. Write each adjective after its sentence number. Do not write the article *the*.

28. The face of Lincoln was strange but powerful. **29.** Hair, coarse and unmanageable, spilled down his wide, high forehead. **30.** His thick eyebrows and heavy eyelids cast shadows over his gray eyes. **31.** Dark rings circled the sad, tender eyes. **32.** Long, deep wrinkles plowed across his large, hollow cheeks and into the short, rough beard on his sturdy chin. **33.** His nose was straight and prominent. **34.** His lips were thick yet delicate. **35.** His look revealed great thoughtfulness and much gentleness.

E. Look at an American one-dollar bill. Then write the paragraph, substituting adjectives for the blanks.

36. The one-dollar bill has a ＿＿ portrait of George Washington. **37.** The President looks ＿＿ and ＿＿. **38.** He has ＿＿ eyes, a ＿＿ mouth, and a ＿＿ jaw. **39.** His ＿＿ clothes are ＿＿. **40.** The portrait has an ＿＿ shape and ＿＿ leaves at the base.

2 Proper and Demonstrative Adjectives

p. 296

A. Write the proper adjective in each sentence.

1. The Hawaiian climate is usually delightful.
2. The Australian wilderness is known as the outback.
3. The Austrian slopes are favorites of skiers.
4. That restaurant serves fine Italian food.
5. French or Middle Eastern food is also available.
6. Some New York shops sell East Indian clothing.

B. Write each proper adjective in this article after its sentence number. Write *none* if a sentence has no proper adjective.

7. Engravings of famous faces appear on the currency of many nations. **8.** Portraits of Queen Elizabeth II are on Canadian dollars and British pounds. **9.** Solemn faces of Norwegian, Swedish, and Danish monarchs can be seen on Scandinavian money. **10.** A German hero may be found on a mark. **11.** On the colorful money of France and Spain, pictures of French and Spanish authors have appeared.

C. Write each demonstrative adjective. Then write the noun it modifies.

   12. These four dictionaries belong to my brother.
   13. Did your father plant those trees?
   14. This book is a Russian novel.
   15. Her aunt made that shelf in one day.
   16. That old red car belongs in a museum.
   17. We discussed those political issues once.
   18. Why is this old sweater so loose?
   19. Be careful on that icy sidewalk.
   20. I found these skates in our attic.
   21. Those last tests were unusually easy.

D. Write each sentence, completing it with the kind of adjective indicated in parentheses.

   EXAMPLE: Who polished (demonstrative) surfboard?
   ANSWER: Who polished that surfboard?

   22. (Demonstrative) knapsacks feel very light.
   23. Has anyone tried (demonstrative) sauerkraut?
   24. We sampled pieces of (proper) bread.
   25. (Proper) winters can be extremely cold.
   26. (Proper) artists made (demonstrative) rings.
   27. Who is (demonstrative) actor?
   28. I ate (proper) dinner at my grandmother's.
   29. Have you seen (demonstrative) sketch?
   30. A (proper) automobile just passed us.
   31. (Demonstrative) students are in the band.
   32. We are reading (proper) poetry.
   33. Take (demonstrative) microscopes to the lab on the second floor.

3 Using Adjectives to Compare   *p. 298*

A. Write each adjective. Label it *comparative* or *superlative*. Then write its positive form(s) after it.

1. richest	**3.** colder	**5.** thinnest	**7.** merrier	**9.** less
2. quicker	**4.** greatest	**6.** hotter	**8.** most	**10.** happier

B. Write the correct word to complete each sentence.

11. That car is the (older, oldest) of the two.
12. That car is the (older, oldest) of the three.
13. Barbara is the (more, most) dependable twin.
14. Keep the (smaller, smallest) of the two pieces.
15. Of the five books, which one is (better, best)?
16. Who is (younger, youngest), Allison or Kelly?
17. Which is (better, best), the book or the movie?
18. I am the (luckier, luckiest) student in America.
19. We are (busier, busiest) today than they are.
20. Both stalks are large, but this is (larger, largest).

C. Write the correct comparative or superlative form of each adjective in parentheses.

21. Noreen has the (bright) eyes we have ever seen.
22. Tear it in two, and give me the (large) piece.
23. Both hats are small, but the red one is (small).
24. Which report is (interesting), hers or his?
25. This is the (expensive) of the two tractors.
26. I have had many bad colds, but this one is the (bad).
27. Of the three birds, the blue one is the (noisy).
28. I feel (cheerful) today than I did last night.
29. It is the (humorous) story I have ever read.
30. My flashlight is dim, but yours is even (dim).
31. Letters are usually (long) than telegrams.
32. Of the two stamps, this one is (valuable).
33. Of the two signatures, yours is (legible).
34. I have (much) mail than you have.
35. This is the (funny) of the two get-well cards.
36. The new telephone is (pretty) than the old one.
37. *E.T.* was the (good) half of the double feature.

D. Write each sentence, using either *than* or *then*.

38. Our cat is cleaner ____ theirs.
39. His paintings are larger ____ her paintings.
40. They studied intensively and ____ took the test.
41. It is now later ____ you think.
42. Proofread your letter and ____ mail it.

4 Words as Different Parts of Speech   *p. 301*

A. Write each underlined word. Label it *adjective* if it modifies a noun. Label it *noun* if it is used as a noun.

1. The cafeteria manager has another surprise.
2. The cafeteria will be painted purple.
3. There are no carrots in their garden.
4. Garden magazines are on the green shelf.
5. The coach revised the basketball schedule for the third time in a week.
6. We played basketball yesterday.
7. The elevator should be repaired soon.
8. The elevator inspector is on the third floor.
9. This parakeet food is expensive.
10. This parakeet talks too much.
11. Butter and other foods are stored in that ice house.
12. These butter churns date from the eighteenth century.
13. The ice wagon hauled ice from the river.
14. A lot of ice was used in the days before refrigerators.

B. Write each underlined word. Label it *adjective* if it modifies a noun. Label it *pronoun* if it is used as a pronoun.

15. Who taught you that trick?
16. That amazed everyone.
17. These are definitely the best bargains.
18. Have you seen those towels?
19. In this picture they look very young.
20. How did this ever happen?
21. That looks like a real emerald!
22. Did the doctor examine both legs?
23. Both should be examined carefully.
24. Each teacher read the composition.
25. Each was impressed with its excellence.
26. All is well in the city tonight.
27. Covers should be on all books.
28. Do you have any transparent tape?
29. I don't have any with me now.
30. This shop has many interesting antiques.
31. That is the oldest rocking chair I've ever seen.

UNIT
SEVEN

USING LANGUAGE
TO

IMAGINE

=== PART ONE ===

Unit Theme   *The Creative Mind*

Language Awareness   Adverbs

=== PART TWO ===

Literature   "The Open Window" by Saki

A Reason for Writing   Imagining

Writing
IN YOUR JOURNAL

WRITER'S WARM-UP ◆ You probably experience creative impulses from time to time. For example, you might have a sudden urge to make up a song, write a poem, or draw a picture. Do you know anyone who seems especially creative? Think of a situation in which you saw creativity at work. Describe the experience in your journal.

GETTING STARTED

Have a classmate name a verb. Can you add a word that describes the verb and begins with the same letter as the verb?

swim *swiftly*   drop *down*   run *rapidly*

1 Writing with Adverbs

Adjectives and adverbs have similar uses in our language. They modify or describe other words in a sentence. Adverbs are used to modify verbs, adjectives, and other adverbs.

Mrs. Ruiz carefully read the passage. (modifies verb)

She has a wonderfully imaginative book. (modifies adjective)

Mrs. Ruiz reads very dramatically. (modifies adverb)

Most adverbs answer one of these questions about the word they modify: *How? When? Where? How often? To what extent?*

How?	She told the story well.
When?	She will read now.
Where?	She put the book away.
How often?	She reads frequently.
To what extent?	She nearly finished the book.

The adverb in each of the following sentences modifies a verb. Notice that an adverb can come before or after the verb it modifies. It can also appear between the parts of a verb phrase.

Soon all of us *will read* the book.
All of us *will read* the book soon.
All of us *will* soon *read* the book.

You can see that an adverb that modifies a verb can appear almost anywhere in a sentence. However, an adverb that modifies an adjective or another adverb usually comes directly before the word it modifies.

Adverbs Modifying Adjectives

quite nice   really enjoyable   completely true

Adverbs Modifying Other Adverbs

so well   quite often   rather carefully

Many adverbs end in *-ly—happily, sadly, warmly*. Remember, though, that some adjectives also end in *-ly*, and that some words can be used as either adverbs or adjectives.

Adverb: I buy the paper <u>daily</u>.
Adjective: I buy the <u>daily</u> paper.

Certain commonly used adverbs are sometimes not recognized as adverbs because they do not end in *-ly*. Four of these adverbs are often used to begin questions: *how, when, where,* and *why.* Twenty more adverbs that do not end in *-ly* are shown in the chart below.

We are <u>almost</u> ready.	You should read <u>more</u>.
Gina has <u>already</u> read it.	I <u>never</u> read that book.
I will <u>also</u> read the book.	She has <u>not</u> seen it.
He <u>always</u> enjoys fantasies.	<u>Perhaps</u> you'll enjoy it.
Did you <u>ever</u> read this?	We <u>seldom</u> hurry.
This will last <u>forever</u>.	We enjoyed it <u>so</u> much.
The book will be <u>here</u>.	I am <u>still</u> reading it.
I <u>just</u> finished that book.	Put the book <u>there</u>.
Jan likes that one <u>least</u>.	The book was <u>too</u> short.
<u>Maybe</u> I'll read it.	Have you read it <u>yet</u>?

Summary ♦ An **adverb** modifies a verb, an adjective, or another adverb. Use adverbs to make your writing more clear and exact.

Guided Practice

Name the adverbs in the sentences. Tell what question is answered by each adverb.

1. Yesterday Randy borrowed a book of science fiction.
2. He sometimes calls it "sci-fi."
3. He is quite particular in his choice of books.
4. Betty Jean had eagerly opened the book to Chapter 1.
5. There she became totally lost in an imaginary world.

Practice

A. Write the adverb in each sentence.

   6. Very creative books are Nora's favorite.
   7. Nora often reads works of fantasy and imagination.
   8. She really enjoyed the Grimm brothers' fairy tales.
   9. She still likes imaginative tales of this type.
  10. Recently she read Richard Adam's *Watership Down*.
  11. Why is it a popular book of fantasy?
  12. The book describes some wonderfully incredible rabbits.
  13. One male rabbit has the rather unlikely name of Hazel.
  14. When did Hazel become worried about their home?
  15. He quickly sets out with some friends to find a new home.

B. Write each underlined adverb. Then write the word or words each adverb modifies. Label the word or words modified as *verb*, *adjective*, or *adverb*.

  16. The rabbits' journey is <u>terribly</u> difficult.
  17. The group <u>finally</u> locates a site for a new home.
  18. They are <u>also</u> looking for new members for their group.
  19. <u>Very</u> <u>often</u> these rabbits struggle with the rabbits of nearby Nuthanger Farm.
  20. The <u>ferociously</u> terrible General Woundwort rules the rabbit warren at that farm.
  21. General Woundwort is <u>almost</u> <u>too</u> strong for Hazel's group.
  22. Hazel and his group <u>never</u> doubt themselves.
  23. The two groups of rabbits meet in an <u>extremely</u> nasty battle.
  24. <u>Soon</u> General Woundwort disappears.
  25. After many adventures, Hazel and his group <u>eventually</u> find a new home.

C. Two words in each sentence end in -*ly*. One is an adverb and one is an adjective. Decide which word in the sentence is modified by each -*ly* word. Then write the adverb.

26. Each evening Nora quietly reads her nightly tale of imagination and fantasy. **27.** Last week she eagerly read about an elderly creature from outer space. **28.** This week she desperately wanted another lovely book. **29.** Nora quickly ran to the stately new library. **30.** A friendly librarian helpfully recommended *The Hobbit,* by J.R.R. Tolkien. **31.** Nora was immediately intrigued by this lively book, the first of a series of related novels. **32.** Another kindly librarian read stories hourly to toddlers. **33.** A weekly program informs readers about newly available books. **34.** New books are constantly displayed in an orderly way. **35.** Borrowers eagerly read the daily announcements on the library's bulletin board.

D. Write each sentence. Complete it with an adverb from the chart on page 351.

36. My brother has read ____ every fantasy book in the library!
37. He ____ misses an opportunity to read.
38. His books are kept ____ on this shelf.
39. ____ has he found a book he didn't enjoy.
40. Has he read any biographies ____?
41. ____ he will appreciate realistic books when he gets older.

E. Write the groups of words below, using an adverb that answers the question in parentheses to complete each phrase.

42. (to what extent?) young boy
43. wrote stories (how often?)
44. put his pencil (where?)
45. (how?) called it finished
46. read it to us (when?)

47. people listened (how?)
48. they responded (how?)
49. praised them (how?)
50. liked it (to what extent?)

Apply ◆ Think and Write

From Your Writing ◆ Read what you wrote for the Writer's Warm-up. List the adverbs you used and the words they modify. Can you add adverbs to any sentences to make your writing more exact?

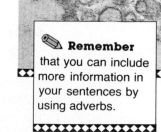

✎ **Remember**
that you can include more information in your sentences by using adverbs.

How many different ways can you complete these sentences?
Harry spoke _____ .   Arturo spoke _____ than Harry.
Gus spoke ____ of all.

2 Using Adverbs to Compare

Adverbs change forms to show comparison in the same way that adjectives do. The degrees of comparison of adverbs are shown below.

Positive Degree: Tom lives <u>close</u> to the library.
Comparative Degree: Eva lives <u>closer</u> to the library than Tom does.
Superlative Degree: Emma lives the <u>closest</u> to the library of all.

How to Form Comparative and Superlative Degrees

Add -*er* or -*est* to the positive form of most one-syllable adverbs.

fast	**late**	**straight**
faster	**later**	**straighter**
fastest	**latest**	**straightest**

Put *more* or *most* before the positive form of most adverbs of two or more syllables.

smoothly	**promptly**	**frequently**
more smoothly	**more promptly**	**more frequently**
most smoothly	**most promptly**	**most frequently**

Become familiar with those adverbs that have irregular forms in the comparative and superlative degrees.

well	**badly**	**much**	**little**
better	**worse**	**more**	**less**
best	**worst**	**most**	**least**

Use the comparative degree to compare two persons or things. Use the superlative to compare three or more.

Comparative: Do you like fantasy <u>more</u> than nonfiction?
Superlative: I like fantasy <u>most</u> of all.

Summary ♦ Many adverbs have three forms—the **positive**, the **comparative**, and the **superlative**.

Guided Practice

Name the comparative and superlative forms of each adverb.

1. little   **2.** fast   **3.** easily   **4.** hard   **5.** quickly

Practice

A. Write the comparative and superlative forms of each adverb.

6. near	**8.** long	**10.** deep	**12.** badly	**14.** clearly
7. well	**9.** bravely	**11.** heavily	**13.** slow	**15.** rapidly

B. Write the correct comparative or superlative form of the adverb in parentheses.

16. Some authors write (imaginatively) than others.
17. Edgar Allan Poe wrote (creatively) than most writers.
18. Which of his many short stories do you like (well)?
19. ''The Fall of the House of Usher'' ends (mysteriously) than any other story on my shelves.
20. I read it the (fast) of all.
21. Did you finish Kipling's *The Jungle Book* (soon) than I did?
22. Kipling describes the jungle animals (realistically) than most writers.
23. Mark Twain's *A Connecticut Yankee in King Arthur's Court* portrays the Middle Ages the (vividly) of all my books.
24. It seems to bring that faraway time (near) to us than any history book does.
25. Which of these authors do you think writes the (well) of all?

C. Write either the comparative or the superlative form of the adverb in each phrase below. Write a sentence using the new phrase.

26. read carefully	**29.** like much	**32.** waited eagerly
27. listen quietly	**30.** soar high	**33.** finished quickly
28. played badly	**31.** stood close	**34.** left soon

Apply • Think and Write

Evaluating a Story ♦ Think of a favorite short story that really impressed you. Describe what it was about the story that makes you remember it. Use different degrees of adverbs to help the reader understand exactly why you liked the story so much.

> ✎ **Remember**
> to use degrees of adverbs to make precise comparisons.

Does the store where this sign appeared have any apples or not?

We haven't no apples today.

3 Using Negatives Correctly

An affirmative sentence can be made negative by the use of just one negative word. If an extra negative word is added, the result is an error called a double negative.

Affirmative (right):	I found the book.
Negative (right):	I found <u>no</u> book.
Negative (right):	I did <u>not</u> find a book.
Double Negative (wrong):	I did <u>not</u> find <u>no</u> book.

Below are commonly used negative words.

neither	nobody	not (n't)	barely
never	none	nothing	hardly
no	no one	nowhere	scarcely

Mistakes sometimes occur with *hardly*, *scarcely*, and *barely*. They are negatives and should not be used with other negatives.

Double Negative (wrong):	I <u>hardly</u> <u>never</u> misplace a book.
Negative (right):	I <u>hardly</u> ever misplace a book.

Many contractions include *n't* in place of the word *not*. Remember that *not* is a negative and should not be used with other negatives.

Double Negative (wrong):	I <u>couldn't</u> enjoy <u>no</u> book more.
Negative (right):	I <u>couldn't</u> enjoy any book more.

> **Summary** ◆ A **double negative** is the incorrect use of two or more negative words in a sentence.

Guided Practice

Name the negative word in each sentence.

1. Few people haven't read Mary Norton's book *The Borrowers*.
2. The Borrowers are not your usual creatures.
3. These tiny people are hardly as big as your hand.

Practice

A. Write the negative word in each sentence.

4. Haven't you ever misplaced something?
5. Perhaps you did not misplace those things at all.
6. Hardly anything escapes the clutches of the Borrowers.
7. None of them use normal furniture or utensils.
8. They are never at a loss for things, however.
9. Couldn't a thimble make a bathtub for a tiny Borrower?
10. Surely nobody would guess a postage stamp could be a rug.
11. Things such as safety pins and postage stamps are scarcely ever missed by their owners.
12. No one but the Borrowers could have taken such things.
13. Nothing escapes their notice.

B. Write the correct word in parentheses.

14. Most people don't (ever, never) see the Borrowers.
15. Borrowers won't let (anyone, no one) see them.
16. In Mary Norton's book there are hardly (any, no) Borrowers left anywhere.
17. These few Borrowers haven't (anywhere, nowhere) to live.
18. The group does not have much time to find (some, no) shelter.

C. Write each sentence, correcting any double negatives you find. If a sentence is correct, write *correct*.

19. For a while the family of Borrowers can't find no place away from human beings.
20. No one will leave the family of Borrowers alone.
21. The Borrowers don't never have special powers.
22. They aren't scarcely different, except in size, from humans.
23. Nobody shouldn't miss this wonderfully imaginative book.

Apply ♦ Think and Write

Imagining Story Characters ♦ Imagine a family of unusual creatures you might create for a story. Write a paragraph describing them. Use some negative words.

✎ **Remember** to be sure you do not use any double negatives.

GETTING STARTED

Try temporarily to tell tricky tongue twisters.
Jolly Jay joyfully jotted jokes in his journal.
The bothersome baby barely babbled banal ballads.

4 Using Adjectives and Adverbs

Many adjectives become adverbs when the suffix *-ly* is added to them. Note the changing forms below.

Adjective: quick   confident   clear
  Adverb: quickly   confidently   clearly

Because such adjectives and adverbs are so similar, mistakes are often made in their use. The most common error is using the adjective when an adverb is needed.

> **Correct:** Arthur Rackham sketched <u>confidently</u>. (not <u>confident</u>)

When you are unsure whether to use an adjective or an adverb, identify the word being modified. If the word that is modified is a verb, use the adverb.

■ **Arthur Rackham** <u>carefully</u> **illustrated many children's books.**

If the word modified is a noun or pronoun, use the adjective.

■ **The pictures are** <u>wonderful</u>.

In the sentence above, *wonderful* is a predicate adjective that modifies the noun *pictures*. The linking verb *are* links the predicate adjective to the subject.

> **Summary** ♦ Verbs are modified by adverbs. Nouns and pronouns are modified by adjectives.

Guided Practice

Tell which word correctly completes each sentence.

1. Arthur Rackham was (famous, famously) as a book illustrator.
2. None of his illustrations were drawn (bad, badly).
3. He drew (skillful, skillfully) and well.
4. Readers waited (devoted, devotedly) for his illustrations.
5. His drawings for *Grimm's Fairy Tales* were (original, originally).

Practice

A. Learn more about Arthur Rackham, the well-known English artist, from the sentences below. Write the adjective or adverb that completes each sentence correctly.

6. Rackham drew (effective, effectively).
7. He (thoughtful, thoughtfully) went about his work.
8. Rackham was (proud, proudly) of his professional work.
9. His work remains (popular, popularly) with people.
10. His imagination was (amazing, amazingly) in its variety.
11. The blending of realism and fantasy is (unusual, unusually).
12. His creatures (routine, routinely) perform common chores.
13. He (skillful, skillfully) used the lines of tree bark and tree branches to add to the feeling of his drawings.
14. The creatures and gnarled trees are (sociable, sociably).
15. Rackham's art was very (creative, creatively).

B. Write an adverb ending in *-ly* to modify the underlined verb.

16. Arthur Rackham <u>drew</u> ＿＿＿ .
17. Rackham ＿＿＿ <u>portrayed</u> the events of the stories.
18. He ＿＿＿ <u>considered</u> the plots and characters of the books.
19. He ＿＿＿ <u>chose</u> many difficult topics and scenes for his work.
20. People <u>responded</u> ＿＿＿ to his drawings.

C. Write an adjective to modify the underlined subject.

21. Rackham's <u>illustrations</u> were ＿＿＿ for years.
22. <u>Readers</u> felt ＿＿＿ looking at them.
23. Rackham's <u>drawings</u> for *Peter Pan* became ＿＿＿ .
24. His <u>works</u> were highly ＿＿＿ .
25. <u>They</u> were ＿＿＿ in style and design.

Apply • Think and Write

Dictionary of Knowledge ◆ Read about the artistic style of Kate Greenaway, another famous illustrator, in the Dictionary of Knowledge. Write a paragraph about the kinds of drawings she made. Use several adjectives and adverbs in your writing.

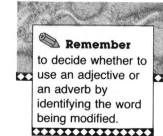

> ✎ **Remember**
> to decide whether to use an adjective or an adverb by identifying the word being modified.

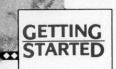

GETTING STARTED

Can you think of other word pairs to substitute for the underlined words in the sentence below?

A real diamond is really expensive.

5 Troublesome Adjectives and Adverbs

Certain adjectives and adverbs are often confused. Study the rules below for using these adjectives and adverbs properly.

Good, Well

Good is an adjective. It modifies a noun or a pronoun.
The Hobbit is a good example of fantasy.

Well is an adverb. It modifies a verb.
The author, J.R.R. Tolkien, writes well.

Well is an adjective when it means "in good health."
I love to read when I feel well.

Real, Really

Real is an adjective that means "actual" or "true."
This is a real first edition of The Hobbit!

Really is an adverb that means "actually" or "truly."
I really enjoyed Tolkien's The Lord of the Rings, too.

Sure, Surely

Sure is an adjective that means "certain."
Are you sure you read all three books in that series?

Surely is an adverb that means "certainly."
Yes, I did and I surely did enjoy them.

Summary ◆ Do not use an adjective when an adverb is needed. Knowing the meanings of confusing adjectives and adverbs can help you choose the right ones to use.

Guided Practice

1. How (good, well) do you feel today?
2. I (sure, surely) will finish *The Hobbit* today.
3. I am (real, really) enjoying the adventures of Bilbo Baggins.

Practice

A. Write each sentence using *good* or *well* where needed.

4. Lewis Carroll was another gifted author who possessed a _____ imagination.
5. How _____ do you know his first delightful book *Alice's Adventures in Wonderland*?
6. He wrote so _____ that even today adults and children are amused by Alice's escapades.
7. It is a _____ story filled with fanciful characters.
8. Are you feeling _____ enough to discuss the book?

B. Complete each sentence with one of the words below.

sure   surely   well   good   real   really

9. Lewis Carroll was an English author whose _____ name was Charles L. Dodgson.
10. *Alice's Adventures in Wonderland* is _____ my favorite book for children.
11. I have always thought it was an especially _____ book.
12. Many parts of the book are _____ wonderful.
13. In it the Red Queen often does not feel _____, so she complains about her health.

C. Write each sentence, correcting any errors in the use of adjectives or adverbs.

14. According to Carroll, Alice behaved good at home.
15. The changes in her behavior are real amusing.
16. I first read the book one day when I did not feel good.
17. It sure became my favorite book because of its incredible creatures and their adventures.
18. I am surely several copies of it are in every library.

Apply ✦ Think and Write

Imagining a Fantasy World ✦ Use your imagination to write two paragraphs describing a fantasy world and its creatures. Try to include in your writing at least four of these words: *good*, *well*, *real*, *really*, *sure*, and *surely*.

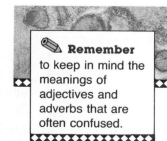

✏ **Remember** to keep in mind the meanings of adjectives and adverbs that are often confused.

Play "Repeat That, Please." Create sentences like these:
Inventors think inventively. Directors give direction.
Teachers hope their students are teachable.

VOCABULARY ✦
Suffixes

A **suffix** is a word part added to the end of a base word. A suffix changes the meaning and sometimes the part of speech of the word to which it is added. Read each sentence below.

1. "What a <u>marvel</u>!" thought Hilda.
2. "I just had a <u>marvelous</u> idea."
3. "I'll treat my sister <u>marvelously</u> and then ask to borrow her dress."

What part of speech is *marvel* in sentence 1? What parts of speech are *marvelous* in sentence 2 and *marvelously* in sentence 3?

Study the six common suffixes in the chart below. Knowing these suffixes can help you analyze the meanings of unknown words.

Suffix	Meaning and Part of Speech	Example
-able	capable of being (adjective)	manageable
-ion	act or result of (noun)	invention
-ize	become; cause to become (verb)	vocalize
-ly	like; in the manner of (adverb)	really
-or	a person or thing that does (noun)	actor
-ous	having or full of (adjective)	glorious

Building Your Vocabulary

State the meaning of each underlined word. Use the base word in parentheses and the chart above for help.

1. The doctors hoped the patient's condition would <u>stabilize</u>. (stable)
2. He walked <u>casually</u> across the street. (casual)
3. The old shack was boarded up because it was not <u>livable</u>. (live)
4. The heat <u>sensor</u> was sensitive enough to detect the body heat of a rabbit. (sense)
5. The thief used all means of <u>deception</u> to win at cards. (deceive)
6. It was a <u>marvelous</u> idea. (marvel)

Practice

A. Write a definition for each underlined word. Use the base word in parentheses and the chart of suffixes for help.

   1. The cook fell asleep and burned the food <u>severely</u>. (severe)
   2. Climbing the steep face of the mountain was quite <u>hazardous</u>. (hazard)
   3. The <u>narrator</u> told the story with great skill. (narrate)
   4. The letter was <u>crudely</u> written. (crude)
   5. Mildred's story was quite <u>believable</u>. (believe)
   6. We called the <u>exterminator</u> to rid the house of termites. (exterminate)
   7. The judge was quick to obtain a <u>conviction</u>. (convict)
   8. We had a <u>measurable</u> amount of rain. (measure)
   9. John's mother is always trying to <u>civilize</u> him. (civil)

B. The suffixes *-ion* and *-or* form nouns when added to verbs. Using these suffixes, form nouns from the underlined verbs to complete the sentences below. Write the sentences.

   10. Stamps that are <u>collected</u> form a ____ .
   11. A person who <u>collects</u> stamps is a ____ .
   12. A person who <u>exhibits</u> stamps is an ____ .
   13. Stamps are <u>exhibited</u> in an ____ .

C. Add *-ly* and *-ize* to the base words below to form adverbs and verbs. Then write a paragraph using some of the words you form.

   civil   **final**   **ideal**   **local**   **real**

Language Corner ◆ Town Names

The suffix *-ton* is used in the names of many cities and towns. Since *-ton* is an old form of *town*, *Kingston* means "King's town." In fact, *-burg(h)* also means "town," and *-ville* means "village."

Name some *-ton*'s, *burg(h)*'s, and *ville*'s in your state.

How to Expand Sentences with Adverbs

In this unit you have learned how adverbs can be used to modify verbs, adjectives, and other adverbs. Because adverbs tell *how, when, where,* or *to what extent,* they can add important details and information to your writing. Notice how adverbs have been added in sentence **2** to expand it and to include more information.

> **1.** Lisa read the rest of the book.
> **2.** Lisa quickly read the rest of the book today.

Example **2** not only tells what Lisa read, it also tells how and when she read it. The addition of the adverbs allows the reader to more clearly understand Lisa's accomplishment.

When you add adverbs to sentences be careful not to use the same adverb too many times in a piece of writing. Overusing an adverb can make sentences annoying to read.

> **3.** Lisa really enjoyed the book and found it really interesting. She really wants to read it again really soon.
> **4.** Lisa really enjoyed the book and found it extremely interesting. She even wants to read it again soon.

Notice that the sentences in example **3** are repetitive and difficult to read because of the overused adverb *really*. By simply changing or eliminating that adverb, the sentences in example **4** are easier to read.

The Grammar Game ♦ How do *you* do it? The verbs below name common actions that are performed every day. Quickly write two or three adverbs to describe how you perform each action.

speak	walk	read	listen
cook	study	play	watch
write	dress	brush	laugh

Working Together

As your group completes activities **A** and **B**, you will find that adverbs will make your writing more interesting and informative.

In Your Group
♦ Invite others to talk. ♦ Agree or disagree in a pleasant manner.
♦ Listen to each other. ♦ Show appreciation for different opinions.

A. Add adverbs to make the sentences below more detailed and interesting. Choose at least two adverbs that give different kinds of information to each sentence.

1. The phone rings during the day.
2. The cast was rehearsing.
3. Dan found the watch.
4. The fog lifted.
5. Kate delivers the mail.

B. Rewrite this paragraph, adding or changing adverbs as needed.

John reads and has books to suggest. He went to the library after school to get a new book. He had heard this book was really good. His friends had said he would really enjoy it. He walked into the library. "Do you have a copy of *The Lord of the Rings?*" he asked the librarian. "I want to read it."

WRITERS' CORNER ♦ Word Choice

If the verb you use in a sentence does not give enough detail, add an adverb to describe it. However, sometimes by choosing a more specific verb, you can replace a vague verb *and* an adverb.

EXAMPLE 1: **"Meet me in the lunchroom after class," he said softly.**

EXAMPLE 2: **"Meet me in the lunchroom after class," he whispered.**

Example **2** does not change the meaning of the sentence, but the use of the more specific verb makes the adverb unnecessary. Read what you wrote for the Writer's Warm-up. Could you have used more specific verbs rather than adding adverbs?

A DREAM   *painting by Minnie Evans*
The North Carolina Museum of History, Raleigh

UNIT SEVEN

USING LANGUAGE TO

IMAGINE

PART TWO

Literature "The Open Window" by Saki

A Reason for Writing Imagining

CREATIVE *Writing*

FINE ARTS ◆ What do you suppose was the dream that prompted Minnie Evans to paint this painting? Try to recreate it. First identify the objects pictured, then make up a story that ties them all together.

CREATIVE THINKING ♦
A Strategy for Imagining

A THOUGHT BALLOON

Imagining is an essential skill for fiction writers. After this lesson you will read a highly imaginative story, ''The Open Window'' by Saki. Later you will use your imagination to write a short story of your own.

Usually, a short-story writer wants the reader to understand the story characters' points of view. The writer plainly describes how the characters think and feel. However, there are times when a writer wants to keep the reader guessing. Consider this as you read the following passage from ''The Open Window.'' Here, Mr. Framton Nuttel has just met the niece of a woman to whom he is paying a visit.

> ''Then you know practically nothing about my aunt?'' pursued the self-possessed young lady.
> ''Only her name and address,'' admitted the caller. . . .
> ''Her great tragedy happened just three years ago,'' said the child. . . . ''Out through that window, three years ago to a day, her husband and her two young brothers went off for their day's shooting. They never came back.''

Can you imagine what Mr. Nuttel must be thinking? Do you know what the niece is thinking? Can you guess?

Learning the Strategy

It is often useful to understand someone else's point of view. For example, imagine a race in which you ran your fastest time ever. You feel you ran well because of your own hard work and talent. Would you be surprised if your coach had a somewhat different idea? How might understanding others' viewpoints affect what you would say to each other after the race? Or imagine you are playing chess with your sister. You've played together often,

CREATIVE THINKING: Point of View

and you have a good idea how she will react to each of your moves. How is understanding her point of view helpful? Or imagine that there is a new girl in your class. She is very good-looking. You assume she is going to be very popular. What would she think if you went up to her and said hello? Can you imagine?

A thought balloon is one strategy for imagining someone else's point of view. For example, put yourself in the place of that new girl in your class. Imagine she sees you approaching and hears you say hello. The thought balloon below shows what she might think. Do you agree? What do *you* think she would think?

Oh, how nice! I was wondering if anyone would speak to me!

new girl

Using the Strategy

A. Imagine that you and your best friend are fooling around in the library. Your friend backs into a book rack and knocks it over. You see the librarian hurrying toward you. Make thought balloons for you, your friend, and the librarian. If you like, draw a cartoon based on your ideas.

B. Reread the passage from ''The Open Window'' on page 368. What, do you suppose, is the point of view of Mr. Nuttel about the disappearance of the three men? What, do you suppose, is the niece's point of view about it? Make a thought balloon for either Mr. Nuttel or the niece. Then read ''The Open Window'' and decide if you were right.

Applying the Strategy

- You have probably never been a librarian. How did you figure out what the librarian's point of view would be for **A** above?
- Have you ever tried to change someone else's point of view? Why?

The Open Window

by Saki

"*My* aunt will be down presently, Mr. Nuttel," said a very self-possessed young lady of fifteen; "in the meantime you must try and put up with me."

Framton Nuttel endeavoured to say the correct something which should duly flatter the niece of the moment without unduly discounting the aunt that was to come. Privately he doubted more than ever whether these formal visits on a succession of total strangers would do much towards helping the nerve cure which he was supposed to be undergoing.

"I know how it will be," his sister had said when he was preparing to migrate to this rural retreat; "you will bury yourself down there and not speak to a living soul, and your nerves will be worse than ever from moping. I shall just give you letters of introduction to all the people I know there. Some of them, as far as I can remember, were quite nice."

Framton wondered whether Mrs. Sappleton, the lady to whom he was presenting one of the letters of introduction, came into the nice division.

"Do you know many of the people round here?" asked the niece, when she judged that they had had sufficient silent communion.

"Hardly a soul," said Framton. "My sister was staying here, at the rectory, you know, some four years ago, and she gave me letters of introduction to some of the people here."

He made the last statement in a tone of distinct regret.

"Then you know practically nothing about my aunt?" pursued the self-possessed young lady.

"Only her name and address," admitted the caller. He was wondering whether Mrs. Sappleton was in the married or widowed state. An undefinable something about the room seemed to suggest masculine habitation.

"Her great tragedy happened just three years ago," said the child; "that would be since your sister's time."

"Her tragedy?" asked Framton; somehow in this restful country spot tragedies seemed out of place.

"You may wonder why we keep that window wide open on an October afternoon," said the niece, indicating a large French window that opened onto a lawn.

"It is quite warm for the time of the year," said Framton; "but has that window got anything to do with the tragedy?"

"Out through that window, three years ago to a day, her husband and her two young brothers went off for their day's shooting. They never came back. In crossing the moor to their favourite snipe-shooting ground they were all three engulfed in a treacherous piece of bog. It had been that dreadful wet summer, you know, and places that were safe in other years gave way suddenly without warning. Their bodies were never recovered. That was the dreadful part of it." Here the child's voice lost its self-possessed note and became falteringly human. "Poor aunt always thinks that they will come back some day, they and the little brown spaniel that was lost with them, and walk in at that window just as they used to do. That is why the window is kept open every evening till it is quite dusk. Poor dear aunt, she has often told me how they went out, her husband with his white waterproof coat over his arm, and Ronnie, her youngest brother, singing, 'Bertie, why do you bound?' as he always did to tease her, because she said it got on her nerves. Do you know, sometimes on still, quiet evenings like this, I almost get a creepy feeling that they will all walk in through that window—"

She broke off with a little shudder. It was a relief to Framton when the aunt bustled into the room with a whirl of apologies for being late in making her appearance.

"I hope Vera has been amusing you?" she said.

"She has been very interesting," said Framton.

"I hope you won't mind the open window," said Mrs. Sappleton briskly; "my husband and brothers will be home directly from shooting, and they always come in this way. They've been out for snipe in the marshes today, so they'll make a fine mess over my poor carpets. So like you men-folk, isn't it?"

She rattled on cheerfully about the shooting and the scarcity of birds, and the prospects for duck in the winter. To Framton it was all purely horrible. He made a desperate but only partially successful effort to turn the talk on to a less ghastly topic; he was conscious that his hostess was giving him only a fragment of her attention, and her eyes were constantly straying past him to the open window and the lawn beyond. It was certainly an unfortunate coincidence that he should have paid his visit on this tragic anniversary.

"The doctors agree in ordering me complete rest, an absence of mental excitement, and avoidance of anything in the nature of violent physical exercise," announced Framton, who laboured under the tolerably wide-spread delusion that total strangers and chance acquaintances are hungry for the least detail of one's ailments and infirmities, their cause and cure. "On the matter of diet they are not so much in agreement," he continued.

"No?" said Mrs. Sappleton, in a voice which only replaced a yawn at the last moment. Then she suddenly brightened into alert attention–but not to what Framton was saying.

"Here they are at last!" she cried. "Just in time for tea, and don't they look as if they were muddy up to the eyes!"

Framton shivered slightly and turned towards the niece with a look intended to convey sympathetic comprehension. The child was staring out through the open window with dazed horror in her eyes. In a chill shock of nameless fear Framton swung round in his seat and looked in the same direction.

In the deepening twilight three figures were walking across the lawn towards the window; they all carried guns under their arms, and one of them was additionally burdened with a white coat hung over his shoulders. A tired brown spaniel kept close at their heels. Noiselessly they neared the house, and then a hoarse young voice chanted out of the dusk: "I said, Bertie, why do you bound?"

Framton grabbed wildly at his stick and hat; the hall-door, the gravel-drive, and the front gate were dimly noted stages in his headlong retreat. A cyclist coming along the road had to run into the hedge to avoid imminent collision.

"Here we are, my dear," said the bearer of the white mackintosh, coming in through the window; "fairly muddy, but most of it's dry. Who was that who bolted out as we came up?"

"A most extraordinary man, a Mr. Nuttel," said Mrs. Sappleton; "could only talk about his illnesses, and dashed off without a word of good-bye or apology when you arrived. One would think he had seen a ghost."

"I expect it was the spaniel," said the niece calmly; "he told me he had a horror of dogs. He was once hunted into a cemetery somewhere on the banks of the Ganges by a pack of pariah dogs, and had to spend the night in a newly-dug grave with the creatures snarling and grinning and foaming just above him. Enough to make any one lose their nerve."

Romance at short notice was her speciality.

Library Link ♦ *You can read other intriguing short stories like "The Open Window" in* The Story-Teller *by Saki.*

Reader's Response

Would you enjoy having Mrs. Sappleton's niece in your class? Explain why or why not.

The
Open Window

Responding to Literature

1. "The Open Window" would work well for a Readers Theatre. Readers read lines from the open book. A reader is needed for each character and a narrator is needed for the parts not spoken by characters. Remember to use your voice expressively to add to the telling of the story.

2. Mrs. Sappleton's niece was imaginative. If you had been the visitor, what story might she have made up about your abrupt departure?

3. Work with a partner to turn this story into a cartoon strip of four frames. Display your work and retell the story together.

Writing to Learn

Think and Imagine ◆ Imagine that Mr. Nuttel rushed from the house and bumped into you. If he had shared his thoughts at that moment, what might he have said? Sketch Mr. Nuttel and yourself. Add a thought balloon for each of you.

Thought Balloon

Write ◆ In the thought balloons, write Mr. Nuttel's words and your response. Use these comments as starting phrases to write a short dialogue between the two of you.

GETTING STARTED

As you tell about something you did recently, have a classmate interrupt you frequently. Describe how you feel.

SPEAKING and LISTENING ♦
Having Conversations

A conversation is an excellent opportunity to express yourself and to learn more about others. Good speaking and listening skills are important whether talking face-to-face or on the telephone. As you study the conversation guidelines below, think of how you might improve your own habits of communication so that you and others get the most from every discussion or conversation.

Speaking with Others	1. Thoughtfulness is the best general rule for a good conversation. Help to introduce yourself and others. 2. Share your ideas briefly and clearly. Encourage others to tell their ideas too. 3. Practice good conversation manners. Avoid comments that are boastful, embarrassing, or offensive. Remain friendly even when you disagree. 4. In a similar manner, begin each phone call with a greeting. Tell who you are and why you are calling. 5. If the person you are phoning is not available, leave a message that includes your name and your phone number.
Listening to Others	1. Be polite. Give the speaker your full attention and show it with eye contact. 2. Don't interrupt or start a side conversation with someone. 3. Show that you are listening carefully by asking questions that focus on the topic. 4. During phone conversations, listen carefully to the caller and, if necessary, take notes on important information. 5. If a telephone call is for someone who is not present, write the message and be certain the person receives it.

Summary ♦ Take an active part in conversations by speaking and listening in a manner that is considerate of others. Apply the same thoughtfulness when you use the telephone.

Guided Practice

Explain whether or not the behavior in each example below shows good conversational manners.

1. "Well, those are a few of my ideas. What do you think, Jim?"
2. "You don't know what you're talking about. Listen to this."
3. "Hello, this is Bill. May I speak to Dotty, please?"

Practice

A. With a partner take turns reading aloud the statements below. Choose the better response to each statement.

    4. "I know you're not through, Lee, but I totally disagree."
        a. "Don't you know how rude it is to interrupt?"
        b. "That's fine, but just let me finish what I'm saying."
    5. "Hi there, I'm Sam. This is a great party, isn't it?"
        a. "It sure is. My name's Toni. Do you know my friend Tom?"
        b. "It's okay, I guess."
    6. "I'd like to leave a message for your sister Tia, please."
        a. "Certainly. Give me your number; I have a pen ready."
        b. "Okay, what is it? If I see her, I'll try to remember it."

B. With classmates, role-play the conversation below. Change it so that each person responds more thoughtfully.

      Rhea: Hi, Dennis. Are you coming to the car wash on Saturday? And what do you . . .
  Dennis: Hey, here comes Carol.
    Carol: Hi, Rhea. The car wash? Yes, I'm . . .
    Rhea: You'd both better come. You never help.
  Dennis: Never mind that, Carol. Let's decide what movie we're seeing tonight.
    Rhea: I want an answer from both of you. Right now!

Apply • Think and Write

Writing Dialogue ♦ Take notes on an interesting conversation you've heard between friends, on television, or in the movies. See if you can develop it into a dialogue for a short story or a scene in a play you might write.

Remember
that courtesy is an important part of any conversation.

GETTING STARTED

Walking in the woods, you sense a presence behind you. A cold, clammy something taps you on the shoulder. You turn around. . . . Continue the story.

WRITING ♦
Elements of a Short Story

Short stories are amazing in their variety. Yet every short story has the same basic elements: character, setting, and plot.

Characters are the people or animals in a story. Most short stories focus on one or two main characters. Sometimes, minor characters are used to help the story along. In "The Open Window," for instance, the main characters are Mrs. Sappleton, Vera, and Mr. Nuttel because the action revolves around them. The lost husband and two brothers function as minor characters; the reader does not get to know them well. Saki, the writer, concentrates on the relationship that develops between the three main characters.

Setting is the time and place in which the story happens. In "The Open Window" the story takes place in a British country house during the early part of the twentieth century. There is always a good reason for the setting a writer chooses—where people are affects what they say and do. The house with "the open window" creates a sense of mystery that Saki wanted to achieve.

Plot is the story plan. It is the action, or sequence of events, and contains the **conflict,** or problem to be solved. Mr. Nuttel, for example, wants a room in a quiet retreat; the plot shows what happens to him. Many plots consist of a beginning, a middle, and an end. First, the writer begins by introducing the setting, the conflict, and the characters. Then, in the middle of the story, the action builds to a **climax,** or turning point. In "The Open Window" the turning point comes when Mr. Nuttel runs from the house in terror. In the end, the writer resolves the problem and ties up loose ends. Saki ends "The Open Window" by revealing that Vera, with her vivid imagination, probably made up the whole story.

> **Summary** ♦ The basic elements of a short story are **character, setting,** and **plot.**

Guided Practice

Tell whether each sentence illustrates character, setting, or plot.

1. The field was still, and the grandstand was silent and empty.

2. The detective kept her distance and stood there silently.

3. This was the clue that could crack the case wide open!

Practice

A. Study this story beginning. Then write three sentences. Tell something that you were able to learn about the character, about the setting, and about the plot.

"I want to go for the ride, right now, now, now!" said five-year-old Kris into the open hood of the car.

"As soon as the oil's changed, dear," said her father from where he lay on the driveway underneath the car. It seemed like the perfect day for both things, fixing the car and riding.

"Can we drive up the beach road?" Kris begged again.

"If you'll hand me the filter wrench now, yes," her father said.

B. Create notes for a story based on what you imagine as you look at one picture below. Write the words *Character, Setting,* and *Plot* on your paper. Make at least one entry for each heading.

C. Use your notes from **Practice B** to explain to a classmate how your entries would fit together to create a story.

Apply • Think and Write

Dictionary of Knowledge • Read about Edgar Allan Poe, America's master of the short story, in the Dictionary of Knowledge. Write a brief paragraph about the kinds of short stories that Poe wrote.

Remember that most short stories have a conflict, or problem to be solved.

Describe your trip to school this morning. Tell about it once, using the pronoun *I*. Then tell about it again, using the pronoun *he, she,* or *they*. With which method are you more comfortable? Why?

WRITING ◆
Third-Person Point of View

As you know, point of view is the vantage point from which a story is told. Earlier you learned about first-person point of view, in which a character in the story tells the story, using the personal pronoun *I*.

Writers often use third-person point of view to write about real people or fictional characters they create. Third-person point of view uses personal pronouns such as *he, she, it,* and *they*. This allows writers to tell the story from someone else's point of view. They tell the story as if they were observing the story and not taking part in it. Saki uses third-person point of view in ''The Open Window.'' Saki, the writer, is not a part of the story; he brings readers into the house and lets them know all about the characters' thoughts and actions.

> Framton Nuttel endeavored to say the correct something which should duly flatter the niece of the moment without unduly discounting the aunt that was to come. Privately he doubted more than ever whether these formal visits on a succession of total strangers would do much towards helping the nerve cure which he was supposed to be undergoing.

If Saki had told the story only from the niece's point of view, for example, then he could not have shared the other characters' thoughts with the reader.

Notice, too, that the story continues after Mr. Nuttel runs away. Since Mr. Nuttel is not telling the story, Saki can tell the reader how it ends.

> **Summary** ◆ Use **third-person point of view** to write about characters you create or people you know. Third-person point of view uses personal pronouns such as *he, she, it,* and *they*.

Guided Practice

Tell whether each statement uses first-person or third-person point of view.

1. She loved to watch the waves breaking up against the cliffs.
2. ''Please hand me the binoculars,'' I said to her quietly.
3. A long time passed as he studied something out beyond the surf.
4. I couldn't tell what it was, and it began to puzzle us both.
5. ''It looks like an old sea chest or trunk,'' she said.

Practice

A. Write whether each passage uses first- or third-person point of view. Explain how you knew the answer.

6. Arthur wanted to scramble down the cliff path right away and pull the sea chest out of the water. He asked Elsa to come with him, but she had always been afraid of heights.

7. ''Then I'll go down and you keep an eye on it,'' I said. Elsa answered with a nod and told me to be careful. I just hoped she wouldn't lose sight of it in the rising tide.

8. By the time he'd pulled the chest up onto the dry beach, Arthur saw that Elsa had made her way down to him. ''Do you think we can get it open? It looks old!'' she shouted.

B. Rewrite this passage, using the third-person point of view. Make any changes you like, but keep the point of view third person.

I felt along the tightly sealed edges of the sea chest. ''I don't know,'' I said to Elsa. ''It's been locked up for centuries.''

Our curiosity was growing by the minute. ''What ship lost the chest? What do you suppose is inside? Just think, Arthur,'' Elsa exclaimed, ''if it's a treasure, we'll be famous!''

''Come on,'' I replied. ''Let's get help and solve this mystery.'' I began to drag the chest down the beach.

Apply • Think and Write

Imagining ♦ What do you imagine Arthur and Elsa will see inside the chest when it is opened? Write a paragraph using the third-person point of view to describe this scene. What is inside? Do they become famous?

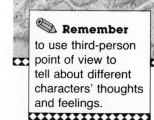

Remember to use third-person point of view to tell about different characters' thoughts and feelings.

Focus on Dialogue in Fiction

Most stories contain **dialogue** — characters talking with one an-other. Generally, dialogue is only one of a number of narrative devices used in a story. In "The Open Window," however, Saki constructs his story almost entirely with dialogue. Look back at "The Open Win-dow" on pages 370–374. Notice how Saki uses his characters' con-versations to develop each of the main elements of the story.

Plot   Traditional short stories consist of a beginning, a middle, and an end. "The Open Window" has such a structure. It begins with dialogue that introduces the aunt, Mr. Nuttel, and the niece Vera in a natural, almost casual way: "My aunt will be down presently, Mr. Nuttel," said a very self-possessed young lady of fifteen...."

Dialogue then carries the story all the way through the middle. The end is signaled by the appearance (in two narrative paragraphs) of three figures approaching in the twilight. Most of the end consists of conversation—mainly Vera's vivid, made-up tale explaining Mr. Nuttel's horror of dogs. It concludes with a line not in dialogue: *Romance at short notice was her speciality*.

Setting   The setting, including the pivotal open window, is shown mostly in dialogue. Vera's imagined scene on the moor is all in dialogue: ''In crossing the moor . . . they were all three engulfed in a treacherous piece of bog. It had been that dreadful wet summer....''

Character   Good dialogue shows the reader directly what the char-acters are like. You learn for yourself by judging their words, not by having the author tell you. Vera's two long speeches show clearly that ''romance'' is her speciality. She likes to tell fanciful tales.

The Writer's Voice ◆ Why, do you think, does Vera want Mr. Nuttel to "wonder" about the house's open window? What makes Vera's second tale — the one about pariah dogs on the Ganges — so effective?

Working Together

Dialogue in fiction can convey a great many aspects of plot, setting, and character. As a group, work on activities **A** and **B**.

In Your Group
♦ Contribute your ideas. ♦ Help the group to stay on the job. ♦ Record people's ideas. ♦ Help the group reach agreement.

A. Discuss the four items below. Use your imagination to convey the same information in four lines of dialogue. Have the group choose the best wording from among the suggestions.

1. Frank's small house is not attractive, but it is comfortable.
2. Frank's friend Nora cannot understand why he bought this unattractive little house instead of the better one he looked at.
3. Frank is very informal and doesn't care for fancy surroundings.
4. Frank decides to give Nora a tour of the tiny house.

B. Build on the dialogue created in activity **A**. With your group, use the notes below to continue the story, changing the facts if you wish. Tell as much of the story as possible with dialogue.

Nora doubts that Frank will be able to make her feel as he does about the old, peeling, isolated house. First, he wants her to see how much land surrounds the place. They walk through a large grove of trees and cross a clear stream. Nora realizes how wild and yet peaceful it is out here away from the city. It is a nice change after her hectic morning in a midtown office.

THESAURUS CORNER ♦ Word Choice

The word in dark type in each of the following sentences does not fit in the context of the dialogue. Use the Thesaurus and Thesaurus Index to find synonyms that are more appropriate.

1. "Wow!" Terry exclaimed. "Mrs. Orr is really **affluent**!"
2. "I'm starved," Sue said. "Is it okay if I **procure** some bread?"
3. "It's a **paramount** prize, all right—a free trip to Italy!"

WRITING PROCESS
IMAGINING

Writing a Short Story

"The Open Window" by Saki is a very famous short story. It tells of Mr. Nuttel's visit to Mrs. Sapperton's house one October afternoon and her niece's explanation of an open window. In it, Saki wove together all the elements of a short story that you have studied: plot, character, and setting. It is told through dialogue. The narrator speaks from third-person point of view.

Know Your Purpose and Audience

In this lesson you will have a chance to weave these elements together in a short story of your own. Your purpose will be to entertain your readers.

Your audience will be your classmates. Later you can have a class read-around or publish your writing in a short story collection.

1 Prewriting

First you need to decide on a topic for your story. Then use an idea-gathering strategy as you get ready to write.

Choose Your Topic ♦ Begin by thinking about the kinds of stories you enjoy. Do you like mysteries, adventures, animal stories, or science fiction? First choose the type of story you will write. Then gather story ideas.

Think About It	Talk About It
What can your story plot be? You might write about searching for a stolen museum piece or escaping from dragons. Make sure your story will capture and keep your readers' attention.	With a partner discuss the kinds of stories you like to read, hear, or see. Talk until both of you decide what type of story you would most like to write.

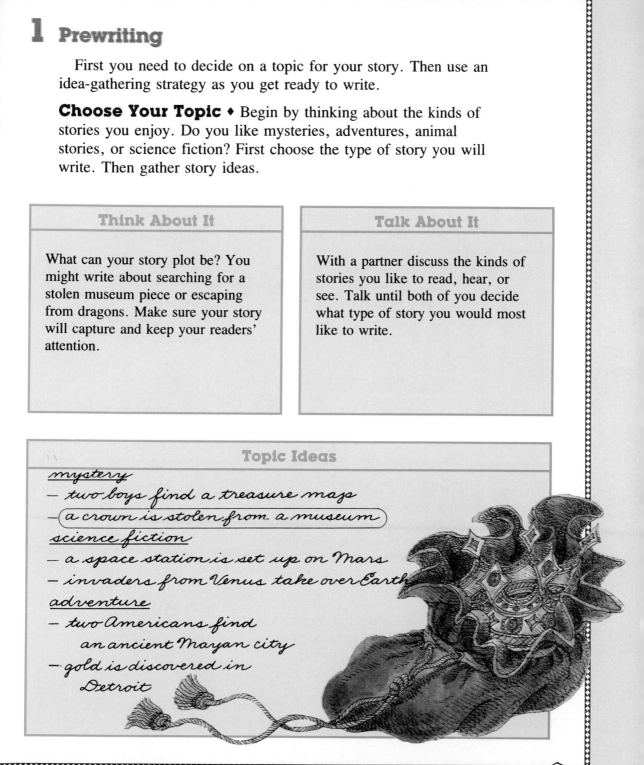

Topic Ideas

mystery
— two boys find a treasure map
— (a crown is stolen from a museum)
science fiction
— a space station is set up on Mars
— invaders from Venus take over Earth
adventure
— two Americans find
    an ancient Mayan city
— gold is discovered in
    Detroit

Choose Your Strategy ◆ How can you develop your story? Here are two strategies that can help. Use the one you prefer.

PREWRITING IDEAS

CHOICE ONE

A Thought Balloon

Think about your main plot idea—for example, looking for a stolen museum piece. Then make a thought balloon for each of your characters. In a balloon, express the character's main point of view about the situation. If you like, sketch out the plot in cartoon form and include the thought balloons.

Model

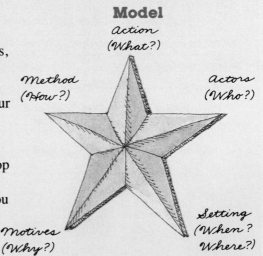

A crown stolen from the museum! There's a reward! If only I could find it!

Max

CHOICE TWO

The Star System

Sometimes it helps to think of your story as a movie with actors, action, sets, and so on. Make a five-pointed star and use it to help you work out the *what*, *who*, *when*, *where*, *why*, and *how* of your story.

Look at each point on the star. Begin with "Action (what?)" and write nonstop for 2 or 3 minutes. Then go all the way around the star, writing as quickly as you can. Be playful and exploratory.

Model

Action (What?)

Method (How?)

Actors (Who?)

Motives (Why?)

Setting (When? Where?)

2 Writing

Now begin to write your story. Most stories follow a pyramid-shaped pattern. To use the pattern, first introduce the main character, setting, and situation (A). Then build events (B) to an important or dramatic point (C), the climax. After the climax, let events fall (D) toward the final outcome, or resolution (E).

Use your prewriting notes to help you construct your story on this pattern. Remember to use dialogue to show what your characters and setting are like and to move the plot along.

Sample First Draft ◆

Junior Detective Camp was for kids who were young crime solvers. Max truged down the street, frowning at the camp brochure. At camp, Max could learn even more than he already knew about lifting fingerprints and following clues.

He really wished he had enough money to go to the detective camp. Suddenly, he bumped into a woman coming the other way.

"Oh, I'm real sorry," said Max "Are you okay?"

"I'm fine," said the woman "But what about you? You look upset."

She seemed so kind that Max blurted out his whole story.

"So you're a junior detective!" said the woman. "did you know that last night the golden crown of King Dumdum was stolen from the Museum where I work?"

"Do they have any clues?" asked Max.

3 Revising

Now that you have drafted your story, you might want to improve it. The following revising strategy may help.

REVISING IDEA

FIRST   Read to Yourself

As you read, decide if you have accomplished your purpose. Did you write a short story? Is it entertaining? Also consider your audience. Will people your own age enjoy your story?

Focus: Have you used dialogue to help develop your characters, setting, and plot?

THEN   Share with a Partner

Ask a partner to be your first audience. Read your story slowly and with expression. Then ask for your partner's responses. These guidelines may help you work together.

The Writer

Guidelines: As you read, notice any places where you feel confused or hesitant. These may need revision.

Sample questions:
- Is my point of view (first or third person) consistent throughout?
- **Focus question:** Where could I use dialogue instead of explanation?

The Writer's Partner

Guidelines: Be honest; say what you really think. Be courteous; say it helpfully and politely.

Sample responses:
- The part I liked best was ____.
- This part might be clearer if you added ____.

Revising Model ◆ Here is the beginning of a short story that is being revised. The marks show the writer's changes.

The writer wanted to introduce the main character in the first sentence.

The writer's partner suggested using dialogue here.

The writer realized that an adverb was correct here.

Sympathetic conveyed the meaning more precisely than *kind*.

The writer added a detail to make the plot clearer.

> Junior Detective Camp was for kids who were *(like max)* young crime solvers. Max truged down the street, frowning at the camp brochure. At camp, Max could learn even more than he already knew about lifting fingerprints and following clues.
> *"How could I ever get enough money for detective camp?" he muttered to himself.* He really wished he had enough money to go to the detective camp. Suddenly, he bumped into a woman coming the other way.
> "Oh, I'm ~~real~~ *realy* sorry," said Max "Are you okay?"
> "I'm fine," said the woman "But what about you? You look upset."
> She seemed so ~~kind~~ *sympathetic* that Max blurted out his whole story.
> "So you're a junior detective!" said the woman. "did you know that last night the golden crown of King Dumdum was stolen from the Museum where *The museum directors are offering* I work? *a big reward.*"
> "Do they have any clues?" asked Max.

Read the revised story beginning the way the writer has decided it *should* be. Then revise your own short story.

Revising Checklist

☐ **Purpose:** Did I write an entertaining short story?

☐ **Audience:** Will readers my own age enjoy my story?

☐ **Focus:** Did I use dialogue to help develop characters, plot, or setting?

Grammar Check ◆ Your writing will read more smoothly if you avoid adjective-adverb confusion.

Word Choice ◆ Do you want a word that conveys a precise meaning? A thesaurus can help you find the right word.

4 Proofreading

Now is the time to check your story for surface errors. A correct copy is a courtesy to your readers.

Proofreading Model ♦ Here is the beginning of the short story. Proofreading changes are in red.

Proofreading Marks

capital letter	≡
small letter	/
add comma	⌄
add period	⊙
indent paragraph	¶
check spelling	⬭

Proofreading Checklist

☐ Did I spell words correctly?

☐ Did I indent paragraphs?

☐ Did I use correct capitalization?

☐ Did I use correct punctuation?

☐ Did I type neatly or use my best handwriting?

Junior Detective Camp was for kids who were *like max* young crime solvers. Max *trudged* trugged down the street, frowning at the camp brochure. At camp, Max could learn even more than he already knew about lifting fingerprints and following clues. *"How could I ever get enough money* He really wished he had enough money to go *for detective camp?" he muttered to* to the detective camp. Suddenly, he bumped into a *himself.* woman coming the other way.

"Oh, I'm *really* real sorry," said Max. "Are you okay?"

¶ "I'm fine," said the woman. "But what about you? You look upset." *sympathetic*

She seemed so kind that Max blurted out his whole story.

"So you're a junior detective!" said the woman. "did you know that last night the golden crown of King Dumdum was stolen from the Museum where *The museum directors are offering* I work?" *a big reward.*

"Do they have any clues?" asked Max.

PROOFREADING IDEA

Handwriting Check Check your handwriting to make sure that the ends of words are as clearly formed as the beginnings. Words that trail off at the end are hard to read.

Now proofread your short story and make a neat copy. Be sure to add a title.

5 Publishing

Stories are meant to be read or told. Here are two ways to share your short story with your classmates and others.

The Junior Detective

Max trudged down the street, frowning at the camp brochure. The Junior Detective Camp was for kids like Max who were young crime solvers. At camp, Max could learn even more than he already knew about lifting fingerprints and following clues.

"How could I ever get enough money for detective camp?" he muttered to himself. Suddenly, he bumped into a woman coming the other way.

"Oh, I'm really sorry," said Max. "Are you okay?"

"I'm fine," said the woman, "but what about you? You look upset."

She seemed so sympathetic that Max blurted out his whole story.

"So you're a junior detective!" said the woman. "Did you know that last night the golden crown of King Dumdum was stolen from the museum where I work? The museum directors are offering a big reward."

"Do they have any clues?" asked Max.

PUBLISHING IDEAS

Share Aloud	Share in Writing
Organize a read-around. Arrange desks in a circle and ask each writer to read his or her story to the group. Ask listeners to tell what they liked best about each story.	Bind your stories together into a book. Choose a title for your collection. Leave blank sheets in the back for readers' comments. Place the collection in the school library.

CURRICULUM CONNECTION

Writing Across the Curriculum Literature

In "The Open Window" Saki put together characters with radically different points of view. You, too, thought about characters' points of view when you wrote your own short story. When you are the audience rather than the author, being able to imagine characters' points of view helps to bring literature to life.

Writing to Learn

Think and Imagine Choose two favorite characters from different pieces of literature. Imagine that these two characters meet. Make a thought balloon for each character in which you write what each thinks of the other.

Thought Balloon

Write Use your thought balloons to help you write a dialogue between the two characters you chose.

Writing in Your Journal

At the beginning of this unit, you wrote about creativity. Then you went on to read about a number of writers and illustrators. Are only some people creative, or can anyone be creative? Explore this question in your journal.

BOOKS TO ENJOY

Read More About It

The High King *by Lloyd Alexander*
In this fifth and final volume of the Prydain cycle,
the author skillfully blends legend, myth, and
fantasy to tell the story of a young pigkeeper who
becomes a hero. **Newbery Award**

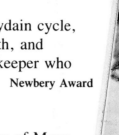

Dragonwings *by Laurence Yep*
Laurence Yep tells us the beautiful story of Moon
Shadow, his father, Windrider, and their struggles to
build a flying machine. The story is set in San
Francisco in the early years of this century and is a
memorable story of immigrant Chinese people who
share a dream.

Book Report Idea Character Report

Have you ever wished that you
lived in another time or place?
The next time you give a book
report, pretend that you do.
Become the main character from
the book.

Give a first-person account of
your role in the book. As much
as possible, try to act in the way
the book character would act.
Even dress like the character.
Tell about the problems you
faced in the book and how they
were resolved. Tell about the
other characters with whom you
interacted.

UNIT REVIEW

Unit 7

Adverbs   *pages 350–361*

A. Write the adverbs in the sentences and the word or words each adverb modifies. Label the word or words modified as *verb, adjective,* or *adverb.*

1. Linda nearly completed the very vigorous marathon.
2. Recently my father wrote about his really enjoyable vacation.
3. The article was just published in a newspaper here.
4. I never knew he could write so well.

B. Write the comparative and superlative forms of each adverb.

5. much
6. early
7. gradually
8. well
9. badly
10. little
11. clearly
12. roughly

C. Write the correct word in parentheses.

13. Why won't (anyone, no one) answer the phone?
14. We scarcely (ever, never) see a whale in these waters.
15. I wouldn't travel (anywhere, nowhere) else.
16. Never place (any, no) clothing over a lamp.

D. Write the correct adjective or adverb to complete each sentence.

17. Some of these chairs were restored (bad, badly).
18. The repairman (careless, carelessly) recaned the seats.
19. Artisans are (particular, particularly) about their work.
20. These workers are highly (competent, competently).

E. Write each sentence, completing it with a word from below.

good   well   sure   surely   real   really

21. Tim's favorite team will ____ be in the playoffs this year.
22. Will the ____ hero please step forward?
23. Hilda felt ____ enough to attend the concert.
24. I am ____ not a professional actor, however.

Suffixes   *pages 362–363*

F. Add a suffix to each word below to change the part of speech of the word. Use the suffixes *-able, -ion, -ize, -or, -ous,* and *-ly.* Write the changed words and the parts of speech.

25. terrible
26. adjust
27. joy
28. contract
29. unusual
30. invent
31. visual
32. fame
33. real

Conversations   *pages 376–377*

G. Read the following telephone conversation. Write whether each person shows good manners. If not, tell what is wrong.

34. Robin: "Hi! I wanted to talk to you about…"
35. Lisa: "Did you hear about what happened to Jackie yesterday?"
36. Robin: "Jackie! Don't tell me you're friends with that phony!"
37. Lisa: (Listening to the radio): "What did you say?"
38. Robin: "Never mind. Listen, I found a great place to skate."
39. Lisa: "That's nice. Talk to you later."

Short Story   *pages 378–379*

H. Read the following short story elements. Write *character, setting,* or *plot,* for each story element.

40. George was only eleven, but he was much taller than all of his friends. "Another basketball?" he said, slumping his shoulders as he looked at his birthday gift.

41. The party room was littered with gift wrappings and ribbons. Brightly colored balloons and streamers hung gaily from the ceiling. The young guests, seated on the floor, surrounded the birthday boy.

42. George opened each birthday gift. The first three gifts were basketballs. George could hardly contain his disappointment. Later George's friends helped him blow out the birthday candles on the cake.

43. George was not eager to open his fourth gift, but he did. It was a gift certificate from a local sporting goods store. "Great!" George thought. "Now I can get the hockey stick I really wanted. And maybe I can exchange the basketballs for other hockey equipment."

LANGUAGE PUZZLERS

Alphabet Acrobatics

How would you complete this adjective-adverb alphabet? (Hint: Use your dictionary for letters like *x*.)

Athletic Abigail acted ably; bright Bertha bounced badly; cautious Carlos crept crazily...

Praise Prowess

Challenge a classmate to a contest of praise. Flatter your friend with real and made-up adjectives. The first player to forget the sequence of adjectives loses.

Player 1: Your turn, magnificent genius.
Player 2: No, your turn, most wonderful champion.
Player 1: No, your turn, dazzling, magnificent genius.
Player 2: No, your turn, world-known, most wonderful champion.
Player 1: No, your turn, splendid-born, dazzling, magnificent genius.
and so on...

Unit 7 Extra Practice

1 Writing with Adverbs

p. 350

A. Write the adverb in each sentence.

1. It rang once.
2. We rushed in.
3. Suddenly I stopped.
4. How did you fix it?
5. Down it came.
6. She scarcely spoke.

B. Write the sentences below. Underline each adverb.

7. Our principal always visits each class twice during the year.
8. They examined their monthly bills quickly.
9. Summer vacations usually go fast.
10. Turn left at the end of the hall.
11. The rain fell steadily in the evening.
12. Bill excitedly opened the package.
13. Walk slowly and listen carefully.
14. The wind really lashed furiously.

C. Each sentence in this article contains an adverb. Write each adverb after its sentence number. Write the word or words that it modifies.

15. In 1983, Lieutenant Colonel Guion S. Bluford, Jr., zoomed skyward on the Space Shuttle. **16.** America's first black astronaut conducted vitally important experiments aboard the *Challenger*. **17.** Complicated problems have always fascinated him. **18.** As a child he loved very difficult puzzles and games. **19.** In school, Guy did well in math. **20.** He organized his junior high school's first math club and was an extremely active member. **21.** At Pennsylvania State University in 1964, he successfully completed its aerospace engineering program. **22.** He promptly joined the Air Force and won his wings at Williams Air Force Base in Arizona. **23.** The Air Force Institute of Technology in Dayton, Ohio, later awarded him a doctorate. **24.** Astronaut Bluford often reminds young people about the value of hard work.

2 Using Adverbs to Compare

p. 354

A. Write each sentence, using the comparative form of each adverb in parentheses.

1. A jet plane can fly (high) than a propeller plane.
2. Which of the two mayors spoke (confidently)?
3. The new doorbell rings (loud) than the old one.
4. Which do you like (much), rice or potatoes?
5. Both secretaries are good typists, but Carlton types (well).

B. Write each sentence, using the superlative form of each adverb in parentheses.

6. Of all the snacks, I like the almonds (little).
7. Which animal in the jungle can run the (fast)?
8. Of all the contestants, Bryan spoke (clearly).
9. Which of the three phonographs played (badly)?
10. Of the three cats, the gray one came (close) to me.

C. Write the correct comparative or superlative form of each adverb in parentheses.

11. Which of those two dogs barks (loud)?
12. Does a submarine travel (smoothly) than a plane?
13. We sat (close) to the exit than they did.
14. Of all the actors, the villain performed (well).
15. The band plays western music (often) than polkas.
16. Did Jill, Michelle, or Linda work the (hard)?
17. Of all the chairs, we liked that one (little).
18. The rain fell (heavily) than we had expected.
19. Why do they write (frequently) than you?
20. The movie ended (soon) than I thought it would.
21. The sky grew dark (fast) than we had expected.
22. The wind blew (briskly) than before.
23. We walked (swiftly) than we had walked before.
24. We needed shelter (urgently) of all.
25. I ran toward a nearby barn (eagerly) of all.
26. Inside, cows mooed (nervously) than before.
27. A small calf mooed (loudly) of all.
28. My friend fell asleep (soundly) than a stone.
29. After the storm, I ventured out (cautiously) than he.

3 Using Negatives Correctly

p. 356

A. Write the negative word in each sentence.

1. Hardly anyone appreciates the telephone directory more than my parents and I. **2.** We can scarcely survive without it. **3.** None of us read it for entertainment. **4.** It has no stories or poems. **5.** It does not have an expensive binding. **6.** It barely fits in our book-case. **7.** Nowhere, however, is there so much valuable information. **8.** The directory never fails us. **9.** Besides addresses and phone numbers, it gives first-aid facts, ZIP codes, and lists of places in our city that nobody should fail to visit. **10.** In my opinion, nothing is more useful than a telephone directory.

B. Write the correct word in parentheses.

11. They don't wish to speak with (anyone, no one).
12. From our seats we (could, couldn't) hardly see.
13. They never go (anywhere, nowhere).
14. We did not select (neither, either) of them.
15. No one wears that kind of hat (no, any) more.
16. Haven't you (ever, never) tasted a mango?
17. Speak louder. We (can't, can) barely hear you.
18. I served carrots, but no one ate (any, none).
19. No, there aren't (any, no) pigeons in that park.
20. It makes (any, no) difference to us.
21. I can't find (no, any) pens.
22. There (were, weren't) none in the store.
23. There weren't (any, none) in my classroom.
24. Now I can't (never, ever) do my homework again!
25. Can't you find a pencil (nowhere, anywhere)?
26. Actually, I hoped no one would (never, ever) think of that.

C. Answer each question below with a complete sentence. Use a negative word in each sentence.

27. Do you have some coins? We have …
28. Did Andy do anything? He did …
29. Did she call either of you? She called …
30. Did it land anywhere near us? It landed …
31. Did they buy some? They bought …
32. Did you hear that noise? I heard …

4 Using Adjectives and Adverbs   *p. 358*

A. Write an adverb ending in *-ly* to complete each sentence. The verb is underlined.

    1. The new announcer <u>speaks</u> _____ .
    2. They <u>skated</u> _____ around the rink.
    3. <u>Seal</u> those envelopes _____ .
    4. Those young trees <u>are growing</u> _____ .
    5. He <u>was approaching</u> us _____ .

B. Write an adjective to complete each sentence. The subject is underlined.

    6. Did that <u>pineapple</u> taste _____ ?
    7. Those huge <u>pillows</u> felt _____ .
    8. <u>Everyone</u> seemed very _____ yesterday.
    9. Their <u>stories</u> always sound _____ .
    10. Today the <u>sky</u> looks _____ .

C. Two words in each sentence end in *-ly*. One is an adverb. One is an adjective. Write the adverb.

    11. Fog drifted soundlessly over the pebbly beach.
    12. Stately pines swayed gently in the breeze.
    13. Hourly the hall echoed with heavenly music.
    14. The nightly news was temporarily interrupted.
    15. Those oily rags are completely useless.

D. Write the correct adjective or adverb in each sentence.

    16. The operator replied (courteous, courteously).
    17. Those new clerks seem (courteous, courteously).
    18. The test looked (easy, easily).
    19. I answered every question (easy, easily).
    20. Who said that we played (bad, badly)?
    21. When we saw the film, we felt (bad, badly).
    22. Everyone remained (silent, silently) for an hour.
    23. They moved (silent, silently) down the stairs.
    24. That food tasted (bitter, bitterly).
    25. Why did they complain so (bitter, bitterly)?
    26. Ellen remained (bitter, bitterly) for days.

5 Troublesome Adjectives and Adverbs

p. 360

A. Write each sentence, using *good* and *well* where needed.

1. She is a ＿＿ writer, and she speaks ＿＿ , too.
2. He likes ＿＿ workers, and he treats them ＿＿ .
3. I always work ＿＿ if I rest ＿＿ .
4. My voice is ＿＿ , but it isn't as ＿＿ as hers.
5. How ＿＿ can a really ＿＿ chef cook?
6. We prepare ＿＿ food, and we serve it ＿＿ .
7. The report is ＿＿ because it is written ＿＿ .
8. If you study ＿＿ , you will do ＿＿ tomorrow.
9. ＿＿ students usually work ＿＿ together.
10. Many ＿＿ athletes do ＿＿ in school.

B. Write the correct adjective or adverb in each sentence.

11. Todd (sure, surely) appreciated my gift.
12. She ran (good, well) in Saturday's race.
13. I was never (real, really) frightened.
14. Why did everybody leave (real, really) early?
15. You (sure, surely) must have seen it.
16. He showed us some (real, really) Swiss watches.
17. I will (sure, surely) have the answer tomorrow.
18. We were (real, really) excited when we won.
19. Are you (sure, surely) about the time?
20. A (real, really) good report card pleases me.
21. She gives a (real, really) interesting tour.
22. Her (real, really) ambition is to become a museum director.

C. Each sentence has one error. Write each sentence correctly.

23. How good did everyone do on the last test?
24. We sure did better than last time.
25. Our parents will be real proud.
26. It sure is wise to study for a test.
27. All the students studied really good.
28. My cousin works for a real large company.
29. Some of the deadlines are sure hard to meet.
30. Terry has always worked good under pressure.
31. Writing real clear reports is an important skill.
32. Hard work sure earns good rewards.

USING LANGUAGE
TO
CREATE

PART ONE

Unit Theme *Famous Poets*

Language Awareness **Prepositions, Conjunctions, and Interjections**

PART TWO

Literature *Poetry*

A Reason for Writing Creating

Writing
IN YOUR JOURNAL

WRITER'S WARM-UP ◆ Poetry is hard to define. It has been called "thought felt." It is said to be "the best words in the best order." Tell what you think each of these definitions might mean. Then write an original definition for poetry in your journal. Explain why your definition captures the meaning of poetry.

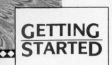
Choose an object in the room but do not name it. See if anyone can guess the object that you are thinking of. Answer questions such as *Is it near the window? Is it in your desk? Is it on the board?*

1 Writing with Prepositions

In the sentence below, the underlined word is a **preposition**. The preposition *of* relates the noun *poet* to the word *feelings*.

■ A poem expresses the feelings <u>of</u> a poet.

The noun or pronoun that follows a preposition is called the **object of the preposition**. A preposition, its object, and any other words that modify the object make up a **prepositional phrase.**

❚ The vivid images <u>in</u> *poems* are often effective.
❚ Poetry attracts many people <u>by</u> its *sounds* and *rhythms*.

In the sentences above, the prepositional phrases are tinted. The prepositions are underlined. The objects of the prepositions are in italics. Notice that in the second example the preposition *by* has more than one object; it has a **compound object.**

Some words can be prepositions or adverbs.

    Adverb: The poet put the book <u>down</u>.
Preposition: My eyes moved <u>down</u> the page.

In the first sentence, *down* is an adverb. In the second sentence, *down* has an object, *page*. Remember that a preposition always has an object. An adverb never does.

You can use prepositional phrases in different positions in sentences to add variety to your writing.

❚ *Throughout the ages,* poetry has influenced people.
❚ Poetry has influenced people *throughout the ages*.

Learn to recognize the commonly used prepositions shown on the next page. Notice that some are made up of two or three words.

> **Summary** ♦ A **preposition** relates a noun or pronoun to another word in the sentence. You can use prepositional phrases to add variety to your writing.

	Prepositions in Prepositional Phrases			
1.	aboard the ship	31.	in front of me
2.	about noon	32.	in spite of the weather
3.	above our house	33.	inside my closet
4.	according to him	34.	instead of art
5.	across the horizon	35.	into Lake Michigan
6.	after any game	36.	like these rivers
7.	against her or me	37.	near the end
8.	along the path	38.	of gold and silver
9.	among three animals	39.	off a steamboat
10.	around the yard	40.	on the deck
11.	at Wilson School	41.	out a porthole
12.	because of him	42.	out of the past
13.	before him or me	43.	outside my door
14.	behind that curtain	44.	over the top
15.	below Washington Street	45.	past Memorial Day
16.	beneath one desk	46.	since that time
17.	beside this bookshelf	47.	through a window
18.	besides music and science	48.	throughout history
19.	between two friends	49.	till summer
20.	beyond my imagination	50.	to a bookstore
21.	but (except) them	51.	toward the street
22.	by Edward Lear	52.	under a cloud
23.	concerning a poem	53.	underneath a bridge
24.	despite difficulties	54.	until 1998
25.	down this avenue	55.	unto us
26.	during that rainstorm	56.	up the Mississippi
27.	except these fans	57.	upon its banks
28.	for those players	58.	with force
29.	from their city	59.	within reach
30.	in Dallas	60.	without hope

Guided Practice

Name the prepositions in each sentence.

1. The word *rhythm* comes from a Greek word for "flow."
2. Rhythm in poetry is the flow of sounds made by language.
3. A poem with a rhyme scheme has words that rhyme at the ends of lines.

Practice

A. Write the preposition in each sentence.

4. The ancient Greeks recited poems at major public events.
5. Religious festivals were not complete without poems, either.
6. Epics, long narrative poems about heroes, were most popular.
7. During the Middle Ages, European poetry flourished.
8. The earliest English epic, *Beowulf*, dates from the 700s.
9. In the poem, the hero Beowulf battles a monster.
10. Troubadours, or poet-musicians, recited poems to the people.
11. Among their favorite subjects were love and knightly deeds.
12. Poems concerning knights were called *romances*.
13. Throughout medieval Europe, poetry was popular entertainment.

B. Write each prepositional phrase, underlining the preposition. Circle the object or objects of the preposition.

14. The Renaissance was a time of renewed interest in art and learning.
15. Renaissance poetry appeared after 1450 in Italy and France.
16. New and intricate forms were developed by Renaissance poets.
17. Poets now wrote in their native languages instead of Latin.
18. Within a few decades, English poetry reflected these changes.

C. Write each sentence, completing it with an appropriate prepositional phrase.

19. Poets write ＿＿＿ .
20. The meaning ＿＿＿ can be interpreted in many ways.
21. The images help us to see the world ＿＿＿ .
22. ＿＿＿ , many people enjoy reading poetry.
23. ＿＿＿ , many great poems have been written.

Apply • Think and Write

From Your Writing • Look back at the sentences you wrote for the Writer's Warm-up. What prepositional phrases did you use? Add prepositional phrases to the sentences to make your writing more complete and to add variety.

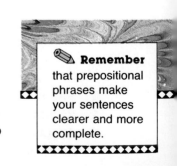

Remember that prepositional phrases make your sentences clearer and more complete.

Think of a short simple sentence such as *I found the poem*. Then see how many prepositional phrases you can add to the sentence.

I found the poem in an old book with a leather cover on the piano.

GETTING STARTED ⟩⟩⟩⟩

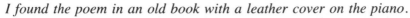

2 Prepositional Phrases as Modifiers

Adjective Phrases Some prepositional phrases function like adjectives. They modify nouns and pronouns. These prepositional phrases are called adjective phrases. They answer the same questions adjectives answer: *What kind? Which one? How much? How many?*

In the examples below, the adjectives and adjective phrases are underlined. Notice that the adjectives and adjective phrases do the same work—they modify the nouns *sonnets* and *techniques*.

Adjectives:	<u>Shakespearean</u> sonnets	<u>poetic</u> techniques
Adjective phrases:	sonnets <u>by Shakespeare</u>	techniques <u>of poets</u>

An adjective phrase follows the noun or pronoun it modifies. More than one adjective phrase can modify the same noun or pronoun.

Shakespeare is the most beloved *poet* of the English language.

Sonnets are *poems* of fourteen lines with a regular rhyme scheme.

Sometimes an adjective phrase modifies a noun that is the object of a preposition.

■ Shakespeare shaped *attitudes* of *people* around the world.

> **Summary** ◆ A prepositional phrase that modifies a noun or pronoun is an **adjective phrase**. Use adjective phrases in your writing to expand your thoughts and add descriptive details.

Guided Practice

Name the adjective phrases and tell which word each phrase modifies.

1. Shakespeare had a keen understanding of human nature.
2. Phrases from his plays and poems are part of our everyday language.
3. Shakespeare had knowledge about many subjects of importance.

Adverb Phrases Not all prepositional phrases function like adjectives. Many function like adverbs. Adverb phrases modify verbs, adjectives, or other adverbs. Like adverbs, they answer questions such as *When? Where?* and *How?*

In the examples below, the adverb phrases are underlined. The words they modify are in italics.

| Shakespeare *was born* in 1564.   (modifies verb)
| He is *famous* for his thirty-seven plays.   (modifies adjective)
| His first poem appeared *sometime* in 1593.   (modifies adverb)

Like an adverb, an adverb phrase may be located anywhere in a sentence.

| Shakespeare produced plays in London.
| In London, Shakespeare produced plays.

A sentence may contain both an adverb phrase and an adjective phrase.

■ Shakespeare wrote during the reign of Queen Elizabeth.
                    adverb phrase   adjective phrase

How can you tell if a prepositional phrase is an adjective phrase or an adverb phrase? Think about the questions that the phrase answers and find the word that the phrase modifies.

Summary ♦ A prepositional phrase that modifies a verb, an adjective, or an adverb is an **adverb phrase**. Adverb phrases can add important details to your writing.

Guided Practice

Name each adverb phrase and tell which word each phrase modifies.

4. Shakespeare's talent was recognized early in his career.

National Portrait Gallery, London

5. In his plays, Shakespeare included short poems and songs.
6. The plays were full of vivid poetic language.

Practice

A. Write the adjective phrase from each sentence and the word it modifies.

7. A cloud of mystery surrounds Shakespeare's early life.
8. Legends about him suggest he was a wild, high-spirited boy.
9. Young Will may have joined a company of traveling actors.
10. The theaters in London were his main training grounds.
11. He eventually became a dramatist without equal.

B. Write the adverb phrase from each sentence and the word or words it modifies.

12. Shakespeare had become a noted playwright by 1594.
13. His historical plays were very popular among his audiences.
14. Then, because of a plague, many theaters closed temporarily.
15. Shakespeare wrote poetry during these months.
16. At this time, poems received more acclaim than plays.

C. Write the prepositional phrase or phrases from each sentence. Identify each as an *adjective phrase* or an *adverb phrase*.

17. Shakespeare used a wide range of settings and characters.
18. Kings, peasants, witches, and ghosts all appear in his work.
19. Shakespeare also experimented with grammar and vocabulary.
20. Into his theater crowded the wealthy and the poor of London.
21. Until 1610, he created two masterpieces a year.

D. Write each sentence, completing it with an adjective phrase or an adverb phrase. Label the phrase *adjective* or *adverb*.

22. ____ the curtain rises.
23. The drama is set ____ .
24. The plot is full ____ .
25. A character ____ speaks out.
26. The tension mounts ____ .
27. An actor performs ____ .

Apply ◆ Think and Write

Dictionary of Knowledge ◆ Read about the Globe Theater in the Dictionary of Knowledge. Write about an audience watching a Shakespearean play in this theater. Underline and label all adjective and adverb phrases that you use.

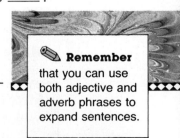

✎ **Remember**
that you can use both adjective and adverb phrases to expand sentences.

Think of a place that you like to visit, but do not name it. Describe the place, using some of the following words: *at*, *to*, *in*, *into*, *beside*, *besides*. See if others can guess the place.

3 Using Prepositions Correctly

The chart below will help you use prepositions correctly.

at	Indicates presence in a place **We were <u>at</u> a poetry reading.**
to	Indicates motion toward a place **We went <u>to</u> the library.**
beside	Means "next to" or "at the side of" **The poems by Emily Dickinson are <u>beside</u> my desk.**
besides	Means "in addition to" **<u>Besides</u> Dickinson, I read works by other poets.**
between	Used when discussing two people or objects **Choose <u>between</u> these two poems.**
among	Used when discussing three or more **Choose <u>among</u> Emily Dickinson's 1,700 poems.**
in	Indicates location within a place **Dickinson lived <u>in</u> the same house all her life.**
into	Indicates motion or change of location **She rarely went <u>into</u> the nearby village.**
different from	Always use *different from*, not *different than*. **Dickinson's poetic style was <u>different from</u> others.**

When the object of a preposition is a pronoun, use an object pronoun.

■ Poetry is important <u>to me</u>.   <u>About whom</u> was this poem written?

When the pronoun is part of a compound object, test for the correct pronoun by using the pronoun alone with the preposition.

■ The poem was written by ~~Arthur and~~ me. (not <u>I</u>)

Summary ◆ Mistakes in usage may occur in choosing a preposition or the object of a preposition.

Guided Practice

Tell which word in parentheses completes each sentence correctly.

1. In her poems, Dickinson explores feelings (among, between) herself and nature.
2. The work of the English poet Elizabeth Barrett Browning was quite different (from, than) Dickinson's.
3. Her best-known poems, *Sonnets from the Portuguese*, express the love between her husband and (she, her).

Practice

A. Write the correct word to complete each sentence.

We were (**4.** at, to) a discussion of Christina Rossetti's poetry. (**5.** Beside, Besides) a light spirit, her famous poem "Goblin Market" has a fast-paced style. Christina was often found (**6.** beside, besides) her brother, Dante. His poetry was somewhat different (**7.** than, from) hers. Many great artists and writers were attracted (**8.** at, to) the Rossetti home.

No Spanish poet has been translated (**9.** in, into) English more than Federico García Lorca. His work is divided (**10.** among, between) ballads and lyrics about nature. Ballads are different (**11.** from, than) lyric poems in that ballads tell a story. (**12.** Besides, Beside) Lorca, Juan Ramón Jiménez is another popular Spanish poet. The Nobel Prize for literature was given to (**13.** he, him) in 1956.

B. Write sentences, using these word groups correctly.

14. strolled into	**18.** beside the bookcase
15. strolled in	**19.** besides the bookcase
16. divided between	**20.** went to
17. divided among	**21.** remained at

Apply • Think and Write

Finding Inspiration • Nature has always inspired poets. Write about a favorite place in nature that inspires you. Use at least ten prepositions from the chart on page 405. Be sure to use the prepositions correctly.

> ✎ **Remember**
> to choose prepositions carefully to make your meaning clear.

4 Writing with Conjunctions

Conjunctions are connecting words. The most common conjunctions are *and*, *but*, *or*, and *nor*. These are called **coordinating conjunctions**. They connect words that do the same kind of work.

Coordinating Conjunctions	
noun + noun	ballads and epics
pronoun + pronoun	he or she
noun + pronoun	Homer and them
adjective + adjective	strange but true
verb + verb	wrote or recited
adverb + adverb	slowly but surely

Coordinating conjunctions can also join groups of words.

> Many legends <u>but</u> few facts exist about the ancient Greek Homer.
> Homer may have written <u>or</u> may have recited his major epics.
> The poems tell about historical events, <u>and</u> they also describe the roles of the gods.

Some conjunctions are made up of pairs of words, such as *both . . . and*, *either . . . or*, *neither . . . nor*. These pairs are called **correlative conjunctions**. Correlative conjunctions, like coordinating conjunctions, join words or groups of words.

> In <u>both</u> the *Odyssey* <u>and</u> the *Iliad*, Homer describes the Trojan War.
> Some believe that Homer could <u>neither</u> write <u>nor</u> see.
> <u>Either</u> Homer <u>or</u> other traveling bards popularized the poems.

> **Summary** ♦ A **conjunction** joins words or groups of words in a sentence. You can use conjunctions to expand your sentences.

Guided Practice

Name the coordinating and correlative conjunctions in each sentence.

1. The poems were composed about 700 B.C. but tell of earlier events.
2. They were recited at religious festivals and read in schoolrooms.
3. Both the history and the religion of ancient Greece were greatly influenced by Homer.

Practice

A. Write the coordinating and correlative conjunctions.

    4. Many poets were inspired by Homer and other ancient Greeks.
    5. Virgil was both a poet and a philosopher of ancient Rome.
    6. His Latin masterpiece, the *Aeneid*, was based on Homer's epics but was still quite original.
    7. Virgil told Rome's history and glorified its future.
    8. Matsuo Basho was a Japanese poet and warrior of the 1600s.
    9. He was a master of haiku, brief but insightful poetry.
    10. Basho could suggest a whole scene or a particular emotion by describing a single detail.
    11. During the 700s, Li Po wandered constantly but contentedly.
    12. This great Chinese poet had neither home nor employment.
    13. His poems describe the scenery and culture of his homeland.

B. Write each conjunction. Label it *coordinating* or *correlative*. Then write the word or words that are joined by the conjunction.

    14. Octavio Paz is both a poet and an essayist.
    15. Mexico's diverse but difficult history influences his work.
    16. Born in Chile in 1889, this woman was a poet and a diplomat.
    17. She was known as either Gabriela Mistral or Lucila Alcayaga.
    18. She won the Nobel Prize and other acclaim for her writing.

C. Write six sentences, using the following conjunctions.

    19. both . . . and   **21.** either . . . or   **23.** or
    20. nor   **22.** neither . . . nor   **24.** but

Apply • Think and Write

Creating a Review Find two poems that you have enjoyed reading. Write sentences that describe what you like about the poems. Underline the conjunctions that you use.

✎ Remember
that conjunctions can combine short, choppy sentences into longer, smoother sentences.

Think of words, such as "Wow!" that express the following emotions: *fear*, *disgust*, *anger*, *happiness*. Say the words and see if listeners can guess the emotions that you are expressing.

5 Writing with Interjections

The seven parts of speech that have been presented are like gears in a machine. They work together to make a sentence meaningful. Each word in this sentence functions as a different part of speech.

■ **Think seriously about this poetry and yourself.**

The verb *think* is modified by the adverb *seriously*. The preposition *about* begins a phrase modifying *think*. *This*, an adjective, modifies *poetry*, a noun. The conjunction *and* joins the pronoun *yourself* to *poetry*. All the words are related grammatically.

The eighth part of speech, the interjection, is used to express feeling or emotion. An interjection has no grammatical relationship to the other words in a sentence. Some common interjections are shown in the chart below.

Interjections				
Ah	Goodness	Hush	Phooey	Well
Aha	Great	Indeed	Really	What
Alas	Help	Mercy	Say	Whew
Brr	Hey	Oh	Terrific	Why
Dear me	Hooray	Ooh	Ugh	Wow

MECHANICS ";?!"

Place an exclamation mark after an interjection that expresses strong emotion. Place a comma after an interjection that expresses mild emotion. See pages 628, 630–637 for more uses of the exclamation mark and comma.

Interjections are used to express many kinds of emotions and feelings. An interjection may express strong or sudden emotion, or it may express mild emotion.

■ **Ha! These poems by Lewis Carroll are hilarious.**

■ **Well, I liked his book, *Alice's Adventures in Wonderland*.**

> **Summary** ♦ An **interjection** expresses feeling or emotion.

Guided Practice

Name the interjection in each sentence.

1. Say! Carroll's poem "Jabberwocky" is full of imaginary words.
2. Goodness! He was a mathematician as well as a poet.
3. Indeed, Carroll's real name was Charles Lutwidge Dodgson.

Practice

A. Write the interjection in each sentence.

4. Aha! Here are those silly limericks by Edward Lear.
5. Wow! Lear was the youngest of twenty-one children.
6. Look at the comic illustrations he drew. Great!
7. Why, he even gave drawing lessons to the Queen of England.
8. Hey, Edward Lear wrote "The Owl and the Pussycat."

B. Write a different interjection for each sentence.

9. _____ , Phillis Wheatley was brought from Africa to Boston as a child slave around 1761.
10. _____ , she began to write poetry at the age of fourteen.
11. _____ , look at her poem about George Washington.
12. _____ , Washington wrote her a letter of thanks for the poem.
13. _____ ! At age twenty, she was given her freedom.
14. _____ ! I want to read you some poems by Gwendolyn Brooks.
15. _____ ! She won a Pulitzer Prize for her poetry.
16. _____ ! I think I misread the last line of that poem.
17. _____ ! In this book, Brooks wrote each poem about a real child.
18. _____ ! Don't write a poem about me!

C. For each emotion named below, write a sentence that expresses that emotion. Use an appropriate interjection from the chart in each sentence.

19. annoyance   **21.** sorrow   **23.** disbelief
20. pain   **22.** impatience **24.** astonishment

Apply • Think and Write

Creating Dialogue • Make a list of interjections that do not appear on the chart. Write a brief dialogue in which two characters use some of these interjections. Read your dialogue to a partner.

✏ **Remember**
that you can use interjections in dialogue as a way to express the feelings of characters.

GETTING STARTED

He pretended to be preoccupied with a prerecorded preview of the preseason game. What's unusual about this sentence? Make up similar sentences of your own.

VOCABULARY ◆
Prefixes from Latin

A **prefix** is a word part added to the beginning of a base word or root. A prefix changes the meaning but not the part of speech of the word or root to which it is added. The word *prefix* itself is formed with a prefix: *pre-* "before" + *fix*. A *prefix*, then, is something that is "fixed before" a word.

What happens to the meaning of *agree* when a prefix is added?

■ Angie will <u>agree</u> with Alan but <u>disagree</u> with Diane.

The prefixes in the chart below are from Latin. Knowing these prefixes will help you to understand the meanings of many words.

Prefix	Meaning	Example
counter-	opposite; against	counterproductive
dis-	not; opposite of; from	disobey, dismiss
in-	not; into	inaction, ingrown
inter-	between or among	interact, interchange
pre-	before	preview, prevent
re-	again; back	refinish, receive
sub-	beneath; under	subsoil, subject

Building Your Vocabulary

Choose prefixes from the chart to make new words from the words below. What does each new word mean?

run	attack	clockwise	marine	judge
come	use	package	state	

The prefix *in-* changes to *im-* when added to words beginning with *m* or *p*. Add *in-* or *im-* to the following words.

plant	mortal	form	movable	pure
side	effective	proper	mature	land

Practice

A. Add a prefix from the lesson to one of the underlined words. Then rewrite the sentence, using the new word.

1. I decided to <u>write</u> the letter <u>again</u>.
2. The monster on the screen looked <u>not human</u>.
3. The scientist <u>mixed between</u> the two chemicals.
4. The television show was <u>recorded before</u>.
5. In January <u>below zero</u> temperatures were recorded.
6. Luis worked hard to <u>pay back</u> the favor.
7. The weights put on one side of the scale <u>balance against</u> those on the other side.
8. We <u>do not agree</u> with their conclusions.

B. Prefixes are often added to Latin roots that are not English words in themselves. These roots become words when a prefix is added. Some of these roots and their meanings are listed below. Combine these roots with the prefixes from the chart on page 416 to form words having the meaning given in the numbered items.

mand: to order   **feit:** to make   **ject:** to throw
     gust: to taste   **cept:** to catch   **spect:** to look

9. to throw in
10. to throw between
11. to throw back
12. to throw under
13. to look in

14. to make against (an imitation)
15. to have an opposite (bad) taste
16. to order back
17. to give an opposite order
18. to catch between

Language Corner ◆ Oxymorons

Do you like *jumbo shrimp*? Have you ever seen *freezer burn*? Have you ever been *clearly confused*? Such figures of speech are called oxymorons. An **oxymoron** brings together two words whose meanings contradict each other.

Find or create more oxymorons.

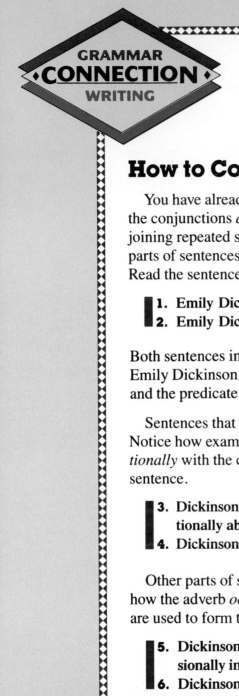

How to Combine Sentences

You have already combined sentences with related ideas by using the conjunctions *and*, *but*, or *or*. You have also combined sentences by joining repeated subjects or predicates. Now you will see how other parts of sentences can be combined to form more efficient sentences. Read the sentences below.

1. Emily Dickinson was a poet. She was American.
2. Emily Dickinson was an American poet.

Both sentences in **1** use words in the predicate that give facts about Emily Dickinson. Example **2** combines the predicate nominative *poet* and the predicate adjective *American* to form one strong sentence.

Sentences that use adverbs in the same way can also be combined. Notice how example **4** combines the adverbs *forcefully* and *emotionally* with the conjunction *and* to form a single, less repetitious sentence.

3. Dickinson wrote forcefully about life. She wrote emotionally about life.
4. Dickinson wrote forcefully and emotionally about life.

Other parts of sentences can be combined in the same way. Notice how the adverb *occasionally* and the prepositional phrase *in her home* are used to form the sentence in example **6**.

5. Dickinson saw only a few close friends. She saw them occasionally in her home.
6. Dickinson saw only a few close friends occasionally in her home.

The Grammar Game ♦ Create your own examples! Write at least four pairs of sentences that can be combined in different ways. Then exchange papers with a classmate and combine each other's sentences.

Working Together

Find out how combining sentences can make your writing more efficient by doing activities **A** and **B** with your group.

In Your Group
◆ Help others follow directions. ◆ Build on other people's ideas. ◆ Summarize after each discussion. ◆ Help the group reach agreement.

A. Combine each pair of sentences below.

1. Emily Dickinson withdrew from society. She withdrew completely.
2. She wrote her poetry at home. She wrote in seclusion.
3. Her poems were short. They were untitled.
4. She wrote about feelings in a universal way. They were feelings of loneliness and anxiety.
5. She ranks among the great American poets. She ranks highly.

B. Rewrite the following paragraph, combining sentences to make the paragraph read more smoothly and efficiently.

Emily Dickinson was a mysterious poet. She was a nineteenth-century poet. Many of her poems were sad. Many were tragic. She was also able to write wittily. She could also write playfully. She probably withdrew from life to contemplate the world. She probably wanted to contemplate it from a distance. She lived in Amherst, Massachusetts. She died in Amherst, too.

WRITERS' CORNER ◆ Sentence Variety

Using different kinds of sentences can make your writing more interesting to read. Can you identify the four kinds of sentences in the paragraph below?

How lonely Dickinson's life seemed! What did she have but her work to keep her company? Although she wrote 1,700 poems, only seven were published during her life. Read some of her poems. You will feel the sadness in her life.

Read what you wrote for the Writer's Warm-up. Did you vary the kinds of sentences you used? If not, can you vary them now?

FROM THE LAKE NO. 1   painting by Georgia O'Keeffe
Des Moines Art Center, Coffin Fine Arts Trust Fund

USING LANGUAGE
TO
CREATE

━━━ PART TWO ━━━

Literature *Poetry*

A Reason for Writing Creating

CREATIVE
Writing

FINE ARTS ◆ In every painting there is a story. What story does this painting tell? Georgia O'Keeffe titled the painting "From the Lake No. 1." What title comes to your mind? Give the painting a title that means something to you.

CREATIVE THINKING ◆
A Strategy for Creating

A CLUSTER MAP

Creating is making up or expressing something that is new or original. Poetry is one kind of creative writing. A narrative poem, for example, tells a story or relates an event. After this lesson you will read some narrative poems, and later, you will write one.

Here is an example from ''The Heron,'' by Theodore Roethke. What event is related in this narrative poem?

> He walks the shallow with an antic grace.
> The great feet break the ridges of the sand,
> The long eye notes the minnow's hiding place.
> His beak is quicker than a human hand.

Like any writer, a narrative poet gathers details to give the reader a fresh, clear image. What are some of the details Roethke told about the heron? How does a poet think of such details?

 Learning the Strategy

Thinking of many ideas about a topic is called elaborating. The ability to elaborate is sometimes equated with creative thinking. The question ''How many uses can you think of for a brick?'' for example, has appeared on creative-thinking tests. How do you think you and your classmates would have scored on that item? Would you be able to break out of the bounds of everyday thinking and come up with some really new ideas?

Many an everyday task is done better if you can be creative. For example, suppose you are part of a debate team. How could elaborating help you prepare your arguments on a topic? Suppose you have been assigned to write a profile about a teacher for the yearbook. How could elaborating be useful?

A cluster map is a strategy for elaborating details or ideas. It is also a strategy for organizing them. Here, for example, is a cluster map you might make for that teacher profile. It contains a topic, subtopics, and details. For the profile, do you see any details that would be interesting to elaborate on further?

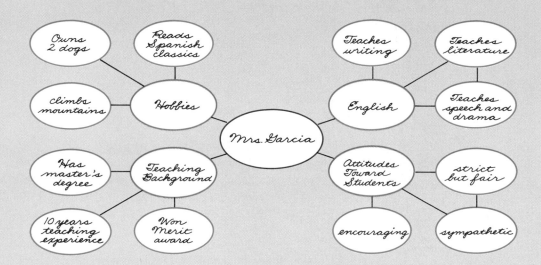

Using the Strategy

A. Think about a toothpick. How could you use it? How many things could be done with it? Think of some usual uses. Then think of as many unusual ones as you possibly can. Make a cluster map. Include even the *silliest* ideas.

B. One poem you are about to read is about an imaginary creature, the Jabberwock. Others are about a heron, some puppies, and the summer air. Choose one of these topics and make a cluster map for it. Include as many subtopics and details as you can. Then read to see what details the poet chose.

Applying the Strategy

♦ What silly ideas did you include in your toothpick cluster? Why is considering silly ideas useful in elaborating?

♦ Elaborate on the following topic: ''Times When Elaborating Would Be a Useful Thing to Do.''

LITERATURE

Poets use different voices to write different kinds of poetry. In these poems, the poets use the narrative, or storytelling, voice to describe an experience or tell a story. Listen to how they use the narrative voice to tell each real or imagined tale.

A soft sea washed around the house,
A sea of summer air,
And rose and fell the magic planks
That sailed without a care.

For captain was the butterfly,
For helmsman was the bee,
And an entire universe
For the delighted crew.
— *Emily Dickinson*

The Heron

The heron stands in water where the swamp
Has deepened to the blackness of a pool,
Or balances with one leg on a hump
Of marsh grass heaped above a musk-rat hole.

He walks the shallow with an antic grace.
The great feet break the ridges of the sand,
The long eye notes the minnow's hiding place.
His beak is quicker than a human hand.

He jerks a frog across his bony lip,
Then points his heavy bill above the wood.
The wide wings flap but once to lift him up.
A single ripple starts from where he stood.

— *Theodore Roethke*

from

Eight Puppies

Between the thirteenth and the fifteenth day
the puppies opened their eyes.
Suddenly they saw the world,
anxious with terror and joy.
They saw the belly of their mother,
saw the door of their house,
saw a deluge of light,
saw flowering azaleas.

They saw more, they saw all,
the red, the black, the ash.
Scrambling up, pawing and clawing
more lively than squirrels, . . .

— *Gabriela Mistral*

Jabberwocky

'Twas brillig, and the slithy toves
    Did gyre and gimble in the wabe:
All mimsy were the borogoves,
    And the mome raths outgrabe.

''Beware the Jabberwock, my son!
    The jaws that bite, the claws that catch!
Beware the Jubjub bird, and shun
    The frumious Bandersnatch!''

He took his vorpal sword in hand:
    Long time the manxome foe he sought—
So rested he by the Tumtum tree,
    And stood awhile in thought.

And, as in uffish thought he stood,
    The Jabberwock, with eyes of flame,
Came whiffling through the tulgey wood,
    And burbled as it came!

      One, two! One, two! And through and through
        The vorpal blade went snicker-snack!
      He left it dead, and with its head
        He went galumphing back.

      ''And, hast thou slain the Jabberwock?
        Come to my arms, my beamish boy!
      O frabjous day! Callooh! Callay!''
        He chortled in his joy.

      'Twas brillig, and the slithy toves
        Did gyre and gimble in the wabe:
      All mimsy were the borogoves,
        And the mome raths outgrabe.

— Lewis Carroll

 ## Reader's Response

✦✦

Which poem would you like to have illustrated and framed for your wall? Explain.

Poetry

Responding to Literature

1. Work with a partner to find real words for the nonsense words in ''Jabberwocky.'' Then read your new poem to another pair of partners.

2. Write a line using a series of words with the same beginning sounds. One example might be *A silky, soft soaring swirl swam in a silent sea*. Trade sentences with a partner. Read aloud the sentence your partner wrote.

3. Choose one poem from this collection. Reread it and then close your eyes and make a mental image of the scene from the poem. Tell a partner what you see. Ask your partner to take notes. Then read the poem aloud and add to those notes any details you both may have missed.

Writing to Learn

Think and Create ♦ Select a poem from this collection to use as the subject for a cluster map. Then reread the poem and record the details you find in it.

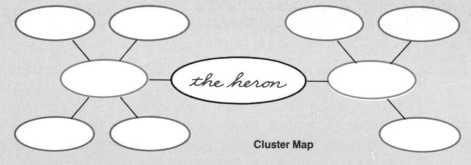

Cluster Map

Write ♦ Use your cluster notes and your own words to write an opinion regarding the message of the poem.

SPEAKING and LISTENING ◆
Choral Reading

When people read aloud together, they make a kind of verbal music. Reading a poem aloud with many voices, or choral reading, is often more fun than reading it alone.

A choral reading allows many speakers to take part, either as solo voices or as part of a chorus. Follow these guidelines for a choral reading activity.

Reading as a Choral Reader	1. Choose a poem you like that lends itself to choral reading. 2. Make a copy of the poem to mark with notes for reading aloud. One copy on a large sheet of paper can be used by the group. 3. Read the poem and divide it into speaking parts. If the poem has characters and dialogue, a character's lines might be assigned to one speaker. Different narrators could read different *stanzas*, or groups of lines. Repeated lines could be said by all. 4. Think about the poem's mood and images. Look closely for the poet's clues to complete thoughts, stops, and pauses. The length of a poem's lines are another clue to reading. 5. Consider how you can use your voice to show the poem's sounds and meaning. Which words, such as end rhymes, would you like to stress? Will you raise or lower your voice to show a change of mood or feeling? Work with others to agree on ways to interpret the poem and mark your copy. 6. Practice reading the poem aloud, both alone and with others. When you speak with a group, avoid a dull, singsong tone by keeping your voice lively. Keep the poem's images in mind as you speak.
Being an Active Listener	1. Listen for the unfolding of the story the speakers are telling. 2. Listen to the voices of the others in your group.

> **Summary** ◆ Select a poem for choral reading and assign speaking parts. Mark a copy of the poem for reading aloud. Study the poem for the poet's clues to meaning and expression. Then practice reading together the interpretation you agreed upon.

Guided Practice

Read this nonsense verse as a choral reading. Before you read, pronounce the underlined nonsense words and imagine each word's meaning. Decide what mood you want your reading to convey.

> **All:** Once on a dark and <u>drimbly</u> night
> When <u>snarecrows</u> <u>wreeled</u> across the moon,
> The <u>Drog</u> and <u>Grompus</u> came to fight
> A duel in the <u>mudgey</u> gloom.
> **Narrator:** They <u>flummeled</u> about 'til the Grompus groaned,
> **Grompus:** "Neither of us can win!"
> **All:** So they <u>whuffled</u> away at the break of day,
> And were never seen again.

Practice

A. With your class, present a choral reading of the nonsense poem "Jabberwocky" on page 426. Make your own copy of the poem and discuss these questions as you mark your copy.

1. This nonsense poem tells a story. What is the story about?

2. How will you divide the poem into speaking parts? Here is one example. Discuss why these parts fit the poem's meaning.

STANZA 1: All	**STANZA 6:** Father (3 lines)
STANZA 2: Father	Narrator 3 (1 line)
STANZAS 3–5: Narrators 1, 2, 3	**STANZA 7:** All

3. Look at the first stanza. How do nonsense words set the scene?

4. List the nonsense words and decide on pronunciations. How will you say words like *snicker-snack* and *whiffling*—words that imitate sounds and actions? Notice the rhyming pattern and rhythm throughout the poem. Which words will you stress?

5. What mood do you want to capture in your reading?

B. Plan a different choral-reading performance of "Jabberwocky." Add music and sound effects and have actors pantomime the actions.

Apply • Think and Write

Dictionary of Knowledge • Choose one of the poems mentioned in the **narrative poetry** entry. Get a copy of the poem you choose from a library and plan a choral reading of it.

✎ **Remember**
to keep your voice active and your ears tuned when reading a poem aloud with others.

Look down at your foot for a minute. Try to picture what it looks like with your shoe off. Then take turns describing your feet in detail.

WRITING ◆
Poets Use Details

Careful observation, selection of details, and imagination are the tools of the poet. Discover how one poet uses these tools to create an unusual image of fir trees.

—from **Les Sapins**

> The firs have pointed caps to wear
> And skirted to the ground they stare
>   Like astrologers
> Over the river where ships steer,
>   Fallen friends of theirs. . . .
>   *—Guillaume Apollinaire*

To this poet, the firs' slender tops and low-hanging branches are details that look like the pointed caps and long cloaks worn by ancient astrologers. The poet shows us this similarity in a simile, a comparison using *like* or *as*: the trees "stare like astrologers." Poet Octavio Paz uses another kind of comparison to picture light.

To Balthus —from **Sight, touch**

> light is a stone that breathes
> by the sleepwalking river,
> light: a girl stretching,
> a dark bundle dawning;
>
> light shapes the breeze in the curtains,
> makes a living body from each hour,
> enters the room and slips out,
> barefoot, on the edge of a knife; . . .
>   *—Octavio Paz*

Octavio Paz uses details he has selected to make imaginative comparisons called metaphors—saying that one thing *is* another. To what does the poet compare light?

Pablo Neruda pictures a child's foot in an imaginative way by using personification—giving human qualities to nonhuman things. What details does the poet use to personify the child's foot as a soldier?

—*from* **To the foot from its child**

The child's foot is not yet aware it's a foot,
and would like to be a butterfly or an apple.

But in time, stones and bits of glass,
streets, ladders,
and the paths in the rough earth
go on teaching the foot that it cannot fly,
cannot be a fruit bulging on the branch.
Then, the child's foot
is defeated, falls
in the battle,
is a prisoner
condemned to live in a shoe.

Bit by bit, in that dark,
it grows to know the world in its own way, ...
—*Pablo Neruda*

Summary ✦ Poets observe details imaginatively, and then use similes, metaphors, and personification to create comparisons.

Responding to Poetry

1. Try to recall a tree you have seen and the details that give character to it. Use a simile or a metaphor to describe it.
2. Octavio Paz says that light "enters the room and slips out, barefoot." What does light do when it enters your room?
3. Personify your feet by drawing a four-frame cartoon strip. Add dialogue in speech balloons to tell what your feet are saying.

Apply ✦ Think and Write

Creative Writing ✦ Look carefully around your classroom or outside and find something to personify. List details about it.

✎ **Remember**
that imaginative comparisons can make the details in your writing more interesting.

What has happened at school lately that might make a good story to tell? Talk about what facts you should include and how you would begin the story.

WRITING ◆
Ballads

Ballads are storytelling poems that were originally sung to music. They are usually composed in rhymed quatrains, or groups of four rhyming lines, that help us remember the story.

Unknown authors composed the old folk ballads, or traditional ballads, which tell of love, brave deeds, and the adventures of the working folk. Literary ballads follow the form of the folk ballad, but are written by one author who tries to stir our feelings with a dramatic tale. The Irish poet William Butler Yeats wrote such a literary ballad, "The Cap and Bells."

The Cap and Bells

The jester walked in the garden:
The garden had fallen still;
He bade his soul rise upward
And stand on her window-sill.

It rose in a straight blue garment,
When owls began to call:
It had grown wise-tongued by thinking
Of a quiet and light footfall;

But the young queen would not listen;
She rose in her pale night-gown;
She drew in the heavy casement
And pushed the latches down.

He bade his heart go to her,
When the owls called out no more;
In a red and quivering garment
It sang to her through the door.

It had grown sweet-tongued by dreaming
Of a flutter of flower-like hair;
But she took up her fan from the table
And waved it off on the air.

'I have cap and bells,' he pondered,
'I will send them to her and die';
And when the morning whitened
He left them where she went by.

She laid them upon her bosom,
Under a cloud of her hair,
And her red lips sang them a love-song
Till stars grew out of the air.

She opened her door and her window,
And the heart and the soul came through,
To her right hand came the red one,
To her left hand came the blue.

They set up a noise like crickets,
A chattering wise and sweet,
And her hair was a folded flower
And the quiet of love in her feet.
                    —*William Butler Yeats*

Summary ◆ Ballads are narrative poems that were original-ly sung. Both **folk ballads** and **literary ballads** are written in rhymed quatrains.

Responding to Poetry

1. Briefly retell the story ''The Cap and Bells'' in your own words. Tell it as if you were talking to a friend.
2. With your classmates, recall and list the folk ballads you know, such as ''John Henry,'' ''Waltzing Matilda,'' and ''On Top of Old Smokey.'' How are these ballads alike and different? You might choose one ballad to sing together to an accompaniment.
3. What historical event have you read about that would make a good ballad? What moment would you choose to tell the story?

Apply ◆ Think and Write

Remember
that you can tell any good story in ballad form.

Creative Writing ◆ Think of a news story that you could retell as a ballad. Make some notes about the main action and characters. Then write the first verse in a rhyming quatrain.

Focus on the Narrative Voice

When poets write about themselves and their feelings, they usually choose the lyric voice — the voice that uses *I*. When poets tell about something happening, they use the **narrative voice**, or storytelling voice. The narrative voice focuses on the events of a story instead of on the writer's thoughts and feelings.

The two poems on this page use the narrative voice. Notice how the poets tell their stories without revealing their own place in the events described.

— *from* Winter Evening

Storm-clouds dim the sky; the tempest
Weaves the snow in patterns wild;
Like a beast the gale is howling,
And now wailing like a child;
On the worn old roof it rustles
The piled thatch, and then again
Like a traveler belated
Knocks upon the window-pane.

— *Alexander Pushkin*
Translated by Avrahm Yarmolinsky

A Pine Tree Towers Lonely

A pine tree towers lonely
In the north, on a barren height.
He's drowsy; ice and snowdrift
Quilt him in covers of white.

He dreams about a palm tree
That, far in the East alone,
Looks down in silent sorrow
From her cliff of blazing stone.

— *Heinrich Heine*
Translated by Aaron Kramer

The Writer's Voice ◆ Where does the narrator seem to be when he tells the story in "Winter Evening"? What contrasting characters and settings does the narrator use in "A Pine Tree Towers Lonely"?

Working Together

The narrative voice in poetry is the storyteller's voice. A narrative poem is a story poem. As a group discuss activities **A** and **B**.

In Your Group
◆ Address people by name.   ◆ Record people's ideas.
◆ Encourage everyone to   ◆ Show appreciation for
participate.   different opinions.

A. While someone in your group reads ''Winter Evening'' aloud, listen for words that describe the sounds of the storm. List these words in order. Then experiment with ways to provide sound effects for such words as *wailing* and *rustles*. Can you think of other storm sounds to add, ones not described in the poem? If so, add them. Finally, have a group of narrators read the poem aloud while a group of sound-effects people provide background. Be sure the sounds do not overwhelm the spoken words of the poem.

B. With your group choose a familiar tree (perhaps one near your school) that you would like to tell about. Or, if you wish, find pictures of interesting trees in books and magazines and choose one of these trees on which to base a story. Have everyone offer ideas about the tree—what kind it is, where it is standing, what event might involve it. As narrators, group members may wish to give the tree thoughts and dreams like those of the lonely pine tree in the poem. Discuss the ideas and as a group agree on those to use in telling the tree's story. Decide on a title for your story poem.

THESAURUS CORNER · Word Choice

Look up the word *hot* in the Thesaurus. Choose three synonyms and use them in three sentences. Describe an event, such as walking across a hot desert. Then choose three antonyms for *hot* and use them in three sentences. Describe a contrasting experience, such as skating on a frozen pond. In each of these sentences, use the narrative voice to tell or describe.

WRITING PROCESS
CREATING

Writing a Poem

Poems are funny or serious, long or short, rhymed or un-rhymed. Poems can be about spring, friendship, love, leather jackets, cars, or colors. Poets write poems in many forms and about many subjects. Sometimes poets write in the narrative voice to tell a story or relate an event.

What's
MY PURPOSE

Who's
MY AUDIENCE

In this lesson you will write a poem using the narrative voice. Your purpose will be to tell a story or relate an event.

Your audience will be your classmates. Later you and your classmates can hold a poetry reading, do a choral reading, or create a poetry display.

1 Prewriting

How can you prepare to write a poem? First decide on a topic. Then use an idea-gathering strategy.

Choose Your Topic ♦ Poets often observe and relate incidents of animal behavior. Think of animals you have encountered or observed. You will write a narrative poem, so think of something that happened with that animal.

Think About It

Perhaps you rescued a cat from a dangerous place. Maybe you saw your friend's parakeet doing acrobatics on its perch. Whatever topic you choose, be sure you like it best of all.

Talk About It

To help spark your memory, talk with a partner about possible topics. Jot down a list of animal events. Which animal or event do you remember most vividly? Circle your choice.

Topic Ideas

animal encounters
— the skunk in the garden
— the pigeons in the park
— the kitten in the swimming pool
— the parakeet that flew away

Choose Your Strategy ♦ Here are two idea-gathering strategies. Read them both. Then use the one you prefer.

PREWRITING IDEAS

CHOICE ONE

First Thoughts

Here is a strategy to help you discover ideas. Write the name of your animal or event. Then write your first impressions about it. Write nonstop for ten minutes. Write descriptive details about the story or event. Does a metaphor or personification come to mind? Do not lift your pen till your time is up.

Model

Kitten
cold air / empty swimming pool
Kitten like a gray cushion
Bright green eyes seem to ask
  a question
Whiskers are stiff white wires
Kitten is lonely, afraid

CHOICE TWO

A Cluster Map

Elaborate on your topic. Write the name of your animal. Add subtopic circles such as events, metaphors, or sensory details. Add detail circles for each subtopic. Think of as many subtopics and details as you can.

Model

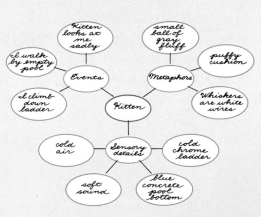

2 Writing

Before you begin, look over your prewriting notes. Look for sensory details and fresh images. With a colored pen underline your best or most creative ideas or phrases. Then decide on the form for your poem. To get ideas, look back at the poems in this unit. Would your story make a good ballad? Do you prefer to write rhymed or unrhymed poetry?

Above all get your ideas down on paper. Don't worry if you can't achieve the effect you want right away. Most poets revise many, many times to create patterns and images that please them.

Sample First Draft ◆

Cold air pinches my cheeks
The pool is empty, or so it seems.
Tired and lonely, I long for summer.
On the blue concrete a small ball
of gray fluff sits.
A weak sound filters through the quite.
Meow. Such a small sound it is. Meow.
I am drawn down the chrome ladder.
the gray puffy cushion is a kitten,
alone afraid abandoned.
Its whiskers are stiff white wires.
Bright green eyes question me,

3 Revising

Revising is "re-seeing." Take a second look at your poem. Play with words and patterns to improve the images and the sound.

REVISING IDEA

FIRST Read to Yourself

Read your poem aloud. Listen to the sounds of the words—the patterns and rhythms. "See" the images you have created. Review your purpose. Have you written a narrative poem? Think about your audience. Will your classmates enjoy listening to your poem?

Focus: Have you consistently used the narrative voice? Have you clearly related an event or told a story?

THEN Share with a Partner

Choose a partner to be your first audience and to respond to your poem. These guidelines may help.

The Writer
Guidelines: Read your poem with expression. Then ask your partner questions.
Sample questions:
• Have I created vivid word pictures? Which part did you like best?
• **Focus question:** Have I used the narrative voice? Did you follow the event or story I was telling?

The Writer's Partner

Guidelines: Be honest, specific, and thoughtful in your responses.

Sample responses:
• I loved your comparison of _____ to _____ .
• Can you add a detail about what you heard?
• You strayed from your story when you told your feelings about _____ .

Revising Model ♦ This narrative poem is being revised. The writer's changes are shown in blue.

Revising Marks

delete ℓ

add ∧

move ⟳

This line about feelings interrupted the narrative.

The writer rearranged this line for a smoother sound.

The writer decided *faint* is more precise and poetic than *weak*.

The prepositional phrase clarifies what draws the poet.

The writer's partner suggested adding this comparison.

Cold air pinches my cheeks

The pool is empty, or so it seems.

~~Tired and lonely, I long for summer.~~

On the blue concrete (a small ball of gray fluff sits.)

faint
A ~~weak~~ sound filters through the quite.

Meow. Such a small sound it is. Meow.

by the mournful cry
I am ~~drawn down the chrome ladder~~∧.

the gray puffy cushion is a Kitten,

alone afraid abandoned.

Its whiskers are stiff white wires.
Its velvety paws are pussy willows.
∧ Bright green eyes question me,

Read the poem as the writer revised it. Then revise your poem.

Revising Checklist

☐ **Purpose:** Did I write a narrative poem?

☐ **Audience:** Will my classmates enjoy my poem?

☐ **Focus:** Did I use the narrative voice consistently? Did I clearly relate an event or tell a story?

Grammar Check ♦ Prepositional phrases can act as adverbs or adjectives to add important details to your writing.
Word Choice ♦ A thesaurus is a source of precise words.

4 Proofreading

Poets often use punctuation and capitalization for effect, breaking the usual writing rules. Read your poem through. Have you used punctuation and capitalization to good poetic effect? Have you used them to make your meaning clear?

Proofreading Model ♦ Here is the poem about the lost kitten. Proofreading changes have been added in red.

Proofreading Marks	
capital letter	≡
small letter	/
add comma	⋏
add period	⊙
check spelling	⬭

Proofreading Checklist

- ☐ Did I spell words correctly?
- ☐ Did I use correct capitalization?
- ☐ Did I use correct punctuation?
- ☐ Did I type neatly or use my best handwriting?

Cold air pinches my cheeks⊙

The pool is empty, or so it seems.

Tired and lonely, I long for summer.

On the blue concrete a small ball
of gray fluff sits.

faint
A weak sound filters through the quite.

Meow. Such a small sound it is. Meow.
by the mournful cry
I am drawn down the chrome ladder.

the gray puffy cushion is a Kitten,

alone, afraid, abandoned.

Its whiskers are stiff white wires.
Its velvety paws are pussy willows.
Bright green eyes question me,

PROOFREADING IDEA

Spelling Check

Cut a window in a note card. Read through it to help yourself concentrate on the spelling of each single word.

Now proofread your poem, add a title, and make a neat copy.

5 Publishing

Here are two ways to share your poem with classmates.

A New Friend
Cold air pinches my cheeks.
The pool is empty, or so it seems.
A small ball of gray fluff sits
    on the blue concrete.
A faint sound filters through the quiet.
Meow. Such a small sound it is. Meow.
I am drawn down the chrome ladder
    by the mournful cry.
The gray puffy cushion is a kitten,
    alone, afraid, abandoned.
Its whiskers are stiff white wires.
Its velvety paws are pussy willows.
Bright green eyes question me,
    "Will you be my friend?"
Forever, friend, forever.
Come with me. We are going home.

PUBLISHING IDEAS

Share Aloud

Share poems at a classroom poetry reading. If you like, wear scarves, berets, peasant skirts, or other bits of costuming. Ask the listeners to choose one or two poems by class members to perform as a choral reading.

Share in Writing

Create a classroom poetry display. Make a decorative border around a bulletin board. Type or copy your poem neatly and mount it on colored construction paper. Read your classmates' poems. Choose a "poet pen pal" and write the poet an appreciative note about his or her poem.

CURRICULUM ·CONNECTION·

Writing Across the Curriculum Composition

You have learned that poets use metaphors. You may have used metaphors when you wrote your own poem. Metaphors are used in all kinds of speech and writing. It is fun to notice when others use them and fun to create them yourself.

Writing to Learn

Think and Elaborate Make a cluster map about yourself. Write your name. Around it cluster phrases about your outstanding features, character traits, interests, and activities.

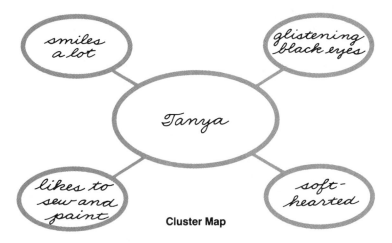

smiles a lot

glistening black eyes

Tanya

likes to sew and paint

soft-hearted

Cluster Map

Write Write metaphors from your cluster map. For example, ''glistening black eyes'' could become ''My eyes are onyxes.'' Write a poem or make a poster about yourself, using your metaphors.

Writing in Your Journal

In the Writer's Warm-up you wrote a definition of *poetry*. Then you read about poets from around the world and across the ages. Did one poet seem more interesting than all the others? In your journal write about who you chose and why.

BOOKS TO ENJOY

Read More About It

Poetspeak: In Their Work About Their Work *edited by Paul B. Janeczko*
This anthology will be of use to anyone who wishes to understand more about poetry and poets. In addition to the best work of contemporary American poets, the editor has collected the poets' reflections of why and how the poems came to be written.

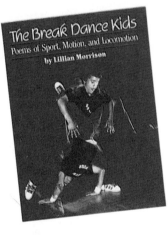

The Break Dance Kids: Poems of Sport, Motion, and Locomotion *by Lillian Morrison*
Lillian Morrison has written a collection of poems about sports, moving, and even riding on a subway. You'll find here poems about running 100-meter races, playing basketball, playing football, jogging, and ice skating.

Book Report Idea An Advertisement

If you would like to persuade others to read a good book, give your next book report in the form of an advertisement.

Short but Sweet ◆ You may have seen ads for books in newspapers or magazines. These ads are quite brief. They contain a few details about characters and plot to catch the reader's attention. The art on the ad should make the reader curious to find out more.

Claudia Kincaid and her brother Jamie have an incredible plan. What happens when the largest art museum in the country becomes their secret home?

A mixture of mystery and mirth you SHOULDN'T MISS!

from the Mixed-up-Files of Mrs. Basil E. Frankweiler

E.L. KONIGSBURG

UNIT REVIEW

Unit 8

Prepositions   *pages 404–411*

A. Write each prepositional phrase. Underline the preposition. Circle the object or objects of the preposition.

1. During the summer I am an assistant camp counselor.
2. The camp is located along the shores of a lake.
3. Throughout the day the campers engage in many activities.
4. Toward the end of the season, they perform in a show.
5. The camp director laughs at our jokes and skits.

B. Write and label each adjective or adverb phrase. Then write the word or words it modifies.

6. Balloon bouquets by Peter adorned the school gym.
7. He is famous for his creative arrangements.
8. A team of student decorators assisted him.
9. By Friday night the gym was transformed.
10. They had worked until the final minutes of the deadline.

C. Write the word that correctly completes each sentence.

11. Barbara's swimming style is different (from, than) others.
12. (Beside, Besides) Barbara, Tina also has a unique style.
13. The girls became competitors (at, to) the team tryouts.
14. The coach had to choose (between, among) Barbara and Tina.
15. Later they both dove (in, into) the pool to cool off.

Conjunctions   *pages 412–413*

D. Write each sentence. Underline the conjunction. Then label it *coordinating* or *correlative*.

16. Ethan enjoyed both the book and the movie.
17. The book told the story movingly but accurately.
18. The movie dramatized and popularized the book.
19. Neither Francis nor I saw the movie.

Interjections *pages 414–415*

E. Write the interjection in each sentence.

20. Phooey! I'll never finish drying all these dishes!
21. Hey, I have a great plan that is sure to work.
22. You are a loyal and good friend, indeed.
23. The practical joker yelled, "Aha! I caught you!"

Prefixes from Latin *pages 416–417*

F. Write a word with a prefix for each group of words.

24. not appropriate
25. unite again
26. below zero
27. take value from

28. register ahead of time
29. not content
30. call back
31. not perfect

Proofreading

G. Proofread each sentence for misspelled words. Write each misspelled word correctly.

32. The wolfs and monkies in the picture are unusual.
33. These to copys aren't very clear.
34. How many printing preses were harmd during the move?
35. You're createing an award for mother-in-laws?
36. The ball skiped along the ground and landed by my tows.

H. Write each sentence, using capital letters correctly.

37. We met the greek ambassador at the athens airport.
38. Many english words come from latin roots.
39. Is your mexican pen pal studying at a french school?
40. dutch chocolates and florida oranges are on sale here.
41. The newport jazz festival is held in rhode island.

I. Write each sentence, using correct punctuation.

42. Ouch What a sharp edge this has
43. Why wasn't the instrument stored in a drawer
44. I've decided to stay in the school band she announced
45. Mike directed a movie and he also acted in it
46. I saw the latest movie but I really didn't enjoy it

·CUMULATIVE· REVIEW

UNIT 1: **Sentences** *pages 4–19*

A. Write each sentence. Underline the simple subject once and the verb twice.

1. The first general meeting will be held in September.
2. Cheryl is the scheduled speaker at this conference.
3. The most important topics of the day are up for discussion.
4. Some members have requested a question-and-answer session.

B. Write and label the compound subject or compound verb in each sentence.

5. Jeffrey's family owns and operates a trucking service.
6. Low rates, courteous service, and trained movers are assured.
7. A single piece or entire contents of homes are moved safely.
8. The movers remove and transport the furniture.

C. Write *simple* or *compound* for each sentence.

9. Follow the crowd to spring registration at the Teen Center.
10. Classes begin next month, but you must register now.
11. The Teen Center offers classes in aerobics and computers.

UNIT 2: **Nouns** *pages 56–65*

D. Write each noun. Label it *common* or *proper*.

12. The state of Arizona has many scenic wonders.
13. The Grand Canyon and the Painted Desert attract many tourists.
14. Deserts and rugged mountains lie outside of Phoenix and Tucson.

E. Write each noun. Label it *singular, singular possessive, plural*, or *plural possessive*.

15. ponies'
16. dancer's
17. Gus's
18. Agnes
19. judges
20. firemen's

UNIT 3: Verbs *pages 118–129*

F. Write and label each direct object and indirect object.

21. Lend me your pen.
22. We brought them home.
23. I will tell you a secret.
24. Kate owes Jim a dollar.

G. Write and label each predicate nominative and predicate adjective.

25. The hero of the day is definitely you.
26. You were generous and courageous during the emergency.
27. The losers might have been Rita and I.
28. You didn't even sound nervous on the telephone.

UNIT 4: Verbs *pages 174–187*

H. Write each underlined verb and label its tense: *present perfect*, *past perfect*, or *future perfect*.

29. Aunt Rosa <u>had witnessed</u> the traffic accident.
30. She <u>has testified</u> under oath in a court of law.
31. The accident victim <u>will have waited</u> a year for this trial.

I. Write the correct form of the verb in parentheses.

32. The kite (rose, raised) quickly on that windy day.
33. I (lay, laid) the cup here yesterday, but now it's gone.
34. Rip Van Winkle had (lain, laid) there for twenty years.

UNIT 5: Pronouns *pages 232–247*

J. Write and label each reflexive or intensive pronoun.

35. We both enjoyed ourselves at the music festival on Saturday.
36. William bought himself a new music cassette afterward.
37. I myself had never heard it.

K. Write the correct pronouns in parentheses.

38. (They, Them) and (we, us) learned about sportsmanship today.
39. Laura and (I, me) shook hands after the game.
40. Will (she, her) score more points than (I, me)?

UNIT 6: **Adjectives**   *pages 294–301*

L. Choose the correct words in parentheses to complete the sentences. Write the sentences.

41. This is the (tastiest, most tastiest) bread in the bakery.

42. This freshly baked roll is (flakier, flakiest) (than, then) the roll I ate yesterday.

43. The baker is (more busier, busier) on holidays.

44. The baked goods here are the (less, least) expensive in the neighborhood.

M. Write whether each underlined word is used as a noun, an adjective, or a pronoun.

45. A <u>carpet</u> specialist can remove stains from a <u>carpet</u>.

46. <u>Construction</u> of the building began today at the <u>construction</u> site.

47. <u>Those</u> are claims from <u>these</u> newspaper advertisements.

48. <u>Some</u> claims are valid, but <u>some</u> are not.

UNIT 7: **Adverbs**   *pages 350–361*

N. Write the comparative and superlative forms of each adverb.

49. gradually	**51.** much	**53.** fast	**55.** deeply
50. smoothly	**52.** noisily	**54.** casually	**56.** little

O. Write the correct word in parentheses.

57. Juan hardly (ever, never) misses basketball practice.

58. My neighbor's child will not stay with (no one, anyone) else but me.

59. Kim can't find (any, no) answers to the crossword puzzle.

60. Isn't there (nothing, anything) to eat in the refrigerator?

P. Write the word in parentheses that correctly completes each sentence.

61. Chad felt (terrible, terribly) about the incident.

62. He was (real, really) sorry that he had lost Ben's wallet.

63. It was (good, well) of him to replace it.

64. Ben listened (careful, carefully) to Chad's apology.

Unit 8: Prepositions *pages 404–411*

Q. Write and label each adjective phrase or adverb phrase.

65. The bridges of our city need major repair.
66. Signs of corrosion appeared in the winter.
67. Repair work will begin by next spring.
68. By next winter bridges with serious problems will be closed.

R. Write the words that correctly complete the sentences.

69. The rules (in, into) his house are different (from, than) our rules.
70. The picture (beside, besides) my bed is dear to (I, me).
71. (Between, Among) all the sites, I enjoyed the museum the most.
72. About (whom, who) was this biography written?

Conjunctions *pages 412–413*

S. Write each conjunction and label it *coordinating* or *correlative*.

73. A strong but determined swimmer swam the English Channel.
74. Gertrude Ederle was the first but not the youngest woman to succeed.
75. Neither she nor the youngest swimmer swam across in both directions.
76. Both Jon Erikson and Philip Rush swam each way.

Interjections *pages 414–415*

T. Write the interjection in each sentence.

77. What! You don't mean that!
78. That's a relief. Whew!
79. Dear me! I never knew!
80. Well, I guess it's fine.

Proofreading

U. Write each sentence, using correct capitalization and punctuation. Write each misspelled word correctly.

81. wow! the largest dance ever held was at a houston show
82. Thousands of peoples were turnd away at the texas gathering
83. Did you know that rodeo's date back to the early days of the north american cattle industry
84. The sport began in new mexico in 1847

Patriotic Phrases

Find nine prepositional phrases in the first verse of our national anthem below. (Hint: *O'er* is a poetic contraction for the preposition *over*.)

Oh, say, can you see by the dawn's early light
What so proudly we hailed at the twilight's last gleaming?
Whose broad stripes and bright stars through the perilous fight
O'er the ramparts we watched were so gallantly streaming.
And the rockets' red glare, the bombs bursting in air
Gave proof through the night that our flag was still there.
Oh, say, does that star spangled banner yet wave
O'er the land of the free, and the home of the brave?

— *Francis Scott Key*

Write down the words to a song that has several prepositional phrases. Write from memory or check a songbook or a record jacket. Have a classmate find and underline all the prepositional phrases.

Skeletal Phrases

Figure out each of these prepositional phrases. (Hint: Only the vowels are missing.)

1. vrthhll
2. bnthths
3. btwns
4. wthtngr
5. frmthmntn
6. ntnnvlp
7. pnthtbl
8. rndthcrnr
9. sncthn
10. ntllnch
11. nthclst
12. tthstr

Unit 8 Extra Practice

1 Writing with Prepositions

p. 404

A. Write the preposition in each sentence.

1. Drive to Oregon.
2. Don't go past us.
3. We work near you.
4. Up a tree it flew.
5. Wait till Friday.

6. Stay off the raft.
7. Live without fear.
8. Down a lane I ran.
9. All of them study.
10. No one but me knew.

B. In this article about the Milky Way, there are ten prepositional phrases. Write each phrase after its sentence number. Underline the preposition once and the object or objects twice.

EXAMPLE: For centuries people have studied the stars.
ANSWER: For centuries

  11. A great band of stars flows across the sky like a river. **12.** For us this is the Milky Way. **13.** In other countries and at other times, it has had different names and meanings. **14.** It has been called a mystical world without struggles, a silvery bridge between earth and heaven, and even a magic serpent with a shiny tail. **15.** One ancient writer thought that all trees and flowers were nourished by its light.

C. Write each sentence, completing it with a prepositional phrase. Select prepositions from the following: *according to*, *because of*, *in front of*, *in spite of*, *instead of*, and *out of*. Underline your prepositional phrase.

16. We finished the assignment on time ____ .
17. The game might be delayed ____ .
18. A friendly crowd was gathering ____ .
19. ____ we might study French.
20. ____ fell a ticket to the concert.
21. ____ it will rain tonight.
22. Tax rates were raised ____ .

2 Prepositional Phrases as Modifiers   *p. 407*

A. This article about the zodiac has ten adjective phrases. Write each phrase after its sentence number. Then write the noun each phrase modifies.

1. Today we have a calendar with twelve months. **2.** The zodiac, with its twelve signs, was a calendar for people in many ancient civilizations. **3.** The zodiac is a band of stars. **4.** The twelve signs of the zodiac are twelve constellations along a wide path in the sky. **5.** The location of each constellation told the people the month of the year.

B. This article about the Milky Way has twenty adverb phrases. Write each phrase after its sentence number.

6. The Milky Way runs endlessly in the sky. **7.** Often it rises over our heads. **8.** Sometimes it rolls along the horizon. **9.** During certain months it flows from east to west. **10.** Occasionally it goes from north to south. **11.** It varies in size and brightness. **12.** Its route can easily be mapped out by the constellations. **13.** The Milky Way drifts out of Cassiopeia and curves under Perseus's feet. **14.** It then moves near Taurus, between Orion and Gemini, past Sirius, and into Argo. **15.** It dips around the Southern Cross, swings through Scorpius and Sagittarius, passes across Cygnus, and settles again at Cassiopeia.

C. This article has twenty prepositional phrases. Write each phrase after its sentence number and label it *adjective* or *adverb*.

16. One of the constellations in the zodiac is Andromeda. **17.** This chain of stars lies between the Milky Way and Pisces. **18.** Andromeda was a beautiful Ethiopian princess in Greek mythology. **19.** One day a monster from the sea stormed into Ethiopia and caused much damage throughout the land. **20.** The people needed an offering for the monster without delay. **21.** With sadness, the people chose Andromeda and chained her to a huge rock near the sea. **22.** Perseus, a son of Jupiter, saved her life. **23.** With his sword he slew the monster and cut the chains from her. **24.** At that moment she selected Perseus for her husband. **25.** Her first son was Perses, the ancestor of the kings of Persia.

3 Using Prepositions Correctly

p. 410

A. Write the correct word to complete each sentence.

1. Many weekend artists were (at, to) our town park Sunday.
2. They set up their easels (beside, besides) the lake.
3. (Between, Among) the footbridge and the boathouse is a small island.
4. Each painted canvas is different (from, than) the others.
5. (In, Into) the lake waddled a family of ducks.
6. They may appear (in, into) several paintings.
7. (Beside, Besides) the painters, there were amateur musicians.
8. We often go (to, at) the park in nice weather.
9. (Between, Among) the park's many attractions is an herb garden.
10. (In, Into) the center of the garden is a fountain.

B. Write a sentence using each word group correctly.

11. traveled to
12. stayed at
13. lived in
14. moved into
15. beside my brother
16. besides my brother
17. decide between
18. decide among

C. Write the correct word to complete each sentence.

19. With (who, whom) will you share first prize?
20. His project is very different (than, from) yours.
21. Did your research reveal anything unusual about (he, him)?
22. That story seems different (than, from) the magazine account.
23. To (who, whom) should my mother make out the check?
24. I don't know anything about (she, her) yet.
25. Between Tom and (I, me) we have ten different models.
26. Our models are very different (than, from) theirs.
27. I enjoyed competing with (he, him) for the first prize at the model contest.
28. With (whom, who) did you see the show?

Practice • Practice • Practice • Practice • Practice • Practice • Practice • Practice • Practice

4 Writing with Conjunctions

A. Write the coordinating conjunction or the correlative conjunctions in each sentence.

1. She and I left.
2. Was it you or he?
3. Be firm but kind.
4. Call Lou and me.
5. Buy or borrow ink.
6. It's dry but cold.
7. Go now or never.
8. Neither they nor we understood it.
9. In that park grow both oaks and elms.
10. Buy either corn or beets.

B. Write each coordinating conjunction or correlative conjunction after its sentence number. Underline the correlative conjunctions.

11. In prehistoric times, people could neither read nor write.
12. There were no alphabets or books, nor did paper or pens exist. 13. The people were illiterate but imaginative. 14. Men and women made the night sky both a library and a calendar.
15. Many of their songs and stories about stars and planets became either myths or superstitions.

C. Write each coordinating and correlative conjunction. Then write the words joined by the conjunctions. Write their parts of speech.

EXAMPLE: Nick or I will come.
ANSWER: or; Nick, I (noun, pronoun)

16. That bird never sings or whistles.
17. She spoke softly and politely.
18. His story was long but funny.
19. The station wagon needed both oil and gas.
20. Neither Linda nor he revealed the secret.
21. Is this elevator going up or down?
22. Divide the work between her and me.

D. Use a comma and a conjunction to combine each pair of sentences.

23. Willa swims well. Paul and Rita swim better.
24. You can fish here. You can fish in the harbor.
25. You can sunbathe here. You can't swim here.
26. Jay swims here. I sail here.
27. Don't go on the beach. Don't go in the water.

5 Writing with Interjections

A. Supply an appropriate interjection for each of the following sentences. Use no interjection more than once.

1. _____ ! Is that a filthy floor!
2. She whispered, "_____ , what a day."
3. "_____ !" the clown kept shouting.
4. _____ ! I dropped the dishes!
5. "_____ ," Valerie said, "I doubt that."
6. _____ ! We won another game!
7. _____ ! It's cold outside!
8. Peter said softly, "_____ , don't cry."
9. "_____ !" screamed the enthusiastic audience.
10. _____ ! You can't go in there!
11. _____ ! This tastes terrible!
12. As the opera ended, everyone shouted "_____ !"
13. _____ , that cool breeze feels good.
14. _____ ! What a storm this is!
15. _____ ! So that's where you were!
16. _____ ! That lizard bit me!
17. _____ , I think I'll go to the library.
18. _____ ! The circus is coming!
19. _____ ! The parking lot is full.
20. The dragon, _____ , turned into a dandelion.

B. Select five of the emotions and situations listed. Write a sentence based on each one. Use an appropriate interjection in each sentence.

21. Thrill (A ride was taken on a roller coaster.)
22. Pain (An elbow has been bumped.)
23. Sorrow (A precious object has been lost.)
24. Impatience (A movie is long and boring.)
25. Disbelief (A strange prediction is made.)
26. Astonishment (Water in a pool is very cold.)
27. Pleasure (An award has been given.)
28. Disgust (A wrong assignment was done.)
29. Exhaustion (Many laps were run on a track.)
30. Happiness (A vacation has begun.)
31. Anger (A friend has broken a valued plaything.)

Practice ◆ Practice ◆ Practice ◆ Practice ◆ Practice ◆ Practice ◆ Practice

UNIT NINE

USING LANGUAGE
TO

RESEARCH

=== PART ONE ===

Unit Theme   *Agriculture*

Language Awareness   **Verbals and Complex Sentences**

=== PART TWO ===

Literature   "Tribute to an Inventor: Cyrus McCormick" by Alice Hengesbach

A Reason for Writing   Researching

Writing

IN YOUR JOURNAL

WRITER'S WARM-UP ◆ Many of us have rather old-fashioned, romantic views of farming as it was practiced in previous decades and centuries. However, modern agriculture is an industry that produces more and more food with fewer and fewer workers. Write in your journal about one aspect of agriculture that you know about.

GETTING STARTED Think of a sentence with an action verb, such as *I paint pictures*. Then try to use a form of the same verb as a different part of speech.
Painting is fun. This painted statue is new.

1 Verbals

A verbal is a verb form used as a different part of speech. The three kinds of verbals are participles, gerunds, and infinitives.

Participles A participle is a verb form that usually ends in *-ing* or *-ed*. A participle is a verbal when it is used as an adjective. Like adjectives, participles can precede or follow the words they modify.

> <u>Wandering</u> tribes once hunted food to survive.
> An ancient tribe, <u>amazed</u> and <u>excited</u>, discovered seeds.

Gerunds A gerund is a verb form ending in *-ing* that is used as a noun. Notice that gerunds can be used wherever nouns are used in sentences.

>   subject   direct object
> ■ <u>Planting</u> promoted the <u>settling</u> of groups.
>   object of a preposition
> ■ People discovered the advantages of <u>harvesting</u>.
>   predicate nominative
> ■ A major challenge was the <u>farming</u> of land without plows.

Infinitives An infinitive is the word *to* plus the basic form of a verb. It can be used as a noun, an adjective, or an adverb.

> <u>To survive</u> was the early farmers' goal.   **(used as a noun)**
> They were eager <u>to tame</u> wild animals.   **(used as an adverb)**
> Livestock gave people food <u>to eat</u>.   **(used as an adjective)**

Do not confuse an infinitive with a prepositional phrase that begins with *to*. A prepositional phrase does not contain a verb.

> ■ Progress came slowly <u>to agriculture</u>.   **(prepositional phrase)**

Summary ♦ A **verbal** is a verb form used as a different part of speech. **Participles**, **gerunds**, and **infinitives** are the three kinds of verbals you can use to add variety to your writing.

Guided Practice

Name each underlined verbal as a participle, gerund, or infinitive.

1. Emerging societies established the first agricultural towns.
2. In ancient Egypt there was not enough rain to grow crops.
3. The raising of crops required irrigation of the land.

Practice

A. Write each participle and the noun it modifies.

> **4.** Persevering farmers pulled their own plows at first.
> **5.** Enlightened workers then used oxen to plow the fields.
> **6.** Soil, used and reused, becomes less productive over time.
> **7.** Certain crops, however, return needed nutrients to the soil.
> **8.** Experimenting Roman farmers soon learned to rotate crops.

B. Write the gerund in each sentence. Label the gerund *subject*, *direct object*, or *object of a preposition*.

> **9.** The Middle Ages was marked by the building of great manors.
> **10.** Caring for the land on these estates required much labor.
> **11.** Fortunately, a new type of harness made harvesting easier.
> **12.** The planting on these manors was very productive.

C. Write the underlined words in each sentence. Label them *infinitive* or *prepositional phrase*.

> **13.** Most settlers came to the thirteen colonies to farm.
> **14.** Indians gave seeds to settlers to help them.
> **15.** Entire families worked hard to survive.
> **16.** In the South, plantations were similar to medieval manors.

D. Write sentences using the following words as indicated.

> **17.** to plant (infinitive) **19.** working (gerund)
> **18.** used (participle) **20.** working (participle)

Apply • Think and Write

From Your Writing • Enhance what you wrote for the Writer's Warm-up. Try adding a gerund, a participle, and an infinitive to your sentences.

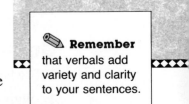

✎ **Remember**
that verbals add variety and clarity to your sentences.

What is your favorite movie? State an opinion about the movie, then see if others can add to your opinion.

The Wizard of Oz was delightful . . . before the wicked witch appeared.

2 Clauses

Phrases and Clauses   A phrase and a clause are both groups of words, but they differ in one important way. A clause has a subject and a verb; a phrase does not.

Phrases	Clauses
during the 1700s	farming methods changed
must have worked	because inventors were successful

Independent and Subordinate Clauses   Every clause has a subject and a verb. An **independent clause** expresses a complete thought. It can stand alone as a simple sentence. A **subordinate clause** does not express a complete thought. The subordinate clause below must be joined to the independent clause to make a sentence. Subordinate clauses are introduced by words such as *since*, *after*, *as*, and *when*.

Independent Clause	Subordinate Clause
Farmers worked by hand	since there were few machines.

Words, Phrases, and Clauses   Like a word, a phrase or a subordinate clause is used as a part of speech in a sentence and is not a sentence by itself. In these examples, each one is used as an adverb.

Word: Farming methods improved <u>rapidly</u>.
Phrase: Farming methods improved <u>during the 1800s</u>.
Clause: Farming methods improved <u>as technology advanced</u>.

Summary ♦ A **clause** is a group of words that has a subject and a verb. Make sure that the subordinate clauses you use are joined to independent clauses.

Guided Practice

Tell whether each group of words is a phrase or a clause.

1. with a crude wooden plow
2. since farmers scattered seeds
3. without scientific knowledge
4. wherever crops were planted

Practice

A. Write each underlined word group and label it *phrase* or *clause*.

   5. <u>During the 1800s</u> an agricultural revolution occurred.
   6. Farming became more productive <u>because of new inventions</u>.
   7. Crop yields increased <u>when a seed drill was invented</u>.
   8. Seeds were scattered by hand <u>before the drill was marketed</u>.
   9. Farmers were excited <u>when the steel plow appeared in 1837</u>.
   10. <u>With John Deere's invention</u> they could plow more land.
   11. <u>After Eli Whitney built his cotton gin</u>, large-scale cultivation of cotton became possible.
   12. <u>Without this device</u> cotton took too much time to clean.

B. Write the subordinate clause in each sentence. Underline its subject once and its verb twice.

   13. In 1834 Cyrus McCormick revolutionized farming when he built his mechanical reaper.
   14. Farms soon expanded since grain could be harvested easily.
   15. Before the reaper was invented, grain was harvested by hand.
   16. Because this method was slow, farmers grew small grain crops.
   17. When farmers used the reaper, they saved valuable time.
   18. As time passed, many other inventions helped the farmer.

C. Write the sentence, completing it with an independent clause (IC) or a subordinate clause (SC) where indicated.

   19. The weather is important to a farmer (SC)
   20. Machines help farmers (SC)
   21. (IC) after a day working on a farm.
   22. Whenever I see a photograph of a farm, (IC)
   23. Farms have many acres of land (SC)
   24. (IC) before certain farming tools were invented.

Apply • Think and Write

Dictionary of Knowledge • In 1793 Eli Whitney invented an important machine, the cotton gin. Read about the history of the cotton gin in the Dictionary of Knowledge. Summarize its importance to farmers in a paragraph. Use at least three subordinate clauses.

✎ **Remember**
that subordinate clauses cannot stand alone.

Imagine a day on a busy farm. Describe the day, beginning each sentence with *before*, *while*, *as*, *after*, or *if*.

3 Complex Sentences

Sentences are classified by the kinds of clauses they contain.

Sentence Type	Clauses	Example
Simple	one independent	Some <u>farms</u> <u>are expanding</u>.
Compound	two or more independent	Some <u>farms</u> <u>are expanding</u>, but fewer <u>farms</u> <u>exist</u>.
Complex	one independent and one or more subordinate	While some <u>farms</u> <u>are expanding</u>, other <u>farms</u> <u>must economize</u>.

A subordinate clause may precede, interrupt, or follow an independent clause in a complex sentence.

> <u>**Wherever you look**</u>, fewer farms are producing more food.
> Fewer farms, <u>**wherever you look**</u>, are producing more food.
> Fewer farms are producing more food <u>**wherever you look**</u>.

Many subordinate clauses begin with a special kind of word called a **subordinating conjunction.** Some common examples are listed below.

after	because	since	when	wherever
although	before	unless	whenever	while
as	if	until	where	

Some of these words can also be used as prepositions. How can you identify them as subordinating conjunctions?

Preposition
<u>since</u> the improvements

Subordinating Conjunction
<u>since</u> the improvements were made

> **Summary** ◆ A **complex sentence** has one independent clause and at least one subordinate clause.

Guided Practice

Tell whether each sentence is simple or complex.

1. The United States has over a billion acres of farmland.
2. Where the land is most fertile, crops are grown.
3. Farmers use modern methods and equipment whenever they can.

Practice

A. Write each sentence and label it *simple* or *complex*. Circle each subordinating conjunction.

4. Wherever you go in our land, you will see farms.
5. As you know, the Midwest is famous for corn production.
6. Farmers in this area fatten hogs with much of the crop.
7. On the Great Plains and in the Northwest, wheat is grown.
8. When the yield is bountiful, surplus wheat is exported.
9. Few dairy farms existed before new methods were developed.
10. Now dairy cows are raised in all regions of our land.

B. Write each sentence and label it *simple*, *compound*, or *complex*. Underline the subject once and the verb twice in each clause.

11. In much of the Southwest, sheep and cattle are raised.
12. When we think of cotton, we think of the South.
13. Farmers in the Southwest can also grow cotton since they practice irrigation.
14. California has many farms, and it leads in farm income.
15. Although they require irrigation, California's valleys are our major producers of fruits, nuts, and vegetables.
16. Florida's main crop is oranges; sugar cane is important too.

C. Write a complex sentence for each subordinate clause.

17. after a farmer plants seeds
18. unless it does not rain
19. before the sun sets
20. if the crop grows

Apply • Think and Write

Making Predictions • Agriculture has advanced rapidly in the last two hundred years. What might farms be like two hundred years from now? Write about a farm of the future, using some complex sentences in your description.

✏️ **Remember** that complex sentences show relationships between ideas.

GETTING
STARTED

Play "One Word at a Time." One person says a word. Others in turn add words to build a sentence. The player who adds a word to complete the sentence may then begin a new sentence.

4 Correcting Sentence Errors

Run-on Sentences   Remember that a run-on sentence occurs when two or more sentences are separated by no punctuation or just a comma. You can correct a run-on sentence by making separate sentences or by writing it as a compound sentence, adding a coordinating conjunction and a comma. You can also sometimes correct it by writing a complex sentence, adding a subordinating conjunction.

> **Run-on:** Farm life appeals to many people it is demanding.
> **Compound:** Farm life appeals to many people, but it is demanding.
> **Complex:** Farm life appeals to many although it is demanding.

Sentence Fragments   A sentence fragment is an incomplete thought written as a sentence. Prepositional phrases, subordinate clauses, and verbals by themselves do not express complete thoughts. They are parts of sentences. Notice how the phrase, clause, and verbal below have been combined with adjoining sentences.

> **Fragment:** Many people left rural areas. Over the years.
> **Correct:** Many people left rural areas over the years.

> **Fragment:** Fewer workers were needed. As farms were mechanized.
> **Correct:** Fewer workers were needed as farms were mechanized.

> **Fragment:** Farmers still work the land. To earn a living.
> **Correct:** Farmers still work the land to earn a living.

Summary ✦ **Run-on sentences** and **sentence fragments** should not appear in written work.

Guided Practice

Identify each sentence error and tell how to correct the sentence.

1. Rural people were once very isolated that isn't the case now.
2. Since highways now link rural communities with cities.
3. Children often live far from school long bus rides are common.

Practice

A. Rewrite each run-on sentence as a compound sentence. Use a coordinating conjunction and a comma.

    4. Farming is an important industry it is one of the oldest.
    5. Agriculture is hard work many farmers work long hours.
    6. A farm is a big investment farm income is often quite low.
    7. Machinery is expensive farmers often share equipment.
    8. Farmers know about science they also need business skills.
    9. Some farms are family-owned big businesses own others.

B. Rewrite each run-on sentence as a complex sentence. Use the subordinating conjunction in parentheses.

    10. Farmers worry about frost it can damage crops. (because)
    11. Farm profits are threatened diseases damage crops. (when)
    12. Droughts may ruin crops they persist. (if)
    13. Farm families will not succeed they cooperate. (unless)
    14. Farms need many helpers harvesting season begins. (whenever)
    15. Few farmers would choose another career farming is difficult work. (although)

C. For each of the following fragments, write a complete sentence.

    16. While some family members care for livestock.
    17. During the planting and harvesting seasons.
    18. When there is free time for families.
    19. At community picnics and dances.
    20. Since animals need constant care.
    21. Because they love the land.
    22. Living on a farm.
    23. To succeed at farming.

Apply • Think and Write

An Outdoor Project • The 4-H program was started in rural areas of our country. Members of 4-H clubs learn a variety of skills, including raising cattle and planting gardens. Write about an outdoor project that you would like to do. Proofread your work to eliminate run-on sentences and fragments.

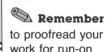

> ✐ **Remember**
> to proofread your work for run-on sentences and sentence fragments.

GETTING STARTED

What are the "miner" mistakes in these sentences: Have you ever been to a *bizarre*? Have you ever had to *steppe* over a *creak*? Have you ever caught the *flue*?

VOCABULARY •
Homophones and Homographs

Homophones are words that sound alike but have different origins, meanings, and spellings. *Right*, *write*, and *rite* are homophones. *Homophone* means "same sound."

Some of the most common words in the English language are homophones. These homophones can cause trouble for writers. The chart below shows six troublesome homophones.

Homophone	Function	Example
their	possessive pronoun	It's *their* turn next.
there	adverb that tells *where*	Put the book *there*.
they're	contraction of *they are*	*They're* almost ready.
to	preposition meaning "toward"	Turn *to* the left.
too	adverb meaning "also"; adverb meaning "overly"	Will she come *too*? The room is *too* cold.
two	one more than one	Ted asked *two* questions.

Homographs are words that are spelled alike but have different origins and meanings. Homographs often, but not always, have different pronunciations. *Tear* meaning "to rip" and *tear* meaning "a drop of liquid from the eye" are homographs. *Bear* meaning "to carry" and *bear* meaning "a kind of animal" are also homographs. *Homograph* means "same writing."

Building Your Vocabulary

Use the homophones in the chart to complete this paragraph.

_____ going _____ visit _____ uncle's farm for _____ days. _____ will be time _____ visit _____ grandparents, _____ .

Think of as many pairs of homographs as you can. Then choose one pair and give the meanings of the two words to the class.

Practice

A. Rewrite the following nonsense paragraphs. Replace the incorrect words with their homophones.

Eye live on a farm. My dad razes corn, or maze, with sum of the biggest colonels yule ever sea. He cells it too a company that makes breakfast serials. Eye help hymn sew the cede when he plants.

Eye have a hoarse with a funny gate. Eye often keep it tide two a steak. Sometimes a heard of dear will grays in the pasture two.

Dad also razes chickens. Chickens are foul, ewe no. His chickens make good friars. The baby chicks go "cheap cheap."

On sonny daze eye like too weighed in the creak in my bear feat. The creak's just a whey down the rode.

B. Many homographs are noun and verb pairs, as *object* is in this sentence: *I object to that object*. Make up sentences, using each homograph below as both a noun and a verb in one sentence.

1. row	**4.** content	**7.** subject
2. reject	**5.** permit	**8.** tears
3. present	**6.** conduct	**9.** compound

C. Write the word that correctly completes each sentence.

10. (Their, They're) leaving for Cairo tomorrow morning.
11. (There, Their) house is over (they're, there) on the hill.
12. (Too, To) many people crowded aboard those (two, too) ships.
13. (It's, Its) (to, too) hot (too, to) run today.
14. (Your, You're) hat is over (their, there) on the counter.

Language Corner ◆ Onomatopoeia

Onomatopoetic words are words that imitate the sounds they name. The words for many animal sounds are imitative: doves *coo*, crows *caw*, cats *meow*.

What words do you associate with the sounds made by these animals?

pigs	**sheep**	**turkeys**
ducks	**donkeys**	**horses**

How to Combine Sentences

As you know, combining sentences with related ideas can make writing smoother, less repetitive, and more effective. Can you see the relationship between the two sentences in example **1**?

> **1. The farmers were hurrying. The farmers harvested their wheat.**
> **2. Hurrying, the farmers harvested their wheat.**

The sentences in example **1** express two actions done by the farmers. By transforming the verb *hurrying* into a participle, these two sentences are combined to form a single sentence in example **2**.

You can also combine related sentences by making one sentence into a subordinate clause. Notice how this is done in example **4**.

> **3. The rain continued. The farmers waited patiently.**
> **4. While the rain continued, the farmers waited patiently.**

Combining sentences with a subordinate clause is especially useful when two sentences have related ideas but one idea is less important than the other. The words *who* and *that* can often be used to combine such sentences, as shown in the examples below.

> **5. Mr. Lane was born on that farm. He has always lived there.**
> **6. Mr. Lane, who was born on that farm, has always lived there.**
> **7. He owns the farm. The farm has been in his family for years.**
> **8. The farm that he owns has been in his family for years.**

The Grammar Game ◆ How would you combine these sentences? Can you combine each pair of sentences below in two different ways?

- His children have studied agriculture. His children would like to farm the same land their ancestors did.
- They have been saving money. They have bought land near the farm.
- Farming is difficult. The children hope to continue the work.

Working Together

As your group completes activities **A** and **B**, you will find that combining sentences makes your writing more effective.

In Your Group

- ♦ Contribute your ideas.
- ♦ Stay on the job.
- ♦ Respond to the suggestions of others.
- ♦ Keep a list of people's ideas.

A. Use a participle or a clause to combine each pair of sentences.

1. Farmers begin their work. Most of us are still sleeping.
2. The farmers were smiling. The farmers were finishing the job.
3. Irrigation is expensive. It has helped many farms.
4. Farmers study weather. They know it is vital to success.
5. Some experts are studying the situation. Some experts expect higher profits for agriculture.
6. Many farms are quite far from the nearest town. Neighbors must help each other out.

B. Rewrite the following paragraph, using a subordinate clause or a participle to combine sentences as needed.

Today's agriculture is highly technical. It is still dependent on the weather. Farmers experience this firsthand. Farmers know that too much or too little rain can be disastrous. Farmers are studying and planning. Farmers are learning more about the weather. They cannot completely control the weather. They can sometimes prevent a disaster.

WRITERS' CORNER ♦ Stringy Sentences

Avoid joining too many sentences or groups of words with the word *and*. Stringy sentences can be difficult to read and understand.

The farmer studied almanacs and weather reports closely, and he changed his timetable for planting some crops and hoped that this would help and also hoped that the crops would be ready to harvest on time.

Break this sentence into shorter, more effective sentences. Then read what you wrote for the Writer's Warm-up. Can you improve any stringy sentences in your writing?

PLANTING POTATOES   *painting by Jean-Francois Millet*
Courtesy, Museum of Fine Arts, Boston

USING LANGUAGE
TO

RESEARCH

=== PART TWO ===

Literature "Tribute to an Inventor: Cyrus McCormick"
by Alice Hengesbach

A Reason for Writing Researching

CREATIVE
Writing

FINE ARTS ◆ Put yourself into Jean–Francois
Millet's painting. Stretch out under the tree in
the background, and listen as the couple speak
to each other. What are they saying? Record
their conversation in your journal.

CRITICAL THINKING ♦
A Strategy for Researching

A GOAL/PLAN/OUTCOME CHART

Researching is gathering information. This information is often the basis of a research report. After this lesson you will read "Tribute to an Inventor," a research report about Cyrus McCormick. Later you will write a research report on a topic you choose.

Research reports are often written about people who have accomplished something out of the ordinary. Cyrus McCormick invented a reaper, a machine that revolutionized agriculture. He was not only an inventor, but a marketing genius. He knew how to make things, and he found out how to sell them. This passage from "Tribute to an Inventor" tells you why.

> Then McCormick decided to try to work out his own design for a reaper. . . . In 1837 he began to work on selling and improving his reaper because the panic of 1837 swept away the family's money.

Cyrus McCormick had a goal: He had to make money. He planned actions to reach his goal: He taught himself how to market his machine. The outcome was success: The reaper changed American agriculture, and McCormick became a millionaire.

◆ Learning the Strategy

Finding out how someone else solved problems to reach a goal may help you reach a goal of your own. For example, if you sometimes feel shy, it might help you to hear an interview with a well-known adult who was shy as a teenager. Imagine that you are having difficulty writing a computer program for a science project. Whom would you turn to for advice? Or imagine that you have invented a new toy called Skate-O-Ski. Is it possible that reading a biography of Cyrus McCormick could help you figure out how to sell it?

Making a goal/plan/outcome chart is one strategy for planning problem-solving behavior. You can chart someone's goal, the actions they took to reach it, and the outcome or outcomes. You can also chart your own goal, actions you plan to take, and—later— what the outcome was. Here, for example, is a chart you might be able to make about your Skate-O-Ski venture. Note that, in this case, the actions taken lead to more than one outcome.

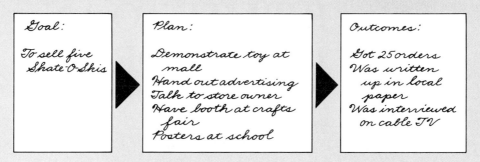

Goal:

To sell five Skate-O-Skis

Plan:

Demonstrate toy at mall
Hand out advertising
Talk to store owner
Have booth at crafts fair
Posters at school

Outcomes:

Got 25 orders
Was written up in local paper
Was interviewed on cable TV

Using the Strategy

A. Think of one aspect of school in which you would like to improve. It may be playing a musical instrument or becoming better organized. Set up a goal/plan/outcome chart. List your goal and at least three actions you can plan to reach it. List the most likely outcome, or leave the outcome box blank and set a reasonable date on which you will fill it in.

B. Many people have ideas for inventions. They may be able to make a working model and even learn how to patent it. Then what? How do you talk people into buying it? How do you manufacture enough to fill orders? On a paper write "How to market and manufacture an invention." Write nonstop for three minutes. Put down every idea that comes to you. Then read "Tribute to an Inventor." See if Cyrus McCormick used any of your ideas to become a millionaire making and selling reapers.

Applying the Strategy

♦ Do you think you will succeed in reaching the goal you set for **A** above? Why or why not?

♦ How could making a goal/plan/outcome chart help you in one of your school subjects?

TRIBUTE TO AN INVENTOR:

Cyrus McCormick

A Report by Alice Hengesbach

"OUR FIELD IS THE WORLD."

LIGHT DRAFT. SUPERIOR DESIGN.

CLEAN AND RAPID CUTTER.

McCormick Harvesting Machine Co., Chicago.

ESTABLISHED 1831.

Cyrus McCormick was born on February 15, 1809, in Rockbridge City, Virginia. He invented a reaping machine that symbolizes the mechanical revolution in agriculture. The machine he invented was not original, and Cyrus used many parts that others before him had developed. However, he was one of the first people to perfect the machine, and he is the one who has been remembered for the invention.

McCormick's father was also an inventor of sorts. He worked for seven years to perfect the reaper, but he couldn't succeed. Cyrus had worked in his father's workshop and soon became interested in building some device that would help farmers. He understood the need because his father was also a farmer.

McCormick's first inventions were the harvesting cradle and the self-sharpening plow, which he patented between the years 1831 and 1833. Then McCormick decided to try to work out his own design for a reaper. This design had a reel to bring the grain within reach of the vibrating cutting blades and a platform on which the grain was collected. There was also a divider which separated the grain to be cut from that which was to be left standing. McCormick continued to improve his product until he was satisfied.

Finally, in 1834, McCormick completed and patented his reaper. After this, McCormick temporarily stopped doing anything further and helped his dad do some farm work. Then in 1837 he began to work on selling and improving his reaper because the panic of 1837 swept away the family's money. At first the reapers didn't sell well; but McCormick had faith in his invention and he continued to advertise anywhere he could. McCormick knew that his reaper was good, and he knew that if the farmers would become familiar with it then there would be more sales, so he decided to go around being his own salesman. It worked. In 1842 nine reapers were sold, in 1843 twenty-nine were sold, and in 1844 fifty were sold.

Then McCormick decided the real need for the reapers was in the Middle West. He made a 3,000 mile trip, going from farm to farm selling his reaper. In 1845 McCormick improved his reaper even more. He then moved his factory to Cincinnati where he could be closer to the farmers who would be wanting the reapers.

He went to Chicago and convinced a man named William Ogden to buy half of his company. Ogden, who was a very rich man, agreed. By 1849 the business was doing so well that McCormick was able to buy back Ogden's share. This kept the business in the McCormick family.

The reapers were improved from year to year and kept up with the advanced mechanical knowledge. That was one of the reasons that the McCormick reaper was so popular. In 1851 the reaper was awarded the grand prize at London's World Fair and at the Paris Exposition.

Later, many people said it was not original, and they challenged his patents and copyrights. These people probably were correct in saying that McCormick's reaper was not original, but by that time the reaper was so successful that this did not affect McCormick very much. McCormick devoted almost his whole life to perfecting and selling the reaper, and fortunately for him, it brought him much success and made him a millionaire many times over by the time he died in 1884.

 ## Reader's Response

If Cyrus McCormick were alive today, would you like to work for him? Explain why or why not.

TRIBUTE TO AN INVENTOR: *Cyrus McCormick*

Responding to Literature

1. With a small group, plan a radio commercial for the McCormick reaper. Include noises, music, and a slogan. Tape your commercial if you can. Share it with the class. Ask others to tell you what they like best about your commercial.

2. Why, do you think, was Cyrus McCormick able to succeed when others had failed to perfect a reaper? List on the chalkboard words you might use to describe McCormick.

3. What would you like to invent? What would it do? How would it work? Make a drawing of your invention. Then present your invention to the class. Tell what it does and how it will contribute to civilization.

Writing to Learn

Think and Plan ◆ Note the various challenges that Cyrus McCormick encountered. Select one of them for a focus. Try to think and plan as McCormick might have done. Prepare a goal/plan/outcome chart that he might have prepared and used.

Write ◆ Write a journal entry as if you were McCormick. Tell how you feel about the outcome of your work.

GETTING
STARTED

Complete the following question with an interesting fact: *Did you know that* _____ ? See if you can "capture" your classmates' attention.

SPEAKING and LISTENING ◆ An Oral Report

You will often be asked to give oral reports to listeners during your school years. In an oral report, you present information about a topic that you have researched. A good oral report must be well organized so that it is easy to follow. To organize your report, divide it into an introduction, a body, and a conclusion.

The introduction should state the main idea of the report. Your introduction should capture your listeners' attention. A humorous statement, an unusual fact, or an interesting question are three ways you can do this.

The body of the report should contain the ideas and details that explain and support your topic. It is helpful to outline the information on index cards, with one card for each main idea. Do not write down everything you want to say. Instead, use phrases that will remind you of important points. (See pages 570–571 for information on outlining.)

The conclusion should briefly summarize the main points of your report.

Use these guidelines when presenting and listening to an oral report.

Giving a Report	1. Before you present your report, underline key points in your note cards. 2. Memorize important parts of your report so you can look at the audience frequently, not always at the note cards. 3. Practice your report before family and friends. 4. Relax as you talk, look at your audience, speak clearly, and vary the tone and stress of your voice. 5. Conclude the report by summarizing main ideas.
Listening to a Report	1. Listen attentively and politely, noting the main idea. 2. Follow the development of the main idea and try to anticipate points the speaker will make. 3. Summarize the speaker's main points from time to time. Take notes if possible.

Summary ◆ Organize an oral report into an introduction, a body, and a conclusion and present it clearly. As a listener, note important points in the report.

Guided Practice

Tell whether each statement would capture listeners' attention in the introduction of an oral report. If not, tell how the statement could be improved.

1. Did you know that dolphins can talk?
2. This report is about the extinction of a bird.
3. Kangaroos are interesting animals.

Practice

A. Write a short introduction for an oral report on one of the following topics. Try to capture an audience's attention and be sure to state your main idea.

4. the results of a school project you worked on
5. a hobby or activity that you enjoy
6. a person in history that you have read about
7. an important farm crop in your state

B. Find a short newspaper or magazine article on a topic that interests you. Read the article aloud to the class. Remind your classmates to listen carefully for the main ideas. When you are finished, see if your listeners can summarize the main points.

C. Develop the introduction you wrote for **Practice A** into a brief oral report, adding a body and a conclusion. Take notes on what you want to say and practice your report. Give your oral report to a group of classmates.

Apply ◆ Think and Write

Evaluating an Introduction ◆ Write an introduction for an oral report on a topic of your choice. Practice the introduction. Then present it to a partner. Have your partner evaluate the oral presentation and give suggestions for improvement.

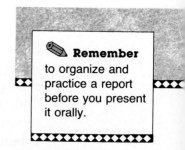

✎ Remember to organize and practice a report before you present it orally.

Think of a question about a topic you would like to learn more about. For example: *How do polar bears survive the long Arctic winters?* Name a few people who you think could answer your question.

STUDY SKILLS ◆
Gathering Firsthand Information

Writing a good report requires a great deal of preparation. The first step is to choose a topic that interests you. Then you must gather information for the report. Although the library is a main source for gathering information, you should also get information firsthand. Interviews and surveys are two methods you can use.

Interviews   In an interview, you gather information from someone who is knowledgeable about the topic that interests you. For example, if you are writing about new methods in farming, you might interview a worker on a modern farm.

Use these guidelines for help in conducting a successful interview.

- Schedule an appointment for the interview.
- Research your topic first and write questions you will ask.
- Include questions such as *Why?* and *How?*
- Listen carefully during the interview and take notes. If the person you are interviewing agrees, you may wish to use a tape recorder in addition to taking notes.
- Review your notes after the interview and verify the facts.

Surveys   You can also get firsthand information from surveys. In a survey, information is gathered from many people by using a questionnaire. Suppose you wanted to find out the types of crops that most farmers grow today. By conducting a mail survey, you could contact many farmers in different geographical areas.

Use these guidelines for help in conducting a survey.

- Clearly state your purpose on the survey questionnaire.
- Write short-answer questions that are easy to tabulate. Questions that require *yes* or *no* answers are best.
- Choose a sample of people and decide whether to conduct the survey by mail, telephone, or personal interview.
- Tabulate, study, and summarize the results of the survey.

Summary ♦ When preparing to write a report, gather information firsthand through interviews and surveys.

Guided Practice

Tell one question you could ask each person about this report topic: How to Start a Farm.

1. a friend's grandfather, who is a retired farmer
2. the owner of a feed and grain store
3. a member of a family that recently moved to a farm

Practice

A. Write three interview questions you could ask each person about the given topic.

    4. a poultry farmer—Raising Chickens
    5. an agricultural school teacher—Agriculture in Asia
    6. a farmer's son or daughter—Family Life on a Farm
    7. a grocery store manager—Buying Food from Farms

B. Choose one of the topics below. Then decide what information about the topic could be gathered by a survey. Write a survey questionnaire that has ten questions.

    8. The Pros and Cons of Farming
    9. Leisure Activities in Rural Areas
   10. Preparing for a Career in Farming
   11. Attending School in a Rural Area

C. Write a survey containing five questions about this topic: Outdoor Activities. Have ten classmates or other friends write answers to the survey on separate sheets of paper. Then tabulate and summarize the results of the survey.

Apply ♦ Think and Write

Interviewing ♦ Practice your interviewing skills. Have a partner play the role of a famous person you would like to interview. Write at least five questions to ask your partner. When you are finished, have your partner evaluate the interview.

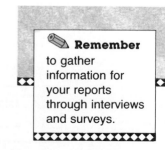

Remember to gather information for your reports through interviews and surveys.

Think of an article in a magazine or newspaper that you have read recently. Tell about a few main ideas from your reading.

STUDY SKILLS ◆
Taking Notes

The library contains many reference sources that can provide useful information for an oral or written report. These sources include nonfiction books, encyclopedias, and other reference books. To learn more about using reference materials, see pages 562–569.

As you gather information from library sources, you need to take useful notes. The notes should contain the main ideas you will cover in your report, along with the facts and details that support those ideas.

A good way to takes notes is to write them on 3″ x 5″ index cards. Each card should contain notes on one main idea and from one source only. You can then group all the cards on one topic together and arrange the cards in the order you choose. Study the card below. It was written for a report on agricultural inventions.

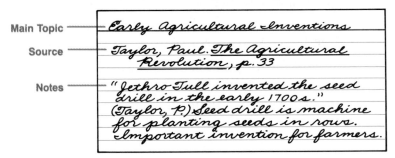

Use these guidelines for taking notes.

◆ Write your notes on index cards, using one card for each main idea.
◆ Write the main idea at the top of each card.
◆ List the source for your information.
◆ Write brief notes in your own words.
◆ If you use quotations, copy the exact words, add quotation marks, and name each person quoted.

> **Summary** ◆ Take notes in your own words on index cards for a report.

Guided Practice

Use this note card to answer the questions below.

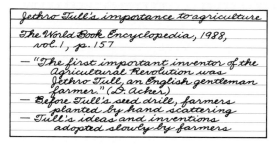

Jethro Tull's importance to agriculture

The World Book Encyclopedia, 1988,
    vol. 1, p. 157

— "The first important inventor of the
    Agricultural Revolution was
    Jethro Tull, an English gentleman
    farmer." (D. Acker)
— Before Tull's seed drill, farmers
    planted by hand scattering
— Tull's ideas and inventions
    adopted slowly by farmers

1. What is the main idea on the note card?

2. What information is given about the source of the information?

3. Why is the first sentence in quotation marks?

Practice

The paragraphs below from *The World Book Encyclopedia* contain information about the inventor John Deere. Read the paragraphs and write notes on index cards about the most important information.

John Deere was an American inventor and manufacturer. In 1837, he invented the first steel plow that efficiently turned the heavy American prairie sod. He became one of the world's greatest plowmakers.

Deere was born in Rutland, Vt. He became a blacksmith's apprentice at the age of 17. In 1836, he opened a blacksmith shop in Grand Detour, Ill. He soon learned that nearby farmers were dissatisfied with their plows. The heavy, gummy prairie sod stuck to the rough surface of the wood or iron moldboard that was used to turn the soil.

Deere built a smooth, hard moldboard out of an old circular steel saw in 1837. . . . Deere and a partner, Leonard Andruss, began making quantities of steel plows. Within 10 years, they were producing 1,000 plows annually.

Apply • Think and Write

Taking Notes • Choose two paragraphs from another textbook to write notes about. Be sure to follow the note-taking guidelines in this lesson.

> ✎ **Remember**
> to take useful notes on your topic before you write a report.

Think of a different way to say this sentence without losing its meaning: *Long before crop irrigation was common practice, the Hohokam Indians dug ditches to carry water to their crops.*

WRITING ♦
Paraphrasing

When you take notes for research reports, it is important to paraphrase, or state in your own words, the information you have read. To paraphrase, you first need to identify the important details you want to include. In the following paragraph, this information is underlined.

> The corn plant was first discovered by Native Americans, and for many generations this fragile food plant was nurtured by them. Native Americans were applying advanced planting techniques to corn long before Europeans traveled to the Americas. Squanto was one Native American known for his planting expertise. It was Squanto who showed Miles Standish and the Puritans how to increase their corn production 300 percent by using fish as fertilizer.

The underlined information in the paragraph above should not be copied word for word unless the words are enclosed in quotation marks. Copying word for word without using quotation marks is a form of stealing ideas known as **plagiarism**. Instead of copying, use the basic ideas and state them in your own words. Notice how these two sentences paraphrase the ideas in the example paragraph.

■ **Before Europeans arrived in America, Native Americans were using advanced methods to raise corn.**
■ **Squanto tripled the Puritans' corn crop with fish fertilizer.**

Summarizing is one kind of paraphrasing. When you **summarize**, you write only the most important ideas in as few words as possible. A summary begins with a statement of the main idea. Supporting sentences then tell the most important facts and details. To summarize a long piece of writing, paraphrase the main idea of each paragraph in a single sentence. Then combine the sentences to form the summary paragraph.

> **Summary ♦ Paraphrasing** is expressing in your own words ideas you have read or heard.

Guided Practice

Paraphrase the following sentences.

1. Corn was cultivated in the Inca civilization of the Andes.
2. Christopher Columbus first introduced corn seeds from the Americas to Europeans.
3. Corn was the main food for American colonists in the 1600s.

Practice

A. Write the following paragraphs. Underline the most important information. Then write notes, paraphrasing the information.

The American colonists were usually successful in farming because they worked hard and had an abundance of farmland. However, this abundance often led to wastefulness. The same kind of crop was planted over and over each season, and the soil's nutrients soon became depleted. Farmers would then simply clear more land and plant again.

The German settlers were the most adept farmers. They rotated crops and added fertilizer to the soil. This enabled them to maintain very productive land for growing their crops.

The crops grown by colonists varied according to the location of the colony. In the Middle Colonies, wheat was the most valuable crop grown and exported. In fact, there was so much wheat that these colonies became known as the "bread colonies." In the Southern Colonies, rice and indigo were the most important crops.

B. Write a summary paragraph of four or five sentences about farming in the American colonies. Use the information from notes you took in **Practice A**.

Apply • Think and Write

Writing a Summary • In a favorite newspaper or magazine, choose an article to read. Take notes about the article, paraphrasing the most important information. Use your notes to write a summary of the article.

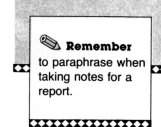

Remember to paraphrase when taking notes for a report.

GETTING
STARTED

Do you know how to plant your own garden? How can you find out?
Name three possible sources of information for this topic.

WRITING ◆
Structuring and Documenting a Report

Once you have gathered sufficient information about your topic, you need to organize the information. Arrange your note cards in the order in which you will present the material. For help in preparing an outline for your report, see pages 570–571.

Your report will have three main parts: an introduction, a body, and a conclusion. The **introduction** briefly tells the subject and main idea of the report. Read the following introduction.

> Fresh water is necessary for all types of outdoor projects, such as gardening. There are three major sources of water that can be used in gardening. Rainfall is the primary source. Surface water from lakes, rivers, and streams is another source. The third major source is subsurface water, which is provided by underground rivers.

The introduction tells you that the purpose of the report is to give information about sources of water used in agriculture.

The **body** of the report gives detailed information about each main topic of your subject. For example, you might devote a paragraph to each of the different water sources named in the above introduction. Each paragraph must then contain a topic sentence and supporting details. Read this paragraph on the topic of rainwater.

> Rainwater is the most important water resource for any home gardening projects. Roof water can be channeled into a barrel by rain gutters and drainpipes. One half inch of rain falling on a ten-by-ten-foot roof area can produce as much as thirty gallons of water.

The function of the **conclusion**, or final paragraph, is to restate all the main points of the report. For example:

> All three water sources—rainfall, surface water, and subsurface water—are necessary for home gardens to flourish. Their conservation and careful management are essential.

The **bibliography** at the end of a report lists all the sources of the information you used. List each source separately on an index card as you write the report. Include the author's name; the title of the article; the name of the book, magazine, or reference book; and the publishing information.

Study the following sample bibliographical entries. Notice that the entries are alphabetized by the author's last name. If there is no author named for an article, alphabetize by the name of the article.

Encyclopedia: Baker, Jerry. "Gardening." The World Book Encyclopedia. 1988 ed.

Magazine: Issacs, F. "How to Grow Great Vegetables." Reader's Digest Apr. 1988: 121–124.

Book: Kelly, John. The All Seasons Garden. New York: Viking Penguin, 1987.

Newspaper: Lacy, Allen. "A Variety of Plants to Suit Any Climate." New York Times 14 Jan. 1988: C10.

Use the following guidelines and the models above for help in writing your bibliography. Follow the models exactly for punctuation, spacing, and indention.

✦ For an encyclopedia article, list the author's name if given (last name first). If not, write the title (in quotation marks), the name of the encyclopedia (underlined), and the year published.

✦ For a magazine article, write the author's name (last name first), the title of the article (in quotation marks), the name of the magazine (underlined), the date, and the page numbers.

✦ For a book, write the author's name (last name first), the title (underlined), place of publication, name of the publisher, and publication date.

✦ For a newspaper article, list the author's name if given (last name first), the title (in quotation marks), the name of the newspaper (underlined), date, section number, and page number.

Summary ✦ A **report** presents information that you have gathered and arranged in a well-organized form.

Guided Practice

Tell whether each sentence is appropriate for the introduction, the body, or the conclusion of a report.

1. Many keep a garden for the simple pleasure of growing food.
2. Thus, whatever your reason for gardening, you will enjoy fresher and often better-tasting food than that purchased at stores.
3. There are several good reasons to keep a vegetable garden.

Practice

A. Write whether the following sentences belong in the introduction, the body, or the conclusion of a report on vegetable gardening.

4. One reason for the popularity of home gardening is the growing fear of pesticides and resulting chemical contamination in store-bought food.
5. Some will conclude that the extra time spent gardening is well worth it, while others will prefer the supermarket.
6. First, it is possible to grow all your salad vegetables with just a few hours of work every weekend.
7. Growing your own vegetables can be a very satisifying activity.
8. However, the advantages and disadvantages of vegetable gardening must be weighed carefully before deciding whether to begin a garden.
9. Another factor is the peace of mind in knowing that only organic materials were used in your garden.

B. Read the following notes. Develop the notes into a paragraph for the body of a report on starting a vegetable garden. Write the paragraph, adding any needed information.

10. Prepare soil before planting.
11. Remove large stones or other debris from garden site.
12. Use shovel; remove grass, plants, and roots from site.
13. Dig up soil to depth of eight to twelve inches; break up, turn over; add nutrients.
14. Before planting, rake soil until fine and smooth.

C. Each bibiliography entry below is either incomplete or written incorrectly. Rewrite the entries that are incorrect, using the correct form. If an entry is incomplete, write what type of information is missing—source, author, page, or date.

15. Food First: Beyond the Myth of Scarcity. Boston: Houghton Mifflin, 1977.
16. McWilliams, Margaret. "Food Supply." 1988 ed.
17. "Drought's Toll on Cannery Row." Hershey, R.D. New York Times 20 Apr. 1988: D1, 8.
18. Cullen, Vincent G. "Sour Pineapples." 6 Nov. 1976: 300.
19. Diet for a Small Planet, New York: Ballantine, 1975. Lappe, Frances Moore.

D. Choose one of the following topics. Then use sources in the library to develop five bibliographical entries for the topic. Refer to the models on page 489 to write the entries correctly.

20. Plants for Flower Gardens
21. Greenhouses for Plants
22. Hydroponics
23. Making a Terrarium

Apply • Think and Write

Dictionary of Knowledge • One of the largest and most valuable research libraries in the world is the Library of Congress in Washington, D.C. Read about the Library of Congress in the Dictionary of Knowledge. Write about why this library is such an important source of information for researchers, teachers, students, and others.

✎ **Remember**
to organize your report carefully and to use a bibliography to document sources.

Focus on Main Idea

The main idea is very important in writing a research report. Your main idea must be the right size — neither too broad nor too narrow.

You get the main idea for a research report by choosing and narrowing a topic. The writer of "Tribute to an Inventor: Cyrus McCormick," which you read earlier, might have started with the idea of "Inventors." But that topic is far too broad; it would take too many pages to develop it properly. On the other hand, the writer might have narrowed the topic too much and tried to write about "McCormick's Addition of the Twine Binder to His Reaper."

Topics that are too broad are more common than topics that are too narrow.

Too Broad   Football, Careers, American Presidents, Travel, Movie Stars, Important News Stories

A narrowed topic represents a main idea, and this main idea is often stated in the title of the report. "Tribute to an Inventor: Cyrus McCormick" clearly shows the main idea of Alice Hengesbach's research report. Notice how the three broad topics "Careers," "American Presidents," and "Travel" from above are narrowed in the titles below.

Narrowed   "A Day in the Life of an Airline Pilot"
"James A. Garfield: An Underrated President"
"Backpacking on the Appalachian Trail"

Research papers often begin with a statement of the main idea. The rest of the paper then sticks to that main idea.

The Writer's Voice ◆ Begin with the too-broad topic of hobbies. Narrow that topic until it is the right size for a research report similar in length to "Tribute to an Inventor: Cyrus McCormick." Compare your main idea with those of your classmates. Are any of them still too broad? Are any of them too narrow?

Working Together

The topic of a research paper — its main idea — often has to be narrowed from a broad, general topic. The main idea should be specific enough to be covered in the number of pages planned. As a group, discuss activities **A** and **B**.

In Your Group
◆ Be sure not to interrupt. ◆ Show appreciation for ideas.
◆ Record the group's ideas. ◆ Help the group finish on time.

A. Discuss the following broad topics. Narrow each one so that it is suitable for a research report like Alice Hengesbach's on pages 476–478. Compare your group's answers with the answers of other groups.

1. Agriculture
2. Women Scientists
3. Popular Music
4. Sports
5. Weather
6. American History
7. Television
8. School

B. With your group, select one of the narrowed topics from activity **A**. Make a list of ideas that would help to develop the topic.

THESAURUS CORNER ◆ Word Choice

Rewrite the following paragraph, changing each word in dark type to a suitable synonym. Use the Thesaurus and Thesaurus Index. Next, underline each verbal you find in the paragraph. Finally, underline twice the one complex sentence.

It is **formidable** to overstate the importance of rice as a food crop. In several European countries, people **fathom** just one word for food, and that word is *rice*. So **momentous** is rice to the Orient that in classical Chinese the words for agriculture and for raising rice are the same. Half the world's population lives wholly or partially on rice, including **opulent** as well as **broke** people.

WRITING PROCESS
RESEARCHING

Writing a
Research Report

Researchers gather information in many ways. When they do *primary research*, they collect their own information from personal experience, observation, surveys, or interviews. When researchers do *secondary research*, they use research someone else has already done. Much of their information comes from library materials.

Whether working from primary or secondary sources, a research writer has one goal—to create a clear, interesting article or report.

Know Your Purpose and Audience

What's
MY PURPOSE

"Tribute to an Inventor," which you read earlier in this unit, is a research report from secondary sources. Its topic was the inventor Cyrus McCormick. Now it's your turn. In this lesson you will write a report from secondary sources about a scientist or an inventor you choose. Your purpose will be to inform your readers.

Who's
MY AUDIENCE

Your audience will be your classmates. Later you can read your reports aloud or create a display for the school lobby.

1 Prewriting

First choose a topic and narrow it to fit the size of your report. Then gather information about your topic.

Choose Your Topic ♦ What general subjects hold your interest? Cars? Movies? Space? Chances are that a number of scientists and inventors made contributions to those fields. Make a list of possible topics; then choose one.

Think About It	Talk About It
Look for "firsts" in different fields. Then choose the one that interests you the most. Narrow your topic to just one aspect of the invention. What do you want to know?	Talk to your classmates about their topic choices. They may have found books or other sources of ideas that you could use. An exciting topic can help make your report better.

Topic Ideas

Luis Alvarez
Marie Curie
Sequoyah
G. W. Carver
Lydia Pinkham
Thomas Edison
Benjamin Franklin

Choose Your Strategy ◆ Read the two information-gathering strategies that follow. Then use the most helpful ideas.

CHOICE ONE

Taking Notes

Research your topic at the library. If you photocopy materials, write the bibliographic information right on the copy. As you read, take notes. Head each card with the topic and source. Be sure to paraphrase the information. Put direct quotations in quotation marks. Organize your notes in the order you will use for your report.

Model

Sequoyah

"Sequoyah," *New Book of Knowledge*, 1985, p. 842.

weekly newspaper started 1828

CHOICE TWO

A Goal/Plan/Outcome Chart

In your report, you will want to tell the scientist's or inventor's goal. You will want to explain the plan of action taken to reach it and the outcome. A goal/plan/outcome chart can help you seek and organize facts to tell that story.

Model

Goal:
To invent a written alphabet for the Cherokee language

Plan:
1. Made one mark for every word
2. Made one mark for every syllable

Outcomes:
1. Didn't work; too many to remember
2. Worked; invented 85 characters

2 Writing

Begin your report with an introduction that names your topic person and states your main idea about him or her. Try to catch your readers' interest in the introduction.

In the body, write paragraphs that tell about your topic person's goal and actions as well as the outcome or outcomes. Your prewriting notes will provide details for these paragraphs.

Finish your report with a conclusion that restates your main idea about your topic person and sums up the information.

Sample First Draft ♦

Many inventors create methods, not machines. A Cherokee named Sequoyah invented a method. He invented the Cherokee alphabet. This alphabet allowed his people to communicate in writing.

Sequoyah was always fascinated by books and writing. He saw american soldiers studying what looked like large white leaves the marks on the leaves seemed to talk to the soldiers. Sequoyah wanted to make talking leaves too. He tried making a different mark for every word he knew. This was too hard to remember then he tried making a different mark for every sylable. This method worked better. After years of effort he created an Alphabet of eighty-five characters.

He taught this alphabet to many people. Soon the Cherokees had a way to write their own language. They quickly produced books and a newspaper.

3 Revising

Revise your report to clarify its meaning. If possible, set it aside for twenty-four hours so that you can consider it more objectively. This strategy may help you revise effectively.

REVISING IDEA

FIRST   Read to Yourself

As you read aloud to yourself, consider your purpose. Did you write a report that gives information about a scientist or inventor based on secondary research? Will your classmates understand and be interested in your report?

Focus: Have you clearly stated your main idea? Does the information in your report support your main idea?

THEN   Share with a Partner

Read your report aloud to a partner. Ask for feedback. These guidelines may help.

The Writer
Guidelines: Listen to your partner's advice but make only the changes you feel are important.
Sample questions:
• Is there anything about my topic that you would like to know more about?
• **Focus question:** Is my main idea clearly stated and supported?

The Writer's Partner
Guidelines: Be honest; give your real opinions. Be polite; speak kindly.
Sample responses:
• I'd be interested in knowing more about _____.
• Could you add something here to support your main idea?

Revising Model ♦ The report below is being revised. The writer's changes are shown in blue.

Revising Marks

delete ℓ

add ∧

move ⟲

The writer combined sentences to make a stronger main idea statement.

The writer's partner wondered when Sequoyah lived.

The writer made this run-on sentence into a complex sentence.

The writer felt that *record* was more precise here than *write*.

The conclusion needed to restate the main idea.

Many inventors create methods, not machines. A Cherokee named Sequoyah invented a method. He invented the Cherokee alphabet. ~~This alphabet~~ *that* allowed his people to communicate in writing. *was born in Tennessee around 1799. He*
Sequoyah ∧ was always fascinated by books and writing. He saw american soldiers studying what looked like large white leaves the marks on the leaves seemed to talk to the soldiers. Sequoyah wanted to make talking leaves too. He tried making a different mark for every word he knew. *Since*
∧ This was too hard to remember ~~then~~ he tried making a different mark for every sylable. This method worked better. After years of effort he created an Alphabet of eighty-five characters.
He taught ~~this~~ alphabet to many people. Soon the Cherokees had a way to ~~write~~ *record* their own language. They quickly produced books and a newspaper. *Sequoyah had made a major ∧ contribution to the Cherokee language.*

Revising Checklist

☐ **Purpose:** Did I write a report giving information about a scientist or inventor based on secondary research?

☐ **Audience:** Will my classmates understand and be interested in my report?

☐ **Focus:** Does my introduction contain a clear main-idea statement? Do the body and conclusion support my main idea?

Now read the report above the way the writer has decided it *should* be. Then revise your own research report.

Grammar Check ♦ Two sentences that run on can often be fixed by combining them as one complex sentence.

Word Choice ♦ Do you want a more precise word for a word like *write*? A thesaurus can help you find exact words.

4 Proofreading

Proofreading gives you an opportunity to fix surface errors and make sure that your report is readable.

Proofreading Model ♦ Look at the report about Sequoyah a second time. The proofreading changes are in red.

Proofreading Marks	
capital letter	≡
small letter	/
add comma	⌄
add period	⊙
indent paragraph	¶
check spelling	⬭

Many inventors create methods, not machines. A Cherokee named Sequoyah invented a method! He invented the Cherokee alphabet. This alphabet allowed his people to communicate in writing. *that* *was born in Tennessee around 1799. He*

Sequoyah was always fascinated by books and writing. He saw american soldiers studying what looked like large white leaves the marks on the leaves seemed to talk to the soldiers. Sequoyah wanted to make talking leaves too. He tried making a different mark for every word he knew. *Since* This was too hard to remember then he tried making a different mark for every (sylable) This *syllable* method worked better. After years of effort he created an Alphabet of eighty-five characters.

He taught this alphabet to many people. Soon *record* the Cherokees had a way to write their own language. They quickly produced books and a newspaper. *Sequoyah had made a major contribution to the Cherokee language.*

Proofreading Checklist

- [ ] Did I spell words correctly?
- [ ] Did I indent paragraphs?
- [ ] Did I use correct capitalization?
- [ ] Did I use correct punctuation?
- [ ] Did I type neatly or use my best handwriting?

PROOFREADING IDEA

Handwriting Check | Check the spacing between your letters and words. Letters and words that are crowded together are hard to read and understand.

Now proofread your report and make a neat copy. Be sure to add a title.

5 Publishing

Make a bibliography for your report. List each source of information. Use the proper form for each entry. Add your bibliography at the end of your report.

The Cherokee Alphabet

Many inventors create methods, not machines. A Cherokee named Sequoyah invented a method that allowed his people to communicate in writing. He invented the Cherokee alphabet.

Sequoyah was born in Tennessee around 1799. He was always fascinated by books and writing. He saw American soldiers studying what looked like large white leaves. The marks on the leaves seemed to talk to the soldiers.

Sequoyah wanted to make talking leaves too. He tried making a different mark for every word he knew. Since this was too hard to remember, he tried making a different mark for every syllable. This method worked better. After years of effort, he created an alphabet of eighty-five characters.

He taught his alphabet to many people. Soon the Cherokees had a way to record their own language. They quickly produced books and a newspaper. Sequoyah had made a major contribution to the Cherokee language.

PUBLISHING IDEAS

Share Aloud

Read your reports aloud. Have the class vote to choose the scientist or inventor they would most like to have known. Cast ballots that include a reason for each voter's choice.

Share in Writing

Display everyone's reports on a bulletin board in the school lobby. Try to include an illustration of each scientist's or inventor's work. Post several sheets of paper for readers' comments.

CURRICULUM
CONNECTION

Writing Across the Curriculum Science

Inventors have contributed to the growth of farm technology. Most inventions are created when someone sees a need and figures out a way to meet it. Many inventors are scientists, but many are not. Do you think you could be an inventor?

Writing to Learn

Think and Plan Think of a product that many people might want or need, such as a homework machine. Then make a goal/plan/outcome chart to help plan it. For *Goal*, write what your invention would do. For *Plan*, write details about how you would make it work. For *Outcome*, describe the success you hope for.

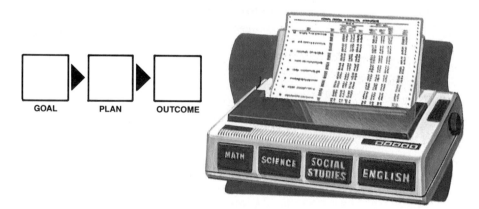

GOAL PLAN OUTCOME

Write Write a proposal to interest a manufacturer in producing your invention. Describe how it works and why it will sell.

Writing in Your Journal

At the beginning of this unit, you wrote about agriculture. Then you read about the development of agriculture. If you don't live on a farm, write in your journal to express your ideas about what farm life might be like. If you do live on a farm, explore your feelings about your future in farming.

BOOKS TO ENJOY

Read More About It

Farms for Today and Tomorrow: The Wonders of Food Production

by Dorothy Shuttlesworth

This is an excellent introduction to the methods and equipment that have made America's farms the most productive on earth.

. . . and now Miguel *by Joseph Krumgold*

Miguel's family have been sheep ranchers for generations. Hard work, strong family ties, and appreciation for nature have brought them success. Now Miguel must overcome obstacles to find his place on the family ranch.   **Newbery Award**

Book Report Idea   Cliffhanger

In the early days of the movies, a film would often end in a "cliffhanger."

Choose Your "Cliff"

Consider giving your next book report as a cliffhanger. Begin by giving some background about the main characters and plot of the book. Then read aloud an excerpt in which the main character is about to experience something exciting. Don't read what finally happens. Encourage your listeners to find out what does happen by reading the book.

UNIT REVIEW

Unit 9

Verbals   *pages 460–461*

A. Write each underlined verbal. Then write whether the verbal is a participle, a gerund, or an infinitive.

1. A <u>caring</u> friend is very important to me.
2. The <u>motivated</u> student wrote a long report.
3. <u>Studying</u> for exams is a challenge to some students.
4. Many students keep notes <u>to study</u>.
5. The teacher gave outlines <u>to guide</u> the students.

Clauses   *pages 462–463*

B. Write *phrase* or *clause* for each underlined word group.

6. <u>Without any effort</u>, the giant picked up the large tree.
7. The wizard rubbed his head <u>when the experiment failed</u>.
8. <u>As the story unfolded</u>, Pam's imagination soared.
9. The genie escaped from the magic lamp <u>within seconds</u>.
10. That character's nose grew longer <u>because he lied</u>.

C. Write each clause in parentheses. Underline its subject once and its verb twice. Then label each clause *independent* or *subordinate*.

11. (If you order now,) you will receive a free gift.
12. Before she sealed the envelope, (she checked its contents.)
13. I wrote with a pencil (since I had no pen.)
14. (I was completely surprised) (when the package arrived.)

Complex Sentences   *pages 464–465*

D. Write whether each sentence is simple or complex.

15. In the back of her mind, Stephanie knew she could win.
16. While they sang the national anthem, Chris eyed the team.
17. As I said before, the best is yet to come.
18. The decisions of the judges are not negotiable or pending.

Correcting Sentence Errors   *pages 466–467*

E. Rewrite each run-on sentence as a compound or complex sentence. Use correct punctuation and the conjunction shown in parentheses.

19. January is promising it signals a new year. (because)
20. I feel so happy snow is on the ground. (when)
21. June is a crucial time I don't worry about my grades. (but)
22. I may not finish my speech the bell rings. (if)

Homophones and Homographs   *pages 468–469*

F. Write the correct homophone shown in parentheses.

23. (Their, They're) on time.   **25.** (Here, Hear) they are now.
24. We arrived (to, too) early.   **26.** Try not to (stare, stair) at anyone.

G. Write each sentence. Underline each pair of homographs. Write whether each homograph is a noun or a verb.

27. The nurse wound a bandage around the patient's wound.
28. Changing a tire can tire you out.
29. The police suspect that the prime suspect has fled town.

Report   *pages 488–491*

H. Write whether each item belongs in the introduction, body, conclusion, or bibliography of a report about Robert Peary.

30. Peary's expeditions between 1893 and 1897 led to some important discoveries about arctic regions.
31. Robert Peary became famous as the discoverer of the North Pole.
32. Huntford, Roland. *The Last Place on Earth*. New York: Atheneum, 1985.
33. After completing his trip, Peary wrote *The North Pole,* a book about his experiences.

Focus on Main Idea   *pages 492–493*

I. Each topic below is too broad. Narrow the topics so that they are suitable for research reports.

34. Sports   **35.** Summer   **36.** History   **37.** Famous People

LANGUAGE PUZZLERS

Sentence Gridlock

Try your hand at making a verbal-sentence grid like the one below. Each sentence must appear twice, and each must contain a verbal.

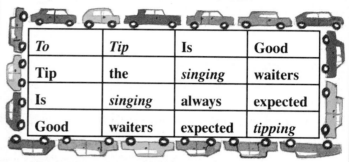

To	Tip	Is	Good
Tip	the	*singing*	waiters
Is	*singing*	always	expected
Good	waiters	expected	*tipping*

Silly Signs

Use verbals to make funny signs like these.

It is unlawful to post signs here.

Reading this sign is forbidden.

Bicycle riding is prohibited on this bicycle path.

Unit 9 Extra Practice

1 Verbals

p. 460

A. Write the participle in each sentence. Then write the noun it modifies.

1. I photographed the rising sun.
2. Unlock the sliding door carefully.
3. We heard some exciting news.
4. My uncle may purchase a used car.
5. That composition does not have one misspelled word.
6. Return the damaged merchandise.
7. A loaded truck entered the yard.
8. The driving rain drenched me.
9. We hiked through the swirling snow.
10. Vida told us an amazing story.

B. Two words are underlined in each sentence. Write the word that is a participle.

11. Beaming, my father unwrapped my gift.
12. The exhausted jogger returned from the park.
13. A local station televised the thrilling game.
14. The startled chipmunk scampered away.
15. They conducted a losing battle.

C. Write the gerund in each sentence below. Then label it *subject*, *direct object*, *predicate nominative*, or *object of a preposition*.

16. Fishing provides many hours of relaxation.
17. My favorite sport is swimming.
18. We saw a filmstrip about mining.
19. Nobody enjoys losing.
20. My counselor suggested a course in typing.
21. That artist also does printing.
22. Their only occupation was farming.
23. Dancing made them famous.
24. They discussed the importance of memorizing.

D. Write the underlined words in each sentence and label them *infinitive* or *prepositional phrase*.

25. Gold was the first metal known <u>to humans</u>.
26. The interest in it seems <u>to remain</u> universal.
27. For centuries people tried <u>to turn</u> base metals into gold in a process called alchemy.
28. Many alchemists spent their lives searching for an easy way <u>to make</u> gold from cheap metals, such as mercury and lead.
29. An interest in alchemy spread from the Greeks and Arabs <u>to the western Europeans</u>.
30. Alchemists in laboratories toiled over smoking pots, or crucibles, hoping <u>to uncover</u> the great secret.
31. <u>To prove</u> their beliefs, they tested nearly every substance known <u>to them</u>.
32. The credit for uncovering basic knowledge about the properties of many important chemicals and compounds belongs <u>to the alchemists</u>.
33. The study of alchemy was not scientific, but it led <u>to the discovery</u> of valuable information.
34. It proved <u>to be</u> the forerunner of chemistry.

E. Write the verbal in each sentence and label it *participle*, *gerund*, or *infinitive*.

35. The people in ancient Greece and Rome always enjoyed the telling of stories about gold.
36. The traveling storytellers often repeated the legend of King Midas.
37. Midas had received a gift for helping Bacchus.
38. Midas was granted the power to turn anything into gold.
39. Laughing, the king touched everything.
40. The greedy king, singing with joy, turned objects into shiny gold in his huge palace.
41. At his golden dinner table, Midas began to notice a serious problem.
42. Eating was now impossible for him.
43. Any food touched turned into gold.
44. Bacchus mercifully prescribed bathing as a cure for Midas's harmful golden touch.
45. The legend of King Midas serves to warn against greed.

2 Clauses

p. 462

A. Write *phrase* if the word group is a phrase. Write *clause* if it is a clause.

1. during the spring
2. when I see rain
3. until help comes
4. if he has money
5. before the class
6. must have been seen
7. we know
8. before she left
9. should have been built
10. someone needs us
11. because I was late
12. until they sparkled
13. at night
14. when she saw them
15. after our test
16. after our test began

B. Write the clause in parentheses. Underline the subject once and the verb twice. Label each clause *independent* or *subordinate*.

EXAMPLE: (They walk) (after they eat).

ANSWER: (They walk) independent, (after they eat.) subordinate

17. (If you can write well now,) (you may become a successful journalist in the future.)
18. (Eliza Poitevent of Pearlington, Mississippi, began her career in journalism) (when she sold some poems to a newspaper in the 1860s.)
19. (She became a literary editor) (after she was hired by the New Orleans *Daily Picayune*.)
20. (While she was employed there,) (she married the publisher of that Louisiana newspaper.)
21. (It became her paper) (when he died in 1876.)
22. (Eliza Poitevent had a serious problem) (because the paper owed money to many people.)
23. (If she could attract more readers,) (the *Daily Picayune* might become profitable.)
24. (Before she went home each day,) (Poitevent wrote the society column for the newspaper.)
25. (Nothing appeared in print) (until it met her high standards for quality and accuracy.)
26. (As the *Daily Picayune* improved,) (the number of its readers grew rapidly.)
27. (When the paper prospered,) (Poitevent returned to writing poems.)

3 Complex Sentences
p. 464

A. Identify each sentence as *simple* or *complex*.

1. Everything has grown rapidly since the rain.
2. Everything has grown rapidly since our town had two inches of rain.
3. We celebrated after we counted the ballots.
4. We had a big party after the last election.
5. They always go where the food is tasty.
6. The store has not opened since the fire.
7. We have not gone there since the new supermarket opened.
8. The flowers bloomed until the snow came.
9. The plants grew until the first frost.
10. We may go if the weather improves.

B. Write each sentence. Underline the subject once and the verb twice in each clause. Label the sentence *simple*, *compound*, or *complex*.

11. Elizabeth Cochrane was born in Pennsylvania in 1867, but she became world famous as Nellie Bly.
12. She was hired by the Pittsburgh *Dispatch* in 1885 and became one of its best reporters.
13. The title of a popular song by Stephen Foster inspired her unforgettable pen name.
14. Nellie Bly, while she worked for the Pittsburgh newspaper, wrote a variety of articles.
15. Some articles described conditions in factories, and others were reviews of plays.
16. When she was only twenty, she was hired by the New York *World*.
17. One of her first assignments was an investigation of a public hospital in New York City.
18. Before she wrote an article on that assignment, Nellie Bly became a patient in that hospital.
19. Because her stories were so vivid and accurate, conditions in the hospital began to improve.
20. As her career with the *World* continued, Nellie Bly wrote many articles about urban problems.
21. She published several books, including *Ten Days in a Mad-House* and *Six Months in Mexico*.

4 Correcting Sentence Errors

p. 466

A. Identify each incorrect word group as a *run-on sentence* or *sentence fragment*.

1. I finished my work then I played chess.
2. Cary was shivering uncontrollably it was cold in his room.
3. During the first act of the comedy.
4. And recited the names of the states.
5. Because we needed that information.
6. The lake changed colors the sun slowly set.
7. If you lose something.
8. The lights went out the movie began.

B. Read the sentences below. If a sentence is a run-on, rewrite it as two sentences. If it is correct, label it *correct*.

9. I found a wallet it was lying on the sidewalk.
10. I looked inside and found an ID card.
11. The owner's name was on it I called him up.
12. He was surprised he came for the wallet.
13. He drove up then I handed it to him.
14. He was relieved to get back his money and credit cards.
15. He offered me a reward for my honesty.
16. I tried to refuse he insisted.
17. Most people are nice they appreciate honesty.

C. Each word group is a sentence fragment. Make each one a sentence by adding your own words. Write sentences about a vacation trip.

18. The vacation of my dreams.
19. Because it looks so wonderful on television.
20. Have ever been there.
21. After buying new suitcases.
22. With everyone in my family.
23. Traveling in comfort on a plane.
24. To stay in a hotel with a large pool.
25. Dining in a colorful restaurant.
26. Would write something every day.
27. About all the unusual sights.
28. Arrive home exhausted.

FOLKLORE

PART ONE

Unit Theme   *African and West Indian Folklore*

Language Awareness   **Subject-Verb Agreement**

PART TWO

Literature   **"Tiger Story, Anansi Story"
retold by Philip Sherlock**

Composition   **The Tradition of Folklore**

Writing
IN YOUR JOURNAL

WRITER'S WARM-UP ◆ What do you know about West Africa and the West Indies? Since some aspects of the culture of those places are now a part of American culture, you may know more than you realize. In your journal tell something about one of these places that you would like to experience firsthand.

Animals in folktales often act like people. Think of five ways that individual animals and groups of animals might act like people.
The spider talks. Elephants laugh.

1 Making Subjects and Verbs Agree

Number means that a word is either singular or plural. In a sentence, a verb must agree in number with the subject noun or pronoun. A subject and verb agree in number when they are both singular or both plural. Study the present-tense verb forms below.

	Singular	Plural
First person	I agree	we agree
Second person	you agree	you agree
Third person	he, she, it agrees	they agree

Notice that a present-tense verb changes its form only in the third-person singular. Subject nouns are always third person, singular or plural. When you speak and write, follow the rules for subject-verb agreement below.

If a subject is a singular noun or a third-person singular pronoun, use the present-tense verb form that ends in *-s* or *-es*.

> **The spider <u>agrees</u> with its friend.**
> **It (or *he*, *she*) <u>agrees</u> to help.**

If a subject is a plural noun or any pronoun other than third-person singular, use the present-tense verb form that does not end in *-s* or *-es*.

> **The spiders <u>agree</u> among themselves.**
> **I (or *you*, *we*, or *they*) <u>agree</u> with the spider.**

Rules for spelling forms of verbs are on page 614.

Summary ◆ A verb needs to agree with its subject in number. When you are proofreading, check for agreement between each subject and its verb.

Guided Practice

Tell which verb agrees with the subject in each sentence.

1. The spider character (call, calls) himself Anansi.
2. Anansi stories (come, comes) from Western Africa.
3. Animals (talk, talks) like people in these stories.

Practice

A. Choose the correct verb in parentheses to complete each sentence about the Anansi stories. Write the verb.

4. Anansi (trick, tricks) other animals with his cleverness.
5. In Anansi folktales, animals (act, acts) like human beings.
6. These stories (describe, describes) human behavior.
7. They (teach, teaches) a lesson about life.
8. This oral literature (reflect, reflects) the people's beliefs.

B. Write each sentence, using the present-tense form of the verb in parentheses.

9. Rosa (read) all kinds of folktales.
10. She always (cheer) for the heroes.
11. Such stories (sparkle) with wisdom.
12. The short, clever plots (entertain) her.
13. Many stories (occur) in nature.

C. Rewrite the following paragraph, using verb forms that agree with the subjects.

14. This book contain several Anansi tales. **15.** Two stories comes from Caribbean countries. **16.** Each Caribbean tale follow the ancient African storytelling formula. **17.** Many people from Trinidad and Jamaica hears these tales. **18.** They proudly traces their heritage of folklore back to Africa.

Apply • Think and Write

From Your Writing • Read what you wrote for the Writer's Warm-up. List three or four subjects with their verbs. Ask a partner to check your list for subject-verb agreement.

Remember
that the subjects and verbs you use need to agree.

Interpret this radio message from a stranded seafaring captain: My motor d____n't work! I h____ no power. The fish a____ biting the boat! My food supply i____ nearly gone!

2 Forms of *be*, *have*, and *do*

The verbs *be*, *have*, and *do* often cause problems in subject-verb agreement because they have irregular forms. The chart below shows which forms to use for different subjects. Notice the difference between the third-person singular and plural forms. The complete conjugation of the verb *be* is shown on page 657.

Forms of *be*, *have*, and *do*				
Singular	**Present**	**Past**	**Present**	**Present**
I	am	was	have	do
you	are	were	have	do
he, she, it or a singular noun	is	was	has	does
Plural				
we	are	were	have	do
you	are	were	have	do
they or a plural noun	are	were	have	do

The present and past-tense forms of these verbs remain the same when they are combined with *n't* to form contractions.

you <u>aren't</u>	the port <u>wasn't</u>	she <u>doesn't</u>
they <u>haven't</u>	we <u>weren't</u>	the island <u>hasn't</u>

To avoid agreement problems with contractions, break them into two words and make the verbs agree with their subjects.

> **Summary** ◆ The verbs *be*, *have*, and *do* have special singular and plural forms. Pay special attention to these verbs when you speak and write.

Guided Practice

Name the correct verb in parentheses.

1. the people (does, do)
2. the culture (is, are)
3. I (hasn't, haven't)
4. you (isn't, aren't)
5. he (doesn't, don't)
6. we (was, were)

Practice

A. Write the correct verb in parentheses and label it *singular* or *plural*.

7. the natives (has, have)
8. the islander (doesn't, don't)
9. my guide (is, are)
10. they (was, were)
11. tourists (isn't, aren't)
12. I (am, is)
13. we (wasn't, weren't)
14. the tribesmen (does, do)
15. the influences (is, are)
16. a nation (hasn't, haven't)

B. Choose the verbs in parentheses that correctly complete the sentences about the heritage of the West Indies. Write the sentences.

17. These islands (is, are) part of the West Indies.
18. Many West Indians (is, are) descendants of African slaves.
19. They (was, were) Ashanti tribesmen from present-day Ghana.
20. African cultural traditions (has, have) influenced islanders.
21. The African influence (is, are) everywhere on the islands.

C. Write each sentence, using the correct present-tense form of the verb in parentheses.

22. Most Caribbean islands (have) an Old-World charm.
23. The four main island groups (be) the Bahamas, the Greater Antilles, the Lesser Antilles, and the Dutch West Indies.
24. Each island (have) a warm climate.
25. The clear, tropical sea (be) an attraction for tourists.
26. (Do) the setting appeal to you?

Apply • Think and Write

Planning a Travel Guide • Work with a partner and plan a travel guide to an imaginary island. Use forms of *be*, *have*, and *do* in your description of the island and its main tourist attractions.

✎ **Remember**
that the verbs *be*, *have*, and *do* have special forms.

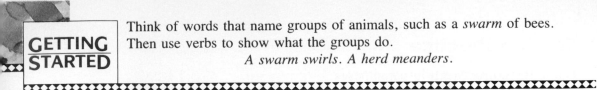

GETTING
STARTED

Think of words that name groups of animals, such as a *swarm* of bees.
Then use verbs to show what the groups do.
A swarm swirls. A herd meanders.

3 Agreement with Collective Nouns

A noun that names a group of people, animals, or things is
called a collective noun. Notice that each collective noun below is
singular in form even though the group it names has many members.

army	chorus	committee	crew	family	group	school
audience	club	convoy	crowd	flock	majority	team

Collective nouns may be used as singular nouns or plural nouns,
depending on the intended meaning of the sentence. Therefore, a
collective noun may be followed by a singular or plural verb.

Use a singular verb when a collective noun refers to a group that is acting as
a single unit.

A *group* <u>shares</u> its home in the forest with Anansi.

In the above sentence, the group is acting as a single unit. The singular verb
shares and the singular pronoun *its* show that the collective noun *group* is
singular in this sentence.

Use a plural verb when each member of the group is acting as an individual.

The *group* often <u>go</u> their separate ways.

In the above sentence, the plural verb *go* and the plural pronoun *their* show
that *group* is plural.

Summary ♦ A **collective noun** names a group but may be
used as a singular noun or as a plural noun.

Guided Practice

Name each collective noun. Tell whether it is singular or plural.

1. The whole group appreciates Anansi's determination.
2. The majority often don't realize Anansi's talents.
3. A crowd usually exclaims its delight at Anansi's triumphs.

Practice

A. Each subject is a collective noun. Write each subject and label it *singular* or *plural*.

4. Our school takes an active interest in African culture.
5. A class writes its book reports on Anansi stories.
6. The drama club gives auditions for the role of the spider.
7. The art committee paint posters of their favorite characters.
8. The faculty give support in their subject fields.
9. An African dance troupe performs at the school each year.
10. The company puts on a show in our auditorium.
11. A small musical ensemble adds its magic.
12. The audience arrive singly or in groups.
13. My family looks forward to these shows.

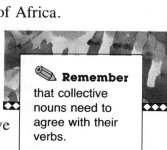

B. Write each sentence, using the correct present-tense form of the verb.

14. A group (travel) together to view African art at the museum.
15. The school (provide) the transportation to the museum.
16. Our crowd (give) its attention to the art historian.
17. The audience (talk) among themselves after the art lecture.
18. The art faculty (praise) their favorite African artists.

C. Write each sentence, using a verb of your choice in the correct form of the verb.

19. A library team _____ their time researching African stories.
20. The staff _____ its support.
21. The Ashanti tribe _____ a remarkable history of its own.
22. A group still _____ in their homes on the Gold Coast of Africa.
23. A family _____ its children to hear the tales of long ago.

Apply • Think and Write

Vocabulary Booster • Find out what groups these collective nouns name: *gaggle*, *kindle*, *exaltation*, *pride*, and *covey*. Write a sentence about the members of each group.

> ✎ **Remember**
> that collective nouns need to agree with their verbs.

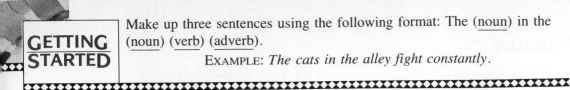

GETTING
STARTED

Make up three sentences using the following format: The (noun) in the (noun) (verb) (adverb).

EXAMPLE: *The cats in the alley fight constantly.*

4 Special Problems of Agreement

You can check subject-verb agreement in your sentences. Focus on the number of the subject, then make the verb agree with it.

Prepositional Phrases   A prepositional phrase coming between a subject and its verb does not affect subject-verb agreement.

■ The *folklore* of many African tribes <u>is</u> interesting.

In the sentence above, the singular verb *is* agrees with the singular subject *folklore*. Do not be confused by the noun *tribes* in the prepositional phrase.

Inverted Word Order   Even when a subject follows a verb, as in an inverted sentence, the verb must agree with the subject. You can check agreement by changing the sentence to normal word order.

■ In their stories <u>was</u> a *lesson*.   A *lesson* <u>was</u> in their stories.

Inverted sentences often begin with *here*, *there*, or *where*. Be careful not to use the contraction for the singular verb *is (′s)* with these words when the subject is plural.

Incorrect: Here's the stories of African folklore.
Correct: Here are the stories of African folklore.

> **Summary** ♦ Find the subject of a sentence and make the verb agree with it.

Guided Practice

Identify the subject of each sentence and name the correct verb in parentheses.

1. The population of people (is, are) diverse in Africa.
2. In the Kalahari desert there (is, are) many Bushmen.
3. The folktales from this region (is, are) unusual.

Practice

A. Choose the correct verb in parentheses to complete each sentence about African folklore. Write the sentence.

4. The forces of nature (is, are) important in African folklore.
5. One tale of the Bushmen tribes (tell, tells) about the origin of the sun.
6. In the tale there (was, were) no sun in the sky.
7. The members of the tribe (look, looks) for a new sun.
8. Where (is, are) the leader of the tribe?

B. Write the subject. Then write *is* or *are* to complete each sentence.

9. The languages of the Bushmen ____ complex and diverse.
10. The speech of these people ____ characterized by clicking sounds.
11. There ____ an average of twenty-five persons in each group.
12. Where ____ other African tribes?
13. The tribes of the Hottentot people ____ also in the Kalahari.

C. Complete each sentence using a present-tense verb. Be sure the subjects and verbs agree.

14. African tales of a tribe
15. Characters in a folktale
16. The heroes of the story
17. Folklore in many countries
18. In one tale there
19. In Africa there
20. Animals in a folktale
21. My favorite tale with animals
22. The plots of folktales
23. In some countries there

Apply • Think and Write

Dictionary of Knowledge • Folklore includes stories, myths, legends, and fables. Read about the animal characters in *Aesop's fables* in the Dictionary of Knowledge. Write sentences about animal characters that have human traits. Include sentences with prepositional phrases coming between the subjects and verbs, and sentences starting with *here*, *where*, or *there*.

✎ **Remember**
that each subject and its verb need to agree in number.

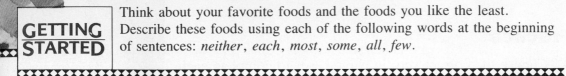

GETTING STARTED

Think about your favorite foods and the foods you like the least. Describe these foods using each of the following words at the beginning of sentences: *neither*, *each*, *most*, *some*, *all*, *few*.

5 Special Problems of Agreement

Compound Subjects Compound subjects joined by *and* need a plural verb. This is true whether the subjects are singular or plural.

- ■ *Beans* and *rice* <u>are</u> traditional foods in the Caribbean Islands.

Singular subjects joined by *or* or *nor* need a singular verb.

- ■ Either a *mango* or a *papaya* <u>is</u> a favorite fruit in Jamaica.

Plural subjects joined by *or* or *nor* need a plural verb.

- ■ Neither *peaches* nor *apricots* <u>are</u> tropical fruits.

If a singular and a plural subject are joined by *or* or *nor*, the verb agrees with the subject closer to it.

- ■ The mangos or the *papaya* <u>is</u> delicious.
- ■ The mango or the *papayas* <u>are</u> delicious.

Singular	
anybody	neither
anyone	nobody
anything	no one
each	nothing
either	one
everybody	somebody
everyone	someone
everything	something

Plural	
both	many
few	several

Singular or Plural		
all	more	none
any	most	some

Indefinite Pronouns As the subject of a sentence, an indefinite pronoun needs to agree with its verb in number. The chart on the left shows that most indefinite pronouns are singular, but a few are plural, and some may be either singular or plural.

Singular: *Each* of the vegetables <u>tastes</u> delicious.
Plural: *Many* <u>taste</u> sweet.

For pronouns that may be singular or plural, look at the word to which the pronoun refers. If the word is singular, the pronoun is considered singular. If the word is plural, the pronoun is plural.

Singular: *Most* of the food <u>is</u> tasty.
Plural: *Most* of the foods <u>are</u> tasty.

> **Summary** ◆ In a sentence with a compound subject or an indefinite pronoun as the subject, the subject and verb need to agree in number.

Guided Practice

Name the correct verb in parentheses for each subject.

1. Steel bands and drums (is, are)
2. Both of them (sounds, sound)
3. A flute or a fife (is, are)
4. Songs or a poem (has, have)
5. Most of the festivals (appear, appears)

Practice

A. Write the correct verb in parentheses for each subject.

6. One of my pears (was, were)
7. Everything (taste, tastes)
8. Bananas or a lime (is, are)
9. A guava or a lemon (has, have)
10. All of the papayas (was, were)

B. Write each sentence, using the correct verb in parentheses.

11. Music and dance (is, are) important in the West Indies.
12. Everyone (likes, like) the Calypso music.
13. Scratch bands or a steel band (are, is) also popular.
14. Both (have, has) interesting rhythms.
15. Most of the instruments (is, are) homemade.

C. Complete each sentence using a present-tense verb. Be sure the verb agrees with the subject.

16. Visitors and students
17. Many of the Europeans
18. Neither an alien nor I
19. Islanders or a tourist
20. Both of the residents
21. Puerto Ricans or Jamaicans
22. No one on the island
23. All of the artists
24. Natives or settlers
25. Some of the history

Apply • Think and Write

Imaginative Description • Imagine you are eating at a Caribbean island restaurant. Write a paragraph describing the food and the atmosphere. Include sentences with each of these constructions: compound subjects joined by *or*; a singular indefinite pronoun as the subject.

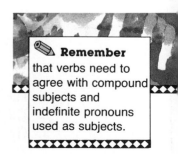

✎ **Remember**
that verbs need to agree with compound subjects and indefinite pronouns used as subjects.

Suppose you are campaign manager for a politician. Would you describe your candidate as *tall* or *lanky*? *Bookworm* or *scholar*? *Proud* or *arrogant*? What other words would you use? Not use?

VOCABULARY ◆
Denotation and Connotation

A word may call forth many meanings. For example, if you called your politician *lanky*, you would be expressing not only the idea of tallness, but also of thinness, awkwardness, and lack of grace.

The *literal*, or exact, meaning of a word is called its **denotation**. A dictionary contains the denotations of words. The positive or negative feeling associated with a word is called its **connotation**. While some words—synonyms—have about the same dictionary meaning, the feelings they bring out often differ in some way. For example, you might consider yourself *brave*, but you probably wouldn't consider yourself *reckless*. You might call yourself *thrifty*, but you wouldn't call yourself *cheap*.

To write or speak well, you must pay attention to the connotation as well as the denotation of words.

Building Your Vocabulary

For each sentence, choose the word with the more negative connotation.

1. The (ambitious, pushy) actor wanted to become a Broadway star.
2. The dog's (hostile, unfriendly) snarl was frightening.
3. The president's face had a (bony, chiseled) appearance.

Practice

A. Write each sentence. Use the word in parentheses that has the more positive connotation.

1. His (task, chore) was to mow the lawn by 4:00 P.M.
2. A (mob, throng) of strikers descended upon the capital.
3. A small (group, gang) of these people talked to the governor.
4. The nobleman loved to (eat, dine) in a splendid fashion.
5. Sharon (smiled, smirked) as she bowed to the audience.
6. It was a(n) (quaint, odd) old house in a quiet neighborhood.
7. John's sister is a (timid, quiet) young girl.
8. The (noise, sound) of the band was heard throughout the park.
9. Mrs. Robinson was known to be a very (strict, firm) teacher.
10. The (scent, odor) of marigolds filled the room.

B. Write the word in each group that has the most negative connotation.

11. loaf, rest, relax
12. brief, curt, concise
13. young, youthful, juvenile
14. unique, different, peculiar
15. low-cost, inexpensive, cheap
16. prying, curious, inquisitive

C. Write two sentences that show the difference in connotation between the synonyms in each pair.

17–18. save, scrimp
19–20. take, grab
21–22. slender, skinny
23–24. speak, chatter

Language Corner ◆ Alliteration

Alliteration is the repetition of the initial sound in two or more words that are used together. For example, "The silvery sea silently swept the sandy shore." Alliteration is often used in poetry; however, it is also used in regular speech and writing.

Make up some brand names that use alliteration. Examples: *Spinelli's Spectacular Spaghetti, Edgar's Exalted Eggnog.*

SPINELLI'S SPECTACULAR SPAGHETTI

How to Combine Sentences

When you combine sentences, be sure that the subject and the verb of your new sentence are in agreement, regardless of their positions in the sentence. Prepositional phrases, for example, are often used to combine sentences with related ideas. Notice that when the two sentences in example **1** are combined in example **2**, the placement of the prepositional phrase between the subject and the verb does not affect their agreement.

1. These myths are from the Caribbean. Many come from Africa.
2. Many myths from the Caribbean come from Africa.

You can also combine sentences by using inverted word order. Notice how changing the placement of the prepositional phrase changes the order of the subject and the verb in example **4**.

3. Many slaves were from Africa. Their <u>myths and legends came</u> with them.
4. With slaves from Africa <u>came</u> their <u>myths and legends</u>.

When you use inverted word order to combine sentences, make sure the verb of your new sentence agrees with the subject—not with any noun or pronoun that comes before the verb.

Combining sentences with repeated subjects or predicates can also cause problems with subject-verb agreement. When you combine sentences and form a compound subject, check to make sure that the subject correctly agrees with its verb.

The Grammar Game ◆ Create your own sentence combinations! Write subjects for four possible sentences. Add a prepositional phrase to each subject. Then exchange papers with a partner and write complete sentences. Check for correct subject and verb agreement.

Working Together

Notice how combining sentences adds interest and variety to your writing as your group works on activities **A** and **B**.

A. Combine each pair of sentences below. Remember to check for subject-verb agreement in your new sentences.

1. African sculpture is widely appreciated today. African paintings are also widely appreciated.
2. African designs impress many artists. These designs are for masks, fabrics, and jewelry.
3. From Africa came music. This was wonderful, rhythmic music.
4. Rituals were brought by Africans. Dance was brought, too.
5. People admire these things a great deal. These people are from many different countries.

B. Rewrite the paragraph below, combining sentences as needed.

Noah's sister is an ethnologist. She is at the university. Her work is important. Her work is with the people of the Caribbean islands. Tape machines record many things for her. She also uses a camera to record many things. She learns about their customs. She learns about their way of life. From her discoveries come new information. She has information about how people live and work.

WRITERS' CORNER ♦ Positioning Words and Phrases

Sometimes you can change the emphasis in a sentence by changing the position of a word or phrase.

EXAMPLE: **The dancer left the stage quickly with a flourish.**

CHANGE: **With a flourish, the dancer quickly left the stage.**

Read what you wrote for the Writer's Warm-up. Do you want to add emphasis to any of your sentences by moving words or phrases?

IBIBIO TRIBE MASK   The Metropolitan Museum of Art
The Michael C. Rockefeller Memorial Collection, Bequest of Nelson A. Rockefeller, 1979

FOLKLORE

PART TWO

Literature   "Tiger Story, Anansi Story"
retold by Philip Sherlock

Composition   The Tradition of Folklore

CREATIVE
Writing

FINE ARTS ◆ Look at the mask in the photograph
at the left. Who wore it? What did the mask
symbolize? Write a description of the person who
wore the mask. Describe both the person and the
occasion on which it was worn.

from

Tiger Story, Anansi Story

retold by Philip Sherlock

There once was a time when all things in the forest were named after Tiger, the strongest of all the animals. Even the stories the animals told in the evening bore Tiger's name. Nothing at all was named after the weakest animal, Anansi the spider. So one evening Anansi went to see Tiger about that.

Tiger listened as Anansi asked for his favor: to name the animals' stories after Anansi. But Tiger hated to name his well-loved stories after such a weak little creature. So Tiger asked Anansi to do two impossible tasks in return for granting his wish.

However, Anansi was more clever than Tiger expected. On Monday, Anansi performed the first task of bringing Tiger a gourd full of bees. Still, the second task was even more difficult than the first one. By Saturday, could Anansi bring Tiger a live Mr. Snake?

The Second Task: Mr. Snake

On Tuesday morning Anansi got up early. How was he to catch Mr. Snake? The question had been buzzing about in his head all night, like an angry wasp. How to catch Mr. Snake?

Perhaps he could trap Snake with some ripe bananas. He would make a Calaban beside the path that Snake used each day when the sky beat down on the forest and he went to the stream to quench his thirst. 'How good a thing it is,' thought Anansi, 'that Snake is a man of such fixed habits; he wakes up at the same hour each morning, goes for his drink of water at the same hour, hunts for his food every afternoon, goes to bed at sunset each day.'

Anansi worked hard making his Calaban to catch Snake. He took a vine, pliant yet strong, and made a noose in it. He spread grass and leaves over the vine to hide it. Inside the noose he placed two ripe bananas. When Snake touched the noose, Anansi would draw it tight. How angry Mr. Snake would be, to find that he had been trapped! Anansi smiled to himself while he put the finishing touches to the trap, then he hid himself in the bush by the side of the track, holding one end of the vine.

Anansi waited quietly. Not a leaf stirred. Lizard was asleep on the trunk of a tree opposite. Looking down the path Anansi could see heat waves rising from the parched ground.

There was Snake, his body moving quietly over the grass and dust, a long, gleaming ribbon marked in green and brown. Anansi waited. Snake saw the bananas and moved towards them. He lay across the vine and ate the bananas. Anansi pulled at the vine to tighten the noose, but Snake's body was too heavy. When he had eaten the bananas Snake went on his way to the stream.

That was on Tuesday. Anansi returned home, the question still buzzing about in his head: 'How to catch Snake? How to catch Snake?' When his wife asked him what he would like for supper, he answered, 'How to catch Snake?' When his son asked if he could go off for a game with his cousin, Anansi replied, 'How to catch Snake?'

A Slippery Hole! That was the answer. Early on Wednesday morning he hurried back to the path in the forest where he had waited for Snake the day before, taking with him a ripe avocado pear. Snake liked avocado pears better even than bananas. In the middle of the path Anansi dug a deep hole, and made the sides

slippery with grease. At the bottom he put the pear. If Snake went down into the hole he would not be able to climb back up the slippery sides. Then Anansi hid in the bush.

At noon Snake came down the path. 'How long he is,' said Anansi to himself; 'long and strong. Will I ever be able to catch him?'

Snake glided down the path, moving effortlessly until he came to the Slippery Hole. He looked over the edge of the hole and saw the avocado pear at the bottom. Also he saw that the sides of the hole were slippery. First he wrapped his tail tightly round the trunk of a slender tree beside the track, then lowered his body and ate the avocado pear. When he had finished he pulled himself out of the hole by his tail and went on his way to the river. Anansi had lost the bananas; now he had lost the avocado pear also!

On Wednesday Anansi spent the morning working at a 'Fly-Up', a trap he had planned during the night while the question buzzed through his head: 'How to catch Snake. How? How?' He arranged it cleverly, fitting one of the slender young bamboo-trees with a noose, so that the bamboo flew up at the slightest touch, pulling the noose tight. Inside the noose he put an egg, the only one that he had left. It was precious to him, but he knew that Snake loved eggs even more than he did. Then he waited behind the clump of bamboos. Snake came down the path.

The Fly-Up did not catch Snake, who simply lowered his head, took the egg up in his mouth without touching the noose, and then enjoyed the egg in the shade of the clump of bamboos while Anansi looked on. He had lost the bananas and avocado pear, and his precious egg.

There was nothing more to do. The question 'How to catch Snake?' no longer buzzed round and round in his head, keeping him awake by night, troubling him throughout the day. The Cal-aban, the Slippery Hole, and the Fly-Up had failed. He would have to go back to Tiger and confess that he could not catch Snake. How Parrot would laugh, and Bullfrog and Monkey!

Friday came. Anansi did nothing. There was no more that he could do.

Early on Saturday morning, before daybreak, Anansi set off for a walk by the river, taking his cutlass with him. He passed by the hole where Snake lived. Snake was up early. He was looking to-wards the east, waiting for the sun to rise, his head resting on the edge of his hole, his long body hidden in the earth. Anansi had not expected that Snake would be up so early. He had forgotten Snake's habit of rising early to see the dawn. Remembering how he had tried to catch Snake, he went by very quietly, limping a little, hoping that Snake would not notice him. But Snake did.

'You there, you, Anansi, stop there!' called Snake.

'Good morning, Snake,' replied Anansi. 'How angry you sound.'

'And angry I am,' said Snake. 'I have a good mind to eat you for breakfast.' Snake pulled half his body out of the hole. 'You have been trying to catch me. You set a trap on Monday, a Cal-aban. Lizard told me. You thought he was asleep on the trunk of the tree but he was not; and as you know, we are of the same family. And on Tuesday you set a Slippery Hole, and on Wednesday a Fly-Up. I have a good mind to kill you, Anansi.'

'Oh, Snake, I beg your pardon. I beg your pardon,' cried the terrified Anansi. 'What you say is true. I did try to catch you, but I failed. You are too clever for me.'

'And why did you try to catch me, Anansi?'

'I had a bet with Tiger. I told him you are the longest animal in the world, longer even than that long bamboo-tree by the side of the river.'

'Of course I am,' shouted Snake. 'Of course I am. You haven't got to catch me to prove that. Of course I am longer than the bamboo-tree!' At this, Snake, who was now very angry and ex-cited, drew his body out of the hole and stretched himself out on the grass. 'Look!' he shouted. 'Look! How dare Tiger say that the bamboo-tree is longer than I am!'

'Well,' said Anansi, 'you are very long, very long indeed. But Snake, now that I see you and the bamboo-tree at the same time, it seems to me that the bamboo-tree is a little longer than you are; just a few inches longer, Snake, half a foot or a foot at the most. Oh, Snake, I have lost my bet. Tiger wins!'

'Tiger, fiddlesticks!' shouted the enraged Snake. 'Anyone can see that the bamboo-tree is shorter than I am. Cut it down you stupid creature! Put it beside me. Measure the bamboo-tree against my body. You haven't lost your bet, you have won.'

Anansi hurried off to the clump of bamboos, cut down the longest and trimmed off the branches.

'Now put it beside me,' shouted the impatient Snake.

Anansi put the long bamboo pole beside Snake. Then he said, 'Snake, you are very long, very long indeed. But we must go about this in the correct way. Perhaps when I run up to your head you will crawl up, and when I run down to see where your tail is you will wriggle down. How I wish I had someone to help me measure you with the bamboo!'

'Tie my tail to the bamboo,' said Snake, 'and get on with the job. You can see that I am longer!'

Anansi tied Snake's tail to one end of the bamboo. Running up to the other end, he called, 'Now stretch, Snake, stretch!'

Snake stretched as hard as he could. Turtle, hearing the shouting, came out of the river to see what was happening. A flock of white herons flew across the river, and joined in, shouting, 'Stretch, Snake, stretch.' It was more exciting than a race. Snake was stretching his body to its utmost, but the bamboo was some inches longer.

'Good,' cried Anansi. 'I will tie you round the middle, Snake, then you can try again. One more try, and you will prove you are longer than the bamboo.'

Anansi tied Snake to the bamboo, round the middle. Then he said:

'Now rest for five minutes. When I shout, "Stretch," then stretch as much as you can.'

'Yes,' said one of the herons. 'You have only six inches to stretch, Snake. You can do it.'

Snake rested for five minutes. Anansi shouted, 'Stretch.' Snake made a mighty effort. The herons and Turtle cheered Snake on. He shut his eyes for the last tremendous effort that would prove him longer than the bamboo.

'Hooray,' shouted the animals, 'you are winning, you are winning, four inches more, two inches more...'

At that moment Anansi tied Snake's head to the bamboo. The animals fell silent. There was Snake tied to the bamboo, ready to be taken to Tiger.

From that day the stories have been called Anansi Stories.

Library Link ♦ *You can read other folktales like "Tiger Story, Anansi Story" in the book from which this excerpt was taken,* West Indian Folk-Tales, *retold by Philip Sherlock.*

Reader's Response

Which part of the tale did you like best? Why?

Tiger Story, Anansi Story

Responding to Literature

1. Read Anansi's story as a Read Around. Choose someone to read the introduction aloud. Then take turns reading from the story. When you read, use your voice to help tell the story.

2. Fables are animal stories that teach lessons. Usually the lesson is stated in a moral. Folktales do not usually state morals, but there are often lessons to be learned. What lesson could be learned from this story? Write a one-sentence lesson for the story. Share it with classmates.

3. If you had told this story, how might you have had Anansi catch Snake? What might have worked? What might have been a funny solution?

Writing to Learn

Think and Analyze ◆ Evaluate these statements and determine your agreement. Use the scale on the left as an indicator.

3 Agree strongly 2 Agree 1 Don't know 0 Disagree	A. Folktales reflect the culture of the people. B. Folktales always contain a series of three events. C. Folktales are only for young children. D. Folktales focus on one character.

Write ◆ In one paragraph, explain the value of folktales in a culture.

Think of a story that someone has told you. What made the story
memorable? How did the storyteller make it interesting?

SPEAKING and LISTENING ◆
The Oral Tradition

Many of the fables, myths, legends, and folktales that we read
today were not always written in books. Originally these tales
were told orally by talented, clever storytellers. The Anansi stories,
for example, were told and shared by storytellers in West Africa.
The stories traveled to the West Indies and eventually reached us in
written form.

Storytellers have given us an oral tradition that connects us to
our past. Oral tradition is the handing down of stories from one
generation to the next by word of mouth. Each new storyteller may
present a different version of a story. For example, there are
hundreds of known versions of the popular folktale ''Cinderella.''

You can continue the enjoyable tradition of storytelling. One of
the best ways to learn storytelling techniques is to tell one of your
favorite folktales. Folktales are good stories to tell because many
have clear simple plots, few characters, and fast-paced action.
They are also usually suitable for all ages.

Use these guidelines for help in telling stories as well as listening to them.

Telling a Story	1. Choose a story that you enjoy. Know the story well before you tell it, but do not memorize the entire story. Take brief notes about important parts of the story. 2. Be sure that the story is appropriate for your audience. A story told to young children, for example, should be fairly short and uncomplicated. 3. Practice the story before you tell it. Then tell it with enthusiasm, involving your audience in the story. 4. In a story with dialogue, give each character a distinctive voice. Also, use gestures for emphasis.
Listening to a Story	1. Listen for the main idea in the story. In your mind, picture the story as it is being told. 2. Listen attentively to appreciate and evaluate the storyteller's style and techniques.

Summary ◆ As a storyteller, choose a story that you enjoy and tell it with enthusiasm. As a listener, picture the story in your mind as it is being told.

Guided Practice

Refer to ''Tiger Story, Anansi Story'' on pages 530–534 to answer the following questions.

1. What words does Anansi keep repeating during the story? Read the words aloud with expression. What does repeating such words as these add to an oral story?

2. Read the dialogue between Anansi and Snake on page 533. What is Snake's mood? Read some of Snake's part aloud, expressing his mood.

3. When does Anansi realize that he can trick Snake at last? Read his words on page 533 aloud, expressing Anansi's slyness.

Practice

A. Write notes for one of the following scenes from ''Tiger Story, Anansi Story.'' Then use the notes to tell that part of the story to a group of classmates.

4. the scene in which Anansi creates a Calaban to try to catch Snake, page 531

5. the scene in which Anansi tries to catch Snake in the Slippery Hole, pages 531–532

6. the scene in which Anansi manages to get Snake tied to the bamboo pole, page 534

B. Choose one of the scenes in **Practice A** to retell in a different way. Include details that create your own unique version of the scene. Tell your version to a partner. Have your partner evaluate your storytelling techniques.

Apply ◆ Think and Write

Storytelling ◆ Write a brief story with Anansi the spider as the main character. Give your story a new plot and different characters. Practice the story, then tell it to the class, using notes to help you remember the story.

✎ **Remember** to tell a story clearly and creatively.

GETTING
STARTED

Name a familiar story you heard as a child, such as "Hansel and Gretel" or "Snow White and the Seven Dwarfs." Describe the scenes that made the story unforgettable.

WRITING ◆
Elements of a Folktale

Folktales are heard in countries all over the world. Most folktales reflect the lives, customs, beliefs, and emotions of the people in their countries of origin. Because folktales were originally told orally among people, many have a conversational tone.

Although they come from different parts of the world, folktales are alike in many ways. They often share the following characteristics.

Purpose   The main purpose of a folktale is to entertain people with an action-packed, suspenseful story. Folktales also teach important values, such as courage and patience. For example, Anansi does not become discouraged when he fails to catch Snake. He is patient and continues to pursue his goal.

Plot and Character   The plots of most folktales develop quickly and are often concerned with some kind of task, challenge, or quest. The plot of "Tiger Story, Anansi Story" is about the tasks Anansi must perform in order to have the stories named after him.

The number three is also significant in many plots. Anansi finally succeeds in catching snake after three failures.

Characters in folktales, whether they are animals or people, usually have only one distinguishing trait. Often they are wise or foolish, good or evil. A common type of character in African folktales is the clever trickster, such as Anansi.

Magic   Folktales usually include magical elements. In the Anansi stories, all the animals can talk, and many have human emotions. Other common magical elements in folktales are magical objects, impossible tasks and trials that are magically accomplished, and wishes supernaturally granted.

> **Summary** ◆ **Folktales** are stories passed down from one generation to the next that share certain common elements.

Guided Practice

Tell whether each description from "Tiger Story, Anansi Story" tells about a magical element, develops the plot, or teaches values.

1. Anansi worked hard making his Calaban to catch Snake.
2. Anansi put the long bamboo pole beside Snake.
3. "Yes," said one of the herons. . . . "You can do it."

Practice

A. Write the element or elements of a folktale that each description illustrates.

    4. An honest, hard-working shoemaker has only enough leather to make one more pair of shoes. During the night, elves make a perfect pair of shoes for him. The next day, a customer pays more than the usual price for the shoes.

    5. A clever cat, dressed in boots, manages to obtain a grand castle for his kind master. He tricks the mean ogre living in the castle.

    6. "Someone has been sleeping in my bed!" Mr. Bear bellowed as he ran and locked the front door of the Bear household.

B. Choose one idea below and write a brief story based on it. Add one or more folktale elements, such as a task, a magical object, or animals that talk.

    7. On a quiet country road, a farmer and his wife see something that stops them instantly.

    8. Gina is not favored to win a gold medal in the swimming meet. However, a secret helper comes to her aid.

    9. On his way to school, Michael stops to help a dog that has been injured.

Apply ◆ Think and Write

Dictionary of Knowledge ◆ The National Storytelling Festival is held each year in the town of Jonesborough, Tennessee. Read about this festival in the Dictionary of Knowledge. Write why you think it attracts people from all over the country to tell tales as well as listen to them. Write what kind of tale you would tell at the festival if you were one of the storytellers.

> ✎ **Remember**
> that folktales have special elements that distinguish them from other types of literature.

Focus on Your Growth as a Writer

Writing takes practice. You can gain practice in many ways. It helps to keep a journal containing ideas for future writing. Above all, you can, and must, write often. Practice brings improvement in writing just as surely as it does in music, sports, and acting.

This lesson suggests some specific ways for you to improve. These are not rules. They are simply bits of common-sense advice that writers through the years have found practical and useful.

Vocabulary   There is no substitute for the right word. Synonyms are not all alike—they have shades of meaning. A Thesaurus, as you have learned, is a valuable tool, but it must be used with care. You should always seek the *exact* word you need.

Grammar   You already know the grammar of English. Otherwise you would be unable to speak it. Now, you should work to develop all the resources of English grammar. That means finding various ways to express an idea — and deciding which one is the *best* way.

Experience and Imagination   The more you see and the more you experience, the more you will have to write about. In other words, you learn by living. But you must also *reflect* on what you see and do. You must use both your intelligence and your creativity.

Confidence   "I can't write" is a complaint made by people of all ages. Except in the rarest of cases, it isn't true. Not only can nearly everyone write, but they can also improve a great deal. You may never win a Pulitzer Prize in literature, but you can learn to write clear, effective prose. You *can* write. Practice!

The Writer's Voice ◆ What kind of writing do you prefer to do? Factual prose? Poetry? Short fiction? Why do you find that kind of writing the most enjoyable? Is it the kind you do best?

Working Together

You can improve your writing by practicing and by working with other writers. Share common concerns and find solutions to common problems as you work with your group on activities **A** and **B**.

In Your Group
♦ Be sure people understand the task. ♦ Volunteer ideas.
♦ Agree or disagree in a pleasant way. ♦ Appreciate other ideas.

A. Below are some problems that writers often experience. Discuss them, adding any that members of your group think are important. Then decide which one of the problems is the most serious or affects the most members. As a group, write a paragraph that explains the problem and offers one or more possible solutions.

1. Getting started — writing that first draft — is the worst part.
2. I start off well, but I can almost never finish what I start.
3. Readers won't be interested in what I want to write.
4. You need a big "message" to write well — and I don't have one.
5. I have an idea for a story, but it's probably been used already.

B. On your own write a paragraph, a full page, a poem, a newspaper column — whatever you wish. Then, when you are finished, share your writing with your group. What do other members see as your greatest *strength* as a writer? Discuss ways to build on that strength.

THESAURUS CORNER ♦ Word Choice

Synonyms are sometimes almost right, but not quite. Use the Thesaurus and Thesaurus Index to find the synonym that is exactly right for each of the words in dark type.

1. By doing his work carefully and well, Kazutaka has proved to be a **prudent** employee.
2. I have a rip in my shirt; could you **overhaul** it?
3. Karen **surmised** that her opponent in the debate did not understand the difficult question.

CURRICULUM
·CONNECTION·

Writing Across the Curriculum   Social Studies

Some folklore and traditions continue to be useful and valuable through the centuries; others become outmoded. Sometimes it is good to evaluate ideas we have come to take for granted.

Writing to Learn

Think and Evaluate   Below are statements from *Poor Richard's Almanac* written by Benjamin Franklin in the 1700s. These statements have become a part of American folklore. Are these ideas by Benjamin Franklin acceptable today? Copy each statement and write a score beside it, based on the evaluation chart at the left.

Hunger is the best pickle.
Love your neighbor, yet don't pull down your hedge.
He that scatters thorns, let him not go barefoot.
Three may keep a secret if two of them are dead.
Now that I have a sheep and a cow, everybody bids me good morrow.

Agree strongly 3 Agree 2 Agree with reservations 1 Disagree 0	Hunger is the best pickle. Love your neighbor, yet don't pull down your hedge. He that scatters thorns, let him not go barefoot. Three may keep a secret if two of them are dead. Now that I have a sheep and a cow, everybody bids me good morrow.

Write   Now that you have evaluated "Poor Richard's" sayings, pick the most interesting one and write what you think it means.

Writing in Your Journal

During this unit you have written about folklore and read about the folklore and folk traditions of West Africa and the West Indies. Every culture and every family have traditions. In your journal write about your favorite family or holiday tradition and why you especially enjoy it.

BOOKS TO ENJOY

Read More About It

Anansi the Spider: Tales from an Ashanti Village *edited by Peggy Appiah*

In these thirteen traditional tales, the crafty Anansi outwits his friends and enemies while surprising and delighting his readers.

Tales from the Story Hat

retold by Verna Aardema

This collection of West African tales by a renowned storyteller is a rich source of both pleasure and information about the folklore of the area.

The Cow-Tail Switch and other West African Stories *collected by Harold Courlander*

In addition to tales about Anansi, the author has collected stories that explain natural phenomena.

Book Report Idea Critic's Card Catalog

Creating a critic's card catalog is a way to keep the information from your classmates' book reports. Each time you report on a book, prepare a card for a classroom card catalog. On the front of the card, list the book's title and author and a brief summary. On the back of the card, however, be a critic. Write an opinion or two of the book. Classmates can use the cards to choose books and later add their opinions to the cards.

Shane by Jack Schaefer

Set in Wyoming in 1889, Shane is a classic Western. A stranger, Shane finds work at the Starrett farm. Young Bob Starrett admires Shane.

UNIT REVIEW

Unit 10

Subject-Verb Agreement   *pages 514–523*

A. Write the verb that correctly completes each sentence.

1. Mrs. Wills (grow, grows) vegetables in her garden.
2. Every spring the gardeners (plant, plants) different seeds.
3. Often it (take, takes) hours to weed and water the plants.
4. We (see, sees) the results of their work months later.

B. Write the correct verb in parentheses and label it *singular* or *plural*.

5. they (isn't, aren't)
6. the leader (does, do)
7. my friends (doesn't, don't)
8. I (am, is)
9. you (was, were)
10. others (wasn't, weren't)
11. I (hasn't, haven't)
12. we (is, are)

C. Write each collective noun. Write whether it is singular or plural.

13. Our company shares its office space with another firm.
14. The family often take separate vacations.
15. The film crew work hard at different jobs on the set.
16. A majority agrees with the mayor's views.

D. Write the subject. Write *was* or *were* to complete each sentence.

17. In the cereal box _____ a small surprise.
18. The setting of many of her mysteries _____ a crime scene.
19. There _____ the long lost photographs.
20. Where _____ the souvenirs from our trip?

E. Write each sentence, using the correct verb shown in parentheses.

21. Neither (know, knows) the answer to that question.
22. Sam and Margo (has, have) sparkling personalities.
23. Both (is, are) extremely popular at school.
24. The contestants or the judge (was, were) incorrect.

Proofreading

G. Proofread each sentence for misspelled words. Write each misspelled word correctly.

25. The mayor's family enjoyed themselfs at the parade.
26. Children's teethbrush are displayed in the store window.
27. It's two early to tell who our next president will be.
28. Place the book about deer on the shelve over their.

H. Each sentence has one incorrect word. Write each sentence correctly.

29. Were you real upset when the game was sold out?
30. I'm glad that I didn't wait in no line.
31. Our audition went good, and we were told to come back.
32. The car was damaged bad in the accident.

I. Write the correct form of each incorrect verb.

33. Tom and I is in the back row in the school picture.
34. You does the actual work while I supervise.
35. Why weren't she at the picnic yesterday?
36. The height of these buildings are within the building code.

J. Write each run-on sentence and fragment correctly.

37. This workbook is helpful I know you could use it.
38. On a week night.
39. The small plane landed abruptly it was out of fuel.
40. Gusting winds from the north.

Denotation and Connotation   *pages 524–525*

K. Write each sentence, using the word in parentheses with the more positive connotation.

41. My parents chose to live in an (old, quaint) house.
42. The suit Juan bought was quite (inexpensive, cheap).
43. Barry's uncle rents a (shack, cabin) for his family each summer.
44. The dinner portions were quite (modest, skimpy) tonight.
45. My sister likes to (save, hoard) all her toys.

CUMULATIVE REVIEW

UNIT 1: Sentences *pages 4–19*

A. Write and label the compound subject or compound verb in each sentence.

   1. Dr. Friedman and Dr. Chung share the same medical offices.
   2. They have evening hours and offer laboratory services.
   3. Competitive fees and excellent treatment are available.

B. Write whether each sentence error is a run-on or a fragment
   Then write the sentences correctly.

   4. Some people wanted Washington to be king, he rejected the idea.
   5. One of the duties of the President.
   6. In addition to Commander in Chief of the armed forces.

UNIT 2: Nouns *pages 56–65*

C. Write each noun. Label it *singular, singular possessive, plural*, or *plural possessive*.

   7. laboratories   **9.** grandchildren's   **11.** policies'
   8. mattress   **10.** Bess's   **12.** teacher's

UNIT 3: Verbs *pages 118–129*

D. Write and label each direct object and indirect object.

   13. Please pass us the papers.   **15.** Please do not take the toys outside.
   14. Dad told Mom the news.   **16.** Can you buy me a snack?

E. Write and label each direct object, predicate nominative and predicate adjective.

   17. The mountaineers began the climb at dawn.
   18. The hike to the base of the mountain was easy.
   19. The leader of the group was Helena.
   20. She was somewhat nervous and fearful before the climb.

Unit 4: Verbs *pages 174–187*

F. Write each underlined verb and its tense: *present, past, future, present perfect, past perfect*, or *future perfect*.

21. Michele and I <u>studied</u> for the test last night.
22. My friends <u>have tried</u> to give me advice, but I never <u>listen</u>.
23. The baseball team <u>had selected</u> a new player for the summer season.
24. Our family <u>will have traveled</u> to many places by next year.
25. George <u>will write</u> about many types of animals in his science report.

Unit 5: Pronouns *pages 232–247*

G. Write and label each reflexive or intensive pronoun.

26. The answering machine turns itself on and off automatically.
27. You yourself must have known that.
28. Did James himself record the message?
29. Diane heard herself on the tape and laughed.

H. Write the correct pronouns in parentheses.

30. You can blame (they, them) or thank (we, us).
31. Did (they, them) take more time than (we, us)?
32. (He, Him) told (we, us) newcomers the password.
33. (She, Her) and Gina gave (I, me) their word.

Unit 6: Adjectives *pages 294–301*

I. Choose the correct words in parentheses to complete the sentences. Write the sentences.

34. Why is this microwave oven (more expensive, expensiver) than the one on display?
35. The heating elements in this stove are (less, least) efficient (then, than) the ones in that stove.
36. The best-selling brand has the (bigger, biggest) fan system of all.
37. The control panel is the (easiest, most easiest) to operate.
38. Of the two models on sale, the red model is (nicer, nicest).

UNIT 7: Adverbs *pages 350–361*

J. Write the correct word in parentheses.

    39. Last night I could not keep my eyes open (any, no) longer.
    40. Mom did not say (nothing, anything) at first.
    41. Hardly (anything, nothing) escapes her or Dad.
    42. They (were, weren't) hardly surprised.

K. Write the word in parentheses that correctly completes each sentence.

    43. My dog Bounce (playful, playfully) barked and chased the ball.
    44. Bounce ran (good, well) and caught up with the ball.
    45. The batter was (real, really) angry at the dog.
    46. The batter was tagged out, and Bounce felt (proud, proudly).
    47. Bounce had (sure, surely) earned his spot on the team.

UNIT 8: Prepositions *pages 404–411*

L. Write and label each adjective phrase and adverb phrase.

    48. The year 1776 began with a bang.
    49. The publication of Thomas Paine's pamphlet rallied everyone.
    50. During the year, colonists assembled in Philadelphia.
    51. The draft prepared by Thomas Jefferson became the official Declaration of Independence.

M. Write the words that correctly complete the sentences.

    52. Against (who, whom) was the American Revolution fought?
    53. What were other important issues (beside, besides) taxation?
    54. Did the French choose (among, between) England and the colonies?
    55. How many amendments are there (in, into) the Bill of Rights?

Conjunctions *pages 412–413*

N. Write each conjunction and label it *coordinating* or *correlative*.

    56. A mule is neither a horse nor a donkey.
    57. A mule is the offspring of a male donkey and a female horse.
    58. Mules are slower but more surefooted than horses.
    59. Both donkeys and mules have long ears.

UNIT 9: Verbals and Complex Sentences *pages 460–467*

O. Write each underlined verbal and label it *participle, gerund,* or *infinitive*.

60. <u>Winning</u> a gold medal in the Olympics is quite an honor.
61. Athletes need the courage <u>to compete</u> on their own.
62. All athletes know the importance of <u>training</u>.
63. One young sprinter, <u>inspired</u> and <u>encouraged</u>, made us proud.

P. Write each clause in parentheses and label it *independent* or *subordinate*.

64. (The dressmaker kept her own hours,) since she worked at home.
65. (When the sewing machine was broken,) she sewed by hand.
66. She made her own patterns (because she was also a designer.)
67. If your clothes need alterations, (she can do the job.)

Q. Write whether each sentence is simple, compound, or complex.

68. The Boy Scouts was founded in England by Sir R. Baden-Powell.
69. While it was founded there in 1908, it started here in 1910.
70. You can consult with your local Scout leader, or you can call the number listed in the telephone book.

UNIT 10: Subject-Verb Agreement *pages 514–523*

R. Write each collective noun. Label it *singular* or *plural*.

71. Another youth group is the Girl Scouts.
72. The membership serve others in the fields of health and art.
73. The friendship committee sends letters to foreign pen pals.
74. In return, the community supports us in different ways.

S. Write the correct verb in parentheses.

75. Here (is, are) the results of the latest survey.
76. Either teachers or the principal (was, were) the writer of this survey.
77. Some of the students (has, have) certain advantages.
78. In their homes (is, are) computers.

LANGUAGE PUZZLERS

Unit 10 Challenge

Collective-Noun Couplets

Write four more rhyming couplets for this zoo poem. Each line should contain one of the collective noun phrases below. Use a singular verb in each first line and a plural verb in the second.

A covey of partridges was guarding its nest
While a pride of lions were getting their rest.

a school of dolphins   a herd of horses
a bevy of quails   a litter of tiger cubs
a drove of cattle   a gaggle of geese
a bundle of hounds   a pack of timber wolves

Sports Chain

The clue to this sports puzzle is a chain of letters. The last letter of each subject is the first letter of the verb in the following sentence. The subject in the last sentence gives the clue for the verb in the first sentence. (Hint: All verbs are in the present tense.)

1. My sisters and Aunt Anne _ _ _ three miles a day.
2. Neither my parents nor I _ _ _ _ _ running.
3. Three miles _ _ a long distance to run.
4. Gymnastics _ _ _ _ _ a better activity for me.
5. The United States _ _ _ _ _ many gymnasts to the Olympics.
6. Our team _ _ _ _ _ all their spare time training for it.
7. The public _ _ _ _ various contributions to the Olympic team.
8. My sisters and my brother _ _ _ _ _ _ _ often.

Unit 10 Extra Practice

1 Making Subjects and Verbs Agree   *p. 514*

A. Write the present-tense verb form that would agree with a third-person singular subject.

1. write
2. hiss
3. study
4. leave
5. wash
6. carry
7. cultivate
8. fix
9. paint
10. echo
11. undergo
12. construct
13. rush
14. hatch
15. worry

B. Write each sentence, using the present-tense form of the verb in parentheses.

16. A large cloud (block) the sun.
17. A bell (signify) the end of the lecture.
18. The little boy (scratch) his mosquito bites.
19. Our new fan (blow) cool air into the living room.
20. The cautious man always (latch) his door.
21. The light (flash) on and off sixty times a second.
22. Warm soda (fizz) more than cold soda.
23. A large maple tree (shade) our house.
24. The airplane (fly) to the east coast every day.
25. The train (move) slowly through the mountains.
26. The catcher (miss) the ball every time.
27. The restaurant (supply) the waiters with uniforms.
28. She (walk) several miles around the lake every day before breakfast.
29. The door (open) by itself.
30. The flower (fill) the room with a beautiful scent.
31. The seal (splash) water at the crowd.
32. Each car (undergo) a series of qualifying laps.
33. The customer (pay) his bill with a check.
34. The painter (mix) her colors carefully.
35. He (play) the guitar, the violin, and the piano like a professional.

2 Forms of *be, have,* and *do*

p. 516

A. Write the correct verb in parentheses. Beside it, write whether it is plural or singular.

1. the dog (has, have)
2. we (is, are)
3. the radio (was, were)
4. the cars (does, do)
5. the games (is, are)

6. they (was, were)
7. the clouds (isn't, aren't)
8. the book (does, do)
9. the pen (is, are)
10. the people (has, have)

B. Write each sentence, using the correct verb in parentheses.

11. The heavy trucks (was, were) in the right lane.
12. The stereo (does, do) not keep me from doing my homework.
13. Your letter (has, have) arrived with the check in it.
14. I (was, were) going to ask you a favor.
15. Two telephones (is, are) enough for this house.
16. You (doesn't, don't) sound like yourself.
17. My friend (has, have) a part-time job.
18. A bad storm (is, are) about to break.
19. The computer (doesn't, don't) make many mistakes.
20. You (do, does) write interesting letters.
21. The key (was, were) misplaced by my neighbor.
22. I (doesn't, don't) know what time the train arrives.
23. The taxi driver (was, were) very helpful.
24. The kittens (has, have) all been fed.
25. Six different people (has, have) told me the show is the best they have seen.
26. It (isn't, aren't) warm enough to eat outside.
27. The runners (was, were) exhausted.
28. The trees (does, do) help conceal the house.
29. The water (wasn't, weren't) clean.
30. The car (has, have) been in the repair shop.
31. My computer system (has, have) a keyboard and a monitor.
32. A monitor (is, are) a display screen.
33. Information (is, are) stored on floppy disks.
34. Disks (is, are) easy to use.
35. Jannell's computer system (has, have) a printer.
36. The printer (do, does) the work of a typewriter.
37. Letters or reports (is, are) typed very quickly.

3 Agreement with Collective Nouns *p. 518*

A. Each subject is a collective noun. Write each subject and label it *singular* or *plural*.

1. Our block committee plans a carnival each spring.
2. The crowd enjoy themselves at a number of attractions.
3. An orchestra entertains throughout the day.
4. Usually our team wins the tug of war.
5. The school lends us several cafeteria tables for the day.
6. The clean-up crew patrols the entire area at dusk.
7. Our youth group help out with different games of skill.
8. My family eat at a variety of food booths.
9. The varsity club sponsors tests of strength and agility.
10. The high school chorus presents a concert at the day's end.

B. Write each sentence, using the correct present-tense form of the verb.

11. A circus troupe (come) to town every summer.
12. A truck convoy (arrive) in the middle of the night.
13. A roustabout crew (erect) the big top at dawn.
14. An acrobatic family (practice) different routines.
15. A crowd (gather) to watch their favorite side shows.
16. The clown army (emerge) from a tiny armored car.
17. An elephant herd (parade) around the ring.
18. A daredevil team (risk) their lives on that stunt.
19. My family (prefer) different acts in the circus.
20. A local group (send) orphans to the circus for free.

C. Write each sentence, using a verb of your choice in the correct present-tense form.

21. The student council ＿＿＿ an annual holiday show.
22. A decorating committee ＿＿＿ a winter scene.
23. Our club ＿＿＿ baked goods.
24. The chorus ＿＿＿ as favorite storybook characters.
25. My class ＿＿＿ to work on advertising.
26. The orchestra ＿＿＿ on the stage.
27. The entire family ＿＿＿ a game together.
28. A crowd of people ＿＿＿ out of the stadium.
29. Our group ＿＿＿ home in several automobiles.

4 Special Problems of Agreement   *p. 520*

A. If the subject in the phrase is singular, write *is*. If the subject is plural, write *are*.

1. Dark clouds in the sky ____
2. The kittens under the chair ____
3. The paint on the walls ____
4. Several horses in the field ____
5. The choice of the judges ____
6. Our costumes for the play ____
7. The color of the flowers ____
8. The heat from the flames ____
9. Many trees on my block ____
10. The noise from the streets ____

B. Write each sentence, using the correct verb in parentheses.

11. Computers of every kind (is, are) useful for communication.
12. Information from computers (makes, make) life easier.
13. Computers in a car (tells, tell) whether anything is wrong.
14. A car with computers even (has, have) the ability to talk.
15. Games of every type (utilizes, utilize) computers.
16. Rides in an amusement park (operates, operate) with the help of computers.
17. Many kitchen appliances (is, are) run by computers.
18. An airplane with several computers (is, are) easier to fly.
19. Computers in every way (affects, affect) our life.
20. The age of computers (has, have) just begun.

C. Write each sentence, using the correct verb in parentheses.

21. On the roof (sits, sit) several large birds.
22. There (flows, flow) a river through the town.
23. Where (does, do) the others want to go?
24. Under the porch (is, are) a rake.
25. What (was, were) the teacher saying?
26. Here (is, are) the papers you asked for.
27. How (does, do) the music sound from across the street?
28. When (has, have) the train ever been on time from Chicago?
29. In the sky (floats, float) several large balloons.
30. On a flagpole (wave, waves) a large flag.

5 Special Problems of Agreement   *p. 522*

A. Write the verb in parentheses that agrees with the subject of the sentence.

 1. Knowledge and information (travels, travel) in a variety of ways.
 2. A signal or a wave (sends, send) information.
 3. Wires or cables (carries, carry) information.
 4. Laser beams and other light sources (is, are) also message carriers.
 5. Waves or electrical signals (creates, create) your television picture.
 6. A telephone or a teletype machine (receives, receive) messages through wires.
 7. Sounds and pictures (is, are) picked up by laser beam from video discs.
 8. Radios or television sets (provide, provides) most people with their information.
 9. Neither magazines nor books (reaches, reach) as many people as television does.

B. Write the correct verb for each of the following sentences.

 10. Most of the road (goes, go) through the hills.
 11. All of the birds (sings, sing) in the morning.
 12. Someone (writes, write) very long letters.
 13. Nobody (wants, want) to be the first to speak.
 14. Each of the cars (looks, look) new to me.
 15. None of the fruit (was, were) ripe.
 16. Something (smells, smell) good enough to eat.
 17. Nothing (feels, feel) as good as a cool breeze.
 18. Most of the food (is, are) gone.
 19. Everyone (is, are) going to the theater.
 20. Each of us (wants, want) a computer.
 21. Most of my friends (has, have) two radios.
 22. Few in the class (takes, take) notes.
 23. Neither of our television sets (is, are) working.
 24. Anything with red (attracts, attract) hummingbirds.
 25. All of the park (is, are) open at dawn.
 26. One in the crowd always (yell, yells) loudly.
 27. Many in our group (has, have) cameras with them.

Acknowledgments continued from page ii.

265: David and Linda Phillips for SB&G. 269: NASA. 271: The Granger Collection. 273: *l*. The Granger Collection; *r*. Rensselear Polytechnic Institute Archives, Troy, New York. 276: Dan De Wilde for SB&G. 280: *l*. © Sam C. Pierson, Jr./ Photo Researchers, Inc.; *r*. J. Moss/H. Armstrong Roberts. 281: *Bert Breen's Barn* © 1975 by Walter D. Edmonds. Used by permission of Little, Brown & Company. **Unit 6** 294: Michael Gallagher/Bruce Coleman. 297: Phil Degginger. 299: Marjorie Kinnan Rawlings Center, Florida. 303: E.R. Degginger. 306: *An October Day* by Winslow Homer. Sterling and Francine Clark Art Institute, Williamstown, Massachusetts. 317: *Osprey's Nest* by Winslow Homer. Sterling and Francine Clark Art Institute, Williamstown, Massachusetts. 321: P. Kresan/H. Armstrong Roberts. 330: Dan De Wilde for SB&G. 335: From *Rascal* by Sterling North, illustrated by John Schoenherr. Illustrations copyright © 1963 by E.P. Dutton. Reproduced by permission of the publisher, E.P. Dutton, a division of Penguin Books USA Inc. **Unit 7** 359: Illustration by Arthur Rackham. 361: Illustration by John Tenniel. 366: *A Dream* by Minnie Evans. The North Carolina Museum of History, Raleigh. 379: IMAGERY for SB&G. 379: NASA. 388: Dan De Wilde for SB&G. 393: *The High King* by Lloyd Alexander. Used by permission of Dell Books, a division of Bantam, Doubleday, Dell Publishing Group, Inc. **Unit 8** 408: *William Shakespeare*, attributed to John Taylor, National Portrait Gallery, London. 411, 412: Culver Pictures. 420: From *The Lake No. 1* by Georgia O'Keeffe. Des Moines Art Center, Coffin Fine Arts Trust Fund. 435: Joe DiStefano/David and Linda Phillips. 440: Dan De Wilde for SB&G. 445: Jacket photo by Martha Cooper from *The Break Dance Kids: Poems of Sport, Motion and Locomotion* by Lillian Morrison. Courtesy William Morrow & Company, Inc., Publishers. **Unit 9** 465: Larry Lefever/Grant Heilman Photography. 467: Jeffrey E. Blackman/The Stock Market of NY. 472: *Planting Potatoes* by Jean-Francois Millet. Courtesy Museum of Fine Arts, Boston. 491: Earth Scenes/E.R. Degginger. 493: E.R. Degginger. 494: The Granger Collection. 498: Dan De Wilde for SB&G. 503: Jacket illustration by Jean Charlot from *...And Now Miguel* by Joseph Krumgold, illustrated by Jean Charlot. Copyright, © 1953 Joseph Krumgold. Reprinted by permission of Harper & Row, Publishers, Inc. **Unit 10** 516: J. Messerschmidt/Bruce Coleman. 519: Robert Frerck/Odyssey Productions. 521: © Peter B. Kaplan/Photo Researchers, Inc. 524: Ed Lettau/FPG. 528: Ibibio tribe mask, The Metropolitan Museum of Art, The Michael C. Rockefeller Memorial Collection. Bequest of Nelson A. Rockefeller, 1979. 543: *The Cow-Tail Switch and Other West African Stories* by Harold Courlander and George Herzog, drawings by Madey Lee Chastain. Copyright 1947 and renewed 1975 by Harold Courlander. Reprinted by permission of Henry Holt and Company, Inc. 566: © Jim Goodwin/ Photo Researchers, Inc. 575: E.R. Degginger. **Dictionary** 577: The Granger Collection. 578: *l*. The Granger Collection; *r*. David Lissy/FPG. 579: *l*. The Bettmann Archive; *r*. © The Cousteau Society, a member supported, non-profit environmental agency. 580: The Bettmann Archive. 581: Historical Pictures Service. 582: *l*. Courtesy Harper & Row, Publishers, Inc. *r*. The Granger Collection. 583: David Doody/Tom Stack & Associates. 584: © Tom Raymond/Fresh Air Photographics. 585: *l*. AP/Wide World Photos; *r*. The Granger Collection. 586: *l*. The Granger Collection; *r*. UPI/Bettmann Newsphotos. 587: *l*. Pat Valenti/Tom Stack & Associates; *r*. N.C. Wyeth Archives, Delaware Art Museum, Wilmington. Every effort has been made to locate the original sources. If any errors have oc-

curred, the publisher can be notified and corrections will be made.

Permissions: We wish to thank the following authors, publishers, agents, corporations, and individuals for their permission to reprint copyrighted materials. Page 26: Excerpts from *Anne Frank: The Diary of a Young Girl.* Copyright 1952 by Otto H. Frank. Reprinted by permission of Doubleday, a division of Bantam, Doubleday, Dell Publishing Group, Inc. Page 74: "Playing the Jug" and "Making a Washtub Bass" from *Kid's America* by Steven Caney. Copyright © 1978 by Steven Caney. Reprinted by permission of Workman Pub. All rights reserved. Page 138: "M.C. Higgins, The Great," a Book Review by Nikki Giovanni. Copyright © 1974 by the New York Times Company. Reprinted by permission. Page 196: Excerpt from *The Black Pearl* by Scott O'Dell. Copyright © 1967 by Scott O'Dell. Reprinted by permission of Houghton Mifflin Company. Page 256: Excerpt from *The Brooklyn Bridge: They Said It Couldn't Be Built* by Judith St. George. Copyright © 1982 by Judith St. George. Reprinted by permission of G.P. Putnam's Sons. Page 310: Excerpt from *The Yearling* by Marjorie Kinnan Rawlings, illustrated by N.C. Wyeth. Reprinted with the permission of Charles Scribner's Sons, an imprint of Macmillan Publishing Co. Text copyright 1938 Marjorie Kinnan Rawlings, copyright renewed © 1966 Norton Baskin. Illustrations copyright 1939 Charles Scribner's Sons; copyright renewed © 1967 Charles Scribner's Sons. Page 424: "A soft sea washed around the house..." by Emily Dickinson. Reprinted by permission of the publishers and the Trustees of Amherst College from *The Poems of Emily Dickinson*, edited by Thomas E. Johnson, Cambridge, Mass.: The Belknap Press of Harvard University Press, copyright © 1951, 1955, 1979, 1983 by The President and Fellows of Harvard. Page 425: From "Eight Puppies" by Gabriela Mistral. Trans. by Doris Dana. Reprinted by permission of Joan Daves. Copyright © 1961, 1964, 1970, 1971, by Doris Dana. "The Heron" by Theodore Roethke from *The Collected Poems of Theodore Roethke*. Copyright 1937 by Theodore Roethke. Reprinted by permission of Doubleday, a division of Bantam, Doubleday, Dell Publishing Group, Inc. Page 430: "Sight, Touch" by Octavio Paz. From *A Draft of Shadows*. Copyright © 1979 by *The New Yorker* magazine. Translated by Mark Strand. Reprinted by permission of New Directions Publishing Corp. Page 431: "To the foot from its child" excerpt from *Extravagaria* by Pablo Neruda. Translation copyright © 1969, 1970, 1972, 1974 by Alastair Reid. Reprinted by permission of Farrar, Straus & Giroux, Inc. Page 434: "A Pine Tree Towers Lonely" by Heinrich Heine. Reprinted with permission from "The Poetry of Heinrich Heine" copyright © 1970 Aaron Kramer. Published by Citadel Press. "Winter Evening" from *The Poems, Prose and Plays of Alexander Pushkin*, edited by Avram Yarmolinsky. Copyright 1936 and renewed 1964 by Random House, Inc. Reprinted by permission of the publisher. Page 476: "Tribute to an Inventor" used by permission of the author Alice Marie Hengesbach. Page 485: Excerpt from "John Deere." Excerpted from *The World Book Encyclopedia*. © 1988 World Book, Inc. Page 530: "The Second Task: Mr Snake" from *West Indian Folk Tales* retold by Philip Sherlock. Copyright © 1966 Philip Sherlock. Reprinted by permission of Oxford University Press. Page 566: Excerpt from "Carlsbad Caverns National Park." Excerpted from *The World Book Encyclopedia*. © 1988 World Book, Inc. Every effort has been made to locate the authors. If any errors have occurred the publisher can be notified and corrections will be made.

556

WRITER'S **REFERENCE BOOK**

Study Skills Lessons	**558**
Dictionary of Knowledge	**576**
Thesaurus	**588**
Reports, Letters, Notes	**608**
Spelling Guide	**613**
Mechanics Lessons	**616**
Diagraming Guide	**648**
Grammar Handbook	**657**
Glossary of Usage	**677**
Writing and Computers	**683**
Index	**691**

Study Skills Lessons

Study Habits

1. **Listen carefully in class.** Make sure you understand what your teacher wants you to do for homework.
2. **Have your homework materials ready.** You will need such items as textbooks, pens, and a notebook.
3. **Study in the same place every day.** You should try to find a quiet and comfortable place where people will not interrupt you. There should be good lighting, a comfortable chair, and a desk or table. Do not have the TV or radio on while studying.
4. **Plan your study time.** Develop a daily study schedule. First decide on the best time of the day for studying, and study at that same time every day. Then plan exactly when you will study each of your subjects. Work on your most difficult subject first, before you become tired. Include time for chores, or household tasks, and recreation. Write down your study schedule, using the one shown below as a guide. Stick to your study schedule.
5. **Set a goal or purpose each time you study.** If, for example, you were going to have an English test, your goal would be to review and understand the material that would be tested. Keep that goal in mind when you study. If you do, you will concentrate better.

Study Schedule

3:30 to 4:00 P.M. —	chores
4:00 to 5:00 P.M. —	sports, flute practice
5:00 to 5:30 P.M. —	study English
5:30 to 6:00 P.M. —	study math
6:00 to 7:00 P.M. —	dinner and free time
7:00 to 7:30 P.M. —	study science
7:30 to 8:00 P.M. —	study social studies
8:00 to 10:00 P.M. —	hobbies, reading, TV

Practice

List the three study habits that you find the most helpful in completing your homework. Be prepared to explain your answer.

Test-taking Tips

Before a Test

1. Prepare for a test by studying your notes and textbook each night. Don't wait until the night before a test to begin studying.
2. Prepare for an essay, or composition, test by thinking about possible test questions. Write your own questions and answers on important ideas from your textbook.
3. Prepare for an objective, or short-answer, test by writing down important information that you will probably have to know. Writing down the information in an orderly way can help you learn it.

During a Test

1. Read or listen to the test directions carefully. Be sure you know what you are to do and where you are to mark your answers.
2. Plan your time. Quickly read all the test questions. Spend more time on the questions that are worth the most points. Don't spend too much time on any one question. Save time to check your answers.
3. Answer the easy questions first. Then answer the questions you are not sure of. If you have a choice of answers, you can narrow your choices by eliminating all the answers you know are wrong. Then select the answer you think is right.
4. Carefully consider the relationships between the words used in an analogy question. An analogy compares two things and shows how they are related. To complete an analogy, determine the relationship between the items in the first pair of words. Then complete the analogy so that the second pair of words has the same relationship.

     EXAMPLE   Circle the correct answer.
     bird:flock::fish: _____
     a. scales   **b.** swim   **c.** school   **d.** pond

Practice

1. Explain what problems might arise as a result of waiting until the night before a test to begin studying.
2. What is the first thing you should do when answering an analogy question?

Parts of a Book

You use your textbook and other nonfiction books to find information for assignments and reports and to study for tests. Most textbooks and other nonfiction books have these four parts: a title page, a copyright page, a table of contents, and an index. Each part provides information that you will need or tells you where to find it.

The **title page** is often the first page of a book. It gives the title, author, publisher's name, and place of publication. The **copyright page** is on the back of the title page. It tells when and by whom the book was published. You should check the copyright date to make sure the book is up-to-date enough for your purpose. A recent book may be needed for topics such as science and current events.

Following the copyright page is the **table of contents**. Study the following portion of the table of contents from a science textbook. It shows that the book is organized into units, chapters, and lessons. Note that the title of Unit Three, "Plants," identifies the general area of study. The chapter titles focus on specific plants, such as "Nonseed Plants." Lesson titles indicate very specific areas of study, such as "Green Algae."

UNIT THREE   PLANTS   144

■ **Chapter 7   NONSEED PLANTS**   *146*
    7-1 Traits of Nonseed Plants   *147*   **7-4 Bryophytes**   *156*
    7-2 Green Algae   *150*   **7-5 Tracheophytes**   *160*
    7-3 Brown Algae and Red
        Algae   *153*

■ **Chapter 8   SEED PLANTS**   *168*
    8-1 Traits of Seed Plants   *169*   **8-4 Roots of Seed Plants**   *177*
    8-2 Gymnosperms   *172*   **8-5 Stems of Seed Plants**   *182*
    8-3 Angiosperms   *174*   **8-6 Leaves of Seed Plants**   *185*

If you are looking for a particular piece of information, the **index** is the place to look. The index, which is found in the back of most nonfiction books, lists in alphabetical order the most important topics covered in the book. Under some main topics, subtopics may also be listed. For example, under *sentence* in the Index of this book, you will find *simple, compound,* and *complex* as subtopics. Next to the topics and subtopics are the pages on which they are discussed. The index helps you find specific topics quickly.

Many textbooks also contain a glossary in the back. The glossary is an alphabetical list of all the important terms used in the book, along with their specialized meanings. The glossary indicates the pages where words are introduced or defined and often gives the pronunciation of difficult words. Note the example below.

Glossary of Terms

gears   Interlocking toothed wheels. *p.*322

generator (jen′ ə rāt′ ər) A device that changes mechanical energy into electrical energy. *p.*419

geothermal (jē′ō thur′ m'l) **energy**   Energy collected from the natural heat of the earth. *p.*560

glaze (glāz)   The layer of ice that forms from rain on objects whose temperatures are below freezing. *p.*550

Practice

A. Write the answers to the following questions.

1. Which part of a book tells you the name of the book as well as the book's author and publisher?

2. What is the copyright date of this textbook?

3. Which part of a book shows how the book is organized?

4. In which part of a book would you look to find a particular piece of information quickly?

5. In which part of a book would you look to find the meaning of an important term used in the book?

B. Use the Table of Contents of this textbook to answer the following questions.

6. How many units are in this textbook?

7. On what page does Unit 2 begin?

8. In which lesson of Unit 2 would you learn about forming possessive nouns?

9. On what page does the literature selection "The Open Window" begin?

10. What is the title of Lesson 3 in Unit 6?

11. How many pages is the literature selection in Unit 5?

12. How many grammar lessons are included in Unit 3?

13. What is the author's name of the literature selection *The Black Pearl* in Unit 4?

Using the Library

To find the information you need in the library, learn to use the card catalog—a file cabinet that contains information cards for all of the books in the library. Some libraries now have computer terminals in addition to the card catalog to help you locate books and information. The listings seen on a computer terminal show the same information as the card catalog but the information is stored in a computer. Often, the computer listing will also tell whether or not the book is currently on loan from the library.

The Card Catalog   The cards in the catalog are arranged in alphabetical order in drawers. On the outside of each drawer is a guide label that shows the beginning letters on the first and last cards inside. For example, a drawer labeled *La–Me* would contain cards for books on Lapland and meteorology, among other topics. Inside the drawer are guide cards to help you locate information.

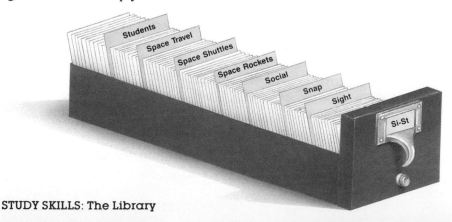

Each nonfiction book usually has three kinds of cards filed in the card catalog: a **title card**, an **author card**, and a **subject card**. Each card gives the same information.

If you know the title of the book you want, look up the title card. Title cards are filed by the first important word of a title. For example, the book *Flying to the Moon* would be found under *Flying*; however, *The Survivors* would be listed under *Survivors*. If you know only the author's name, look up the last name on an author card. If you are doing research on a particular subject, such as space travel, look for a subject card labeled *space travel*.

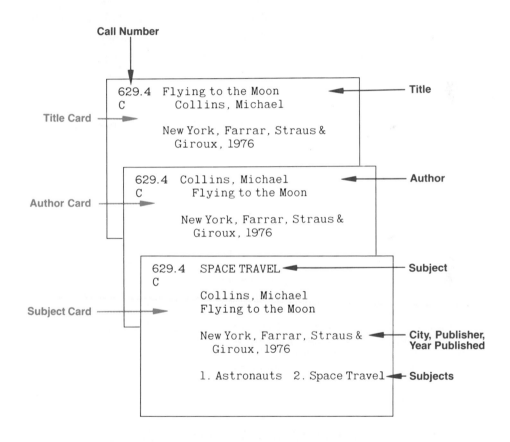

You may also find cross-reference cards in the card catalog. A cross-reference card will direct you to another subject heading that lists books you can use. If you look up *space shuttles*, you may find a cross-reference card that says, "See reusable space vehicles."

The Arrangement of Books   It is also important to learn how books are arranged on the library shelves. Books in the library are shelved systematically. Fiction books are found in their own section. They are arranged alphabetically by the author's last name. Biographies are also often in a special section. These books are arranged alphabetically by the last name of the main person in the book.

To find any nonfiction book in the library, you need to know its **call number**. The call number of a book appears on the side or spine of the book. It also appears in the upper lefthand corner of its cards in the card catalog. Nonfiction books are shelved numerically, according to their call numbers. One of two numerical systems is used. Most libraries use the **Dewey decimal system**, which places all nonfiction books within ten categories, or subject areas. The following chart shows the number ranges of the Dewey decimal system and their corresponding subject areas.

Numbers	Subjects
000–099	**General Works** (reference works such as the encyclopedias, atlases, almanacs)
100–199	**Philosophy** (includes psychology)
200–299	**Religion** (includes myths)
300–399	**Social Sciences** (includes education, government, folktales, fairy tales)
400–499	**Language** (includes the thesaurus, foreign language versions of the dictionary)
500–599	**Science** (includes mathematics, biology, chemistry, physics)
600–699	**Technology** (includes medicine, engineering, aviation, farming)
700–799	**The Arts** (includes painting, music, sports)
800–899	**Literature** (includes plays, poetry, essays, television scripts, but not fiction)
900–999	**History and Geography** (includes travel)

Each subject is divided further into more specific topics. For example, *the arts* (700's) is divided into categories such as *architecture* (720's), *painting* (750's), and *music* (780's). Each book within a category has a call number that includes the initial of the author's last name. The **Library of Congress system** uses a different combination of numbers and letters in its call numbers.

Practice

A. Write which card you would look for—title, author, or subject—to find each of the following. Then write the word under which the card would be alphabetized.

1. A book by Pura Belpré
2. A book called *A Treasury of Poems*
3. A Mexican-American cookbook
4. *Who's Who of American Women*
5. Books by Myra Cohn Livingston

B. For each book title, write the number range under which it would appear in the Dewey decimal system.

EXAMPLE: *Travels in Africa*
ANSWER: 900–999

6. *Whales and Porpoises*
7. *The World Book Encyclopedia*
8. *Poetry in Our Time*
9. *Vietnamese Folktales*
10. *Psychological Testing*
11. *Square Dancing*
12. *Spanish-English Dictionary*
13. The Bible
14. *The Government of the U.S.A.*
15. *Spacecraft*
16. *Great Lakes Country*
17. *Drama and the Stage*
18. *Atmospheres of Earth and the Planets*

C. Go to the card catalog or computer terminal and write a title, author, and call number for each of the following.

19. A book about ancient Rome
20. A biology book
21. A book about travel
22. A book about modern governments
23. A collection of essays
24. A biography about Franklin D. Roosevelt
25. A book about the history of the United States
26. A collection of poetry

Encyclopedia

An **encyclopedia** is a collection of articles that give detailed facts about a variety of topics. Encyclopedia articles are arranged in alphabetical order within books, or volumes. Each volume lists on its spine the number of the volume and the beginning letters of its first and last entries. At the top of each page of the volume are guide words showing the first and last entries on the page.

Cross-references in an article (for example, **Cave** below) refer the reader to other related articles in the encyclopedia. Illustrations give concrete examples of topics mentioned in the article. Captions further explain the illustrations. Read the article below from the *World Book Encyclopedia*.

Carlsbad Caverns National Park is a chain of huge underground caves in southeastern New Mexico. Stalactites and stalagmites, in white and pastel shades, form shapes like Chinese temples, heavy pillars, and lacy icicles (see **Stalactite; Stalagmite**). One large chamber, called the Big Room, is 4,000 feet (1,200 meters) long and 625 feet (191 meters) wide. At one point, the ceiling is 285 feet (87 meters) high. The caverns became a national park in 1930. For area, see **National Park System** (table: National parks).

Many passages in the caverns have been explored, but unexplored areas still exist. Two levels, at 750 feet (229 meters) and 829 feet (253 meters) underground, may be reached by trail from the natural entrance, or by elevator. On the lower level, visitors may view an unopened passage which has been explored as deep as 1,100 feet (335 meters). One part of the caverns contains millions of bats which fly out at dusk in warm weather in search of insects. Paintings on the cave's entrance wall show that Indians once used the cave.

The limestone in the caverns is believed to have formed in a shallow inland extension of the ocean about 200 million years ago. When the Rocky Mountains were formed about 60 million years ago, the cavern area rose above sea level and water began hollowing out the limestone to form the caves.   HERBERT E. KAHLER

See also **Cave** (table); **New Mexico** (picture: Stalactites)

Carlsbad Caverns National Park in New Mexico is famous for its spectacular underground landscape of stalactites and stalagmites. The caves are made of hollowed-out limestone.

Practice

1. List two interesting facts about the caverns.
2. Where in the encyclopedia would you look to find the area of the Carlsbad Caverns National Park?

Atlas

An **atlas** is a book of maps. It may contain maps of cities, states, countries, and continents. Some maps show geographical features, such as mountains and rivers. Others show features such as roads, points of interest, climate, or population. Look at this map of a region, or a part, of the United States. The map **key**, or **legend**, labeled *The South Central States*, explains what the symbols on the map mean. The small map in the lower-left corner is an **inset** map. It shows the location and size of the South Central region in relation to all the states except Alaska and Hawaii.

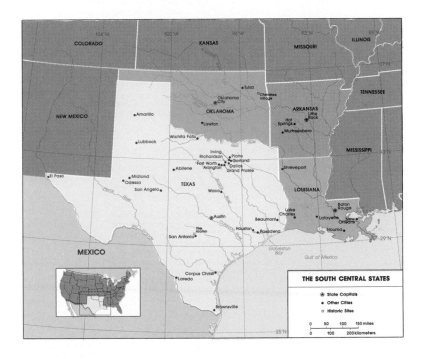

Practice

Use the map to answer the following questions.

1. What states make up the South Central states?
2. What is the capital of Louisiana?
3. How many historic sites are shown on the map?
4. What South Central States are bordered by Missouri?
5. What bay is located on the Texas coast?

Almanac

Yearly **almanacs** contain both timely and general information on a variety of subjects, especially politics, geography, and the economy. An almanac is a good source of information on current events, sports, weather, population figures, and awards for books, films, and music. The almanac index is the quickest guide to the location of a subject. The almanac articles below give key facts about the cities of Los Angeles and San Francisco, California.

Los Angeles, California

Population: 3,022,247; **Pop. density:** 6,380 per sq. mi.; **Pop. growth:** +0.5%; **Pop. over 65:** 10.6%; **Pop. under 35:** 58.1%; **Area:** 465 sq. mi.; **Employment:** 1,472,090 employed, 8.9% unemployed; **Per capita income:** $13,417.
Transportation: 1 major airport; 4 railroads; major bus carrier service; major freeway system. **Communications:** 19 TV stations; 71 radio stations. **Medical facilities:** 822 hospitals and clinics; 409 nursing homes. **Educational facilities:** 11 universities and colleges; 1,642 public schools; 800 private schools; 61 public libraries. **Further information:** Chamber of Commerce, P.O. Box 3696, Terminal Annex, Los Angeles, CA 90051.

San Francisco, California

Population: 691,637; **Pop. density:** 14,760 per sq. mi.; **Pop. growth:** −5.1%; **Pop. over 65:** 15.4%; **Pop. under 35:** 51.7%; **Area:** 46 sq. mi.; **Employment:** 370,775 employed, 6.4% unemployed; **Per capita income:** $17,875.
Transportation: 1 major airport; intra-city railway system; 2 railway transit systems; bus and railroad service; ferry system; 1 underwater tunnel. **Communications:** 7 TV stations; 45 radio stations. **Medical facilities:** 29 hospitals; 1 major medical center. **Educational facilities:** 4 universities and colleges; major public library system. **Further information:** Chamber of Commerce, 465 California Street, San Francisco, CA 94104.

Practice

Use the almanac articles to answer these questions.

1. What is the population of Los Angeles, California?
   What is the population of San Francisco, California?
2. Which city has more universities and colleges?
3. How many public libraries are there in Los Angeles?
4. What is the population density of Los Angeles? What is the population density of San Francisco?
5. What is the difference in square miles between the areas of Los Angeles and San Francisco?

Readers' Guide

Periodicals are newspapers and magazines that are published at regular intervals, such as daily, weekly, or monthly. If you need magazine articles to complete research for a report, use the *Readers' Guide to Periodical Literature.* Articles are arranged alphabetically by subject and by author. Entries may be divided by subheadings. Some entries have cross-references (marked *See* or *See also*) referring to related articles. When you know what periodical you want, fill out a request form and the librarian will give you either the periodical itself or a reproduction of it from microfilm.

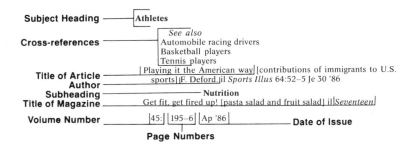

Abbreviations in the above entry include *il* for *illustrated, Je* for *June,* and *Ap* for *April.* A complete list of abbreviations is found in each volume.

Practice

Use this *Readers' Guide* entry to answer the questions.

```
Cats
    Cats, D. Carlinsky, il Seventeen 45:168–9+ Ap '86
    What's special about my cat. C. Jakobson, il Glamour 84:206+ Ap '86
        Anecdotes, facetiae, satire, etc.
    Why cats are causing the decline of civilization. J. Gorman, il Discover
        7:18+ Ap '86
        Diseases and pests
    Mystery disease stalks older cats [feline hyperthyroidism] J. Raloff. Sci
        News 129:166–7 Mr 15 '86
        Photographs and photography
    Ernie and Tony [T. Mendoza's photographs] N. Schreiber, il Pop Photogr
        93:21 Je '86
Cats, Wild
        See also
        Bobcats
        Leopards
        Pumas
```

1. Which magazine has a humorous article about cats?

2. Which magazine has an article on cats on one page?

3. Under what heading are articles about pumas?

4. What is the date of the *Science News* magazine?

Outlining

It is always a good idea to make a plan before you start to write a composition or a report. Your plan should follow outline form. An **outline** organizes material into main ideas, supporting ideas, and supporting details.

By the time you write an outline, you will have decided on the subject you will cover. If you did research, you will have main ideas or topics on your note cards. The cards should be arranged so that all the information on each main topic is together. Look at your note cards and decide in which order you will present the topics. Next, decide which subtopics to include under each main topic and in what order the subtopics should be presented. Finally, choose and arrange the supporting details under each subtopic.

Now you are ready to write the ideas from your note cards in outline form.

In an outline all main topics are preceded by Roman numerals. Subtopics, or supporting ideas related to the main topics, are preceded by capital letters. Supporting details are set off by Arabic numerals.

There are two kinds of outlines. One has full sentences and is called a **sentence outline**. The other has topics and is called a **topic outline**.

An outline follows a logical and rigid structure. Study the chart below and the sample outline on the following page to learn how to write a topic outline.

How to Write an Outline
1. Center the title at the top of the outline.
2. You must write at least two items at each level of the outline. For example, there must be at least two main ideas, labeled I and II.
3. Place a period after each numeral or letter.
4. You should indent each new level of an outline.
5. Each Roman numeral, capital letter, and Arabic numeral should be in line with others of its kind.
6. Capitalize the first word of each item.

What Makes a Successful Astronaut?

I. How astronauts are chosen
  A. Physical qualities needed
  B. Personality traits needed
  C. Education needed
  D. Career training needed

II. How astronauts are trained
  A. Physical training
    1. Fitness training
    2. Survival skills training
  B. Psychological training
    1. Teamwork
    2. Space flight stress
    3. Emergency procedures
  C. Flight training
    1. Military aircraft
    2. Spacecraft
  D. Scientific training

Practice

A. Refer to the sample topic outline above to write the answers to the following questions.

1. What is the title of the report outlined above?
2. What are the two main topics?
3. How many subtopics does topic II have?
4. How many details are included under "Flight training"?
5. Which subtopic under topic II has no details listed?

B. Arrange the main topics, subtopics, and details below into a topic outline titled ''Folk Art.''

6. Painting
7. Kinds of folk art
8. Anonymous craftworkers
9. Edward Hicks
10. Known folk artists
11. Sculpture
12. People who created folk art
13. Decorative utensils
14. Household objects
15. Grandma Moses
16. Amateurs working for fun
17. Quilts

Using a Dictionary

A dictionary aids in finding, pronouncing, and understanding words. The sample entry below is from the Dictionary of Knowledge, which begins on page 576.

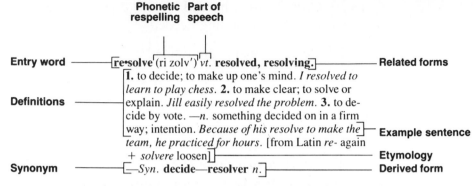

Entry word   This shows the spelling and syllable divisions of a word.

Phonetic respelling   This shows how a word is pronounced. It is given in symbols that stand for certain sounds. For example, the symbol ō stands for the long o sound heard in *bold*. The Pronunciation Key on page 576 tells the sound for each symbol. Stress marks (′) indicate syllables that are spoken with more force.

Part of speech   This label is abbreviated, such as *adv.* for *adverb*.

Related forms   Plurals of nouns, principal parts of verbs, and comparatives and superlatives of adjectives and adverbs are shown when the spelling of the base word changes.

Definitions   The meanings are grouped by part of speech and numbered.

Example sentence   This shows the word in use and clarifies meaning.

Etymology   This is a word history, and it appears in brackets.

Synonym   This is a word that has a similar meaning to that of the entry word. Its label is abbreviated as *Syn.* Antonyms, labeled *Ant.,* are given for some entry words.

Derived forms   These are related forms of the word that are made by adding a suffix to the base word that changes its part of speech.

Practice

A. Write the answers to the questions, using the entry on page 572.

1. Which syllable of the entry word is spoken with more force?
2. From what language does *resolve* come?
3. How many meanings are given for *resolve* as a verb? as a noun?
4. How many example sentences are included in the entry?
5. For which meaning could the following be an example sentence? *They set out on their journey with great resolve.*

Aids to Finding Words   To find words quickly, think of a dictionary as having three parts: front, *a–g*; middle, *h–p*; and back, *q–z*. *Calf* would be in the front part, *lap* in the middle, and *ramp* in the back.

Remember that dictionary entry words are arranged in alphabetical order and guide words show the first and last entry words on a page.

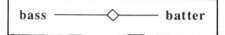

Practice

B. Write each word. Then write *front, middle,* or *back* to show in which part of a dictionary it would be found.

6. volume	**9.** envelope	**12.** medium
7. gelatin	**10.** oilskin	**13.** redeem
8. kayak	**11.** tedious	**14.** fumble

C. Think of the words *desert* and *detail* as guide words. Write *on, before,* or *after* to show where each word would be found.

15. detain	**18.** design	**21.** dessert
16. derrick	**19.** desolate	**22.** destiny
17. deserve	**20.** detach	**23.** depress

D. For each word below write an appropriate pair of guide words.

EXAMPLE: patio   **ANSWER:** patio; onion, patriot

24. friendship	**26.** glossary	**28.** thesaurus
25. practical	**27.** literary	**29.** dictionary

Study the sample dictionary entries below. You will use them as you complete **Practice E** and **F** on page 575.

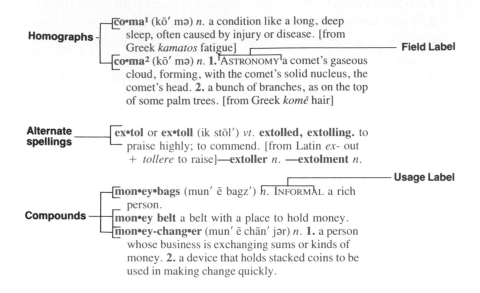

Homographs —
co•ma[1] (kō′ mə) *n.* a condition like a long, deep sleep, often caused by injury or disease. [from Greek *kamatos* fatigue]

co•ma[2] (kō′ mə) *n.* **1.** ASTRONOMY a comet's gaseous cloud, forming, with the comet's solid nucleus, the comet's head. **2.** a bunch of branches, as on the top of some palm trees. [from Greek *komē* hair] — **Field Label**

Alternate spellings —
ex•tol or ex•toll (ik stōl′) *vt.* **extolled, extolling.** to praise highly; to commend. [from Latin *ex-* out + *tollere* to raise] —**extoller** *n.* —**extolment** *n.*

Usage Label

Compounds —
mon•ey•bags (mun′ ē bagz′) *n.* INFORMAL a rich person.

mon•ey belt a belt with a place to hold money.

mon•ey-chang•er (mun′ ē chān′ jər) *n.* **1.** a person whose business is exchanging sums or kinds of money. **2.** a device that holds stacked coins to be used in making change quickly.

Homographs   These are words that are spelled alike but have different meanings and origins. They have separate entries followed by superscripts, such as ¹ and ².

Compounds   Words that are compounds are written in three ways. Some are written as single words (*moneybags*), some as a hyphenated word (*money-changer*), or as two separate words (*money belt*).

Field Label   This label identifies a meaning of a word that is used in a specialized field of knowledge.

Usage Label   This label identifies a word or word meaning that is used only in certain situations.

When you are writing, you may need to know how to divide a certain word at the end of a line. Dots, or bullets, appear between the syllables of a dictionary entry word. They tell you how the word can be divided at the end of a writing line. A one-syllable word such as *strength* cannot be divided, and a single letter such as the *a* in **a•gain** or the *y* in **curl•y** cannot be left alone on a line.

To check spelling, think of the possible spellings for a word's beginning sounds and look under each of these. Suppose that a gardener told you about plants that had names with these sounds: (floks) and (fil ə den′ drən). To spell the names of these plants, you might look for words beginning with the letter *f*, but you would not find the plant names. You would need to think of another way to spell the first sound and look under *ph* as in *photograph*. Then you would find the names: *phlox* and *philodendron*.

Sometimes a dictionary lists two spellings for a word. Both are correct. Although the first spelling given is preferred, you may safely use either spelling: **theater** or **theatre**. Occasionally a British spelling is given: **vapor** or *British* **vapour**.

Practice

E. Write the answer to each question, using the entries on page 574.

    30. Write the entry number for the meaning of *coma* in this sentence: *Why are soap-opera characters in comas so often?*
    31. Write the spelling that is preferred: *extoll* or *extol.*
    32. Write the compound that is written as two separate words.
    33. Write the compound that is used only in informal speech.

F. Use the Dictionary of Knowledge to answer the questions below.

    34. How can these words be broken at the end of a line of writing: *azalea, imminent, adversary, cite?* (Mark the divisions with hyphens, as in this example: *atomic, atom-ic.*)
    35. Which word is spelled incorrectly, and how should it be spelled: *albeit, duly, lagune, self-possession?*
    36. What part of speech is the word *pinnacle?*
    37. Which syllable of the word *indolent* is stressed?
    38. Which word means ''a downpour'': *fathom* or *deluge?*

Dictionary of Knowledge

This Dictionary of Knowledge has two kinds of entries, **word entries** and **encyclopedic entries**. Many of the word entries in this dictionary are taken from the literature pieces found throughout this book. You might use these entries to help you understand the meanings of words. You will use the encyclopedic entries in two "Apply" sections in each unit.

Word Entries ♦ These entries are just like the ones found in the ordinary dictionaries you are familiar with. Each entry includes such elements as pronunciation respellings, definitions, and example sentences.

Encyclopedic Entries ♦ These entries resemble encyclopedia articles. Each entry provides interesting information about a particular topic or person.

Abbreviations Used in This Dictionary

adj.	adjective	n.	noun	Syn.	Synonym
adv.	adverb	pl.	plural	vi.	intransitive verb
Ant.	Antonym	prep.	preposition	vt.	transitive verb
conj.	conjunction	pron.	pronoun		

Full pronunciation key* The pronunciation of each word is shown just after the word, in this way:
abbreviate (ə brē′ vē āt).

The letters and signs used are pronounced as in the words below.

The mark ′ is placed after a syllable with a primary or heavy accent as in the example above.

The mark ′ after a syllable shows a secondary or lighter accent, as in **abbreviation** (ə brē′ vē ā′ shən).

SYMBOL	KEY WORDS	SYMBOL	KEY WORDS	SYMBOL	KEY WORDS	SYMBOL	KEY WORDS
a	ask, fat	ô	law, horn		o in collect	t	top, hat
ā	ape, date	oi	oil, point		u in focus	v	vat, have
ä	car, father	⊙o	look, pull	b	bed, dub	w	will, always
		ōō	ooze, tool	d	did, had	y	yet, yard
e	elf, ten	yoo	unite, cure	f	fall, off	z	zebra, haze
er	berry, care	yōō	cute, few	g	get, dog		
ē	even, meet	ou	out, crowd	h	he, ahead	ch	chin, arch
				j	joy, jump	ŋ	ring, singer
i	is, hit	u	up, cut	k	kill, bake	sh	she, dash
ir	mirror, here	ʉr	fur, fern	l	let, ball	th	thin, truth
ī	ice, fire			m	met, trim	*th*	then, father
		ə	a in ago	n	not, ton	zh	s in pleasure
			e in agent	p	put, tap		
o	lot, pond		e in father	r	red, dear		
ō	open, go		i in unity	s	sell, pass	′	as in (ā′b'l)

*Pronunciation key adapted from *Webster's New World Dictionary, Basic School Edition,* Copyright © 1983 by Simon & Schuster, Inc. Reprinted by permission.

ad•ver•sar•y (ad′ vər ser′ ē) *n.*, *pl.* **adversaries**. a person who is against another; an enemy or opponent. *My adversary defeated me in the marathon race.* — *Syn.* **enemy**. — *Ant*. **comrade**.

Ae•sop's fa•bles (ē′ səps fā′ b'ls)

Aesop's fables are a collection of stories originally told by a Greek man named Aesop, who lived in the sixth century B.C. The fables were passed along orally from generation to generation for many years. They were eventually written down and translated into other languages by various writers. As a result, there are different versions of the fables.

Each of Aesop's fables teaches a moral, or lesson, and most of the characters are talking animals with human characteristics. For example, in the fable "The Fox and the Grapes," the hungry

fox tries to pull sweet grapes off a high vine. When he fails, he proudly walks away saying, "I thought those grapes were ripe, but I see now they are quite sour."

In another fable, "The Birds, the Beasts, and the Bat," there is a war between birds and beasts. A bat joins the war but changes sides according to which group is winning. When the birds and the beasts finally resolve their conflict, the bat finds that he has no friends on either side.

al•be•it (ôl bē′ it) *conj.* although; even though. *He is clever, albeit not a genius.* [from Middle English *al be it* al(though) it be]

al•man•ac (ôl′ mə nak)

An almanac is a book or pamphlet of useful information. Almanacs are usually published once a year. They often contain facts about the days, weeks, and months of the year; the motions of heavenly bodies, such as the sun and moon; tidal movements; weather; geography; history; and governments.

One of the earliest almanacs in the United States was "Poor Richard's Almanac," first published by Benjamin Franklin in 1733. It contained mainly astronomy information, poetry, and lists of roads. Franklin also contributed many proverbs, or short sayings, that became very popular.

Today's almanacs may also include world maps, biographies of famous people, statistics about many countries, and world athletic records.

an•tic (an′ tik) *adj.* odd and funny; laughable. *The clown's antic movements delighted the crowd.* —*n.* a playful or silly act or trick; a prank. *We enjoyed the juggler's antics.* — *Syn.* **comic**. — *Ant.* **grave**.

a•zal•ea (ə zāl′ yə) *n.* a shrub having narrow, pointed leaves that are shed each season, and flowers of various colors. *The azaleas are in bloom.*

a	fat	**i**	hit	**oi**	oil	**ch**	chin	ə = a *in* ago
ā	ape	**ir**	here	**oo**	look	**sh**	she	e *in* agent
ä	car, father	**ī**	bite, fire	**o͞o**	tool	**th**	thin	i *in* unity
e	ten	**o**	lot	**ou**	out	***th***	then	o *in* collect
er	care	**ō**	go	**u**	up	**zh**	leisure	u *in* focus
ē	even	**ô**	law, horn	**ur**	fur	**ng**	ring	

B

bol•ster (bōl′ stər) *n.* a long, narrow pillow or cushion. *The snowy hills were like white, fluffy bolsters—vt.* to prop up, as if with a bolster. *Her letter bolstered my confidence.*

C

ca•pit•u•la•tion (kə pich′ ə lā′ shən) *n.* the act of capitulating; conditional surrender. *The capitulation of one side was necessary for victory.* — *Syn.* **resignation.** — *Ant.* **resistance.**

chor•tle (chôr′ t'l) *vi.* **chortled, chortling.** to chuckle in a loud, gleeful way. *Mei chortled at the cartoons.*

cite (sīt) *vt.* **cited, citing. 1.** to order to come to a law court. **2.** to mention or quote. *In her report, she cited two articles from a magazine.* **3.** to mention for praise. *The mayor cited the firefighter for bravery.*

Co•han, George M. (kō han′, jôrj′ əm) 1878–1942

George Cohan was born in Providence, Rhode Island, and became one of the most famous theatrical performers in the United States. He began his career in vaudeville, a type of stage entertainment with a variety of acts, including comedy and singing. Cohan was a member of his family's performance group.

By the time he was twenty-three, Cohan had written and starred in his own play, *The Governor's*

Son. Cohan wrote or produced over fifty plays and musicals. He also wrote many famous songs, including the World War I tune "Over There." For this effort, he received a Congressional Medal. Other classic American songs that he wrote include "Give My Regards to Broadway" and "You're a Grand Old Flag."

Cohan's life story, *Yankee Doodle Dandy*, was filmed in 1942. Cohan was played by the actor James Cagney. Today a statue of Cohan stands in the heart of New York City's Theater district.

com•mun•ion (kə myōō′ yən) *n.* **1.** a sharing of things in common. **2.** a close relationship with deep understanding; fellowship. *The communion between the two friends was inspiring.*

con•duc•tor, mus•i•cal (kən duk′ tər, myōō′ zi k'l)

A musical conductor is the person who leads the performance of an orchestra. The conductor of an orchestra has many responsibilities. The conductor must first select music for the orchestra. Before leading an orchestra, a conductor must study a composer's work in order to interpret the meaning in each piece. The conductor must then see that all sections of the orchestra know their parts well.

At rehearsals, the conductor listens carefully for any problems in the music's rhythm, tone, solo passages, or other areas that might hinder the orchestra's performance. The conductor then strives to make the orchestra play as a unified group, while also trying to bring out the best in each section of the orchestra.

The conductor also has the orchestra experiment with different ways of playing the same music. This individual interpretation is what finally determines the true quality of a conductor's work.

con•spir•a•cy (kən spir′ ə sē) *n., pl.* **conspiracies.**
secret planning with others to do something that is unlawful or wrong, especially against a government or a public personage.

cot•ton gin (kot′ ′n jin)

A cotton gin is a farm machine that was invented by Eli Whitney in 1793. It was one of the chief inventions of the early Agricultural Revolution.

The cotton gin enabled farmers to process cotton plants faster. Before the cotton gin was invented, workers had to separate the cotton seeds from the fibers by hand. This difficult, slow method required many workers in the field, and most farmers struggled to make a profit.

The first cotton gin was a simple box with rows of rotating teeth to comb the seeds out of the fibers. Workers cranked the machine while feeding cotton through it. The fibers were then separated while special ginning ribs kept the seeds from passing through.

The cotton gin has evolved through the years since Whitney's first design. Modern cotton gins use electricity and are several stories tall.

coun•cil (koun′ s'l) *n.* **1.** a group of people called together to talk things over or settle questions. **2.** a group of persons elected by citizens to make laws for and manage a town or city. *At its regular meeting, the town council discussed the need for more parking space at the shopping mall.* [<Old French *concile* < Latin *concilium* < *com-* together + *calare* to call]

Cou•steau, Jacques-Yves (kōō stō′, zhäk ēv) 1910–
Jacques-Yves Cousteau is a noted French oceanographer, author, and filmmaker. After serving in France's navy, Cousteau became interested in underwater exploration. He helped to invent the aqualung, also known as self-contained underwater breathing apparatus (or *scuba* gear). This equipment allows divers to move about freely under the water for long periods of time. Cousteau also developed other important equipment for underwater use, including the first underwater diving station and an underwater observation vehicle.

Many of Cousteau's research projects have been supported by private organizations, such as the National Geographic Society. Through these projects, Cousteau has traveled all over the world. His research ship, the *Calypso*, has its own laboratories and diving vehicles. In the Mediterranean Sea, he has searched for the remains of the lost island of Atlantis. In Antarctica, he has studied the wildlife and ecology of the continent.

cut•lass (kut′ ləs) *n., pl.* **cutlasses.** a short, curved sword with a sharp edge on one side. *The pirate drew his cutlass for the battle.*

a	fat	**i**	hit	**oi**	oil	**ch**	chin	ə = a *in* ago
ā	ape	**ir**	here	**oo**	look	**sh**	she	e *in* agent
ä	car, father	**ī**	bite, fire	**ōō**	tool	**th**	thin	i *in* unity
e	ten	**o**	lot	**ou**	out	***th***	then	o *in* collect
er	care	**ō**	go	**u**	up	**zh**	leisure	u *in* focus
ē	even	**ô**	law, horn	**ur**	fur	**ng**	ring	

Dictionary of Knowledge

Dictionary of Knowledge

D

del•uge (del′ yo͞oj) *n.* **1.** a great flood. **2.** a heavy rain; a downpour. **3.** a rush or flood of anything. — *vt.* **deluged**, **deluging**. to flood; to inundate. *Phone calls deluged her at the office.*

de•lu•sion (di lo͞o′ zhən) *n.* **1.** a deluding or misleading. **2.** a false or mistaken belief, especially when it is a sign of mental illness. *The explorer's delusion led him in the wrong direction.*—**delusional** *adj.*

dis•tinc•tive (dis ting′ tiv) *adj.* making distinct or different from others. *Her distinctive attire made her stand out in the crowd.*—*Syn.* **unique.** —*Ant.* **common.**—**distinctively** *adv.*

du•ly (do͞o′ lē *or* dyo͞o′ lē) *adv.* as due; in a way or at a time that is right or fitting. *James was duly honored for his bravery.*

E

en•deav•or or British **en•deav•our** (in dev′ ər) *v.* to try hard; to make an effort; to strive. *I endeavor to improve my grades.*—*n.* an effort or try.

ex•tract (ik strakt′) *vt.* **1.** to pull out something by trying hard. **2.** to get by squeezing or pressing. **3.** to manage to get. *He extracted the meaning from the paragraph.* — *n.* (eks′ trakt) **1.** a strong substance that has been extracted from something. **2.** a section of a book or other work that has been chosen as for quoting.

F

fath•om (fath′ əm) *n.* a length of six feet, used as a unit of measure for the depth of water. *John swam two fathoms below the surface of the water.* — *vt.* **1.** to measure the depth of. **2.** to understand completely. *I cannot fathom my recent dream.*

fleet•ing (flēt′ iɴg) *adj.* passing swiftly; not lasting. *He gave me a fleeting glance.*

flout (flout) *v.* to pay no attention to in an insulting or mocking way; treat with scorn; to *flout* someone's advice.

foi•ble (foi′ b'l) *n.* a small fault or weakness in a person's character.

foist (foist) *v.* to cheat or use tricks in passing something off as a fine or genuine thing; to *foist* a false diamond on someone.

fo•ment (fō ment′) *v.* to excite or stir up trouble of some sort; to *foment* a riot.

fon•dant (fon′dənt) *n.* a soft, creamy candy made of sugar, often used as a filling for other candies.

fools•cap (fo͞olz′ kap) *n.* a large size of writing paper, about 13 by 16 inches.

Ford, Hen•ry (fôrd′, hen′ rē) 1863–1947

Henry Ford established the Ford Motor Company and invented the Model T, one of the first automobiles in the United States. The Model T appeared in 1908.

Ford also pioneered improvements in mass production methods for producing automobiles. His cars were produced "from the ground up" in a moving assembly line. A conveyor belt moved the frame of the car through the plant. Workers on each side built the car by adding parts that had been brought to them by other conveyor belts in the plant. This method helped reduce production costs. The Model T was originally priced at $850.00, but had dropped to $250.00 by 1926. This cost reduction enabled more Americans to purchase automobiles.

Ford produced millions of vehicles faster than they had ever been built. Other industries soon adopted his method of mass production.

G

gal•lant•ry (gal′ ən trē) *n.*, *pl.* **gallantries.** **1.** great courage. *The gallantry of the captain was appreciated by his men.* **2.** very polite behavior, especially toward women. **3.** a polite act or remark.

gar•goyle (gär′ goil) *n.* a decoration on a building in the form of a strange, imaginary creature. It usually has a channel to let rainwater run off through its mouth.

gar•nish (gär′ nish) *v.* to decorate; especially to decorate food to make it look better or taste better; to *garnish* ham with parsley.—*n.* something used in garnishing.

gar•ret (gar′ it) *n.* the room or space just below the slanting roof of a house; attic.

gen•o•cide (jen′ə sīd) *n.* any deliberate attempt to kill, or program planned to destroy, all the people of a certain nation, race, ethnic group, etc.

Globe The·a·ter (glōb thē′ ə tər)

The Globe Theater was a playhouse in London, England, that was built in 1599. The plays of William Shakespeare and others were first presented at the Globe.

Scholars believe that the Globe may have been an outdoor theater. It probably had no main roof over the audience but contained a three-sided gallery built around an open courtyard. The stage, over which a flag flew on performance days, reached into the courtyard. Behind the stage were doorways and balconies. The balconies were often used as part of the setting in a play. For example, in Shakespeare's *Romeo and Juliet*, Juliet stood on the balcony to talk to Romeo, who spoke to her from the garden below.

In 1613 the Globe Theater burned down when a cannon misfired during Shakespeare's play *Henry VIII*. It was soon rebuilt but was torn down in 1644 to make room for needed housing.

glock·en·spiel (glok′ ən spēl) *n.* a musical instrument with tuned metal bars in a frame, played with one or two hammers.

gneiss (nīs) *n.* a rock that has a coarse grain and looks like granite.

gnu (n$\overline{oo}$ *or* ny$\overline{oo}$) *n.* a large African antelope with a head like an ox and a long tail.

Green·a·way, Kate (grēn′ ə wā, kāt′) 1846–1901

Kate Greenaway was an English illustrator of children's books. She became famous mainly for her work in watercolor paints. She painted children, flowers, and gardens in a gentle style, using delicate blues and greens.

Before illustrating books, Greenaway became known for her valentines and Christmas-card drawings. Some of Greenaway's first work appeared in a children's magazine, *Little Folks*. In 1879 she won acclaim for the children's book *Under the Window*. This book included her wonderful drawings as well as poetry she had written. Other children's books that Greenaway illustrated were *The Language of Flowers* and *Marigold Garden*.

gon·do·la (gon′ də lə *or* gon dō′lə) *n.* **1.** a long, narrow boat with high, pointed ends, used on the canals of Venice. **2.** a railroad freight car with low sides and no top. **3.** a cabin fastened to the underside of a balloon or airship. **4.** a car held from and moved along a cable, for carrying passengers.

gou·lash (g$\overline{oo}$′ läsh) *n.* a beef or veal stew seasoned with paprika.

gourd (gôrd *or* goord) *n.* **1.** a vine with large fruit containing many seeds. Gourds belong to the same family as the squash and pumpkin. **2.** the fruit of this vine, not fit for eating but often dried and used for cups, bowls, etc.

grack·le (grak′ 'l) *n.* a kind of blackbird that is a little smaller than a crow.

a fat	i hit	oi oil	ch chin	ə = a *in* ago
ā ape	ir here	oo look	sh she	e *in* agent
ä car, father	ī bite, fire	o͞o tool	th thin	i *in* unity
e ten	o lot	ou out	*th* then	o *in* collect
er care	ō go	u up	zh leisure	u *in* focus
ē even	ô law, horn	ᵤr fur	ṅg ring	

Green•field, El•o•ise (grēn′ fēld, el′ ō ēz) 1929—
Eloise Greenfield is an American author. She was born in Parmele, North Carolina, but she moved to Washington, D.C. as an infant. Greenfield is known for writing in a wide variety of literary forms. She has written biographies of civil-rights activist Rosa Parks (1973) and singer Paul Robeson (1975), two novels — *Sister* (1974) and *Talk About a Family* (1978), and a volume of poetry called *Honey, I Love: And Other Love Poems* (1978). Greenfield has also written children's books such as *Bubbles* (1972) and *I Can Do It by Myself* (1978), and has edited books, including *Double Action Short Stories* (1973).

Greenfield's many talents have brought her numerous awards. She says that her goal is "to give children words to love, to grow on." Of writing, she says it is "talent combined with skills." Her desire is to create literature in which black children can see themselves and their place in history. She says she wants to write books for all children that they can "live in" while they read.

gru•el (grōō′əl) *n*. a thin, watery food made by cooking oatmeal or other meal in milk or water. It is often fed to sick people.

guer•ril•la or **gue•ril•la** (gə ril′ə) *n*. a member of a small group of fighters who are not part of a regular army. They usually make surprise raids behind the enemy's lines.

guf•faw (gə fô′) *n*. a loud and rough laugh.—*v*. to laugh with such a laugh.

gu•ru (gōō′ rōō′ *or* goo rōō′) *n*. **1.** a leader who is highly respected by a group of followers. **2.** a Hindu teacher.

gus•set (gus′it) *n*. a small piece shaped like a triangle or diamond, set into a skirt, glove, etc. to make it stronger or roomier.

gut•ta•per•cha (gutə pur′ chə) *n*. a substance like rubber, made from the milky juice of certain tropical trees. It is used inside golf balls, in dentistry, etc.

Haw•thorne, Na•than•iel (hô′ thôrn, nə than′ yəl) 1804–1864
Nathaniel Hawthorne is recognized as one of America's greatest writers of fiction. Hawthorne was descended from an influential family that first arrived in Colonial America in 1603.

Hawthorne grew up in Salem, Massachusetts. Though he was expected to enter the business world after college, he chose to be an author and spent many years reading and writing in seclusion. His first novel, *Fanshawe* (1828), was published anonymously at his own expense.

Disappointed in his initial efforts at writing books, Hawthorne retreated briefly to the mountains of Vermont. There he kept a notebook and jotted down his observations of places, people, ideas for stories, and phrases that he heard. Throughout his career Hawthorne wrote in notebooks, and many of the ideas he wrote down were the seeds for later novels and short stories.

Hawthorne's first truly successful novel was *The Scarlet Letter*, a masterpiece that remains a classic in American literature today.

helms•man (helmz′ mən) *n*., *pl*. **helmsmen**. the person who steers a ship. *The helmsman obeyed the directions from the captain.*

hilt (hilt) *n* . the handle of a sword or dagger. *The hilt of the dagger was pure gold.*

hith•er•to (hi*th*′ ər tōō) *adv*. until this time; to now. *William had been hitherto unsuccessful in trying to get his book published.*

I

im·mi·nent (im′ ə nənt) *adj.* likely to take place soon; about to happen. *The clouds indicated that a rainstorm was imminent.* [from Latin *imminere* to project over, threaten] — **imminence** *n.* — **imminently** *adv.*

im·promp·tu (im promp′ tōō) *adj., adv.* without preparation or thought ahead of time; offhand. *His impromptu remark surprised us.* [from Latin *in-* + *promptu* in readiness]

in·do·lent (in′ də lənt) *adj.* not liking work; lazy. *The indolent student did not finish his schoolwork.* —**indolence** *n.*

in·fir·mi·ty (in fur′ mə tē) *n.*, *pl.* **infirmities.** weakness or sickness. *Dan's infirmities kept him from playing football.*

L

la·goon (lə gōōn′) *n.* **1.** a shallow lake or pond, especially one that joins a larger body of water. **2.** the water that is surrounded by an atoll. **3.** an area of a shallow salt water cut off from the sea by sand dunes. *The lagoon remained calm during the storm.*

Li·brar·y of Con·gress (lī′ brer′ ē uv kong′ grəs)

The Library of Congress is one of America's most important historical archives. It ranks as one of the world's greatest reference libraries.

The library was formally established in 1800. In 1815 Congress purchased the library of Thomas Jefferson. These six thousand volumes nearly doubled the size of the library. Today its collections include approximately twenty million books and millions of films, photographs, maps, musical compositions, recordings, and engravings. Rare manuscripts — including some of the first books ever printed — journals, and other historical memorabilia are also stored within the library. The library also provides books in braille for the blind.

Although the library's main responsibility is to assist the United States Congress, it also serves as the national library. Scholars, other libraries, teachers, students, and the general public may use its extensive services.

M

mel·an·chol·y (mel′ ən kol′ ē) *adj.* **1.** sad and gloomy. *Jill felt melancholy after the sad movie.* **2.** causing sadness or gloom. — *n.* sadness or a tendency to be sad and gloomy. — *Syn.* **unhappiness.** — *Ant.* **joy.**

mus·ter (mus′ tər) *vt.* **1.** to bring or come together; to gather. **2.** to gather up; to summon. *Bill mustered all his strength for the game.*—*n.* **1.** a gathering together, as of troops for inspection. **2.** the persons or things gathered. **3.** the list of soldiers, sailors, etc. in a unit. [from Latin *monstrare* to show]

N

na·dir (nā′ dər) *n.* **1.** the point in the heavens directly opposite the zenith and directly beneath where one is standing. **2.** the lowest point. *He had reached the nadir of his hopes.*

name·sake (nām′ sāk) *n.* a person with the same name as another; especially, a person named after another.

Nar·cis·sus (när sis′əs) a beautiful youth in a Greek legend, who fell in love with his own reflection in a pool and was changed into the narcissus plant.

a fat	**i** hit	**oi** oil	**ch** chin	ə = a *in* ago
ā ape	**ir** here	**ōō** look	**sh** she	e *in* agent
ä car, father	**ī** bite, fire	**ōō** tool	**th** thin	i *in* unity
e ten	**o** lot	**ou** out	**th** then	o *in* collect
er care	**ō** go	**u** up	**zh** leisure	u *in* focus
ē even	**ô** law, horn	**ur** fur	**ŋ** ring	

Dictionary of Knowledge

nar•cis•sus (när sis′ əs) *n., pl.* **narcissus** or
narcissuses. a plant that grows from a bulb and
has white, yellow, or orange flowers.

nar•ra•tive po•e•try (nar′ ə tiv pō′ ə trē)

Narrative poetry tells a story. The story may
be long or short, simple or complex, but it is
told in some poetic form.

There are different kinds of narrative poetry.
In epic poetry the stories tell about the deeds of
heroes. For example, the Anglo-Saxon epic poem
Beowulf tells of the adventures of the warrior-hero
Beowulf, who battles with a dragon and monsters.

Another form of narrative poetry is the folk, or
popular, ballad. Folk ballads tell brief stories.
Such poems probably began as folktales and were
given poetic form by professional bards, or
singers.

The subject matter of folk ballads stems from
the everyday lives of the common folk. The story
in a folk ballad is usually quite simple and direct
and develops mainly through dialogue. Two
popular early Scottish ballads are "Bonny Barbara
Allan" and "Get Up and Bar the Door." Popular
American ballads include "Lewis and Clark"
by Rosemary and Stephen Vincent Benét,"Abraham
Lincoln" by Mildred Plew Meigs, and "Casey
Jones" (author unknown).

nar•whal (när′wəl *or* när′hwəl) *n.* a small whale of
the arctic. The male has a long tusk sticking out
from its upper jaw.

nas•tur•tium (nə stur′ shəm) *n.* a plant with a
sharp smell and red, yellow, or orange flowers.

Na•tion•al Sto•ry•tell•ing Fes•ti•val (nash′ ə n′l stôr′
ē tel iṅg fes′ tə v′l)

The National Storytelling Festival was
established in 1973 in Jonesborough, Tennessee.
The annual festival is sponsored by the National
Association for the Preservation and Perpetuation
of Storytelling. The festival usually takes place
over a weekend and features many renowned
storytellers from all over the United States.

People who attend the festival may hear a
variety of stories, including folktales from around
the world, fairy tales, family stories, and musical
stories. Some of the talented storytellers at the
festival may include Jackie Torrance, known as
"The Story Lady;" Bill Harley, who plays a guitar
while he tells many of his stories; Brenda Wong
Aoki, who combines ancient Japanese theater with
classic legends and folktales from Japan; and
Bernard Bragg, a deaf storyteller who performs
"Wonders of a Soundless World" using sign,
mime, and poetry accompanied by voice
narration.

No•bel Peace Prize (nō′ bel′ pēs′ prīz)

The Nobel Peace Prize is one of six Nobel Prize awards presented each year. It is awarded in Oslo, Norway. Swedish scientist Alfred Nobel (1833–1896) created the prizes to encourage and reward creativity in scientific, political, and literary endeavors, among others. The Peace Prize consists of a cash award, a gold medal, and a scroll.

Traditionally, each recipient accepts the award at a formal ceremony held in Oslo. Recipients include Theodore Roosevelt (1906) for negotiating peace in the Russo-Japanese War; Martin Luther King, Jr. (1964) for his work in the American civil-rights movement; and Mother Teresa (1979) for aiding the poor in India.

────────── **P** ──────────

parch (pärch) *vt.* **1.** to roast or dry with great heat. **2.** to make dry and hot. **3.** to make very thirsty. *The sun parched the hills.* — *Syn.* **scorch**. — *Ant.* **moisten**.

pat•ent (pat′ ′nt) *n.* **1.** the right given to someone by a government to be the only one who may make and sell a new invention, or use a new method, for a certain number of years. **2.** the paper giving such a right. **3.** the invention or new method protected by such a right.—*vt.* to get a patent for. *The inventor patented his new machine.*—*adj.* **1.** protected by a patent. **2.** easy to see or recognize; plain; evident.

pen•e•trat•ing (pen′ ə trāt iṅg) *adj.* that can penetrate; keen or sharp. *James had penetrating thoughts on the subject.*

pin•na•cle (pin′ ə k'l) *n.* **1.** a pointed top, as of a mountain; a high peak. *The mountain climber tried to scale the rocky pinnacle.* **2.** the highest point. **3.** a slender, pointed tower or steeple.

pli•ant (plī′ ənt) *adj.* **1.** easily bent; pliable. *We made a box out of the pliant cardboard.* **2.** adaptable or compliant.—**pliancy** *n.*—**pliantly** *adv.*

Poe, Ed•gar Al•lan (pō′, ed′ gər al′ ən) 1809–1849

Edgar Allan Poe was an American poet, short-story writer, and literary critic. Through his short stories "The Gold-Bug" and "The Murders in the Rue Morgue," Poe became one of the first writers to make criminal investigation the subject of short stories. He is known as the father of modern mystery and detective fiction. Poe was a talented editor of magazines as well.

Poe's most productive fiction-writing period was between 1837 and 1845. His first collection of short stories, *Tales of the Grotesque and Arabesque*, appeared in 1840. His greatest public recognition came in 1845 when his tale "The Gold-Bug" sold 300,000 copies, and his poem "The Raven" received wide acclaim.

Poe's short stories are known for their suspenseful, eerie, and sometimes frightening plots.

a fat	**i** hit	**oi** oil	**ch** chin	**ə** = a *in* ago
ā ape	**ir** here	**oo** look	**sh** she	e *in* agent
ä car, father	**ī** bite, fire	**ōō** tool	**th** thin	i *in* unity
e ten	**o** lot	**ou** out	***th*** then	o *in* collect
er care	**ō** go	**u** up	**zh** leisure	u *in* focus
ē even	**ô** law, horn	**ur** fur	**ṅg** ring	

Pul·it·zer, Jo·seph (pool′ it sər, jō′ zəf) 1847–1911

Joseph Pulitzer was an American newspaper editor and publisher. Pulitzer was born in Hungary, emigrated to Boston in 1864, and became a United States citizen in 1867. Among other jobs, Pulitzer served in the Union Army and was a reporter on a St. Louis newspaper. He graduated from law school and later owned papers in St. Louis and New York.

Pulitzer's newspaper ideas eventually brought together many features now commonly used in American daily newspapers. These include the sports section, the comics, and illustrations.

The Pulitzer Prizes that are given each year in journalism, literature, and music were established by Pulitzer to reward individual achievements in these areas. For example, Pulitzer Prizes in journalism are given in a number of categories, including distinguished reporting on subjects such as sports, business, education, and science. In literature, one of the prizes given is for a distinguished book on the history of the United States.

The first Pulitzer Prizes were awarded in 1917. Each recipient receives an established cash award.

R

rash·er (rash′ ər) *n.* **1.** a thin slice of bacon or ham to be fried or boiled. **2.** a serving of such slices.

rat·tan (ra tan′) *n.* **1.** the long, slender stems of a kind of palm tree, used in making wicker furniture, baskets, etc. **2.** a cane or switch made from one of these stems. **3.** this palm tree.

Raw·lings, Mar·jo·rie Kin·nan (rô′ lin̂gs, mär′ jə rē kin′ ən) 1896–1953

Marjorie Kinnan Rawlings was an American author best known for her book *The Yearling*. Rawlings began her writing career as a journalist. However, she received acclaim for her short stories, such as "Jacob's Ladder" and "Gal Young 'Un," and decided to devote her career to writing novels.

Some scholars believe that Rawlings got her idea for *The Yearling* from Max Perkins, a noted editor at Scribner's publishing house in New York. Perkins suggested that Rawlings write a novel about the places and people she knew in rural Florida, where she eventually settled.

The success of *The Yearling* was followed by other novels and short stories, including "The Sojourner" in 1953. Rawlings spent many years living and writing in Cross Creek, Florida. Her book, *Cross Creek*, tells of her experiences in this rural area.

re·frain[1] (ri frān′) *vi.* to keep from doing something; to hold back. *I refrained from laughing too loud.*

re·frain[2] (ri frān′) *n.* a phrase or verse that is repeated from time to time in a song or poem. *The chorus sang the refrain twice.*

re•solve (ri zolv′) *vt.* **resolved, resolving**. **1.** to decide; to make up one's mind. *I resolved to learn to play chess.* **2.** to make clear; to solve or explain. *Jill easily resolved the problem.* **3.** to decide by vote. — *n.* something decided on in a firm way; intention. *Because of his resolve to make the team, he practiced for hours.* [from Latin *re-* again + *solvere* loose] — *Syn.* **decide** — **resolver** *n.*

——————— S ———————

sci•ence mu•se•ums (sī′ əns myo͞o zē′ əmz)

Science museums are generally divided into two types — pure science museums and applied science museums. A pure science museum, such as the National Museum of Natural History in Washington, D.C., exhibits rocks, animal species, plants, fossils, and other objects and things found in nature.

In an applied science museum, you will find exhibits related to science in industry as well as to technological developments. Many of the exhibits show how various machines can make work easier. In fact, most of the exhibits are three-dimensional and encourage visitor participation. For example, in the Musuem of Science and Industry in Chicago, you can go aboard a submarine, tour a coal mine, and walk down a replica of a street from 1910.

self-pos•ses•sion (self′ pə zesh′ ən) *n.* full control over one's own actions and feelings; composure. *Marie's self-possession won her the promotion at her job.* — **self-possessed** *adj.*

——————— U ———————

un•du•ly (un do͞o′ lē *or* un dyo͞o′ lē) *adv.* beyond what is proper or right; too much. *Ray was unduly upset by the argument.*

——————— W ———————

whit•tle (hwit′ 'l) *vt.* **whittled, whittling**. **1.** to cut thin shavings from wood with a knife. **2.** to carve by doing this. **3.** to make less bit by bit. *He whittled away at the problem.*

Wy•eth, N.C. (wī′ əth, en sē) 1882–1945

N.C. Wyeth was an American painter and illustrator. Wyeth became known for his illustrations in classic juvenile books, including the 1939 edition of Marjorie Kinnan Rawlings' *The Yearling* and Robert Louis Stevenson's *Treasure Island.*

Newell Convers Wyeth was born in Needham, Massachusetts, and studied art in Boston. He then went to Chadds Ford, Pennsylvania, to study with the noted illustrator Howard Pyle.

The illustrations that Wyeth created for books enabled readers to visualize important parts of the stories. He combined vivid images with free expressiveness. The results were illustrations that told the stories by themselves. Wyeth also painted landscapes and created large murals for public buildings in Washington, D.C, New York, Boston, and other cities.

Wyeth's son Andrew and grandson Jamie have carried the family artistic tradition; both are well known today for their individual painting styles.

a	fat	i	hit	oi	oil	ch	chin	ə = a *in* ago
ā	ape	ir	here	o͞o	look	sh	she	e *in* agent
ä	car, father	ī	bite, fire	o͞o	tool	th	thin	i *in* unity
e	ten	o	lot	ou	out	*th*	then	o *in* collect
er	care	ō	go	u	up	zh	leisure	u *in* focus
ē	even	ô	law, horn	ur	fur	ñg	ring	

Dictionary of Knowledge

Thesaurus

A thesaurus contains lists of synonyms and antonyms. You will use this Thesaurus for the thesaurus lesson in Unit 1 and for the Thesaurus Corner in each Writing Connection lesson in this book. You can also use the Thesaurus to find synonyms to make your writing more interesting.

Sample Entry

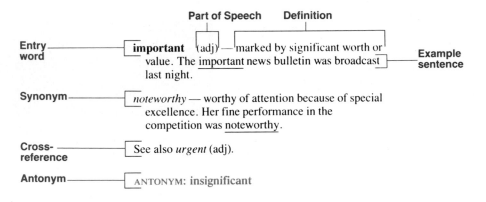

How to Use the Thesaurus Index

To find a word, use the Thesaurus Index on pages 589–593. All entry words, synonyms, and antonyms are listed alphabetically in the Index. Words in dark type are entry words, words in italic type are synonyms, and words in blue type are antonyms. A cross-reference (marked "See also") lists an entry that gives additional synonyms, related words, and antonyms. The page number tells you where to find the word that you are looking for.

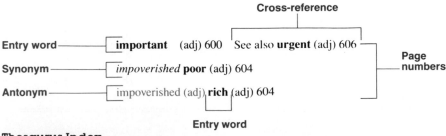

THESAURUS INDEX
A list of all the words in this thesaurus

A

accept **believe** (v) 594
accomplish **win** (v) 607
achieve **win** (v) 607
acquire **buy** (v) 595
acquire **give** (v) 598
acute **urgent** (adj) 606
address **talk** (v) 606
adjacent **far** (adj) 597
adjacent **near** (adj) 603
adjoining **near** (adj) 603
affluent (adj) **poor** (adj) 604
affluent **rich** (adj) 604
afraid **brave** (adj) 594
answer (v) **ask** (v) 594
anxiety **fear** (n) 597
appear **disappear** (v) 596
apprehend **know** (v) 601
article **object** (n) 603
articulate **say** (v) 605
artifact **object** (n) 603
ask (v) 594
association **group** (n) 598
auction (v) **buy** (v) 595
author **write** (v) 607

B

band **crowd** (n) 596
bankrupt (adj) **rich** (adj) 604
be in stitches **laugh** (v) 601
believe (v) 594
benevolent **kind** (adj) 600
big-league **important** (adj) 600
bleach **clean** (v) 596
blistering **hot** (adj) 599
blunder **mistake** (n) 602
bold **brave** (adj) 594
boldness **fear** (n) 597
bordering **near** (adj) 603
brave (adj) 594
bravery **fear** (n) 597
break (v) 595
break (v) **fix** (v) 595
bring home the bacon **win** (v) 607
broke **poor** (adj) 604
bunch **crowd** (n) 596

burning **hot** (adj) 599
burst (v) **fix** (v) 598
buy (v) 595
buy **believe** (v) 594

C

cabin **house** (n) 600
call (v) 595
call **say** (v) 605
careful (adj) 595
careless **careful** (adj) 595
castle **house** (n) 600
cautious **careful** (adj) 595
chancellor **leader** (n) 601
chat **talk** (v) 606
cheer **call** (v) 695
chief **important** (adj) 600
chuckle **laugh** (v) 601
clean (v) 596
close (adj) **far** (adj) 597
close **near** (adj) 603
cold **hot** (adj) 599
collapse (v) **fix** (v) 598
comfortable **easy** (adj) 597
comfortable **rich** (adj) 604
commander **leader** (n) 601
compassionate **kind** (adj) 600
compelling **urgent** (adj) 606
complicated **easy** (adj) 597
comprehend **know** (v) 601
confidence **fear** (n) 597
conscientious **careful** (adj) 595
contaminate **clean** (v) 596
contribute **give** (v) 598
corral **win** (v) 607
correspond **write** (v) 607
cottage **house** (n) 600
courage **fear** (n) 597
courageous **brave** (adj) 594
cowardly (adj) **brave** (adj) 594
crack (v) **fix** (v) 598
crawl **move** (v) 603
crew **group** (n) 598
crisp **hot** (adj) 599
critical **urgent** (adj) 606
crowd (n) 596
   See also **group** (n) 598

crucial **urgent** (adj) 606
cruel **kind** (adj) 600
crush **crowd** (n) 596
cry (v) **laugh** (v) 601

D

dash **move** (v) 603
debate **talk** (v) 606
debilitated (adj) **strong** (adj) 605
decimate **break** (v) 595
deliberate **careful** (adj) 595
deliver **give** (v) 598
depart **disappear** (v) 596
despot **leader** (n) 601
destitute **poor** (adj) 604
destitute **rich** (adj) 604
destroy **break** (v) 595
device **object** (n) 603
difficult **easy** (adj) 597
difficult **hard** (adj) 599
dirty (v) **clean** (v) 596
disappear (v) 596
disbelieve **believe** (v) 594
discontinue **move** (v) 603
discreet **careful** (adj) 595
dispute (v) **believe** (v) 594
distant **near** (adj) 603
doctor **fix** (v) 598
doohickey **object** (n) 603
double-barreled **important** (adj) 600
doubt (v) **believe** (v) 594
dread **fear** (n) 597
drop **lose** (v) 602
dry-clean **clean** (v) 596
dwelling **house** (n) 600

E

easy (adj) 597
easy **hard** (adj) 599
effortless **easy** (adj) 597
emerge **disappear** (v) 596
endow **give** (v) 598
energetic **strong** (adj) 605
energetic **weak** (adj) 607
error **mistake** (n) 602
evaporate **disappear** (v) 596
expire **disappear** (v) 596

F

facile **hard** (adj) 599
fade out **disappear** (v) 596

fail **lose** (v) 602
fail (v) **win** (v) 607
faint **weak** (adj) 607
fainthearted **brave** (adj) 594
fall **lose** (v) 602
fall (v) **win** (v) 607
far (adj) 597
far **near** (adj) 603
faraway **far** (adj) 597
faraway **near** (adj) 603
far-off **far** (adj) 597
fathom **know** (v) 601
fear (n) 597
fearful **brave** (adj) 594
fearlessness **fear** (n) 597
feeble **strong** (adj) 605
filter **clean** (v) 596
find (v) **lose** (v) 602
fix (v) 598
fix (v) **break** (v) 595
flock **group** (n) 598
flop **lose** (v) 602
flop (v) **win** (v) 607
flow **move** (v) 603
follower **leader** (v) 601
forceful **strong** (adj) 605
foreboding **fear** (n) 597
forfeit (v) **win** (v) 607
formidable **easy** (adj) 597
fragile **weak** (adj) 607
frail **strong** (adj) 605
frail **weak** (adj) 607
fright **fear** (n) 597
frigid **hot** (adj) 599
frosty **hot** (adj) 599
frown (v) **laugh** (v) 601
frozen **hot** (adj) 599
funk **fear** (n) 597
furnish **give** (v) 598

G

gab **talk** (v) 606
gadget **object** (n) 603
gain (v) **give** (v) 598
gain (v) **lose** (v) 602
get **buy** (v) 595
get **know** (v) 601
giggle **laugh** (v) 601
give (v) 598
glower (v) **laugh** (v) 601
grasp **know** (v) 601
great **kind** (adj) 600
grill **ask** (v) 594

group (n) 598
   See also **crowd** (n) 596
guffaw **laugh** (v) 601
gutsy **brave** (adj) 594

H

halt (v) **move** (v) 603
hard (adj) 599
hardy **strong** (adj) 605
hardy **weak** (adj) 607
harsh **kind** (adj) 600
hasty **careful** (adj) 595
have down pat **know** (v) 601
have no doubt about **believe** (v) 594
hefty **hard** (adj) 599
heroic **brave** (adj) 594
high rise **house** (n) 600
hike **walk** (v) 606
hold (v) **lose** (v) 602
holler **call** (v) 595
horde **crowd** (n) 596
hot (adj) 599
hot as a furnace **hot** (adj) 599
house (n) 600
howl **call** (v) 595
humane **kind** (adj) 600

I

immediate **far** (adj) 597
immediate **near** (adj) 603
implement **object** (n) 603
important (adj) 600
   See also **urgent** (adj) 606
impoverished **poor** (adj) 604
impoverished (adj) **rich** (adj) 604
imprudent **careful** (adj) 595
inconsequential **important** (adj) 600
inconsiderate **kind** (adj) 600
indiscreet **careful** (adj) 595
individual (n) **group** (n) 598
inferior **poor** (adj) 604
inherit **give** (v) 598
inhumane **kind** (adj) 600
inquire **ask** (v) 594
inscribe **write** (v) 607
insignificant **important** (adj) 600
instrument **object** (n) 603
interrogate **ask** (v) 594

J

judicious **careful** (adj) 595

K

keep (v) **lose** (v) 602
kind (adj) 600
kingpin **leader** (n) 601
KO **break** (v) 595
know (v) 601

L

laborious **easy** (adj) 597
laugh (v) 601
laugh it up **laugh** (v) 601
launder **clean** (v) 596
leader (n) 601
leery **careful** (adj) 595
listless **strong** (adj) 605
listless **weak** (adj) 607
loaded **rich** (adj) 604
long-distance **far** (adj) 597
lose (v) 602
lose **win** (v) 607
lumber **walk** (v) 606
luscious **rich** (adj) 604

M

magnanimous **kind** (adj) 600
malevolent **kind** (adj) 600
manageable **easy** (adj) 597
mansion **house** (n) 600
market (v) **buy** (v) 595
materialize **disappear** (v) 596
melt **disappear** (v) 596
mend (v) **break** (v) 595
mend **fix** (v) 598
merciless **kind** (adj) 600
migrate **move** (v) 603
miscalculation **mistake** (n) 602
misjudgment **mistake** (n) 602
misplace **lose** (v) 602
misprint **mistake** (n) 602
mistake (n) 602
mistrust (v) **believe** (v) 594
misunderstand **know** (v) 601
mob **crowd** (n) 596
momentous **important** (adj) 600
monarch **leader** (n) 601
moneyed **poor** (adj) 604
move (v) 603
   See also **walk** (v) 606
multitude **crowd** (n) 596
muscular **strong** (adj) 605
mutter **say** (v) 605

N

near (adj) 603
near **far** (adj) 597
nearby **far** (adj) 597
nearby **near** (adj) 603
needy **poor** (adj) 604
needy (adj) **rich** (adj) 604
negligent **careful** (adj) 595
neighboring (adj) **far** (adj) 597
neighboring **near** (adj) 603
not to be sneezed at **important** (adj) 600
noteworthy **important** (adj) 600

O

object (n) 603
obtain **buy** (v) 598
obtain **give** (v) 598
opulent **poor** (adj) 604
opulent **rich** (adj) 604
orchestra **group** (n) 598
outlying **far** (adj) 597
outlying **near** (adj) 603
overhaul **fix** (v) 598
overheated **hot** (adj) 599
oversight **mistake** (n) 602

P

pace **walk** (v) 606
pack **group** (n) 598
painless **easy** (adj) 597
paramount **important** (adj) 600
pause (v) **move** (v) 603
penniless **poor** (adj) 604
petty **important** (adj) 600
philanthropic **kind** (adj) 600
phobia **fear** (n) 597
plain (adj) **rich** (adj) 604
pollute **clean** (v) 596
poor (adj) 604
poor (adj) **rich** (adj) 604
powerful **weak** (adj) 607
powerless **strong** (adj) 605
powerless **weak** (adj) 607
premier **leader** (n) 601
present **give** (v) 598
president **leader** (n) 601
pressing **urgent** (adj) 606
presume **believe** (v) 594
prevail **win** (v) 607
procure **buy** (v) 595
procure **give** (v) 598
progress **move** (v) 603

propel **move** (v) 603
prosperous **poor** (adj) 604
prosperous **rich** (adj) 604
provide **give** (v) 588
prudent **careful** (adj) 595
purchase **buy** (v) 595
purify **clean** (v) 596
put into words **say** (v) 605
put through the third degree **ask** (v) 594

Q

question **ask** (v) 594
question (v) **believe** (v) 594
quiz **ask** (v) 594

R

ramble **walk** (v) 606
rap **talk** (v) 606
ravage **break** (v) 595
receive **give** (v) 598
reckless **careful** (adj) 595
recognize **know** (v) 601
recondition **fix** (v) 598
reconstruct **fix** (v) 598
record **write** (v) 607
recover **lose** (v) 602
relinquish **lose** (v) 602
remote **far** (adj) 597
remote **near** (adj) 603
removed **near** (adj) 603
repair (v) **break** (v) 595
repair **fix** (v) 598
report **talk** (v) 606
request **ask** (v) 594
residence **house** (n) 600
respond **ask** (v) 594
restore **fix** (v) 598
retain **lose** (v) 602
rich (adj) 604
rich (adj) **poor** (adj) 604
rigorous **easy** (adj) 597
rolling in money **rich** (adj) 604
rugged **hard** (adj) 599
ruin **break** (v) 595

S

say (v) 605
    See also **talk** (v) 606
scalding **hot** (adj) 599
scowl (v) **laugh** (v) 601
scream **call** (v) 695
scribble **write** (v) 607

sell (v) **buy** (v) 595
service **fix** (v) 598
shout **call** (v) 595
shriek **call** (v) 595
shriek **laugh** (v) 601
simple **easy** (adj) 597
simple **hard** (adj) 595
slipup **mistake** (n) 602
smudge (v) **clean** (v) 596
snap (v) **fix** (v) 598
snicker **laugh** (v) 601
soft **easy** (adj) 597
soft (adj) **hard** (adj) 599
soft (adj) **strong** (adj) 605
soil (v) **clean** (v) 596
solid **hard** (adj) 599
split (v) **fix** (v) 598
spunky **brave** (adj) 594
stain (v) **clean** (v) 596
sterilize **clean** (v) 596
stern **hard** (adj) 599
sticky **hot** (adj) 599
stop (v) **move** (v) 603
strenuous **easy** (adj) 597
strict **hard** (adj) 599
stride **walk** (v) 606
strong (adj) 605
strong (adj) **weak** (adj) 607
strong as a bull **strong** (adj) 605
sturdy **strong** (adj) 605
sturdy **weak** (adj) 607
subordinate (n) **leader** (n) 601
subsidize **give** (v) 598
succumb **lose** (v) 602
superficial **important** (adj) 600
superior (adj) **poor** (adj) 604
suppose **believe** (v) 594
surmise **believe** (v) 594
sweltering **hot** (adj) 599
sympathetic **kind** (adj) 600

T

take (v) **give** (v) 598
take down **write** (v) 607
talk (v) 606
   See also **say** (v) 605
team **group** (n) 598
telephone **call** (v) 595
terror **fear** (n) 597
think **believe** (v) 594
thoughtless **careful** (adj) 595
throng **crowd** (n) 596

timid **brave** (adj) 594
timorous **brave** (adj) 594
titter **laugh** (v) 601
torrid **hot** (adj) 599
tough **strong** (adj) 605
traipse **walk** (v) 606
travel **move** (v) 603
triumph **win** (v) 607
trivial **important** (adj) 600
troupe **group** (n) 598
trudge **walk** (v) 606
trust **believe** (v) 594

U

unable to make ends meet **poor** (adj) 604
unafraid **brave** (adj) 594
underprivileged **poor** (adj) 604
understand **know** (v) 601
unimportant **important** (adj) 600
unimportant **urgent** (adj) 606
unkind **kind** (adj) 600
unmanageable **easy** (adj) 596
urgent (adj) 606
   See also **important** (adj) 600
utter **say** (v) 605

V

valiant **brave** (adj) 594
vanish **disappear** (v) 596
vend **buy** (v) 595
vigorous **strong** (adj) 605
vigorous **weak** (adj) 607

W

walk (v) 606
   See also **move** (v) 603
wanting (adj) **rich** (adj) 604
wash **clean** (v) 596
weak (adj) 607
weak **strong** (adj) 605
wealthy **poor** (adj) 604
wealthy **rich** (adj) 604
whisper **say** (v) 605
win (v) 607
win (v) **lose** (v) 602
worthless **important** (adj) 600
wreck **break** (v) 595
write (v) 607

Y

yap **say** (v) 605

A

ask (v)–**1** to question; to call on to answer. Our teacher will ask us questions about the homework assignment. **2** to request something of someone. Ask the librarian to help you find the book.

interrogate–to question systematically. The detective will interrogate the witness.

inquire–to ask about someone or something. I will inquire about the price of tickets.

question–to ask of or about. Did the doctor question the nurse about the test results?

quiz–to question carefully. Our history teacher will quiz us on ancient Greece.

request–to ask for. The pilot of the private plane has requested permission to land.

grill [informal]–to question with intensity. The police officer will grill the suspect.

put through the third degree [idiom]–to question unmercifully. After coming home very late from school, Mark was put through the third degree.

ANTONYMS: **answer (v), respond**

B

believe (v)–to accept with trust and faith; to have a firm conviction of the reality of something. I believe that the climate of our area is changing.

accept–to receive as true or satisfactory. I accept his explanation for the delay.

presume–to suppose to be true without any proof. We presume that all the arrangements for the trip have been made.

suppose–to have as an opinion; to believe. I suppose that what she said about the earthquake is true.

surmise–to imagine on slight proof to be true; to guess. I surmise that the storm has delayed the arrival of the flight.

think–to have an opinion. I think that we must protect the wilderness areas of the world.

trust–to rely on the honesty or truthfulness of. Do you trust his judgment on the subject?

buy [slang]–to accept as true. Do you buy the ridiculous explanation that he just gave you?

have no doubts about [idiom]–to believe totally. I have no doubts about the safety of this automobile.

ANTONYMS: **disbelieve, dispute (v), doubt (v), mistrust (v), question (v)**

brave (adj)–having or displaying courage. The brave fire fighters entered the burning building.

bold–fearless when facing danger. The bold rider urged her horse over the difficult jump.

courageous–possessing or characterized by bravery. The courageous individual dove into the icy water to save a child who had fallen from the bridge.

heroic–marked by courage and daring. The mountain climber made a heroic effort to reach the summit.

unafraid–without fear. The seriously ill patient faced the operation unafraid.

valiant–having or exhibiting valor; courageous. Although in extreme pain, the valiant marathon runner stayed in the race.

spunky [informal]–spirited; brave. The spunky individual refused to let anything get her down.

gutsy [slang]–courageous. Trying to steal home is a gutsy play in baseball.

ANTONYMS: **afraid, cowardly (adj), fainthearted, fearful, timid, timorous**

break   (v)–to reduce to pieces with sudden or violent force. Please do not break that valuable vase.

decimate–to destroy a large portion of. Spraying the area with a pesticide will decimate the insect population.

destroy–to break into pieces; to ruin. Lack of sufficient rainfall can destroy farm crops.

ravage–to damage greatly; to destroy. The fire ravaged an entire city block.

ruin–to destroy; to devastate. Certain stains can ruin a shirt.

wreck–to destroy or ruin. Improper maintenance procedures can wreck a power lawn mower.

KO [slang]–to knock out or destroy. Nothing can KO me faster than the flu.

ANTONYMS: **fix (v), mend (v), repair (v)**

buy   (v)–to acquire ownership of something by the payment of money. My sister will buy a new coat tomorrow.

acquire–to gain possession of. A motion picture studio acquired the movie rights to that popular novel.

get–to obtain possession of. I will get a loaf of bread and a quart of milk at the store.

obtain–to attain usually through planned action. Judy will obtain two tickets to the basketball game.

procure–to obtain or acquire. The stockbroker will procure one-hundred shares of the stock of that company.

purchase–to obtain through the payment of money. Where did you purchase those tennis shoes?

ANTONYMS: **auction (v), market (v), sell (v), vend**

C

call   (v)–to say; to cry out or shout. The team captain called the plays.

cheer–to shout support of or praise. The fans at the basketball game cheer every time the home team scores a basket.

howl–to give a long mournful cry. The crowd howled when the football team fumbled the ball.

scream–to make a loud, piercing cry. Some of the passengers screamed when the plane jolted because of severe turbulence.

shout–to cry out suddenly and loudly. Almost everyone applauded and shouted after the pianist had finished playing.

shriek–to make a shrill sound. The parrot shrieked when I came near.

telephone–to communicate with someone by telephone. I will telephone my best friend tonight.

holler [informal]–to shout loudly. When angry, the coach can really holler.

careful   (adj)–having caution; showing concern over what one says or does. A pedestrian should always be careful when crossing a street.

cautious–extremely careful; not taking any chances. A cautious driver never tailgates.

conscientious–careful to do whatever is right; scrupulous. A conscientious student hands in homework assignments on time.

deliberate–done on purpose; thought over ahead of time. He made a deliberate effort to improve his grades.

discreet–careful in action or speech; prudent. Being discreet, she did not tell

careful (*continued*)

anyone about the confidential information.

judicious–having good judgment; sensible. A judicious physician tries not to alarm a patient.

prudent–showing wisdom; thoroughly planning ahead of time. A prudent individual saves some money for the future.

leery–wary, suspicious. The police were leery of the suspect's story.

ANTONYMS: **careless, hasty, imprudent, indiscreet, negligent, reckless, thoughtless**

clean   (v)–to free from dirt or impurities. When will you go upstairs and clean your room?

bleach–to remove stains or make lighter in color. Can you bleach those towels?

dry-clean–to clean clothes with naphtha, or the like, and little or no water. You must dry-clean that stained suit jacket.

filter–to pass a liquid or gas through a porous mass in order to separate out matter or impurities. My cousin's fish tank has a device that filters all of the water.

launder–to wash clothes with water. I will launder all of my shirts today.

purify–to clear from material imperfection. A huge plant purifies the city water supply.

sterilize–to free from living germs or microorganisms, as by heating. Hospital personnel will sterilize all the surgical instruments that will be used in the operation.

wash–to clean by using a liquid such as water. When should I wash this dirty floor?

ANTONYMS: **contaminate, dirty (v), pollute, smudge (v), soil (v), stain (v)**

crowd   (n)–a large number of people collected together. A crowd gathered near the stadium entrance.

band–a number of persons or animals acting together. A band of scientists worked ceaselessly to find a cure for the disease.

crush–a group of people crowded together. The crush of people jammed the subway train during rush hour.

horde–a loosely organized crowd. A horde of students left the school building at the end of the day.

multitude–a large group of people. A somber multitude gathered near the site of the mine cave-in.

throng–a great number of people. A loud cheer arose from the throng at the stadium.

bunch [informal]–a group of people. That bunch always sticks together.

mob [slang]–a lawless crowd of people. The angry mob started to move toward city hall.

See also *group* (n).

D

disappear   (v)–to pass from sight; to cease existing. The freight train disappeared as it rounded the curve.

depart–to leave or go away. The plane will depart for Honolulu in about an hour.

evaporate–to change from liquid or solid into vapor; to disappear. Soon after the heavy rain, all the water evaporated from the street.

expire–to terminate; to come to an end. The time left in the first half of the game expired.

melt–to change from solid to liquid; to dissolve. These mild March temperatures are melting the ice on the pond.

vanish–to disappear quickly; to cease existing. The brilliant golden sunset vanished into darkness.

fade out [slang]–to disappear gradually. The singer's popularity began to fade out about a year ago.

ANTONYMS: **appear, emerge, materialize**

E

easy (adj)–**1** not difficult to do or obtain. Learning to speak French was easy for me. **2** free from pain or worry. Vacationing at this tropical island is certainly the easy life.

comfortable–having ease. I certainly feel comfortable in this soft reclining chair.

effortless–needing or showing little exertion; easy. The runner in the lead has an effortless stride.

manageable–capable of being handled or controlled. That simple task is certainly manageable.

painless–without physical or emotional distress or suffering. The tooth extraction was painless.

simple–free of complications; easy to do or understand. Fortunately, the directions for assembling the model airplane were simple.

soft–requiring little effort. Stacking these boxes is a soft task.

cushy [slang]–requiring little difficulty; comfortable. I wish I had a cushy job like yours.

easy as pie [idiom]–not difficult. For me, riding a bicycle is easy as pie.

ANTONYMS: **complicated, difficult, formidable, laborious, rigorous, strenuous, unmanageable**

F

far (adj)–not near; remote in time or space; distant. They moved to a far country.

distant–not near; far away in time or space. I wonder if everyone will be able to travel to other planets in the distant future.

faraway–remote; located at a great distance. I would like to travel to faraway places.

far-off–located far away, distant. He gazed across the wheat fields toward the far-off mountains.

long-distance–over or for a long distance. My uncle made a long-distance telephone call to Fairbanks, Alaska.

outlying–distant or far from the center. The meteorologist said the outlying suburbs would receive more snow than the city.

remote–far away; far removed in space or time. There are no paved roads in that remote wilderness area.

ANTONYMS: **adjacent, bordering (adj), close (adj), immediate, near (adj), nearby (adj), neighboring (adj)**

fear (n)–an unpleasant emotion caused by belief that danger is present or near. As he glanced down from the steep mountain path, my friend was suddenly overcome by fear.

anxiety–uneasy or painful thoughts about what might happen. My anxiety over the upcoming history test continues to grow.

dread–to look forward to with great fear. I dread our class trip to the snake farm.

foreboding–a warning or prediction of coming evil; an omen. She boarded the plane even though she had a foreboding that something bad would happen during the flight.

fright–sudden fear; terror. The sound of the door slamming shut behind him gave him a fright.

phobia–a persistent abnormal fear of a certain thing. She has a phobia about elevators.

terror–a state of great fear. We felt terror as we watched the tornado approach.

fear *(continued)*

funk [informal]–a state of fear; a depressed state of mind. The gloomy weather left me in a blue funk.

ANTONYMS: **boldness, bravery, confidence, courage, fearlessness**

fix   (v)–to repair or mend. Can you fix my broken guitar?

mend–to repair; to put into good shape again. I will mend these torn socks.

overhaul–to examine and make any necessary repairs. Even though the automobile mechanic overhauled the engine last month, the automobile still is not running right.

recondition–to restore to a good condition; renovate. The mechanic will recondition the automobile in order to make it perform as if it were brand new again.

reconstruct–to build or construct again; to restore. The carpenters will reconstruct that dilapidated old house.

repair–to fix by putting together what is broken or by replacing a part. Someone must repair the broken refrigerator quickly before all of the food spoils and we have absolutely nothing to eat.

restore–to bring back to an original condition; to renew. I will restore the finish on this old table.

service–to repair or perform maintenance on. Airlines periodically service the engines on each of their airplanes.

doctor [informal]–**1** to repair. We doctored the leaning wooden fence. **2** to alter or tamper with. The dishonest executive doctored the company records.

ANTONYMS: **break (v), burst (v), collapse (v), crack (v), snap (v), split (v)**

G

give   (v)–to hand over as a gift; to grant

by formal action. I will give my brother a new camera for his birthday.

contribute–to give in common with others. I will certainly contribute to the fund for the new children's hospital.

deliver–to hand over; to carry and give out. We must deliver this package to Los Angeles.

endow–to give money or property in order to provide an income. The wealthy person generously endowed the hospital.

furnish–to provide with something necessary. The sponsor will furnish uniforms for the baseball team.

present–to give to; to offer formally. The principal will present the awards during the assembly.

provide–to supply what is needed or wanted. The volunteers will provide transportation to anyone who wants to attend the football game Saturday afternoon.

subsidize–to assist with a grant of money. Does the government subsidize commuter bus lines that do not make a profit?

ANTONYMS: **acquire, gain (v), inherit, obtain, procure, receive, take (v)**

group   (n)–a usually comparatively small number of persons, animals, or things together. A group of children played in the sandbox.

association–a group of people with a common purpose. The recreation association of our town has done much for everyone.

crew–the people needed to work a ship. The crew of a cruise ship includes chefs and doctors.

flock–a group of animals of one kind keeping or herded together. A flock of geese just flew over the horizon.

orchestra–a group of musicians, including string players, organized to perform together. The symphony orchestra played Beethoven's Fifth Symphony at our high school auditorium.

team–a group of persons joined together in a certain activity. A team of mountain climbers is on its way up Mt. Everest.

troupe–a band, especially of actors, dancers, or other entertainers. The city ballet troupe will perform *Swan Lake* next month.

pack [informal]–a set or number of persons or things together. Do you think that everything you just heard was a pack of lies? See also *crowd* (n).

ANTONYM: individual (n)

H

hard (adj)–**1** not easy to penetrate. The thick ice on the lake is frozen hard. **2** difficult to do. Painting that lattice fence is hard. **3** unyielding to influence. He is a hard person when it comes to accepting excuses.

difficult–not easy to do or understand. It is very difficult for me to read that handwriting.

formidable–difficult to overcome or to deal with. Inclement weather can be a formidable challenge for airplane pilots.

rugged–having a rough and uneven surface; covered with rough edges. This rugged gravel road is filled with dangerous ruts.

solid–neither gaseous nor liquid; put together strongly; hard, firm. The solid form of water, ice, is lower in density than the liquid form of water.

stern–strict, harsh, severe. A stern person does not smile very often.

strict–careful in following a rule or in making other people follow it. My English teacher is strict when it comes to handing in homework assignments on time.

hefty [informal]–considerable; having bigness or bulk. Reshelving all of the books in our school library is a hefty job.

ANTONYMS: easy, facile, simple, soft

hot (adj)–**1** having a temperature that is relatively high. It is really hot outside. **2** having the sensation of high bodily heat. The fever from the illness made him feel extremely hot and uncomfortable.

blistering–capable of causing blisters; extremely hot. After playing baseball all morning, the blistering heat was too much to endure.

burning–hot; being on fire; affecting with heat. Immediately after running the race, Sue was overcome by a burning sensation.

overheated–warmed beyond a safe or desired point. The overheated car was parked on the shoulder of the highway.

scalding–hot enough to burn with hot liquid or steam. Don't drink that scalding coffee.

sweltering–oppressively hot. On that sweltering summer day, thousands of people headed for several of the local beaches.

torrid–parched with heat; scorching. The torrid heat caused some people to become dizzy.

sticky [informal]–hot and humid. In sticky weather like this, I cannot stop perspiring.

hot as a furnace [idiom]–having unbearable heat. The tennis court is hot as a furnace today.

ANTONYMS: cold, crisp, frigid, frosty, frozen

Thesaurus

house (n)–a building in which one or more families live. Jessica lives in the blue house on the corner just one block from my house.

cabin–a roughly built small house. There are many cabins in the wooded area that surrounds the lake.

castle–a large building or set of buildings with thick walls and battlements for defense. Many medieval castles can be found in Europe.

cottage–a small house, especially in the country or suburbs. We stayed at a cottage near a picturesque lighthouse.

dwelling–the place in which a person lives; a house. We live in a modest dwelling on Maple Avenue.

high rise–a building having many stories. We live in an apartment in the new high rise on Brinker Street.

mansion–a large, imposing house. Some movie stars live in impressive mansions in Beverly Hills.

residence–the place where a person lives; a home. Did your sister take up residence in Colorado yet?

I

important (adj)–marked by significant worth or value. The important news bulletin was broadcast last night.

chief–of greatest importance or significance. The chief member of the crew on a plane is the pilot.

momentous–very important; consequential. The anniversary celebration was a momentous occasion.

noteworthy–worthy of attention because of special excellence. Her fine performance in the competition was noteworthy.

paramount–superior to all else. The final exams are of paramount significance.

big-league [informal]–something outstanding of its kind. Linda gave a big-league performance in the play last Wednesday evening.

double-barreled [slang]–important; having a dual purpose. The lawyer asked the witness a double-barreled question.

not to be sneezed at [idiom]–of considerable importance. His chances in the race are not to be sneezed at.

See also *urgent* (adj).

ANTONYMS: **inconsequential, insignificant, petty, superficial, trivial, unimportant, worthless**

K

kind (adj)–having a gentle and considerate nature; tending to be helpful. A kind person usually manages to find time to help others.

benevolent–wanting to promote the happiness of others; disposed to doing good. The benevolent king was kind to all of his subjects.

compassionate–sympathetic; desiring to help those that suffer. The compassionate nurse comforted the severely injured accident victim by reassuring him.

humane–merciful; compassionate; not cruel. A humane person treats animals, as well as people, with kindness.

magnanimous–noble of mind; free from mean acts; generous in forgiving. In a magnanimous gesture, the senator who had just lost the election asked everyone to support his victorious opponent.

philanthropic–kind and helpful toward people in general; charitable. The philanthropic organization in our town raised enough money to build a new senior citizen center.

sympathetic–showing kind feelings toward other people. My sympathetic friend always lifts my spirits when I feel sad.

great [slang]–noble; kind and generous. Your brother is a great guy to pay for our hot dogs.

ANTONYMS: **cruel, harsh, inconsiderate, inhumane, malevolent, merciless, unkind**

know   (v)–**1** to have understanding of the facts of. I know the geography of North America quite well. **2** to be acquainted with. I know that person very well.

apprehend–to become aware of; to perceive. He clearly apprehended the risks involved in skydiving.

comprehend–to understand the nature or meaning of something. I cannot comprehend her complex report about lasers.

fathom–to fully understand. I cannot fathom the vastness of outer space.

grasp–to lay hold of with the mind; to understand. Can you grasp the meaning of what I am saying?

recognize–to be aware of someone or something as previously known. Do you recognize that television personality?

understand–to grasp the meaning of. I understand why we must conserve all natural resources.

get [slang]–to understand. I get what you mean.

have down pat [idiom]–to understand something quite well. I have the entire plan down pat.

ANTONYM: **misunderstand**

L

laugh   (v)–to show happiness or scorn with a smile and a chuckle or a very loud sound. I laughed uncontrollably at the joke that she told me.

chuckle–to laugh quietly or inwardly. I happily watched and chuckled when my dog danced excitedly with my slipper between its teeth.

giggle–to laugh in a silly manner. The two children giggled almost every time they glanced at each other.

guffaw–to laugh coarsely and loudly. When I dropped my ice-cream cone into my lap, all of my companions guffawed.

shriek–to utter a sharp, shrill, loud sound. When her parents first showed the young girl her new bicycle, she shrieked with delight.

snicker–to laugh in a partly suppressed and often disrespectful manner. The two political opponents frequently snickered at each other's remarks during the televised campaign debate.

titter–to laugh in a partly suppressed manner because of nervousness. The two children tittered when the famous actor approached them.

laugh it up [slang]–to act happy by use of laughter. I hope you guys will laugh it up when I tell my funny story.

be in stitches [idiom]–to laugh uncontrollably. You will be in stitches when you hear that comedian do his monologue.

ANTONYMS: **cry (v), frown (v), glower (v), scowl (v)**

leader   (n)–someone who has commanding authority or influence. The leader of a symphony orchestra is called a conductor.

chancellor–the prime minister or other high official in some European countries. Who is the chancellor of West Germany?

leader *(continued)*

commander–someone in an official position of control. The naval commander has just issued new orders.

despot–**1** a ruler having unlimited power and authority. A despot can put laws into effect without anyone else's approval. **2** one who exercises power abusively or oppressively. The despot proclaimed that nearly all private property would now belong to the government.

monarch–someone, such as a queen or king, who rules over a kingdom or empire; usually a hereditary leader. In some countries a monarch exercises only limited authority.

premier–the prime minister or other chief officer. I saw the premier of the Soviet Union on the television newscast last night.

president–the chief officer of a governmental body; the chief officer of an organization such as a corporation or an institution. The president of the company announced that profits were up ten percent from the previous year.

kingpin [informal]–the most important person. Without doubt their all-star center fielder is the kingpin of the team.

ANTONYMS: **follower, subordinate (n)**

lose　(v)–**1** to fail to win or obtain. Do you think that the football team will lose more than four games this season? **2** to be unable to find; to fail to keep. It seems as if I always lose pens and pencils.

fail–to be unable to do or become what is attempted, expected, or desired. I have never failed to get a good grade in all of my school subjects.

fall–to come down from a higher place. Our team will fall from first place if it loses the game.

misplace–to put in a wrong place. I must have misplaced my wristwatch; I can't find it.

relinquish–to release; to give up; to stop holding physically. The governor relinquished his authority to his newly elected successor.

succumb–to give way or yield to superior strength or overpowering appeal. The dieter succumbed to temptation and devoured some extra rolls and butter with dinner.

flop [informal]–to utterly fail. The new musical play flopped after just one performance.

drop [slang]–to lose. The New York Yankees dropped last night's game to the California Angels.

ANTONYMS: **find (v), gain (v), hold (v), keep, recover, retain, win (v)**

M

mistake　(n)–**1** a misunderstanding of the meaning of something. My mistake was in not realizing the impact that lack of sufficient rainfall can have upon a harvest. **2** a wrong action, judgment, or thought. While driving to the airport, my father made a mistake by turning off of the highway at the wrong exit.

blunder–a careless or stupid mistake. How could I commit the blunder of not putting my name on my test paper?

error–something done that is incorrect or wrong; something that is not the way it should be. I made an error by putting too much fertilizer on the lawn.

miscalculation–a mathematical error such as in addition or subtraction. When I added the column of numerals, I made a miscalculation.

misjudgment–a wrong or unjust opinion or estimate. Thinking that this class would be easy was a terrible misjudgment on my part.

Thesaurus

misprint–an error in printing. The
misspelled word on the very first page of
that book is a misprint.

oversight–a failure to notice or to think of
something; an error. Not checking the
weather forecast before planning the
picnic was an oversight on my part.

slipup [informal]–a mistake; an error. Do
you think you can do what I ask without
any slipups?

move   (v)–**1** to change or cause to change
the position or place of; to put in motion;
to keep in motion. A bulldozer will
move that large pile of rocks. **2** to
advance or proceed; to make progress.
The construction project is moving on
schedule.

crawl–to move slowly by pulling the body
across the ground. I saw the snake crawl
behind the rock.

dash–to move with a sudden speed. The
runner dashed across the finish line.

flow–to move in a current or a stream. The
molten lava flowed slowly down the
mountainside.

migrate–to move from one place or locality
to another. Some animals migrate from
mountain slopes to valleys for winter
protection and food.

progress–to move forward; to go ahead; to
advance. We make progress by working
very hard and avoiding any unnecessary
conversation.

propel–to push or drive forward or onward
by means of a force. Powerful engines
propel the space shuttle into orbit.

travel–to journey; to move from one place
to another. We will travel to Florida
during our vacation this year.

See also *walk* (v).

ANTONYMS: **discontinue, halt (v), pause
(v), stop (v)**

N

near   (adj)–not distant in time, place, or
degree; close. Please remember that I
will wait for you at the near entrance to
the theater.

adjacent–laying close or near;
neighboring; having a common border.
The supermarket is adjacent to the
pharmacy.

adjoining–being next to or in contact with;
touching. There is a door between the
two adjoining rooms in this apartment.

bordering–touching at the boundary;
nearby. The bordering property is for
sale.

close–having little space between; near.
When in a movie theater, you should be
aware of a close exit in case of fire.

immediate–close or near; near at hand.
Many exotic birds can be found right in
the immediate vicinity.

nearby–close by; near. The nearby
mountains are about ten-thousand feet
high.

neighboring–being near; bordering;
adjacent. Although the neighboring
town is larger in area than ours it does
not have as many people.

ANTONYMS: **distant, far, faraway,
outlying, remote, removed**

O

object   (n)–**1** something that can be seen,
touched, or otherwise sensed. That
metal object must weigh about five
pounds. **2** a person or thing toward
which action, feeling, or thought is
directed. The object of the geological
study is the Grand Canyon.

article–a particular item or thing. This
article of clothing is quite expensive.

object *(continued)*

artifact–a usually simple object made by human skill. Those pieces of pottery are artifacts of an ancient civilization.

device–something made for a particular use or special purpose; a mechanism. What is the name of the device that a plumber uses to clean out clogged pipes?

gadget–a small mechanical or electronic device. An electric pencil sharpener is a handy gadget to have around.

implement–a useful piece of equipment; a tool or utensil. A plow is, of course, an extremely important farm implement.

instrument–**1** something used to do something; a tool. Surgical instruments of various kinds are utilized during an operation. **2** a device that produces musical sounds. I think that the instrument we are now listening to is an oboe.

doohickey [informal]–a gadget or thing whose name is unknown or forgotten. Hand me the doohickey that goes on this faucet.

P

poor (adj)–**1** lacking money or property; having few things or nothing at all; needy. Many poor people have very little to eat. **2** not good in quality or value; lacking something necessary. This soil is too poor for agriculture.

destitute–lacking things that are necessary such as food, clothing, and shelter. Destitute people cannot afford new clothes.

impoverished–extremely poor. The impoverished family worried from day to day about food and other necessities that many people take for granted.

inferior–lower in quality; below average; of little value or merit. Purchasing an inferior automobile may lead to costly repairs.

needy–poverty-stricken; not having enough necessities to live on. Some charitable organizations give food and clothing to needy people.

penniless–not having any money; extremely poor. Having lost my wallet at the airport, I found myself penniless.

underprivileged–not having many of the advantages that most people have, especially because of poor social or economic status. The underprivileged people of some nations have horrible living conditions.

broke [slang]–penniless; without money. I can't buy tickets for the game because I'm broke.

unable to make ends meet [idiom]–not having enough money. With so many bills to pay this month, I'm unable to make ends meet.

ANTONYMS: affluent (adj), moneyed, opulent, prosperous, rich (adj), superior (adj), wealthy

R

rich (adj)–**1** having an abundance of money, land, goods, or other material possessions. The rich fashion designer lives in a penthouse in New York. **2** having great value or quality; sumptuous. The rich decor increased her enjoyment in the meal she was served.

affluent–having a generous supply of material possessions; wealthy. The affluent attorney owns condominiums in Florida.

comfortable–having enough money to be content or secure. Maybe we are not wealthy, but at least we are comfortable financially.

luscious–very delicious to taste or smell; richly sweet. I savored every bite of that luscious peach dessert.

opulent–displaying wealth often to the point of showing off; luxurious. The opulent home of the millionaire impresses every visitor.

prosperous–having economic well-being; successful; thriving. The computer industry is certainly prosperous in this country.

wealthy–extremely affluent; rich. The wealthy investor just purchased bonds worth $1,000,000.

loaded [informal]–having a large amount of money. She must be loaded to have been able to buy that diamond-studded necklace.

rolling in money [idiom]–extremely well-off financially. Some professional tennis players are so rich they are rolling in money.

ANTONYMS: bankrupt (adj), destitute, impoverished (adj), needy (adj), plain (adj), poor (adj), wanting (adj)

S

say (v)–to speak, state, or express in words; to communicate. I often say things without thinking.

articulate–to speak distinctly; to express in clear and effective words. When speaking before a large group of people, a person must articulate every word so that everyone can hear what is said.

call–to say, especially with a loud voice; to shout. The coach called the players to the bench.

declare–to make known publicly or formally; to state strongly. The senator declared at the press conference that she would run for reelection.

mutter–to speak words indistinctly or with a low voice and with the lips partly closed; to murmur angrily. The child muttered something when told to stop climbing the very high fence.

utter–to give forth as a sound; to express in words; to speak. He finally uttered what was on his mind.

whisper–to speak very softly or low, especially to avoid being overheard. Kristen whispered that she knew who the culprit was.

yap [slang]–to talk or chatter idly and insistently. Some people always yap about what they do.

put into words [idiom]–to speak; to express verbally. Sometimes I cannot put into words how I feel.

See also *talk* (v).

strong (adj)–having much power or force; healthy; vigorous; able to last or endure. Only a very strong person can move that heavy piece of furniture.

energetic–full of the power to do work; eager to do work. The energetic youngster did household chores and homework immediately after school.

forceful–having much strength; powerful or vigorous. Lisa's composition made a forceful statement about the great amount of food wasted in the cafeteria.

hardy–able to withstand the cold weather of winter, or able to bear other adverse conditions. I was told that these hardy chrysanthemums can survive extremely cold winter temperatures.

muscular–of, relating to, or influencing the muscles; having well-developed muscles. Occasional muscular strains are common occurrences in athletics.

sturdy–firmly built; strong and stout. That rickety wooden bridge is not very sturdy.

strong *(continued)*

tough–firm but flexible and not brittle; difficult to cut, tear, or chew. Some animals have <u>tough</u> protective hides.

vigorous–strong and active both physically and mentally; having much strength or active force. That <u>vigorous</u> couple plays three sets of tennis almost every day even though they both work.

strong as a bull [idiom]–possessing great strength or toughness. That professional football player is <u>strong as a bull</u>.

ANTONYMS: debilitated (adj), feeble, frail, listless, powerless, soft (adj), weak

T

talk (v)–to speak; to use words; to exchange words or engage in conversation. Do you think that I <u>talk</u> too much?

address–to deliver a formal speech to; to speak directly to. At the assembly our principal <u>addressed</u> all of the students.

chat–to talk in an informal and familiar way. During dinner my sister and I <u>chatted</u> about homework among other things.

debate–to discuss the reasons for and against something; to argue a topic in a public meeting. The two candidates for mayor <u>debated</u> various issues during a one-hour telecast.

report–to give an account of something seen, heard, read, done, or considered; to relate or tell. I <u>reported</u> the traffic accident I had seen to the police.

gab [informal]–to talk in a rapid and thoughtless manner; to talk too much. That person <u>gabs</u> all the time about almost anything and everything.

rap [slang]–to talk openly and frankly. My dad and I <u>rapped</u> about school all evening.

See also *say* (v).

U

urgent (adj)–calling for immediate action or attention; pressing; important. The governor made an <u>urgent</u> request for financial aid for the flood victims.

acute–seriously in need of urgent attention; threatening. The <u>acute</u> housing shortage in this area must be addressed immediately.

compelling–that drives or urges with force. The <u>compelling</u> reason I have for staying home is to finish my book report on time.

critical–important or indispensable for the weathering of a time of difficulty or danger. There is a <u>critical</u> need at this time to reach all of the motorists stranded in the snow.

crucial–very important; essential for resolving a crisis. It is <u>crucial</u> that the supplies reach them no later than tonight.

pressing–requiring immediate attention; critical. There are several <u>pressing</u> deadlines I must deal with today.

See also *important* (adj).

ANTONYM: unimportant

W

walk (v)–to go on foot; to advance by steps. Tom <u>walked</u> to the house.

hike–to take a long walk, especially for pleasure or exercise. Maryann and I <u>hiked</u> in Yellowstone National Park.

lumber–to move along heavily or clumsily. The defeated team <u>lumbered</u> off the field.

pace–to walk with slow or measured steps. The worried captain <u>paced</u> the deck.

ramble–to wander about aimlessly. People <u>rambled</u> through the shopping mall all day.

Thesaurus

stride–to walk with long steps. The guest speaker strode into the auditorium.

trudge–to walk wearily or with effort, but steadily or persistently. The exhausted troops trudged through the deep mud.

traipse [informal]–to walk about aimlessly or needlessly. That guy traipses all over the countryside.

See also *move* (v).

weak (adj)–not having strength; deficient in some way; lacking intensity. I was too weak to budge that heavy table.

faint–not clear; hardly perceptible; lacking in amount, loudness, or intensity. I barely heard a faint voice somewhere off in the distance.

fragile–easily broken or damaged. Be careful with those fragile crystal glasses.

frail–not very strong; weak; delicate. The frail individual had to be helped up the steps.

listless–seeming too tired to care about anything; lacking the inclination to be active. I was so listless from that virus that I could hardly move.

powerless–without strength or force; unable to produce an effect. The king was powerless in the face of so many foes.

ANTONYMS: energetic, hardy, powerful, strong (adj), sturdy, vigorous

win (v)–to gain a victory in a contest; to succeed; to get possession of by work or fortune. You cannot win unless you try.

accomplish–to succeed in completing; to carry to conclusion. The task was accomplished in two days.

achieve–to carry out successfully; to accomplish. Wendy achieved a school record at the track meet.

prevail–to win the victory; to gain supremacy through strength or superiority. In the end our strong defense prevailed.

triumph–to be victorious; to prevail. Many people are working so that medical research will triumph over disease.

corral [informal]–to capture or secure. Our football team corralled the state championship.

bring home the bacon [idiom]–to win. Let's get out on that field and bring home the bacon!

ANTONYMS: fail (v), fall (v), flop (v), forfeit (v), lose

write (v)–to make letters, words, or symbols on a surface with an instrument such as a pen; to be the author of. Write your name.

author–to write or compose. She authored many excellent novels.

correspond–to write letters to each other. Although my friend lives hundreds of miles away, we correspond often.

inscribe–to write or engrave on stone, metal, or other material. The names of the class officers were inscribed on the plaque.

record–to set down in writing so as to retain for future use; to register permanently. The secretary recorded what was said during the meeting.

scribble–to write or draw carelessly; to write illegibly. I scribbled these notes so quickly that I can hardly read them.

take down [idiom]–to write out what is spoken. Take down everything I say to you.

Reports, Letters, Notes

Book Reports

A **book report** contains a description of a book and your judgment about it. It is a way of sharing your thoughts about a book with others.

There are three parts to a book report: the introduction, the body, and the conclusion. In the **introduction**, tell the title and author. State whether the book is fiction or nonfiction and give some information about the author.

In the **body** of the report, briefly summarize the book so that readers will be able to judge whether or not they might find the book interesting. If the book is fiction, briefly describe the characters, setting, and plot, but don't give away the ending.

In the **conclusion** of the report, give your reasons for either recommending or not recommending the book.

Introduction —

The Adventures of Tom Sawyer is a novel by Mark Twain, one of America's greatest authors. Twain, whose real name was Samuel Clemens, grew up in Hannibal, Missouri, on the Mississippi River. In this book Twain tells what life on the river was like.

Body —

The story takes place during the nineteenth century in St. Petersburg, a small town along the Mississippi River. The main character of the book is, of course, Tom Sawyer. As the story progresses you can see Tom's character change from that of a mischievous boy to a person who cares about other people. The book also has many other interesting characters, especially Becky Thatcher, a girl whom Tom really likes.

Although this book was written over one hundred years ago, its story is still exciting today. Tom has many suspenseful adventures; a creepy cemetery, a mysterious cave, and a buried treasure all play important roles in the plot.

Conclusion —

I highly recommend The Adventures of Tom Sawyer. I liked the book because of its characters and the author's understanding of human nature. It truly is difficult to put the book down once you are caught up in Tom's story. If you enjoy lots of action and stories about the feelings and problems of other young people, you will like this book.

Friendly Letters

A **friendly letter** is a personal letter. In a friendly letter, you write more informally than you do in a business letter. Write as if you were talking to a friend. Write about your own interests or experiences, but choose them according to your audience — the person to whom you are writing. Include specific details so that your letter will be more interesting and appealing. If you are replying to a letter, answer any questions the person may have asked.

Study the five parts of the friendly letter below.

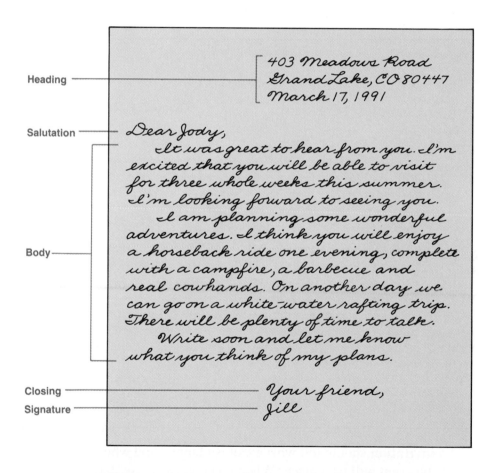

Heading

403 Meadows Road
Grand Lake, CO 80447
March 17, 1991

Salutation

Dear Jody,

Body

    It was great to hear from you. I'm excited that you will be able to visit for three whole weeks this summer. I'm looking forward to seeing you.
    I am planning some wonderful adventures. I think you will enjoy a horseback ride one evening, complete with a campfire, a barbecue and real cowhands. On another day we can go on a white-water rafting trip. There will be plenty of time to talk.
    Write soon and let me know what you think of my plans.

Closing

Your friend,

Signature

Jill

Letters should be written as neatly as possible. You may use tinted paper, but white paper of good quality is always suitable. If the letter is handwritten, blue or black ink should be used. Center the letter on the page. Keep equal margins on the sides and on the top and bottom.

Social Notes

A **social note** is a short letter usually written to thank someone for something or to invite someone to a special occasion. A social note is also written to accept or decline an invitation. A **bread-and-butter note** is a special thank-you note written when you have stayed overnight at the home of a friend or a relative. Write a thank-you note promptly.

A social note is similar in form to a friendly letter and has a heading, salutation, body, closing, and signature. Sometimes a social note includes only the date in the heading. Study the thank-you note below.

May 29, 1991

Dear Uncle Glen,
    Thank you so much for the subscription to _Photography_ magazine. It was the perfect gift. Can you believe the first issue arrived on my birthday?
    Before I had a chance to read it, John was already sitting at the table, reading an article. I am sure the magazine will be a help when I start my photography class.
    Once again thanks for the gift.

Love,
Katie

An **invitation** should tell what event is planned and where and when the event will take place. When you receive an invitation, you may see the initials R.S.V.P. written at the bottom. They stand for French words that mean "please respond." You should reply to such an invitation as soon as possible by sending a note of acceptance or regret.

Business Letters

A **business letter** may request information, clarify a problem, place an order, or state an opinion. It should be written in a clear and concise manner. A business letter has six parts instead of the five in a friendly letter. A business letter includes an inside address — the name and address of the person or company to whom the letter is sent. Study the letter below. Notice that a colon is used after the salutation in a business letter.

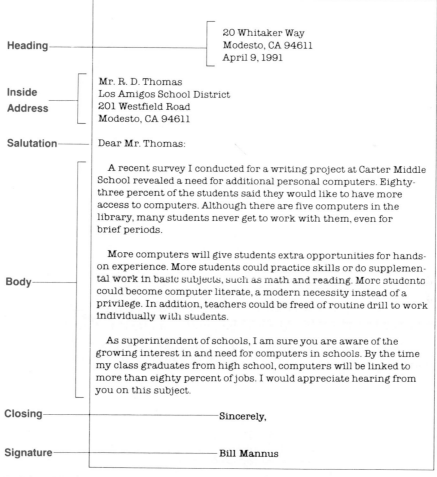

Heading

20 Whitaker Way
Modesto, CA 94611
April 9, 1991

Inside Address

Mr. R. D. Thomas
Los Amigos School District
201 Westfield Road
Modesto, CA 94611

Salutation

Dear Mr. Thomas:

Body

A recent survey I conducted for a writing project at Carter Middle School revealed a need for additional personal computers. Eighty-three percent of the students said they would like to have more access to computers. Although there are five computers in the library, many students never get to work with them, even for brief periods.

More computers will give students extra opportunities for hands-on experience. More students could practice skills or do supplemental work in basic subjects, such as math and reading. More students could become computer literate, a modern necessity instead of a privilege. In addition, teachers could be freed of routine drill to work individually with students.

As superintendent of schools, I am sure you are aware of the growing interest in and need for computers in schools. By the time my class graduates from high school, computers will be linked to more than eighty percent of jobs. I would appreciate hearing from you on this subject.

Closing

Sincerely,

Signature

Bill Mannus

White paper is appropriate stationery for business letters. If you do not type, write the letter neatly in blue or black ink. Be concerned about the physical appearance of your business letter. Neatness counts and creates a good impression. Center the letter properly on the page and keep equal margins.

Preparing Letters for Mailing

When you have finished writing a letter, make sure you fold it neatly. It is also important to address and stamp the envelope correctly so that the letter will reach its destination.

Folding a Letter   Friendly letters are usually written on stationery that is about 6″ x 8″. The envelope usually measures 3½″ x 6½″. Follow the diagram below to fold a friendly letter.

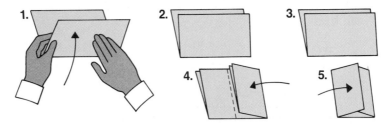

A business letter should be written on 8½″ x 11″ paper. The envelope usually measures 4½″ x 9½″. Follow the diagram below to fold a business letter.

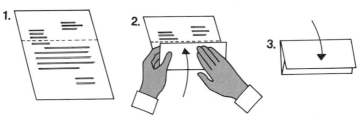

Addressing an Envelope   Every envelope must have a mailing address and a return address. The mailing address includes the receiver's name, street address, city, state, and ZIP code. The return address gives your name and complete address. Study the model envelope below for the position of each address.

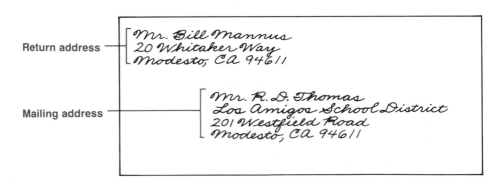

Return address

Mr. Bill Mannus
20 Whitaker Way
Modesto, CA 94611

Mailing address

Mr. R. D. Thomas
Los Amigos School District
201 Westfield Road
Modesto, CA 94611

A Guide to Spelling

The English language has more than 250,000 words. This large number of words makes learning to spell a very challenging task. Because many English words have been borrowed from other languages, there is often more than one way to represent a sound in English.

As a result, learning to spell can be difficult. However, the following guidelines will help you to become a better speller.

* Look carefully at words when you read. Try to see each letter. Do this not only for new words but for familiar words, too.

* Pronounce words carefully when you speak. Some English words are not pronounced the way they are spelled. Frequently mispronunciation leads to misspelling. For example, a student who mispronounces *library* as *"liberry"* will probably also misspell the word.

* Use a dictionary to check the spelling of words. If you are not sure how a word begins, list all the logical possibilities. Then look up each possibility until you find the word. In addition to improving your spelling, the dictionary will help you use and pronounce words correctly.

* Maintain a list of personal spelling words in a notebook. If you are like most people, there are certain words that you misspell over and over. List these words alphabetically in your spelling notebook. Review them frequently.

* Learn to spell long or difficult words syllable by syllable. Since a syllable has only a few letters in it, it is easy to spell. Once you learn to spell each syllable, put them together.

* Use memory aids to help you remember the spelling of words that are especially troublesome. Usually, you will have to make a memory aid for each word that causes you trouble. For example, I *labor* in the *laboratory*.

Proofread all your writing carefully for spelling errors. During this stage of the writing process, it is necessary to reread all your words and correct any misspellings.

Rules for Spelling

Know the rules for spelling. Some of these rules are listed below.
Learn these rules and use them when you write.

1. If a word ends in *e*, usually drop the *e* when you add a suffix that
begins with a vowel.

VERBS lease leasing

2. If a word ends in a vowel and *y*, keep the *y* when you add a suffix.

NOUNS turkey turkeys **VERBS** pay paying

3. If a word ends in a consonant and *y*, change the *y* to *i* when you add
a suffix unless the suffix begins with *i*.

NOUNS cherry cherries **VERBS** pry prying
ADJECTIVES muddy muddier muddiest

4. If a word ends in one vowel and one consonant and has one
syllable or is stressed on the last syllable, double the last consonant
when you add a suffix that begins with a vowel.

NOUNS swim swimmer **VERBS** refer referring

5. When you choose between *ie* and *ei*, use *ie* except after *c* or for a
long *a* sound. (Exceptions: *leisure, either, seize, weird*)

thief shriek receive neighbors

6. The suffix *-s* can be added to most nouns and verbs. If a word ends
in *s, ss, sh, ch, x,* or *zz* , add *-es*.

NOUNS	bus	buses	**VERBS**	hiss	hisses
	bush	bushes		punch	punches
	ax	axes		buzz	buzzes

7. If a word ends in a single *f* or *fe*, usually change the *f* to *v* when you
add *-s* or *-es*.

calf calves   wife wives

8. The letter *q* is always followed by the letter *u* in English words.

quarter inquire request

Words Often Written

The words most often used by students in Grades 1 through 8 are, in alphabetical order, *a, all, and, be, but, for, go, had, have, he, I, in, is, it, like, me, my, of, on, said, she, so, that, the, then, there, they, to, was, we, went, when, with, would,* and *you.*

The list below contains words that were used most often in samples of writing done by students your age. Have you ever paid attention to the words *you* use most frequently?

1. beautiful		26. love	
2. before		27. might	
3. being		28. name	
4. both		29. parents	
5. brother		30. person	
6. cat		31. popular	
7. city		32. pretty	
8. class		33. probably	
9. clothes		34. reason	
10. couldn't		35. rich	
11. country		36. road	
12. different		37. same	
13. each		38. show	
14. father		39. sister	
15. favorite		40. still	
16. few		41. story	
17. girl		42. test	
18. give		43. that's	
19. grade		44. turn	
20. hard		45. until	
21. I'll		46. wasn't	
22. kids		47. water	
23. later		48. week	
24. live		49. white	
25. lived		50. wouldn't	

Mechanics Lessons

Capitalizing Names and Titles

A proper noun names a particular person, place, or thing. It is always capitalized. A common noun is the general name of a person, place, or thing. A common noun is not capitalized.

Capitalizing Proper Nouns

Capitalize the names of people.
    Rosa Nogales   Alfred P. Wilson, Jr.
    Adele B. Barbour   Anthony Costello, Sr.
 Middle initials and the abbreviations *Jr.* and *Sr.* should be capitalized.

Capitalize titles or abbreviations that come before the names of people.
    Dr. Sarah M. Frost   Doctor Sarah M. Frost
    Mr. Jason Randolph   Mrs. Helen McNeal
    Sargent Paul Williams   Professor S.A. Ruíz
 Capitalize A.D. and B.C. Capitalize A.M. and P.M.
    Norsemen were exploring the waters of America before A.D. 1000.
    Julius Caesar was born in 100 B.C.
    We begin at 9:00 A.M. and end at 5:00 P.M.

Capitalize the titles *President* and *Vice-President* when referring to officials of the United States.
    The President signed the treaty.
    The Vice-President entered the room.
 Do not capitalize other titles unless they appear before a person's name.
    The mayor of Chicago will be there.
    We welcomed Mayor Brady to our town.
    The professor hurried to class.

Capitalize words showing family relationships when used as titles or as substitutes for a name.
    Uncle Fred and Aunt Marcia moved to Baltimore.
    I asked Mother to come.
 Do not capitalize these words if they are preceded by a possessive noun or pronoun.
    My aunt and uncle moved to Baltimore.
    Jennifer's sister is coming to visit.
    My mother visited them.

Practice

A. Write the word groups using correct capitals.

1. thomas malley, jr.
2. 8:00 a.m.
3. aunt rose
4. gov. pauline smith
5. professor perry
6. grandmother edoga
7. a.d. 512
8. cousin kay
9. uncle dominick
10. mrs. nina showner
11. 28 b.c.
12. mr. j.k. louis
13. president harding
14. cousin louisa
15. mayor t.j. harris
16. 11:00 p.m.

B. Write each sentence using correct capitals.

17. Our neighbors are mr. and mrs. arnold craig.
18. Their children are arnold, jr., and joan.
19. The letter was dated a.d. 1860.
20. Did mother come to the party?
21. They set the alarm for 6:00 a.m.
22. The meeting was addressed by senator lund.
23. In 44 b.c. julius caesar was slain.
23. Does uncle arthur still live in Vermont?
25. Our family physician is dr. martin driscol.
26. She met president johnson in Miami.
27. The students greeted superintendent park.
28. The concert ends at 11 p.m. tonight.

C. After each sentence number, write the words that should be capitalized.

29. arnold craig and his family took an automobile trip.
30. Before leaving, mrs. frances craig packed clothes, their son arnie purchased film, and his sister joan bought stamps for sending postcards.
31. At 7:00 a.m. they drove to Philadelphia to see historic sites.
32. The craigs visited the University of Pennsylvania, which was founded in a.d. 1756.
33. Later joan sent a postcard to her aunt, and arnie sent one to their neighbors, dr. sarah m. frost and derrick g. frost, sr.
34. Soon they would arrive at the house of grandmother and grandfather craig.

Capitalizing Geographical Names

Capitalizing Proper Nouns
Capitalize names of cities, states, countries, and continents.

Cities:	Tel Aviv, Boston, Juneau, Los Angeles
States:	North Dakota, Minnesota, Vermont, Ohio
Countries:	Dominican Republic, Belgium, Egypt
Continents:	South America, Africa, Asia

Capitalize names of bodies of water and other names found on maps.

Bodies of Water:	Lake Erie, Red Sea, Amazon River, Gulf of Mexico, Atlantic Ocean
Other Map Features:	Mammoth Cave, Cape Horn, Iberian Peninsula, Rock Creek Park, Mount Everest

Do not capitalize unimportant words such as *of* or *on* with proper nouns.

Great Wall of China, Croton-on-Hudson
Isthmus of Panama, Southend-on-Sea

Capitalize names of buildings, monuments, and bridges.

Buildings:	World Trade Center, Sears Tower
Monuments:	Taj Mahal, Grant's Tomb, Fort Sumter
Bridges:	Golden Gate Bridge, Walt Whitman Bridge

Capitalize names of streets and highways.

Streets:	Memorial Drive, Madison Avenue, Ely Place, Franklin Street Shady Lane, Ford Avenue
Highways:	Pennsylvania Turnpike, Route 44, Santa Ana Freeway, Garden State Parkway New York Thruway, Sunrise Highway

Capitalize names of sections of the United States.

Mona was born in the Midwest.
The South is known for its citrus products.
We visited our friends in the North.

Do not capitalize directions of the compass.

The Craigs headed south on their trip.
Our store is located west of Broadway.
My grandparents live south of Boston.

Practice

A. Write each sentence using correct capitals.

> EXAMPLE: Is mount kilimanjaro in kenya or somalia?
> ANSWER: Is Mount Kilimanjaro in Kenya or Somalia?

1. In new mexico we visited carlsbad caverns.
2. Beyond the rocky mountains is the pacific ocean.
3. Civilizations grew in the nile delta.
4. Is peru east or west of the andes mountains?
5. Rainfall is precious in the southwest.
6. The sprague hotel is on north street.
7. In london she visited the british museum and st. paul's cathedral.
8. Much of his art work is in paris.
9. The city of pittsburgh is west of scranton.
10. The statue of liberty came from france.
11. The gobi desert touches china and mongolia.
12. When did she visit independence hall?
13. The virgin islands lie in the caribbean sea.
14. Major Powell explored the colorado river.
15. He left ellesmere island for the north pole.
16. Captain James Cook explored the continents of australia and north america.
17. He also explored the waters of the st. lawrence river, botany bay, and the great barrier reef.

B. After each sentence number, write the words that should be capitalized.

18. Having left the suburbs of philadelphia, the Craigs crossed both the brandywine river and the susquehanna river on their way to baltimore, maryland.
19. First they visited fort mchenry, which lies on the patapsco river, an inlet of chesapeake bay.
20. Later they went to the baltimore streetcar museum and the national aquarium.
21. The next morning they went to the flag house.
22. In the afternoon they drove on the baltimore-washington expressway on their way to washington, d.c.
23. They will end their trip near the gulf of mexico.

Capitalizing Other Names

Capitalizing Proper Nouns
Capitalize names of clubs, organizations, businesses, and institutions.

Clubs: Elks, Rotary, Springfield Glee Club
Organizations: American Bar Association
Businesses: Ajax Food Co., Don's Gas Service
Institutions: Williams College, Tulane University

Do not capitalize words such as *school, college,* or *theater* unless they are used as names.

> After high school I entered Colby College.
> What college did you attend?
> I attended Newton High School.

Capitalize brand names but not the products.

> Cleanall soap, Fudd automobiles,
> Prove polish, Naturo juice,
> Sharpee scissors, Crown combs

Capitalize the names of days, months, and holidays.

Days: Tuesday, Friday, Thursday
Months: October, June, February
Holidays: Thanksgiving Day, Veteran's Day

Do not capitalize the names of seasons.

> In the autumn the foliage is quite pretty.
> Many birds migrate in the spring.

Capitalize names of languages, races, and nationalities.

Languages: French, German, Chinese
Races: Asian, Polynesian
Nationalities: Greek, Italian, Bolivian

Do not capitalize names of school subjects except languages or those followed by a number.

> She took history, Spanish, and Algebra II.
> My favorite subjects were Latin and economics.

Capitalize names of historical events, periods, or documents.

Events: Revolutionary War, Louisiana Purchase
Periods: Renaissance, Bronze Age
Documents: Bill of Rights, Magna Charta

Practice

A. Write the word groups using correct capitals.

1. declaration of independence
2. french II and english history
3. harlem renaissance
4. age of enlightenment
5. iris soap
6. massachusetts institute of technology
7. girl scouts of america
8. cherry microcomputers, inc.
9. smith college
10. thursday, april 1
11. mother's day
12. latin, greek, and early egyptian
13. league of women voters
14. american wax and dye company
15. boston tea party
16. coast guard
17. great depression
18. middle ages
19. black river playhouse
20. olympic games

B. After each sentence number, write the words that should be capitalized.

21. On tuesday, the day before the fourth of july, the Craigs visited the smithsonian institution in Washington, D.C.
22. That afternoon, in the library of congress, they saw the constitution of the united states and the bill of rights.
23. "We studied these documents in our american history class," said Arnie.
24. In the evening the Craigs heard the gonzaga high school band, the howard university glee club, and a pianist from american university at the john f. kennedy center for the performing arts.
25. Before they went to sleep, Arnie and Joan each drank a glass of cold sweepes ginger ale.
26. The following day the Craigs toured several art museums at which they saw dutch and german paintings, persian rugs, and italian sculpture.

Capitalizing First Words and Certain Parts of Speech

Capitalizing First Words

Capitalize the first word of a sentence.

> **A**t night the city lights shone brightly.
> **T**oo many cooks spoil the broth.

Capitalize the first word in a line of poetry.

> **B**y the rude bridge that arched the flood,
> **T**heir flag to April's breeze unfurled,
> **H**ere once the embattled farmers stood
> **A**nd fired the shot heard round the world.

Not all poets use capital letters to begin lines of poetry. This is particularly true of modern poets.

Capitalize the first word of a direct quotation.

> Marcia said, "**P**lease serve the potatoes first."
> "**I**t is good to be home," Jim said.

Do not capitalize the first word of an indirect quotation.

> John said that <u>he</u> would do as Marcia had asked.
> Lana replied that <u>she</u> had to feed the horses.

Capitalize the first words and the names or titles of people addressed in letter salutations.

> **D**ear **H**enry, **D**ear **S**ir, **D**ear **M**adam,
> **D**ear **M**iss **D**unn, **D**ear **D**ad, **D**ear **R**osa,

Capitalize only the first word in letter closings.

> **L**ove,   **Y**ours truly,   **S**incerely yours,
> **F**ondly,   **B**est regards,   **V**ery truly yours,

Capitalizing Certain Parts of Speech

Capitalize the pronoun *I*.

> "What a sight **I** saw!" exclaimed Miriam.
> "You and **I** will take photographs," stated Chris.

Capitalize proper adjectives.

> We met the **N**orwegian ambassador.
> The **R**ussian exchange student was my friend.
> We visited historic **E**uropean cities.

Practice

A. Write the sentences, using capital letters. Some are lines of poetry.

> **EXAMPLE:** he took a final test in english prose.
> **ANSWER:** He took a final test in English prose.

1. the farmer's tractor was stuck in the soft mud caused by so much rain this spring.
2. a few people in my class know russian history.
3. "o friends!
   with whom my feet have trod."
4. "where are the car keys?" asked Maria.
5. "true ease in writing comes from art, not chance
   as those move easiest who have learned to dance."
6. this french cheese is delicious with the bread that my dad bought at the italian bakery.
7. earlier this year i visited my british cousin.
8. the grocery store sells kenyan coffee, swiss chocolate, and hawaiian pineapples.
9. "dear sir," began the applicant's letter.
10. hector said, "i will try out for the track team and the football team this season."
11. "life has loveliness to sell,
    all beautiful and splendid things,"
12. tom's letter to me ended with "very truly yours."

B. Joan Craig sent a postcard to her Aunt Doris. Write her message using correct capitals.

dear aunt doris,

    we are now in Williamsburg, Virginia. mother took us to see many of the old houses. dad said, "i would like to go, but i really don't feel well." then he said, "perhaps I will be able to join you tomorrow."

    in one house we met the british ambassador who quoted some lines by the poet Longfellow:

        "all houses wherein men have lived and died
        are haunted houses."

    mom says to say hello and that she wishes you could be here with us.

your niece,
Joan

Capitalizing Other Titles

The titles of written works, movies, and works of art are capitalized in writing. Certain religious terms are also capitalized.

Capitalizing Other Titles

Capitalize the first word and all important words in titles.

Books:	The Yearling, A Tale of Two Cities
Stories:	"The Cask of Amontillado"
Articles:	"The Reluctant Dragon"
Poems:	"The Skeleton in Armor," "Annabel Lee"
Magazines:	Popular Mechanics, Time
Plays:	The Skin of Our Teeth, Hamlet
Newspapers:	St. Louis Post-Dispatch
Movies:	Star Wars, American Gothic
Paintings:	Mona Lisa, Black Beauty
Works of Music:	Aida, "Yesterday"

Unimportant words, such as articles, coordinating conjunctions, and prepositions, are usually not capitalized unless they are the first word in the title.

Gone with the Wind
A Light in the Forest

Capitalizing Certain Religious Terms

Capitalize words referring to the Deity, the holy books, religions, and denominations.

Deity:	God, Allah, the Father
Holy Books:	the Bible, the Torah
Religions:	Christianity, Islam
	Judaism, Buddism
Denominations:	Roman Catholic, Baptist

Do not capitalize the word *god* when referring to deities in ancient mythologies.

Odin, the god of art and culture, was a very important figure in Scandinavian mythology.
Many constellations take their names from the gods and goddesses of ancient myths.

Practice

A. Write the word groups using correct capitals.

1. *to sir with love* (movie)
2. "the rime of the ancient mariner" (poem)
3. *washington post* (newspaper)
4. *all quiet on the western front* (book)
5. *carmen* (work of music)
6. *christina's world* (painting)
7. "sea cucumbers are not a menace" (article)
8. *journal of medicine* (magazine)
9. "the most dangerous game" (story)
10. *you can't take it with you* (play)
11. "stopping by woods on a snowy evening" (poem)
12. *bamboo tree in the wind* (painting)

B. Write each sentence with correct capitals.

13. The ecumenical society meets here on Sunday.
14. We watched *i love lucy* on TV last night.
15. Angie has played the lead parts in *a doll's house, our town,* and *the tempest.*
16. In some religions god is called jehovah.
17. His article, called "how the mind works," was printed in *science* magazine.
18. We read an excerpt from her story "south of the border" in *newsweek* magazine.
19. There was an article in *time* about the bible.
20. Maria loves the song the "st. louis blues."
21. I'm reading the book *johnny tremaine.*
22. The koran is the holy book of islam.
23. The class saw *the sound of music* yesterday at Radio City Music Hall.
24. Longfellow wrote "the wreck of the hesperus."
25. He stood and sang "the star-spangled banner" at the opening ceremonies last week.
26. *"the lion, the witch, and the wardrobe* is an exciting book," said Mrs. Barker.
27. My favorite paintings by the American artist, Winslow Homer, are the *herring net* and *on a lee shore.*
28. My family really enjoys the bill cosby show on TV.

Writing Numbers

Writing Out Numbers
Write out numbers that are made up of fewer than three words. Out of **one hundred** stamps **ninety-four** were left. The workers counted **437** new job applications. There were only **nine** jobs available.
Write out a number that begins a sentence or rewrite the sentence. **Three hundred fifty** sheep grazed nearby. In the meadow grazed **350** sheep.
Write out ordinal numbers. Ordinal numbers are the names for numbers such as *first, tenth,* and *fifth*. The **third** person to arrive received a prize. Rita was the **first** person up to bat. Abraham Lincoln was the **sixteenth** President.
Write out approximate times of day. We'll meet at **quarter past seven** and walk to the movies. I finish my chores by **half past four**.
Express exact times as numerals. The red alert signal sounded at **3:51** A.M. Almost everyday at **4:30** P.M., Pat walks the dog.
In dialogue write out all numbers except dates. Minerva said, "All **seven hundred two** students graduated on May **30, 1981**."

Writing Numbers as Arabic Numerals
Write dates as numerals. The Martians landed on October **12, 1999**. Walt Whitman published *Leaves of Grass* in **1855**.
Write divisions of written material as numerals. Chapter **4**   lesson **19**   line **12**   item **42** Unit **2**   section **10**   Volume **6**   question **5**
Write house numbers and room numbers as numerals. Raul lives at **41** Walnut Street in Room **301**. Room **24** at **19** Pines Road is for rent.

Practice

A. Write each sentence, using correct number forms.

  1. 75 couples attended the dance.
  2. On July sixth we ate salmon and fresh peas.
  3. Mrs. Argent lives at ten Mulberry Street.
  4. Did you find any errors on page nine?
  5. Wilmer asked, "Will 7 of you come with me?"
  6. Every 3rd student raised a hand.
  7. Chapter four is the shortest in the book, and Chapter twenty is the longest.
  8. Our meeting was originally scheduled for June tenth, but it has been postponed until July sixth.
  9. Is Room sixty-five or Room sixty-seven yours for the conference?
  10. Item six on page fourteen is incomplete.
  11. Spring arrives officially at two seventeen A.M.
  12. Nikki dated her letter May ninth, 1983.
  13. Alexander the Great lived in the 4th century.
  14. All 32 scouts earned their 15 merit badges before leaving for summer camp.
  15. We should be there by 4 o'clock on January twenty-third, nineteen hundred eighty-five.
  16. All students were required to read Unit nine, Chapter five, and answer questions one, two, and three.

B. Write the correct number forms after each sentence number.

  17. The Craigs left at 2 o'clock on July third, 1983.
  18. 1st they drove to Philadelphia, then to Baltimore, and 3rd to Washington, D.C.
  19. They had to fill the car with 20 gallons of gasoline, and they refilled it 2 more times on the way.
  20. In Washington the Craigs visited old friends at forty-eight Tyson Street.
  21. Chapter 3 of the Williamsburg guide book pointed out three hundred seventy-eight places of interest to visit.
  22. The Craigs will arrive at Williamsburg by four P.M.
  23. They would return home on August tenth, 1983.
  24. This was the 2nd vacation they had taken in 5 years.

End Marks

Periods   Use a period at the end of a declarative sentence. A declarative sentence makes a statement.

> Bismarck is the capital of North Dakota.
> Eli Whitney invented the cotton gin.

Use a period at the end of an imperative sentence. An imperative sentence makes a command or request.

> Don't pull the dog's tail. (a command)
> Please open the window. (a request)

Use a period after abbreviations and initials. Use periods with A.M. and P.M.

> Dr. Mary M. Clarke lives in Blakestown.
> Jill met me at 3:15 P.M. on Hillside Avenue.
> The bell rang at 9:00 A.M. today.

Question Marks   Use a question mark at the end of an interrogative sentence. An interrogative sentence asks a question.

> When was Thomas Edison born?
> Who won the World Series in 1964?
> Did you find the movie interesting?

Exclamation Marks   Use an exclamation mark at the end of an exclamatory sentence. An exclamatory sentence expresses strong feeling.

> My books are falling!
> He won first prize in the contest!

Use an exclamation mark at the end of an imperative sentence that expresses strong feeling.

> Watch out for the puddle!
> Be careful of the wet paint!

Summary ♦ **End marks** are punctuation marks that show where a sentence ends.

Practice

A. Write the sentences using the correct end marks.

1. Mom used to collect matchbook covers
2. How long ago was that
3. She was a teenager
4. Wow! That was a long time ago
5. Don't be rude
6. The matchbook covers had flowers printed on them
7. Mom organized them by type of flower
8. She also arranged them by color
9. How many did she finally collect
10. She collected a few hundred
11. You've got to be kidding
12. How did she get so many
13. She found some She traded with friends, too
14. Please tell me how I can start a collection
15. It's easy You have enough records to open a store
16. Have you seen Tom's collection of bird art
17. He has over two hundred items, including figurines, posters, and paintings
18. He has a wire sculpture of a great blue heron that is four feet tall
19. Amazing, I'd really like to see that
20. Shall I call and see if we can visit him Friday

B. Write the paragraph with the correct end marks.

Do you know anything about stamp collecting It is a hobby that is very popular all over the world In the first place, the study and collection of stamps is called philately It probably was started in Great Britain in 1840 In that year the British government produced the first official postage stamp Imagine owning one of those original stamps It would be worth thousands and thousands of dollars Stamp collecting is an enjoyable hobby, even if your stamps are not worth a fortune There are so many different stamps that it is probably best to limit the ones you collect For example, you might choose to collect the stamps of just one country Which country would you choose Of course, rare stamps are the most highly prized since they are difficult to locate

Commas That Separate

Commas in a Series   Unlike an end mark, a comma stands for a pause in a writer's thought. If you read without pausing, you will be confused. A comma makes writing easier to understand.

Use a comma to separate items in a series. A series is made up of three or more items. The items may be single words or groups of words.

> Dan is allergic to strawberries, fish, and oranges.
> I ate my lunch, rode my bike, and walked two miles.
> Many teachers, parents, and students attended the meeting.

Do not use a comma after the last item in a series.

> Lori, Brad, and Dale were at home today.
> I saw a wren, a cardinal, and a crow today.
> Books, pens, and cards were on sale.

Commas in Compound Sentences   Use a comma before the conjunction that joins the parts of a compound sentence.

> The magician performed many dazzling tricks, and her
>   daughter assisted her.
> We wanted to go to the ball game, but the game was canceled
>   because of the storm.

Do not use a comma before a conjunction in a short compound sentence.

> The dog barked and it yelped.
> They sang and they danced.
> The tree split and it fell.

Do not use a comma to separate a compound verb.

> The singer bowed to the audience and sang again.
> The tennis player jumped and hit the ball.
> The student listened and took notes at the meeting.

> **Summary** ◆ Use a **comma** to separate items in a series and to separate the parts of a compound sentence.

Practice

A. Write each sentence, adding commas where necessary. If a sentence needs no commas, write *correct*.

1. Many people collect stamps, coins, or autographs.

2. Others collect cans strings or ticket stubs.

3. Amy collects and sells mugs.

4. She also collects thimbles spoons and music boxes.

5. She wants to start more collections but she has run out of shelf space.

6. Tia collects statues of glass china wood and metal and keeps them on shelves in her room.

7. Animal statues are very popular and she adores them.

8. Mr. Burke collects and repairs owl statues.

9. He likes owls but he cannot collect real ones.

10. Plastic, clay, and crystal owls appear on his shelf.

11. Some of my friends collect baseball cards and they trade special cards with each other.

12. Jeff Pedro and Pam are always searching for new cards to add to their collections.

B. Write each sentence, adding commas where needed.

13. People collect magazines and they don't throw them out.

14. Collectors of *National Geographic* magazine have issues from the sixties fifties and even the forties!

15. Old issues turn up in doctors' dentists' and lawyers' offices.

16. Old copies have outdated information but collectors do not care.

17. Many collectors compete for these old copies and they try to find the oldest copies.

18. They advertise for these old issues of *National Geographic* and they attend conventions.

19. Very old issues are valuable but what real collector would want to sell his or her treasured magazines?

20. Probably no one will want to collect *Pet Rock News Fly-Fishing Weekly* or *Great Sardine Recipes*.

21. Some people believe computers may turn printed matter into antiques and they save *any* magazine.

22. Do you think that magazines books and newspapers may soon become items of the past?

Commas for Appositives and Nouns of Direct Address

Appositives   Use commas to set off most appositives. Appositives explain the meaning of nouns that directly precede them. Appositives often include prepositional phrases.

> Ed, my friend, lives upstairs.
> Juneau, the capital of Alaska, is by the water.
> The Pauls, our neighbors, are moving.
> Have you been to Porto's, the new restaurant?

Do not use commas with an appositive when it is part of a proper name or when it is needed to identify the noun it follows.

> Richard the Lion-Hearted   his friend Tony
> Alexander the Great   my Aunt Maryellen

Nouns of Direct Address   Use commas to set off nouns of direct address. You often use a person's name when you speak. The person's name is called a noun of direct address. It may appear anywhere in a sentence.

> Mr. Diaz, may we go to the beach tomorrow?
> I do not know, Sue, if I can come to the party.
> Is something on your mind, Barry?

A noun of direct address may also be a nonspecific name that refers to a person.

> Excuse me, Sir, but could you tell me what time it is?
> Waiter, may we have a menu?
> Are you coming to the game, my friend?

When a noun of direct address appears in the middle of a sentence, it is both preceded and followed by commas.

> Did you enjoy the movie, Barry, or did it bore you?
> May I join you, Grandma, on your walk?
> Wait, Miss, you dropped your scarf.

Summary ♦ Use commas to set off appositives and nouns of direct address.

Practice

A. Write each sentence, adding commas where necessary. If a sentence needs no commas, write *correct*.

1. Class this is Mrs. Helen Parker our guest speaker.
2. She has brought a package with her that she will share with you today.
3. It contains an unusual collection boys and girls.
4. Class it is nice to be here.
5. Jill my niece first started this collection a long time ago when she was only seven years old.
6. She once asked me, "Aunt Helen why do only boys collect cards?"
7. "What do you mean Jill?" I asked.
8. "Baseball cards are collected mostly by boys."
9. "Jill girls collect baseball cards, too."
10. "Girls want cards about female athletes."
11. Mrs. Parker our visitor began to explain what causes some baseball cards to be more valuable than others.
12. My friend Kim wants to collect baseball cards.

B. Write each sentence, adding commas where necessary. Underline each appositive.

13. Some U.S. Treasury Department medallions for 1982 have Louis Armstrong the jazz musician on them.
14. Numismatists coin collectors will enjoy them.
15. Medallions are like coins but are larger.
16. Another difference is that medallions are made of gold a precious metal.
17. United States coins metal money are not made of gold.
18. The places that make coins mints are forbidden to make coins from gold.
19. The Bureau of the Mint an agency of the Treasury Department is in charge of producing money and medals.
20. There are mints in San Francisco, Philadelphia, and Denver three of America's largest cities.
21. Gold bullion gold in the shape of bars is kept at Fort Knox in Kentucky.
22. The Secretary of the Treasury a member of the President's Cabinet is director of the bureau.

Commas After Introductory Words and to Set Off Interrupters

Introductory Words   Use a comma after words such as *yes, no well,* and *why* at the beginning of a sentence.

> Yes, I think you're right.
> Why, I didn't recognize him!
> Well, here we are at last.
> No, he looks very different.

Interrupters   Parenthetical expressions are interrupting words that are added to a sentence for extra emphasis or clarity. Some parenthetical expressions are listed below.

of course	by the way	I suppose (guess, hope,
after all	to be fair	think)
however	for example	to tell the truth
in fact	in addition	in my opinion
indeed	furthermore	to say the least
therefore	besides	on the other hand

Parenthetical expressions may appear anywhere in a sentence.

> On the other hand, you are hardworking.
> That movie, in my opinion, was wonderful.
> The gift was thoughtful, to say the least.

Parenthetical expressions can be dropped from a sentence without changing its meaning.

> Kyle, after all, won the election fairly.
> Kyle won the election fairly.

When a parenthetical expression is in the middle of a sentence, it is both preceded and followed by commas.

> He is, therefore, the new leader.

Summary ◆ Use a comma after introductory words and to set off words or expressions that interrupt the sentence.

Practice

A. Write each sentence, adding commas where necessary.

1. Yes there are people who collect old schoolbooks and other educational memorabilia

2. Many such collectors by the way are not teachers.

3. In fact many collectors do not keep old texts for their educational value.

4. Old textbooks after all have much to offer.

5. Of course we can learn about people in the past.

6. In addition I like the old-fashioned printing and the manner in which the pages are designed.

7. In fact some of the subjects are the same as ours.

8. Many things have changed however.

9. Well textbooks are no longer illustrated with woodcuts.

10. In my opinion these textbooks are valuable.

B. Write each sentence, adding commas where necessary. If a sentence needs no commas, write *correct*.

11. Well I didn't know that old comic books can be valuable, or I wouldn't have thrown mine out!

12. My brother and I kept our *Classic Illustrated* and *Superman* comics for many years.

13. Our mother on the other hand was not interested.

14. In fact she could not wait for us to get rid of them.

15. She did not enjoy reading comics very much.

16. She was we guessed not thrilled about having to dust and arrange large piles of comics.

17. To tell the truth we did have too many.

18. Yes the day came when even we thought we had too many.

19. There was a question of age after all.

20. I mean the age of the comics as well as our ages.

21. Many comics had yellowed for example.

22. In addition many pages were torn or loose.

23. We could not have kept all of them of course.

24. We should have held on to some of them.

25. To be honest I sometimes still get the urge to read them.

26. Comics to say the least are entertaining.

27. Furthermore some of them can be quite informative.

28. Collecting comic books in my opinion is an interesting and stimulating hobby.

Other Uses of Commas

Commas in Dates and Addresses Use a comma to separate items in dates and addresses.

> March 17, 1977
> Sunday, April 17, 1983
> 24 West Elm Street, Brockton, MA 02401

Notice that you do not use a comma between the state and the ZIP code in an address. The ZIP code number should be written a few spaces after the state unless it is included in a sentence.

Use a comma after the last part of a date or an address when they are included in a sentence.

> April 23, 1616, was the day William Shakespeare died.
> A bill from 44 Yale Avenue, Tulsa, OK 74136, came
>   today in the mail.
> Our mailing address is 5 Oak Lane, Mayville, ND 58257.

Do not use a comma between the month and the year if no specific day is given.

> December 1985   May 1957
> July 1908   October 1941

Commas with Letter Parts Commas are used with certain parts of a letter. Use a comma after the salutation of a friendly letter.

> Dear José,   Dear Justin,
> Dear Aunt June, Dear Lizbeth,

Use a comma after the closing of a friendly or a business letter.

> Love,   Yours truly,
> Sincerely yours, Cordially yours,

Summary ✦ Use a comma to separate items in dates and addresses. Use a comma with certain letter parts.

Mechanics Lessons

Practice

A. Write each sentence, adding commas where necessary.

1. On February 9 1964 Mom was one of the thousands who welcomed the Beatles to New York New York.
2. Mom was born on June 27 1946 in the Bronx New York.
3. She spent the major part of her childhood years at 840 Grand Concourse Bronx NY.
4. Paul McCartney was born on June 18 1942.
5. He was born in Liverpool England.
6. Ringo Starr was born in July 1940 and John Lennon was born in October 1940.
7. George Harrison's birthdate is February 23 1943.
8. Mom and some friends went to Atlantic City New Jersey to see the Beatles in August 1964.
9. On June 4 1968 and September 7 1970 Mom went to St. John's Wood London England to look for Paul McCartney.
10. John Lennon died December 8 1980 in New York.

B. Write Randi's letter, adding commas where needed.

February 14 1988

Dear Shawn

The reason I did not answer your letter earlier is that you sent your letter to my old address. We do not live at 212 Hill Road Reading PA 19610 anymore. Our new address is 8422 Lyons Place Philadelphia PA 19142.

Thanks very much for the beautiful stamps from the Caribbean. Did you get the stamps in San Juan Puerto Rico or in the West Indies? Did you visit there in December 1987 or was it in January 1988? I have already carefully positioned the stamps in my new album.

You will be interested to know that I received a postcard from Cassie dated Saturday December 16 1987. "Affectionately yours," was the closing she used!

I am really looking forward to our skiing trip which is planned to begin on March 16 1988. Could you bring along any photographs that you took on your Caribbean vacation? I would really enjoy seeing them.

Yours truly
Randi

Quotation Marks

Direct Quotations   A direct quotation is enclosed within quotation marks. It is often separated from the rest of the sentence by a comma. Use a comma *after* a quotation and *inside* the quotation marks if the quotation begins a sentence. Do not use a comma if the quotation ends with a question or an exclamation mark.

> "The library is closed today," said Andy's mother.
> "Are you sure of that?" asked Andy.
> "That is disappointing news!" Miki exclaimed.

A direct quotation begins with a capital letter. Use a comma *before* a quotation and *outside* the quotation marks if the quotation ends a sentence. Periods should be placed inside closing quotation marks.

> Toni said, "My report card is in my book."
> Elia replied, "The rain has stopped."

Place a question mark or an exclamation mark inside the closing quotation marks if it is part of the quotation. Otherwise place it outside.

> "What time is it?" Lilia asked.
> Alicia exclaimed, "What a beautiful baby!"
> Did you say, "I am too tired to go out"?

Do not use quotation marks with an indirect quotation.

> **Indirect:** Marc suggested that we raise money.
> **Direct:** Marc said, "Let's raise money."

Quotation Marks with Titles   Use quotation marks to enclose titles of works like those listed below.

> **Short stories:** "The Car"   **Songs:** "Yesterday"
> **Poems:** "The Road Not Taken"   **Chapters:** "First Fear"

Summary ♦ Use **quotation marks** to enclose a person's exact words.

Practice

A. Write each sentence, adding quotation marks where necessary.

1. What's in your collection of strange but true facts today? asked Wendy.
2. Paul said, Let's see if we can master the worst tongue twister in the entire world.
3. I'd like to hear that, Wendy remarked.
4. The sixth sick sheik's sixth sheep's sick, Paul said.
5. Wendy exclaimed, I can't even say it slowly!
6. Here are some more facts, Paul said browsing through the book with great fascination.
7. The *Apollo 9* astronauts sang a song in space on March 8, 1969, Paul said.
8. This chapter in the book is called Unique Facts About Everything You Ever Wondered.
9. Happy Birthday is a song frequently sung in different languages around the world.
10. Paul said, Of course, we all remember that Thomas Jefferson had red hair.
11. Wendy said that she was tired of strange facts and would rather listen to a story.

B. Write each sentence, adding quotation marks and commas where necessary.

12. Paul read the short story Wonderful Words.
13. Paul said that *apple* is one of the oldest words in the English language.
14. Wendy said Yes, and Mandarin is spoken by at least 660 million people, more than any other language.
15. That's right, and English is next Paul continued.
16. Paul said that millions of people speak English.
17. Wendy added English contains about 490,000 words.
18. Did you like the word with twenty-nine letters, which is one of the longest words in English? Wendy asked.
19. Quick, pronounce it for me teased Paul.
20. She laughed Pick one of the other 489,999 words.
21. I prefer floccinaucinihilipilification Paul said.
22. Finally Wendy said that she couldn't bear to listen to any more strange but true facts.

Divided Quotations

Divided Quotations   A speaker's words may be divided into parts by other words. If the second part of the divided quotation is a separate sentence, begin it with a capital letter, and enclose it with quotation marks.

> "It is warm outside," said Lou. "I do not need a coat."
> "It is almost summer," Beth exclaimed. "I can't wait!"
> "What time is it?" Sasha asked. "We need to go."

Do not begin the second part of a divided quotation with a capital letter if that part is not a separate sentence. Put a comma after the first part of the quotation, and enclose that part with quotation marks. Begin the second part of the quotation with a small letter, and enclose that part with quotation marks also.

> "He is," said Lynn, "at the bus stop in the morning."
> "Well," Terry said, "it is about time you came."
> "Where were you," Henry asked, "last night?"

Dialogue   A conversation between two people is a dialogue. Start a new paragraph each time another speaker begins talking.

> *Deltiologist* is the word for today," said Sue.
> "I know what that means," replied Chad. "You are talking about a place to buy sandwiches, right?"

Do not put quotation marks around every sentence spoken by the same person. Put quotation marks around the entire uninterrupted speech.

> Sue laughed and said, "You are funny, Chad. That is a delicatessen! A deltiologist collects postcards!"
> "Well," Chad responded humorously, "isn't a delicatessen a shop that collects smoked fish, cold cuts, cheeses, salads, and relishes? That means I almost had the right answer!"
> "You certainly can twist words and meanings around," said Sue chuckling. "I really enjoy it. Tomorrow, you will have another opportunity to identify a word."

Summary ♦ Sometimes a direct quotation is divided into two or more parts.

Practice

A. Write each sentence, adding quotation marks, commas, and capital letters where necessary.

1. Then said José there is a man in California who owns more than 1,000 different credit cards.
2. He must have a very large wallet Stacey laughed to be able to carry so many credit cards.
3. Never mind that José responded. can you imagine the size of his monthly bills?
4. Actually Stacy said that is probably a very inexpensive and unique hobby.
5. Just how José questioned do you figure that?
6. After all Stacy explained it costs only the yearly fee for each card, if a card has one.
7. That is true José agreed but it is expensive if you buy things.
8. In addition José added it could actually be very expensive if many of the cards do have a yearly fee.
9. Plastic cards said Stacy do not seem like money.
10. You are right José said. paper money is special.
11. Actually, what I would miss replied Stacy would be seeing the presidents on the bills.
12. Did you know that before money was invented José asked people used to trade with each other to get the things they wanted?

B. In the following dialogue, write each quotation as a divided quotation.

"Did you hear about the dentist who kept all the teeth he had pulled for thirty-six years?" asked José.

"Why did he do that? Was he going to make a necklace?" asked Stacy.

"Once he pulled them, I guess he thought they were his," replied José.

Stacy remarked, "Maybe that is true. After all, what could the patients do with the teeth?"

"What could he do with more than two million teeth?" questioned José.

"Well, I am sure he made a world record," said Stacy.

"Perhaps he wanted to be in the *Guiness Book of World Records*," José suggested.

Italics and Underlining

The titles of books, magazines, newspapers, movies, plays, paintings, and operas should be underlined in handwriting or in typing. This is true also for names of planes, trains, and ships. In printed materials these titles and names appear in *italics*.

Books: *The Secret Garden*
The Phantom Tollbooth

Newspapers: *The New York Times*
Wall Street Journal

Magazines: *Newsweek*
National Geographic

Operas: *Madame Butterfly*
The Magic Flute

Plays: *Othello*

Movies: *Star Wars*

Paintings: *The Starry Night*

Ships: the *Flying Cloud*

Summary ◆ **Italics** are letters that lean to the right in printed material—*italics*. In writing, these words are underlined.

Practice

A. Write the following titles and names. Use underlining for italics.

1. The Outsiders (book)
2. E.T.: The Extra-Terrestrial (movie)
3. Splash (movie)
4. Boston Globe (newspaper)
5. Sports Illustrated (magazine)
6. Amahl and the Night Visitors (opera)
7. Junior Scholastic (magazine)
8. Old Ironsides (ship)
9. Romeo and Juliet (play)
10. Beacon Journal (newspaper)
11. Roots (book)
12. Sunflowers (painting)
13. The Elephant Man (play)
14. Elektra (opera)
15. Lady Sings the Blues (movie)
16. The Hobbit (book)
17. Daily News (newspaper)
18. Sirius (ship)
19. Country Music (magazine)
20. Andes of Ecuador (painting)

B. After each sentence number, write the words that should be printed in italics. Then underline them.

21. I walked to the Louvre Museum in Paris, France, carrying my copy of the International Herald Tribune.
22. I saw the famous painting Arrangement in Gray and Black No. 1: Portrait of the Painter's Mother, commonly called Whistler's Mother, by James Whistler, an American.
23. Later I saw Bizet's opera Carmen at the Paris Opera House, a world-famous theater.
24. The only thing I saw that did not need translation was the Marx Brothers' film A Night at the Opera.
25. Someday I would like to return to Europe and cruise on the Mediterranean in a ship such as the Golden Odyssey.

Semicolons and Colons

Semicolons   Use a semicolon to join independent clauses in a compound sentence when the clauses are not joined by a conjunction such as *and, but, or,* or *nor*.

> Leslie read a book; then she visited her friend Sam.
> It was raining; Taro didn't take his umbrella.

Colons   Use a colon as shown below for time, after salutations, and before lists.

Time:	10:45 P.M. 6:17 A.M. 4:00 P.M.
Salutation:	Gentlemen: Dear Ms. Goldman:
List:	To operate the elevator proceed as follows: press button labeled Close Door, press button for your floor, press Start button.

When you write a list of items in a sentence, try to use a phrase such as *the following* or *as follows*. This phrase will help you use colons correctly.

> We were told to do as follows: run, jump, and hop.
> Use the following items: pens, ink, and paper.

Do not use a colon immediately after a verb or a preposition. Either leave out the colon or reword the sentence.

Wrong:	According to his horoscope, Chris's lucky days are: Tuesday, Friday, and Saturday
Right:	According to his horoscope, Chris's lucky days are Tuesday, Friday, and Saturday.
Right:	According to his horoscope, Chris's lucky days are as follows: Tuesday, Friday and Saturday.

Summary ◆ Use a **semicolon** to join the parts of a compound sentence when conjunctions are not used. Use a **colon** between the hour and the minute in time, after the salutation of a business letter, and before a list of items.

Practice

A. Write the sentences, adding semicolons where needed.

1. Dr. John Chung spoke he told of his amazing collection of antique books for children.
2. The valuable collection of antique children's books was guarded no one could touch them.
3. Few children's books existed before 1650 even one century later not many were printed.
4. Early children's books did not entertain they simply preached.
5. Today that is not true children's books are fun.

B. Write the sentences, adding colons where necessary.

6. Dr. Chung began his presentation at exactly 3 30 this afternoon in the school's auditorium.
7. He talked about several things nursery rhymes, jokes and riddles, and educational books.
8. Authors of children's books included the following the brothers Grimm, Hans Christian Andersen, and Andrew Lang.
9. Dr. Chung left at 6 15 on his way to his next talk.
10. In the next several weeks, he will be giving talks in these cities Tulsa, Boston, and Reno.
11. The following of my friends really enjoyed his talk Kim, Delia, and Che.

C. Write the sentences correctly using semicolons and colons. Add any necessary words.

12. Many early children's books were printed in: New York, London, and Boston.
13. The early books were often instructional they consisted of the alphabet, spelling, or arithmetic.
14. Some of these books were: *Jack Jingle, The Good Child's Illustrated Alphabet*, and *The Tragical Death of an Apple Pie*, an alphabet book.
15. *American Pictorial Primer*, of about 1825, helped children learn: reading, spelling, and character.
16. Many of these first books for children weren't fun they were useful in helping children become familiar with books.

Apostrophes

Use an apostrophe with the possessive form of a noun. The possessive form of a noun shows ownership.

To write the possessive form of a singular noun, add an apostrophe and *s* (*'s*).

boy	boy's	person	person's
Maria	Maria's	Mrs. Simmons	Mrs. Simmon's
cat	cat's	sailor	sailor's

To write the possessive form of a plural noun that ends in *s* add only an apostrophe (*'*).

workers	workers'	babies	babies'
runners	runners'	students	students'
poets	poets'	coaches	coaches'

To write the possessive form of a plural noun that does not end in *s*, add an apostrophe and *s* (*'s*).

women	women's	people	people's
mice	mice's	children	children's
sheep	sheep's	oxen	oxen's

Use an apostrophe with a contraction. Some letters are left out when the two words are combined. The apostrophe takes the place of those letters.

Some contractions are formed by combining verbs with the word *not*.

is not	has not	do not
isn't	hasn't	don't

Contractions are also formed by combining nouns or pronouns with verbs such as *am*, *is*, *have*, or *will*.

I am (I'm)	she will (she'll)	we would (we'd)
he had (he'd)	you have (you've)	who is (who's)

Summary ♦ **Apostrophes** show ownership and the omission of letters in contractions.

Practice

A. Write the possessive form of each noun.

1. men	**7.** oxen	**13.** rhinoceros
2. family	**8.** singers	**14.** Mr. Hess
3. dog	**9.** Sonia	**15.** horses
4. teachers	**10.** painter	**16.** children
5. girl	**11.** writers	**17.** lawyer
6. sheep	**12.** knees	**18.** mice

B. In the sentences below write each group of underlined words as either a contraction or a possessive form with an apostrophe.

> **EXAMPLE:** Ken <u>has not</u> seen <u>the shoes of his sister</u>.
> **ANSWER:** hasn't, his sister's shoes

19. <u>The camera of my friend</u> <u>does not</u> take good pictures without a flash attachment.

20. <u>I am</u> going to the museum to see <u>the paintings of the artists</u>.

21. <u>The contributions of the alumni</u> <u>are not</u> enough to pay for a new addition to the school.

22. <u>Who will</u> go to <u>the picnic of the fire fighters</u> at Mountainview Park on Saturday?

23. <u>They had</u> given many performances to <u>the delight of their fans</u>.

24. <u>Have not</u> any of the guests arrived at <u>the party of Billy</u>?

25. <u>The house of Mr. Jones</u> <u>could not</u> have been located any closer to the river.

26. When she goes to the library, <u>she will</u> return <u>the library books of her sister</u>.

27. <u>The letter of his brother</u> <u>did not</u> arrive until 4:15 P.M. the day before yesterday.

28. <u>Is not</u> the day after tomorrow the day of <u>the recital of the renowned pianist</u>?

29. I hope the new <u>camera of his sister</u> <u>did not</u> get lost on their last trip.

30. <u>We would</u> travel for miles across the grassy, fertile plains before seeing any <u>houses of farmers</u>.

31. <u>Who is</u> going to decorate and serve refreshments at the <u>birthday party for the children</u>?

32. The mayor of Penville <u>has not</u> responded yet to the <u>concerns of the citizens</u> about enlarging the library.

Diagraming Guide

Sentence Parts

A **diagram** is a line drawing that explains something. Just as an architect uses a diagram to show the structure of a building, you can use a diagram to show the structure of a sentence.

A sentence diagram is made up of horizontal, vertical, and slanting lines. Each word is placed at a certain location on the diagram to show its use in the sentence. Diagraming sentences will strengthen your ability to identify parts of speech and sentence structure.

Subjects and Verbs   The simplest sentence diagram shows a subject and a verb. Both the subject and the verb are placed on a horizontal line. They are separated by a crossing vertical line. If a sentence has a verb phrase, the entire phrase appears on the horizontal line.

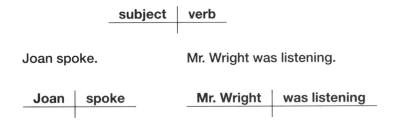

Joan spoke.   Mr. Wright was listening.

To diagram an interrogative sentence, put the subject before the verb. To show the subject of an imperative sentence, put *you* in parentheses in the subject place.

May I go?   Leave!

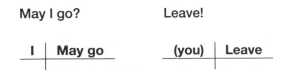

Notice that a sentence diagram shows the capital letters of a sentence but not the punctuation.

Compound subjects and compound verbs are diagramed on separate horizontal lines. The conjunction that joins the subjects or verbs is written on a vertical broken line linking the horizontal lines.

You and I should go.   It blinks, beeps, or hums.

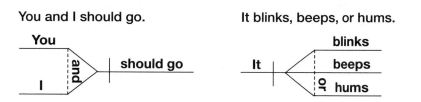

Adjectives and Adverbs   All sentences have a subject and a verb. Most sentences also have adjectives and adverbs. These parts of speech can be shown in a sentence diagram.

In a sentence diagram an adjective is written on a slanting line connected to the noun or pronoun the adjective modifies. When more than one adjective modifies a word, each is written on a separate slanting line. The articles *a, an,* and *the* are also diagramed in this way.

Three cars passed.   A tall blond man waved.

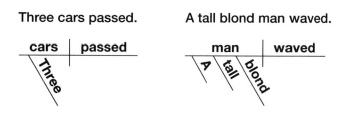

Adverbs, like adjectives, are diagramed on slanting lines. If an adverb modifies a verb, it appears directly below the verb.

We ran quickly.   The child stood there quietly.

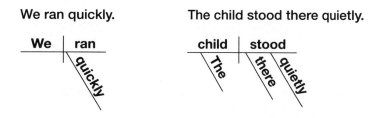

Diagram an adverb modifying an adjective or an adverb on a slanting line attached to the word modified.

A really strange thing happened.

Kate laughs very loudly.

As you have seen, conjunctions are placed on broken lines between the words they connect.

The young but lame pony limped slowly and painfully.

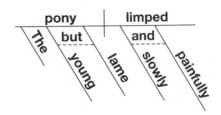

Prepositional Phrases   A prepositional phrase is diagramed below the word it modifies. The preposition is placed on a slanting line connected to the word modified. Its object is placed on a horizontal line connected to the slanting line.

The boys in the red balloon soon returned.
They traveled over two tall mountains.

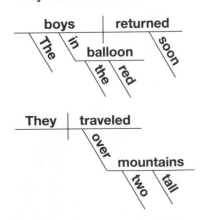

Other Sentence Parts   A direct object appears on the horizontal line after the verb. It is separated from the verb by a short vertical line that does not cross the horizontal line.

The trainer finally found the lost tiger.

An indirect object is placed on a horizontal line below the verb. A slanting line connects the indirect object to the verb.

That doctor gave the school a computer.

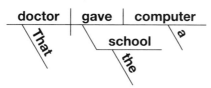

Predicate nouns, predicate pronouns, and predicate adjectives are placed on the horizontal line after the verb, just like direct objects. However, they are separated from the verb by a line that slants backward toward the subject and that does not cross the horizontal line.

James is the pitcher.   The girl in the picture is she.
                The stew tasted delicious.

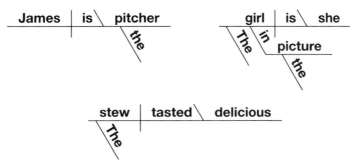

Practice

A. Diagram each sentence.

1. Birds were singing.
2. Grass grows.
3. Go!
4. Do hurry.
5. Did they run?
6. Will Emma sing?
7. We have finished.
8. Have they been eating?
9. Jay listens.
10. He might have heard.

B. Diagram each sentence. Remember to write each conjunction on a broken line.

11. Biff barked and growled.
12. Dad will write or call.
13. You and they must agree.
14. He and I argued.
15. Mona or Myra dances.

C. Diagram each sentence. Place each adjective and adverb below the word it modifies.

16. The hot air shimmered steadily.
17. The nervous young puppy was behaving poorly.
18. Did the class sing clearly?
19. Only one child could speak persuasively.
20. The small girl skates so gracefully.
21. We worked hard but barely finished.
22. Listen carefully and quietly.
23. Two very fine artists were painting quite busily.
24. Did young Madge ski very slowly?
25. Tom should arrive rather early.

D. Diagram each sentence. Be sure each prepositional phrase is placed below the word it modifies.

26. The purple mountains towered in the distance.
27. Shrubs with big yellow berries grew nearby.

28. A large flag hung from the window.
29. The ring with nine diamonds should be in a safe.
30. The costumes for the green monsters are stored inside the small gymnasium.

E. Diagram each sentence. Be sure your diagrams indicate which words are direct objects; indirect objects; and predicate nouns, pronouns, and adjectives.

31. Is Ms. Gray the new teacher?
32. Rod sent Cliff a secret message.
33. Ella and Clay seem undecided.
34. Bruce could not finish the puzzle.
35. Show me the hidden staircase.
36. The actors definitely were we.
37. The clever coach gave the runner a signal.
38. The players and the fans are happy.
39. Our third President is the author.
40. Has Mr. Warner already given Alice the trophy.?

F. Diagram each sentence. The following sentences contain various sentence parts and parts of speech that you have studied in this section.

41. A thing of beauty is a joy forever.
42. Tom and Fred worked quickly and efficiently.
43. The terrible flood destroyed thousands of homes.
44. Its chief feature was a long, clear, high note.
45. Anyone can catch a firefly in his or her hand.
46. Mrs. Pringle and her lawyer showed the mayor a copy of the petition.
47. The weary campers gave the brave ranger a loud cheer of thanks.
48. The writer of the almost illegible message was unfortunately I.
49. Two angry cats clawed and yowled.
50. In the morning give her your old but unused hat.

Compound and Complex Sentences

The sentences you have diagramed so far have been simple sentences. A simple sentence, as you remember, has only one subject and one verb, although each may be compound. You can use the same diagraming techniques that you have learned to diagram more complicated sentences. In this section you will study how to diagram compound and complex sentences.

Compound Sentences   A compound sentence is made up of two or more independent clauses joined by a conjunction or a semicolon. (For a review of compound sentences, see pages 16–17.) Each independent clause in a compound sentence is diagramed like a simple sentence. The first clause is diagramed above the second. The clauses are joined by the conjunction as shown below.

We thoroughly enjoyed the band, but the singer could barely carry a tune.

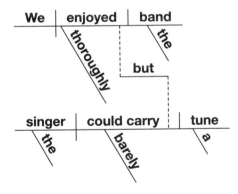

Notice that the line that connects the two independent clauses is drawn from verb to verb. If the clauses are joined by a semicolon, a broken line connects the two verbs.

Complex Sentences   A complex sentence contains two or more clauses. However, only one clause is independent. The other clause or clauses are subordinate. (To review subordinate clauses and complex sentences, see pages 462–465.)

When diagraming a complex sentence, diagram the independent clause first. Then diagram the subordinate clause below the independent clause. You should be able to identify the subordinate clause by the subordinating conjunction—such as *after, because, before, if, since, while,* or *where*—that begins the clause.

Connect the verbs of the two clauses with a slanting broken line. Write the subordinating conjunction on the slanting line. Study the diagrams of the complex sentences that follow.

He kept his pet outside, since it was an elephant of
   some size.
If you like elephants, visit him.

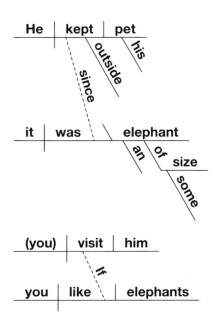

Practice

A. Diagram each compound sentence.

1. The journey was long, and the wind was cold.
2. They won the game, but we will win the match.
3. Should I send Jill the mango, or may I eat it?
4. Jane was ill, but the other actors rehearsed.
5. Each actor must learn his or her part, or the play will be a complete failure.
6. In the early morning we fished, and later we explored the lighthouse.
7. You must hurry, or you will miss the bus.
8. Everyone agrees with your conclusions, but can anything be done in three days?
9. I took my camera to the picnic, but I forgot the film.
10. The solution is simple, or I would not have discovered it so quickly.

B. Diagram each complex sentence.

11. If you need any help, call me.
12. I must study now because my test is tomorrow.
13. If wishes were horses, beggars would ride.
14. She left before anyone could ask her any more questions.
15. While she worked, the dentist hummed softly.
16. They will repair your shoes while you wait.
17. When all danger of frost had passed, we planted the tomatoes in a sunny spot.
18. After I told my teacher the plot, I began work on the story.
19. This season was a complete success for our team because we won the state championship.
20. Before the phone rang twice, Sophie answered it.

Grammar Handbook

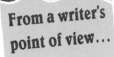

From a writer's point of view...

I create vivid word pictures and make my writing more interesting and colorful for my readers by using adjectives to add definitive details.

▶ **adjective** An adjective modifies a noun or pronoun.

> **A narrow river flows through the western part of town.**

proper adjective A proper adjective is formed from a proper noun.

> **an Australian outback   a New York newspaper**

predicate adjective A predicate adjective follows a linking verb and describes the subject of the sentence.

> **These books are quite worthwhile to readers.**

demonstrative adjective The demonstrative adjectives *this*, *that*, *these*, and *those* point out the nouns they modify. When *this*, *that*, *these*, and *those* stand alone, they are pronouns, not adjectives.

> **This ship looks gigantic.** (demonstrative adjective)
> **Can any ship be larger than that?** (demonstrative pronoun)

comparison of adjectives Many adjectives have three forms, or degrees of comparison: **positive**, **comparative**, and **superlative**.

From a writer's point of view...

Using various forms of adjectives helps to make interesting comparisons.

♦ Add *-er* and *-est* to most one-syllable adjectives and many two syllable adjectives. Some spelling changes may occur.

Positive	Comparative	Superlative
sharp	sharper	sharpest
big	bigger	biggest

♦ Use *more* and *most* with some two-syllable adjectives and with all adjectives of three or more syllables.

Positive	Comparative	Superlative
careful	more careful	most careful
generous	more generous	most generous

♦ Some adjectives have irregular forms in the comparative and superlative degree.

Positive	Comparative	Superlative
good	better	best
bad, ill	worse	worst
much, many	more	most
little	less	least

♦ Use the comparative degree to compare two.

An elk is <u>faster</u> than a horse.

♦ Use the superlative degree to compare more than two.

The cheetah is the <u>fastest</u> animal of all.

♦ Do not use double comparatives or superlatives.

She wrote <u>better</u> (not <u>more</u> <u>better</u>) nature stories than news articles.

articles   The words *a*, *an*, and *the* are special adjectives called articles. Because *the* refers to specific persons, places, or things, it is called a **definite article**. Because *a* and *an* refer to any person, place, or thing, they are called **indefinite articles**.

<u>the</u> **river**   <u>a</u> **river**   <u>an</u> **ocean**

▶ **adverb**   An adverb modifies a verb, an adjective, or another adverb.

Mrs. Ruiz <u>carefully</u> *read* the passage. (modifies verb)
She wrote a <u>wonderfully</u> *imaginative* book. (modifies adjective)
Mrs. Ruiz reads <u>rather</u> *dramatically*. (modifies adverb)

comparison of adverbs Many adverbs have three forms, or degrees of comparison: **positive**, **comparative**, and **superlative**.

From a writer's point of view...

Using adverbs helps make my writing clear and informative. I can use degrees of adverbs to make precise comparisons.

♦ Add *-er* or *-est* to the positive form of most one-syllable adverbs.

Positive	Comparative	Superlative
fast	faster	fastest
late	later	latest

♦ Put *more* or *most* before the positive form of most adverbs of two or more syllables.

Positive	Comparative	Superlative
smoothly	more smoothly	most smoothly
frequently	more frequently	most frequently

♦ Some adverbs have irregular forms in the comparative and superlative degree.

Positive	Comparative	Superlative
well	better	best
badly	worse	worst
little	less	least

♦ Use the comparative degree to compare two persons or things. Use the superlative to compare three or more.

Comparative: **Eva lives <u>closer</u> to me than Tom does.**
Superlative: **Emma lives <u>the closest</u> of all to me.**

▶ **appositive** An appositive explains the meaning of a noun that directly precedes it. Use commas to set off most appositives.

Watson, <u>Bell's assistant</u>, received the first phone call.

▶ **clause** A clause is a group of words that has a subject and a verb. There are two types of clauses, **independent** and **subordinate**.

independent clause An independent clause expresses a complete thought. It can stand alone as a simple sentence.

The child was very young.

subordinate clause   A subordinate clause does not express a complete thought. It must be joined to an independent clause to make a sentence.

<u>When he was a child</u>, he lived in the South.

▶ **conjunctions**   A conjunction joins words or groups of words in a sentence.

coordinating conjunctions   Coordinating conjunctions join words that do the same kind of work. The most common coordinating conjunctions are *and*, *but*, *or*, and *nor*.

Mexico's diverse <u>but</u> difficult history influences Octavio Paz's work.

correlative conjunctions   Some conjunctions are made up of pairs of words, such as *both ... and*, *either ... or*, *neither ... nor*. These pairs are called correlative conjunctions.

Octavio Paz is <u>both</u> a poet <u>and</u> an essayist.

subordinating conjunctions   Subordinating conjunctions introduce many subordinate clauses.

We were present <u>when</u> Paz read his poetry.

Common Subordinating Conjunctions				
after	because	since	when	wherever
although	before	unless	whenever	while
as	if	until	where	

▶ **contraction**   A contraction is a shortened form of two words. An apostrophe replaces a letter or letters.

We <u>won't</u> need hotel reservations because <u>we're</u> staying with friends.

▶ **direct object**   The direct object receives the action of the verb. It answers the question *Whom?* or *What?*

Television shows employ <u>writers</u>.

▶ **double negative** An affirmative sentence can be made negative by the use of just one negative word. A double negative is the incorrect use of two or more negative words in a sentence.

> **I did <u>not</u> find a book. (*Not* I did<u>n't</u> find <u>no</u> book.)**

▶ **indirect object** The indirect object usually comes before the direct object. It tells to whom or for whom the action of the verb is done.

> **We asked the <u>editor</u> many questions.**

▶ **interjection** An interjection expresses feeling or emotion.

> **<u>Great</u>! Our field trip is tomorrow.**
> **<u>Well</u>, I don't want to go.**

▶ **noun** A noun names a person, place, thing, or idea.

> **<u>Woodie Guthrie</u> was a <u>songwriter</u>.** (person)
> **He was born in <u>Oklahoma</u> in <u>1912</u>.** (place)
> **He sang and played the <u>guitar</u>.** (thing)
> **He achieved <u>greatness</u>.** (idea)

singular noun A singular noun names one person, place, thing, or idea.

> **A musical <u>conductor</u> leads an <u>orchestra</u>.**

plural noun A plural noun names more than one person, place, thing, or idea.

> **Voice <u>coaches</u> give singing <u>lessons</u>.**

common noun A common noun is the general name of a person, place, or thing.

> **A famous <u>ballerina</u> visited our <u>school</u>.**

proper noun A proper noun names a particular person, place, or thing.

> **<u>T.S. Eliot</u> was born in <u>St. Louis, Missouri</u>.**

possessive noun   A possessive noun shows ownership.

Many <u>actors'</u> roles require them to be good dancers.

♦ To write the possessive form of a singular noun, add an apostrophe and *s* (**'s**).

Bob   Bob<u>'s</u> pen   the actor   the actor<u>'s</u> costume

♦ To write the possessive form of a plural noun that ends in *s*, add only an apostrophe (**'**).

actors   actors<u>'</u> lines   bosses   bosse<u>s'</u> orders

♦ To write the possessive form of a plural noun that does not end in *s*, add an apostrophe and *s* (**'s**).

**children   children<u>'s</u> dances
women   women<u>'s</u> songs**

collective noun   A collective noun names a group of people, animals, or things.

**army   committee   family   team
crowd   flock   group   majority**

▶ **phrase**   A phrase is a group of words that does not have a subject and a verb.

during the 1700s   must have worked

▶ **preposition**   A preposition relates a noun or pronoun to another word in the sentence.

The story <u>about</u> the spider was <u>of</u> special interest <u>to</u> Gretchen.

object of the preposition   The noun or pronoun that follows a preposition is the object of the preposition.

Poets write *about* many <u>themes</u>.

prepositional phrase   A preposition, its object, and any other words that modify the object make up a prepositional phrase.

<u>From the deck</u>, I saw a dolphin.

From a writer's point of view...

Using carefully chosen prepositions helps make my writing clear and specific.

♦ A prepositional phrase that is used as an adjective to modify a noun or pronoun is an **adjective phrase.**

> **Shakespeare had a keen *understanding* of human nature.**

♦ A prepositional phrase that is used as an adverb to modify a verb, an adjective, or an adverb is an **adverb phrase**.

> **Central America *borders* on Mexico.**

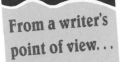

From a writer's point of view. . .

Prepositional phrases can expand my sentences and add important details and variety.

▶ pronoun   A pronoun takes the place of a noun or nouns.

> ***John Roebling* was the builder of the *Brooklyn Bridge*. He died before it was completed.**

personal pronoun   Personal pronouns have different forms to show person.

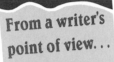

From a writer's point of view. . .

Pronouns help me avoid repeating the same nouns over and over again.

Person	Singular	Plural
First (the person speaking)	I, me, my, mine	we, us, our, ours
Second (the person spoken to)	you, your, yours	you, your, yours
Third (the person or thing spoken about)	he, him, his, she, her, hers, it, its	they, them, their, theirs

antecedent   An antecedent is the word or words to which a pronoun refers. The antecedent for every pronoun should be clear, and the pronoun should agree with its antecedent in both gender and number.

> **If his plan works, the *inventor* will become famous.**

subject and object pronouns   Some pronouns have different forms, or cases. The form of a pronoun is determined by how it is used in a sentence.

♦ The subject pronouns are *I, you, he, she, it, we, they*, and *who*. Use subject pronouns as subjects of verbs and as predicate nominatives.

> **He visited an old factory.   The tour guide was she.**

♦ The object pronouns are *me*, *you*, *him*, *her*, *it*, *us*, *them* and *whom*. Use object pronouns as direct objects, indirect objects, and objects of prepositions.

The librarian gave <u>them</u> to <u>him</u>.

possessive pronoun   A possessive pronoun shows ownership.

<u>His</u> radio is broken.   **The camera is <u>hers</u>.**

interrogative pronoun   An interrogative pronoun asks a question. The interrogative pronouns are *who*, *whose*, *whom*, *which*, and *what*.

<u>Who</u> invented the phonograph?

demonstrative pronoun   A demonstrative pronoun emphatically points out its antecedent. The demonstrative pronouns are *this* and *that* (singular), and *these* and *those* (plural).

<u>That</u> was *Thomas Edison*.   **<u>Those</u> were his *notes*.**

reflexive and intensive pronouns   The reflexive and intensive pronouns are *myself*, *yourself*, *himself*, *herself*, *itself*, *ourselves*, *yourselves*, and *themselves*. A **reflexive pronoun** refers to a noun or pronoun in the same sentence, usually the subject. An **intensive pronoun** emphasizes another word in the sentence.

Reflexive: **The climbers pulled <u>themselves</u> up with a rope.**
Intensive: **We met the President <u>himself</u>.**

indefinite pronoun   A pronoun that does not always refer to a particular person, place, or thing is called an indefinite pronoun.

<u>Everyone</u> is invited to visit the White House.
<u>Many</u> of the public rooms are open for tours.

▶ **sentence** A sentence is a group of words that expresses a complete thought. Always capitalize the first word in a sentence and use correct end punctuation. There are four kinds of sentences.

declarative sentence A declarative sentence makes a statement and ends with a period (.)

Anne Frank kept a fascinating diary.

interrogative sentence An interrogative sentence asks a question and ends with a question mark (?).

Can you illustrate your diary?

imperative sentence An imperative sentence gives a command or makes a request. It ends with a period.

Write something about yourself.

exclamatory sentence An exclamatory sentence expresses strong feeling. It ends with an exclamation mark (!).

What a beautiful morning it is!

simple sentence A simple sentence has one subject and one verb, either or both of which may be compound.

Samuel Pepys <u>was</u> **an English public official in the late 1600s.**
Writers **and** *politicians* <u>research</u> **and** <u>admire</u> **his career.**

compound sentence A compound sentence consists of two or more simple sentences. You can join simple sentences with the conjunction *and, or, but,* or *nor* or with a semicolon. Place a comma before the conjunction unless the sentence is very short.

Samuel Pepys served in Parliament, and he also wrote a famous diary.
His diary tells a personal story; it also is a historic record.

complex sentence   A complex sentence has one independent clause and at least one subordinate clause.

> **Crops are grown <u>where the land is most fertile</u>.** (The subordinate clause is underlined.)

sentence error: fragment   A sentence fragment is an incomplete thought written as a sentence. Prepositional phrases, subordinate clauses, and verbals by themselves do not express complete thoughts.

> Fragment: **The design for hundreds of inventions.**
> Correct: **Leonardo's notebooks contain the design for hundreds of inventions.**

sentence error: run-on sentence   A run-on sentence occurs when two or more sentences are separated by no punctuation or just a comma. Correct a run-on sentence by making separate sentences or by writing it as a compound sentence.

> Run-on: **Leonardo da Vinci trained as a painter he was an excellent observer.**
> Correct: **Leonardo da Vinci trained as a painter, and he was an excellent observer.**

▶ **subjects and predicates**   The subject is the part of a sentence that names someone or something. The predicate tells what the subject is or does.

complete subject   The complete subject is all the words in the subject part of a sentence.

> **<u>Young Theodore Roosevelt</u> went to Egypt with his family.**

simple subject   The simple subject is the main word or words in the complete subject. It is usually a noun or a pronoun.

> **A young <u>woman</u> from New England wrote a historic journal.**

compound subject   A compound subject is two or more simple subjects that have the same verb.

> **Theodore Roosevelt** and **John Muir** *valued* natural resources.

subject of imperative sentence   The subject of an imperative sentence is understood to be *you*, although the word *you* is not used.

> **(You)** *Do* not *talk* **loudly in the library.**

complete predicate   The complete predicate is all the words in the predicate part of the sentence. It tells what the subject is or does.

> **Captain James Cook <u>discovered the southeast coast of Australia in 1770.</u>**

simple predicate, or verb   The simple predicate is the main word or words in the complete predicate. It is always a verb.

> **Catherine *<u>lived</u> with her father and younger sister*.**

compound verb   A compound verb is two or more verbs that have the same subject.

> **Robert <u>hiked</u> and <u>climbed</u> in Yellowstone National Park.**

▶ **subject-verb agreement**   A verb needs to agree with its subject in number. Number means that a word is either singular or plural. A subject and verb agree in number when they are both singular or both plural.

♦ If a subject is a singular noun or a third-person pronoun, use the present-tense verb form that ends in *s* or *es*.

> **The *teacher* <u>reads</u> with his students.**
> *He* (or *she, it*) <u>reads</u> some poetry.

♦ If a subject is a plural noun or any pronoun other than third-person singular, use the present-tense verb form that does not end in *s* or *es*.

The *students* <u>read</u> their writing to themselves.
I (or *you*, *we*, or *they*) <u>read</u> some poems aloud.

♦ The verbs *be*, *have*, and *do* have special singular and plural forms.

Forms of *be*, *have*, and *do*				
Singular	**Present**	**Past**	**Present**	**Present**
I	am	was	have	do
you	are	were	have	do
he, she, it or a singular noun	is	was	has	does
Plural				
we	are	were	have	do
you	are	were	have	do
they or a plural noun	are	were	have	do

collective nouns   A collective noun may be used as a singular noun or plural noun, depending on the intended meaning of the sentence. Therefore, a collective noun may be followed by a singular or plural verb.

The *group* <u>shares</u> its findings with the entire committee.
The *group* often <u>go</u> their separate ways.

compound subjects   Compound subjects joined by *and* need a plural verb. This is true whether the subjects are singular or plural.

Beans and *rice* <u>are</u> traditional foods in the Caribbean Islands.

♦ Singular subjects joined by *or* or *nor* need a singular verb.

Either a *mango* or a *papaya* <u>is</u> a favorite fruit in Jamaica.

♦ Plural subjects joined by *or* or *nor* need a plural verb.

Neither *peaches* nor *apricots* <u>are</u> tropical fruits.

♦ If a singular and a plural subject are joined by *or* or *nor*, the verb agrees with the subject closest to it.

The *mangos* or the *papaya* <u>is</u> delicious.
The *mango* or the *papayas* <u>are</u> delicious.

indefinite pronoun   As the subject of a sentence, an indefinite pronoun needs to agree with its verb in number. Most indefinite pronouns are singular, but a few are plural, and some may be either singular or plural.

Singular: ***Each* of the vegetables <u>tastes</u> delicious.**
Plural: ***Many* <u>taste</u> sweet.**

♦ For pronouns that may be singular or plural, look at the word to which the pronoun refers. If the word is singular, the pronoun is considered singular. If the word is plural, the pronoun is plural.

Singular: ***Most* of the food <u>is</u> tasty.**
Plural: ***Most* of the foods <u>are</u> tasty.**

inverted word order   Even when a subject follows a verb, as in an inverted sentence, the verb must agree with the subject.

In their stories <u>was</u> a *lesson*.

♦ Inverted sentences often begin with *here*, *there*, or *where*. Be careful not to use the contraction for the singular verb *is* (**'s**) with these words when the subject is plural.

Incorrect: **Here<u>'s</u> the stories of African folklore.**
Correct: **Here <u>are</u> the stories of African folklore.**

▶ **verb**   A verb expresses action or being.

> **Guglielmo Marconi built the first radio in 1895.**
> **Radio broadcasting was experimental until 1920.**

action verb   Some verbs show action that is visible. Other verbs show action that cannot be seen. These verbs are action verbs.

> **Many people heard about the new invention.**

state-of-being verb   Verbs that state that someone or something exists are called state-of-being verbs. The most common state-of-being verbs are forms of the verb *be*: *am*, *is*, *are*, *was*, *were*, *being*, and *been*.

> **Baseball games and election results were the first broadcasts.**

helping verb and main verb   When a verb is more than one word, the most important word is the main verb. Any verb that is not the main verb is the helping verb. A helping verb works with the main verb to express action or being.

> (helping) (main)
> **Television has transformed the communication industry.**

Helping Verbs							
am	were	have	could	shall	may	was	did
is	be	has	do	should	might	been	would
are	being	had	does	will	must	can	

verb phrase   A verb phrase is made up of a main verb and one or more helping verbs.

> **By 1950 the number of TV sets had soared to six million.**

active voice   A verb is in the active voice when the subject performs the action.

> The fierce shark <u>intimidated</u> the small cowfish.

passive voice   A verb is in the passive voice when the subject receives the action.

> The small cowfish <u>was intimidated</u> by the fierce shark.

▶ verbal   A verbal is a verb form used as a different part of speech. The three kinds of verbals are **participles**, **gerunds**, and **infinitives**.

participle   A participle is a verb form used as an adjective. It usually ends in *ed* or *ing*.

> Waving *flags* inspire the patriotism of a nation's citizens.

gerund   A gerund is a verb form ending in *ing* that is used as a noun.

> The <u>using</u> of flags began in Greece. (subject)
> Europeans began the <u>designing</u> of flags in the Middle Ages. (direct object)

infinitive   An infinitive is the word *to* plus the basic form of a verb. It can be used as a noun, an adjective, or an adverb.

> <u>To survive</u> was the early farmer's goal. (noun)
> They worked <u>to tame</u> wild animals. (adverb)
> Livestock gave people food <u>to eat</u>. (adjective)

linking verb   A linking verb connects the subject with a word or words in the predicate.

> *Radio* <u>remained</u> the major *source* of entertainment for years.

Forms of *Be*	Other Linking Verbs
am, is, are, was, were, being, been	appear, become, feel, grow, look, remain, seem, smell, sound, stay, taste, turn

predicate nominative   A predicate nominative is a noun or pronoun that follows a linking verb and renames or identifies the subject of the sentence.

> *Tourism* is an important <u>business</u>.

predicate adjective   A predicate adjective follows a linking verb and describes the subject of the sentence.

> This *author* is quite <u>creative</u>.

transitive verb   A verb that has a direct object to complete its meaning is a transitive verb.

> Her books <u>entertain</u> *readers*.

intransitive verb   A verb that has no direct object is an intransitive verb. A linking verb is always intransitive.

> She also <u>writes</u> very clearly.

principal parts   The principal parts of a verb are its basic forms. They are the present, the past, the past participle, and the present participle.

Present	Past	Past Participle	Present Participle
sail	sailed	(have) sailed	(are) sailing

tense   The tense of a verb shows time.

present tense   The present tense expresses an action taking place now.

> Coral reefs <u>form</u> from tiny animals.

past tense   The past tense expresses an action that took place in the past.

> Many reefs <u>formed</u> off the Florida coast.

future tense   The future tense expresses an action that will occur in the future. It is formed by adding the helping verb *will* or *shall* to the present.

> More coral reefs <u>will form</u> in time.

present perfect tense   The present perfect tense expresses an action that occurred at an indefinite time in the past and may still be going on. It is formed with the helping verb *have* or *has* and the past participle of the main verb.

> Many reefs <u>have formed</u> over hundreds of years.

past perfect tense   The past perfect tense expresses an action that happened before another past action. It is formed with the helping verb *had* and the past participle.

> This coral reef <u>had formed</u> long before divers came here.

future perfect tense   The future perfect tense expresses an action that will be finished before a stated time in the future. It is formed with *will have* or *shall have* and the past participle.

> Before long, another reef <u>will have formed</u> across the bay.

regular verb   Most verbs are regular verbs. Their past and past participles are the same and are formed by adding *-ed* to the present. The present participle is formed by adding *-ing* to the present.

> **jump**   **jumped**   **(have) jumped**   **(are) jumping**

♦ Some regular verbs require spelling changes when *-ed* and *-ing* are added to the present.

> | dive | dived | have dived | are diving |
> |------|-------|------------|------------|
> | deny | denied | have denied | are denying |
> | clap | clapped | have clapped | are clapping |

irregular verb   An irregular verb does not form its past and past participle by adding *-ed*. Some irregular verbs follow patterns when forming their principal parts; others do not.

♦ Some irregular verbs form the past participle by adding *-en* to the past.

Present	Past	Past Participle	Present Participle
break	broke	(have) broken	(are) breaking
choose	chose	(have) chosen	(are) choosing

♦ Some have the same present and past participle.

come	came	(have) come	(are) coming
run	ran	(have) run	(are) running

♦ Some have the same past and past participle.

bring	brought	(have) brought	(are) bringin
feel	felt	(have) felt	(are) feelin

♦ Some have the same present, past, and past part

burst	burst	(have) burst	(are) b
cost	cost	(have) cost	(are)

Glossary of Usage

Conjugation of the Verb *Be*

Principal Parts: be, was, (have) been, being

Present	Past	Future
I am	was	will (shall) be
she, he, it is	was	will be
we are	were	will (shall) be
you, they are	were	will be

Present Perfect	Past Perfect	Future Perfect
I, we have been	had been	will (shall) have been
she, he, it has been	had been	will have been
you, they have been	had been	will have been

Conjugation of the Verb *Have*

Principal Parts: have, had, (have) had, having

Present	Past	Future
I, we have	had	will (shall) have
you, they have	had	will have
she, he, it has	had	will have

Present Perfect	Past Perfect	Future Perfect
I, we have had	had had	will (shall) have had
you, they have had	had had	will have had
she, he, it has had	had had	will have had

Conjugation of the Verb *Do*

Principal Parts: do, did, (have) done, doing

Present	Past	Future
I, we do	did	will (shall) do
you, they do	did	will do
she, he, it does	did	will do

Present Perfect	Past Perfect	Future Perfect
I, we have done	had done	will (shall) have done
you, they have done	had done	will have done
she, he, it has done	had done	will have done

Usage Problems

a	An indefinite article used before a word beginning with a consonant sound We need <u>a</u> vacation. It is <u>a</u> hot day.
an	An indefinite article used before a word beginning with a vowel sound We saw <u>an</u> eagle. The bus leaves in <u>an</u> hour.
accept	A verb that means "to receive" or "to agree to" Who will <u>accept</u> the award?
except	As a preposition, means "excluding" or "but" Everyone <u>except</u> Meg can come.
ain't	Avoid this word in your speaking and writing; it is not standard English.
at	Indicates presence in a place We were <u>at</u> a meeting.
to	Indicates motion toward a place We went <u>to</u> a meeting.
bad	An adjective used to modify a noun or a pronoun It was a <u>bad</u> road. We felt <u>bad</u> about losing.
badly	An adverb used to modify a verb This area needs rain <u>badly</u>.
beside	A preposition that means "next to" or "at the side of" Put the package <u>beside</u> the stairs.
besides	As a preposition, means "in addition to" <u>Besides</u> soccer, Tim also plays baseball.
between	Used in discussing two people or things Divide the work <u>between</u> her and him.
among	Used in discussing three or more Divide it <u>among</u> all the students.

bring	Means "to lead or carry toward the speaker"
	<u>Bring</u> the book here.
take	Means "to lead or carry away from the speaker"
	<u>Take</u> your coat with you when you go.
different from	*Different from* is generally preferred over *different than*.
	Your answers are <u>different from</u> mine.
fewer	Refers to number; means "not as many"
	This bus holds <u>fewer</u> people than that one.
less	Refers to size or degree; means "not as much"
	We spent <u>less</u> time traveling this year.
good	An adjective used to modify a noun or a pronoun
	The report is <u>good</u>. She is a <u>good</u> student.
well	An adverb used to modify a verb
	He writes <u>well</u>.
	An adjective when it refers to a person's health
	I do not feel <u>well</u> today.
hisself, theirselves	Do not use these forms in your speaking and writing; they are incorrect. Use *himself* or *themselves*.
	Sam taught <u>himself</u> to skate. (Not *hisself*)
in	Indicates location within one place
	We played football <u>in</u> the park.
into	Indicates motion or change of location
	The ball fell <u>into</u> the lake.
its	Possessive form of the pronoun *it*
	The tree has lost <u>its</u> leaves.
it's	Contraction of *it is* and *it has*
	<u>It's</u> time to begin the race.

learn	Means "to gain understanding"
	Our dog <u>learns</u> tricks quickly.
teach	Means "to instruct"
	Ms. Ellis will <u>teach</u> us to use the computer.
let	Means "to permit"
	Please <u>let</u> me borrow your pen.
leave	Means "to place," "to go away from," or "to allow to remain"
	<u>Leave</u> the book on the shelf.
	We must <u>leave</u> the party early.
lie	Means "to rest" or "to recline"
	Don't <u>lie</u> in the sun too long.
lay	Means "to put something down" or "to place"
	<u>Lay</u> your report on the desk.
rise	Means "to get up" or "to go up"
	Because of the drought, food prices will <u>rise</u>.
raise	Means "to lift" or "to move something higher"
	<u>Raise</u> your hand if you can help.
shall, will	For the future and future perfect tenses, *shall* was once preferred with the first person (I <u>shall</u> go) and *will* was used with the second person and third person (you, they <u>will</u> go). Today this distinction is not usually made, and *will* is acceptable with the first person also.
	I <u>will</u> ride my bike to school tomorrow.
sit	Means "to move into a seat" or "to be in a place"
	Dad likes to <u>sit</u> in that chair.
set	Means "to put or place something"
	<u>Set</u> the plant in the sun.

than	A conjunction often used when making comparisons
	She ran faster <u>than</u> I did.
then	An adverb that tells when
	Alan read the book; <u>then</u> he saw the movie.
this here, that there	Do not include the *here* and *there*; they are unnecessary
	<u>This</u> story is my favorite. (Not *this here* story)
their	Possessive form of the pronoun *they*
	They left <u>their</u> bikes by the fence.
there	An adverb that tells where
	Please put the papers <u>there</u>.
	A word used to begin a sentence in which the verb comes before the subject
	<u>There</u> is a call for you.
they're	Contraction of *they are*
	<u>They're</u> going to the concert.
theirs	A possessive pronoun that can stand alone
	Our dog is not as old as <u>theirs</u>.
there's	Contraction of *there is* and *there has*
	<u>There's</u> plenty of food for everyone.
to	A preposition that means "toward"
	We walked <u>to</u> the beach after dinner.
	A word used to begin an infinitive
	They were anxious <u>to</u> leave.
too	An adverb that means "also"
	Will she come <u>too</u>?
	An adverb that means "very" or "excessively"
	This title is <u>too</u> long.
two	The number between one and three
	The race is <u>two</u> miles long.

try and, try to	*Try and* is often used in informal English; however, *try to* is preferred, especially in formal English. Try to be here by noon. (not *try and*)
use (to), used (to)	Do not omit the *-d*; *used* is a past form, used with an infinitive. Margaret used *to live* in New Jersey. (Not *use to*)
whose	Possessive form of the pronoun *who* Do you know whose book this is?
who's	Contraction of *who is* and *who has* Do you know who's at the door?
your	Possessive form of the pronoun *you* Bring your friends with you.
you're	Contraction of *you are* You're late for the meeting.

Writing and Computers

Along with an imagination, the best friend a writer can have is a computer. It's easy and fun to prewrite, write, revise, and proofread a piece of writing on a word processor. Then, when you've made all the changes, it takes only a few minutes to print a final copy.

Monitor · Keyboard · Modem · Printout · Printer · Mouse

Catch the Computer Bug

If you've never used a computer, you may feel just the way a lot of people feel. You may feel nervous or even a little scared. Many people think that computers are difficult and complicated. Some even think that computers are smart! But a computer is just a machine. The only trick you need to know is how to tell it what to do. You need to know how to put your writing into it. Then you need to know how to give it commands so that the computer can help you do your revising and proofreading tasks.

Every computer is slightly different. But each comes with a manual, or handbook, that tells you how to give the commands. Use the manual for help. This list of computer terms, and the chart of computer commands that follows it, will help you understand the directions in your manual.

Computer Terms

Address: numbers or words that label a document or file to show where it is located on the computer's permanent storage.

Backup: a copy of a document that is made to protect the original. The backup is often stored on a floppy disk.

Character: a single letter, numeral, or space. The word *dog* has three characters; so does the number *134*.

Command: an order, such as PRINT or SAVE, that the user gives to the computer.

Computer program: a list or system of instructions that tells the computer what to do; software.

Cursor: the blinking line or square on the screen that shows where the next typed character will appear.

Disk: a magnetic object on which information is stored (See *floppy disk* and *hard disk*).

Document: one or more pages of written material, such as a short story, a report, an essay, or a poem.

Edit: to change what you type into the computer; to revise.

Floppy disk: a small plastic disk used to save and store documents. Sometimes this is called a diskette.

Floppy Disk

Font: any one of various styles of letters that a computer is equipped to use in order to print output.

Format: to prepare a blank floppy disk for use (also called *initialize*).

Function: an operation that the computer does on command, such as SAVE, DELETE, or REPLACE.

Function key: a key that is pushed to tell the computer to do a certain function, such as CUT.

Hard copy: text that is printed out from the computer onto paper.

Hard disk: an internal section of the computer where information is kept in permanent storage. This differs from memory, which is temporary storage of information that is being used at the moment.

Hardware: the machine, including the monitor, computer, and keyboard.

Input: information, including text, numbers, and so on, that the user types into the computer.

Keyboard: part of the computer used to input information. Resembles a typewriter keyboard.

Load: to transfer information from an information storage device, such as a disk, into a computer's memory.

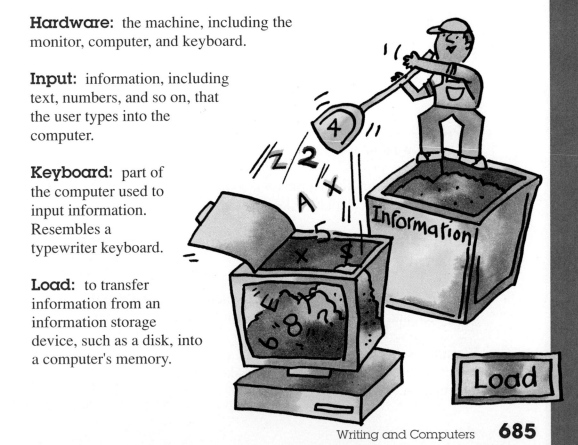

Memory: the part of the computer where programs and text are temporarily stored while they are in active use.

Menu: a list of functions. The user opens the menu, selects a function, and tells the computer to do it.

Modem: the device that allows computers to communicate over telephone lines.

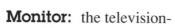

Monitor: the television-like screen on which input and output can be viewed.

Output: text that the computer displays, on the screen or in hard copy.

Printer: the device that prints output in hard copy.

Printout: a copy of your writing made by the printer.

Program: a disk that contains a group of instructions that tells the computer what to do.

Software: programs that run on a computer to allow it to do word processing, math calculations, and so on.

System: the combination of hardware and software that allows the computer to work.

Terminal: includes the keyboard, which loads input into the computer, and the monitor, where output is viewed.

Virus: a set of instructions, hidden in a computer system, that leaves copies of itself in other programs or disks and can erase stored information.

Computer Commands

Cut ▶ Tells the computer to take out, or "cut," a highlighted piece of text.

Delete ▶ Tells the computer to back up one space with the cursor and to remove the character in that space.

Find ▶ Tells the computer to find a certain word within the text.

New ▶ Tells the computer to open a new, blank page so that the user can begin a new document.

Open (or Load) ▶ Tells the computer to open a certain document, identified by its address (or file name).

Paste ▶ Tells the computer to insert a word or group of words in a certain place in the document.

Print ▶ Tells the computer to print out the document in hard copy.

Quit ▶ Tells the computer to close a document.

Return ▶ Tells the computer to move the cursor to the next line of text.

Save ▶ Tells the computer to save a document by putting it into permanent storage.

Shift ▶ Tells the computer to use a capital letter.

Tab ▶ Tells the computer to indent a line of text, as for a paragraph indent.

The Key to Typing

The hardest part of writing on a computer can be learning how to type. The first step is learning which fingers hit which keys. Use the finger diagram below to practice typing "The quick brown fox jumped over the lazy dog." Make sure your fingers are curved and that your hands are parallel to the keyboard. It may be slow going at first, but with practice you'll soon be typing like a pro.

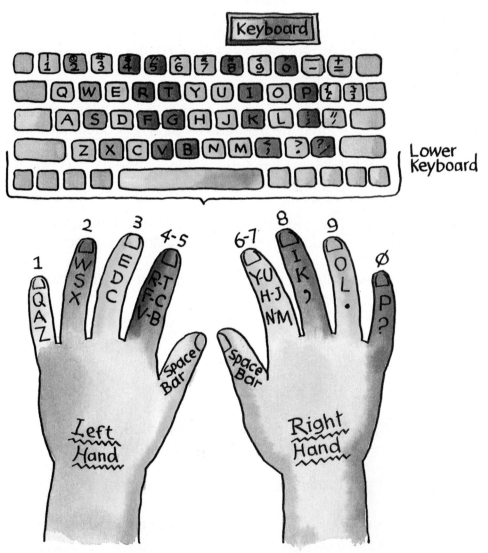

Word Processing

Writing with a computer can make it easier to

- choose topics to write about
- discover your ideas
- organize your ideas
- write your first draft
- revise your writing
- correct your mistakes
- share your writing with others

A word processing program makes the writing process more efficient. The program you use will tell you how to use the computer to enter, save, edit, and print your work. Check your software manual for special features that will help you write. Some programs can catch spelling errors. Others have drawing features (called graphics) that you can use to add pictures or borders to your pages.

Word processing programs cannot do the following things:

- think
- get ideas
- choose the best words
- organize your work
- spell words as you write
- punctuate correctly

You are still in charge of the writing, and you still need to use all of your language skills.

Ready, Set, Write!

Now you are ready to prewrite, write a first draft, revise, and proofread a piece of writing. Follow these steps.

Create a File and First Draft A file is a group of related documents. In a cardboard file folder, you might keep such related papers as prewriting ideas, a first draft, revision, and final copy of a story. A computer can also keep a file for you, but your documents will be stored in computer memory, not on paper. To begin a file:

- ◆ Tell the computer to open a new document.
- ◆ Give the document an address, or name. Some computers ask you to label a document with words; others, with a series of numbers or letters. For example, you might use *SHORTSTOR.DR1*, meaning "short story, draft 1."
- ◆ Now set your margins, font size, and spacing format. (Most papers should be typed double-spaced.)
- ◆ Type a list of ideas, words that describe your topic, or questions about your topic.
- ◆ Type your first draft. Tell the computer to SAVE your work.
- ◆ When your document is complete, follow the directions in your manual for creating a file. Give it an address, or name, such as *SHORTSTOR.FILE*. Put your draft in the file. Take a break! Then begin to revise.

Revise and Proofread Your Draft Now the fun begins! You'll have no more messy papers with arrows, cross-outs, and scribbles in the margins when you revise on a computer. You do the thinking; let the computer do the work! To begin revising:

- ◆ Make a computer document copy of your first draft.
- ◆ Label the new document *short story revision* or *SHORTSTOR.REV*. Save your original draft for reference. Use the new copy for revisions.
- ◆ Move the cursor to a place that needs revision. Give the computer a command. For example, you might tell it to CUT a sentence, move it to another place in your paper, and PASTE the sentence in.
- ◆ Check your writing for errors and correct them.

Make a copy of your document. Decide how to share your writing.

Index

Abbreviations
usage, 248–249
Action verbs, 118–119, 124–125, 162, 165
Addresses
in business letters, 611, 612
on envelopes, 612
in friendly letters, 609, 612
Adjectives
and adverbs, 358–359
articles, 294–295, 336, 341
comparative, 298–300, 336, 345–346
definition of, 6–7, 294–295
degrees of comparison, 298–300, 341, 345
demonstrative, 296–297, 336, 341, 344, 345
infinitives as, 460–461
nouns used as, 301, 336, 341, 347
overused, 305
participles as, 460–461
phrases, 407–409
predicate, 128–129
prepositional phrases as, 407–409
pronouns used as, 301, 336, 341, 347
proper, 296–297, 336, 340, 344–345
review of, 6–7, 343, 547
sentence combining with, 418–419
superlative, 298–300, 336, 345–346
using, in writing, 294–295, 297, 300, 301,
304–305
Adverb phrases, 407–409
Adverbs
and adjectives, 358–359, 394, 400
comparative, 354–355, 394, 398, 450
definition of, 6–7, 350–353
degrees of comparison, 354–355
infinitives as, 460–461
with -ly, 350–353, 358–359, 400
overused, 364–365
and prepositions, 404–406
prepositional phrases as, 407–409, 526–527
review of, 6–7, 394, 397–398, 547
sentence combining with, 418–419
superlative, 354–355, 394, 398, 450
using, in writing, 350–353, 355, 364–365
Agreement
with compound subjects, 522–523
with indefinite pronouns, 242–243
in inverted sentences, 520–521, 526–527
pronoun–antecedent, 234–235
subject-verb, 514–515, 516–517, 518–519,
520–523, 526–527, 544, 554–555
Alliteration, 525
Almanac, 568

Among, between, 410–411
Analogies, 559
Anne Frank: The Diary of a Young Girl, translated
by B. M. Mooyaart, 26–31
Antecedents of pronouns, 234–235
Antonyms, 20–21. *See also* Thesaurus
Apollinaire, Guillaume, from "Les Sapins," 430
Apostrophes
in contractions, 236–237, 516–517, 646–647
in possessive nouns, 64–65, 646–647
Article
definite, 294–295
indefinite, 294–295
Asking Questions, 212. *See also* Prewriting
strategies.
At, to, 410–411
Atlas, 567
Audience for writing, Introduction 4, 34–35,
36–37, 96, 152, 210, 272, 326, 384, 436, 494
definition of, 34–35, 36–37, 96

Ballads, 432–433
Be
agreement with subject, 516–517, 520–521, 522–523
conjugation of, 516–517, 552
as helping verbs, 120–121, 174–175
as linking verbs, 122–123, 128–129
as main verbs, 118–119, 120–121, 122–123
Beside, besides, 410–411
Between, among, 410–411
Bibliographies, 41, 105, 161, 219, 281, 335, 392,
445, 503, 543
writing, for reports, 488–491
Black Pearl, The, by Scott O'Dell, 196–201
Books
bibliographies, 41, 105, 161, 219, 281, 335, 392,
445, 503, 543
parts of, 560–561
reference, 484–485
titles of
capitalization of, 488–491, 624–625
underlining, 488–491, 642–643
See also Library.
Books to Enjoy, 41, 105, 161, 219, 281, 335, 393,
445, 503, 543
Book reports, 41, 105, 161, 219, 281, 335, 393, 445,
503, 543, 608
Book Review of *M. C. Higgins, the Great*, by Nikki
Giovanni, 138–141
Brainstorming, 274. *See also* Prewriting strategies.
Brand Names, 130–131
Bread-and-butter note, 610
British English, 249

Brooklyn Bridge: They Said It Couldn't Be Built, The, by Judith St. George, 256–261
Business letters, 611–612

Caney, Steven, "Jug Bands," from *Kids' America*, 74–79
"Cap and the Bells, The," by William Butler Yeats, 432
Capitalization
　of abbreviations, 616–617
　in direct quotations, 204–205, 622–623
　of first word of sentence, 4–5, 622–623
　of geographical names, 618–619
　of names, 616–617, 618–619, 620–621
　in poetry, 622–623
　proofreading mark for, 102, 158, 216, 278, 332, 390, 442, 500
　of proper adjectives, 296–297, 622–623
　of proper nouns, 58–59, 616–617
　of religious terms, 624–625
　review of, 616–617, 618–619, 620–621, 622–623, 624–625
　in salutations and closings, 622–623
　of titles for people, 624–625
　of titles of written works, movies, works of art, 488–491, 624–625
Card catalog, 562–565
Carroll, Lewis, "Jabberwocky," 424–427
Character, 270–271, 378–379, 382–383, 538–539
Character Sketch, 264–265
Choosing and Narrowing Topics, Strategies for
　interview partner to discover hidden favorites, 97
　listing actions you've seen animals perform, 437
　listing everything you know how to do, 97
　listing firsts in interesting professional fields, 495
　listing meaningful shows you've seen, 153
　listing story types and plots, 385
　listing your favorite places, 327
　make a list of people you admire, 273
　recalling memorable events, 211
　talk about it
　　with classmates, 153, 327, 437
　　with a partner, 97, 211, 273, 385, 437
　think about it, 97, 153, 211, 273, 327, 385, 437, 495
　visualize, 327
Choppy Sentences. *See* Revising sentences.
Classifying, A Strategy for, 254–255
Classifying, Writing Process, 272–279
Clauses
　definition of, 462–463
　distinguishing from phrases, 462–463, 504
　independent, 462–463, 464–465, 504
　subordinate, 462–465, 470–471, 504
Clichés, 130–131
Climactic order in paragraphs, 88–91

Clincher sentences of paragraphs, 82–83
Clipped Words, 67
Cluster Map, 137, 141, 154, 423, 427, 438. *See also* Thinking Strategies.
Coherence of paragraphs, 92–93
Collective nouns, 189, 518–519
Collective Words, 189
Colons, 644–645
Commands. *See* Sentences; Imperative sentences.
Commas
　in addresses, 612
　in compound sentences, 16–17, 22–23, 464–465, 630–631
　in dates, 636–637
　after interjections, 414–415, 634–635
　after introductory words, 634–635
　with letter parts, 636–637
　proofreading mark for, 102, 158, 216, 278, 332, 390, 442, 500
　in quotations, 640–641
　in a series, 630–631
　to set off appositives, 632–633
　to set off complex sentences, 464–465
　to set off interrupters, 634–635
　to set off nouns of direct address, 632–633
Common Nouns, 58–59
Compare/Contrast, 254–255, 261, 266–267, 274, 283, 308–309, 315. *See also* Thinking skills.
Comparison
　of adjectives, 298–300
　of adverbs, 354–355
Comparison and contrast paragraph/essay, 266–267, 272–279
Complex sentences, 464–465, 505, 511
　using, in writing, 464–465
Composition 40, 444. *See also* Writing.
Compound objects, 404–406
Compound predicate, 14–15. *See also* Compound verbs.
Compound sentences, 16–17, 464–465, 505
Compound subject, 14–15
Compound verbs, 14–15, 522–523
Compounds, 66–67
Computers, 562–565, 683–690
Conclusion paragraph, 488–491, 608
Conference, A, 98. *See also* Prewriting strategies.
Conjugation, 176–179
Conjunctions
　in compound objects, 412–413
　in compound predicates, 14–15, 412–413
　in compound sentences, 22–23, 412–413, 418–419
　in compound subjects, 14–15, 412–413, 522–523
　coordinating, 412–413, 446, 451, 456, 522–523
　correlative, 412–413, 446, 451, 456
　definition of, 6–7, 412–413
　review of, 6–7, 456, 547
　subordinating, 462–463, 464–465, 470–471
　using, in writing, 412–413, 456, 470–471

Connections
between grammar and writing, *See* Grammar and Writing Connection.
between reading and writing, *See* Reading and Writing Connection.
Connotation, 524–525, 545
Context Clues, 302–303, 337
Contractions, 236–237, 248–249, 516–517
Conversations, 204–205, 415, 382–383, 395
Cooperative Learning, 22–23, 38–39, 68–69, 94–95, 132–133, 150–151, 190–191, 208–209, 250–251, 270–271, 304–305, 324–325, 364–365, 382 383, 418–419, 434–435, 470–471, 492–493, 526–527, 540–541
Coordinating conjunctions, 412–413, 446
Correlative conjunctions, 412–413, 446
Creating, A Strategy for, 422–423
Creating, Writing Process, 436–443
Creative Thinking. *See* Thinking Strategies.
Creative Writing, 25, 71, 135, 193, 253, 307, 367, 421, 473, 529
Critical Thinking. *See* Thinking Strategies.
Curriculum Connection, 40, 104, 160, 218, 280, 334, 392, 444, 502, 542

Dates,
commas in, 636–637
Declarative sentences, 4–5, 42
Definite article, 294–295
Demonstrative adjectives, 296–297
Demonstrative pronouns, 238–239, 296–297
Denotation, 524–525, 545
Describing, A Strategy for, 308–309
Describing, Writing Process, 326–333
Description
details for, 318–319, 322–323, 430–431
using adjectives for, 318–319
using figurative language, 430–431
words for the senses, 318–319, 430–431
writing, 326–333
Details
in descriptive paragraphs, 318–319, 322–323
in poems, 430–431
sensory, 318–319, 337, 430–431
in supporting sentences, 322–323, 484–485
using, in writing, 318–319, 322–323, 430–431
Dewey decimal system, 563
Diagraming, 648–656
Dialogue
in literature, 382–383
punctuation of, 204–205, 640–641
writing, 204–205, 221, 382–383, 415
Dickinson, Emily, untitled poem, 424–427
Dictionary, 572–575. *See also* Thesaurus.

Dictionary of Knowledge, 576–587
using the, 7, 37, 61, 93, 127, 145, 183, 207, 241, 269, 300, 319, 359, 379, 409, 463, 491, 521
Direct objects, 124–125, 126–127, 339, 449
Directions
giving, 80–81
listening to, 80–81
Do
agreement of, with subject, 516–517
conjugation of, 516–517, 552
Double negatives, avoiding, 356–357

Editing. *See* Proofreading; Revising.
"Eight Puppies," by Gabriela Mistral, 425–426
Elaborating, 141, 422–423. *See also* Thinking Skills.
Encyclopedias, 566
End marks, 4–5, 628–629
English, history of, 67, 249, 303, 363
Entry words. *See* Dictionary; Thesaurus.
Envelopes, addresses on, 612
Essay, 272–279
Etymology, 67
Evaluating media, 152–159
Exclamation marks
as end marks, 4–5, 628–629
after interjections, 414–415
Exclamatory sentences, 4–5, 42

Fact and opinion, 150–151, 163
Fiction
The Black Pearl, by Scott O'Dell, 196–201
The Yearling, by Marjorie Kinnan Rawlings, 310–315
Figurative language, 320–321, 337, 430–431
Fine Art, 24–25, 70–71, 134–135, 192–193, 252–253, 306–307, 366–367, 420–421, 472–473, 528–529
First draft, sample, 99, 155, 213, 275, 329, 387, 439, 497
First-person point of view, 208–209
First Thoughts, 438. *See also* Prewriting strategies.
Folktale
"Tiger Story, Anansi Story," retold by Philip Sherlock, 530–535
Folktale, elements of, 538–539
Form in poetry, 436–443
Form for writing, 36–37
Formal language, 248–249, 283
Friendly Letters, 609, 612
Future tense. *See* Verbs, future tense.
Future perfect tense. *See* Verbs, future perfect tense.

Gender, agreement of pronouns, 234-235
Gerunds, 460-461
Giovanni, Nikki, Book Review of *M.C. Higgins, the Great*, 138-141
Glossary, 677-682
Goal/Plan/Outcome Chart, 72-73, 79, 98, 474-475, 479, 496. *See also* Thinking Strategies.
Good, well, 360-361
Grammar and Writing Connection
  How to Combine Sentence Parts, 22-23
  How to Combine Sentences, 418-419, 470-471, 526-527
  How to Expand Sentences with Adjectives, 304-305
  How to Expand Sentences with Adverbs, 364-365
  How to Revise Sentences with Nouns, 68-69
  How to Revise Sentences with Pronouns, 250-251
  How to Revise Sentences with Verbs, 132-133, 190-191
  See also Revising sentences.
Grammar Checks
  avoid confusion with adverbs and adjectives, 389
  correcting run-on sentences with complex sentences, 499
  using clear antecedents of pronouns, 277
  using prepositional phrases to add details, 441
  using specific nouns, 101
  using specific and varied verbs, 215
  using verbs in the active voice, 157
  using vivid adjectives, 331
Grammar Handbook, 657-676

Handwriting. *See* Proofreading Checklist.
Have
  agreement with subject, 516–517, 552
  conjugation of, 516–517, 552
Health. *See* Writing across the curriculum.
Heine, Heinrich, "A Pine Tree Towers Lonely," 434
Helping verbs. *See* Verbs, helping.
Hengesbach, Alice, "Tribute to an Inventor: Cyrus McCormick," 476–479
"Heron, The," by Theodore Roethke, 425
History of English, 67, 249, 303, 363
Homographs, 468–469, 505
Homophones, 468–469, 505
How-to Article, writing, 96–103

Idioms, 130–131
Imagining, A Strategy for, 368–369
Imagining, Writing Process, 384–391
Imperative Sentences, 4–5, 12–13, 42
In, into, 410–411

Indefinite articles, 294–295
Indefinite pronouns, 242–243
  agreement with verbs, 520–521, 522–523
Indenting, 82–83
  proofreading mark for, 102, 158, 216, 278, 332, 390, 442, 500
Independent clauses, 462–463
Indirect objects, 126–127, 163, 339, 449
Infinitives, 460–461
Informal language, 248–249, 283
Informing, A Strategy for, 72–73
Informing, Writing Process, 96–103
Intensive pronouns, 240–241
Interjections, 414–415, 447, 451, 457
  definition of, 6–7, 414–415
Interrogative pronouns, 238–239
Interrogative sentences, 4–5, 42
Interviewing, 482–483
Intransitive verbs, 124–125, 162, 169
Introduction paragraph, 488–491, 608
Inverted word order in sentences 12–13, 526–527
Invitations 610
Irregular verbs. *See* Verbs, irregular.
Italics 642–643
Its, it's, 236–237

"Jabberwocky," by Lewis Carroll, 426
Journal, writing in a, Introduction 2, 3, 5, 11, 23, 38–41, 55, 57, 69, 104–105, 117, 119, 133, 160–161, 173, 175, 191, 206–207, 218–219, 221, 231, 233, 251, 280–281, 293, 295, 305, 334–335, 349, 353, 365, 392–393, 403, 406, 419, 444, 459, 461, 471, 502, 513, 515, 527, 542
"Jug Bands," from *Kids' America*, by Steven Caney, 74–79

Language Corner, 20–21, 66–67, 130–131, 188–189, 248–249, 302–303, 362–363, 416–417, 468–469, 524–525
Lay, lie, 186–187
"Les Sapins," from, by Guillaume Apollinaire, 430
Letter
  addressing envelopes for, 612
  business, 611, 612
  friendly, 609, 612
  of opinion, 147
  social notes, 610
Library, using a, 562–565
Linking verbs. *See* Verbs, linking.
Listening
  active, 80–81, 202–203, 428–429
  carefully, 32–33

closely, 80–81, 316–317, 428–429, 480–481
critical, 32–33, 142–145, 262–263
anticipating ending, 480–481
asking questions, 80–81, 316–317, 376–377
for details, main idea, 316–317, 536–537
in a discussion, 32–33, 262–263
to directions, 80–81
eye contact, 80–81, 376–377
for fact and opinion, 142–145, 262–263
giving others time, 262–263
to learn, 80–81
maintaining polite attention, 32–33, 80–81, 202–203, 262–263, 376–377, 480–481, 536–537
to poetry, 428–429
recognizing propaganda techniques, 142–145
repeat order of directions to yourself, 80–81
as a response to literature, 31, 79, 141, 201, 261, 262–263, 315, 375, 427, 479, 535
for sensible progressions, 142–145, 202–203, 428–429
and sharing opinions, 32–33, 262–263
to take notes, 480–481
on the telephone, 376–377
visualizing, 316–317
to your writing, 100, 156, 214, 276, 330, 388, 440, 498
See also Cooperative Learning; Partner, working with a; Peer Conferencing; Speaking; Speaking and Listening; Working Together.

Literature
bibliographies, 41, 105, 161, 219, 281, 335, 393, 445, 503, 543, 488–491
character, setting, plot in, 270–271, 378–379, 382–383, 538–539
clarity in, 94–95
descriptive details in, 318–319, 322–323, 430–431
dialogue in, 204–205, 382–383
listening as a response to, 31, 79, 141, 201, 261, 315, 375, 427, 479, 535
mood in, 324–325
narrative voice in, 434–435
point of view in, 208–209, 380–381
space order in, 322–323
speaking as a response to, 31, 79, 141, 201, 261, 315, 375, 427, 479, 535
thinking skills related to, 31, 79, 141, 201, 261, 315, 375, 427, 479, 535
writer's voice in, 38–39
writing as a response to, 31, 79, 141, 201, 261, 315, 375, 427, 479, 535
See also Fiction; Nonfiction; Poems; Stories; Thinking Skills; Thinking Strategies.

Literature in Your World, Introduction I

Lower–case letters,
proofreading mark for, 102, 158, 216, 278, 332, 390, 442, 500

Main idea
listening for, 536–537
in notes, 484–485, 486–487
of an outline, 570–571
of paragraph, 82–83, 84–85, 86–87, 92–93, 148–149, 492–493
Main verbs. *See* Verbs, main.
Mass Media
evaluating, 152–159
reviewing, 152–159
viewing television critically, 142–145, 152–159
Mechanics, 616–647. *See also* Capitalization; Punctuation.
Media review, 152–159
Mental Movie, A, 328. *See also* Prewriting strategies.
Metacognition, 40, 73, 104, 137, 160, 195, 218, 255, 280, 309, 334, 369, 392, 423, 444, 475, 502, 542
Metaphors, 320–321, 337, 430–431
Mistral, Gabriela, "Eight Puppies," 424–427
Mood, 324–325
Mooyaart, B. M., translator, *Anne Frank: The Diary of a Young Girl*, 26–31

Narrating, A Strategy for, 194–195
Narrating, Writing Process, 210–217
Narrative personal, 210–217
Narrative voice in poetry, 434–435
Negative words, 356–357, 399
Neruda, Pablo, from "To the foot from its child," 431
Nonfiction
Anne Frank: The Diary of a Young Girl, translated by B. M. Mooyaart, 26–31
Book Review of *M. C. Higgins, the Great*, by Nikki Giovanni, 138–141
The Brooklyn Bridge: They Said It Couldn't Be Built, by Judith St. George, 256–261
"Jug Bands," from *Kids' America*, by Steven Caney, 74–79
"Tribute to an Inventor: Cyrus McCormick," by Alice Hengesbach, 476–479
Note taking, 484–485
Nouns
collective, 189, 518–519, 553
common, 58–59, 106, 109, 112, 448
compound, 66–67
definition of, 6–7, 56–57
of direct address, 632–633
gerunds, 460–461
infinitives as, 460–461
letters and numerals as, 626–627
plural, 56–57, 60–61, 62–63, 109, 113, 518–519

possessive, 64–65, 109, 115
  apostrophes in, 64–65, 646–647
as predicate nominatives, 128–129
proper, 58–59, 106, 109, 112
  capitalization of, 58–59, 616–625
review of, 6–7, 222, 546
as simple subjects, 10–11
singular, 56–57, 222, 518–519
spelling of, 60–61, 62–63, 114
using, as adjectives, 6–7, 301
using, in writing, 56–57, 59, 61, 63, 65
Number, agreement
  of collective nouns, 518–519
  of pronouns, 234–235, 242–243, 514–515
  of verbs, 514–515, 520–521

Object
  compound, 404–406
  direct, 124–125, 126–127
  indirect, 126–127
  of prepositions, 404–406
Object pronouns, 244–245, 246–247
  in prepositional phrases, 407–409
O'Dell, Scott, *The Black Pearl*, 196–201
Onomatopoeia, 469
"Open Window, The," by Saki, 370–375
Opinion
  fact and, 142–143, 150–151, 163
  letter of, 146–147
Oral Language. *See* Speaking; Listening; Speaking
    and Listening.
Order. *See* Order of importance; Time order; Space
    order; Word order.
Order of importance, 88–91, 148–149
Order of impression, 322–323
Organizational patterns for paragraphs
  climactic order, 88–91
  order of importance, 88–91
  order of impression, 322–323
  space order, 88–91, 322–323
  time order, 88–91, 94–95
Outlining, 570–571
Oxymorons, 417

Paragraphs
  choosing and narrowing topics for, 492–493
    See also Choosing and narrowing topics,
      strategies for.
  clincher sentences of, 82–83
  coherence, 92–93
  comparison/contrast, 266–267, 283

definition of, 82–83
descriptive, 322–323
developing
  by examples, 86–87
  by facts, 84–85
  by reasons, 148–149
explanatory, 86–87
indenting, 82–83
main idea in, 82–83, 84–85, 86–87, 148–149,
    492–493
order of ideas in, 88–91, 148–149, 322–323
organizing, 88–91, 148–149, 322–323
persuasive, 146–147
supporting sentences in, 82–83, 84–85, 86–87,
    148–149
topic sentence in, 82–83, 84–85, 86–87, 148–149
unity in, 92–93
writing, 13, 17, 82–83, 84–85, 86–87, 88–91,
    92–93, 148–149, 239, 241, 265, 266–267,
    321, 323, 357, 359, 361, 363, 379, 381, 487,
    523
  See also Writing Process.
Paraphrasing, 484–485, 486–487
Parenthetical expressions, 634–635
Participles, 460–461, 470–471
Partner, working with a, Introduction 6, 4–5,
    100, 141, 145, 156, 214, 235, 276, 315,
    330, 375, 388, 427, 440, 483, 498, 515,
    517, 535
Parts of a Book, 560–561
Parts of Speech
  review of, 6–7, 42, 46–47
  See Adjectives; Adverbs; Conjunctions;
    Interjections; Nouns; Prepositions; Pronouns;
    Verbs.
Past participle. *See* Verbs, past participles
Past perfect tense. *See* Verbs, past perfect tense.
Past tense. *See* Verbs, in past tense.
Paz, Octavio, from "Sight, touch," 430
Peer Conferencing, Introduction 6, 23, 39, 69, 95,
    100, 133, 151, 156, 191, 209, 214, 251, 271,
    276, 305, 325, 330, 365, 383, 388, 419, 435,
    440, 471, 493, 498, 527, 541
Periodicals, 569
Periods
  ending sentences, 4–5, 628–629
  proofreading mark for, 102, 158, 216, 278, 332,
    390, 442, 500
  See also Punctuation.
Personal narrative, 210–217
Personal pronouns, 232–233, 234–235
Personification, 320–321, 337, 430–431
Persuading, A Strategy for, 136–137
Persuading, Writing Process, 152–159
Persuasive strategies, 146–147, 163
Phrases
  adjective, 407–409
  adverb, 407–409
  definition of, 462–463

distinguishing from clauses, 462–463, 504, 509
positioning, 526–527
prepositional, 404–406, 407–409
verb, 120–121, 122–123
"A Pine Tree Towers Lonely," by Heinrich Heine, 434
Plagiarism, 486–487
Plot, 378–379, 382–383, 395, 538–539
Poems
    "The Cap and Bells," by William Butler Yeats, 432–433
    "Eight Puppies," by Gabriela Mistral, 424–427
    "The Heron," by Theodore Roethke, 424–427
    "Jabberwocky," by Lewis Carroll, 424–427
    from "Les Sapins," by Guillaume Apollinaire, 430–431
    "A Pine Tree Towers Lonely," by Heinrich Heine, 434–435
    from "Sight, touch," by Octavio Paz, 430
    from "To the foot from its child," by Pablo Neruda, 430–431
    untitled poem by Emily Dickinson, 424–427
    from "Winter Evening," by Alexander Pushkin, 434–435
Poetry
    ballad form in, 432–433
    capital letters for titles of, 622–625
    figurative language, 430–431
    form, 432–433, 436–443
    listening to, 428–429
    lyric, 434–435
    metaphor, 430–431, 436–443
    narrative voice in, 434–435, 436–443
    personification in, 430–431
    quatrains, 432–433
    quotation marks for titles of, 638–639
    rhyme, 432–433
    simile, 430–431, 436–443
    voice, 436–443
    writing, 430–431, 436–443
Point of view, in literature, 208–209, 380–381
Point of view, 194–195, 201, 212, 368–369, 375, 386. *See also* Thinking skills.
Possessive nouns, 64–65
Possessive pronouns, 236–237
Predicate adjectives, 128–129, 170–171, 339
Predicate nominatives, 128–129, 170–171, 339
Predicates
    complete, 8–9, 10–11, 42, 47–48, 108
    compound, 14–15, 43, 50–51, 108
    simple, 10–11, 48–49
Prefixes, (*counter-, dis-, in-, inter-, pre-, re-, sub-*), 416–417, 447
Prepositional phrases
    as adjective phrases, 407–409, 446, 451
    as adverb phrases, 407–409, 446, 451
    definition of, 404–406
    positioning, 526–527
    sentence combining with, 418–419, 526–527

Prepositions
    and adverbs, 404–406
    definition of, 6–7
    object of, 404–406, 446
    in prepositional phrases, 404–409, 446
    review of, 6–7, 446, 453, 549
    sentence combining with, 418–419
    using, in writing, 404–406, 455
Present participle. *See* Verbs, present participle form.
Present perfect tense. *See* Verbs, present perfect tense.
Present tense. *See* Verbs, present tense.
Prewriting as a step of the writing process, Introduction 4, 97, 153, 211, 273, 327, 385, 437, 495
    definition of, 97
Prewriting strategies, Introduction 4,
    Asking Questions, 212
    Brainstorming, 274
    Cluster Map, 154, 438
    A Conference, 98
    First Thoughts, 438
    A Mental Movie, 328
    The Star System, 386
    Taking Notes, 496
    A Team Review, 154
    Thought Balloon, 212, 386
    Goal/Plan/Outcome Chart, 98, 496
    Venn Diagram, 274, 328
Principal parts. *See* Verbs.
Problem Solving, 72–73, 79, 98, 474–475, 479, 496. *See also* Thinking skills.
Pronouns
    as adjectives, 301
    antecedents of, 234–235, 282, 286, 340
    and contractions, 236–237
    definition of, 6–7, 232–233
    demonstrative, 238–239, 282, 288, 296–297
    indefinite, 242–243, 283, 289, 340
    intensive, 240–241, 282, 340, 449
    interrogative, 238–239, 282, 288–289
    nominative case of, 244, 283
    object, 244–247, 283, 290, 340
    objective case of, 244, 283
    personal, 232–233, 285
    possessive, 236–237, 282, 287, 340
    as predicate nominatives, 128–129
    reflexive, 240–241, 282, 289, 340, 449
    review of, 6–7, 282–283, 285, 547
    sentence combining with, 250–251
    subject, 244–245, 246–247, 283, 290
    using, in writing, 232–233, 235, 237, 239, 241, 243, 245, 247
Proofreading Checklist, 102, 158, 216, 278, 332, 390, 442, 500
Proofreading marks, 102, 158, 216, 278, 332, 390, 442, 500

Proofreading strategies, Introduction 7
focusing on beginnings and endings, 216
handwriting hints
clear word endings, 390
letter spacing, 500
one thing at a time, 102
placing ruler under each line, 332
reading backwards, 278
reading through a window, 442
trading with a partner, 158
using Proofreading Checklist, 102, 158, 216, 278,
332, 390, 442, 500
using proofreading marks, 102, 158, 216, 278,
332, 390, 442, 500
using your best handwriting, 102, 158, 216, 278,
332, 390, 442, 500
Proofreading as a step of the writing process,
Introduction 7, 102, 158, 216, 278, 332, 390,
442, 500
definition of, 102
Propaganda techniques, 142–145
Proper adjectives, 296–297
capitalization of, 296–297, 622–623
Proper nouns
capitalization of, 58–59, 616–617
geographical names, 58–59, 618–619
names, 58–59, 616–617, 618–619, 620–621,
622–623
religious terms, 624–625
titles for people, 622–623
titles of written works, movies, works of art,
58–59, 624–625
Publishing as a step of the writing process,
Introduction 7, 103, 159, 217, 279, 333, 391,
443, 501
definition of, 103
Publishing strategies, Introduction 7
creating a class bulletin board, 501
creating a class chart, 279
creating a class poetry display, 443
creating a class short story collection, 391
creating a how-to column for the school
newspaper, 103
creating a media review column for the school
newspaper, 159
having a poetry reading, 443
holding a class awards ceremony, 217
holding a class/team read-around, 279, 391
holding a mock-television show, 159
holding a vote for the most interesting personality,
501
letting a younger class illustrate descriptions, 333
making a class book, 391
reading aloud to a younger class, 333
reading your writing aloud, 103, 159, 217, 279,
333, 391, 443, 501
reviewing a partner's work using exclamatory
words, 217

Punctuation
apostrophes, 646–647
in business letters, 611, 612
colons, 611, 644–645
commas, 16–17, 22–23, 204–205, 488–491,
630–631, 632–633, 634–635, 636–637
end marks, 4–5, 628–629
exclamation marks, 4–5, 628–629
in friendly letters, 609, 612
italics, 642–643
periods, 4–5, 488–491, 628–629
question marks, 4–5, 628–629
quotation marks, 204–205, 488–491, 638–639
semicolons, 16–17, 644–645
underlining, 488–491, 642–643
Purpose for writing, Introduction 4, 34–35, 36–37,
96, 152, 210, 272, 326, 384, 436, 494
definition of, 34–35, 36–37, 96
Pushkin, Alexander, from "Winter Evening," 434

Quatrains, 432–433
Question marks, 4–5, 628–629
Questionnaires, 482–483
Questions. *See* Sentences; Interrogative sentences.
Question Wheel. *See* Thinking Strategies.
Quotation marks
for direct quotations, 204–205, 638–639
with titles, 488–491, 638–639

Raise, rise, 186–187
Rawlings, Marjorie Kinnan, *The Yearling*, 310–315
Reader's Guide to Periodical Literature, The, 569
Reading and Writing Connection
Focus on Character Traits, 270–271
Focus on Clarity, 94–95
Focus on Dialogue in Fiction, 382–383
Focus on the Main Idea, 492–493
Focus on Mood, 324–325
Focus on the Narrative Voice, 434–435
Focus on Opinions, 150–151
Focus on Point of View, 208–209
Focus on a Writer's Voice, 38–39
Focus on Your Growth as a Writer, 540–541
Real, really, 360–361
Reasons, persuading, 146–147, 148–149,
152–159
Reference materials, 20–21, 484–485, 566–569,
572–575
See also Almanac; Atlas; Dictionary;
Encyclopedia; *Readers' Guide to Periodical
Literature*; Thesaurus.

Reflexive pronouns, 240–241
Reports
  book, 41, 105, 161, 219, 281, 335, 393, 445, 503, 543, 608
  structure of, 488–491, 505
Reports, Letters, Notes, 608–612
Requests. *See* Sentences; Imperative sentences.
Researching, A Strategy for, 474–475
Researching, Writing Process, 494–501
Research Report, 492–493, 488–491, 494–501
Response to Literature, 30, 31, 78, 79, 140, 141, 200, 201, 260, 261, 314, 315, 374, 375, 426, 427, 478, 479, 534, 535. *See also* Literature; Speaking; Listening; Writing.
Revising as a step of the writing process, Introduction 6, 100, 101, 156, 157, 214, 215, 276, 277, 330, 331, 388, 389, 440, 441, 498, 499
  definition of, 100
Revising Checklist, 101, 157, 215, 277, 331, 389, 441, 499
Revising marks, 101, 157, 215, 277, 331, 389, 441, 499
Revising sentences
  with adjectives, 304–305, 418–419
  with adverbs, 364–365, 418–419
  with compatible ideas, 418–419
  choppy sentences, 23
  with exact nouns, 68–69
  with exact pronouns, 250–251
  expand with adjectives, 304–305, 418–419
  overused adjectives, 305
  overused adverbs, 364–365
  overused verbs, 132–133
  sentence combining, with *and*, 22–23, 418–419
  stringy sentences, 471
  using varied sentences, 190–191, 418–419
  with verbs in correct tense, 190–191
  word choice, 365
Revising Strategies, Introduction 6
  character dialogue, 215, 388
  clearly stating main idea, 498
  describing steps clearly, 100
  details contributing to mood, 330, 331
  details keeping plot clear, 389
  listening to your writing, Introduction 6, 100, 156, 214, 276, 330, 388, 440, 498
  peer conferencing, 100, 156, 214, 276, 330, 388, 440, 498
  reading to yourself, Introduction 6, 100, 156, 214, 276, 330, 388, 440, 498
  revealing character traits, 276
  sharing with a partner, Introduction 6, 100, 156, 214, 276, 330, 388, 440, 498
  sounding smooth, 441
  state and support your opinion, 156
  using examples, 277
  using logical order to describe, 101
  using narrative voice, 440
  using Revision Checklist, 101, 157, 215, 277, 331, 389, 441, 499
  using revising marks, 101, 157, 215, 277, 331, 389, 441, 499
  using supporting details, 499
  writing in first–person point of view, 214
Rhyme, 432–433
Roethke, Theodore, "The Heron," 425
Run-on sentences, 18–19, 466–467

Saki, "The Open Window," 370–375
Science. *See* Writing across the curriculum.
Semicolons, 16–17, 644–645
Sensory details, 318–319, 337, 430–431
Sentence combining. *See* Grammar and Writing Workshops.
Sentence fragments, 18–19, 466–467
Sentences
  agreement of subject and verb, 514–515, 516–517, 518–519, 520–523, 526–527, 549, 551
  capitalization of first word in, 4–5, 622–623
  clincher, 82–83
  combining, 22–23, 68–69, 132–133, 190–191, 250–251, 304–305, 364–365, 418–419, 470–471, 526–527
  complex, 464–466, 504, 510
  compound, 16–17, 22–23, 43, 51–52, 68–69, 464–467, 470–471, 526–527
  declarative, 4–5, 42, 45
  diagraming, 648–656
  end punctuation of, 4–5, 628–629
  exclamatory, 4–5, 42, 45
  expanding, with modifiers and prepositional phrases, 418–419, 526–527
  fragments, 18–19, 43, 52–53, 466–467
  imperative, 4–5
    subject of, 12–13
  interrogative, 4–5, 42, 45
  inverted, 12–13, 526–527
  kinds of, 4–5, 42, 45
  parts of speech in, 6–7, 42, 46–47
  predicates in
    complete, 8–9, 10–11
    compound, 14–15
    simple, 10–11, 338
  review of, 546
  revising. *See* Revising sentences.
  run-on, 18–19, 52–53, 466–467, 505, 511
  simple, 16–17, 43, 51–52, 108, 465–466
  subjects in
    complete, 8–9, 10–11
    compound, 14–15, 448, 522–523
    simple, 10–11, 338, 448
  supporting, 82–83, 84–85, 86–87, 148–149

topic, 82–83, 84–85, 86–87, 148–149
variety, 190–191, 418–419
word order in, 12–13, 49
writing, 4–5, 9, 15, 19, 59, 61, 63, 121, 123, 125, 127, 129, 179, 183, 185, 187, 207, 235, 237, 243, 245, 247, 297, 300, 301, 319, 409, 411, 413, 465, 467, 483, 491, 517, 519, 521, 523
Set, sit, 186–187
Setting, 378–379, 382–383, 395
Sherlock, Philip, retold by, "Tiger Story, Anansi Story," 530–535
Short stories
"The Open Window," by Saki, 370–375
"Tiger Story, Anansi Story," retold by Philip Sherlock, 530–535
Short story, elements of, 378–379, 384–391, 395, 538–539
"Sight, touch," from, by Octavio Paz, 430
Similes, 320–321, 337, 430–431
Simple sentences, 16–17, 465–466, 510
Slang, 248–249
Social Notes, 610
Social Studies. See Writing across the curriculum.
Space order, 88–91, 322–323
Speaking
appropriateness for audience, 536–537
ask if there are any questions, 80–81
be polite, 32–33, 262–263, 376–377
brainstorming, 274
discussions, 32–33, 262–263
dramatize your actions, voice, 80–81, 202–203, 316–317, 428–429, 480–481, 536–537
giving and following directions, 80–81
having confidence in your personal views, 32–33
keeping focused, 32–33, 202–203
make eye contact, 80–81, 202–203, 480–481, 536–537
memorizing the important parts, 480–481, 536–537
practice first, 32–33, 80–81, 428–429, 480–481, 536–537
preparing, 32–33, 428–429, 480–481, 536–537
reading poetry, 428–429
reading your writing aloud. See Revising as a step of the Writing Process.
relax, 80–81, 480–481
as a response to literature, 31, 79, 141, 201, 261, 315, 375, 427, 479, 535
sharing opinions. See also Revising as a step of the Writing Process.
speak clearly, 142–145, 202–203, 376–377, 428–429, 480–481
summarizing the main ideas, 480–481
support your opinion with facts, 142–145, 262–263, 480–481
telling about an incident, 202–203
using appropriate details, facts, 80–81, 202–203, 316–317, 480–481
using the telephone, 376–377
using visual aids, 80–81, 316–317
visualize, 316–317, 428–429
See also Listening; Partner, working with a; Peer conferencing; Speaking and Listening; Working Together.
Speaking and Listening
to classify, 262–263
to create, 428–429
to describe, 316–317
to express yourself, 32–33
to imagine, 376–377
to inform, 80–81
to narrate, 202–203
the oral tradition, 536–537
to persuade, 142–145
to poetry, 428–429
to research, 480–481
See also Listening; Speaking.
Spelling
homographs, 468–469
homophones, 468–469
plural nouns, 60–61, 62–63
possessive nouns, 64–65
proofreading marks for, 102, 158, 216, 278, 332, 390, 442, 500
rules for, 613–615
verbs, 174–175
Star System, The, 386. See also Prewriting strategies.
Statements. See Declarative sentences.
State-of-being verbs, 118–119, 122–123, 162, 165
Stories. See Personal narrative; Short stories; Fiction.
Story
characters, 264–265, 270–271, 378–379, 382–383, 538–539
elements of a, 378–379, 382–383, 384–391, 538–539
plot, 378–379, 382–383, 538–539
setting, 378–379, 382–383
time order, 94–95
title of a
capitalization, 488–491, 624–625
quotation marks, 488–491, 638–639
writing a, 378–379, 384–391
Strategies
for choosing and narrowing topics. See Choosing and narrowing topics, Strategies for.
for prewriting. See Prewriting Strategies.
for proofreading. See Proofreading Strategies.
for publishing. See Publishing Strategies.
for revising. See Revising Strategies.
for thinking. See Thinking Strategies.
for writing. See Writing Strategies.
Stringy sentences. See Revising sentences.
Study Habits, 558

Study Skills
almanac, 568
analogies, 559
atlas, 567
card and computer catalogs, 562–565
choosing and narrowing a report topic, 492–493
dictionary, 572–575
encyclopedia, 566
library, using, 562–565
outlining, 570–571
paraphrasing, 484–485, 486–487
parts of a book, 560–561
periodicals, 569
The Reader's Guide to Periodical Literature, 569
study habits, 558
taking notes, 484–485, 486–487
taking tests, 559
thesaurus, 20–21
Study Skills Lessons, 558–575
Subject pronouns, 244–245, 246–247
Subjects
agreement of, with verbs, 514–515, 516–517, 518–519, 520–521, 522–523, 526–527
complete, 8–9, 10–11, 42, 47–48, 222
compound, 14–15, 43, 50–51, 522–523
of imperative sentences, 12–13
simple, 10–11, 48–49, 222
Subordinate clauses, 462–463, 464–467, 470–471
Subordinating conjunctions, 462–463, 464–467, 470–471
Suffixes, (*-able, -ion, -ize, -ly, -or, -ous*), 362–363, 395
Summarizing information, 486–487
Supporting details, 484–485
Supporting sentences in paragraphs, 82–83, 84–85, 86–87, 92–93, 148–149
Sure, surely, 360–361
Surveys, 482–483
Synonyms, 188–189, 221. *See also* Thesaurus.
as context clues, 302–303
definition of, 188–189
in a thesaurus, 20–21

Taking notes, 484–485, 486–487, 496. *See also* Prewriting strategies.
Taking Tests, 559
Team Review, A, 154. *See also* Prewriting strategies.
Tenses. *See* Verbs, tenses of.
Thank-you notes, 610
Their, there, they're, 236–237, 468–469
Thesaurus, 588–607. *See also* Dictionary.
definition of, 20–21
parts of, 20–21, 43
using, in writing, 20–21
Thesaurus Corner, word choice, 39, 95, 151, 209, 271, 325, 383, 435, 493, 541

Thinking Skills
creative
elaborating, 136–137, 141, 154, 422–423, 427, 438
point of view, 194–195, 201, 212, 368–369, 375, 386
critical
compare/contrast, 254–255, 261, 274, 308–309, 315, 328
problem solving, 72–73, 79, 98, 474–475, 479, 496
Thinking Strategies
creative
Cluster Map, 136–137, 141, 154, 422–423, 427, 438
Thought Balloon, 194–195, 201, 212, 368–369, 375, 386
critical
Goal/Plan/Outcome Chart, 72–73, 79, 98, 474–475, 479, 496
Venn Diagram, 254–255, 261, 274, 308–309, 315, 328
Third-person point of view, 208–209, 380–381
Thought Balloon, 194–195, 201, 212, 368–369, 375, 386. *See also* Thinking Strategies.
"Tiger Story, Anansi Story," retold by Philip Sherlock, 530–535
Time order, 88–91, 94–95
Titles
of books, stories, poems, 638–639, 642–643
To, at, 410–411
"To the foot from its child," from, by Pablo Neruda, 431
To, too, two, 468–469
Topic sentences, 82–83, 84–85, 86–87, 148–149
Topics
choosing and narrowing, 492–493, 505
in an encyclopedia, 566
See also Choosing and narrowing topics, Strategies for.
Town Names, 363
Transitive verbs, 124–125, 162, 169
"Tribute to an Inventor: Cyrus McCormick," by Alice Hengesbach, 476–479

Underlining book titles, 642–643
Unity of paragraphs, 92–93
Untitled poem by Emily Dickinson, 424–427
Usage
adjectives, 358–359
comparison of, 298–300
adverbs, 358–359
comparison of, 354–355
at, too, 410–411
be, 516–517
beside, besides, 410–411

between, among, 410–411
collective nouns, 518–519
different from, 410–411
do, 516–517
double negatives, 356–357
good, well, 360–361
have, 516–517
homophones, 468–469
in, into, 410–411
its, it's, 236–237
lay, lie, 186–187
negative words, 356–357
pronoun
    antecedents, 234–235
    indefinite, 242–243
    intensive, 240–241
    interrogative, 238–239
    possessive, 236–237
    reflexive, 240–241
    subject and object, 244–245, 246–247
raise, rise, 186–187
real, really, 360–361
set, sit, 186–187
subject-verb agreement, 514–515, 516–517,
    518–519, 520–521, 522–523, 526–527
    with compound subjects, 522–523
    with indefinite pronouns, 520–521, 522–523
    in inverted sentences, 520–521, 526–527
sure, surely, 360–361
their, there, they're, 236–237, 468–469
to, too, two, 468–469
verbs
    irregular, 180–183
    principal parts of, 174–175, 180–183
    tenses of, 176–179

Venn Diagram, 254–255, 261, 274, 308–309, 315,
    328. *See also* Thinking Strategies.
Verb phrases, 120–121, 122–123, 184–185
Verbals
    definition of, 460–461
    gerunds, 460–461, 504
    infinitives, 460–461, 504, 507
    kinds of, 460–461, 504, 507, 549
    participles, 460–461, 470–471, 504, 507
    as adjectives, 460–461, 507
Verbs
    action, 118–119, 122–125, 162, 165
    in active voice, 184–185, 220, 228
    agreement with subject, 514–515, 516–517,
        518–519, 520–521, 522–523, 526–527
    be, 118–119, 120–121, 122–123, 516–517
    compound, 14–15, 222
    conjugation of, 176–179, 516–517
    definition of, 6–7, 118–119
    direct object of, 124–125, 126–127, 162

do, 516–517
    in future perfect tense, 176–179, 220, 339
    future tense, 176–179, 220
    have, 120–121, 516–517
    helping, 120–121, 174–175
    indirect object of, 126–127, 163, 169
    infinitive, 460–461
    intransitive, 124–125, 162, 169
    irregular, 180–183, 220, 227
    linking, 120–125, 128–129, 162, 167–168
    main, 120–121, 122–123, 162, 166
    overused, 133
    in passive voice, 184–185, 220, 228
    past participles, 174–175, 184–185
    in past perfect tense, 176–179, 220, 339
    in past tense, 174–175, 176–179, 220
    phrases, 120, 166–167
    with predicate nominatives or predicate adjectives,
        128–129, 163, 170–171
    present participles of, 174–175
    in present perfect tense, 176–179, 220, 339
    in present tense, 174–175, 176–179, 514–515
    principal parts of, 174–175, 180–183, 220, 225
    regular, 174–175
    review of, 6–7, 546–547
    as simple predicates, 10–11
    state-of-being, 118–119, 122–123, 162, 165
    tenses of, 174–175, 176–179, 190–191, 514–515
    transitive, 124–125, 162, 169
    troublesome pairs of, 186–187, 229
    used as different parts of speech, 460–461
    using, in writing, 118–119, 121, 123, 125, 127, 129,
        175, 179, 183, 185, 187, 461
Vocabulary
    compounds, 66–67
    connotation, 524–525
    context clues, 302–303
    denotation, 524–525
    history of English, 67, 249, 303, 363
    homographs, 468–469
    homophones, 468–469
    idioms, 130–131
    prefixes, 416–417
    shades of meaning, 188–189
    suffixes, 362–363
    synonyms, 188–189
    thesaurus, 20–21
Voice, 38–39
Voice in poetry, 434–345

Well, good, 360–361, 401
What is a Writer?, Introduction 1
"Winter Evening," by Alexander Pushkin, 434
Word Choice, 39, 95, 101, 151, 157, 209, 215, 271,
    277, 325, 331, 383, 389, 435, 441, 493, 499,
    541

Word History, 67, 249, 303, 363

Word Meaning, 21

Word order in sentences, 12–13

Working Together, 23, 39, 69, 95, 133, 151, 191, 209, 251, 271, 305, 325, 365, 383, 419, 435, 471, 493, 527, 541

Writers' Corner, 23, 69, 133, 191, 251, 305, 365, 419, 471, 527

Writer's Warm–up, 2–3, 54–55, 116–117, 172–173, 230–231, 292–293, 348–349, 402–403, 458–459, 512–513

Writing
addresses on envelopes, 612
with adjectives, 294–295, 297, 300, 301
with adverbs, 350–353, 355
audience for, 34–35, 36–37, 96, 152, 210, 272, 326, 384, 436, 494
a book report, 41, 105, 161, 219, 281, 335, 393, 445, 503, 543, 608
a character sketch, 264–265
choosing appropriate form, 36–37
comparison/contrast paragraph/essay, 266–267, 272–279
with conjunctions, 22–23, 412–413
with descriptive details, 318–319, 322–323, 326–333, 430–431
dialogue, 204–205, 415, 640–641
an explanatory paragraph
with figurative language, 320–321, 430–431
a friendly letter, 609, 612
a how–to article, 96–103
an invitation, 610
in a journal, Introduction 2, 3, 5, 11, 23, 40–41, 55, 57, 69, 104–105, 117, 119, 133, 160–161, 173, 175, 191, 206–207, 218, 231, 233, 251, 280, 293, 295, 305, 334, 349, 353, 365, 392, 403, 406, 419, 444, 459, 461, 471, 502, 513, 515, 527, 542–543
letter, 147
a media review, 152–159
with nouns, 56–57, 59, 61, 63
paragraphs, 13, 17, 82–83, 84–85, 86–87, 88–91, 92–93, 148–149, 239, 241, 265, 266–267, 321, 322–323, 357, 359, 361, 379, 381, 487, 523
a persuasive article, 35, 146–147, 152–159
poetry, 433, 436–443
with prepositions, 404–406
with pronouns, 232–233, 235, 237, 239, 241, 243, 245, 247
with proper nouns, 58–59
purpose for, 34–35, 36–37, 96, 152, 210, 272, 326, 384, 436, 494
questions, 482–483
a report, 488–491, 494–501

as a response to literature, 31, 79, 141, 201, 261, 315, 375, 427, 479, 535
sentences, 4–5, 9, 15, 19, 59, 61, 63, 121, 123, 125, 127, 129, 179, 183, 185, 187, 207, 235, 237, 243, 245, 247, 297, 300, 301, 319, 409, 411, 413, 465, 467, 483, 491, 517, 519, 521, 523
and sentence combining. *See* Grammar and Writing Workshops.
as a step of the writing process, Introduction 5, 99, 155, 213, 275, 329, 387, 439, 497
a story, 384–391
a thank-you note, 610
with verbs, 118–119, 121, 123, 125, 127, 129, 174–175, 179, 183, 185, 187, 460–461

Writing across the curriculum
Art, 280
Composition, 40, 444
Literature, 160, 392
Music, 104
Science, 334, 502
Social Studies, 218, 542

Writing in Your World, Introduction 1

Writing Process. (Choosing and narrowing topics, prewriting, writing, revising, proofreading, and publishing are taught in each Writing Project.)
Classifying: Writing a Comparison Essay, 272–279
Creating: Writing a Poem, 436–443
Describing: Writing a Description, 326–333
Imagining: Writing a Short Story, 384–391
Informing: Writing a How–to Article, 96–103
Narrating: Writing a Personal Narrative, 210–217
Persuading: Writing a Media Review, 152–159
Researching: Writing a Research Report, 494–501

Writing Strategies, Introduction 5,
beginning with topic sentence, 329
deciding on poem's form, 439
knowing your purpose and audience, 96, 152, 210, 272, 326, 384, 436, 494
nonstop writing, 213
using an organizational outline, 99, 155, 497
using point-by-point or block comparison, 266–269, 275

Writing to Learn, 31, 40, 79, 104, 141, 160, 201, 218, 261, 280, 315, 334, 375, 392, 427, 444, 479, 502, 535, 542

Yearling, The, by Marjorie Kinnan Rawlings, 310–315

Yeats, William Butler, "The Cap and Bells," 432–433

You, **understood as subject of imperative sentence**, 12–13